GLAS

Jacques Derrida

English Translation

by John P. Leavey, Jr.,

and Richard Rand

University of Nebraska Press   Lincoln and London

Preparation of this volume was made possible in
part by a grant from the Program for Translations
of the National Endowment for the Humanities, an
independent federal agency. Publication was also
supported by a grant from the National Endowment
for the Humanities.

First paperback printing: 1990

Most recent printing indicated by the first digit below:

1 2 3 4 5 6 7 8 9 10

First published in France as *Glas,* © Éditions
Galilée, 1974

The paper in this book meets the minimum require-
ments of American National Standard for Information
Sciences—Permanence of Paper for Printed Library
Materials, ANSI Z39.48-1984. ∞

Library of Congress Cataloging-in-Publication Data
Derrida, Jacques.
Glas.
Translation of: Glas.
1. Hegel, Georg Wilhelm Friedrich, 1770-1831.
2. Genet, Jean, 1910—86.   I. Title.
B2948.D4613   1986   193   85-28877
ISBN 0-8032-1667-X (alkaline paper)
ISBN 0-8032-6581-6 (pbk.)

Note to the Translation

The translation of *Glas* was a joint effort. Richard Rand provided the first draft translation of the column on Jean Genet and I of the column on Hegel. I then integrated and reworked both columns for accuracy, continuity of language, and stylistics.

For the critical apparatus to the translation, that is, explanations of particular terms and their translations, commentary on individual lines, and the location of all cited passages, as well as introductory essays, the reader is referred to *Glassary*, by John P. Leavey, Jr., with an essay by Gregory L. Ulmer and a foreword by Jacques Derrida. *Glassary*, also published by the University of Nebraska Press, is the complement of this translation and indicates all references to it by page and line number.

The translation follows these textual principles: German terms within parentheses are Derrida's citations or emphases. German terms with translation alternatives or explanations within square brackets are Derrida's. German terms alone within square brackets are the translators' addition for clarity. French terms within square brackets are likewise the translators'.

I would like to thank the following: Dr. Susan Mango and the Translations Program of the National Endowment for the Humanities for a grant that allowed full-time work during 1980–81; the University of Florida's Division of Sponsored Research, College of Liberal Arts and Sciences, and English Department for their support of other parts of this project; Clark Butler for making available to me his translation of the Hegel letters before publication by Indiana University Press; Indiana University Press for permission to cite from *Hegel: The Letters*, trans. Clark Butler and Christiane Seiler, with commentary by Clark Butler (Indiana University Press, 1984); Barbara Fletcher for her help in the early stages of the translation; and Marie A. Nelson for her time, good spirits, and patience in typing and correcting the entire manuscript—without her this project would still not be finished.

I would also like to acknowledge the support that Paul de Man and John Sallis gave this translation from its inception. J. Hillis Miller has always been available and helpful with any problems that might arise. He made this work possible. Gilbert Debusscher was kind enough to review parts of the translation and answer questions on particular passages in the French. Finally, I want to thank Jacques Derrida himself. His friendship, patience, and generous answers to my many questions continually guided me in this translation.

J. L.

what, after all, of the remain(s), today, for us, here, now, of a Hegel?

For us, here, now: from now on that is what one will not have been able to think without him.

For us, here, now: these words are citations, already, always, we will have learned that from him.

Who, him?

His name is so strange. From the eagle it draws imperial or historic power. Those who still pronounce his name like the French (there are some) are ludicrous only up to a certain point: the restitution (semantically infallible for those who have read him a little—but only a little) of magisterial coldness and imperturbable seriousness, the eagle caught in ice and frost, glass and gel.

Let the emblanched [*emblémi*] philosopher be so congealed.

Who, him? The lead or gold, white or black eagle has not signed the text of *savoir absolu*, absolute knowledge. Even less has the red eagle. Besides, whether *Sa* is a text, has given rise to a text, whether it has been written or has written, caused writing, let writing come about is not yet known.

Sa from now on will be the siglum of *savoir absolu*. And *IC*, let's note this already since the two staffs represent each other, the Immaculate Conception. A properly singular tachygraphy: it is not first going to dislocate, as could be thought, a code, i.e., what we depend [*table*] on too much. But perhaps, much later and more slowly this time, to exhibit its borders

Whether it lets itself be assigned [*enseigner*], signed, ensigned is not yet known. Perhaps there is an incompatibility (rather than a dialectical contradiction) between the teaching and the signature, a schoolmaster and a signer. Perhaps, in any case, even when they let themselves be thought and signed, these two operations cannot overlap each other [*se recouper*].

Its/His [*Sa*] signature, as thought of the remain(s), will envelop this corpus, but no doubt will not be contained therein.

This is—a legend.

remain(s) to be thought: it (*ça*) does not accentuate itself here now but will already have been put to the test on the other side. Sense must conform, more or less, to the calculi of what the engraver terms a counterproof

Not a fable: a legend. Not a novel, not a family romance since that concerns Hegel's family, but a legend.

The legend does not pretend to afford a reading of Hegel's whole corpus, texts, and plans [*desseins*], just of two figures. More precisely, of two figures in the act of effacing themselves: two passages.

"what remained of a Rembrandt torn into small, very regular squares and rammed down the shithole" is divided in two.

As the remain(s) [*reste*].

Two unequal columns, they say distyle [*disent-ils*], each of which — envelop(e)(s) or sheath(es), incalculably reverses, turns inside out, replaces, remarks, overlaps [*recoupe*] the other.

The incalculable of *what remained* calculates itself, elaborates all the *coups* [strokes, blows, etc.], twists or scaffolds them in silence, you would wear yourself out even faster by counting them. Each little square is delimited, each column rises with an impassive self-sufficiency, and yet the element of contagion, the infinite circulation of general equivalence relates each sentence, each stump of writing (for example, *"je m'éc . . ."*) to each other, within each column and from one column to the other of *what remained* infinitely calculable.

Almost.

Of the remain(s), after all, there are, always, overlapping each other, two functions.

The first assures, guards, assimilates, interiorizes, idealizes, relieves the fall [*chute*] into the monument. There the fall maintains, embalms, and mummifies itself, monumemorizes and names itself—falls (to the tomb(stone)) [*tombe*]. Therefore, but as a fall, it erects itself there.

I

Two very determined, partial, and particular passages, two examples. But perhaps the example trifles with the essence.

First passage: religion of flowers. In *Phenomenology of Spirit*, the development of natural religion always has the form of a syllogism: the mediate moment, "plant and animal," includes a religion of flowers. Flower religion is not even a moment or station. It all but exhausts itself in a passage (*Übergehen*), a disappearing movement, the effluvium floating above a procession, the march from innocence to guilt. Flower religion would be innocent, animal religion culpable. Flower religion (a factual example of this would come from Africa, but above all from India) no longer, or hardly, remains; it proceeds to its own placement in culpability, its very own animalization, to innocence becoming culpable [*coupable*] and thus serious. And this insofar as the same, the self (*Selbst*) has not yet taken place, has given itself, still, only (in) its representation (*Vorstellung*). "The innocence of the *flower religion*, which is merely the self-less representation of self, passes into the seriousness of warring life, into the guilt of *animal religions*; the quiet and impotence of contemplative individuality pass into destructive being-for-self."

"*Die Unschuld der* Blumenreligion, *die nur selbstlose Vorstellung des Selbsts ist, geht in den Ernst des kämpfenden Lebens, in die Schuld der* Tierreligion, *die Ruhe und Ohnmacht der anschauenden Individualität in das zerstörende Fürsichsein über.*"

always look sideways toward India in order to follow this enigmatic passage, which passes very badly, between the Far West and the Far East. India, not Europe, nor China. A kind of historic strangulating bottleneck. Contracted as Gibraltar, "a sterile and costly rock," the pillars of Hercules whose history belongs to that of the Indies route. In this somewhat shifting channel, the East-West-Euroafrican panorama infinitely narrows. A point of becoming.
The rocky point has often changed name, nonetheless. The promontory has been called Mons Calpe, Notre-Dame-du-Roc, Djebel Tarik (Gibraltar)

Second passage: the phallic column of India. The *Aesthetics* describes its form in the chapter on "Independent or Symbolic Architecture." It is said to have spread toward Phrygia, Syria, and Greece where, in the course of the Dionysiac celebrations (according to Herodotus as cited by Hegel), the women were pulling the thread of a phallus that thus stood in the air, "almost as big as the rest of the body." At the beginning, then, the phallic columns of India,

The other — lets the remain(s) fall. Running the risk of coming down to the same. Falls (to the tomb(stone)) — two times the columns, the waterspouts [*trombes*] — remain(s).

Perhaps the case (*Fall*) of the *seing*.

If *Fall* marks the case, the fall, decadence, failure or fissure, *Falle* equals trap, snare, springe, the machine that grabs you by the neck [*cou*].

The *seing* falls (to the tomb(stone)).

The remain(s) is indescribable, or almost so: not by virtue of an empiric approximation, but rigorously undecidable.

"*Catachresis* . . . n. 1. Trope wherein a word is diverted from its proper sense and is taken up in common language to designate another thing with some analogy to the object initially expressed; for example, a tongue [*langue*], since the tongue is the chief organ of spoken language; a looking glass . . . a leaf of paper. . . . It is also a catachresis to say: ironclad with gold; to ride a hobby-horse. . . . 2. Musical term. Harsh and unfamiliar dissonance.
"—E. Κατάχρησις, abuse, from κατά, against, χρῆσις, usage."

"*Catafalque* . . . n. Platform raised as an honor, in the middle of a church, to receive the coffin or effigy of a deceased. . . .
"—E. Ital. *catafalco*; Low Latin *catafaltus*, *cadafaldus*, *cadafalle*, *cadapallus*, *cadaphallus*, *chafallus*. According to Du Cange, *cata* derives from the Low Latin *catus*, a war machine called *cat* after the animal; and, according to Diez, from *catare*, to see, to regard; after all [*du reste*], finally, these two etymologies merge, since *catus*, cat, and *catare*, to regard, share the same root. There remains *falco*, which, given the variants of the Low Latin where *p* appears, can be only the German word *balk* (see BALCONY). *Catafalque* is the same word as *scaffold* (see that word [*échafaud*])."

"*Cataglottism* . . . n. Term from ancient literature. The use of abstruse words.
"—E. Καταγλωττισμὸς, from κατά, indicating abstruse, and γλῶσσα, word, tongue, language (see GLOSS [*glose*])." Littré.
The ALCs sound, clack, explode [*éclatent*], reflect and (re)turn themselves in every sense and direction, count and discount themselves, opening—here (*ici*)—in the stone of each column a variety of inlaid judas holes, crenels, Venetian shutters [*jalousies*], loopholes, to see to it not to be imprisoned in the

enormous formations, pillars, towers, larger at the base than at the top. Now at the outset—but as a setting out that already departed from itself—these columns were intact, unbreached [*inentamées*], smooth. And only later (*erst später*) are notches, excavations, openings (*Öffnungen und Aushöhlungen*) made in the columns, in the flank, if such can be said. These hollowings, holes, these lateral marks in depth would be like accidents coming over the phallic columns at first unperforated or apparently unperforatable. Images of gods (*Götterbilder*) were set, niched, inserted, embedded, driven in, tattooed on the columns. Just as these small caverns or lateral pockets on the flank of the phallus announced the small portable and hermetic Greek temples, so they broached/breached the model of the pagoda, not yet altogether a habitation and still distinguished by the separation between shell and kernel (*Schale und Kern*). A middle ground hard to determine between the

there, behind the absolute of a *déjà*, an *already*, what is there

"*Hauptsächlich in Indien nun gingen von dieser Art der Verehrung der Zeugungskraft in der Form der Zeugungsglieder auch Bauwerke in dieser Gestalt und Bedeutung aus; ungeheure säulenartige Gebilde, aus Stein, wie Türme massiv aufgerichtet, unten breiter als oben. Sie waren ursprünglich für sich selber Zweck, Gegenstände der Verehrung, und erst später fing men an, Öffnungen und Aushöhlungen darin zu machen und Götterbilder hineinzustellen, was sich noch in den griechischen Hermen portativen Tempelhäuschen, erhalten hat. Den Ausgangspunkt aber bilden in Indien die unausgehölten Phallussäulen, die sich später erst in Schale und Kern teilten und zu Pagoden wurden.*"
Correspondences: the moment immediately following both the flower religion and the phallic columns, a moment that relieves them forthwith as it were, is Memnon, the resonating colossal statue (*kolossale Klangstatue*) that produces a *Klang* under the incidence of the sun's rays. The *Klang* announces the end of the flower religion and the phallic columns, but is not yet voice or language. This ringing, sonorous light reverberating as on a stone bell [*cloche*] is already no longer mute, but not yet speaking (*nur Klang und nicht Sprache*). These structural correspondences can be verified among all the descriptions of *Klang* in the *Aesthetics*, the *Phenomenology of Spirit*, the *Philosophy of Nature*, etc.

column and the house, sculpture and architecture.

So no one can live there. Whether dead or alive. It is neither a house nor a burial place. Who contemplates such a structure, who can do so, one wonders. And how can an altar, a habitat, or a burial monument, town planning [*urbanisme*] or a mausoleum, the family and the State, find their origins there?

Let me admit—a throw of the d(ie) [*coup de dé*]—that I have already chosen these two very compressed passages, this angle or odd channel in order to introduce, strictly, in/to Hegel's name.

Between the words, between the word itself as it divides itself in two (noun and verb, cadence or erection, hole and stone), (to) insinuate the delicate, barely visible stem, an almost imperceptible cold lever, scalpel, or *stylus*, so as to enervate, then dilapidate, enormous discourses that always end, though more or less denying it, in attributing an author's rights: "that (*ça*) comes (back) to me," the *seing* belongs to me.

The stake of the signature — does the signature take place? where? how? why? for whom? — that will be treated practically, in passing: an indispensable preliminary to the explanation of (for example "literary") formality with all the muscled

colossus, tattoos in the folded flesh of a phallic body that is never legible except in banding erect, legends as well for the stones of the *Balcony* or the brothel. Irma indicates to the chief of police that his "image does not yet conform to the liturgies of the brothel." He protests: "My image is growing bigger and bigger, I assure you. It's becoming colossal. [Like the "gigantic phallus," the "prick of great stature" whose form the chief cop is later urged to adopt.] . . . You've got secret judas holes in every partition [*cloison*]. Every wall, every mirror, is rigged. . . . You don't need me to tell you that brothel tricks are mainly mirror [*de glaces*] tricks. . . ." If you could tour around this column, you will head back to *The Balcony*, to read there ("THE ENVOY: It's reading or the Image that counts. History was lived so that a glorious page might be written, and then read." Farther on, Roger repeats the sentence and adds: "It's reading that counts. . . . CARMEN: The truth: that you're dead, or rather that you don't stop dying and that your image, like your name, resounds to infinity."), in the "stones" that "say," "familiarly," death upright, the bordel [*le claque*], the sound of bells [*cloches*], the apotheosis, the tomb as pedestal [*socle*], the mausoleum, the prelate's neck [*cou*], the collapse [*dégringolade*] of the Immaculate Conception, and so on, the letters and steps [*marches*] of "glory." For the first and last time, and as an example, here you are as if *forewarned* by this text of what clacks here—and decomposes the cadaver of the word (balc, talc, alga, clatter [*éclat*], glass, etc.) in every sense. You will have to do the work that remains on your own, and accuse yourself, as does he, as the one who writes, in your own tongue. At least. "*Perhaps I wanted to accuse myself in my own tongue.*" You will also have to work the word tongue like an organist

judges who interrogate it from apparently extrinsic instances (question about the classified—biographical, historical, economic, political, and so on—sub-

Einführung, as German philosophers say, introduction *into* Hegel. *Einführung* demands the accusative and so indicates the active movement of penetration. Not to stay here at or be content here with the skirt of the Hegelian thicket. Not to stop immediately in all the difficulties, intrinsic or extrinsic, intrinsically extrinsic—and supplementary—that the decision of such a stroke [*coup*] instigates. There have been many introductions to Hegel for sale and generally available. And the problem of the introduction in/to Hegel's philosophy is *all* of Hegel's philosophy: (the) *already* posed throughout, especially in his prefaces and forewords, introductions and preliminary concepts. So, already, one would be found entrained in the circle of the Hegelian beginning, sliding or endlessly atrip there. I mark the decision and interrupt the vertigo with a fictive rule [*règle*]: this operation—the *glas* of Sa, *glas* as Sa—is addressed to those who have not yet read, heard, or understood Hegel; this perhaps is the most general situation, in any case mine here and now.

In order to work on/in Hegel's name, in order to erect it, the time of a ceremony, I have chosen to draw on one thread. It is going to seem too fine, odd, and fragile. It is the law of the family: of Hegel's family, of the family in Hegel, of the concept family according to Hegel.

In the major expositions of the *Encyclopedia* or the [*Elements of the*] *Philosophy of Right*, the "objective spirit" is developed in three moments: abstract right (*Recht*), morality (*Moralität*), and *Sittlichkeit*—a term translated in various ways (ethics, ethical life, objective morality, *bonne moeurs*), but I won't try to translate it in my turn. (One day, elsewhere, I'll tell why I love this German word.) Now within *Sittlichkeit*, the third term and the moment of synthesis between right's formal objectivity and morality's abstract subjectivity, a syllogism in turn is developed.

Its first term is the family.
The second, civil or bourgeois society (*bürgerliche Gesellschaft*).
The third, the State or the constitution of the State (*Staatsverfassung*).

Even before analyzing these dialectical syllogisms and the architectonics to which they give rise, we see the stake and the interest of this familial moment. Its interpretation directly engages the whole Hegelian determination of right on one side, of politics on the other. Its place in the system's structure and develop-

ject). As for general textuality, perhaps the *seing* represents the case, the place for (topically and tropically) overlapping the intrinsic and the extrinsic.

Initialing the margin, the incessant operation: signing in the margin, exchanging the name against a revenue, paring down, trying to reduce the margin and letting oneself be rushed into the angles—daedalian frame.

Case and scrap [*recoupe*]. What remains of a signature?

First case: the signature belongs to the inside of that (picture, relievo, discourse, and so on) which it is presumed to sign. It is in the text, no longer signs, operates as an effect within the object, plays as a piece in what it claims to appropriate or to lead back to its origin. The filiation is lost. The *seing* is defalcated.

Second case: the signature holds itself, as is generally believed, outside the text. The signature emancipates as well the product that dispenses with the signature, with the name of the father or of the mother the product no longer needs to function. The filiation again gives itself up, is always betrayed by what remarks it.

In this double case the secreted loss of the remain(s) overlaps itself. There would be only excrement. If one wanted to press, the whole text (for example, when it signs itself Genet) would gather itself in such a "vertical coffin" (*Miracle of the Rose*) as the erection of a *seing*. The text re(mains)—falls (to the tomb), the signature re(mains)—falls

ment, in the encyclopedia, the logic, and the Hegelian ontotheology, is such that the displacements or the disimplications of which it will be the object would not know how to have a simply local character.

Before attempting an active interpretation, verily a critical displacement (supposing that is rigorously possible), we must yet patiently decipher this difficult and obscure text. However preliminary, such a deciphering cannot be neutral, neuter, or passive. It violently intervenes, at least in a minimal form: the choice of this place and this moment, the family, in the Hegelian systematics.

This choice is far from being innocent. Not only does it result from theoretical ulterior motives [arrière-pensées], undoubtedly also from some unconscious motivations that must be put in play and to work without any preliminary theorizing about it being possible.

The concept family very rigorously inscribes itself in the system: within the *Encyclopedia* and the *Philosophy of Right*, those final forms that are subsequent to the great *Logic*. Must the analysis be limited to this final and systematic placement?

The analysis can be limited in two ways. One could be satisfied with making the most of these last texts, or one could consider that we can read everything preceding as a development teleologically oriented, without rupture, without essential displacement, toward this final accomplishment.

One can dream of a channel between these two limits that as a matter of fact are only one. But there is no pure solution, no solution in principle [de principe] to such a problem.

What always remains irresoluble, impracticable, nonnormal, or nonnormalizable is what interests and constrains us here. Without paralyzing us but while forcing us on the *course* [démarche]: zigzagging, oblique to boot, jostled by the bank [rive] to be avoided, like a machine during a difficult maneuver. by à-coups, fits and starts, jolts, little successive jerks, while touching, tampering with the borders

We cannot feign to begin with the chronological beginning, pretty much with *The Life of Jesus*: there's no sense in privileging here the law of temporal or narrative unfolding that precisely has no internal and conceptual sense. This already has a resonance with Hegel's teaching. And at the limit, even if we accepted proceeding in that way, somewhere we would have to anticipate, even were it the end of the first sentence of the first text.

(tombs)—the text. The signature remain(s) resides and falls (to the tomb), the signature remain(s) house and tomb. The text labors to give the signature up as lost [en faire son deuil]. And reciprocally. Unending overlap [recoupe] of noun and verb, of the proper name and the common noun in the case of the cast-off [rebut].

The great stake of literary discourse—I do say discourse: the patient, crafty, quasi animal or vegetable, untiring, monumental, derisory too, but on the whole holding itself up to derision, transformation of his proper name, *rebus*, into things, into the name of things. The thing, here, would be the looking glass [glace], the ice [glace] in which the song sets, the heat of an appellation that bands itself erect [se bande] in the name.

Genet has often feigned to define the "magnifying" operation of his writing by the act of nomination. The allegation seems frequent enough that we could suspect it of a certain refrain-effect [effet de rengaine].

What is a refrain?

Of what does the act of "magnifying" nomination consist? Of giving the form of a common noun to a proper name? Or of the inverse? In both cases one (un)names, but is this, in both cases, to appropriate, expropriate, reappropriate? What?

What is a thing? What is the name of a thing?

Genealogy cannot begin with the father.

Anticipation or precipitancy (the risk of the precipice and the fall [*chute*]) is an irreducible structure of reading. And teleology does not only or always have the appeasing character one wants to give it. It can be questioned, denounced as a lure or an effect, but its threat cannot be reduced.

With the *telos* can also be found the cliff [*l'à-pic*]. Where one can get a foothold or fall (to the tomb).

In positing the teleological necessity *in effect* we are already in(to) Hegel. He did nothing but powerfully unfold the consequence of this proposition.

So we can neither avoid nor accept as rule or principle teleological anticipation, neither accept nor avoid as rule or principle the empirico-chronological delay of the narrative, the *récit*.

A bastard course.

Is there a place for the bastard in ontotheology or in the Hegelian family? That is a question to be left to one side, to be held on the margin or a leash when entering a true family or the family of truth. No doubt the question is not so exterior to that of the *Klang*; at least, without corresponding with the Hegelian concept of exteriority, its exteriority presses another exteriority toward the question's center.

A bastard path, then, that will have to feign to follow naturally the circle of the family, in order to enter it, or parcel it out [*partager*], or partake of [*partager*] it as one takes part in a community, holy communion, the last supper scene, or part [*partager*] it as one does by dissociating.

I shall say no more about procession or method. As Hegel would say, they will speak of (for) themselves while marching.

I begin with love.

This concept does not leave much room, despite appearances, for chitchat, or for declaration.

It is constructed in the third part of the *Philosophy of Right*, the part treating *Sittlichkeit*, after the first two parts had treated respectively abstract right and morality. *Sittlichkeit* relieves [*relève*], in departing from, *Moralität*. These two words are difficult to translate and even as words, if not as concepts, difficult to distinguish. Hegel explains himself here on a certain arbitrariness. And he does so by way of showing: (1) that he adhered to distinguishing the signifier from the concept, (2) that he did not entrust to etymology

For the moment, let's drop [*laissons tomber*] his personal case. When Genet gives names, he both baptizes and denounces. He gives the most: the name is not, as it seems on the first approach, a thing encountered in nature or acquired in commerce. The name seems produced, one time only, by an act without a past. There is no purer present, no generosity more inaugural. But a gift of nothing, of no thing, such a gift appropriates itself violently, harpoons, "arraigns" [*arraisonne*] what it seems to engender, penetrates and paralyzes with one stroke [*coup*] the recipient thus consecrated. Magnified, the recipient becomes somewhat the thing of the one who names or surnames him, above all if this is done with a name of a thing.

"I was chaste.

"Armand was away on a trip. Although I heard that he was sometimes called by other names, we shall keep this one. Am I myself not up to my fifteenth or sixteenth name, including Jean Gallien, my current one?" It will be necessary to hollow out the arbitrariness of this name—Gallien—if not of this siglum J.G. And what if this random pseudonym formed something like the matrical first name of the text?

As for the siglum in *Funeral Rites* it is J.D. Jean D. "The escutcheon with a capital D embroidered in silver had been, for a day, the family's blazon." "My contact with the concrete wounds my sensibility cruelly: the black escutcheon adorned with the silver-embroidered 'D' that I saw on the hearse. . . ." The capital D, to which falls representing the family name, does not perforce revert to the father. In any case, it concerns the mother, and she is the one to benefit from its title, "the mother was ennobled by this escutcheon on which the capital D was embroidered in silver." As for the one who organizes the *Funeral*—i.e., literary—*Rites* of J.D., is one to say it is the author, the narrator, the narratee, the reader, but of what? He is at once the double of the dead (*colossos*), the one who remains alive after him, his son, but also his father and his mother. "The star of my friendship rose up larger and rounder into my sky. I was pregnant with a feeling that could, without my being surprised, make me give birth [*accoucher*] to a strange but viable and certainly [*à coup sûr*] beautiful being, Jean's being its father vouched for that."

He has always been afraid that someone would steal his death, and since this could not fail to happen to someone who has only one of them, he has, in advance, occupied all the places where that (*ça*) dies. Well played? Who makes, who says, the dead better

the right to regulate a concept's content. What a word properly means (to say) cannot be known by referring back to some would-be primitivity or authentic primordiality. This did not prevent him from playing with dictionaries in a productive and genetic, verily poetic, way. That the same word or two words of analogous root can have two conceptually different, verily opposite, significations proves that a word is never a concept. Which immediately disqualifies the etymological instance, at least as philosophical, logical, conceptual recourse. Hegel says this at the end of the Introduction, when according to the proceeding of all his systematic expositions, he presents the schema of the internal division, of self-differentiation as self-determination and self-production of the concept. When the *Einleitung* (introduction) becomes *Einteilung* (division). Then he explains the passage from *Moralität* to *Sittlichkeit* and tries to justify the almost arbitrary choice of these two words. Because this choice is arbitrary, the translations fluctuate. "*Moralität* and *Sittlichkeit*, which perhaps usually pass current as synonyms (*die gewöhnlich etwa als gleichbedeutend gelten*), are taken here in essentially different senses (*sind hier in wesentlich verschiedenem Sinne genommen*). Yet even commonplace thinking (*Vorstellung*)

Kant's critique of practical philosophy organizes the whole *Philosophy of Right*: it insures the passage from *Moralität* to *Sittlichkeit*. For Hegel, Kant cannot, does not want to, think the possibility of *Sittlichkeit* and so cannot, nor want to, for reasons to be analyzed (with or without Hegel), think this essential moment of *Sittlichkeit* that the family is. So there would not be any Kantian concept of the family, any philosophical, logically deducible, and rigorously assignable concept that escapes the chitchat of an empiric anthropology. There is no Kant family in the sense that there is a Hegel family: what the latter implies—love, (monogamous) marriage, and above all the child—would be inconceivable to Kant. Save by empiric and extrinsic accident: like a bastard.

At the end of his life, Hegel responds to a natural son come to be acknowledged: I know I had had something to do with your birth, but previously I was the accidental thing, now I am the essential one

seems to be distinguishing them; Kant generally prefers to use the word *Moralität* and, since the principles of action in his philosophy are always limited to this concept, they make the standpoint of *Sittlichkeit* completely impossible, in fact they explicitly [*ausdrücklich*, formally] nullify and spurn it. But even if *Moralität* and *Sittlichkeit* meant the same thing (*gleichbedeutend*) by derivation (*ihrer Etymologie nach*), that would in no way hinder them, once they had become different words, from

being used for different concepts."

Is the question of vocabulary here marginal?

Hegel has not skirted the problem of philosophical language, of philosophy's tongue. Is it a natural language (tongue) or a formal one?

Here the important thing is that Hegel has not separated this question from a family question.

The thing: magnificent and classed, at once raised above all taxonomy, all nomenclature, and already identifiable in an order. To give a name is always, like any birth (certificate), to sublimate a singularity and to inform against it, to hand it over to the police. All the police forces in the world can be routed by a surname, but even before they know it, a secret computer, at the moment of baptism, will have kept them up to date.

To "arraign" is to ask for identity papers, for an origin and a destination. It is to claim to recognize a proper name. How do you name without arraigning? Is that possible?

When Genet gives his characters proper names, kinds of singularities that are capitalized common nouns, what is he doing? What does he give us to read beneath the visible cicatrix of a decapitalization that is forever threatening to open up again? If he calls Mimosa, Querelle, Divine, Green-Eyes, Culafroy, Our-Lady-of-the-Flowers, Divers,

sibylline effect of arbitrariness in the immaculate choice, in the conception of syllables that name and open glory. The convention dethrones and crowns [*couronne*] at once. The ablation of the first name, the surname alone doing the job, accumulates the powers of the overlap, remarks and abolishes, to the point of infinity, oneness in the common, scatters it in the namelessness of the variable and diversifiable, from the moment the singular individual—a prisoner under common law—is named Divers. A nomination more solemn, more inaugural, and also more institutive, when the thesis of the name erects the attribute, the adjective, the epithet, what is not yet even the name of the thing but the supervening accident that unnecessarily adds itself to the substance

I begin by accumulating the results of his analysis: the family speaks and does not speak; it is family starting from the moment it speaks—passing from *Klang*, if one likes, to *Sprache*, from resonance to language [*langue*]—but it destroys itself as family the moment it speaks and abandons *Klang*. Like natural language, like language in general, it ceases to be what it is the moment it posits itself as such; it denies itself as nature in becoming what it is naturally, just like (the) nature itself (of the remain(s)) after all.

The Jena texts describe the development of the family within the *Volksgeist*, the spirit of a people. The family is essentially spiritual. And language too: "Only as the product or work (*Werk*) of a people is speech the ideal [*ideale*] *existence of the spirit.*" So spiritual language is natural as well. Belonging to the people, the family then is always speaking; there is no biological family. But the language it speaks is not, at least so it seems, formal or arbitrary. Nevertheless, by reason of the structure of language's internal development, what is elaborated there destroys itself in that very elaboration or rather submits itself to the process [*procès*] of the *Aufhebung*, relieves itself.

there is no family without *Geist*, no *Geist* without family. *Geist, esprit,* spirit: at once the possibility of repetition (tradition, history) and of breath [*souffle*] holding itself back in the sonorous vibration (inspiration, expiration). *Geist* is also consonant with death according to Hegel, spiritual life with natural death. In order to hear, to understand something according to the spirit, smell some expiration, some expiring repetition.

Let this not prevent using the same words for different concepts, and in order to betray language, homonyms and false etymologies for analogous concepts.

Thus words are unchained. They drive the dictionary wild. Language [*langue*] has not taken place, has no place, has no sure place. Discourse is the giver of sense, but as a guidebook—or an informer—comes to betray a network. *Traditio* hands over, delivers (*livre, überliefert*) the sense, but in order to lose the institution in the repetition. The (last supper) scene of language must always be made to depend on one too many [*Il faut toujours tabler la scène de la langue sur un de trop*]. The opposition (language/discourse) denounces itself, itself and all the others

In positing itself as a system of natural signs, as existing in exteriority, language raises itself to the concept (ideal interior signification) and from then on denies itself as a system of natural signs.

The thing (the referent) is relieved (*relevée, aufgehobene*) in the sign: raised, elevated, spiritualized, magnified, embalmed, interiorized, idealized, named since the name accomplishes the sign. In the sign, the (exterior) signifier is relieved by signification, by the (ideal [*idéel*]) signified sense, *Bedeutung*, the concept. The concept relieves the sign that relieves the thing. The signified relieves the signifier that relieves the referent. "In this way, then, speech is reconstructed (*rekonstruiert*) in a people, in that although it is the ideal [*ideelle*] nullification (*Vernichten*) of the external, it is itself *something outward* (ein Äusseres) that must be nullified (*vernichtet*), relieved (*aufgehoben werden*), in order to become meaningful language (*um zur bedeutenden Sprache zu werden*), toward what it is in

and can always detach itself from the substance, in order to fall (to the tomb). What is the epithet? What is its status? In other words, how is status conferred on it? And what if, inversely, all status were from the epithesis? "The fact that his name was Divers conferred on him an earthly and nocturnal dream quality sufficient to enchant me. For one isn't called Georges Divers, or Jules or Joseph Divers, and that nominal singleness set him on a throne, as if glory had recognized him when he was still in the children's hell. The name was almost a nickname, royal, brief, haughty, a convention. And so he galloped in and took possession of the world, that is, of me. And he dwelt within me. Henceforth, I enjoyed him as if I were pregnant with him" (*Miracle of the Rose*). "Nominal singleness" stiffens, tightens the name, in one single piece, toward the point or the infinite. This singleness reduces the classifying gap [*écart*] between the name and the first name. One's own proper, sublime, glorious body is gathered into an organless vocable. And is signed in a monogram. "The black escutcheon adorned with the silver-embroidered 'D,'" the "ivy monograms" of the *Funeral Rites* form the ideal of the *seing*. Querelle de Brest "took his knife and cut a highly stylized design of his initials into the humid bark of an acacia. . . . Querelle kept a double watch on himself. . . . thought offered up to the Holy Virgin. Around his own altar, Querelle embroidered a protective veil, with his own monogram on it, equivalent to the gold-thread on blue altar cloths, the celebrated: M."

and so on, does he violently uproot a social identity, a right to absolute proprietorship? Is that the most effective political operation, the most significant revolutionary practice? Or else, but this is the refrain of contraries ceaselessly overlapping, does he baptize them with the pomp and the sacredness—glory

the word *glory* he uses proportionally, almost as often as the translator of the Gospel, of whom he is in sum the most destructive parodying double. I see him work (over) the Gospels and all the mythological texts, of which he is a connoisseur and which he inhabits particularly by name, like a miner who is not sure of getting out from the depths of the earth alive, and who, in his gallery, essays explosions, blastings. *Gallery*, however, must be deciphered; the gallery speaks, writes. On its legendary walls. Writes to him, says much to him. Why (what was he going to do there?) is he so fond of galleries? Not only those that keep you, orient you, and

(it)self according to its concept (*zu dem, was sie an sich, ihrem Begriffe nach ist*); thus language is in the people, as a total other (*als ein total Anderes*) than itself, and becomes totality when it is relieved (*aufgehoben*) as other, and comes to fruition in its concept."

Language accomplishes itself, thus becomes signifying only by relieving within itself the (sensible, exterior) signifier, traversing it and denying it with a view to the concept. With a view also to its very own proper concept of language. Language becomes language only by deleting/conserving itself in the concept. *Traditio* is *Aufhebung*. Language rejoins its own proper concept only by going to the end of what induces it, by going to the end of its own proper internal negativity, according to a schema of the essence as negativity that verifies itself and unceasingly elaborates itself.

This becoming (*traditio*) of language, or rather of the linguistic, produces itself then in the heart [*sein*] of a people, of a people's spirit that would not be posited without this becoming. Linguistic negativity is not reduced either to the rooting or the uprooting of a language with regard to the ground of the historical community. Uprooting, denaturalization, explantation of a language achieves the rooting essence of language. Language belongs to a people as finite totality: thus it is a "natural language," a finite, particular, determinate language. But it ceases to be such as soon as it posits itself as such; it achieves its essence as "natural" language only by recovering from this [*s'en relevant*], by relieving the natural limits of its system, by de-limiting, de-bordering, overflowing itself toward the concept's universality. Language then is immediately universal language that destroys within itself natural language.

The dialectic of language, of the tongue [*langue*], is dialectophagy.

Without this overflow of language, of the tongue that swallows itself and eats itself, that is silent, tongue-tied, or dies, that also vomits a natural remain(s)—its own—it can neither assimilate nor

without the conception of the concept, it is a dead language, writing, and defunct speech, or resonance without signification (*Klang* and not *Sprache*). An affinity here between *Klang* and writing. Insofar as the *Klingen* of *Klang* resists, withstands conception, it plays for the Hegelian logos the role of mute or mad sound, a kind of mechanical automaton that triggers

make equal to the universal power of the concept, language would not be language— a living language hears, understands itself. Language would not be what it is in (it)self, conformably to its concept (*Begriff*), to what in it conceives itself, grasps, takes possession of itself, catches and comprehends itself, elevates itself, leaves with one wing stroke [*d'un coup d'aile*] the natal ground and carries off its natural body.

A people's natural language becomes what it is, thinks itself, exposes itself as what it was to be, what it will have had to

threaten you in the bosom [*sein*] of the earth, but also those for which one lays oneself open to the theater, those that architecture associates with boxes [*loges*], homes [*logis*], balconies, all the galleries of language, all the constructions of simulacra to one side [*à l'écart*], all the dissimulated shelters, more or less fake, in the corners: ". . . the most meager shelter became habitable. I would sometimes adorn it with an artful comfort drawn from what was peculiar to it: a box [*loge*] in the theater, the chapel of a cemetery, a cave, an abandoned quarry, a freight car and so on. Obsessed by the idea of a home [*logis*], I would embellish, in thought, and in keeping with its own architecture, the one I had just chosen. While everything was being denied me, I would wish I were meant for the fluting [*cannelures*] of the fake columns that ornament facades, for the caryatids, the balconies, the freestone, for the heavy bourgeois assurance which these things express" (*The Thief's Journal*).

is his word—that he always confers on nomination?

The statement, "I wanted them to have the right to the honors of the Name," is multiplied, metamorphosed endlessly, to the point of obsessing the totality of the corpus. The given proper (sur) name relieves the head that falls (to the tomb) on the scaffold, but simultaneously redoubles, through the decision to nominate, the arbitrariness of the sentence, consecrates and glorifies the fall, cuts one more time, and engraves — on a literary monument. Swooping down like a capital sentence and a last judgment, the surname sounds better, bursts your tympanum with its tocsin. All this will have resounded in the striking [*frappe*] of a signature.

"*Tocsin* . . . n. 1. The noise of a bell [*cloche*] that is rung with hasty and redoubled strokes [*coups*]. . . . 'One says *to ring the tocsin* . . . but it is better to write *toquesin*; and if, moreover, by adding a *g* one writes *toquesing*, one

be, by becoming other than itself, making itself artificial, rational, universal, the moment the people dies as natural people. A people dies as natural people in universalizing its own products through language and labor. Language and labor, in the Jena field of analysis, sound the end of the natural people by positing the people as such, by permitting the people to make itself recognized and named as such.

and operates itself without meaning (to say) anything.

Fall, in this case, of the tongue [langue]

Now this passage within a people's language had already opened the path from the family to the people. The movement by which the family posits itself as such, gives itself a head, regroups itself into a family of families, a sort of hierarchized clan that becomes a people, this movement is also an *Aufhebung*, the retention of what slips away [*s'écoule*] as it slips away. This sort of historic screen [*claie*] or floodgate [*écluse*] does not let pass what passes or lets pass what does not pass.

In order to explain Hegel's disqualification of etymology and his assuming a certain arbitrariness in the use of words, one must therefore take charge of and the consequence of all his theory of language and, in this theory, of the whole procession of the negative (the *Aufhebung*). So no longer is there any opposition that holds, no longer any obligation to choose between natural language and formal language. Natural language bears and affects [*touche*] within itself the sign of its own death; its body is suited for resonating and in so doing for raising its natural corpse to the height of the concept, for universalizing and rationalizing it in the very time of its decomposition.

This dialectical law bends and reflects itself, applies itself to its very own statements, to its very own metalinguistic effects, for example to that seemingly singular signifier that is called *Aufhebung* in German and that permits designating, Hegel delights greatly in this, a law of essential and speculative universality in the heart [*sein*] of a natural language, of a people's language. A people that has the *Aufhebung* in its throat denies itself as a particular people, strangles and depopulates itself, but in order to extend further its imperium and deploy infinitely its range.

Aufhebung is not the sole example of this law. Is it even, an example?

Remain(s), then, the general question: how can the idiom of a familial generation think itself, that is, deny itself while erecting itself in the universality of the speculative type?

It (*Ça*) would begin with love.

Love is an essential predicate of the concept family, that is, of an essential moment of *Sittlichkeit*.

How is the passage (*Übergang*) from *Moralität* to *Sittlichkeit* induced? In *Moralität*, a subjective instance of the Kantian type,

Ascension of the glorious body, after forty days.

"He uttered, for the first time, following the name Baillon, the words: 'Known as Our-Lady-of-the-Flowers.' Our-Lady was given the death penalty. The jury was standing. It was the apotheosis. It's all over. When Our-Lady-of-the-Flowers was given back to the guards, he seemed to them invested with a sacred character, like the kind that expiatory victims, whether goat, ox, or child, had in olden times and which kings and Jews still have today. The guards spoke to him and served him as if, knowing he was laden with the weight of the sins of the world, they had wanted to bring down upon themselves the benediction of the Redeemer. Forty days later, on a spring evening, the machine was set up in the prison yard. At dawn, it was ready to cut. Our-Lady-of-the-Flowers had his head cut off by a real knife. And nothing happened. What would be the point? There is no need for the veil of the temple to be ripped from top to bottom because a god gives up the ghost. All that this can prove is the bad quality of the cloth and its deterioration. Though it behooves me to be indifferent, still I would not mind if an irreverent scapegrace kicked through it and ran off shouting about the miracle. It's flashy and would make a very good framework for the Legend."

will come closer to the etymology; for it is a Gascon word, composed of toquer, in place of which we say to touch or strike, and of sing, which signifies bell, and mainly a big bell, since we willingly ring the biggest bell when afraid.' H. Est, Precellence, p. 186.

"—E. Toquer, and the Lat. signum, taken, in the Middle Ages, in the sense of bell." Littré

The one who names, denames — the great denominator officiates very close to the scaffold, at the moment when *that falls (to the tomb)* (*ça tombe*).

the Good, the universal substance of freedom (no freedom without relation to the Good and vice-versa), still keeps its abstract form. Reciprocally, moral conscience, the exigence of universal objectivity, remains formal and virtual, therefore immoral. It does not overflow its own one-sided subjectivity. It becomes the contrary of what it is (immoral) to the very extent it remains enclosed in its own proper side. Kant thus retains *Moralität* in the heart [*sein*] of a certain one-sided abstraction. The Good on one side, moral conscience on the other stay separate, facing, taking account of, but inaccessible to, each other. So they are not yet what they are. They are not "explicitly posited (*gesetzt*)" as what however they are in (them)selves. This position, this being posited (*Gesetzwerden*), they attain only in their negativity. "That is to say, in their *one-sidedness* (einseitig), when each must not have in it what it is *in itself*—the Good without subjectivity and a determinate character, and the determining principle, subjectivity without the being in itself— and when both build themselves into a totality for itself, they are relieved (*aufheben*), and thereby de-posed (*herabsetzen*), reduced to moments, to moments of the *concept* which becomes manifest as their unity. . . ."

The two sides face each other without the ability to rejoin or complete themselves, like two abstract halves or partitions of one same spiritual body. They must deny their one-sidedness in the concept, must reconstitute in it their menaced or morseled oneness.

The first synthesis that permits binding [*lier*] them or reading [*lire*] them together, thinking them as the flanks of one and the same continuous piece [*tenant*], their first integration (*Integration*), is *Sittlichkeit*. In *Sittlichkeit* the Idea of freedom becomes actually present, is no longer only in the head of subjective individuals. "The fact that this Idea is the *truth* of the concept of freedom is something which, in philosophy, must be *proved* [an object of demonstration, *ein Bewiesenes*], not adopted from feeling or elsewhere. The deduction [of these moments] is contained only in the fact that right and the moral self-consciousness [the first two moments of the philosophy of right] both display in themselves their regression to this Idea as their *outcome*, their *result*. Those who hope to be able to dispense with proof and deduction in philosophy show thereby that they are still far from knowing the first thing about what philosophy is. On the rest argue (*reden*) they may, but in philosophy they have no right to join in the argument if they wish to argue without the concept."

Sittlichkeit—the family constitutes its first moment—is thus the idea of freedom,

the beginning—before it the *déjà*, the already—befalls, as always, by the instance of the [*au titre du*] result. The rebound of the *already* should not leave any remain(s). In speculative dialectics, the result is not a remain(s), the remain(s) does not result. At least as remain(s). If it could result, it would relieve its remnance [*restance*]. A

That institution, a law posing the name while deposing the head, does not dispense with a neck [*cou*].

The division becomes only a little more complex when the denominator (the Cratylean nomothete) institutes or erects himself in his own proper signature.

Colossal habitat: the masterpiece.
He bands erect in his *seing*, but also occupies it like a sarcophagus.

The form of the name—a place of solitary confinement — eats the body and holds it upright.

Glory again, with which the syllabary is initiated, in the future perfect, in the publishing contract, signed with the institution (family and city), that is, with the funeral rite, the burial organization. Tearing up the contract, the literary operation reverts to no more than confirming it indefatigably, in the margin, with a siglum. "There is a book entitled *I'll Have a Fine Funeral*. We are acting with a view to a fine funeral, to formal obsequies. They will be the masterpiece, in the strict sense of the word, the major [*capitale*] work, quite rightly the crowning glory of our life. I must die in an apotheosis, and it doesn't matter whether I know glory before or after my death as long as *I know* that I'll have it, and I shall have it if I sign a contract with a firm of undertakers that will attend to fulfilling my destiny, to rounding it off." At the moment of the "theatrical stunt [*coup*]," in *Funeral Rites*, when they "slid" the coffin onto the catafalque—"the conjuring away of the coffin"—before its reduction, as with the coffin of "*Saint-Osmose*" (a fictive letter about the Golden Legend—published in Italian) into a box of matches, "Jean's death was duplicating itself in another death." The dead Jean whose corpse is banded erect and who therefore takes "the shape and consistency of a milk-almond in its cloths and wrappings," "a soft, compact almond," is watched over, written, banded erect by the other, by the friendship gone to the head of the other ("my friendship went to my head (as one says: reseda goes to my head)"), who "'love[s] the executioner,'" wants to make "'love with him, at dawn!'" And who also bands erect.

doubtlessly inevitable consequence of an *al-ready* conceived as origin, beginning, ground in the sense of presentation

but of freedom as the Good living, present, and concrete in the present (*vorhandenen*) world, which implies an actual elaboration (*Wirklichkeit*), action, operation (*Handeln*). In that moment there, the concrete substance of morals (*Sittlichkeit*), such as it is produced and remains in the *Vorhandensein* of the world, exceeds the *Meinen* (according to Hegel's wordplay between the opining self's subjective wavering and the "my own, mine"); constrains the subjective caprice and the floating velleity (*Belieben*); and takes on stability in laws, in organizations that last (*Einrichtungen*), in *institutions*.

The stability, the permanence of the transsubjective institution overflows, de-borders, individuals, imposes itself on them, enchains them, to be sure, but with the force and dignity of the rational. The institution erects its freedom in the individual and makes that freedom stand upright. The individual subject is not subject to that institution as to the empirical force of the natural elements, the sun, the moon, mountains and rivers. In *Sittlichkeit* the authority of laws is "infinitely higher, because natural objects conceal rationality under the cloak of contingency and exhibit it only in their utterly *external* and *singularized* way." This rationality no longer conceals itself, but on the contrary unveils itself in the institution.

In the family, love forms the first moment of this rationality. There is no love nor family in physical or biological nature. *Logos*, reason, freedom are love's milieu. The *Encyclopedia* states it precisely: in the animal kingdom, generation, the sex relationship, the process of copulation that, like a syllogism's copula, gathers together the genus with itself—they all engulf individuals in a death straight out [*sans phrase*]. Unlike the human, rational family, animal copulation does not give rise to any higher determination. Animal copulation leaves behind itself no monument, no burial place, no institution, no law that opens and assures any history. It names nothing. "The genus preserves itself only through the perishing of the individuals, which fulfill their determination [destination, *Bestimmung*] in the process of generation, and in so far as they have no higher determination than this, pass on to death."

But death does not appear to them as such. On the contrary, the limit that *Sittlichkeit* imposes on empiric subjectivity, finally its very death, opens the relation of subjectivity to its own substantial freedom. Mortality is experienced in *Sittlichkeit* as a freedom-effect. Individual subjectivity finds in *Sittlichkeit*'s apparently suppressive objectivity (its right, its police, its prisons, its penal colonies) the condition of its freedom, of its truth, of its essentiality. What

Next, in drawing on "What Remained . . . ," let us not forget that the "vertical coffin" described a prison cell ("I entered one of those narrow cells, a vertical coffin"): ". . . nothing tender, no affection. Neither in regard to that form assumed by the other — or its prison. Or its tomb [*sa tombe*]? On the contrary, I tended to

The other also bands erect. In front of him, in front of flowers, in front of nothing. "In the presence of the flowers I banded erect, and it made me feel ashamed, but I felt that I could oppose the stiffness of the corpse only with the stiffness of my verge. I banded erect and desired nobody." The other also bands erect, such is the question of the noun (in all genders and kinds) and the verb. Banding erect in front of the flower and the corpse of his double, a colossal homonym itself erected in its theatrical adversity, is what can only be observed from a certain angle, also a certain lacuna in the tongue [*langue*], which we must now try to recognize. All writing is perhaps caught, enclosed in this scene that one could still try to name. For the first name is not sufficient to classify it. Nor the noun. The one has to band the other erect

show myself as pitiless with it as I was with that form that answered to my name and wrote these lines."

Between the two effects of that so-called literature of theft, betrayal, denunciation, is there a decision to be made? Expropriation or reappropriation? Decapitation or recapitation? Dissemination or recapitulation, recapitalization? How are we to cut through to a decision?

Apparently, yielding to the Passion of Writing, Genet has made himself into a flower. While tolling the *glas* (knell), he has put into the ground, with very great pomp, but also as a flower, his proper name, the names and nouns of common law, language, truth, sense, literature, rhet-

"The executioner follows close behind me, Claire! The executioner's by my side. . . . They'll all be wearing crowns, flowers, oriflammes, banners. They'll toll the knell [*glas*]. The burial will unfold its pomp. It's beautiful, isn't it? . . . The executioner's lulling me. I'm being ac-

"The *right of individuals* to be *subjectively destined* [*determined*] *to freedom* is fulfilled ([*hat seine*] *Erfüllung*) when they belong to an actual ethical order (*sittlichen Wirklichkeit*), because their *conviction of their freedom* finds its *truth* in such an objective order (*Objectivität*), and it is in an ethical order (*Sittlichen*) that they are *actually* (*wirklich*) in possession (*besitzen*) of *their own* essence (*ihr eigenes Wesen*), their own *inner* universality" (*Philosophy of Right*).

denies and cuts [*coupe*] subjectivity of/from itself is also what raises and accomplishes it.

The proper essence, the property, the propriety of individual subjectivity, far from restricting itself to that and simply choking [*étrangler*], appropriates it-self, becomes what it is, possesses itself in the form of its contrary or negation. It possesses itself in that form: *besitzen* is extremely powerful, and this sense of possession, of private property, of goods or of a having that constructs the whole problematic of the family must not be effaced. The subjective appropriates itself in *Sittlichkeit*'s objectivity; the individual possesses itself in the institution's generality; freedom in a law's obligatory regularity. This appropriation that, in order to keep upright, to have constancy, essence, existence, substance, makes it necessary to be raised into its contrary, this appropriation is also an interiorization and an idealization: a magnification, since here the ideal causes growth, enlargement. Negativity erects one in the other. Here dialecticalness is marked by *Sittlichkeit*'s objectivity (*Objektivität*) being at the same time the inner universality (*innere Allgemeinheit*) of the individual subject, of the proper name thus positing and recognizing itself in that universality.

We have not yet come to the family. Only to the general concept *Sittlichkeit* that defines the general field in which something like a family upsurges.

Is it by chance that, in the paragraphs of the *Philosophy of Right* that present the concept *Sittlichkeit*, even before it is a question of family, an almost proverbial or legendary citation appeals to the father and to the son's education? It is a Remark following a paragraph. Education is also a constituting/deconstituting process of the family, an *Aufhebung* by which the family accomplishes itself, *raises itself* in destroying itself or falling (to the tomb) as family. *As* family: the *as*, the *comme*, the *as such* of the essentiality, of the essential property or propriety, since it raises only in crossing out, is itself the *as* only insofar as other than what it is; it phenomenalizes the phenomenalization it discovers only in engulfing that phenomenalization in darkness or causing it to be engulfed. The *as* appropriates itself only in expropriation.

The father loses his son like that (*comme ça*): in gaining him, in educating him, in raising him, in involving him in the family circle, which comes down, in the logic of the *Aufhebung*, to helping him leave, to pushing him outside while completely retaining him. The father helps his son, takes him by the hand in order to

oric, and, if possible, the remain(s).

Or so at least it appears. And this would have begun with poisoning the flowers of rhetoric or poetics. Parodied, altered, transplanted, these quickly begin to rot, to resemble those mortuary wreaths [*couronnes*] that are thrown over the walls of the cemetery. These flowers are neither artificial nor entirely natural. Why say "flowers of rhetoric"? And what would the flower be when it becomes merely one of the "flowers of rhetoric"?

claimed. I'm pale and I'm going to die." At the moment of the *glas*, let oneself be lulled. By an executioner. Let oneself be lulled, verily be given the breast [*sein*] by an executioner: by the one who, do not forget, enables having a name. The name is given near the scaffold. The one who gives the name and the *seing* brings his blade next to your neck [*cou*]. To divide you. And with the same gesture, he transforms you into a god. Now one has only one executioner —as one has only one mother—and it is therefore the first. And whatever draws near his blade, never castrating in the present in order to elaborate the decapitation, will (should) have to be, like the mother, like an infant, virgin. Like Solange in *The Maids*, Our-Lady-of-the-Flowers "loved his executioner, his first executioner. . . . Exactly what is an executioner? A child dressed as a Fatal Sister, an innocent . . . a poor, a humble fellow."

In *Saint Genet*, the question of the flower, the anthological question, is, among others, infallibly avoided. Along with those of "psychoanalysis" and "literature," by the most agile and intelligent reading in phenomenological ontology of the epoch, in the French style. One development, however, just misses this question. Note that it starts in this way: "There

destroy the family in accomplishing it within what dissolves it: first bourgeois or civil society (*bürgerliche Gesellschaft*), then the *State* that accomplishes *Sittlichkeit* in "relieving the family and bourgeois society," in magnifying them.

Here is the remark: an out-of-place hors d'oeuvre, like a citational example, then like an addition to a philosophical and speculative paragraph, finally because its content is "familial," borrowed from a particular determination of *Sittlichkeit*. Now *Sittlichkeit*, for the moment, is defined only in a preliminary and general way. This anticipation cannot be insignificant.

"When a father inquired about the best method of educating his son in ethical conduct (*seinen Sohn sittlich zu erziehen*), a Pythagorean replied: 'Make him a *citizen of a state with good laws* (*eines Staats von guten Gesetzen*).' (The phrase has also been put in the mouth of others.)"

in his hand, in the manuscript, Hegel adds this —it will not be found in the French translations: "Others—i.e. Socrates." By right of the legend, taking into account the system, I work here then with the handwritten or oral remarks added by Hegel, as it were, in the margin of his principal text. I work *mit Hegels eigenhändigen Notizen und den mündlichen Zusätzen* unavailable in French (and incomplete in the English). Readers concerned about philological and editorial authentifications will always be able to protest or consider them fictions. The burden of proof devolves on those readers

This remark illustrates the general law, the law of the law: individual subjectivity accomplishes in truth its freedom in the universality of *Sittlichkeit* that denies that subjectivity.

The family is the first moment of this process. The first of the syllogism's three moments (family, bourgeois society, State) articulates itself in three moments or instances that are going to accomplish that first moment by denying it: marriage, family property, the education of children. But the dialectical unity of these three moments, what makes the family be what it is in its outburst, the unity of its syllogistic self-destruction, is love. A felt unity, or rather a unity that feels, a unity to be felt, a unity of self-feeling (*sich* empfindende Einheit), a unity that feels itself.

To know what love is, then, one needs to know what *feeling* is, or what self-feeling is.

But that will truly not be known before knowing what love is, that is, what the family is. One only feels (oneself) in the family.

What is the family?

"The ethical (*sittliche*) substance, as containing independent self-consciousness united with its concept, is the *actual spirit* (wirkliche Geist) of a family and a people."

Spirit can attain its actuality only in the family and the people. It would remain abstract, would strangle itself in singularity. The Remark of this paragraph adds that one must not raise oneself "atomistically" from singularity considered as a foundation (a non-

remains the simple possibility of *not* reading him. That is the only risk he runs, and it is a big one. But, in the last analysis, whether he is read depends *on him*, on him alone." Verily. Two figures of the flower are then reduced to the most conventional semantic content, crushed, in the course of the dissertation, between an ontological reading and a poetico-rhetorical one, each of which verifies its homology with the other: "The structure of the poetic sentence very accurately reflects the ontological structure of saintliness." Whether it is a matter of the flowers with which the poor old woman is covered ("'perhaps my mother'"), or of a "logical" paradox of the type "'the gardener is the loveliest rose in his garden,'" the question, as Sartre puts it, of knowing why the flower is "the poetic object par excellence" shifts between a pre-Heideggerian misontologism and a vague Mallarméism. There is evoked the "'vibratory disappearance'" and the flower absent from all bouquets; "therein lies all the poetry of Genet."

"Such a flower always bears its double within itself, whether it be seed or type . . . and by virtue of the repetition in which it endlessly puts itself into *abyme*, no language can reduce in (it)self the strict-ure of an anthology. This supplement of a code which traverses its own field, endlessly displaces its closure, breaks its line, opens its circle, and no ontology will have been able to reduce it." (Offered with grafts, white mythology

But what is poetry, once the flower is "the poetic object par excellence"? What is rhetoric, if the flower (of rhetoric) is the figure of figures and the place of places? How is this *effect* of transcendental excellence to be read, how is it elaborated? Why does the flower dominate all the fields to which it nonetheless belongs? Why does it stop belonging to the series of bodies or objects of which it forms a part?

spiritual point of view), but must proceed from spirit as the synthesis of the singular and the universal. The concept of the Idea is spirit, but spirit as it knows itself and is actual (*als sich Wissendes und Wirkliches*). Now it can know itself and become actual only insofar as it objectifies itself. This objectification (*Objektivierung*) produces itself through the "form of its moments (*durch die Form seiner Momente*)." In becoming an object for itself, spirit issues from, goes out of, itself. But it does so in order to remain (in) itself, to return to and become equal to itself. Here this very general procession of the Hegelian spirit has *Sittlichkeit* for its principal stage or station.

But as every sally of the spirit outside itself has the general form of its other, to wit, nature; as nature is the spirit outside itself but also a moment of the spirit's return to self, so *Sittlichkeit* will entail this naturalness. That will be a spirit-nature. Its naturalness will resolve itself, reabsorb itself, spiritualize itself in proportion as *Sittlichkeit* will develop itself through the form of its moments, will exhaust the inner negativity that works (over) it, will produce itself by denying itself as nature. Each of its three moments will mark a progress in this relief [*relève*] of the naturalness. *Wirklichkeit*, actuality, the *Wirken* of *Wirklichkeit* will be the operation of the negativity reappropriating the spirit, bringing it back home to itself, (close) by [*auprès de*] itself, through its ethical objectification. Having denied itself in naturalizing itself and objectifying itself,

why is the reconstitution of a Hegelian process written more easily in the future? Narrative ease? Pedagogical ease? Why does a philosopher so hard on narrative, on *récit*—he always opposes it to the concept—why does he incite us to use a kind of conceptual narration?

When Hegel is explained, it is always in a seminar and in telling students: the history of the concept, the concept of history.

Rearing (the student), in French *élève*: that is the word I am treating here, like the thing, in every sense.

Rearing (the student), *l'élève*. What is *élever* in general (*élevage, élévation, élèvement, breeding, elevation, education, upbringing*)? Against what is rearing (*une élève*) practiced? To what is it answerable [*De quoi relève-t-elle*]? What does it relieve? What is *relever une élève*, relieving a rearing?

There is some lightness in all this. The dream of the eagle is alleviating. Wherever it (*ça*) falls (to the tomb). And is sublimating.

When a future is used for the student, it is a grammatical ruse of reason: the sense that reason will have meant (to say) is, in truth, the future perfect, the future anterior. The encyclopedic version of the greater *Logic* (circular pedagogy, for the student) narrates itself in the future perfect

spirit will deny its negation by returning to itself through the less and less abstract form (*Form*) of its moments. The spirit's general at-home-with-itself is not the family at-home-with-itself. The latter however is a determinate representation of the former, and this representative relation precisely opens the question.

Love is in sight: it cannot be thought in its concept (the concept of self-feeling that is not affected by it) without taking into account this relieving negativity. If *Sittlichkeit* is a relieving naturalization

The flower is *(de)part(ed)*. It holds, from its being-(de)part(ed), the force of a transcendental excrescence that only makes it seem such (transcendental) and that no longer even has to be deflowered. Practical deconstruction of the transcendental effect is at work in the structure of the flower, as of every *part*, inasmuch as it *appears* or grows [*pousse*] *as such*.

Question of the plant, of *phuein*, of nature, and of what elsewhere, the reference being taken from a certain taboo, was named verginity. How can a part take part, be party to?

This therefore could have started with the parodic, altering, rotting poisoning, by an anthological dose, of the soil of ontological truth, where the prose and poetry, rhems and poems have grown. Besides, the taste for and the handling of poison are declared throughout the text. The text is nourished by them. And if I tell you from now on that *glas* is a kind of poisoned milk, you will find the dose too strong and the image dissonant. So it is not yet the time.

Let us restrict ourselves: the *glas* that is raised and resounds on the surface of some page — already — between "lilacs" and "explosions [*éclats*]," also announces, while

"This century is certainly the century of poison, . . . and my taste for poisons, the appeal they have for me. . . . but the doctors gave me an emetic and, after analyzing my vomit. . . ." He is therefore condemned for having introduced poison into prison, for having caused "a dangerous medication to enter the prison by fraud." This *glas* can be read as the interminable analysis of vomit, of a nausea [*écœurement*] rather, by which I am affected and which causes me to write

of spirit, and if each of its moments partakes of this process, the first moment will also be the most natural. It will be the most natural form of the spirit as *Sittlichkeit*: it is the family; it is love in the circle or, this comes down to the same thing, the symbolic triangle of the family. In the objectifying movement of the actual spirit, Hegel in effect discerns three moments:

"(A) ethical (*sittliche*) spirit in its *natural* (naturliche) or immediate phase—the *Family*.

"This substantiality loses its unity (*geht in den Verlust ihrer Einheit . . . über*), passes over into division (*Entzweiung*), and into the phase of relation, i.e. into

"(B) *Bourgeois* (Civil) *Society*—an association of members as *self-subsistent individuals* in a *universality* which, because of their self-subsistence, is only *formal*. Their association is brought about by their *needs*, by the *legal system*—the means to security of person and property (*Eigentums*)—and by an *external organization* for attaining their particular and common interests. This *external state*

"(C) is brought back to and welded into unity in the *Constitution of the State* (Staatsverfassung) which is the end (*Zweck*) and actuality (*Wirklichkeit*) of both the substantial universal order and the public life devoted thereto."

Such are the three moments, dialectically linked together, by which *Sittlichkeit* penetrates, permeates, and gathers itself together, goes back home to its own proper substance. Most often, and for good reasons, interest is taken in the movement's last two phases (bourgeois society and the State). The problems of right, of politics, of political economy appear therein under a thematic form recognizable from a distance. But such a privilege has no philosophical foundation. If, to compensate for this, we stay a longer time in the family, that will only be in order to make a problematic pertinence within the whole field appear in the family. And not at all, obviously, in order to displace any privilege.

In the additive Remark in the margin of the preceding paragraph, Hegel enumerates, in notes barely written out, the traits of opposition between the family and the State. The most general opposition, the law of opposition, is the opposition between the law and its other. In the State, attention goes to the law, to the universal—the State is *a* universal (ein *Allgemeines*)—that, as law, is the same for all (*das Gleiche für alle*), indifferent to subjective desire. For the family as such, insofar as it is not yet proceeding toward bourgeois society and toward the State, the equal and the universal (*das Gleiche, das Allgemeine*) of the law count less than the subjective difference between "love and fear."

How does the equality of legality come to the family? In other words, come to what feels-self? In other words, to nature? to immediacy?

The following paragraph: "The family, as the *immediate substan-*

covering it with flowers, the death of every code, "The Man Condemned to Death":

myself [*m'écrire*]: "Je m'ec."

Your mouth is a dead woman's where your eyes are of roses

. . .

The glittering frost . . .

. . .

That crowned your forehead with thorns of the rosebush

. . .

Despite your frozen [*glacés*] tears . . .

. . .

. . . will you steal the keys

. . .

From where you sow, royally, the white enchantments,
This snow on my page, in my silent prison:
The dread of it, the dead among the violet blossoms,
Death with her cocks! . . .

. . .

A dazzling pimp carved [*taillé*] from an archangel
Working it up [*Bandant*] over the bouquets of carnations and
    jasmines

. . .

Be the young girl with the pure radiant neck [*cou*],
Or, if you dare, be the child of lovely lyrics
Dead within me long before the axe chops off my head.

Fair child of honor crowned with lilac!
Bend over my bed, let my rising cock
Smack your golden cheek. Listen, your killer lover
Is telling you his story in a thousand explosions.

He's singing that he once had your body and your face,
Your heart that a massive rider's spurs
Will never open.

tiality of spirit, is specifically characterized by *love*, which is spirit's *feeling* of its own unity [feeling itself, sensible to itself, as feeling (*sentiment*) of self, *seine sich* empfindende *Einheit*]. Hence in a family, one's frame of mind [consciousness, *Gesinnung*] is destined (*Bestimmung*) to have self-consciousness of one's individuality *within this unity* as the absolute essence in and for (it)self, with the result that one is in it not as a person for (it)self but as a *member-participant* (Mitgleid)."

So love—relation of the *Mitgleid*, of the member articulated to the family body—determines the unity of self-feeling as the family's self-adherence. But what permits the family to constitute itself, to hold on to itself is also what keeps it in naturalness and would prohibit it, by itself alone, to proceed toward bourgeois society and the State. By itself alone, the affect would prevent the family from denying itself as family, then of relieving itself; at the same time [*du même coup*] the affect would deny the family the affect itself. As always, the choice takes place only between two negations of self. Economy—the law of the house—ought to arrange itself in order to insure its expenses.

For, as affect (*Empfindung*), love still belongs to nature. It is the natural of spirit. From this perspective, Hegel always limits its value: love *remains* in the spirit's being-outside-self. Love returns to it, goes back there, to be sure; but as such, in its own proper instance, it develops as if on a staircase. It is like a stair [*une marche*]. Rather a ramp, a movement's winding upward, for love always already carries itself beyond each station. Love is only ascent and so has no proper instance on which to stop and consider itself within itself. This figure of the ramp has a general bearing for the whole of speculative dialectics. Whence the impossibility of stopping a concept's determining limit.

Staircase: one stair against another.

What is sought here is a staircase that is not Hegelian, a slightly silly way of saying another staircase of the spirit from which to understand, to climb up and down, to dismantle the Hegelian course [*démarche*].

No longer can one even say, "it (*ça*) begins or ends with love." "I begin with" or "I end with" equals: "the I begins where it (*ça*) has not begun, or where it (*ça*) has begun before the I believes" and "the I ends where it (*ça*) continues to begin again," already.

A Remark to the preceding paragraph: "Love means in general terms the consciousness of my unity with another, so that I am not in selfish isolation but win my self-consciousness as the renunciation of [*Aufgebung*, the dispossession of] my being-for-self and through knowing myself (*Mich-Wissen*) as the unity of myself with another and of the other with me."

". . . *sondern mein Selbstbewusstsein nur als Aufgebung meines Fürsichseins gewinne*. . . ."

Flowers, culled with the dead, always for covering the coffin, the verge's rigid body, the virgin's too, and the mother's. Theft of flowers, their flight in(to the) place of verginity [*Vol des fleurs au lieu de la verginité*]. To steal the keys, to fly into pieces, to splatter, peal of bells [*Voler les clés, voler en éclats, voler en éclaboussures, volée de cloches*].

> To steal, to fly your blood-splattered sky
> And to make a single masterpiece with the dead
> Culled here and there in the meadows, the hedges. . . .

Such apparently conventional flowers, pearls abyssed by mortuary wreaths [*couronnes*], are already worth their weight in sperm and phallus: that death cuts from nature, whence — already—the signature

"O come my rosy sky, O my blond basket!
. . .
Come pour into my mouth a little heavy cum."

that engraves or grafts the artificial flower. Pastiche and postiche, an inversion of values for fucking yourself. Always to be cut—cuttable-culpable [*coupables*]—the flower the sex will get their erection from the postiche.

> "Who carved a Wind Rose in the plaster?
> . . .
> A consoling hell peopled with handsome soldiers,
> Naked to the waist, and from their reseda skivvies
> Pull up those heavy flowers whose odor strikes me
>   like thunder."

(What I ought to let fall (to the tomb), with each cutting [*coupe*], from all the letters of the text—of the law that is verified there—should, after the event [*après coup*], resound, if not be summarized, explode [*éclater*] in *glas*'s. I cut into the "complete works." I tailor [*taille*] another text there, a little as he tailors his pimp into a banding-erect archangel. But why an archangel? Which one? What does he announce?)

The movement described is thus the relief [*la relève*] of a dispossession, the *Aufhebung* of an *Aufgebung* by which I find again in the other what I *lose of myself*. But this repossession has already begun to make love pass on beyond itself, and the family into the law, and so on. The remark immediately turns on itself (*sondern, aber*, but, but): "But love is feeling, i.e. ethical life in the form of the natural. In the State, feeling no longer is [in the form of the natural]; there we are conscious of unity as law; there the content must be rational and known to us. The first moment in love is that I do not wish to be for me an independent person and that, if I were, then I would feel lacking and incomplete (*mangelhaft und unvollständig*). The second moment is that I attain myself in another person, that I count in the other for what the other in turn attains in me."

"Die Liebe ist aber Empfindung. . . ."

So these two moments divide *the* moment of love; they divide, parcel out, work (over) the inside of the family's essential kernel. Contradiction: I do not wish to be independent; I do not wish to be what I am; I experience [*ressens*] autarky as a lack. But what I count for in love, the price of what I dispossess myself of is fixed by what the other finds in me. I am only as much as I count for something (*ich gelte*). *I count for something for the other*, a formula about which we would have to agree before concluding any deal [*marché*] whatsoever, good or bad. I speculate here, like the other, in order to derive some profit from a contract between love as narcissism and speculative dialectics.

This contradiction is unintelligible; its economy surpasses understanding; no formal logic can master or resolve it. Its actual solution does not return to the intellect (*Verstand*), to the instrument of a formal [*formelle*] analysis.

That does not entrain love in irrationality, on the contrary. Love plays, on the contrary, in the gap [*écart*] between understanding and reason. Love's—and so here the family's—dialectical contradiction surpasses understanding only in order to resolve itself in actual rationality. ". . . I count in the other for what the other in turn attains in me. Love, therefore, is the most unheard-of contradiction [extraordinary, prodigious, monstrous contradiction: *ungeheuerste Widerspruch*]; the understanding cannot resolve it since there is nothing more stubborn (*Härteres*) than this *punctuality* of self-consciousness which is denied and which nevertheless I ought to possess as affirmative (*affirmativ*). Love is at once (*zugleich*) the producing (*Hervorbringen*) and the resolving (*Auflösung*) of this contradiction. As the resolving of it, love is unity of an ethical type [the appeasing concord: *die sittliche Einigkeit*]."

This can already be verified on the "lofty foremast [*haute vergue*]" of "A Song of Love," above "O my black Continent my robe of great mourning!" enjoining "clusters" and "gloves" with which the postiche becoming will be elaborated, a "windflower" in a "scarf" or a necktie knotted to a tree, an "angel of ivy" or a "little girl curled up," like liana and all the wisteria [*glycines*] of the corpus, around an erect tree,

the text is composed in liana and ivy. It is first gleaned. Gleaning ("norm. *lianne*; Berry, *glene*; génev. *glenne*") is rolled up, woven and braided like liana ("Norm. *liaune*, the name for clematis; *lianne*, gleaning. This word seems to come from *lier* [to bind, to link], and to be another form of *lien* [bond, link]") around an already standing [*déjà dressée*] column; it gives its form to all textual chains, to all sexual couplings. "A few days later, Divers did the very same operation and thus tugged at all my nerves, which wound about him and climbed lovingly over his body." ". . . I wanted to give my body the suppleness of osier so as to twine round him, though I wanted to warp [*se voiler*], to bend over him" (Stilitano is the column here). "The boy I was at fifteen [was] twined in his hammock around a friend." Twisted [*torsé*] text. Always one, at least, verily a torso [*torse*] to be described.
To glean in Littré's etymology again (in order to play, poetics): "E. Génev. *glener, glainer*; picard, *glainer*; Berry, *glainer, glener*, provenç. *grenar* . . . low Lat. *glenare*. . . . Diez notes the etymology indicated by Leibniz: kimry, *glain, glân*, clean; to which he adds the Scandinavian *glana*, clarify; so that *to glean* properly would be to clean. This is possible but not very satisfying; so one must not lose sight of the low Lat. *geliba, gelima, gelina*, sheaf, handful [*poignée*]; Anglo-Saxon, *gelm, gilm*, handful. Here the sense is satisfying, and the variations in the consonant leave room for the transformation. Uncertainty then remains between an etymology good for the form, less good for sense; another good for sense, less good for the form. The Provençal *grenar* seems to be an accidental form, and not to be connected in any way to *granum*, grain."

the color rose, the rose, above all the "petals" ("hemmed petal," "pearly petal") whose name displaces its own letters, condenses and defoliates, decomposes endlessly, analyzes itself: everywhere, in the

In the *simul*, the *zugleich*, the *du-même-coup*, the at-once, the in-the-same-stroke, the producing and the resolving of the contradiction do not remain together in the stroke. The *zugleich* is immediately divided, unbalanced, breaking the symmetry, the *même-coup* worked (over) by two unequal forces: the resolving—also the dissolving—bests the producing. But only in order to announce or prepare another stroke: the resolving is already in the act of producing another unheard-of contradiction in which the *zugleich* will separate from itself in order to reason against understanding.

play of the p's, the farts [*pets*], the faggots [*pédales*]; enjoined, as well, a frost [*gel*], a neck [*col*], a throat [*cou*], a collar [*cou*], a "Hand that hastens in vain cut off," of which you could follow, interminably, beyond the "first poems," what would be called an elaboration. It will be necessary, of course, to reread all these words at least once.

The one who signs "The Man Condemned to Death" offers himself, already, *déjà*,

(to) read the *déjà* [*already*] as a siglum. When I sign, I am already dead. I hardly have the time to sign than I am already dead, that I am already dead. I have to abridge the writing, hence the siglum, because the structure of the "signature" event carries my death in that event. For which it is not an "event" and perhaps signifies nothing, writes out of a past that has never been present and out of a death that has never been alive. To write for the dead, out of them, who have never been alive: this is the desire (formulated for example in *The Studio of Alberto Giacometti*, but unceasingly refrained [*rengainé*] elsewhere) that is interrogated and resounds here as *glas* in order finally to insinuate [*laisser entendre*] the unheard, the illegibility of an *already* that leads back to nothing *present* any more, even were it past. The "I am therefore dead. I am a dead man who sees his skeleton in a mirror . . ." of the *Miracle of the Rose* is not just one proposition among others. Everywhere that it is repeated, cashed, retailed, detailed, divided, it imparts a writing- (or *already*-)stroke [*coup d'écriture (ou de déjà)*] to all the forces that cling to the present, to truth as presence. The past is no longer a past present, nor the future a present to come. And all the values depending on that axiom are stopped by the siglum. They no longer function already, they are defunct in advance. Even here

I shall stop on this stair [*marche*]; I want to stress it. I am not following for now [*l'instant*] the deduction of the concept family, of its three moments: monogamous marriage, the property of goods, the education of children or the dissolution of the family.

Leaving the completed system (*The Philosophy of Right*) as a seedling, I go down again toward the first steps of its constitution, the texts of Frankfurt, Jena, the *Phenomenology of Spirit*. But I am also going to try not to transform love and the contradiction of the family affect into a privileged guiding thread [*fil*], verily into a *telos* or ideal model [*régulateur*]. I am interested in the experience, not the success or the failure [*échec*]. The circle is not practicable; or avoidable.

under his proper name—his *glas*—an anthological basket. *Déjà*, al-

To the question *"qu'appelle-t-on penser?"* *"qu'est-ce qui s'appelle penser?"* "what is called thinking?" one can respond only with an impracticable and unavoidable circle, since the very literalness of the question's statement is not displaced.

To think is to call, to name oneself.

How does one think, that is, how is one called outside or apart from the family name? And how is the family thought outside the circle or the trinitarian triangle?

The question of the method that works (over) your reading inscribes already the family name. It is a family question.

The family is a *party to* the system of the spirit: the family is both a part and the whole of the system.

The whole system repeats itself in the family. *Geist* is always, in the very production of its essence, a kind of repetition. Coming to, after losing itself in nature and in its other, spirit constitutes itself as absolute spirit through the negative process of a syllogism whose three moments are *subjective spirit* (anthropology, phenomenology of spirit, psychology), *objective spirit* (right, morality, *Sittlichkeit*), and *absolute spirit* (art, religion, philosophy). Each of the three moments of the three moments itself includes three syllogistic moments. So the family is the first moment of the third moment of objective spirit, *Sittlichkeit's* first moment. Family forms its still most natural instance and accomplishes itself by destroying itself in three stages: marriage, patrimony, education.

In the stage of this initial floodgate [*écluse*], a first methodological temptation: after recognizing love in its dialectical contradiction as the most "stubborn" rational kernel of the family structure, if this metaphor of metaphor can be risked, one could go back toward the works of the young Hegel, toward the so-called youthful works, toward the philosophy of love and life in the texts on Christianity. What is found in them in effect is presented at once as a germ and as an ensemble of the system's invariant traits. A germ one could legitimately consider that Hegel has let grow, develop itself, raise itself, teach itself, run through its cycle and accomplish its *Bestim-*

as you know, that can be said this way only in French. There the question is, exactly. *"Was heisst Denken"* gives rise to another literal chain: neither closed nor simply open to this one. The relation of one to the other is not translation but transformation. A labor relation, fitting with floodgates [*éclusant*], sluices. The relation never takes place right here, but elsewhere.

Another form of the same question: can a family name be translated? Strangulation: the singularity of the general, the classification of the unique, the tightening structure of a grip in which the concept conceives, limits, and delimits itself. The strangulating bottleneck (seizure/disseizure) is named (called) in the concept.

The passion of the proper name: never to let itself be translated —according to its desire—but to suffer translation—which is intolerable to it. To want to reappropriate itself, to take again into its belly all the world's tongues come to lick its surface the moment, exposed, pronounced, the proper name has commonly engaged itself in the concept or the class

ready, be careful about this, does not signify that the signature will always be gathered, summarized, announced in its siglum beforehand. This already marks an entirely different thing. *Toquesing*:

> Let the sky awaken, the stars flower,
> Let the flowers not sigh, the belltower sound,
> And the black grass greet the dew [*rosée*] that morning
> Will drink in the fields. I alone, I am going to die.
>
> O come my rosy sky, O my blond basket!
> Visit in his night your man condemned to death.
>
> . . .
>
> The milkman's cans, a bell [*cloche*] in the air
>
> . . .
>
> My God, I'm going to croak without once being able
> To hold you close to my cock and my heart!

What does the *glas* of the proper name signify? Sooner: does that (*ça*) signify?

The phallic flower is cuttable-culpable. It is cut [*se coupe*], castrated, guillotined, decollated, unglued. Sooner: it *appears* only on the scaffold, is what is defalcated there, what is removed and left to fall. This appearing, this luminous phenomenon—decorporated—of the flower, was glory:

mung, the destination or the determination that called it, in which it is called (thus affording itself to be thought) from itself to itself. A complex of invariant traits because between the germ and the adult concept something does not change and lets itself be identified without any possible doubt. The youthful works on Christianity—and notably on the Last Supper scene—would be read, for example, as the teleological preformation of the completed system. Nothing in the author would prohibit this. On the contrary, he has multiplied the propositions on teleology, on the system as the development of a germ.

So one can operate according to his rule [*sa règle*]. We shall do that. But this obedience to the rule of a detour will make us pay a price that it is still too soon to calculate.

The family is marked twice.

It is a determinate, a most narrowly particular moment. Its place is inscribed in the encyclopedia and in history as the history of spirit. A finite moment, the family is never passed through more than once.

But simultaneously another account of the family must be taken, on another ledger, another charter. This determinate moment of the family, this finiteness *figures* (for now I leave a very large opening for this word) the system's totality. A certain familial schema, a certain family (last supper) scene *suits* the system's infinite totality. The system's infinite totality thinks, produces, and reflects itself in that scene.

Will one rashly say that the finite family furnishes a metaphoric model or a convenient figuration for the language of philosophical exposition? A pedagogical ease? A good way to speak of abstract things to the student [*élève*] while playing with the familiarity of family significations? Even then what the absolute familiarity of a signification is must be known. If that can be thought and named without the family. Then one needs to ascertain that the finite family in question is not infinite already, in which case what the alleged metaphor would come to figure would be already in the metaphor.

How does the family remark itself?

A very late text analyzes *the determination of spirit*. The spirit thinks and at the same time is conscious of itself. I know the object only insofar as I know myself; I also think it while thinking myself thinking it. In that I am a man and not an animal. "In other words, I only know an object in so far as I know myself and my own determination through it, in so far as whatever I am is also an object for me, and I am not just this or that, but only what I know. I know my object, and I know myself; the two are inseparable." Consequently, the content of spirit, inasmuch as it knows itself knowing some other thing, this content is spiritual. Its content never simply stands outside itself; it does not impose itself on itself

the attack of the word *glory* must be well understood, well heard. A machine for calculating reading would doubtlessly confirm this; along with *gallery, galley*, and a few others, it is one of the author's preferred words. It falls three times, for example, on a page explaining "the death on the scaffold which is our glory" and why "secretly choose decapitation." Glory always springs from a "decollated head" (which is why it "is not human" but "celestial"—to divinize you): "Each of them knew that the moment his head fell into the basket of sawdust, and was taken out (by the ears) by an assistant whose role seems to me strange indeed, his heart would be garnered by fingers gloved with modesty and carried off in a youngster's chest [*poitrine*] adorned like a spring festival. I thus aspire to celestial glory . . ." which lodges not far from the chest, from the heart, certainly, but also not far from the bosom [*sein*] and the throat. Which may well explain already, but to be reasoned out [*à raisonner*] later on, the contiguity of the *milkman* [laitier] and the *bell* [cloche] in "The Man Condemned to Death"

Our-Lady-of-the-Flowers opens up with the archive of all the heads that have just fallen, condemned to death. "Weidmann appeared before you," virgin like a nursling or a nun, head enveloped in diapers or wedding veil [*voile d'hymen*], new-born, a royal mummy, "his head swathed in white bands, a nun and yet a wounded pilot, fallen into the rye. . . ." Remark everything, especially the rye [*seigle*]. "His handsome face, multiplied by the presses, swept down upon Paris. . . ." But in letting itself fall, the head was already relieved. It upsurges, is erected precisely, decidedly in this case. To be decapitated is to appear—banded, erect: like the "head swathed" (Weidmann, the nun, the aviatior, the mummy, the nursling) and like the phallus, the erectile stem—the style—of a flower.

When a flower opens up, "blows [*éclôt*]," the petals part [*s'écartent*], and then there rises up what is called

from the outside. To know is to appropriate oneself, to produce or reproduce the known. One should not even say that spirit does not have any content outside itself, an object of which it would be only the knowing form. One must say: what cannot have any content outside itself, what in advance interiorizes all content, even were it infinite or rather in infinitizing it, that is what calls itself spirit, conceives or grasps itself as spirit. *Geist* repeats itself. So spirit alone can conceive spirit. As such, it has no outside limit; thus it is the free and the infinite.

Infinite freedom, the other name of spirit inasmuch as it gives itself its own proper element and so stands "(close) by itself." It can only be near itself, gathered together with itself, bound to itself by itself, completely compressed against itself by itself. It is free, infinitely so, only by remaining close to itself, as if it kept itself awake by murmuring its very own proper name. "Thus the spirit by nature always stays (close) by itself (*bei sich*) or free."

How does this "being-(close)-by-self" of the spirit represent itself? Why does it detach itself within the family hearth itself, in the center of its own circle? Why would being (close) by self come down to "being with one's family," infinitely or indefinitely with one's family?

Let us proceed slowly.

Free and infinite in itself, spirit has no absolute opposite. At least its opposite cannot be absolute. Absolute, that would be spirit. Habitually, Hegel says in the same passage, matter is posited as the spirit's opposite. Matter is not free. It weighs, it goes toward the bottom.

It falls (to the tomb).

But there is a law to its weight, its gravity. If the gravity and the dispersion of matter to the outside are analyzed, one should recognize there a tendency, an effort tending toward unity and the gathering of self. A tendency toward the center and unity, matter then is spirit's opposite only inasmuch as it remains resistant to this tendency, inasmuch as it is opposed to its own tendency. But to be opposed to its own tendency, to itself, to matter, it must be spirit. And if it yields to its tendency, it is still spirit. It is spirit in any case; its essence is nothing but spiritual. There is no essence but spiritual. So matter is weight or gravity as the search for the center, is dispersion as the search for unity. Its essence is its nonessence: if it

one can try to displace this necessity only by thinking—but what is called thinking?—the remain(s) outside the horizon of essence, outside the thought of being. The remain(s)

complies with that, it rejoins the center and unity, is no longer matter, and begins to become spirit, for spirit is center, unity bound to self, rolled up close by and around self. And if it does not rejoin its essence, it remains (matter) but no longer has any essence: it does not remain (what it is).

the *style*. The stigma designates the highest part, the *summit* of (the) style.

After the roll-call of the men condemned to death, Weidmann, Angel Sun, Pilorge, from the first page: "I learned only in bits and pieces of that wonderful blossoming [*éclosion*] of dark and lovely flowers: one was revealed to me by a scrap of newspaper; another was casually alluded to by my lawyer; another was mentioned, almost sung, by the prisoners—their song became fantastic and funereal (a *De Profundis*), as much so as the plaints which they sing in the evening, as the voice which crosses the cells. . . ."

But this voice only arrives the moment it "breaks," when it carries the trace of a "break," perhaps like a bell [*cloche*], the "bell" that is "unleashed" for a child on the same page.

The flower opens out, achieves, consecrates the phenomenon of death in an instant of *trance*. The trance is that kind of limit (trance/partition), of unique case, of singular experience where nothing comes about, where what surges up collapses "at the same time," where one no longer can cut through to a decision between the more and the less. Flower, trance: the *simul* of erection and castration. Where one bands erect for nothing, where nothing bands erect, where the mere nothing "bands erect."

"*Trance* . . . n. Great apprehension of an evil thought to be near at hand. . . .
"— E. Wallon, *transs*, *glas* tolled for death; Span. and Portug. *trance*, hour of death, decisive moment; Ital. *transito*, passing away; from the Lat. *transitus*, passage. In French, *transe*, which meant any vivid, painful emotion, stems from *transir* (see this word)." Littré

n'este pas [does not come-to-essence], as one translates by making use of a crutch, an *ersatz*, or a prosthesis (*west nicht*).
Even so, one must cross the dialectical step [*pas*], the dialectical no [*pas*]

"Speculative philosophy has shown that freedom is the one authentic truth of spirit. Matter (*Materie*) possesses gravity in so far as it is impelled (*Trieb*) to move toward a central point [the midpoint: *le milieu, Mittelpunkt*]; it is essentially composite [*zusammengesetzt*, gathered together], and consists entirely of discrete parts which all tend (*streben*) towards a centre (*Mittelpunkt*); thus matter has no unity. It is made up of (*Aussereinander*) separate elements and searches for (*sucht*) its unity; it thus endeavours to relieve itself (*sich selbst aufzuheben*) and seeks its own opposite (*Gegenteil*). If it were to succeed, it would no longer be matter, but would have ceased to exist as such (*als solche untergegangen*); it strives towards ideality, for unity is its ideal existence [*ideell*]. Spirit, on the other hand, is such that its centre is within itself; it too strives (*strebt*) towards its centre, but it is itself this centre. Its unity is not something external; it always finds it within itself, and exists in itself and (close) by itself (*bei sich*). Matter has its substance outside itself; spirit, on the other hand, is being-(close)-by-itself (*das Beisichselbstsein*) which is the same thing as freedom. For if I am dependent, I am beholden to something other than myself, and cannot exist without this external other thing. I am free if I am (close) by myself (*bei mir selbst bin*)."

here is confirmed the essential—and not only the figurative—affinity between the movement of relief (*relève, Aufhebung*) and rearing (the student) (*l'élève*) in general: *élévation, élèvement, élevage*, elevation, breeding, education, upbringing. Airy ascent of the concept. *Begriff* grasps and sweeps upward, opposes its force to everything that falls (to the tomb). *Begriff* is necessarily victorious. Victory does not devolve upon it; the *Begriff* is what wins. Hence its imperial character. The concept wins against matter that can hold its own against the concept only by relieving itself, only by denying itself in raising itself [*s'élevant*] to spirit. The concept also wins against death: by erecting even up to the tomb. The burial place raises itself.
Let us not approach too quickly Hegel's burial place, about which we will have to concern ourselves later

Thus: spirit is. Alone. Its contrary, matter, is only inasmuch as it is not what it is, inasmuch as, in order to be what it is (falling weight and the tendency of dispersion to unity), it becomes what it is not: spirit. Spirit is. Alone. Being is being (close) by self. Weight and dispersion, the essence of matter, could not qualify an essence. Matter has no essence; its essence is its contrary, its essence is not having an essence. Dispersion, like weight (nonunity and nonideality), has no essence. *Thus* is not. Being is idea.

Thus: to be, matter will-already-have-become spirit. And since matter will have been nothing before becoming spirit, spirit will always have preceded or accompanied itself up to the procession's

Not that the mere nothing is.

Perhaps we can say *there is* [il y a] the mere nothing (that bands erect).

No sooner than *there is* [il n'y a], there bands erect (an impersonal complement) in a past that was never present (the signature — already [*déjà*] — denied [*nia*] it always): *it banded erect* [il banda] (an impersonal

to band (erect), *bander*, is always to close up [*serrer*], to gird (banded erect: girt), to tighten, with a band, a girdle [*gaine*], a cord, in a bond [*lien*] (liana, ivy [*lierre*], or lash). "*Band . . . n. . . .* E. Wallon *baine*; Namurian, *bainde*; rouchi, *béne*; picard, *benne*; Provenç. and Ital. *benda*; Spanish, *venda*; from the old high Germ. *binda*; mod. Germ. *binden*, to bind; Sanskrit, *bandh*, to bind. Compare the Gaelic *bann*, a band, a bond." Higher up: "They nursed their children without swaddling them, neither binding them up in bands nor in swaddling clothes,' Amyot." Littré, whose whole article has to be read, in order at least to put into relief there [*y relever*] that bands, in printing terms, are "pieces of iron attached to the two tongues in the middle of the press's cradle, on which the train rolls." Double contra sense, at least, of the word *banded (erect)*. What is called bandaging [*panser*]

complement) is equal to *it bound* [il lia]. Lock [*Serrure*].

A certain mere nothing, a certain void, then, erects.

The bells [*cloches*] were unleashed a moment ago [*il y a un instant*].

Now reconstitute the chain that sets all the *glas* machines in motion (you will fit all its pieces together later on), its annuli, its links: the erection (of the cuttable-culpable flower), the liana's undulation (or the ivy's: here, the lashes), the rhetorical reading of lilies and of the bed (here, the coffin lying on the virgin mother [*mère*]), the unsheathed bell that strikes a *seing*—and it all flows out like milky sperm,

so *Geist* can only repeat itself, repeat its own spiriting (away) [*souffle*], inhaling/exhaling itself. Effluvium or sublimate, the repetition of a spiriting (away) maintains itself above what falls (to the tomb), above matter. Such repetition unfolds the infinite freedom of an auto-affection. Between self and self, in the being (close) by self, what can prevent the spirit from repeating? The hands can be bound and the tongue cut out [*couper*], all the possibilities of action and auto-affection limited, but how could *Geist* be prevented from repeating? This operation, which one would not know how to decide whether it is internal or external, spontaneous or accidental, is spirit's last refuge—its supreme irony—against all repressive constraints. But this operation is nearly nothing, and yet matter must ferment (all this awaits us near the burial place), but the ferment, the heat that decomposes matter, is it not yet, already, the spirit preparing a beautiful repetition? It must first, because of that, forget itself

Spirit's being-(close)-by-self actively produces itself through an unlimited negativity. Spirit becomes for-itself, (close) by itself, only in actively denying all that limits its freedom from the outside. Its essence is active, dynamic, negative: "When the spirit strives (*strebt*) towards its own center, it strives to perfect (*vervollkommen*) its own freedom; and this striving is fundamental to its nature. To say that spirit exists would at first seem to imply that it is a completed entity (*etwas Fertiges*). On the contrary, it is by nature

activity: the place of man (*vir*). The pure activity of the spirit—the spirit produces itself—a little farther on induces the spirit's assimilation to the father who produces or gives himself, by doubling himself, a son. I am my father my son and myself. My name is my father. But the giving-producing-doubling-himself insinuates into the pure activity an inner division, a passivity, an affect that obscurely breaches/broaches the father's paternity and begins to ruin all the determinations and oppositions that form a system with it. All the family significations then set about passing (away) in each other, and nothing can stop them. Such is the play of spirit with itself, as soon as it begins to stretch, strain itself. For *Streben*, striving, tending, as was just seen, forms its essence. Its play immediately ruins and slackens the spirit

end. Matter precedes or remains (first or last) only as spirit: in raising or erecting what falls (to the tomb).

What is the relation between this being-(close)-by-self (another way of saying being) and the family?

When one says that spirit is—alone—that it has its own proper essence, its own proper center, and its own proper unity in itself, that is not a simple and tautological affirmation. This proposition is speculative in the Hegelian sense of the word; it states the dialectical identity of identity and nonidentity. This proposition is

active (*Tätiges*), and activity (*Tätigkeit*) is its essence; it is its own product (*Produkt*), and is therefore its own beginning and its own end. Its freedom does not consist in static being (*ruhende Sein*), but in a constant negation of all that threatens to destroy [*aufzuheben*] freedom. The activity of spirit is to produce itself, to make itself its own object, and to gain knowledge of itself; in this way, it exists for itself. Natural things do not exist for themselves; for

this reason, they are not free. The spirit produces and realises itself in the light of its knowledge of itself; it acts in such a way that all

"in little continuous jerks" (it is written like that (*comme ça*)).

Enjoyment's simul:

"I approach, my heart racing wildly, and discover nothing, nothing but looming emptiness, sensitive and proud like a tall foxglove!" And just after the embalmer's emblem, an exclamation point—"I do not know, as I have said, whether the heads there are really those of my guillotined friends, but I have recognized by certain signs that they—those on the wall—are thoroughly supple, like the lashes of whips, and rigid as glass knives, precocious as child pundits and fresh as forget-me-nots, bodies chosen because they are possessed by terrible souls.

"The newspapers are tattered by the time they reach my cell, and the finest pages have been looted of their finest flowers, those pimps, like gardens in May. The big, inflexible, strict pimps, their members in full bloom—I no longer know whether they are lilies or whether lilies and members are not totally they, so much so that in the evening, on my knees, in thought, I encircle their legs with my arms — all that rigidity floors me and makes me confuse them, and the memory which I gladly give as food for my nights is of yours, which, as I caressed it, remained inert, stretched out; only your verge, unsheathed and brandished, went through my mouth with the suddenly cruel sharpness of a steeple [*clocher*] puncturing a cloud of ink, a hatpin a breast [*sein*]. You did not move, you were not asleep, you were not dreaming, you were in flight, motionless and pale, frozen [*glacé*], straight, stretched out stiff on the flat bed, like a coffin on the sea [*mer*], and I know that we were chaste, while I, all attention, felt you flow into

one no longer knows *stricto sensu* — what figure to recognize

its knowledge of itself is also realised. Thus everything depends on the spirit's self-consciousness; if the spirit knows that it is free, it is altogether different from what it would be without this knowledge. For if it does not know that it is free, it is in the position of a slave who is content with his slavery and does not know that his condition is an improper one. It is the felt sensation (*Empfindung*) of freedom alone which makes the spirit free, although it is in fact always free in and for itself."

Spirit is always—already—free as spirit, but it remains for spirit to be what it will have been: to create the phenomenal experience of its freedom, to appear to itself as such, to free itself, to free its freedom. Nothing more painful, despite the appearance—but the evil here is appearance—than this return to self and this freeing of freedom. That is first produced in matter's becoming-alive, its becoming-life. In life, the spirit that had lost itself, dispersed according to the exteriority of matter, begins to relate itself to itself. First under the form of *self-feeling*. This instance of self-feeling, which predicates love as well, gives itself first in an immediate, natural, and external way (feeling) in animality. Human feeling is still animal. The animal limitation, I feel it as spirit, like a negative constraint from which I try to free myself, a lack I try to fill up. This tension, this tendency to free myself from feeling, I share it with all the living. Hegel calls this *Trieb*. Here *Trieb* cannot be translated, as has been done, by *desire* or *drive* [pulsion]. Let us say *pressure* [poussée] in order to decide nothing yet.

Man passes from feeling to conceiving only by suppressing the pressure, what the animal, according to Hegel, could not do. Ideality, as thought of the universal, is born and then bears the mark of a suppression of the pressure: the violent interruption between pressure and satisfaction, between the animal moment and the spiritual moment of life, death in the natural life, natural death as the spirit's life. The family is announced.

"The most immediate knowledge spirit can have of itself when it assumes the shape of a human individual is that it is capable of *feeling* (fühlend). No objectivity is yet present here (*Hier ist noch keine Gegenständlichkeit vorhanden*). And we simply feel ourselves determined in some particular way. I then try to distinguish between myself and this determinate quality (*Bestimmtheit*), and set about creating an internal division within myself. Thus, my feelings are split up into an external and an internal world. But at the same time my determinate nature enters a new phase, in that I have a feeling of deficiency (*mangelhaft*) or negativity; I encounter a contradiction within myself which threatens to destroy (*aufzulösen*) me. But I nevertheless am (*Ich bin aber*); this much I know, and I balance this knowledge against my feeling of

some would be tempted to hold on to the inversion: *I am but*. But what? *I am nevertheless*

me, warm and white, in little continuous jerks. Perhaps you were playing at coming. At the climax, you were lit up with a quiet ecstasy, which enveloped your blessed body in a supernatural nimbus, like a cloak that you pierced with your head and feet."

In little continuous jerks, the sequences are enjoined, induced, glide in silence. No category outside the text should allow defining the form or bearing [*allure*] of these passages, of these trances of writing. There are always only sections of flowers, from paragraph to paragraph, so much so that anthological excerpts inflict only the violence necessary to attach importance [*faire cas*] to the remain(s). Take into account the overlap-effects [*effets de recoupe*], and you will see that the tissue ceaselessly re-forms itself around the incision [*entaille*].

a paraph is the abbreviation of a paragraph: what is written on the side, in the margin

What was elaborated while rotting, under the foxgloves, the lilies or the forget-me-nots, was an interment: that of Divine, who will therefore not have surprised us, two pages further on. "Decaying flowers," violets, of which the bouquet, lest we forget, becomes an umbrella, and vice versa: the umbrellas are *like* bouquets, and

the umbrella [*parapluie*], like all figures in para (lightning rod [*paratonnerre*], parachute, screen [*paravent*]), is an ab-

25

(or *I am in the mean-time*) seduces even more

negation or deficiency. I survive and seek to relieve (*aufzuheben*) the deficiency, so that I am at the same time *pressure* (Trieb). The object towards which my pressure is directed is accordingly the means by which I attain satisfaction and the restoration (*Wiederherstellung*) of my unity. All living things are endowed with pressures. We are therefore natural beings, and all our pressures are of a sensuous character. Objects, in so far as I am drawn to them by pressure, are means of integration, and this is the general basis of theory and practice alike. But in our intuitions of the objects to which our pressures are directed, we are dealing directly with externals and are ourselves external. Our intuitions are discrete units of a sensuous nature, and so also are our pressures, irrespective of their content. By this determination (*Bestimmung*), man would be no different from the animals; for pressures are not conscious of themselves. But man knows himself, and this distinguishes him from the animals."

The leap from animality to humanity, as the leap from feeling to thinking, takes its impulse in a suppression of the pressure. Like the animal, man has pressures, but he can himself inhibit, suppress, restrain, bridle, contain them. This negative power—let one not hasten to name it repression—is his very own. In this power man becomes conscious and thinking. The process of idealization, the constitution of ideality as the *milieu* of thought, of the universal, of the infinite, is the suppression of the pressure. Thus *Aufhebung* is also a suppressive counterpressure, a counterforce, a *Hemmung*, an inhibition, a kind of anti-erection.

Hegel links up: inseparable from suppression, idealization is just as much the relation of spirit to itself as the relation of father to son in a trinitarian structure.

"But man knows himself, and this distinguishes him from the animals. He is a *thinking* (denkend) being. Thought, however, is knowledge of universals, and it simplifies the content of experience, so that man too is simplified by it so as to become something inward and ideal [*Ideelles*]. Or, to be more precise, I am this inwardness and simplicity, and the content of my experience only becomes universal and ideal [*ideell*] if I proceed to simplify it.

"What man is in reality (*reell*), he *must* also be in ideality (*ideell*). Since he knows the real (*Realen*) as the ideal (*Ideellen*), he ceases to be merely a natural being at the mercy of immediate intuitions and pressures which he must satisfy and produce. This knowledge leads him to suppress (*hemmt*) his pressures; he places the ideal [*Ideelle*], the realm of thought, between the demands (*Drängen*) of the pressure and their satisfaction. In the animal, the two coincide; it cannot sever their connection by its own efforts—only pain or fear can do so. In man, the pressure is present before it is satisfied and independently of its satisfaction; in bridling or giving rein to

then the bouquets are *like* umbrellas. Also, a staircase, lest we forget, leads to death. Divine's. Stony monumentalization, against which the burst [*éclat*] of names resounds. The procession [*théorie*] of queens, "girl-queens and boy-queens, the aunties, fags, and nellies" proceeds, a host of flowers, in an even movement.

solutely threatening apotrope. Protection and aggression pass into each other, reverse themselves unceasingly in their veiled relation to truth. The supplement's always reversible function. *The Screens* are full of umbrellas. Scene six: *"In front of the screen, an open umbrella is resting, but upside down. A blazing [éclatant] sun is painted on a very blue sky."*

"The stairway [*escalier*] leading up to it [Divine's attic] plays an important role today. It is the antechamber, sinuous as the corridors of the Pyramids, of Divine's temporary tomb. This cavernous hypogeum looms up, pure as the bare marble arm in the darkness which is devouring the queen [*cycliste*] to whom it belongs. Coming from the street, the stairway mounts to death. It ushers one to the final resting place. It smells of decaying flowers and already of the odor of candles and incense. It rises into the shadow. From floor to floor it dwindles and darkens until, at the top, it is no more than an illusion blending with the azure. This is Divine's landing. While in the street, beneath the black haloes of the tiny flat umbrellas which they are holding in one hand like bouquets, Mimosa I, Mimosa II, Mimosa the half-IV, First Communion, Angela, Milord, Castagnette, Régine—in short, a host, a still long litany of creatures who are glittering [*éclatés*] names—are waiting, and in the other hand are carrying like umbrellas, little bouquets of violets which make one of them lose herself, for example, in a reverie from which she will emerge bewildered and quite dumbfounded with nobility, for she (let us say

his pressures, man acts in accordance with *ends* and determines himself in the light of a general principle. It is up to him to decide what end to follow; he can even make his end a completely universal one. In so doing, he is determined by whatever representations he has formed of what he is and what he wills. It is this which constitutes man's independence: for he knows what it is that determines him. Thus he can take a simple concept as his end—for example, that of his own positive freedom. The representations of the animal are not ideal [*Ideelles*] and have no true actuality; the animal therefore lacks this inner independence. As a living creature, the animal too has its source of movement within itself. But it can only respond to those external stimuli to which it is already inwardly susceptible; anything that does not match its inner being simply does not exist for it. The animal divides itself in two (*entzweit sich*) from itself and within itself. It cannot interpose anything between its pressure and the satisfaction of its pressure; it has no will and knows no inhibition (*Hemmung*). Its stimulation comes from within itself and presupposes an immanent development. Man, however, is independent, not because he is the initiator of his own movement, but because he can inhibit this movement and thereby break his immediacy and naturalness."

The animal's self-mobility is absolute only insofar as it remains an external or sensible automatic working, a pure constraint as for the spirit. Inhibiting the animal self-mobility in himself, man frees the self-mobility of the spirit, freedom.

a powerful and ample chain from Aristotle, at least, to our day, it binds ontotheological metaphysics to humanism. The essential opposition of man to animal—or rather to animality, to a univocal, homogeneous, obscurantist concept of animality—always serves the same interest there. The Animal would not have Reason, Society, Laughter, Desire, Language, Law, Repression. Of the three wounds to anthropic narcissism, the one Freud indicates with the name Darwin seems more intolerable than the one he has signed himself. It will have been resisted for a longer time

That is explained—the style is almost a seminar's— by the seed or semen. Or by the germ. Which immediately intervenes after the analysis of pressure. The germ (*der Same*) is also, as germ, the ontotheological figure of the family.

This concept (of) germ (*Same*, semen, seed, sperm, grain) regularly enters on the scene in speculative dialectics, in places and regions of the encyclopedic discourse that are at once homologous and distinct, whether of the vegetal, biological, anthropological, or the onto-logical order in general. Among all these orders, speculative dialectics assures a system of figurative correspondences.

From where would these figures export themselves? What would be their own proper place?

The figure of the seed (let us call it thus provisionally) is immediately determined: (1) as the best representation of the

First Communion) remembers the article, thrilling as a song come from the other world, from our world too, in which an evening paper, thereby embalmed, stated: 'The black velvet rug of the Hotel Crillon, where lay the silver and ebony coffin containing the embalmed body of the Princess of Monaco, was strewn with Parma violets.'"

Follow the cortege interminably, you will see all the accidents "magnify," the "trails of slime," "the weighty magnificence of the barbarian who tramples choice furs beneath his muddy boots. . . . Merely to have mentioned him is enough for my left hand in my torn pocket to . . . the plaster cast that Divine herself made of his cock, which was gigantic when erect [*bandait*]. . . . I can't stop praising him until my hand is smeared [*s'englue*] with my liberated pleasure. . . . in short, all the queens, imprinted a tendril-like movement to their bodies and fancied they were enlacing this handsome man, were twining about him. Indifferent and bright as a slaughterhouse knife, he passed by, cleaving them all into two slices which came noiselessly together again."

The thyrsus, the thyrsanthus, which was at first a cutting or penetrating weapon, here informs both the text and its "object."

Are you going to fall precipitously into the trap?

spirit's relation to self, (2) as the circular path of a return to self. And in the description of the spirit that returns to itself through its own proper product, after it lost itself there, there is more than a simple rhetorical convenience in giving to the spirit the name father. Likewise, the advent of the Christian Trinity is more than an empiric event in the spirit's history.

". . . thereby break his immediacy and naturalness.

"The root (*Wurzel*) of human nature is that man can think of himself as an *ego* (*Ich*). As a spirit, man does not have an immediate existence but is essentially returned-home-to-self (*in sich Zurück-gekehrtes*). This movement of mediation (*Ver-mittelung*) is an essential moment of the spirit. Its activity consists in transcending and negating its immediacy so as to return upon itself (*Rückkehr in sich*); it has therefore made itself what it is by means of its own activity. Only the returned-home-to-self is subject, real actuality. Spirit exists only as its own result. The example of the seed (*die Vorstellung des Samens dienen*) may help to illustrate [or clarify: *zur Erläuterung*] this point. The plant begins with the seed, but the seed is also the result of the plant's entire life, for it develops only in order to produce (*hervorzubringen*) the seed. We can see from this how impotent life is (*die Ohnmacht des Lebens*), for the seed is both the origin and the result of the individual; as the starting point and the end result, it is different and yet the same, the product of one individual and the beginning of another. Its two sides fall asunder like the simple form (*Form*) within the grain [of wheat: *Korn*] and the whole course of the plant's development.

"Every individual has an example (*Beispiel*) even closer to hand in the shape of his own person. Man is what he should be only through education [formation, culture: *Bildung*] and discipline (*Zucht*); what he is immediately is only the possibility of being (that is, of being rational, free), only the destination (*Bestimmung*), obligation. The animal's formation is soon complete (*fertig*); but this should not be seen as a blessing bestowed on the animal by nature. Its growth (*Wachstum*) is merely a quantitative increase in strength (*Erstarken*). Man, on the other hand, must make himself what he should be; he must first acquire everything for himself, precisely because he is spirit; in short he must throw off the natural. Spirit, therefore, is its own proper result."

Dialectical paradox: natural living being, life as nature develops by itself without freedom insofar as its self-mobility is finite. It does not go out of itself, it does nothing but develop the germ: the quantitative increase without interruption, without relation to the outside and the absolute other. As natural necessity following its

mediation: the return (close) by self that overcomes the division and the loss. The relief of the two in(to) the three, unity's self-return. The father divides himself, goes out of himself into his son, recognizes himself in the son, and finds himself again, recounts himself in his revenue

And translate that The Flower, which signifies (symbolizes, metaphorizes, metonymizes, and so on) the phallus, once caught in the syntax of the cuttable-culpable, signifies death, decapitation, decollation? Anthologos signifying the signifier signifying castration?

That would be to arrest once again, and in the name of the law, of truth, of the symbolic order, the march of an unknown: its *glas*, which is in action here.

To try once more to arrest it, as in 1952, when, at the exit from prison, the ontophenomenologist of the liberation

liberation—under this title, first and at the least, must be thought the avoidance of psychoanalysis and Marxism in the name of freedom, of the "original choice," and of the "existential project." "Such is the case of the child Genet. . . . It was, I think, Genet's optimism that kept him from adopting this conclusion in reality [to kill himself like that "punished child who chastizes his mother by depriving himself of dessert"]. I mean thereby to designate the very orientation of his freedom. . . . He has chosen to live; he has said, in defiance of all, I will be the Thief. I deeply admire this child who grimly *willed* himself at an age when we were merely playing the servile buffoon. So fierce a will to survive, such pure courage, such mad confidence within [*au sein du*] despair will bear their fruit. Twenty years later, this absurd determination will produce the poet Jean Genet. . . . But when a systematized, hardened sulking holds out for ten years, thirty years, when it is at the root of the most singular, the most beautiful poetic work, when it changes into a world system, into an occult religion, then it must singularly transcend the level of a simple childish reaction, a man's freedom must be thoroughly involved in it. . . . If we want to understand what he is today and what he writes, we must go back to this original choice and try to give a phenomenological description of it."

insisted on handing back to you, right into

own bent, without freedom, its self-mobility is then the result of something other than self, is the result of something else precisely because it remains enclosed within itself and has no relation to self as to the other. No doubt the natural living being divides itself in two; but since this division is not absolute, the animal has no absolute relation to itself. Or to the other. Neither self nor other. That is why there is no natural family, no father/son relation in nature.

The qualitative leap would be brought about with the human individual: radically dividing itself, the human individual is conscious of itself as the other. No longer having, by the fact of this division, its natural movement in itself, it constitutes itself by its *Bildung*, its culture, its discipline, its symbolic formation. Paradoxically, it is, more than the plant or animal, its own proper product, its own son, the son of its works. More than the plant or animal, the human individual is descended from its own germ. It conceives itself. Because it has interrupted the natural pressure and deprived itself of self-mobility, it has given itself law. It names itself, autonamedly [*autonommément*].

But of this self-production, as the inhibiting negation of natural self-mobility, the human individual, the particular, finite individual, as such, is only an *example*. And the (human) father/son relation is only a (finite) example of the infinite father/son relation, of the relation of infinite spirit freely relating to itself as to its own rebound [*ressaut*], its own resource. Just as there was a leap [*saut*] into negativity, between the negativity of the natural (plant, animal) *Entzweiung* and that of the spiritual or human *Entzweiung*, between the relief *in* nature and the relief *of* nature in the *finite* spirit, so there is a dialectical leap that is the absolute rebound of the result, between the *Aufhebung* of the finite spirit and that of the infinite spirit. Just as—so: the analogy or the proportion depends on what the finite *is* as the passage to the infinite.

Whence Hegel's exemplary rhetoric, the exemplarist proceeding of his rhetoric: of his rhetoric as the technique of figures and as the form of argumentation.

After attaching value [*fait cas*] to the human individual as an example (*Beispiel*) of the infinite spirit's movement and the result's rebound, Hegel passes on to the infinite movement of the rebound itself, to the infinite spirit that itself can no longer be an example, since it is not finite. At least it can no longer play the role of an example, if the example is a particular case in a whole or a homogeneous series. It can be an example if the example is the exemplary ideal, the absolute sense of which the finite examples are precisely only approximating samples [*exemplaires*]. This passage from the example to the exemplariness of the example, this passage from the finite to the infinite can sometimes be given aspects of rhetoric and of the mode of exposition. This is *in truth* the ontologic of the

your hand, to a safe place, the "keys" to the-man-and-the-complete-work, their ultimate psychoanalytico-existential signification.

The echo drags on at length ("This is the key to his conduct and his disorders. . . . The Other than self. Here we have the key to Genet. This is what must be understood first: Genet is a child who has been convinced that he is, in his very depths, *Another than Self.* . . . Our certainty of ourself finds its truth in the Other.").

The fence was then as blind to the sexual figure of the key as to his own ability to be on the lookout [*faire gâfe*] if it fell into bad hands. General enough to introduce into the transcendental structures of the ego, it was as effective and as undifferentiated as a passkey, a universal key sliding into all signifying lacunae.

A note from Jacques Lacan's *Ecrits* (Genet is one of the very rare "French writers," modern or otherwise, not to figure in the Index of Names Cited) names this object "that we could not designate better

so what signs Genet would be there only to make the example, the case, of a universal structure, which would give us its own key. When one speaks of a *case*, the doctor, the judge, the prof, the guard, and the lawyer are already in consultation. One sees the robes and the uniforms and the sleeves bustle about. And the neckties. Some years earlier, François Mauriac wrote "The Case of Genet." Some years later, Bataille's verdict: "*Genet's Failure* [échec]." What signs is also interested, but literally and that is something else entirely, in the case of the key [*clé*]. How that (*ça*) is enchained, opened, falls (to the tomb) and sounds. And how the case can falsify, rather force, a dialectical law, a lock [*une serrure*] that should nonetheless open to all. Attacked from a certain angle

than by calling it the universal phallus (just as we say: universal key)."

passage, the reason of the finite that posits itself as such only by passing into the infinite. In the finite the examples (*Beispielen*) can be substituted for each other, and that is why they are examples, particular cases classed according to the general law. This substitution is the freedom of play, of the play among the examples. This freedom is finite. Play here is made possible by finitude, but finitude relieves itself.

In the case—unclassable—of the absolute spirit (God), (no) more play in that sense.

The case of God, can that be said? Can the name of God be classed?

If there were a case of God, if God could be taken as an example, that would mean that one takes God for a finite body, that one is mistaken in making God fall outside what God is, that one takes God for another. God, if he is God, if one thinks what is being said when one names God, can no longer be an example of the *Aufhebung*. God is the infinite, exemplary, infinitely high *Aufhebung*. God is no longer an example, and the play of substitution can no longer be brought about [*s'opérer*].

But cannot God—of himself—fall into the finite, incarnate himself, become his own proper example, play with himself as the infinite becoming finite (death) in order to reappropriate his infinity, to repeat the spirit, that is, to have a son-man who is his own proper seed, his own proper product, his own proper result, his best yield [*revenu*]?

So only the figure of Christ can regulate the productive exchange—amortization and gain—between rhetoric and ontologic. Investment [*Investissement*: financial and cathectic] of the Holy Family, or rather of the Trinity:

"The most sublime [raised, elevated, relieved, eminent: *das erhabenste Beispiel*] example is to be found in the nature of God himself; strictly speaking (*eigentlich*), this is not a genuine example in the sense of one casual instance among others (*ein Beispiel (Bei-her-spiel)*)), but rather the universal, truth itself, of which everything else is an example (*Beispiel*). It is true that the older religions also referred to God as Spirit; but this was no more than a name which could not as yet contribute [grasp: *gefasst*] anything towards explaining the nature of spirit. In the Jewish religion too, the spirit was at first represented (*vorgestellt*) only in general terms. In Christianity, however, God is revealed (*offenbart*) as Spirit. In the first place, he is the Father, power (*Macht*), abstract universal (*abstrakt Allgemeines*), which is still veiled, enveloped (*eingehüllt*) within itself. Sec-

"an untranslatable play on words" right and accurately note the translators. This wordplay is not one wordplay among other possible ones. It is the play that makes all plays possible: the play of the infinite with itself, the exemplary play that plays more—or less—than every other. It plays less by playing more. It plays with itself without the limit and without the rule [*règle*] it gives itself. Which in

This transcendental key, the condition of all determined signifiers and the concatenation of the chain, was prescribed and inscribed, but as a piece and an effect in the text, was enchained, entrained in the *Miracle of the Rose*. It falls (to the tomb) then, accusing itself, under the pen. "All burglars will understand the dignity with which I was arrayed when I held my jimmy, my 'pen.' From its weight, material, and shape, and from its function too, emanated an authority that made me a man. I had always needed that steel verge. . . .

". . . The two wedges . . . lightened it and gave it that air of a winged prick [*bite*] by which I was haunted. I slept beside it, for the warrior sleeps armed."

Let's cut very short, act very quickly: this prick I sleep next to is less the father's, as one would think, than the Virgin Mary *herself*. I do *not* say that it is *not* the father's, I say "less than." But to know how the father's is written, one still has to elaborate, induce, in order to glide better.

Thus, in (the) place of the flower, the anthographic, marginal and paraphing text: which no longer signifies.

the same stroke [*du même coup*] infinitely limits the play

ondly, he is an object for himself, an other than himself, a dividing himself in two (*ein sich Entzweiendes*), the Son (*der Sohn*)."

The Christian God manifests the concrete spirit, which still remained veiled and abstract in Judaism; but he manifests this only by becoming father. The father—the Jewish God certainly was one—remains an abstract universal form, as long as he has no acknowledged son. A father without a son is not a father. He manifests himself as concrete spirit—and not just anticipated, represented, *vorgestellt*—only by dividing himself in his seed that is *his* other, or rather that is himself as the object for himself, the other for him and that then returns to him, in which he returns to himself: his son [*fils*].

As this son is infinite—the son of God—he is not the other of God. He gives to God his image. But as this son of God is man—finite—he is God separated from himself and appearing himself as the passage from the infinite to the finite, from the finite to the infinite. God knows and recognizes himself in his son. He assists (in) his death, burial, his magnification, his resurrection. The knowledge relation that organizes this whole scene is a third, a third term, the element of the infinite's relation to self: it is the holy spirit. This medium obtains the element of *familiarity*: God's familiarity with his very own seed, the element of God's play with himself. The (infinite) exemplar gives itself and makes the (finite) exemplar return to it. The infinite father gives himself, by self-fellation, self-insemination, and self-conception, a finite son who, in order to posit himself there and incarnate himself as the son of God, becomes infinite, dies as the finite son, lets himself be buried, clasped in bandages he will soon undo for the infinite son to be reborn.

". . . a dividing himself in two, the Son. But this other than himself is equally himself immediately; he knows himself and intuits himself in that—and it is this self-knowledge and self-intuition which constitutes the third element, the Spirit itself."

The spirit is neither the father nor the son, but filiation, the relation of father to son, of son to father, of father to father through the mediation of the son, of son to son through the mediation of the father. The spirit is the element of the *Aufhebung* in which the seed returns to the father.

"In other words, the Spirit is the whole, and not just one or other of the elements for itself. Or to put it in terms [defined, expressed, *ausgesprochen*] of feeling (*Empfindung*), God is eternal love, whose nature is to have the other as its own (*das Andere als sein Eigenes zu haben*). It is this trinity [this tripleness, *Dreifaltigkeit*] which raises Christianity above the other religions. If it did not have this Trinity, the other religions might well provide more material for thought than it does. The Trinity is the speculative part (*das*

The *glas*'s, such as we shall have heard them, toll the end of signification, of sense, and of the signifier. Outside which, not to oppose the signature, still less to appose, affix it to that, we remark the signature that through its name, in spite of what is thereby named, no longer signifies.

In *no longer* signifying, the signature

what is a signature? And what becomes of the language of flowers in it? The question must find a form that can accommodate, for example, the following propositions: (1) *Miracle of the Rose*: ". . . the flowers spoke . . . ," (2) "I do not think they [flowers] symbolize anything" (*Funeral Rites*).

What then, under these conditions, is a "book laden with flowers" (*Our-Lady-of-the-Flowers*)? A bed, of course, that is, as shall be perceived later on, some pages, the skeleton of J. D. that "had been laid out on a bed of roses and gladioli" (*Funeral Rites*), and that they would like to eat with dialectophagous words: "I am his tomb." "I was hungry for Jean." "I shall never keep close enough to the conditions under which I am writing this book. Though its avowed aim is to tell of the glory of Jean D., it perhaps has more unforeseeable secondary aims."

I am only good for embalming.

If, then, there is no language of flowers, if the flower is in (the) place of zero signification, how can this symbolic zero *take hold* in a jungle of signs and figures belonging to the natural tongue, to nature, to the physical, to the physical tongue, as a mother tongue that is necessarily foreign to it? A question again of *phusis* as *mimesis*. It also comes down to knowing how to be done with what we eat. The work of mourning as work of the tongue, of the teeth, and of saliva, of deglutition too, of assimilation and belching. The end of Jean refers to the Last Supper scene [*Cène*]. ". . . the tomb, he needs light for two thousand years! . . . and food for two thousand years. . . . (*She shrugs her shoulders.*) Oh well, everything's in working order, and dishes have been prepared. Glory means descending into the tomb with tons of victuals!" (*The Balcony*).

Spekulative) of Christianity, and it is through it that philosophy can discover the Idea of reason in the Christian religion too."

But just as Christianity represents and anticipates itself only in its *Vorstellung*, in Judaism, so the absolute religion Christianity is remains the *Vorstellung* of *Sa* as philosophy. *Vorstellung*'s structure opens the scene of the holy family onto *Sa*.

Thus Christianity offers the example of a *naturally speculative* religion. Philosophy—speculative dialectics—will have been the truth of this religious representation of the speculative. Just as German, the naturally speculative tongue in certain of its traits, relieves itself by itself in order to become the universal tongue, so a historically determinate religion becomes absolute religion, and an absolute religion relieves its character of representation (*Vorstellung*) in order to become absolute truth. This explains how Hegelian philosophy—through and through a philosophy *of* religion—could be read as an effect of Christianity as well as an implacable atheism. Religion accomplishes itself and dies in the philosophy that is its truth, as the truth of past religion, of the essence as thought past (*Gewesenheit*) of the Christian religion.

Truth—the past-thought—is always the death (relieved, erected, buried, unveiled, unbandaged [*débandée*]) of what it is the truth of.

The position of the father, filiation such as we have just read it, also *in truth* interprets itself as the position of the dead father. The

quoin of the Last Supper (scene) and judas. *Totem and Taboo* has just inscribed the Orphic origin of the doctrine of original sin, the relation between Christ and Dionysus-Zagreus cut into morsels: "There can be no doubt that in the Christian myth the original sin was one against God the Father. If, however, Christ redeemed mankind from the burden of original sin by the sacrifice of his own life, we are driven to conclude that the sin was a murder. The law of talion, which is so deeply rooted in human feelings, lays it down that a murder (*ein Mord*) can only be expiated by the sacrifice of another life: self-sacrifice points back to (*weist zurück*) blood-guilt. And if this sacrifice of one's own life brought about reconciliation with God the Father, the crime to be expiated can only have been the murder of the father (*der Mord am Vater*).

"In the Christian doctrine, therefore, men were acknowledging in the most undisguised manner (*am unverhülltesten*) the guilty primaeval deed (*zu der schuldvollen Tat der Urzeit*), since they found the fullest atonement for it in the sacrifice of this one son. Reconciliation with the father was all the more complete (*um so gründlicher*) since the sacrifice was simultaneously accompanied by a total renunciation of the women on whose account the rebellion against the father was started. But at that point the psychological fatality of ambivalence demanded its rights. The very deed in which the son offered the greatest possible atonement to the father brought him at the same time to the attainment of his wishes against the father. He himself became God, beside, or, more properly, in place of, the father (*neben, eigentlich an Stelle des Vaters*). A

If flowers figure "infernal props," it is because, signifying nothing, they are nonetheless the support of, but forever withdrawn from, the whole text, all determinations. ". . . they were beginning to exist for me with their own existence, with less and less the help of a support: the flowers" (*Miracle of the Rose*). Such is the relationship of the miracle to the text. That is, to a remain(s) that is the remain(s) of nothing, that does not remain at peace. That above all is not a result, in the sense of speculative dialectics.

"THE QUEEN: But it was I who did everything, who organized everything. . . . Remain(s). . . . What is. . . .

"(*Suddenly a burst of machine-gun fire*)" (*The Balcony*).

You see, but you cannot see, you are necessarily blind to the fact that flowers, not themselves shown, hardly even promised, are constantly being stolen, filched, swiped from you. In the *Journal*: "'The burial. We need flowers. . . .'

"'Go swipe some flowers with his pals. . . .'

"At night, with two friends, he pilfered some flowers from the Montparnasse cemetery. . . .

"They went looking for roses with a flashlight. . . . A joyous intoxication made them steal [*voler*], run [*courir*] and joke among the monuments. 'You can't imagine what it was like,' he said to me."

no longer belongs to or comes from the order of signification, of the signified or the signifier.

Thus, dingdong [*Donc*]—what emits a tolling of the knell, *un coup de glas*, is the fact that the flower, for example, inasmuch as it signs, no longer signifies anything.

Falls (to the tomb), remain(s).

Neither a noun nor a verb in any case.

The *seing* does not suffer to be illegible in this respect. If, at least, reading means (to say) to decipher

son-religion displaced the father-religion (*die Sohnesreligion löst die Vaterreligion ab*). As a sign of this substitution [of this ersatz, *Zum Zeichen dieser Ersetzung*] the ancient totem meal was revived in the form of communion, in which the company of brothers ate the flesh and blood of the son—no longer the father—obtained sanctity thereby and identified themselves with him. . . . The Christian communion, however, is at bottom a new setting-aside (*Beseitigung*) of the father, a repetition of the deed that must be expiated."
What is the difference between this viewpoint (the gaze of judas) and that of speculative dialectics, concerning the most unveiled truth? What is, at table, at dinner, the gap [*écart*] between Judas and the one who is the truth? Who holds here the truest discourse? What place then returns to a Judas. But can the discourse of truth leave the table?
Verily

life of the spirit as history is the death of the father in his son. The relief of this death always has the sense of a reconciliation: death will have been able to be only a free and violent act. History is the process of a murder. But this murder is a sacrifice: the victim offers himself. A scandal that a finite tribunal cannot understand at all: a victim would thus have tendered to the murderers, at the same time as his body, the instrument of the crime.

a sense or to refer to something. But this illegibility that takes form by falling (from my hand, for example), that scrambles and broaches signification, is that without which there would not be any text. A text "exists," resists, consists, represses, lets itself be read or written only if it is worked (over) by the illegibility of a proper name. I have not—not yet—said that the proper name exists, or that it becomes illegible when it falls (to the tomb) in the signature. The proper name resounds, losing itself at once, only in the instant of its *debris*, when it is broken, scrambled, jammed, while touching, tampering with the *seing*.

What is the function of this Christian model? In what sense is it exemplary for speculative onto-theology? Can this model be circumscribed and displaced as a finite and particular structure, bound to given historical conditions? Can a history different from the one represented here be interrogated? Can the horizon be changed? the logic?

which is done notably starting from *The Origin of the Family, Private Property, and the State*. Engel's title reproduces the first and the last moment of the Hegelian *Sittlichkeit* and deports the analysis outside the Western Christian center on the basis of Bachofen's and Morgan's works on family ethnology

Within the system, the program of the so-called youthful works on Christianity will have been the law. With a scope as powerful and invariable as the first words of John's Gospel on the history of the West.

Concerning the family, one can follow a very precise homology between the system's first schemas and those of the final period.

The passage from Judaism to Christianity is interpreted as the advent of love, in other words, of the family, as

You are still *on the stairway*, on the way to a crypt that always expects you to come in advance of just what it seems to conceal. "It was then that we began to exchange the love letters in which we spoke of ourselves, of plans for robberies, of prodigious jobs [*coups*] and, above all, of Mettray. He signed his first letter 'Illegible,' as a matter of caution, and I began my reply with 'Dear Illegible.' Pierre Bulkaen will remain for me the indecipherable. It was always on the stairway, where he waited for me, that we handed each other the slips of paper."

the relief of formal and abstract morality (*Moralität*) (in that respect Kantianism is, structurally, a Judaism). This passage sets to work an ontotheological theory of the figure, an ontotheological rhetoric and semiotic that belong by full right to the very content of the discourse.

Wasn't there then any family before Christianity? Before Christianity, the family had not yet posited itself as such. The family announced, represented, anticipated itself. Love was not yet at the hearth of the family. The true father/son relation awaited Christianity, monogamy too, such as it will be defined in the *Philosophy of Right*. From Christ on, love is substituted for right and abstract duty: in general and not just in the relations between spouses.

The Spirit of Christianity: "Similarly, over against dutiful fidelity in marriage and the right to divorce a wife, Jesus sets love. Love excludes the (culpable) desire not forbidden by that duty and, except in one case, suspends this permission to divorce, a leave contradictory to that duty."

Jesus suspends, lifts the permission save in one case. Here the German word for suspend or lift is *aufheben*. Jesus suspends the permission only inasmuch as it still belongs to abstract right. In truth he suspends and relieves abstract right into love.

We are not going to ask ourselves here *what is* this operation? Since the ontological question (what is it? what is? what does being mean (to say) and so on) unfolds itself here only according to the process [*processus*] and structure of *Aufhebung*, confounds itself with the absolute of the *Aufhebung*, one can no longer ask: what is the *Aufhebung*? as one would ask: what is this or that? or, what is the determination of such and such a particular concept? Being is *Aufhebung*. *Aufhebung* is being, not as a determinate state or the determinable totality of beings [*étant*], but as the "active," productive essence of being. So the *Aufhebung* cannot form the *object* of any determined question. We are continually referred back to this, but that reference [*renvoi*] refers to nothing determinable.

It is impossible, for example—but the example also relieves itself—to understand the advent of the *true* family (love and monogamy), of the Christian family, without taking account of the *Aufhebung* of abstract right. Loving being reconciles itself despite injury, without taking account of right, of the judge, and of the one who judges the right (*nicht vom Richter ihr Recht zumessen*), without any regard [*sans égard et sans regard*] for right (*ohne alle Rücksicht auf Recht*). A handwritten note adds: "Love even requires the *Aufhebung* of right that is born of a separation (*Trennung*), a lesion (*Beleidigung*); love requires reconciliation (*Versöhnung*)."

The schema of the *Philosophy of Right* is in place: love as the relief of right and abstract morality, that is, of a split between objectivity and subjectivity.

The *Miracle of the Rose* is what had begun (at Fontevrault, its cells in the form of a "vertical coffin" in the "ivy") with setting on an anthotropical stage, though sideways, the graft(ing) of the proper name so as to leave it apparently as a seedling, as if one had to be on the lookout [*faire gâfe à*] not to fetter anything in it (that (*ça*) is always written like that (*comme ça*): the grand style of the flower seems in the open air not to touch it the very moment that (*ça*) elaborates the most). A graft does not supervene upon the proper. The proper begins with finding in the graft its bursting [*éclat*]: its appearing or its blowing [*éclosion*], but also its morseling.

The name of the person who seems to affix, append here his *seing* (Genet) is the name, as we know (but how and from where do we know?), of his mother. Who then would have given birth according to a kind of immaculate conception.

The mother's name would be—commonly—the name of a plant or a flower, except for one letter, the fallen s, dropped [*l's tombé*], or to cicatrize its fall [*chute*], for a circumflex. Covering the space between [*l'entre-deux*] the lips or displaced letters—in (the) place of s—with a stretched, pointed sheet, a tent, or pyramidal nonument [*monumanque pyramidale*].

The handwritten note has been deleted, but it is in accord with the whole context that constantly confirms it. It intervenes immediately after the proposition on love as the *Aufhebung* of conjugal rights and duties as such.

In the (Judaic) order of abstract right and duty, of the objective law, the duty of fidelity, fidelity as duty went together with the right to separate oneself from one's wife. But the duty as such does not forbid the desire of infidelity; it only forbids, in objectivity, the act of infidelity. The love that Jesus opposes to this objective law suspends even up to the unfaithful desire. At least he excludes (*ausschliesst*) this desire at the same time that he suspends (*aufhebt*) the permission (to separate from one's wife) inasmuch as it is contrary to fidelity. The interdict bearing on infidelity is maintained, but at the same time abolished [*supprimé*]: this is no longer an interdict bearing from the outside, in a heteronomic way. It belongs to the spontaneity of love; it is assumed in desire's freedom, in the autonomy of a desire that no longer desires what it cannot have or only desires what it can have, desires what it has. The vulgar translation of the *Aufhebung*: nothing coming from the outside forbids you from cheating on your wife, but

discourse, here, of course, of man for man

you no longer want to since you love her. Then the permission for you to separate from her, an authorization contrary to the duty of fidelity, remains suspended (*aufgehoben*) as it were by the past, but you no longer realize it since you no longer want to.

The interiorization of the interdict, the interiorization of the objective law (right and duty) by love, the assimilation digesting the objective debt and abstract exchange, the devouring of the limit is then the *Aufhebung*'s *economic* effect. Economic: subjectivized, the interdict is in a certain way lifted; I am freer since I am no longer subject to any outside interdiction. Economic: my satisfaction, at least as consciousness, is adjusted to [*réglée sur*] my desire; I do what I desire, I am faithful because I desire it and nothing else.

But would the economy do nothing but interiorize an interdict? but domesticate it in freedom's being close by self?

The economic effect is more complex. To say that the interdictive limit has simply passed from the outside to the inside, without being transformed in this passage, would require that desire, in Christian marriage, be limited, and first of all limited to a finite being. Now that is not at all the case. The finite crosses itself toward the infinite. No longer is one limited to loving a finite being: one loves a finite being as infinite. In passing inside, the limit becomes infinite: so there is no longer any finite limit, no longer any limit or, what comes down to the same, there is an

Genêt names a plant with flowers—yellow flowers (*sarothamnus scoparius*, *genista*; broom, *genette*, *genêt-à-balais*, poisonous and medicinal, as distinct from the dyer's broom, *genista tinctoria*, *genestrolle*, dyer's greenweed, woodwaxen, an herb for dying yellow); *genet* a kind of horse. Of Spain, a country of great importance in the text.

If all his literature sings and weaves a funerary hymen to nomination, Genet never sets any value, noblesse oblige, on anything but naming himself.

He rides horse(back) on his proper name. He holds it by the bit [*mors*]. Like a Spanish grandee or a circumflex. But also like a child in his father's saddle.

The cavalier phantasm presides over the great inner scene and takes possession of all the senses. Feigning perhaps to give "my" "illegible name" for reading. Illegible name, hence positively legible.

Miracle of the Rose: "'You're going by? Where are you going? . . . And besides, I don't like your tone. Take your hands out of your belt . . .'

"I was on horseback.

"Even when I am very calm, I feel as if I were being swept by a storm which may be due to my mind's stumbling over every unevenness of surface because of its rapid pace, or to my desires, which are violent because they are almost always suppressed, and when I live my inner scenes, I have the intoxication that comes from always living them on horseback, on a rearing and galloping steed. I am a horseman. It is since I have known Bulkaen that I live on horseback, and I enter the lives of others on horseback as a Spanish grandee enters the Cathedral of Seville.

infinite limit. Conjugal desire is free because it is subject to an infinite law.

The family according to (Christian) love is infinite. This family is already what could be called the speculative family. Now the speculative family follows the infinitely circular course of the father/son filiation: the infinity of desire, of marriage, and of the inner law holds itself between the father and the son. Except for a short detour, with the insignificant exception of an inessentiality (the wife here is as it were matter), the essence of speculative marriage, with all the systematic consequences that can be inferred from this, consecrates the union of father and son.

One column in the other.

The exception, the only case (*Fall*) where the right to separate oneself from one's wife is maintained, where the suspense is suspended, the *Aufhebung* relieved, occurs when the wife *has taken the initiative*, when "the wife has bestowed her love on another." According to Jesus, "the husband may not remain a slave to her."

No doubt the speculative family achieves its destination only with Christ. But this proposition is not simple. To achieve its destination is to relieve itself and go out from itself. Christianity itself achieves itself only by relieving itself in(to) its philosophical truth. Then one would have to specify that with Christianity the speculative family breaches/broaches itself, begins to come to itself, to love, and to the true marriage that constitutes the family as family. The first moment of *Sittlichkeit* would be inaugurated by Christ. This does not form a simple proposition either: the upsurging of Christianity announced itself. There is *family* before *the* (Christian) family. So one must interrogate this circular and teleological structure of the before and after, this speculative reading of the future perfect that puts the family before itself.

Immediately before Christianity there is Judaism: at once family and nonfamily, nonfamily as the not-yet-there of the already-there, the family's being-there *not consisting*, only consisting in dissolving itself in its passage.

The Christian thesis, the axial thesis that replaces the Jewish thesis by opposing it, overturns mastery. In substituting love for mastery, for the Jewish relations of violence and slavery, Jesus founded the family. The family has constituted itself through him: "To the Jewish idea of God as their Lord (*Herrn*) and Governor (*Gebieter*), Jesus opposes a relationship of God to men like that of a father to his children." Such is the "exact antithesis" that gives to the family its infinite foundation.

Before the antithesis that comes to place itself in place of the thesis, there was family nonetheless. Judaism was not only what preceded the advent of the speculative family, what resisted it up to

My thighs grip the flanks, I spur my mount, my hands tighten on the reins.

"Not that it happens quite that way, I mean not that I really know I'm on horseback, but rather I make the gestures and have the spirit of a man on horseback: my hand tightens, I toss back my head [*ma tête se relève*], my voice is arrogant. The sensation of riding a noble, whinnying animal overflowed into my daily life and gave me what is called a cavalier look and what I considered a victorious tone and bearing.

"The guard reported me, and I was brought up before the warden. . . ."

Not to arrest the career of a Genet. For the first time I am afraid, while writing, as they say, "on" someone, of being read by him. Not to arrest him, not to draw him back, not to bridle him. Yesterday he let me know that he was in Beirut, among the Palestinians at war, encircled outcasts. I know that what interests me always takes (its/his) place over there, but how to show that? He almost never writes anymore, he has interred [*enterré*] literature like no one, he leaps wherever that explodes (*ça saute*) in the world, wherever the absolute knowledge of Europe takes a

"Your heart that a massive cavalier's spurs / will never open," my slashed paraph that parades in freedom like a wild animal, "A curious beast would appear if each of my emotions became the animal it evokes: anger [*colère*] growls under my cobra neck [*col*], the same cobra swells up what I do not dare to name; my cavalry, my merry-go-rounds are born of my insolence. . . ."
Concerning the "fear of metamorphoses," and above all of animals, *The Thief's Journal* makes the point that "it is not mere rhetoric which requires the comparison."
Begin, then, to approach the unnameable crypt and the studio of Alberto Giacometti, where such a wound of the paraph takes on animal form. You will have already suspected that if the signature is all that at once, it is neither a thing, nor a flower, nor an animal. Remain(s) to (be) know(n) if there is any

36

a certain point. Judaism had constituted a certain natural family in relieving already another family more natural still. The value of nature must be handled very prudently. Nature is not a determinate essence, a unique moment. It overlays [*recouvre*] all the forms of the spirit's exteriority to self. Nature appears then—while progressively disappearing therein—in each stage of the spirit's becoming. For example, for having broken with the natural-biological group, the human family is no less the natural, the most natural moment of *Sittlichkeit*, and so on. In this sense, the family is always natural, even the Christian family. But the Christian family relieves a natural family, the Jewish family, that itself relieves a more natural family. And each relief breaks with what it relieves, leaves between the other and itself a kind of margin that constitutes the truth of the other as the (past) essence whose truth the relief, for its part, gives to be read.

There was—then—a Jewish family deprived of love; this family has itself broken with a more primitive and natural family.

Here begins the legendary discourse on/of the eagle and the two columns.

On castration and dissemination, a question going back to the flood.

Like Condillac, like Rousseau, Kant and some others, Hegel resorts to a kind of theoretical fiction: the recital of a catastrophic event reconstitutes the ideal-historic origin of human society. And this recital reinscribes the Biblical narration with eyes fixed on a network of philosophemes. For it to run [*ça marche*], the two texts must indeed somewhere be homogeneous.

The flood is the loss of the state of nature (*Verlust des Naturzustandes*). Before the flood (*Flut*) man lived in natural harmony with nature. The flood tears man, uproots him from nature, destroys the beautiful unity. Ever since then man nurses an infinite, monstrous disbelief (*ungeheuerste Unglaube*) toward nature. No longer his mother, nature has taken back or poisoned all the resources of protective belief (*Glauben*) she had given or promised. Of this mother we keep only some obscure traces (*sind uns nur wenige dunkle Spuren aufbehalten worden*). Till then, she had shown herself "friendly or tranquil (*freundlich oder ruhig*)," in "the equipoise (*Gleichgewicht*) of her elements"; now she responds to humanity's faith (*Glauben*) with "the most destructive, invincible, irresistible hostility." The mother turns against man, dismantles herself, causes havoc.

Thus, in the flood man conceives the plan to control in his turn what had sheltered, protected, nourished him. Saying that he conceives the plan to master, to defend himself with an apotropaic gesture from what, numbing, lulling his belief with an equal and

blow [*coup*], and these (hi)stories of *glas*, *seing*, flower, horse ought to make him shit.

How right he is. This is what I want to show by deporting you as swiftly as possible to the limits of a basin, a sea, where there arrive for an interminable war the Greek, the Jew, the Arab, the Hispano-Moor. Which I am also (following), by the trace [*Que je suis aussi, à la trace*].

If all this eloquence about the signature in the form of a horse makes him shit, too bad. The *seing* also falls (to the tomb) like excrement under seal [*sous scellé*].

To magnify *the turd* [l'étron], to glorify what falls cut (*stronzo, stronzare, strunzen*) under the saddle [*sous la selle*], to erect the stallion [*étalon*], the standard [*étalon*] of his signature, or to cause the erection to fall from the horse, the king from the throne—all that would be equivalent.

Remain(s) — to (be) know(n) — what causes shitting.

Now—the cavalier scene ("I was on horseback") brings along in its procession, in little continuous jerks, at the trot, the two pages that follow, where, as if by chance, at Fontevrault (which "has its roots in the vegetable world of our children's prison"), in the "center of the circle," stands "the can into which the men shit."

It is a pureblood, an Arabian this time, a sort of erected hole one mounts like a horse, a throne, the cone of a volcano. The erection in abyss, that is how

37

regular movement, had fallaciously promised him symbiosis, that is saying too much: one could be content with saying that he has begun to conceive—nothing else.

In all the senses of that word. Noah is the concept. By a bad wordplay, Jewish-Greek, à la Joyce, and mixing in a little gallicism (Noé), one would say noesis.

In effect, in order to control maternal nature's hostility in her unleashed waters, she had to be thought, conceived, grasped. Being thought is being controlled. The concept marks the interruption of a first state of love. Her son says to nature: you don't love me, you don't want me to love you, I'm going to think you, conceive you, control you. The concept busies itself around a wound. "If man was to hold out against the aggressions of a nature now hostile, nature had to be mastered (*beherrscht*); and since the whole divided in two (*das entzweite Ganze*) can be divided only into idea and actuality (*in Idee und Wirklichkeit*), so also the supreme unity of mastery (*Beherrschung*) lies either in being-thought (*Gedachten*) or in being-actual (*Wirklichen*)."

Noah chose to gather together the world torn apart, to reconstitute in sum the *Gleichgewicht* in the being-thought. He has chosen to make his ideal-thought (*gedachtes Ideal*) come to be, to divinize it in a way, and to oppose to it all the remain(s) of nature as nature thought, that is mastered (*als Gedachtes, d. h. als Beherrschtes*). Therefore the ideal thought (God) "promised" Noah to place the elements at his service, to hold them back in their limits, so that no flood could come to submerge humanity. This kind of alliance with the father reestablishes by contract the natural *Gleichgewicht* that nature had broken by unleashing its waters. The ark was able to float, carrying in its flanks, on the deck or at the bottom of the hold, the exemplary living ones.

The noetic response to the mother's murderous aggression is accompanied from then on, such is its singularity, by a cult of life (*Zōē*). Man was forbidden to kill man. In breaking this rule [*règle*] one loses life oneself. Such is the contract of thought with itself, that is, with God. God, in compensation, grants man mastery (*Herrschaft*) over the plants and the animals. Putting one or the other to death, the unique authorized destruction of the living, sanctions the exchange. But in return the living must be honored, and it remains forbidden to consume the blood of animals, which still contains their soul or life (it is the same thing in Hebrew, and the *Spirit of Christianity* follows here Genesis 9 : 4 very closely).

To the rupture of the maternal *Gleichgewicht*, another response could be made.

Not the quelled flanks of a floating dwelling but the erection of a warlike tower.

Like Noah, Nimrod ripostes to the natural violence by making the thought, the *Gedachtes*, be. Like Noah, he also imposes the law

that (*ça*) signs and how that (*ça*) gets into the saddle and how that (*ça*) reigns, how that (*ça*) is jammed, how that (*ça*) signs and that (*ça*) reigns. *Genêts* grow very close to volcanoes. "At the center of the circle is the can into which the men shit, a recipient three feet high in the form of a truncated cone. It has two ears, one on each side, on which you place your feet after sitting down, and a very low backrest, like that of an Arab saddle, so that when you drop your load you have the majesty of a barbaric king on a metal throne. When you have to go, you raise your hand, without saying anything; the assistant makes a sign, and you leave the line, unbuttoning your trousers, which stay up without a belt. You sit on the top of the cone with your feet on the ears and your balls [*couilles*] hanging. The others continue their silent round, perhaps without noticing you. They hear your shit drop into the urine, which splashes [*gicle*] your naked cheeks. You piss and get off [*descend*]. The odor rises up. When I entered the room, what struck me most was the silence of the thirty inmates and, immediately, the solitary, imperial can, center of the moving circle.

". . . 'One . . . two! One . . . two!'

"It is still the same guttural voice, a big shot's voice, that issues from a throat encumbered with oysters which he can still spit violently in the face of a jerk [*cloche*]. It is the same cry and voice he had at Mettray."

The "inmate," the "circle of inmates" who stand up straight, resembling one another and substituting for one another in silence like letters on the page, one in place of another, one counting for another, the glob that resounds in cadence off the walls of the grotto like a moiled, guttural, hard and coated *glas*, the glory of solid excrement raised in the incorporeal song

of the living. But unlike Noah, he does not proceed under the sign of peace: he unleashes in his turn a tyrannical violence, distrust, war; he founds a society united by force, and the law of the living is the law of the strongest. Instead of opposing to the sea just what the sea carries still sitting on it, rocked [*bercé*] by it, the ark, he faces it, jostles it, and cleaves it with one gigantic tower. Here Hegel follows the indications of Moses, which agree with Josephus' *Antiquities of the Jews*: "For he [Nimrod] had resolved to build a tower (*Turm*) which was to be far higher than the waves and streams (*Wasserwogen und Wellen*) could ever raise themselves (*sich auftürmen*) and in this way to avenge the downfall (*Untergang*) of his forefathers (according to another tale, Eupolemos in Eusebius [*Praeparatio evangelica* ix 17], the tower was to have been built by the very survivors of the flood)."

By the turn [*tour*] of a contract, Noah had delegated mastery to a more powerful one; Nimrod himself has repressed, bound hand and foot, tamed the hostile power (*dass er selbst sie bändigte*). But in both cases it is a question of a "forced peace" with the sea. The split is consummated by a war and reproduces the cleavage by which nature, promising maternal protection and in truth unfolding the worst threat, is separated from itself.

To this warlike, rigid, avenging apotropaic, Hegel already opposes the Greek response to the flood: not a forced peace but a peace of harmonious friendship, of reconciliation. And this peace is not concluded or imposed by a leader, but by a happy couple: neither Noah nor Nimrod reconciled himself with the enemy as did a very beautiful couple (*ein schöneres Paar*), Deucalion and Pyrrha, when after the flood they invited men to renew their friendship with the world, with nature, when they made them forget the need and hatred in the joy and enjoyment [*jouissance*], when they concluded a peace of love, when they became the root stock of a beautiful nation and made of their time the mother of a newborn nature, which was going to preserve the flower of its youth (*und ihre Zeit zur Mutter einer neugeborenen, ihre Jugendblüte erhaltenden Natur machten*).

So the Jew remains stiff, on edge, taut in his opposition to maternal nature. He is ugly, offers ugliness as his spectacle, is "lacking" the "spirit of beauty (*Geist der Schönheit*)." He remains cut in two, and the

remain(s) that all this is done with stones, Nimrod's tower and the insemination of a new rootstock:
"After the flood, which left them at the top of Parnassus, both of them, Deucalion and Pyrrha, created human beings by throwing stones over their shoulder. Whereas Pyrrha created women, Deucalion created men."
How does the stone become a child? the flower an animal? innocence culpable? Phenomenology of spirit: "Innocence, therefore, is merely non-action

of the odor while everything "drops [*descend*]," falls in, hangs, prompting the liquid baton to squirt [*gicler*] out on high, toward the naked cheeks—all this is a mobile glossary, more active through the words missing, through all that he robs from your pocket the moment you loaf about like a tourist in the text, your eyes fixed on what the native really wants to show you, carelessly, about his operation. After the hit [*coup*], it will be too late.

So the *Miracle of the Rose* cultivates the grafts of the proper name. Battle, labor, digging [*Lutte, labeur, labour*], with catastrophic turns [*retours de batons*], waves of repression, against the desire to reconstitute, out of the *seing* of the virgin, the genealogical force. In morseling the name, dissociating it, making it unrecognizable in glorious deeds [*coups d'éclat*: strokes of *ec* there], one also extends it, makes it gain ground like a clandestine occupation force. At the limit, of the text, of the world, there would remain nothing more than an enormous signature, big with everything it will have engulfed in advance, but pregnant with itself alone.

A necessarily undecidable, if not contradictory, movement. An economy of loss ($\rightarrow$ breast [*sein*] $\leftrightarrow$ child $\leftrightarrow$ excrement $\leftrightarrow$ penis $\rightarrow$). The signature keeps nothing of all it signs.

Plant the *genêt* there, the cavalier inscription falls off it, the funerary monument is a plant *à genêt*: that writes, i.e., speaks without an accent.
"Moments later, likewise muffled, but remote, a voice, which sounded to me like that of the inmate, cried out:

(*Nichttun*), like the mere being of a stone (*das Sein eines Steines*), not even that of a child."

As interpreted by Hegel, the Greek flood has more affinity than the Jew with the spirit of Christianity: reconciliation, love, and the founding of a family. The opposition of Jew and Greek is pursued, precisely regarding the family. The contrast between Abraham on the one hand, Cadmus and Danaus on the other, reproduces in its signification the contrast between Noah or Nimrod on the one hand, Deucalion and Pyrrha on the other.

Abraham abandons Chaldaea, his native land, in the company of his father. Then in the level plains of Mesopotamia (*in den Ebenen Mesopotamiens*), he repeats and aggravates the break. He wants to become a leader and make himself absolutely independent. He breaks with his family (*riss er sich auch . . . vollends von seiner Familie los*). And that in a decisive, nearly arbitrary way, without having been injured or driven out, without having suffered the least of those pains that answer some injustice or cruelty; those pains would still testify to a wounded but living love, a love trying to find again a new fatherland in order "to flourish . . . there." No, without the least affection, the least affect, has Abraham torn apart *die Bande*, the bonds of communal life and thus breached/broached his history and engendered the history of the Jewish people. "The first act which made Abraham the root-father of a nation (*Stammvater einer Nation*) is a splitting (*Trennung*) which snaps the ligaments of communal life and love (*die Bande des Zusammenlebens und der Liebe*). The entirety of the relationships in which he had hitherto lived with men and nature, these beautiful relationships of his youth (Joshua xxiv. 2), he spurned."

The Jew does not love beauty. Suffice it to say that, nothing else, he does not love.

Undoubtedly, Abraham raises: a genealogical tree, a family, a people, a nation. But whose lineage, as it were, never touches the earth. It takes root nowhere, never reconciles itself with nature, remains foreign everywhere. Cadmus and Danaus had also abandoned their fatherland, but their departure had been motivated, had taken the form of a battle. After that they had searched for

very tragedy of his cut [*coupure*] is ugly, abominable. "The great tragedy (*Trauerspiel*) of the Jewish people is no Greek tragedy; it can rouse neither terror nor pity, for both of these arise only out of the fate which follows from the inevitable slip of a beautiful being (*schönen Wesens*); it can arouse horror (*Abscheu*) alone. The fate of the Jewish people is the fate of Macbeth who stepped out of nature itself, clung to alien Beings, and so in their service had to trample and slay everything holy in human nature, had at last to be forsaken by his gods (since these were objects and he their slave) and be dashed to pieces on his faith itself."

"'Regards to your fanny [*à ta lune*] from my prick!'

"The guards in the office heard it too but didn't bat an eyelash. Thus, as soon as I arrived I realized that no convict's voice would be clear. It is either a murmur low enough for the guards not to hear, or else a cry muffled by a thickness of walls and anguish.

"As soon as each of us gave his name, age, occupation, and distinguishing marks, and signed with the print of his forefinger, he was taken by a guard to the wardrobe. It was my turn:

"'Your name?'

"'Genet.'

"'Plantagenet?'

"'Genet, I tell you.'

"'What if I want to say Plantagenet? That (*Ça*) upset you?'

"'. . .'

"'Given name?'

"'Jean.'

"'Age?'

"'Thirty.'

"'Profession?'

"'No profession.'

"The guard gave me a dirty look [*coup d'œil méchant*]. Perhaps he despised me for not knowing that the Plantagenets were interred in Fontevrault, that their coat of arms—leopards and the Maltese Cross—is still on the stained-glass windows of the chapel."

Second movement of the crowd on the theoretical agora.

Departed are those who thought the flower signified, symbolized, metaphorized, metonymized, that one was devising repertories of signifiers and

another land in order to be "free" and to "love." Abraham, he "did *not* want to love, did *not* want to be free to love."

He does not carry his Lares with him, like the Greeks, he forgoes the hearth, the home, every residence, every at-home sedentariness. He does not stay, not even (close) by himself. Desert, nomadism, errance with herds on an arid and "boundless" (*grenzenlosen*) land. No place of his own. A conflict with nature, a struggle for him to get hold of water, a war with foreign nations he penetrates and undertakes to control. "The same spirit which had carried Abraham away from his kin led him through his encounters with foreign nations during the rest of his life; this was the spirit of self-maintenance in strict opposition to everything—the being-thought (*Gedachte*) raised to be the unity dominant over the nature which he regarded as infinite and hostile (for the only relationship possible between hostile entities is mastery (*Herrschaft*) of one by the other)."

What comes and deposits itself in the Abrahamic cut? Two remarks on this subject:

(1) Errance, the war with nature and nations, the ruse, the control, the violence do not dissolve the Jewish family. On the contrary, the Jewish family constitutes itself in isolation, the jealous closure of its identity, the fierceness of its endogamy. Abraham will have cut his bonds with his family and father only in order to become the stronger father of a more determinate family. What remains of/from the cut becomes stronger.

In order to remark the isolation, to reinforce the identification, to call itself a family (a family less natural than the preceding but still too natural by the very fact that it opposes nature): circumcision.

Circumcision is a determining cut. It permits cutting but, at the same time and in the same stroke [*du même coup*], remaining attached to the cut. The Jew arranges himself so that the cut part [*le coupé*] remains attached to the cut. Jewish errance limited by adherence and the countercut. The Jew is cutting only in order to treat thus, to contract the cut with itself.

"*Er hielt an seiner Absonderung fest, die er auch durch eine sich und seinen Nachkommen auferlegte körperliche Eigenheit auffallend machte.*" "He [Abraham] steadily persisted in cutting himself off from others, and he made this conspicuous by a physical property imposed on himself and his posterity."

With this symbolic castration that Hegelian discourse lightly glides over, Abraham associates endogamy: "Even his son he forbade to marry any Canaanitish woman but made him take a wife from his kinsfolk, and they lived at a great distance from him."

anthic figures, classifying flowers of rhetoric, combining them, ordering them, binding them up in a sheaf or a bouquet around the phallic arch (*arcus*, *arca*, ἀρχή, which trap you fall into doesn't matter).

Departed then are, save certain exceptions, duly so considered, the archeologists, philosophers, hermeneuts, semioticians, semanticians, psychoanalysts, rhetoricians, poeticians, even perhaps all those readers who still believe, in literature or anything else.

Those still in a hurry to recognize are patient for a moment: provided that it be anagrams, anamorphoses, somewhat more complicated, deferred and diverted semantic insinuations capitalized in the depths of a crypt, cleverly dissimulated in the play of letters and forms. Genet would then rejoin this powerful, occulted tradition that was long preparing its coup, its haywire start from sleep, while hiding its work from itself, anagrammatizing proper names, anamorphosing signatures and all that follows. Genet, by one of those movements in (n)*ana*, would have, knowing it or not—I have my own views about this, but that doesn't matter—silently, laboriously, minutely, obsessionally, compulsively, and with the moves of a thief in the night, set his signatures in (the) place of all the missing objects. In the morning, expecting to recognize familiar things, you find his name all over the place, in big letters, small letters, as a whole or in morsels deformed or recomposed. He is no longer there, but you live in his mausoleum or his

41

(2) Opposing himself to hostile, infinitely aggressive nature and humankind, Abraham behaves as a master. Through his infinite opposition, he reaches that thought of the infinite the Greek lacks. In this sense the spirit of Judaism elaborates a negativity or an abstraction indispensable to the production of Christianity. The desert, nomadism, and circumcision delimit the finite. The finite overflows and unbungs itself there. But in the same stroke, by founding Jewish law through this passage to mastery's abstract infinite, Abraham (a historic, finite, determinate being) submits himself to infinite control. He becomes its slave. He can tame nature only by contracting a relation with the infinite mastery of an all-powerful, jealous, violent, transcendent master, the God of the Jews. Abraham is not the master that he is, since he also has a master, since he is not the mastery that he disposes of by contract. As finite subject, he is under the infinite force that is loaned, entrusted him. Constructed, raised on this slave relation, "he could love nothing," only fear and cause to fear.

He could not even love his son. Just as he imposes on himself the sign (or simulacrum) of castration, he is constrained to cut himself off from his son, or at least to engage the operation that remained, it too, a simulacrum of sacrifice. His son was his only love (*einzige Liebe*), "the one mode of immortality he knew." His disquiet was appeased only when he undertook to assure himself that he could overcome this love and kill his son "with his own hand."

Circumcision and the sacrifice of Isaac are analogous gestures. Problems of reading that must be taken note of here.

The two operations conjugated under the concept "simulacrum of castration" appear on the same page. Although they are not fortuitously set apart in advance by Hegel from all the traits and events of the Abrahamic gesture, we must recognize that

(1) the two operations are not immediately placed in relation with each other. But they are, according to a short mediation, related to each other with a single jerk by the Hegelian interpretation. Both signify the curtailing, the cut, the transcendence, the absence or the subordination of love. All of that comes to (ful)fill the concept of castration. Is more and something else said when the word castration is pronounced? A question all the sharper since castration has an essential economic relation here with the simulacrum and does not let itself be thought as a real "event," in the current sense of these words.

(2) Hegel puts forward neither the concept nor the word castration. Taking into account everything that has happened since Hegel on that matter, do we read in the text that Hegel reads, in the one he writes as well, something that he himself, verily Abraham, could not read? Apparently and in many regards that is not very contestable. The word "castration," the very rapidly recon-

latrines. You thought you were deciphering, tracking down, pursuing, you are included. He has affected everything with his signature. He has affected his signature. He has affected it with everything. He himself is affected by it (he will even be decked out, later on, with a circumflex). He has tried, he himself, properly, to write what happens between the affect and the *seing*.

How does one give the *seing* to an affect? How does one do it without a simulacrum to attract the attention of all? By postiches, fetishes, pastiches? And finally, will one ever know whether the *seing* has arrived at signing, whether the signature has arrived at its text, whether the text has itself arrived at a proper name. Visibly dreaming about becoming, so as to resound, his own proper (*glas*), to attend *his own* interment after giving birth to himself or performing his own decollation, his own ungluing, he would have been watchful to block up all that he writes in the forms of a tomb. Of a tomb that comes down to his name, whose stony mass no longer even overflows the letters, yellow as gold or betrayal, like the *genêt*. Letters without a pedestal, a contract with writing as a funeral rite.

More precisely, the contract does not have the burial (place) as its object. Burial is not an event to come, foreseen by a contractual act. Burial is the signature of the contract. So much so that in determined places—those that seem to interest us here—this so-called literature of betrayal would itself betray itself; con-

stituted chain, the style of deciphering, the selection of lexemes, all that stands out clearly [*tranche*]. If Hegel had thought that (*ça*), he would have done and said as much (*comme ça*).

But these differences, however important, are not enough to confer a rigorous status on the gap [*écart*] between the two readings. They can be secondary, external, nonconceptual. From the conceptual perspective, what is a difference of style or rhythm, verily of narrative space?

Not insignificantly, the concept reduces the difference to nothing.

Once the difference is reduced, is something, some other thing added to Hegelian discourse by relating the Abrahamic figure to castration, verily to self-castration, supposing some such thing exists? Is something else or more being done than placing them, like Hegel, in relation to the process of the *Aufhebung*, of truth, of the law? One cannot fail to recognize that Hegel proposes a powerful systematic articulation of them. I have always said that, Hegel would respond to the doctors of castration. Besides, what do all of you understand by castration? Here we are not concerned with a real event but with an economic simulacrum: the property is constituted by castration's *le vraiment feint*, its truly feigned (circumcision and the interrupted sacrifice of Isaac). The doctors agree. Hegel: if we are not concerned with a real event, all of you must talk at great length, even spin tales, in order to describe or fulfill the conceptual structure of what you name castration; you must recount a legend, make a whole network of significations intervene; frankly speaking, you must make the whole world of signification intervene, beginning with the relief, truth, being, law, and so on. That is what I have done since the works on Judaism and Christianity up to the philosophy of right and passing through the encyclopedia and the greater logic. And all of you cannot even understand what you want to say by castration if you do not take charge of all the idealism of speculative dialectics.

And that is true.

So it is not certain that something more or different from Hegel is being said, that something more or different from what he himself read is being read when the word castration and other similar things are put forward. It is not certain that one conceptually intervenes in his logic. To do that, one would have to displace conceptually the conceptual articulation—for him manifest—between *Aufhebung*, castration, truth, law, and so on. Forces resistant to the *Aufhebung*, to the process of truth, to speculative negativity must be made to appear, and as well that these forces of resistance do not constitute in their turn relievable or relieving negativities.

In sum a remain(s) that may not be without being nothingness: a remains that may (not) be.

cealing, stealing the signature would have its stoolie in the text.

Verily [*Voire*].

This word will henceforth come down to saying the truth (*verus*, *voirement*), but also the undecided suspense of what remains on the march or on the margin within the true, but nevertheless not being false in no longer being reduced to the true.

Elsewhere defined: *le vraiment feint*: the truly feigned, the true lies fine.

"What Remained of a Rembrandt" develops over its two columns a theory or an event of general equivalence: of subjects—"every man *is worth* another"—of terms, of contraries exchanged without end, of the "*je m'éc. . .*" ("*je m'écoulais*," "I was flowing" in my body, in the body of the other). *S'écouler*, to flow: a syntagm, relayed through "*écœurement*" (disgust), the "exchanged regard," the "feeling of *s'écouler*" (flowing), "*je m'étais écoulé*" (I had been flowing), "*j'écrivais*" (I was writing), *je m'écrivais* (I was writing myself) in "*tant d'écœurement*" (so much disgust), so much "sadness"—(the word returns six times in fewer than ten pages), of the infinite exchange between two columns that regard themselves in reverse.

X, an almost perfect chiasm(us), more than perfect, of two texts, each one set facing [*en regard*] the other: a gallery and a graphy that guard one another

That is not easy. From the *viewpoint* of the concept, that is foreseeably impossible.

The question is *of the order of the concept*. One must question the order of the concept or, better still, must question the form of the question that is arranged in the conceptual instance in general.

So here it is a matter of the relation or the nonrelation between castration and the concept, between castration and truth.

A desert question that must be left time to wander thirsty.

Abraham could love nothing. His heart was cut off from all (*sein von allem sich absonderndes Gemüt*)—a "circumcised heart." Hegel makes no allusion to the fact that the sacrifice of Isaac had been interrupted—by the one who was going to grant the benefit of the operation. But he does note the economic advantage, the amortization of the sacrifice engaged: more than the beloved son of a father to whom he has offered his son, Abraham becomes the *Gunst*, the *Günstling*, the single favorite of God, and this favor is hereditary. Abraham reconstitutes a family—which has become much stronger—and an infinitely privileged nation, raised above the others, separated from the others. But the privilege of this mastery stays abstract, thus simultaneously inverts itself into its contrary: this privilege implies an absolute slavery with respect to God, an infinite heteronomy. The Jewish reign is a reign of death; it destroys the life of other national families, commands from out of its very own death, symbolized by the submission to a transcendent, jealous, exclusive, miserly, presentless god. The Jew is dead, castrated: by his father who thus is not a good father, thus not a father. From out of this position, he kills, transforms to dead, that is, materializes everything he touches and everything not his own. He brings into play his death or castration in order to enslave (always the question of knowing—who plays dead better). Ever since his own castration, he castrates. He petrifies, makes everything ugly, transforms everything into matter. His castration is a materialist arm or weapon. A materialist and warlike people with the Medusa'ing power:

"How could they have an inkling of beauty who saw in everything only matter?"

"Control (*Beherrschung*) was the only possible relationship in which Abraham could stand to the infinite world opposed to him; but he was unable himself [as a finite individual] to realize this control, and it therefore remained ceded to his ideal [God]. He himself also stood under his ideal's mastery (*Herrschaft*), but the idea was present in his spirit, he served the idea, and so he enjoyed his ideal's favor (*Gunst*); and since its divinity was rooted in his contempt for the whole world, he became its one and only favorite (*ganz allein der Günstling*). Hence Abraham's God is essentially different from the Lares and the national gods. A family which reverences its Lares, and a nation which reverences its national god, has admittedly also isolated itself, partitioned (*geteilt*) what is

and disappear from view. But the pictures are written, and what (one) writes (oneself) is seen regarded by the painter.

The word "regard" that opens the right column fixes you again at the end of the left column. You think you are the one who regards, and it is the text of the picture (Rembrandt) that oversees and informs against you, sketches and denounces you—what? from elsewhere. "The remain(s), all the remain(s), seemed to me the effect of an optical error provoked by my appearance itself necessarily faked. Rembrandt was the first to denounce me. Rembrandt! That severe finger that brushes aside [*écarte*] showy rags and shows . . . what? An infinite, an infernal transparency."

In order to see you must therefore reverse the perspective and the remain(s), so as to give yourself the *right distance* [recul]. *"You do not really have the right distance in the museum at Cologne. You have to place yourself diagonally, at an angle. It is from there that I regarded him, but with the head below—my own—turned upside down, so to speak. Blood flowed to my head, but how sad was that laughing face!"*

Now this double theory (or double column taking note of the general equivalence of subjects or contraries) describes the text, describes itself as it feigns to recount some pictures, some *"works of art,"* as the suspense of the *verily*: remain(s) beyond the true and the false, neither entirely true nor entirely false. That (*Ça*) is stretched between two subjects absolutely independent in their distress but nonetheless interlaced, interwoven, entwined like two lianas orphaned from their tree.

unitary, and shut the rest out of its god's share (*Teile*). But, while doing so, it has conceded the existence of other shares; instead of reserving the immeasurable to itself and banishing others therefrom, it grants to others equal rights with itself; it recognizes the Lares and gods of others as Lares and gods. On the other hand, in the jealous God of Abraham and his posterity there lay the horrible demand that he alone and this nation be the only ones to have a God.

"But when it was granted to his descendants to reduce the gap separating their actuality from their ideal, when they themselves were powerful enough to realize their idea of unity, then they exercised their mastery (*herrschten*) mercilessly with the most revolting and harshest tyranny, that utterly extirpated all life; for it is only over death that unity hovers. Thus the sons of Jacob avenged with satanic atrocity the outraging of their sister even though the Shechemites had tried to make amends with unexampled generosity. Something alien had been mingled (*gemischt*) with their family, had willed to fasten a bond (*Verbindung*) with them and so to disturb their segregation. Outside the infinite unity in which nothing but they, the favorites (*Lieblingen*), can share, everything is matter—the Gorgon's head transformed everything to stone—a stuff, loveless, with no rights, something accursed which, as soon as they have power enough, they treat as accursed and then assign to its proper place if it attempts to raise anything {a finger, voice, protestation]."

"... ist alles Materie— das Haupt der Gorgo verwandelte alles in Stein—, ein lieb- und rechtloser Stoff, ein Verfluchtes, das denn, sobald die Kraft dazu da ist, auch so behandelt, ihm, das sich regen wollte, seine Stelle angewiesen wird."

The head of Medusa, one of the three Gorgons, is between dashes. Like the Gorgon, the Jew materializes, petrifies everything he sees and everything that regards him, that raises, for example the eyes, toward him. An analogous accusation had been hurled against Socrates, and the analogy affords many readings.

Hegel does not exploit further this small phrase between dashes. This phrase seems to effect, on the surface, a sort of conventional, illustrative, and pedagogical mythological recourse. Just that and nothing more. A Greek mytheme nevertheless seems to him pertinent for describing a figure of Judaism. One could ask oneself, in Hegel's terms or otherwise, about the general and prephilosophical power of a mytheme born of a strongly determinate culture, which is opposed even, should the case arise, to that of Judaism.

So Hegel makes the Gorgon upsurge and maintains her between dashes, as between parentheses or brackets. In the same way he had, in passing, situated circumcision and Isaac's sacrifice.

"But *what is* the stone, the stoniness of the stone? Stone is the phallus. Is that any   An effect of the wide open mouth. Convergence:

High up on the left: "Only those kinds of truths, those that are not demonstrable and are even '*false*,' those that we cannot, without absurdity, conduct to their extremes without going to their negation and our own, those are the truths that ought to be exalted by the work of art. They will never have the chance or the mischance of being applied someday. May they live through the song they have become and sustain."

On the right, toward the middle: "*As a matter of course everything I just said has some importance only if you accept that everything was almost false. . . . Now I have been playing.*"

Remain(s) — the almost? Lower down, at the end of the right column: "*And as a matter of course every work by Rembrandt makes sense—at least for me—only if I know that what I have just written was false.*" But if I only know it. Remain(s) to (be) know(n).

It was a matter of what lets itself be discovered, verily withdrawn "*under the skirts,*" "*under the fur-trimmed mantles,*" "*under the painter's extravagant robe,*" where "*the bodies do do their functions.*"

Twofold anatomy lesson in the margins, and in the margin of margins.

answer? Is that saying anything if the phallus is in fact the thing's concealing, its stealing? And what if, occupying no center, having no natural place, following *no path of its own*, the phallus has no signification, eludes every sublimating relief (*Aufhebung*), extracts the very movement of signification, the signifier/signified relation, from all *Aufhebung*, in one direction or the other, both types coming down ultimately to the same? And what if the 'assumption' or denial of castration should also, strangely enough, come down to the same, as one can *affirm*? In that case, apotropaics would always have more than one surprise up its sleeve. In this connection, it would be apropos to slate for a rereading Freud and the scene of writing, the march that opens and closes it, the signification of the phallus, the short analysis of *Das Medusenhaupt* ('To decapitate = to castrate. The terror of Medusa is thus a terror of castration that is linked to the sight of something.' Freud goes on to explain that what turns to stone does so for and in front of the Medusa's severed [*coupée*] head and wide-open mouth, for and in front of the mother insofar as she reveals her genitals. 'The hair upon Medusa's head is frequently represented in works of art in the form of snakes, and these once again are derived from the castration complex. It is a remarkable fact that, however frightening they may be in themselves, they nevertheless serve actually as a mitigation of the horror, for they replace the penis, the absence of which is the cause of the horror (*dessen Fehlen die Ursache des Grauens ist*). This is a confirmation of the technical rule according to which a multiplication of penis symbols signifies castration (*Vervielfältigung der Penissymbole bedeutet Kastration*). The sight of Medusa's head makes the spectator stiff with terror, turns him to stone. Observe that we have here once again the same origin from the castration complex and the same transformation of affect! For becoming stiff (*das Starrwerden*) means an erection. Thus in the original situation it offers consolation to the spectator: he is still in possession of a penis, and the stiffening reassures him of the fact. . . . If Medusa's head takes the place of a presentation (*Darstellung*) of the female genitals, or rather if it isolates their horrifying effects from their pleasure-giving ones, it may be recalled that displaying the genitals is familiar in other connections as an apotropaic act. What arouses horror in oneself will produce the same effect upon the enemy against whom one is seeking to defend oneself. We read in Rabelais of how the Devil took to flight when the woman

the Jew effects (on) himself a simulacrum of castration in order to mark his own-ness, his proper-ness, his property, his name; to found the law he will suffer in order to impose it on others and to constitute himself as the favorite slave of the infinite power. By first incising [*entamant*] his glans, he defends himself in advance against the infinite threat, castrates in his turn the enemy, elaborates a kind of apotropaic without measure. He exhibits his castration as an erection that defies the other.

The logical paradox of the apotropaic: castrating oneself *already*, always already, in order to be able to castrate and repress the threat of castration, renouncing life and mastery in order to secure them; putting into play by ruse, simulacrum, and violence just what one wants to preserve; losing in advance what one wants to erect; suspending what one raises: *aufheben*. The relief is indeed the apotropaic essence of life, life as apotrope. Now being is life; being is *Aufhebung*. The Medusa provides for no off-scene [*hors-scène*]. She sees, shows only stony columns.

Judaic destiny, however, is only one example on the scene.

So it is true that the flower signifies, symbolizes, figures, and rhetoricizes, and further that Genet anagrammatizes his own proper(ty), sows more than any other, and gleans his name over whatever it falls [*tombe*]. Gleaning equals reading.

Verily, for that is not all. If this (double) signifying and anagrammatical operation were possible, absolutely practicable or central, if the irrepressible desire that activates it were effected (by death or by life, here they come down to the same thing), there would be neither text nor remain(s). Even less so this text here. The summary would be absolute, and it would be carried off, would remove itself with the stroke of a wing [*un coup d'aile*].

Objection: where do you get that *there is* text, and after all, remain(s), for example this text here or this remain(s) here?

There is does not mean (to say) *exists*, *remain(s)* does not mean (to say) *is*. The objection belongs to ontology and is unanswerable. But you can always let-fall-(to the tomb) [*laisser-tomber*]. And at least not take into account this remain(s) here. This regards you from elsewhere.

There is what counts: the operation in question engages several proper names. And *glas*, a profusion of names sleeps in those letters.

showed him her vulva. The erect male organ also has an apotropaic effect, but thanks to another mechanism. To display the penis (or any of its surrogates) is to say: "I am not afraid of you. I defy you. I have a penis." Here, then, is another way of intimidating the Evil Spirit.'), and the remain(s). In lapidary fashion, one could lay out the infinitely opened and turned-back chain of these equivalents: stone—falls (to the tomb)—erect—stiff—dead, etc. Dissemination will always have threatened signification there."

But the example relieves itself in(to) the ontological.

The Jew could secure himself mastery and carry death everywhere in the world only in petrifying the other by becoming stone himself. Playing so not too badly, he has become Medusa to himself. But he does not exist, that one (he), the Jew, before having become Medusa to himself.

So it (Ça) has become Medusa to itself before him.

The Jew is a stone heart. He is insensible. Now feeling, sensing (Empfinden), has been determined as the hearth, the living unity of being as family. There is no true family where *feeling* has let itself be anesthesized, cut, denied or petrified: no true Jewish family, and first of all because no relation of familiarity was possible between the Jew and his God.

This insensibility, this incapacity to form a true family is not an empiric trait; it is a structural law that organizes the Judaic figure in all the forms and places of its manifestation. For example, contrary to what could be expected, Joseph's and Jacob's sedentarization does not interrupt the effects of this law. Mastery remains slavery here. This relation persists even in the manner in which the Jews live then their liberation, the moment Moses comes to offer it to them.

Hegel specifies: that is unintelligible to us. We would not know how to grasp with our understanding (*mit unserem Verstande*) the Jew's becoming-free. That depends on the overflowing, the de-bordering, of the intellectual order. The irruption of the infinite, then of reason, rages like a passion in the Jewish destiny. But the irruption remains abstract and desert; it does not incarnate itself, does not concretely, actually unite itself to the forms of understanding, of imagination, or of sensibility.

Such is the insensibility of the Jews. It catches, as in ice or glass, all their history, their political practice, their juridical and family organization, their ritual and religious procedures, their very language and their rhetoric.

For example, since the liberation of the Jews by Moses is inaccessible to the understanding (*Verstand*), if not to reason (*Vernunft*), one could believe that, for want of rational discourse, a form of imagination (*Phantasie*) has been, would have been, able to represent the phenomenon adequately.

This time the theoreticians of the *ana*—are in for discouragement because the proper names overlap themselves when they sow [*sément*], just as the semes pervert themselves when they overlap themselves.

Thus the flower (which equals castration, phallus, and so on) "signifies"—again!—at least overlaps virginity in general, the vagina, the clitoris, "feminine sexuality," matrilinear genealogy, the mother's *seing*, the integral *seing*, that is, the Immaculate Conception. That is why flowers no longer have anything symbolic about them. "They symbolized nothing."

Demonstration. For castration to overlap virginity, for the phallus to be reversed into the vagina, for alleged opposites to be equivalent to each other and reflect each other, the flower has to be turned inside out like a glove, and its style like a sheath [*gaine*]. *The Maids* pass their time reflecting and replacing one sex with the other. Now they sink their entire "ceremony" into the structure of the glove, the looking glass, and the flower. The onset is supported by the signifier "glove." *Glove* is stretched as a signifier of artifice. First words: "Those gloves! Those eternal gloves!" They will have been preceded only by the stage direction indicating "flowers in profusion" and a hairdresser's looking glass, to which Claire turns her back. But these gloves are not only artificial and reversible signifiers, they are almost fake gloves, kitchen gloves, the "dish-gloves" with which, at the close of the ceremony, the strangling of Madame is mimed, and

An impossible adequation: when Moses comes to talk to the Elders about his plan of liberation, he cannot speak the language of intellect to them, nor that of sensibility either. If the Jews have rebelled, it is not because their heart (*Gemüt*) revolted against the oppression (*Unterdrückung*), not because they felt any nostalgia for pure air and freedom. They have not freed themselves in order to be free, but in order to proceed from one place of seclusion to another. They have no sense of freedom. How did they let themselves be convinced? Neither by intelligence, nor by sensibility.

By imagination? Yes and no.

Yes, because Moses, still in the grips of enthusiasm, in effect acts on their imagination (*Phantasie*). No, because, by reason of this cut [*coupure*] between infinite reason and the determinate orders of understanding, imagination, and sensibility, the appeal to imagination remains abstract, disordered [*déréglé*], artificial, inadequate. The intermediate schema of an incarnation is wanting.

This inadequation explains how the Jew is incapable of comprehending a concrete symbol and how he is insensible to art. The *Aesthetics* makes a place for Hebrew poetry, but under the category of the *negative* sublime: an impotent, crushed, overwhelmed effort for expressing the infinite in the phenomenal representation.

When Moses proposes to the Jews to set themselves free, his rhetoric is forcefully cold and artificial. He resorts to artifices, to ruses (*Künsten*) of eloquence. He dazzles more than touches or convinces. A stranger to the symbol, to the concrete and felt union between the infinite and the finite, the Jew has access only to an abstract and empty rhetoric. That is why he writes very badly, as if in a foreign language. The split between the infinite and the finite blinds him, deprives him of all power to represent to himself the infinite concretely. His iconoclasm itself signifies the coldness of his heart: seeing in the sensible representations only wood and stone—matter—he easily rejects them as idols.

It is always the same law: they deal only with stone, and they have only a negative relation with stone. They do not even think death as such, since they relate only to it. They are preoccupied only with the invisible (the infinite subject is necessarily invisible, insensible), but since they do not see the invisible, they remain in the same stroke [*du même coup*] riveted to the visible, to the stone that is only stone. They deal only with some invisible and some visible, with some insensible and some sensible, but they are incapable of seeing the invisible, of feeling the insensible, of feeling (such is the mediatizing, agglutinating function of feeling) the invisible in the visible, the insensible in the sensible, of letting themselves be affected by their unity: love and beauty, the love of beauty open to this unity of the sensible and the nonsensible, of the finite and the infinite. "The infinite subject had to be invisible, since everything visible is a being limited (*ein Beschränktes*). Before

which, in sum, circulate between places (the kitchen and Madame's bedroom). *The Maids* are gloves, the gloves of Madame. They are also called "angels." At once castrated and castrating (spiders or umbrella case), full and void of the phallus of Madame that Madame does not have, they exchange their first names and transform them unceasingly into adjectives or common nouns:

"CLAIRE [*calmly*]: I beg your pardon, but I know what I'm saying. I'm Claire. And ready. I've had enough. Enough of being the spider, the umbrella-case, the shabby, godless nun, without a family! I've had enough of having a stove for an altar."

So the ceremony continues between two pairs of gloves being turned unceasingly inside out before a looking glass. "I've had enough of this frightening mirror."

But between these pairs of gloves, flowers, only flowers, too many flowers. Their displacement is like the law, the metronome as well, nearly inaudible, the lateral cadence, dissimulated, of each gesture. Madame's two onsets pass through flowers. The one mimed by Claire, at the beginning of the (re)presentation, and then, in the middle, the "real" entrance onstage of Madame. In both cases, flowers forewarn of death. Again announced with a *je m'éc*:

(1) "CLAIRE [*she's fixing herself up in the looking glass*]: You hate me, don't you? You crush me with your attentions, your humility, your gladioli and reseda. [*She stands up and with a lower tone.*] We're loaded down, uselessly. There are too many flowers. It is deadly. [*She looks at herself again.*]"

(2) "MADAME: More and more. Horrible gladioli, such a sickly rose, and mimosa! . . . One lovely day I shall collapse [*je m'écroulerai*], dead beneath your

during the leaving of Egypt, Yahweh preceded the Jews and showed them the way. Two columns: a column of fire during the night, a column of clouds during the day. "The pillar of cloud never failed to go before the people during the day, nor the pillar of fire during the night" (Exodus 13:22).

Moses had his tent [his tabernacle], he showed to the Israelites only fire and clouds which kept the eye busy on an undetermined play of continually changing shapes without fixing it on a form." Free play without form, a natural and sublime play at once, but without formal determination, an infinite play but without art, pure spirit and pure matter. "An idol (*ein Götterbild*) was just stone or wood to them; it sees not, it hears not, etc.—with this litany they fancy themselves wonderfully wise; they despise the idol because it does not manage them, and they have no inkling of its deification (*Vergöttlichung*) in the enjoyment of beauty or in the intuition of love."

Christianity will have precisely performed this relief of the idol and of sensible representation in(to) the infinite of love and beauty.

Such a blind secession paralyzes art, word, rhetoric. But first it has fractured the structure of the tabernacle.

The tabernacle gives its name and its place to the Jewish family dwelling. That establishes the Jewish nation. The Jewish nation settles in the tabernacle, adores therein the sign of God and his covenant. At least such would be believed.

Now the tabernacle (texture of "bands" whose excess we must continually reuse, Exodus 26) remains a signifier without signified. The Jewish hearth forms an empty house. Certainly, sensible to the absence of all sensible form, the Jews have tried to produce an object that gave in some way rise, place, and figure to the infinite. But this place and this figure have a singular structure: the structure encloses its void within itself, shelters only its own proper interiorized desert, opens onto nothing, confines nothing, contains as its treasure only nothingness: a hole, an empty spacing, a death. A death or a dead person, because according to Hegel space is death and because this space is also an absolute emptiness. Nothing behind [*derrière*] the curtains. Hence the ingenuous surprise of a non-Jew when he opens, is allowed to open, or violates the tabernacle, when he enters the dwelling or the temple, and after so many ritual detours to gain access to the secret center, he discovers nothing—only nothingness.

No center, no heart, an empty space, nothing.

One undoes the bands, displaces the tissues, pulls off the veils, parts [*écarte*] the curtains: nothing but a black hole or a deep regard, without color, form, and life. It is the experience of the powerful Pompey at the end of his greedy exploration: "Though there was no concrete shape (*Gestalt*) for feeling (*Empfindung*), devotion and reverence for an invisible object had nonetheless to be given direction (*Richtung*) and a boundary (*Umgrenzung*) inclusive

flowers. Since it's my tomb you are preparing, since you've been accumulating funeral flowers in my room for several days!"

In both cases, the gladiolus, *gladiolus*, little glaive, of the iris family (Provençal: *glaviol*; to the common gladiolus other therapeutic and nutritional powers have often been accorded; the gladiolus of the harvests

extract from the V. Wartburg, after the article *glacées* and before the articles *glans*, *glarea*, which will be profitably consulted:

gladiŏlus schwertlilie.

"I. Fr. *glaïeul* 'gladiolus' (seit 13. jh., R 16, 600), afr. *jagleux* (pl., 13. jh., Gdf; Galeran), *jaglol* Antid Nic, afr. mfr. *glagol* (Esc; Cotgr 1611), afr. *glagel* HMond, mfr. *glageul* Modus, *glageur* Modus, *jageul* Modus, *glagou* Cotgr 1611, aflandr. *glagiot* (15. jh.), apr. *glaujol* (hap.), *glaugel* (pr. 14. jh.), *glongol* (1397, Pans), Colembert *gläžœ* Viez 55, pik. boul. *glajeu*, Formerie id. G 17, Noyon *glaju*, Dém. 'id.; iris pseudacorus', norm. *glajeul* 'glaïeul', Bray. yèr. havr. *glageux*, Thaon *glǫdyœ* 'iris pseudacorus', *glādyœ*, Vire *liageu*, hag. *głažœ* (pl. -œr) 'glaïeul', Guern. *głažœr* 'yellow flag', Jers. *gliageu* 'glaïeul', *glajeur* Z 13, 391, *bliagieu*, Canc. *glageu*, nant. *glajou*, saint. *liajou*. . . . Agen *graoujol*, *glaoujol*; Péz. 'nautilus, edible mollusk'; cogl. *głaižœ* 'horse-collar made with dried aquatic plants' ABret 18, 473.

"Ablt.—Afr. *glaioloi* m. 'place planted with gladioli' (13. jh., Gdf; R 11, 143).—Apik. *glaiollat* (ca. 1330).—Mfr. *glaioleure* f. 'iris tincture' (Reims 1340).—Afr. *jaglolé* 'which has the color of iris' (1260), *glagolé* (Douai 1400).—Apik. *glaiolé* 'strewn with gladioli, verdure, flowers in gen. (of a hall)' Bueve 2; *englaiolé* (ca. 1200—15. jh., Gdf; Bueve 3 b).

"II. Nfr. *gladiole* f. 'glaïeul' (Boiste 1829—Besch 1858.—Ablt. Nfr. *gladiolé* 'arranged in the manner of gladioli (of another plant)' (seit Besch 1845, auch 1901, Huysm); *gladiolage* 'particularity of writing that causes the height of letters to diminish from the beginning to the end of a word' (seit Lar 1930; Bonn).

. . .

"4) Der ersatz von *-a-* durch *-au-* findet sich auch bei GLADIUS. Es liegt wohl einfluss eines andern wortes zugrunde. In lt. handschriften und glossaren, die vor

of the object. This, Moses provided in the Holy of Holies of the Tabernacle and the subsequent Temple. After Pompey had approached the most interior place of the Temple, the center (*Mittelpunkt*) of adoration, and had hoped to discover in it the root of the national spirit, to find indeed in one central point the life-giving soul of this remarkable people, to gaze on a Being [an essence, *Wesen*] as an object for his devotion, on something significant (*Sinnvolles*) for his veneration, he might well have been, on entering the secret [the family and secret intimacy, *Geheimnis*] mystified (*getäuscht*) before the ultimate sight and found what he searched for in an empty room (*in einem leeren Raume*)."

The Jewish *Geheimnis*, the hearth in which one looks for the center under a sensible cover [*enveloppe*]—the tent of the tabernacle, the stone of the temple, the robe that clothes the text of the covenant—is finally discovered as an empty room, is not uncovered, never ends being uncovered, as it has nothing to show.

That the absolute familiarity of the *Geheimnis* proper is thus empty of all proper content in its vacant center would signify that the Jewish essence is totally alienated. Its ownness, its property would be infinitely foreign to itself.

So he cannot enjoy (this). Since everything is obtained through the favor of a transcendent and separate God, what the Jew enjoys is under the seal of expropriation. What I enjoy does not belong to me. My life and my body are not mine. Hegel recalls that every firstborn could be put to death: "Consecrate all the first-born to me, the first issue of every womb . . ." (Exodus 13). Since the human body belongs to God, it had to be kept clean [*tenu propre*], but like a disguise [*travestissement*], like the livery of a servant. The Jew bears everything as a gift, rather a loan: garment, livery, name. The Jewish people identifying itself with one of the tribes from which it received its appellation was God's classed property, the manager or the servant of that domain. It administered God's goods and property, defended his rights, organized itself in the hierarchy from the most humble servant to the minister. This last one would not be considered the guardian of the secret (*Bewahrer des Geheimnisses*) but only of secret or family things (*nur der geheimen Dinge*) detached, in order to represent it, from the inaccessible secret. The *Geheimnis* is not even at the disposal of the leader who remains a minister of God.

Their ownness, their property remains foreign to them, their secret secret: separate, cut, infinitely distant, terrifying. "The secret proper was itself something wholly alien (*Das Geheimnis selbst war etwas durchaus Fremdes*), something into which a man could not be initiated; he could only be dependent on it. And the concealment (*Verborgenheit*) of God in the Holy of Holies had a significance quite different from the secret (*Geheimnis*) of the Eleusinian gods. From the pictures, feelings, enthusiasm, and devotion of Eleusis,

dem 11. jh. liegen, finden sich mehrfach schreibungen wie *glavdius, claudius, gaudio*, welche offenbar die ältesten belege für diese formen mit -*au*- sind. Vgl. Birt, Der Hiastus bei Plautus; Marburg 1901, s. 279.

"**gladius** schwert.

"1. 1. a. Awald. *glai* 'sword', *glay* 'lance' Chayt, alyon. *glaio* R 30, 224.—Ablt. Apr *esglaiar* 'to kill with a weapon' GirBorn, *desglaiar* Gir Born.

"b. Apr. *glai* m. 'fright' (13. jh.).—Ablt. Apr. *esglaiar* 'to frighten, intimidate' Kolsen 171, hdauph. *eiglayé* 'v. a. to surprise, delight; v.r. to be surprised, to roar with laughter [*rire aux éclats*]', mdauph. *ęyglayá*, bdauph. *esglayá*, Queyr. *esglayar* 'to frighten', lang. *esglajá*. Bdauph. *esglayá* 'frightened', Alais *esglaiat*. Apr. *esglai* 'fright; sorrow; uproar', 'fear [*crainte*] SHon, Queyr. 'fear [*frayeur*]', castr. *eglach*, Carlat *esglach* 'excitement [*émoi*] Delh 155, Teste *esglady* 'fear pushed to madness'. Mdauph. *ęyglayá* f. 'astonishment, hearty laughter', bdauph. *esglayado*. Mdauph. *ęyglayáyre* 'the one who surprises, who causes laughter'; *ęyglayamēn* 'astonishment, outburst of laughter'.

"c. Apr. *glai* m. 'ice [*glace*]' (hap.).—Ablt. Dauph. *eiglayé* 'glide, to have a slide [*faire une glissade*]' Ch, hdauph. *ęyglayé*; *eiglayada* 'glissade'.

"2. Fr. *glai* m. 'glaïeul' (Ben SMaure—1709, s. Trév; Gdf; Chrestien; Gace; Escoufle; Mon Guill; Enf Guill; Molin; JLemaire; Tristan H), judfr. *glaid* Rs, anam. *glare* Haust Méd, Cherb. *gliai* 'iris faetidissima' Joret Fl, Troyes *glas* 'glaïeul' Gr, Esternay *glai* 'iris', HMarne *gyę* ALF 1599 p 28, *gla* ALF Suppl p 128, Marne *glę* 'reed' ALF 1166 p 135, Vouth. *diâ* 'glaïeul', Brillon, Dombras *glâ*, Cum. gaum. 'iris', Metz *gya* 'glaïeul', Isle *gyọ*, saun. *dya*, Brotte 'yellow flag', Gruey *dyē*, bress. *diê*, Plancher *hya, gya*, Châten. *iâ, iaî*, fourg. *ła*, Schweiz *glé*, rhod. *glai* 'glaïeul', St-AndréV. *glays* ALLo 332, périg. *glai*; afr. *lai* 'place where gladioli are growing' Gerbert, *glai* Gloss Douai 244, alütt. *glay* (ca. 1380), nfr. *glai* 'mass of gladioli forming an island in a pond [*étang*]' NM rust 2, 582—Besch 1858). . . .

"Ablt.—Afr. *glaie* f. 'glaïeul' (lothr. ca. 1220), *glalie* Gl Vat 1020, mfr. *glage* Baïf, *glaye* 'iris' (Cotgr 1611; Oud 1660), Esternay *glaje* 'glaïeul, iris, etc. (t. coll.)', Reims *glages* 'large plants, on the edge of ditches and rivers' S, Rethel 'pile of gladioli', Guign. *glage* 'rush', périg. *glèio* 'reed' M, Chabrac *glayę*, Puyb. *głoyę* RPGR 5, 263.—Rhod. *glaujo* f. 'iris', périg. *glauso* 'glaïeul'.—Maug. *głavart* 'yellow flag'.—Mfr. *glaitel* 'glaïeul' (Cotgr 1611; Oud 1660). . . . Afr. *glageure* 'strewn' Ruteb, Cum. Chatt. 'all verdure spread on the path of a high personnage, in part. on the route of the Corpus Christi procession', Brillon *glaïures*.—Agn. *deglagier* 'to fell'

from these revelations of god, no one was excluded; but they might not be spoken of since words would have desecrated them. But of their objects and actions, of the laws of their service, the Israelites might well chatter (Deuteronomy xxx. 11), for in these there is nothing holy. The holy was always outside them, unseen and unfelt (*ungesehen und ungefühlt*)."

How could one have a secret?

Absolute expropriation makes the secret of the sacred inaccessible to that very one holding its privilege. In this absolute alienation, the holder of the inaccessible can just as well peacefully manage its effects or phenomena, can chatter about them, manipulate them. The invisible remains invisible, out of reach; the visible is only the visible. Simultaneously the most familiar, secret, proper, near, the *Heimliche* of the *Geheimnis* presents itself as the most foreign, the most disquieting (*unheimliche*).

One cannot even decide the expropriation, cut through to a decision regarding castration, or run after its truth. A system's undecidability is here more powerful than the value of truth. Like this text of Hegel, *Das Unheimliche* should de-border, should have de-bordered the opposition, verily the dialectic, of the true/nontrue.

To make a political discourse bear this problematic chain, is that to limit the extent of this chain? Is that to narrow the field of a general question elaborated after all [*au reste*] in other places?

Hegel, for example, and his discourse, depends on truth. Whence the political accusation hurled against the Jew.

The Jew cannot become, as such, a citizen; he cannot have any true laws of State. Why?

Hegel holds a dialogue with Mendelssohn, author of *Jerusalem oder über religiöse Macht und Judentum*, 1783, a philosopher of the Enlightenment, a Jewish philosopher of the Enlightenment for whom Judaism was not a revealed *religion* but a revealed *law*; this law prescribes acts but enriches our knowledge with nothing. Hegel seems to approve: the Jewish religious laws provide us no knowledge, no consciousness, no eternal truth. "Mendelssohn reckons it a high merit in his faith that it proffers no eternal truths. There is one God, that is what stands on the summit of the State's laws. . . ." That cannot be called truths, save to say that there is no more profound truth for the slave than the affirmation by which he has a master. But Mendelssohn is right not to call this truth. Since God does not manifest himself, he is not truth for the Jews, total presence or parousia. He gives orders without appearing. "Hence the presence of God (*Dasein Gottes*) appears to the Jews not as a truth but as a command (*Befehl*)." The Jews were slaves, and one cannot be a slave to a truth or beauty: "How could they have an inkling of beauty who saw in everything only matter? How could

Edm.—Afr. *sorglaigier* 'overwhelm [*accabler*]' (hap.).

"II. 1. Apr. *glazi* m. 'sword; every cutting weapon' (13.—14. jh.), Cantal *glasi* 'sword', lim. *glaize*. Übertragen apr. *glazi* 'massacre, carnage'; *mort de glazi* 'sudden death', *glazi* (Lv; SFR 7, 168); périg. *glase* 'glaïeul'.—Ablt. Apr. *glazier* 'adj. one who takes up arms; cruel, bloodthirsty; m. massacre'; *glazios* adj. 'murderous'.

"2. Bigorre, Gers *glasi* 'to frighten'. Pr. *glàri* m. 'grief'.—Apr. *esglasiat* 'possessed by the devil' Jaufre, 'terrible (of a blow [*d'un coup*])' (hap.), pr. *eiglariá* 'possessed, demoniac; enraged, alarmed', mars. *esglariat* 'filled with trepidation, hot-tempered, beside oneself [*hors de soi*], troubled' A, *aiglariat* A, St-Simon *eglosiat* 'terrified'. Gers, bearn, *esglasiá* 'to frighten'. Gers *esglásio* f. 'terror'. BAlpes *eiglári* m. 'sudden disquiet mixed with fear', Alais *esglari* 'fright'. Barc. *esglarir* 'to frighten'.—Apr. *deglaziar* 'to kill with a weapon'.—Apr. *aglaziar*; *aglaziador* 'assassin'.—Apr. *englasiat* 'possessed by the devil' Jaufre. Ariège *englasi* 'to frighten' Am. Toulouse *englázi* m. 'fright' G, Tarn, castr. id.; Puiss. *englas* 'fear'.

"III. 1. Afr. mfr. *glaive* m. f. 'lance, javelin' (12.—14. jh., Gdf; Gay; Chrestien; R 21, 292; Beneit Th; Arch 97, 441; Edm; Huon Abc; Perc; Fille Ponth; Tournai 1280, RF 25, 132; Eust; Beaum Cout; Ibn Ezra; Perl), *glavie* Brendan 1713, *claive* Perl, *glave* Veng Rag, *clave* Veng Rag, judfr. *groibe* (1100, RSt 1, 186), mfr. *gleve* 'small pike' (St-Quentin 1340), *glave* 'lance' (14. jh.), apr. *glavi* (lang. 14. jh., Lv; Bonis), *clavi* CCons Albi. Übertragen mfr. *glaive* m. 'soldier armed with a lance' (14. jh., Gdf; Runk), apr. *glavi* (14. jh., Lv; Millau 1359, Doc 113).—Mfr. nfr. *glaive* 'sword' (seit 15. jh.), mfr. *glave* (Molin; Mist). Bellau *glievo* 'cutting [*tranchant*]'; faria *gliâve* 'knife', bellau *diâvo*. . . .

"Ablt.—Mfr. *glavelot* 'small pike' (14. jh.).—Mfr. *glaviot* 'kind of dagger (or pike?)' (15. jh., Gay).—Nfr. *glaivataire* 'angel that bears the glaive' (1891, Huysm). . . .—Mfr. *glavieur* 'gladiator' (1531, Mir. hystorial XIV, 36, Db).—Afr. *glavoier* 'to pierce with a *glaive*' (13. jh.).—Afr. mfr. *deglaiver* v. a. 'to kill by the glaive' (13.—15. jh., Gdf; TL; Gaimar 3000); afr. *deglaveis* 'massacre' Wace. Afr. mfr. *desglavier* 'to kill by the glaive'. . . .

"2. Afr. *glaive* m. 'massacre, carnage' (norm. 12. jh.); 'epidemic, calamity' (ca. 1210—1380, Gdf; Ilvonen), St-Omer to die *à glave* 'en masse (in times of epidemic)' (1790), pic. St-Pol id. (dazu pic. *aglaver de soif* 'to be very thirsty'; Manche *églavé* 'starved to death' Dm); Lille it rains *à glave* 'in torrents', Metz *e gläf*; flandr. Tourc. *a glafe* 'in profusion, much [*beaucoup*]'. . . .

"2. Fr. *gladiateur* 'man made to fight in the amphitheatre, for the people's amusement (according to the ancient Romans)' (seit 13. jh.); nfr. 'duellist, hired killer, swordsman' (Retz 1646—Lar 1872); 'esp. the Dauphin's'

they exercise reason and freedom who were only either mastered or masters?"

Strangers to reason and freedom, the Jews no more then had any rational laws. The absence of obligation is not a sign of freedom, indeed on the contrary. The Jews have no political obligation because they have no concept of freedom and of political rationality. It is the reign of violence. This unfettering does not correspond to a liberation or to some political progress: would the Eskimos have the right to consider themselves superior to the Europeans because they pay no excise on wine nor taxes on agriculture?

Once more the analogy between Greek and Jew is limited to appearance. As for property rights and family goods (second moment of the family syllogism in the *Philosophy of Right*), the first texts on the spirit of Christianity bring certain dispositions of the Mosaic law closer together with such rules [*règles*] established by Solon and Lycurgus. In both cases one wants to put an end to the inequality of riches. "Socialist" laws tend to neutralize a disproportion that threatens political freedom. Both legislations put in place a complete judicial process [*processus*]: it is necessary to prevent the theft [*vol*] that allows one family to enrich itself beyond certain limits.

But the Greek process founds right and politics, constitutes family subjects as citizens. The Jewish process, on the contrary, scoffs at right and politics: in order to limit the property right and thus of expropriation/appropriation, it foresees in effect that a family's goods belong to it for always. The one who has had to sell his goods or his person because he is in need "was to enter on his real rights again in the great jubilee year, and in other cases on his personal rights in the seventh year." This is in effect foreseen in Leviticus. Likewise, the one who had inherited excess fields was not their owner, only the manager, and was to restore the supplement on a determined date. This system of compensation, despite its appearance, denies civil right such as Hegel interprets it. Civil right supposes family property. As the *Philosophy of Right* will confirm, there can be internal public right only if the property of family goods and the right of inheritance are intangible. Now Mosaic law limits the right of inheritance and the right of property in subjecting them to an *external* rule. The proper [*Le propre*] is determined from the outside, equalized, levelled by extrinsic measures. The family name becomes secondary; it falls to the rank of subject accident, "Thus family goods depended rather on something acquired from the outside than on what was most peculiarly the family's own (*Eigentlichsten*), on a characteristic otherwise indelible, i.e., on one's descent from certain parents." The evil, then, is a radical expropriation that constitutes property as management or administration, possession as loan [*en prêt*], and then the name lent to an enterprise, the *prête-nom*.

(Boiste 1829—Lar 1872).—Nfr. *gladiatrice* 'woman who fights with the sword' (Balzac G; Prévost, s. Trév 1771). . . .
"5. Nfr. *gladié* 'in sword-form, with sharp edges (bot. t.)' (seit Boiste 1803)."

The sword or the *gland* [acorn, glans] in the phoneme, the *glas* in the phenomenon. Panglossia. Is there gl in every *natural* tongue [*langue*]? gl . . . ph . . . lt (Ça) shines [*brille*] and shatters [*se brise*]

used to pass for an aphrodisiac and emmenagogue).

In one single case, the reseda, a yellow flower (*reseda lutea, luteola*) that furnishes even the yellow color, and to which medicinal and apotropaic virtues used to be attributed. The frocks, of "The Man Condemned to Death" in particular, are "reseda." In both cases, the threat is also a defense, it forewarns, the flower that kills embalms, the weapon barricades (*gladiolus, reseda morbis*): "I had a terrible decision to make, for it meant breaking the barrier of flowers, fighting my way into the realm of the fabulous.

according to Pliny, reseda was supposed to deflate the tumor, and prevent it from swelling or growing bigger, provided its application was accompanied with the formula: *reseda morbis*

". . . I stood . . . looking perfectly natural so that neither the guard nor the flowers would suspect what I was up to" (*Miracle of the Rose*). *The Maids*: "CLAIRE: . . . I act underneath, camouflaged by my flowers, but you are helpless against me. . . . SOLANGE: Madame thought she was protected by her barricades of flowers. . . . I'm going back to my kitchen. There I find again my gloves and the odor of my teeth. The silent belch

Here the Hegelian interpretation concerns a certain "spirit" of Mosaic law. In its letter, one sees poorly what in effect distinguishes Mosaic law from the disposition envisaged by Solon and Lycurgus. But the same literality will have, according to Hegel, a completely different spirit in the Greeks: and first of all a spirit and nothing else, an inner sense animating the law of the inside. The limitation of property is destined to prohibit violence, to guarantee the citizen's freedom, to see to it that every subject finds itself in itself and not a foreigner in the city. For that reason every subject has to have its own proper goods [*son bien propre*].

In this sense all Greeks are citizens; no Jew has any true citizenship, any true right of the city. Hegel cites Leviticus: "You can alienate (*veräussern*) nothing, for the land belongs to me, you are foreigners and the nationals of a foreign nation (*Einheimische von fremder Nation*) with me."

If one follows this value of the proper, of property (*propriété, Eigen, Eigenheit, Eigentum*), one must conclude that the free citizen's independence and quality go on a par with private property. "Among the Jews, the source lay in the fact that they had no freedom and no rights, since they held their possessions only on loan and not as property (*nicht als Eigentum*), since as citizens they were all nothing. The Greeks were to be equal because *all* were free, independent; the Jews equal because *all* were incapable of independence."

So there is no "for itself," no Jewish being-(close)-by-self.

A question of the letter. Hegel refers to the spirit of the law and acknowledges that the only thing that counts for him is the legislator's intention. If in the Jewish "legislator's soul," in his "intention (*Absicht*)," the question were truly, as in the Greeks, limiting the inequality of riches and assuring the citizen's freedom, there would be a whole system of other converging measures. Hegel says he does not find these in Mosaic law. So the Jews are all slaves of an invisible sovereign: between them and their sovereign, no legal and rational mediation, only heads of tribes appearing or disappearing according to the state of forces. The powers are real, not juridical. There are indeed empiric powers, officials or "scribes (*Schreiber*)." But the scribes are not guided by the spirit of a law. They obey empirical rules, precepts, and commandments (*Befehle*). Their writing is heteronomic. And as this literality remains empiric, the prescription can always be violated when the situation of forces permits or requires it. The process of Pharisaism. "In the case of the Israelites having a sudden notion to be ruled by a king like other peoples, Moses gave only a few commandments (*Befehle*), some so fashioned that the monarchical power could

for a sound understanding of this "silent belching," one must remember that Solange is the one who pronounces the word here and who claims the thing: further on, she complains that "the *glas* tolls" for her, and that her hangman lulls her. All this happens not very far away from the stove of the Holy Virgin, to be sure, but is forced to pass first through a bell [*cloche*], a glottis, and a throat. Like toxic milk, if you wish, and the milkman, he who poisons the desire of the three women, is never very far from the tocsin. Unusual sound, the very rarity of the association (tocsin-milkman, tocsin-morning, tocsin-delight) confirms the distant but powerful constraint of agglutination ("Her morning milkman, her messenger of dawn, her delicious tocsin, her pale and charming master. That's all finished. Take your place for the ball.").
Like a spermatic pharmakon that you spit out again. This play, encumbered with gladioli, is also the spitting stage [*le stade du crachat*]. "Everything, yes everything that comes out of the kitchen is spit! Go. And take away your spittings! . . . I've told you, Claire, with*out* spit. Let it sleep in you, my child. . . . Do you think I find it pleasant to know that my foot is enveloped by the veils of your saliva?" This foot induces—the whole text.
"SOLANGE: . . . The game! Will we even be able to go on with it? And if I have to stop spitting on someone who calls me Claire, my spittings are going to choke me! My spurt of saliva is my spray of diamonds! . . . CLAIRE: . . . Spit in my face! Cover me with mud and filth. . . . Cover me with hate! With insults! With spit!" Whom, what does one want "to cover" in this way, with a "veil," with a drape or a winding sheet, with flowers or spit? And what, in the *glas*, is induced from spit? What more

of the sink. You have your flowers, I my sink."

Thus the flower plays the part of a kind of counter-poison poison. One negative works against the other.

Madame's exit, like her entrance, also marks a flower's return: a ceremonial [*de gala*] poison that one would have to vomit right off. "MADAME: You want to kill me with your tea [with phenobarbital], your flowers, your recommendations. . . . Tea! Poured into the ceremonial tea set! . . . Take away these

abide by them or not as it pleased, others with no bearing whatever (not even only in general) on the founding of a constitution or of any popular rights against the kings. What rights could be felt to be in danger for a people which had none and in whom there was nothing left to oppress?"

Thus there is an abyss between the divine all-powerfulness and the empiric unleashing of forces. No law comes to schematize the abyss that leaves the dead letter to the scribes.

Hence the failure [*échec*] of Moses. A double failure: he unjustly died for having disobeyed only once, for having marked his independence "when he struck one single unbidden blow (*in einem einzigen unbefohlenen Schlag*)." And the structure in question left room for only one *Schlag*. Then Moses did not succeed in *raising* the Jew, in grasping him and uprooting him above his literal and servile earthboundness, in bearing him away toward the heights of freedom. The Mosaic *Aufhebung* has not taken off.

There is nothing accidental in this failure, this fall [*chute*]; the Jewish figure does not submit to weight as a contingent event. It does not fall, it has fallen. That is its essential mark. Moses' failure has not reached the Jews. Judaism is constituted starting from it, as the impossibility of Moses to raise his people, to educate and relieve (*erheben* and *aufheben*) his people.

To raise the Pharisaic letter of the Jew would also be to constitute a symbolic language wherein the literal body lets itself be animated, aerated, roused, lifted up, benumbed by the spiritual intention. Now the Jew is incapable of this in his family, his politics, his religion, his rhetoric. If he became capable of it, he would no longer be Jewish. When he will become capable of it, he will have become Christian.

Moses, the dead Jew, the Jew whose death comes from a blow [*coup*] and fixes the figure of Judaism, Moses was conscious or preconscious of this limit. And to say this, he uses, Hegel recalls, a "comparison" (*Vergleichung*).

The *Vergleichung* has more than one import: in itself, in the correction or the complement that Hegel allots it, and finally because it remarks the rhetoric or rather the rhetorical impotence of Judaism, the figural weakness of a people incapable of appropriating and raising the letter.

The *Vergleichung* explains the failure, the fall [*chute*], or chasm. It is found in Deuteronomy 32: "In the regard (Deuteronomy xxxii. 11) cast over his political life, he [Moses] compares (*vergleicht*) the way in which his God had led the Jews, through his instrumentality, with the behavior of the eagle (*des Adlers*) which wishes to train its young to fly—it continually flutters its wings over the nest, takes the young on its wings, and bears them forth thereon."

flowers. Take them home with you. . . . Madame escapes! Take these flowers away from me!"

Reciprocally, specularly, Madame, each of whose maids successively occupies her place, poisons the maids with her flowers. Madame is (a) good (maid) insofar as she poisons. "The apartment is poisoned." "CLAIRE [*remaining alone*]: For Madame is a maid, and good! . . . With her goodness, Madame poisons us. For Madame is a maid, and good. . . . She showers us with faded flowers. Madame prepares our teas. . . ."

In both cases, the *pharmakon* is a hymen, that is to say, immediately its contrary: "MADAME: . . . And those flowers that are there to celebrate the contrary of a wedding!"

In both cases, where "who threatens the other? Eh? You hesitate?" is never known, the most natural flowers are the most artificial, like the virginity of the Holy Virgin, whose altar, hearth, stove, case [*le foyer, le fourneau, le fourreau*] watches over the entire scene. "CLAIRE: That's right. Let's skip over our devotions to the plaster Holy Virgin, our kneelings. We won't even talk about paper flowers. . . . [*She laughs.*] Paper flowers! And the branch of holy boxwood! [*She points to the flowers in the room.*] Look at those corollas open in my honor! I am a more beautiful Virgin, Claire."

Much further on, it is also a question of Madame's womb, stove, case: "We'll never be able to replace Madame. . . . For us, Madame's wardrobe is like the chapel of the Holy Virgin. When we open it . . . SOLANGE [*curtly*]: The tea is going to get cold. CLAIRE: We'll open both doors, on our festival days. . . . Madame's wardrobe is sacred. It's her great hanging-closet!"

And each maid asks the other to carry her within herself, like Madame's

penis. Naturally, the   they would have liked to strangle her.

Thus is the eagle set forth in Moses' *Vergleichung*. Hegel begins by reproducing the statement. He transcribes Deuteronomy rather accurately. Then he completes and corrects in order to throw the stone back again, to renew it. In every logic it is necessary to be stone in order to transform the other into stone. Like the Gorgon, the Jew petrifies the other. Hegel said this; now he marks that the Jew is stone himself. His discourse is not only rhetorical, but of rhetoric, on the subject of rhetoric. "Only the Israelites did not complete this beautiful image (*Bild*); these young never became eagles. In relation to their God they rather afford the image of an eagle which by mistake warmed stones, showed them how to fly and took them on its wings into the clouds, but whose weight can never become flight [*vol*], whose borrowed warmth never burst [*éclata*] (*aufschlug*) into the flame of life."

The logic of the concept is the eagle's, the remain(s) the stone's. The eagle grasps the stone between its talons and tries to raise it.

The Jew falls again; he signifies what does not let itself be raised—relieved perhaps but denied from then on as Jew—to the height of the *Begriff*. He holds back, pulls the *Aufhebung* toward the earth. The case of the Jew does not refer to a past event. He indicates the system of a figure in the synchrony of the spirit. He is even what as such resists history, remains paradigmatic: "All the subsequent circumstances of the Jewish people up to the mean, abject, wretched circumstances in which they still are today, have all of them been simply consequences and developments of their primordial destiny. By this destiny—an infinite power which they set over against themselves and could never conquer—they have been maltreated and will be continually maltreated until they reconcile it by the spirit of beauty and so relieve (*aufheben*) it by reconciliation."

For the relief of this destiny, of this death stone [*pierre*], one must await Our-Lady, the Messiah, another Last Supper scene, another Rock, Peter [*Pierre*], this time living, the Church that builds itself on him, a certain Holy Family.

The difficulty of the march continues to worsen.

More visibly still, one enters the analyses of Christianity and of the Christian family elaborated by the young Hegel as the conceptual matrix of the whole systematic scene to come. There are engendered not only the whole philosophy of religion, the description of revealed religion in the *Phenomenology of Spirit*, certain fundamental interpretations of the *Philosophy of Right*, and so on. The announced zigzag will be necessary, but the indispensable anticipation will become as rare as possible. Precipitancy is too easy.

But the question of the bearing [*démarche*], the teleology or not of the reading, does not let itself be evaded. And it finds itself *already* posed, within the "younger" elaborations, precisely as an ontological question, a question of the ontological.

author of these paper flowers insists that the flowers in this piece (the room [*pièce*], the chamber, in the play [*pièce*]), and in this ceremony (representation, "evening," in the performance [*représentation*]), be "real flowers." This is "How to play *The Maids*": "false trains, false frills, the flowers will be real flowers, the bed a true bed. The director must understand, for I cannot altogether explain it all, why the room should be the almost exact copy of a feminine room, the flowers true, but the dresses monstrous. . . ."

They mimed the strangling of Madame, the (hi)story of banding her erect (of making her band erect) and of finally reaching her great hanging-closet, or, what comes down to the same thing, in getting rid of her, they come to the other, Monsieur (or) The milkman. So many figures of the lulling executioner that represent one another, that detach one another to what makes the winded [*essoufflé*, dispirited] text pant, the text running after a *seing* it can never touch, never tamper with. The invisible lover of the Maids, the man with the "delicious tocsin" who makes Madame drool, could not have another vocation. There is a galactic law there that one will see applied from now on, from a certain angle, to all cases. This law initiates into the mother thus first named. What has to be closed here is the angle in which to bandage [*panser*] together a neck [*cou*] and a peniclitoris. That a strangling bands erect, how much so, it must—

The lulling executioner, the one who gives the poisoned breast [*sein*] to Solange, that is to say, by rotation or circular spit, to Claire and to Madame, who spend their time being caught in the looking glass, that executioner is represented solely by each term of the identifying and specular trio. Which one should not hasten to define as homosexual: the fourth excluded, discounted, decapitated, always invisible but never absent, always absent but never without effect, represented by the acorn [*gland*] fallen from the tree, the gloves, the gladiola or the gobs of spit, the executioner cut off from the stage [*scène*], the Monsieur or the Milkman (phallic homologs) appear at the heart [*sein*] of what they seem to set in motion

It is the question of the *Wesen* (essence) and of the copula *is* as a question, the relation or name of father-to-son.

To know for example whether the "later" texts can be treated as the descendant and akin consequence, filiation, the product, the son of the youthful elaborations that would be the system's paternal seed; to know whether the second, following, consequent or consecutive texts are or are not the same, the development of the same text, this question is posed in advance, reflected in advance in the analysis of Christianity. It is the question itself of Christianity staged as the Last Supper scene [*mise en cène*].

The Father *is* the Son, the Son *is* the Father; and the *Wesen*, the essential energy of this copulation, its unity, the *Weseneinheit* of the first and the second, is the essence of the Christian Last Supper scene. The spirit of Christianity is rather the revelation of the essentiality of the essence that permits in general copulating in the *is*, saying *is*. Unification, conciliation (*Vereinigung*), and being (*Sein*) have the same sense, are equivalent in their signification (*gleichbedeutend*). And in every proposition (*Satz*), the binding, agglutinating, ligamentary position of the copula (*Bindewort*) *is* conciliates the subject and the predicate, laces one around the other, entwines one around the other, to form one single being (*Sein*). The *Sein* is constituted, reconstituted starting from its primordial division (*Urteil*) by letting itself be thought in a *Bindewort*.

Now this conciliation that supposes—already—a reconciliation, that produces in a way the ontological proposition in general is also the reconciliation of the infinite with itself, of God with himself, of man with man, of man with God as the unity of father-to-son. All the "youthful works" elaborate the demonstration of the father's presence in the son, the end of the opposition in the heart [*sein*] of the divine, the necessity of the copula in the following proposition stating the possibility of the speculative family, such as it will be maintained in its concept up to the *Philosophy of Right*: "The child is the parents themselves," or "the united beings separate again, but in the child the conciliating unification (*Vereinigung*) has become unseparated (*ungetrennt*)."

Thus is opened and determined the space in which the ontological (the possibility of *Wesen*, *Sein*, *Urteilen*) no longer lets itself be unglued or decapitated from the family. And par excellence from the question of the father-to-son, this figural value of the "par excellence" accentuating [*accusant*] what it excludes.

Consequently, even before wondering whether the ontological project was first a Greek event from which Christianity would have developed an outer graft, one must be certain that, for Hegel at least, no ontology is possible before the Gospel or outside it.

Then the bond announced between the question of the copula and the question of the family also bears this consequence: if one

only under the nonspecies of a writing, quasi anonymous, without signature. A writing that will never return, by some proper or circular course, to its own place. For this writing has no place and its nonplace has no determinable contour. This has to do with the intrigue of a letter denouncing Monsieur, in which the maids hope and fear that their writing will be recognized. "Your denunciations, your letters, it's working out [*marche*] admirably. And if they recognize your writing, it's perfect. . . . The game is dangerous. I'm sure we've left traces. . . . I see a host of traces I'll never be able to efface. And she, she walks around in the middle of what she tames. She deciphers it. She places the end of her rosy foot on our traces." "MADAME: . . . Who moved the key to the secretary again? . . . Who could send these letters? . . . Monsieur will know how to unravel the mystery. I wish someone would analyze the writing and would know who could pull off such an intrigue. . . . Did anyone telephone?"

What would the Immaculate Conception have to do [*voir*] with those little letters?

The work of art, the ungraspable flower, more natural and more artificial than any other, is the *Miracle of the Rose*.

tries to articulate an apparently "regional" (sociological, psychological, economico-political, linguistic) problematic of the family onto an ontological problematic, the place that we have just now recognized cannot be gotten around [*incontournable*].

If *Sein* cannot be what it is, cannot posit itself, become and unfold itself, manifest itself without traversing Christianity's destiny, that is first because *Sein* must determine itself as subjectivity. Being perhaps lets itself be re-covered and dissembled, bound or determined by subjectivity (Heidegger), but that is, for Hegel, in order to think itself. First in Christ.

Jesus' revolution consisted in opposing the subjective principle, that is the principle of freedom, to the enslavement of objective laws or more precisely of objective commandments. Each time Jesus transgresses one of these commandments, for example a prescription of Jewish ritual, he does so in the name of man, subjectivity, and the heart. Thus, on the Sabbath day he cures a

the miracle of the hand: Jesus restores to a man the use of a hand of which he was deprived: "On the same day [the Sabbath] Jesus healed a withered hand (*eine verdorrte Hand*)."
"For the son of man is lord of the sabbath. And passing on from there he went into their synagogue, and behold, there was a man with a withered hand. And they questioned him, saying: Is it lawful to heal on the sabbath? They meant to bring a charge against him. But he said to them: Will there be one of you who owns one sheep, and if it falls down a hole on the sabbath, will not take hold of it and pull it out? How much better a man is than a sheep. Then he said to the man: Stretch out your hand. And he stretched it, and it became sound, like the other. But the Pharisees went outside and began plotting against him to destroy him."

man's withered hand.

Not that Jesus opposed to the heterogeneous and heteronomous objectivity of the commandments the formal universality of the law or of a *you must* [tu dois] in the Kantian sense. In that case, the Jewish split would only be displaced, and interiorized. The tyrant of the outside would become a domestic tyrant. The (Kantian) autonomy would remain apparent; it would be its truth in a severe and implacable heteronomy.

Hegel does not doubt the possibility of autonomy. Parodying Kant and *Religion Within the Limits of Reason Alone*, turning his own sentence against him, Hegel displaces the difference: the profound heteronomy of the Kantian *you must* would see to it that between the Shaman of the Tungus, between the prelates of the European Church, the Mongol or the Puritan on the one hand, the man of formal duty on the other, the difference would not be between slavery and freedom. The first simply have their master outside themselves, and the second within himself, as his own proper

This time, Harcamone's *glas* is scattered among eglantine and wisteria [*glycines*]. Harcamone is going to die. One recalls the "eglantine bush" next to the place where he "fell on top of [the little girl]" and ended up cutting her throat after talking "into the child's neck." And the wisteria overflowing the sites of a mimed crucifixion. It — the wisteria — becomes the christic body.

eglantine: one of the popular names for the columbine, also known as Our-Lady's seal [*sceau*], or again, Our-Lady's glove. Presumably, this plant took its Latin name (*aquilegia, aquilea*) from the fact that its nectaries had the curved profile of an eagle's beak or again from the fact that it made one's sight as piercing as an eagle's (*aquila*).
An eagle, male, white eagle, black eagle, Ganymede's eagle, dominates the whole corpus, regularly swoops down on it, from behind, holds it tightly [*le serre*] and in its claws bands it erect, screws it, the beak in the neck [*cou*]. One can say an eagle, female or heraldic [*une aigle*].

Touched by grace under the eye of a Perdoux. "I was suddenly [*tout à coup*] touched by the smell of roses, and my eyes were filled with the sight of the wisteria at Met-

Flight/theft [*vol*] without reference, textual fiction, pure letters in the ear or throat. Eagle: tattoo in the *Miracle of the Rose*. Eagle: chimera—associated, in *The Balcony*, with the unicorn, since it has two heads. Eagle: absence of content and weightiness, sublime elevation, flier's/thief's theft/flight [*vol du voleur*] become light and dreaming of being called — somewhat — Ganymede: "I shall be light. I shall have no further responsibility. I shall gaze over the world with the clear regard that the eagle imparted to Ganymede" (*Thief's Journal*). The flight/theft of his empire—polysemy

tray. As you know, it was at the end of the Big Square, toward the lane, against the wall of the custodian's office. I said it was entangled in the thorns of a bush of tea roses. The trunk of the wisteria was enormous, twisted with suffering. It was fastened to the wall by a wire [*fils de fer*] network. Some of the overgrown

death, as a "pathological" love in the strict sense this word has in Kant. The Kantian autonomy is pathological.

Now in preaching love, Jesus proposes neither laws nor a transgression of laws: he recommends a relief, an *Aufhebung* of the law, of the law's formal legality. Nevertheless the legality abolishes and fulfills itself in one blow [*coup*]: "This spirit of Jesus, a spirit raised above morality (*über Moralität erhabene Geist*), is visible, immediately opposed to the laws, in the Sermon on the Mount, which is an attempt, trying in numerous examples, to strip the laws of legality (*das Gesetzliche*), of their legal form (*Form von Gesetzen*). The Sermon does not preach reverence for the laws; on the contrary, it exhibits that which fulfils (*erfüllt*) the law but relieves (*aufhebt*) it as law and so is something higher than obedience to law and makes law superfluous." Jesus does not preach the dissolution (*Auflösung*) of the law but on the contrary the fulfillment of what they lack (*Ausfüllung des Mangelhaften der Gesetzte*). In raising itself above the frigid formal universality, living love describes then the great syllogistic movement of the *Philosophy of Right*: objective morality (*Sittlichkeit*), the third moment that begins with the family (and in the family with love), arises in the relief of abstract right and of formal subjective morality. The schema very quickly puts itself in place: one can understand the principles of the philosophy of right, can grasp again its conceptuality, only in the echo of this historico-speculative event that was The Sermon on the Mount.

> "Do not think that I have come to abolish the Law or the Prophets. I have come not to abolish but to complete. Indeed, I say to you, until the sky and the earth are gone, not one iota or one end of a letter must go from the Law, until all is done."

The Sermon seems to proceed by "paradoxes": that is, in truth the "reconciliation" that forms its central motif comes to overcome all the oppositions congealed by Judaism. In the eyes of the logic of Judaism, the reconciliation seems unthinkable: "a different genius, a different world" in which the opposites are no longer opposed (law and nature, universal and particular, duty and inclination, subject and object, and so on) or in any case are no longer opposed in that sort of indifference and positive immorality characterizing the Jew or the Kantian subject. Jesus is opposed to the formal and thus indeterminate, indifferent opposition. So he opposes one "or else" (*das Oder*) to another: for example, the opposition of virtue and vice has been opposed to the opposition of rights or duties to nature. "In love all thought of duties vanishes (*wegfällt*)." At the same time the ancient opposition is accomplished, fulfilled, de-bordered by a richer principle. *Pleroma* (πλήρωμα) will have been the name of this de-bordering fulfillment of synthesis.

branches were supported by a forked post. The rosebush was attached to the wall by rusty nails. Its leaves were gleaming and

> "A girl may be a Maid, but she no less has her periods [*règles*]. . . . Joan of Arc mounted the stake . . . and remained exposed with that rusty rose at cunt level." Elsewhere, still in the *Miracle of the Rose*, the game is closed in the following way by the chain of roses and the chain of steel binding the hands of Harcamone: "I put the rose into the false pocket that was cut in my jacket." The rose is always more or less a postiche, as is the pocket, which is false: both cut themselves out of a cloth. We shall speak again about the cutting [*taille*] of the rose and about sizes and cutting [*taille*] in general. Rose, which is neither simply a noun nor simply an adjective, neither an assured masculine nor an assured feminine, can also be played as a proper name. Dissimulated, for example, in the foreign tongue, Warda's, (Warda means rose) that works (over) her mouth all the time. Warda cleans her teeth, all day long, with a hatpin [*épingle à chapeau*] she calls her style. She is the one who does not believe in the truth. The play is set in a sort of rose garden full of nettles whose owner tries to increase his size with a postiche belly and postiche ass [*cul*] (with cushions, with a small cushion). "THE VOICE: . . . Madame, I love only your belly, where for nine months I took the rosy form that the rose of your womb let fall on the tiled floor . . ."

the flowers had all the tints of flesh. . . . and it was in front of the mingled wisteria and rosebush that M. Perdoux, the head of the shop, used to make us halt. The roses, in the figure, shot whiff

> the essence of the rose is its nonessence: its odor insofar as it evaporates. Whence its effluvial affinity with the fart [*pet*] or the belch: these excrements do not stay [*se gardent*], do not even take form. The remain(s) remain(s) not. Whence its interest, its lack of interest. How could ontology lay hold of a fart? It can always put its hand on whatever remains in the john [*aux chiottes*], but never on the whiffs let out by roses. So the anthropy of a text that makes roses fart must be read. And yet the text does not itself altogether disappear, not altogether as quickly as the farts that blast, prompt,

The living and conceptual signification of life as love is the pleroma.

The pleroma's overabundance throws off balance the principle of equivalence, commerce, the economy of exchange that regulates *justice*: I give you what you give me, take from you what you take from me, I return blow for blow [*coup pour coup*] to you. Castration, according to justice, is justice. Castration is not only something one exchanges (an eye for an eye, a tooth for a tooth). Castration is the very principle of exchange. It castrates, equalizes or lops off [*élague*] the pleroma; it tends to maintain two forces, two erections, two pressures at the same height. Somewhere castration is in check, like justice, as soon as an inequality appears. But castration takes its revenge in the same stroke [*du même coup*]: isn't the inequality of heights castration itself? Castration is indifference, castration is (the) difference. In being opposed to positive justice does Christ suspend or aggravate castration? Does he permit or forbid erection? Both no doubt; both operations must be read at once, since he relieves. He castrates on one side and thinks the end of castration on the other.

"An eye for an eye, a tooth for a tooth, say the laws. Retribution (*Wiedervergeltung*) and the equivalence (*Gleichheit*) in the retribution is the sacred principle of all justice (*Gerechtigkeit*), the principle on which any constitution of state must rest. But Jesus in general demands the surrender (*Aufgebung*) of rights, the elevation (*Erhebung*) above the whole sphere of justice or injustice by love, for in love there vanish not only rights but also the feeling of inequality and the you-must of this feeling that demands equality, i.e., the hatred of enemies."

Pleroma, the rupture of the principle of equivalence, the at least apparent imbalance of the economy of exchange, the dissymmetry between the opposables. Both Xs must not take account of one another, or reflect, record, inscribe themselves equally one in the other. That is how Hegel interprets the "your left hand must not know what your right is doing (*Lass die linke Hand nicht wissen, was die rechte tut*)." This does not mean, as is currently believed: don't try to get approval when you act according to duty, don't know what you do in order to leave it unknown, in the dark and without publicity. Nor any longer does this mean: be satisfied with being aware of what good you do without seeking the recognition of others. In fact the simple awareness of doing good is already an inner applause and a kind of economic recompense, an equivalence for itself of the benefit I feign to renounce when it comes from others. The good conscience (*gute Gewissen*) maintains the circle of exchange. I recover with one hand what I give with the other, each

spirit (off) [*soufflent*] the text. *The Screens*, which can be experienced as the enormous parade of a fart produced from the very first word ("Rose!"), remain, reread themselves, repeat themselves [*se répètent*]. This suspension between the remain(s) and the non-remains of the remain(s), this suspension of the text that retards a bit—nothing must be exaggerated—absolute dissipation, could be named effluvium. Effluvium generally designates decomposing organic substances, or rather their product floating in air, that kind of *gas* hanging over marshes for awhile, and a kind of magnetic fluid also. So the text is a gas; for the origin and the stake [*enjeu*] of the word, one hesitates, but this comes back to the same thing, between spirit (*Geest, Geist*) and fermentation (*gäschen*).
If there is a sense to the problem of repetition, it is then that one. And to read it, the exhalation must be sniffed out

after whiff at our faces. No sooner was I visited by the memory of the flowers than there rushed to my mind's eye the scenes I am about to relate.
"Someone opened Harcamone's door."

What is happening here with the eyes? Is it a matter of worn-out [*usées*] metaphors? "My eyes were filled with the sight of the wisteria," "there rushed to my mind's eye the scenes I am about to relate."

If, no doubt, they open themselves at once [*d'un coup*], the scenes were no less elaborated from a great distance. For a long time, expert, loving, diligent hands have caressed the surface of the fabric [*tissu*], undone the folds, passed under the lining, unfastened, unbuttoned. Speaking all the while, telling you stories. With eyes shut, or turned elsewhere.

hand holds the ledger of the other, masters and annuls the difference between both operations. A higher calculus without remain(s): what consciousness wants to be.

To be somewhere unconscious, on one side, of what is in the act of developing on the other, to dissociate absolutely one hand from the other, such is the condition for breaking the exchange in the pleroma and for making appear the fraud, the simulation, the totalizing lure of the good conscience. Such is the Hegelian interpretation of the "your left hand must not know what your right is doing."

But what forms the specific Christian characteristic of this interpretation is not only the promise of a relief that will come to compensate the dissymmetry, is not only the expectation of an infinite reconciliation that will again appease the inequality. That is because the rupture of the equivalence takes here, in this determinate moment, the form of an essentially culpable consciousness, culpable [*coupable*] and self-accusing, self-mutilating in all its blows [*coups*]. To the good conscience of the Pharisee content with the duty done, keeping with one hand what he gives with the other, Hegel opposes the gaze of the publican who strikes his breast. "The consciousness of the Pharisee (a consciousness of duty done), like the consciousness of the young man (the consciousness of having truly observed all the laws—Matthew xix. 20), this good conscience, is a hypocrisy (*Heuchelei*) because (*a*) even if it be bound up with the intention of the action, it is already a reflection on itself and on the action, is something impure (*ein Unreines*) not belonging to the action; and (*b*) if it is a representation (*Vorstellung*) of the agent's self as a moral man, as in the case of the Pharisee and the young man, it is a representation whose content is made up of the virtues, i.e., of limited things enclosed in their

the gift [*don*] without counterpart, verily without benefit, resolves itself into appearance in the talk that Jesus has with the Young Man and that Hegel nevertheless opposes to the miserly logic of exchange. The spiritual or symbolic benefit reconstitutes the annulus and makes the Prodigal Son a profound miser. Is the sequence disjointed [*décousue*]? A little after the discourse on the eunuchs ("Not all can accept this saying, but those to whom it is given. For there are eunuchs who have been so from their mother's womb, and there are eunuchs who have been made sexless by other men, and there are eunuchs who have made themselves sexless for the sake of the Kingdom of Heaven. Let him who can accept, accept."), having laid his hands on the small children that must be allowed to come to him because the kingdom of heaven belongs to them, Jesus addresses the Young Man who wonders what he is lacking, since he has observed all the commandments: "If you wish to be perfect, go sell what belongs to you and give it to the poor, and you shall have a treasury in heaven ..." (Matthew 19).

This handling of the fabric does not furnish to sight anything that might be perception or hallucination. If a good definition of phantasm were available, one might be able to tell whether this writing is of a phantasm. In everyday language, one would say a dream. But the text itself obliges us to draw on this language: this dream is a dream within another dream, and within the dream of another. That, the miracle of the rose, which can take place only in a text, as text, implies a certain chaining of the critical body.

Point of view. Scenes that violently *fill* the view or *rush* the mind's eye produce the blindness necessary for the theater. The point of view envelops or blinds itself. There is first of all the point of view of the one that feigns to be the narrator: "Someone opened Harcamone's door. He was sleeping on his back. First, four men penetrated his dream. Then he awoke. Without getting up, without even raising his torso, he turned his head to the door. He saw the black men and understood immediately, but he equally realized very quickly that, in order to die in his sleep, he must not disrupt [*briser*] or destroy the state of dreaming in which he was still entangled. He decided to maintain the dream. . . ."

The one who seems to feign being the narrator only sees Harcamone's point of view by following the four black men in their break-in and thus penetrating Harcamone in contraband, by introducing himself clandestinely into his "dream," and thus in downshifting multiplies the point of view to infinity.

matter, within their given circle, and which therefore are one and all incomplete, while the good conscience, the consciousness of having done one's duty, hypocritically claims to be the whole (*sich zum Ganzen heuchelt*)."

Striking his breast, breaking by culpability the whole economy of equivalence, dividing the good conscience that reappropriates the whole: to this pleroma, to this revolution in the circle of the restricted economy, to this humiliation without counterpart, a dissymmetry on the other side is going to answer. Forgiveness of sins is also raised above the law, that is, above the principle of reciprocity.

An example near which Hegel stays for a long time: that of "the famous and beautiful sinner, Mary Magdalene."

The traits of the narration are borrowed from several Gospels. The occasion to recall that the factuality of the narratives, *récits*

Marie Magdelan were his mother's first names (Maria Magdalena Louisa, born Fromm), Marie his daughter's (Susanna Maria) and his wife's (Maria Helena Susanna). Hegel's daughter died almost immediately after her birth (1812). On a trip to Dresden (1821), he writes to his wife. As usual, he spoke to her about the picture galleries he systematically toured on each of his travels. Particularly about a painting by Holbein the Younger, *Madonna of Burgomaster Meyer*. He always took the original—that he regularly saw in Berlin—for a copy and the copy that he had just seen in Dresden for the original. "I went of course to the gallery and among the paintings inspected dear old friends. Above all I was anxious to see the painting by Holbein of which we saw a copy in Berlin, and I paid special attention to the particulars which I had already noted in Berlin, namely the complexion of the middle figure among the three female figures, the nose of the mayor, and the child on Mary's arm. Considering these particulars, it was immediately clear to me that the figures in the Berlin painting, as beautiful as it is, taken for itself, were made by an understudy. Visibly, the child in the painting here is sickly. It is obviously—and I in this am completely convinced of the correctness of what was indicated by the local inspector—supposed to be a dead child of the donee which they see in the Heavenly Mother's arm, and which in this embrace sends down to them a message of consolation and resignation to the divine will. The accuracy of this interpretation is confirmed by the child in the middle at the bottom, which is almost standing and which here is most beautiful. I have no doubt at all that the painting in Berlin is a skillfully made copy, but one in which there is above all a lack of spirit."

And the following year, the same day he writes to Goethe the extensive letter on colors (15 September 1822):
"Good morning, dear Maria, from the sunshine of Marianburg, i.e. Magdeburg, whose maid [*Magd*] is Holy Mary, to whom the Cathedral is or was dedicated.
"... It is more difficult to get out of Magdeburg than into it. ..."

Who dreams? Whom? Who writes? What? Who signs the miracle of the red rose? Who signs under this text that no less has its period, its rules [*ses règles*]?

Will there be bleeding [*saigner*]?

The question can be left suspended for a while at least. The risk is to die before having finished writing one's *glas*.

Remain(s) to (be) know(n)—in the name of what, of whom, to refuse to die asleep.

"He decided to maintain the dream." The miracle of the rose—let us wait for it, because it is the very object of the detour—will be produced since the dream of the other: Harcamone of gold (sleeps).

As always, the burst of the tale [*l'éclat du récit*] had resounded in advance; within itself, hence as close to silence, in the citation of self or other, as snow grazing a sensitive golden bell [*cloche*]. From higher up: "The magnificence of my tale springs naturally (as a result of my modesty too and of my shame at having been so unhappy) from the pitiable moments of my entire

(*Erzählungen*), the variations concerning places, times, circumstances change nothing in the conceptual intent (*Ansicht*) and that "nothing is to be said {judged, decided, *gesprochen*} about the actual facts (*Wirklichkeit*)," about the factual reality [*réalité événementielle*] of the facts. The question for Hegel is not "setting aside all the facts," as Rousseau proposed to do in the narrative of the origin: rather, in the manner of *Religion Within the Limits of Reason Alone*, the question is to look in the Biblical text for a semantic web of philosophemes or prephilosophemes. The facts were or were not such as they are told; what counts is the interpretation drawn from them from what they will have become: philosophy. The truth of Christianity is philosophy.

So the "beautiful example" is that of Mary the sinner who overtakes Jesus in the course of a meal with the Pharisees. She throws herself at his feet, sobs [*sanglote*], bathes his feet in tears, drys them with her hair, kisses them, and embalms them with a pomade, anoints them with an ointment, with a balm (*salbet sie mit Salben*), "with authentic and costly spikenard (*mit unverfalschtem und köstlichem Nardenwasser*)." When the righteous Simon sees her drown her faults and drink reconciliation, he concludes from this that she is a sinner and that if Jesus were a seer (*Seher*) he would know this. Jesus pardons her. Because she has loved much, to be sure. But above all, Hegel says, because she has made something "beautiful" for Jesus: "this is the only moment in the whole story of Jesus that induces the name of beautiful."

To what beauty was Jesus sensitive? To that of the overflowing of love, certainly, to the kisses, the tears of tenderness, but above all, let us believe Hegel on this, to that perfumed oil, to that chrism with which she coats his foot. It is as if in advance she took care of his corpse, she adored it, pressed it gently with her hands, soothed it with a holy pomade, wrapped it with strips [*bandelettes*] the moment it begins to stiffen. This whore who behaves like a virgin

equivalences: "One of the Pharisees invited him to a meal. When he arrived at the Pharisee's house and took his place at table, a woman came in, who was a sinner in the town. She had heard he was dining with the Pharisee and had brought with her an alabaster jar of ointment. She waited behind him at his feet, weeping, and her tears fell on his feet, and she wiped them away with her hair; then she covered his feet with kisses and anointed them with the ointment.
"When the Pharisee who had invited him saw this, he said to himself, If this man were a prophet, he would know who this woman is that is touching him and what a sinner she is. Then Jesus took him up and said, 'Simon, I have something to say to you.' 'Speak, Master,' was the reply. 'There was once a creditor who had two men in his debt; one owed him five hundred denarii, the other fifty. They were unable to pay, so

life. Just as the Golden Legend flowered from a banal condemnation to torture two thousand years ago, just as Botchako's singsong voice blossomed [*éclosait*] into the velvet corollae of his rich rippling voice, so my tale, which issues from my shame, becomes exalted and dazzles me."

Once he has been condemned to torture, Harcamone the Christ escapes into sleep; he sleeps, watched over, cared for and fattened by society like a *pharmakos* or a scapegoat. "Each day the trusty took better care of him than the day before. His face grew a little fuller. He was acquiring the majesty of glutted dictators.

"As the fatal moment approached, I felt Harcamone getting more and more tense, carrying on an inner struggle, seeking to escape from himself in order to escape from there. To break loose, to leave, to flee through the fissures, like a golden vapor! But he had to transform himself into a golden powder. Harcamone clung to me. He urged me to find the secret. And I raked up all my memories of miracles, known or unknown, those of the Bible, of mythologies, and I sought the likely explanation, the kind of simple conjuring trick [*tour de passe-passe*]. . . ."

So everything happens [*se passe*] while Harcamone is asleep. And, to read the legend, the Golden Fleece glistens near the heart of the dream. Around the collar [*col*], the neck [*cou*]: is a necklace [*collier*]. This necklace, by the privilege, in a word, it has of giving rise to decollation, of assigning to the executioner the parting line (circumcision or castration), represents the most threatening adornment [*parure*] or parade, the one that forms, in advance, of the body, a part.

To write, for Genet: to know how to carry, to include the neck (*cou*

he pardoned them both. Which of them will love him more?' 'The one who was pardoned more, I suppose,' answered Simon. Jesus said, 'You are right.' Then he turned to the woman. 'Simon,' he said, 'you see this woman? I came into your house, and you poured no water over my feet, but she has poured out her tears over my feet and wiped them away with her hair. You gave me no kiss, but she has been covering my feet with kisses ever since I came in. You did not anoint my head with oil, but she has anointed my feet with ointment. For this reason I tell you that her sins, her many sins, are forgiven her, because she loved much. But one who is forgiven little loves little.'"

This passage from the Gospel according to Saint Luke is followed, as you know, by a description of the feminine entourage of Jesus and the Twelve, then by the parable of the four seeds. In Matthew, the narrative of the anointing at Bethany ("'When she poured this ointment on my body, she did it to prepare me for burial.'") immediately precedes Judas's betrayal

(*Die schüchterne, sich selbst genügende stolze Jungfräulichkeit*) "'has embalmed me in advance,' Jesus says, 'for my burial' ('*Sie hat mich', sagt Jesus, 'im voraus auf mein Begräbnis gesalbt.*')." The oily-like balm made the body of Christ glisten [*reliure*], a kind of funereal glory caresses it. A shiny, yellow, and waxy stain in a very somber picture. Destined for virginity, the prostitute stays beside the Son of God. The weeping woman also melts over [*fond sur*] him like a candle.

The extreme of love inundates, the pleroma always gives cause [*matière*] for unction.

Love is the pleroma of the law. But the logic of the pleroma leaves nothing in repose. What is fulfilled with love still lacks something, is lame somewhere. "Love itself is still an incomplete nature."

An account of this can be given only by restaging (a last supper scene) the relation of father to son.

In recalling that this relation has been established by Christianity, Hegel appeals against love—still lacking—to its pleroma, the religious. The religious reestablishes in its rights an objectivity that love had suspended. The force of love that had succeeded in relieving the opposition (subject/object for example) limits itself, encloses itself again, above all if love is happy, in a kind of natural subjectivity. There the religious causes an infinite object to break in.

All this consum(mat)es itself, passes through the mouth. A long detour is necessary.

"To the Jewish idea of God as their Master and Sovereign Lord, Jesus opposes the relationship of God to men like that of a father to his children.

"Morality (*Moralität*) relieves (*hebt auf*) domination (*Beherrschung*) into the circles of what has come to consciousness; love

"And when he was on his feet, upright in the middle of the cell, his head, neck [*cou*] and entire body emerged from the lace and silk which are worn, in the most trying moments, only by the diabolical masters of the world, and with which he was suddenly adorned. Without growing an inch, he became huge, overtopping and splitting the cell, filling the Universe, and the four black men shrank until they were no bigger than four bedbugs. The reader has realized that Harcamone was invested with such majesty that his clothes themselves were ennobled and turned to silk and brocade. He was clad in patent leather boots, breeches of soft blue silk, and a shirt of old blond lace, the collar [*col*] of which was open on his splendid neck [*cou*] that supported the collar [*collier*] of the Order of the Golden Fleece. Truly, he came in a straight line, and by way of the sky, from between the legs of the captain of the galley."

What was he going to do there, the tom thumb [*le petit poucet*] who shoots up "without growing an inch [*d'un pouce*]" in the boots or "between the legs" of the galley captain? Who leads to the children's prison? to Guiana? In the *Journal*, "lead by the ogre, Roger sowed little white pebbles."

But the galley captain is not the galley, which carries this giant tom thumb here on the sea [*la mer*], coming to her "in a straight line, and by way of the sky," as if by immaculate conception. *Galley*, would that be the noun or the floating first name borne by the holy mother [*la sainte mère*]? or laid on her? at least her siglum that she would let us touch, summarize, suck on again, make it ring in the mouth?

Covered with algae ("velvet algae," "azure algae") with glaireous "spit," with "wet flowers," engorged with gold, with uncoffined cadavers or with unornamented coffins, "The Galley" (a poem about Harcamone, facing the *Miracle of the Rose*) carries these lines in its flanks: "Clusters of poisoners hung high from the riggings / The prisoners jacking off mixing their ages. / From the Great Sleep a sleeping child came back / Stark naked and spotted all over with spewed sperm. / And the most agonizing of the trimmed sail's sighs [*sanglots*], / . . . a star's . . . / . . . a young guy's . . . lips, / . . . the damages."

The galley lulls like an executioner. Borne itself by the sea [*la mer*], the galley carries everywhere but also makes the condemned galley slave [*galérien*] work without end. From the body of the galley that holds him locked up, from its flank, the galley slave exhausts himself over his oar. In cadence he attacks the surface of the sea [*la mer*] that glistens [*brille*], herself; he makes a

relieves the limits of the circle of morality; but love itself is still an incomplete nature."

Anticipation of the *Philosophy of Right*: love (the felt unity of the family) relieves subjective morality that had itself relieved abstract right or domination; but love (the family) is still nature, the first moment of an incomplete *Sittlichkeit*, and so in its turn will have to be relieved.

When Hegel says that Jesus opposes to the Jewish figure of God the relation of a father to his children, what discourse is in question? A discourse of Jesus, certainly, and one that Hegel assumes or reproduces. But what form of discourse? Symbol, figure, metaphor, comparison? An analogy of an infinite relation (implying God) with a finite relation (father/children)? But the "infinite" relation also implies finite terms, creatures. So the very possibility of the question is uncertain. In order to make its presuppositions appear, one must first take account of what Hegel himself says about comparison in the Last Supper scene.

What then consum(mat)es itself?

The opposition between the contraries (universality/particularity, objectivity/subjectivity, whole/part, and so on) resolves itself in love.

Love has no other: love your neighbor as yourself does not imply that you must love your neighbor as much as you. Self-love is "a word without sense (*ein Wort ohne Sinn*)." Love your neighbor as one (*als einen*) who is you or "that you is (*der du ist*)." The difference between the two statements is difficult to determine. If self-love had no sense, what would it mean (to say) to love the other as one that you is? Or who is you? One can love the other only as an other, but in love there is no longer alterity, only *Vereinigung*. Here the value of *neighbor* (*Nächsten*) foils this opposition of the I to the You as other.

If love has no other, it is infinite. To love is necessarily to love God. One can love only God. To love God is to *feel self* [*se sentir*] in the whole of life "with no limits, in the infinite (*schrankenlos im Unendlichen*)."

Love, the sensible hearth of the family, is infinite, or it does not exist.

No longer can one rigorously distinguish between a finite family and an infinite family. The human family is not *something other* than the divine family. Man's father-to-son relation is not *something other* than God's father-to-son relation. Since these two relations are not distinguishable, above all not opposed, one cannot pretend to see in one the figure or metaphor of the other. One would not know how to compare one to the other, how to feign knowing what can be one term of the comparison before the other.

mark there, finds support there, but the movement is endless, the element is equal to itself, re-forms itself, impassible, engulfs the wake [*sillage*] or scours [*écume*] the sigla, shines, remain(s)

p) cutting stroke. To draw with a song the course of a blade that, erecting the text, makes it fall on the other side and so precipitates two inseparable heads, one the exalted, the brandished, the aureolated, the other what resembles and reflects it, to a near margin that renders the balance undecidable and announces the cost [*coût*] of the operation very quickly: a *glas* that no longer dies away.

You can always keep the necklace. Or, in any case, believe in it. You will have to sell this belief again in the marketplace of what is called literature.

But you can take interest in what I am doing here only insofar as you would be right [*auriez raison*] to believe that—*somewhere*—I do not know what I am doing (I exclude something and am excluded from it: an "I'm removed" or "I'm crushed" [*un "je m'écarte," ou "je m'écrase"*]). Nor what activates itself here. And what equals being scaffolded [*s'échafauder*].

Why make a knife [*couteau*] pass between two texts? Why, at least, write two texts at once? What scene is being played? What is desired? In other words, what is there to be afraid of? who is afraid? of whom? There is a wish to make writing ungraspable, of course. When your head is full of the matters here, you are reminded that the law of the text is in the other, and so on endlessly. By knocking up the margin—(no) more margin, (no) more frame—one annuls it, blurs the line, takes back from you the

One cannot know, outside Christianity, what *is* the relation of a father to his son, verily (but let us hold this extension in reserve) to his children. One cannot even know, we are coming to this, what is the *is* in general outside Christianity. Such is the Hegelian thesis on the spirit of Christianity, that is, on rhetoric.

Thus the question of the figure seems very fleeting.

Love no longer opposes itself: thus it has no object. Not even a religious object. The disappearance of the object poses the question—the question of rhetoric in particular—as the question of consuming destruction [*consumation*]. At Christ's table.

Jesus' good-by to his friends, at the Last Supper, is a "love-feast" (*Feier eines Mahls der Liebe*). The most visible, the closest form of this is the position of the preferred disciple, John, on the breast [*sein*] of Jesus.

Love is not yet the "strictly . . . religious" adoration addressing itself to a determinate object, to a form with contours, facing the worshiper, without confusion. In order that an object become detached, stand out, and that such a form appear, in order that a finite representation of the infinite be cut out, show up, the opposition must intervene, to be sure, but so must the imagination (*Einbildungskraft*) as well. It produces a finite object, an image of the infinite. Religion is the adoration of this image (*Bild*). But love does not yet have access to religion, because this opposition between the finite and the infinite has not taken place in love, has not yet or no longer taken place. So the Last Supper, the love-feast, does not belong to a religious space. All of the acts at the Last Supper manifest love; love itself is present (*vorhanden*), near at hand there, but only by right of feeling (*Empfindung*). No image (*Bild*), no figure, no schema becomes detached or stands out here in order to unite feeling to representation, sensibility to concept. "The feeling (*Gefühl*) and the representation (*Vorstellung*) of the feeling are not unified (*vereinigt*) by the productive imagination (*Phantasie*). Yet in the love-feast there is also something objective in evidence, to which feeling is linked but with which it is not yet united into *one* unique image (ein *Bild*). Hence this eating (*dies Essen*) hovers [*schwebt*, floats] between a common table (*Zusammenessen*) of friendship and a religious act, and this hovering makes it difficult to characterize distinctly its spirit."

What then is Jesus doing when he says while breaking the bread: take this, this is my body given for you, do this in memory of me? Why already memory in the present feeling? Why does he present himself, in the present, before the hour, as cut off from his very own body and following his obsequy [*obsèque*]? What is he doing when he says in picking up the cup: drink all of you, this is my blood, the blood of the New Testament, of the new contract entered into with religious pomp, shed for you and for so many others in remission of their sins, do this in memory of me? Memory

standard rule [*règle*] that would enable you to delimit, to cut up [*découper*], to dominate. You are no longer let know where the head of this discourse is, or the body, the neck [*cou*] is dissimulated from you so that you cannot bear your own.

So do not rely on the proper name that is always worn like a chain or a necklace. Genet has arranged the necklace of the Golden Fleece over all his text, but not far from "between the legs of the captain of the galley." (*Galley*, moreover, is a strange word that literally bears everywhere.) Diabolical master of the world, he has arranged the necklace with infinite craftiness [*ruse*]. Necessarily finite, that is.

It is not enough to be crafty, a general theory of the ruse *that would be part of it* must be available. Which comes down to making a confession, unconscious, to be sure. The unconscious is something very theoretical.

If I write two texts at once, you will not be able to castrate me. If I delinearize, I erect. But at the same time I divide my act and my desire. I—mark(s) the division, and always escaping you, I simulate unceasingly and take my pleasure nowhere. I castrate myself—I remain(s) myself thus—and I "play at coming" [*je "joue à jouir"*].

Finally almost.

(Ah!) you're (an) ungraspable (very well) remain(s).

Fetter(s), then, understands two times.

here is *Gedächtnis*; Hegel has often insisted on the kinship between memory and thought (*Denken*). Think me, Jesus says to his friends while burdening their arms, in advance, with a bloody [*sanglant*] corpse. Prepare the shrouds, the bandages, the oily substance.

What is he doing, the anointed of the Lord? Is he using a signifier? a symbol? an image? What about the *this* when he holds out the bread and the wine? When he speaks of food and funeral in place of his body, his individuality, his finiteness?

There it is not a question of a sign, a comparison, or an allegory. In the sign, the relation between the signifier and the signified, between the sign (*Zeichen*) and the designated (*Bezeichnetes*) remains a relation of conventional exteriority. What links the members of signification to each other still remains an objective ligament (*Verbindung, Band*). For example, when an Arab drinks a cup of coffee with a stranger, he enters with him into a contract of friendship. This common action "binds" the Arab, and this bond commits him to showing himself faithful and helpful. "The common eating and drinking here is not what is called a sign. The ligament (*Verbindung*) between the sign and the designated is not itself spiritual, is not life, but an objective ligament (*ein objektives Band*); the sign and the designated are strangers to one another, and their ligament remains outside them in a third term; their ligament is only a thought ligament. To eat and drink with someone is an act of communion (*Vereinigung*) and is itself a felt communion, not a conventional sign." In communion, the third term disappears, is properly consum(mat)ed. The sign is gulped down.

That is already true for the Arab. Now something more still happens in transubstantiation. This more, to state it briefly, is a certain judicative proposition of the type *S is P* (this is my body, the wine is blood, the blood is spirit) and a certain intervention of the father in the discourse.

To be sure, the banquet forms an act of friendship. The disciples bind themselves to him and to each other, think themselves together. There it is not a question of a "mere sign," but of a felt experience (*Empfindung*). Religion has not yet appeared, since there is no object as such. Nonetheless religion announces itself and shows a glimpse of itself, when Jesus adds something more to this common consum(mat)ing. What? What is this more (*das Weitere*)? A declaration, an explanation, a discursive manifestation, an *Erklärung* that explains, states in the form of *S is P*, and from then on constitutes an objective judgment, an objectivity that opens, even though incompletely, the religious space. He says, "*Dies ist* (*ceci est*, this is) my body (*mein Leib*). *Hoc est enim corpus meum, touto estin to sōma mou to uper umōn didomenon*, this is my body given for you." The apparition of the ligament, of the copula (couple), and of *the pair* produces an object exceeding the interiority of feeling. This judicative declaration, plus the fact of *parceling out* (*Austeilung*), of

For if my text is (was) ungraspable, it will (would) be neither grasped nor retained. Who, in this economy of the undecidable, would be punished? But if I linearize, if I line myself up and believe—silliness—that I write only one text at a time, that comes back to the same thing, and the cost of the margin must still be reckoned with. I win and lose, in every case, my prick.

In Plato's teaching, the pharmacy had distilled this effect under the label of the glyph or of the glyphic *coup*. This remark within the groove of writing, overflowing the piece from both sides, remained entirely tautological, since *glyph* means (to say) *coup*. And scalp.

What is the fleece. The golden fleece. Apart from a *genêt*, of course.

The golden fleece surrounds the neck, the cunt, the verge, the apparition or the appearance of a hole in erection, of a hole and an erection at once, of an erection in the hole or a hole in the erection: the fleece surrounds a volcano.

The borders of the hole the fleece hides or delimits are certainly those of a pit, and what the four black men find at the heart of Harcamone's heart, at the heart of the rose, is a "shadowy pit" ("At the very

double posture. Double postulation. Contradiction in (it)self of two irreconcilable desires. Here I give it, accused in my own tongue, the title DOUBLE BAND(S), putting it (them) into form and into play practically. A text laces [*sangle*] in two senses, in two directions. Twice girt. Band contra band

genêt is also said to inhabit the brim of the volcano. Leopardi's *La Ginestra*, the *odorata ginestra*, grows "su l'arida schiena / del formidabili monte / Sterminator Vesevo." The exergue is taken from Saint John. And there a *genêt* flower is found that is "patient in the deserts," in the "fields that are strewn/ With unbreeding ashes, sealed down with lava / turned hard as stone / and echoing to each visting foot." The burning lava flows like milk "Dall'inesausto grembo," from the inexhaustible breast [*sein*]. The "yielding *genêt*" that inclines its "innocent head" will not have chosen

dividing, in order to consum(mat)e them together, the bread and the wine, expels feeling outside itself and makes it "in part objective (*zum Teil objektiv*)." Undoubtedly Hegel plays here on *Austeilung* and *Teil* as he does elsewhere on *Ur-teil* (judgment and primordial division: judgment corresponds to a primordial division of being, of *Sein*, into subject and predicate, the copula couples, mates [*accouple*] the pair, draws closer in the same ligament (*Band*) the thing and the attribute thus becoming party again to *Sein*). The moment, through this parceling out and this predication (*das Weitere, die Erklärung Jesu*), the disciples are dealing with definite objects (this is that), their friendship, their union in the one they recognize as their midpoint and master (*in ihrem Mittelpunkte, ihrem Lehrer*) becomes more than sensible, more than internal. Their friendship, their union is visible, evident on the outside (*sichtbar*), objectified, like the very thing it is. No longer is it just "represented (*vorgestellt*)" in an "image (*Bild*)" or an "allegorical figure."

Nevertheless this object is not an object like any other. This very thing does not give itself "in person" like any other. On one side feeling becomes objective, but on the other side the bread, the wine, and the sharing [*partage*] are not "purely objective." There is something more to them than what is seen. It is a question of a "mystical action" that can be understood only from within. From the outside, only bread and wine are seen. In the same way, when two friends part company and break an annulus of which each keeps a fragment, the third party who does not participate in their contract sees only two metal morsels without symbolic power. The annulus does not form itself again.

What then is the nature of this surplus, this more (*dieses Mehr*)? Presupposed throughout, this *Mehr* does not take itself into account, cannot give rise to an objective calculus, to a discursive explanation. It does not relate itself to any "objects." The relation it enters without ever belonging there, no analysis can account for according to the ways of comparison or analogy. No explanatory statement (*Erklärung*) can say here, "this is equal to that," "this does not equal that." The *Mehr* in question is neither equal nor unequal to any object; it is *as* nothing, it resembles, reassembles itself with nothing like the *as* (*Gleichwie*) (*Dieses Mehr hängt nicht mit den Objekten, als eine Erklärung, durch ein blosses Gleichwie zusammen . . .*). The question here is not one of saying "just as"; the *just as* cannot envelop, think love. It is not as if one were saying: just as the particular, divided, singular morsels (*vereinzelten Stücke*) you eat are from *one and the same* bread, just as the wine you drink, you drink it from *one and the same* cup [*coupe*], so you are divided or separated, particulars (*Besondere*), cut off [*coupés*] from one another, but in love, in spirit, you are *one* (*eins*), one and the same *being* (*Sein*), together. Just as all of you have your part of this bread and this

border of this hole, which was as black and deep as an eye, they leaned forward and were seized by an unknown kind of vertigo."), but also the borders of the capital erection, the trunk, the pyramid or the cone of a volcano.

Around the spitting gulf, the inexhaustible eructation of letters in fusion, the fleece (ἔριον), the fleece *pubien*

its "abode" and its "birthplace." "Fortune" alone has decided it. "SAÏD. The woman the birds in the sky shit above so you become a stone statue. Piazza Leopardi in Verona, I saw you there one day at four o'clock in the morning, under the shit of doves and naked. Magnificent in the daylight . . ." . . . To Roger Blin: "For a few seconds, he has been known to wander off to Piazza Leopardi in Verona, or to the rue Saint-Benoit."

---

the text is the golden fleece: a precious object, detached by a sort of scalping. The galley would go by the name here of Argo.

Writing remains modest because it is caught in a fleece. A propos modesty, "braiding," "weaving," and "felting," Freud proposes a model natural to the feminine technique of the text: the hairs that dissimulate the genitals and above all, in the woman, the lack of a penis. And he claims to be disarmed in the case where this hypothesis would be taken for a fantasy or an *idée fixe*.

Smear these hairs, make them shine, make them gluey with drool, spit, milk, and you will have a kind of textual veil. The *Thief's Journal*, for instance, envelops everything in that. "I barely recognized him . . . but hardly had he opened his mouth for a more softly uttered phrase than I saw there again, veiling it, the white spit, and through the strange mucosity which formed it, though staying intact, I recognized, between his teeth, the Stilitano of old." Worm [*ver*] and cocoon, the apotrope of the culprit [*coupable*]: "Within his shame, in his own drool, he envelops himself, he weaves a silk which is his pride. This is not a natural garment. The culprit has woven it to protect himself, woven it purple to embellish himself."

A fleet of screens [*paravents*] with purple sails, purple veils [*voiles pourpres*], a fleet ready for the attack, the defense, a fleet guarding itself at the prow and the poop, gold spurs for the parade.

wine, so all of you participate in my sacrifice. The same thing for all the *as*'s, all the *Gleichwie*'s.

In that case, the question is indeed that of the party taking part. What is a *morsel*—literally: what does one place (get) under one's teeth?—since one can no longer reckon with nothing?

Except [*Sinon*] with such incalculable enjoyment.

The ligament, the synthesis, the *Zusammenhang*, the tension that holds the objective bit [*mors*] and the subjective bit together, the bread and the persons, for example, is not the ligament "of the compared with a comparison (*des Verglichenen mit einem Gleichnis*)." Here we do not have a "parable" in which "the compared (*Verglichene*) is set forth as severed, as separate (*als geschieden, als getrennt*)." Nor a comparison (*Vergleichung*) that requires thinking the equality of dissimilars (*das Denken der Gleichheit Verschiedener*). On the contrary, in this copulation, in this binding (*Verbindung*), diversity falls (*fällt die Verschiedenheit weg*) and with it the very possibility of a comparison, of an equation. The equal disappears, but this end of the equal is not reasoned as the subsistence of the unequal. Heterogeneous parts remain, to be sure, but tied up, attached, enveloped in each other in the most intimate way. "*Die Heterogenen sind aufs innigste verknüpft.*" So the act of *verbinden* does not merely signify the upsurging of an objectivity through the operation of a holy copula; it also annuls the opposition of the dissimilars, effaces the discontinuity of all objectivity. Here all the difficulties of transubstantiation and of the Eucharist, such as they work (over) for example Cartesian rationalism and the logic of Port-Royal, give themselves to be read on the bias [*par la bande*].

Feeling, enjoyment itself (*Genuss*) are induced by this copulation without any proper object of its own. More precisely by a penetration (*Durchdringen*).

Here the father intervenes.

Jesus not only says, "the wine is blood"; he also says, "the blood is spirit." The common cup [*coupe*], the fact of drinking together, of swallowing in one gulp [*d'un seul coup*] the same liquid substance, is in spirit a new bonding (*der Geist eines neuen Bundes*). This spirit thus extends itself in the covenant and penetrates (*durchdringt*) "many." Thirsty, many come to drink of this, in order to gain height there and raise themselves (*zur Erhebung*) above their sins. The present of the cup that makes copulation possible in the covenant, that present is not given, is not present. It presents itself only in the expectation of another coupling that will come to fulfill, accomplish (*vollenden*) what is announced or broached/breached here. One day one will drink, as one is already acquiring a taste for this, for the father himself, in his kingdom: "in a new life, in the kingdom of my father I shall drink again with you."

That is why this operation is not a useful sacrifice—of an objective usefulness at least—exchanging something against an-

*The parade always stays behind [*derrière*].*

Derrière: every time the word comes first, if written therefore after a period and with a capital letter, something inside me used to start to recognize there my father's name, in golden letters on his tomb, even before he was there.

A fortiori when I read *Derrière le rideau* [*Behind the Curtain*].

Derrière, behind, isn't it always already behind [*déjà derrière*] a curtain, a veil, a weaving. A fleecing text: "One of my other lovers adorns his intimate fleece with ribbons. Another once wove a tiny crown of daisies for the tip of his friend's prick. A phallic cult is fervently celebrated in private, behind the curtain [*derrière le rideau*] of buttoned flies. If a rich imagination, availing itself of the disturbance, should turn it to account, just imagine what festivals—to which plants and animals will be invited—will ensue, and from them, above them, what spirituality! I arrange in Java's hairs the feathers that escape at night from the punctured pillow. The word balls [*couilles*] is a roundness in my mouth" (*Thief's Journal*).

ne weaves, braids, preens, *tricks out* its writing. Within it everything is sewn [*se coud*], fit out with, makes way, on the borders, for all flowers. The gulf hides its borders there. In the weaving of this dissimulation, the erection is produced only in *abyme*.

The tangled tracing of its filial filaments assures *at once* (impossible castration decision) sewing *and* overlap cutting again [*la couture* et *la recoupe*]: of the mass of flowers as a phallic upsurging *and* a vaginal concavity (small *glas* grown, summarized in between, at the back of the glottis), intact virginity *and* bleeding castration, *taille* (clipping and size) of a rose, of "the red rose of monstrous size and beauty" that will soon open up into a "shadowy pit."

other under the form of an object. This operation comes down to letting onself be penetrated (the word "*durchdringen*" occurs three times) and to establishing one's identity. Jesus' identifying penetration in his disciples—first John, the beloved disciple; the Father's in Jesus and through him in his disciples—John first; subjective in a first time, then objective, becomes subjective by ingestion. Consum(mat)ing interiorizes, idealizes, relieves.

A remarkable reflection: Hegel *compares* this penetrating resubjectivation to the very movement of the tongue. More precisely, he proposes to read that movement as the tongue's, as language's, hearing-understanding-oneself-speak in reading. More precisely still, its absolute murmur in reading in a low voice. The voice kills, the absolutely restrained voice annihilates the signifier's objective exteriority. The letter and the word disappear the moment they are heard-understood within and first very simply grasped, understood-included. Provided it name, it engage a discourse, the movement of the tongue is analogous to the copulation at the Last Supper scene.

This whole analogon takes form, stands up, makes sense [*tient debout*], and lets itself be grasped only under the category of categories. It relieves itself all the time. It is an *Aufhebung*.

Of blood.

"Not only is the wine blood but the blood is spirit. . . . The blood is the connection, the relation between them and the wine which they all drink out of the same cup and which is for all and the same for all. All are drinking together; a like emotion (*ein gleiches Gefühl*) is in them all; all are penetrated, permeated (*durchdrungen*) by the like spirit (*vom gleichen Geiste*) of love. If they are made alike simply as recipients of an advantage, a benefit, accruing from a sacrifice of body and an outpouring of blood, then they would only be united in a like concept (*im gleichen Begriff*). But because they eat the bread and drink the wine, because his body and his blood pass over into them, Jesus is in them all, and his essence (*sein Wesen*), 'as love,' has divinely penetrated (*durchdrungen*) them. Hence the bread and the wine are not just an object for the understanding. The action of eating and drinking is not just a self-unification brought about through the annihilation of food and drink, nor is it just the feeling of merely tasting food and drink. The spirit of Jesus, in which his young disciples (*seine Jünger*) are *one* (eins), has become present as object, an actuality, for external sense. Yet the love made objective, this subjective element become a thing, reverts once more to its nature, becomes subjective again in the eating. This return may perhaps in this respect be compared (*verglichen*) with the thought that in the written word becomes a thing and recaptures its subjectivity out of an object, out of something dead (*aus einem Toten*), when we read. The comparison (*Vergleichung*) would be more pertinent if the written word, in silent reading, by

The *erion*—fabric of writing and pubic fleece—is the maddening, atopical place of the *verily*: more or less (*than the*) truth, more or less (*than the*) veil. The *erion* derides everything said in the name of truth or the phallus, sports the erection in the downy being [*l'être à poil*] of its writing. Derision does not simply make the erection fall; it keeps the erection erect but does so by submitting the erection to what it keeps the erection from, already, the crack of the proper no(un) [*du non propre*]. Apotropaic incantation of the reseda, derisory erection of the gladiolus.

Gravely, imperturably, the author splits with laughter [*se poile*]. He also rows with the application of a sweet gale (*galé*

you do not yet perceive the word "*galérien*." What must be avoided is underlining, hammering at, putting into relief [*relever*] those words or letters in a text whose style glides over the important syllables, grazes, buggers [*effleure*] each part of its body, buries, effaces the essences, which end up being equal to each other, muffling the sounds at the base of the tongue, in the crypt of the palate [*palais*]. Everything must float, suspended, then resound elsewhere after the event [*résonner après coup*] for the first time. As if coming from a grotto that is almost closed:

". . . the collar was open on his splendid neck that supported the collar of the Order of the Golden Fleece. Truly, he came in a straight line, and by way of the sky, from between the legs of the captain of the galley. Perhaps because of the miracle of which he was the place and object, or for some other reason—to give thanks to God his father—he put his right knee on the floor. The four men quickly took advantage and climbed up his leg and sloping thigh. They had great difficulty, for the silk was slippery [*glissait*]. Halfway up the thigh, forgoing his inaccessible and tumultuous fly, they encountered Harcamone's hand, which was lying in repose. They climbed on to it, and from there to the arm, and then to the lace sleeve. And finally to the right shoulder, the bowed neck [*cou*], the left shoulder and, as lightly as possible, the face. Harcamone had not

being understood, vanished as a thing, just as (*so wie*) in the enjoyment (*Genuss*) of bread and wine not only is a feeling (*Empfindung*) for these mystical objects aroused, not only is the spirit made alive, but the objects vanish as objects. Thus the action seems purer, more appropriate to its end, in so far as it gives spirit only, feeling only, and robs the understanding of its own (*das Seinige*), i.e., annihilates the matter (*Materie*), the soulless (*das Seelenlose*)."

The understanding's very own (*das Seinige*) does not disappear except as the finite object, that is, as object, as insufficiently reappropriable (soulless, inanimate matter).

Hegel defines by a comparison the return to subjectivity in the act of consum(mat)ing. Here the comparison with reading must define just what escapes—he had barely told us above—the comparative structure. The comparison's necessity perhaps provokes the ceaseless relapse [*rechute*] of what should escape that structure, but this fate is itself relieved: the comparison receives its possibility from a spiritual analogy that always draws upward.

Attaching importance [*Faire cas*], once more, to the stone. In the present relief of the Last Supper, sublimation (idealization-interiorization-animation-subjectivation, and so on) even works on the stone.

Twice, the stone, love frozen in stone.

But this time the stone, the stone of love opposed to Christian sublimation, the stone that does not let itself be relieved, is the Greek and not the Jewish stone.

Here the movement is necessarily complicated by the fact that the stone always falls (entombs) again. Remain(s).

The Last Supper scene certainly accomplishes a consuming destruction of love that Greek plastic art cannot attain: a split again, in the Greek, between stony matter and the interiority of love. But the Christian consuming destruction will also divide itself. A new split will dupe by itself this Christian destruction in order to appeal to another relief, *Aufhebung* first in the heart [*sein*] of Christianity, then *Aufhebung* of Christianity, of the absolute revealed religion in(to) philosophy that will have been its truth.

Here are the Greek stones, stones other than Epimetheus's or Pyrrha's, but always on the trail of a delay. ". . . the soulless (*das Seelenlose*). When lovers sacrifice before the altar of the goddess of love and the prayerful breath of their emotion fans [animates or spiritualizes, *begeistert*] their emotion to a white-hot flame, the goddess herself has entered their hearts, yet the stone image remains standing in front of them (*das Bild von Stein bleibt immer vor ihnen stehen*). In the love-feast, on the other hand, the corporeal vanishes and only living feeling is present (*vorhanden*)."

moved, except that he was breathing through his half-open mouth. The judge and the lawyer wormed their way into the ear and the chaplain [*aumônier*] and executioner dared enter his mouth. They moved forward a little along the edge of the lower lip and fell into the gulf. And then, almost as soon as they passed the gullet, they came to a lane of trees that descended in a gentle, almost voluptuous slope. All the foliage was very high and formed the sky of the landscape. They were unable to recognize the essences, for in states like theirs one can no longer distinguish particular features: one passes through forests, tramples down flowers, climbs over stones. What surprised them most was the silence . . ."

rien) convict, a galley slave, driven to write by orders received at the back, threatened by the whip if he stops.

The miracle is that that (*ça*) sings, that that (*ça*) pricks, that that (*ça*) bands erect like a lyre.

So the *erion* will have been able to bloom [*éclore*] like a flower. In botany, erianthus designates an organism furnished with villous and fleecy flowers. Thus one can no longer decide, and that is the whole *interest* of writing, whether or not there is a style beneath the fleece. One also says, ἔριον τῆς ἀράχνης, the thread [*fil*] and the web of the spider, of the phallic or castrating mother, of the tarantula or the great spider

before the appearance of the fleece, the lecture on femininity puts the spider into its web ("in some classes of animals the females are the stronger and more aggressive and the male is active only in the single act of sexual union. This is so, for instance, with the spiders." Abraham, who weaves the thing around the phallic mother—"the spider's web represents pubic hair [*la toison pubienne*]"—and the *Unheimliche*, also recalls the suction by which the spider, or the incestuous mother, kills its victim.) and poses the problem of the *pharmakon* in galactic terms. "The fear of being poisoned is also probably connected with the withdrawal of the breast [*sein*]. Poison is nourishment that makes one ill." Milk, a poison contra poison, is also treated as the source of jealousy. Which would come back to our question: what is the excess of zeal around the signa-

But the spirituality of the Christian Last Supper consum(mat)es its signs, does not let them fall outside, loves without remain(s). This assimilation without leftover [*sans relief*] also satisfies itself. The destruction of the object keeps love in sight of the religion to which this destruction prohibits love any access. Religion always binds itself to an object. Love is still too subjective; it still marks Christianity, in the moment of the Last Supper, with an inner split. Then, when religion will be born, the existence of the object, the institution, the stone [*pierre*, Peter, rock] of the Church will provoke another fission, will appeal to another reconciliation, beyond religion and the religious family.

Love—remains interior. Speaking of the relief of objectivity and of the superiority of the Christian feast, Hegel names neither Plato's banquet nor a certain feast of the stone statue [*festin de pierre*]. "But just this kind of objectivity [*diese Art von Objektivität*; the stone image is in question] is totally relieved (*ganz aufgehoben wird*), whereas feeling remains (*bleibt*); this kind of objective mixing rather than a unification, such that love becomes visible in something, attached to something that is to be annihilated—that is what does not let this action become a religious one."

Consum(mat)ed without remain(s), the mystical object becomes subjective again but ceases thereby even to be the object of religious adoration. Once inside, the bread and the wine are undoubtedly subjectivized, but they immediately become bread and wine again, food that is digested, naturalized again; they lose their divine quality. They would lose it as well, it is true, in not being digested. Their divinity stands, very precariously, between swallowing [*engloutissement*] and vomiting; and it is neither solid nor liquid, neither outside nor in.

The moment the thing becomes thing again because consum(mat)ed—the thing is essentially consum(mat)ed, the process of consum(mat)ing constitutes it as thing rather than breaching/broaching it as such—the thing can be compared again with the Greek statuary of love, the moment the stone becomes dust again. Then Hegel again takes up the references to the statues of Apollo and Venus. As long as they have a form, their friable matter, their "breakable stone (*zerbrechlichen Stein*)" can be forgotten; then appeal is made to its immortal element; one is penetrated with love. But if the statue falls into ruin and if it is still said, "This is Apollo, this Venus," the dust I have before me and the divine image in me can no longer be reassembled. The value of the dust lay in the form. After the disappearance of the form, the scattered dust again becomes the principal thing. Meditating, worshiping thought cannot appeal to the dust, but only, through it, to self-recollection. The same applies for the mystical bread. Once eaten, although this time the destruction is internal, the bread swallows up [*engloutit*] with itself the possibility of a properly religious adoration. Whence

ture? Can one be jealous of something other than a *seing*? Such a question galvanizes and vulcanizes everything.

The *glas* also has to do with a war for the signature, a war to the death—the only one possible—in view of the text, then (dingdong), that finally, obsequently, remains no one's. *Glas* is written neither one way nor the other, the one counting on the other to relieve the double's failure, the colossus the column, the column the colossus. *Glas* strikes between the two. The place the clapper will, necessarily, have taken up, let us name it *colpos*. In Greek, *colpos* is the mother's [*de la mère*], but also the nurse's, breast [*sein*], as well as the fold [*pli*] of a garment, the trough of the sea [*repli de la mer*] between two waves, the valley pushing down into the breast [*sein*] of the earth

that eats her male.

One of the two Erigone's, the daughter of Icarius, slept with Dionysus, who laid her for a goatskin of wine for Icarius. Some shepherds, thinking they were poisoned by the wine, kill Icarius, and a baying hound, Marra, discovers the place of the paternal cadaver deprived of burial. The hound guides Erigone there, and she hangs herself from a nearby tree. The revenge of Dionysus:

the Christic scene, the sacrifice of the scapegoat, at the end of the *Miracle*, is slightly preceded, almost accompanied, doubled, by a Dionysian revel [*fête*]. There Harcamone is far from the Lord. The *pharmakon* suspends, apostrophizes the contraries, brings them together by dis-tancing them. "The execution of Métayer was a revel, it began with immolation and continued with orgiastic frenzy. In short, I think that those children's joy was of a Bacchic order, a kind of drunkenness caused by certain cruelties so intense that the joy could be expressed only by a hoarse but also musical laugh. . . . Flowers are gaiety and some are sadness become flowers. . . . And the whole Colony composed one enormous Harcamone. . . . Can it be that this monstrous thicket of vipers which had enticed so many boys withered in its prime [*fleur*]?" And if you follow, up to Harcamone's decapitation, the writing's tentacular and Medusa'ing movements, you will never be finished with them. Since this is a writing of decapitation, it has no

the mourning, the feeling of loss, of regret (*Bedauern*), of split (*Scheidung*) that seizes the young friends of Christ when the divine has melted in their mouths. Today's Christians still experience that feeling. The imminent loss of Christ, the quasi-presence of his corpse are felt [*sensibles*] precisely at the end of the meal, "after enjoying the supper (*nach dem Genuss des Abendmahls*)."

The religious does not put up with this feeling of impotence and division after the enjoyment. After a "genuinely" religious action, the soul must be appeased, that is, must continue to enjoy itself. The Last Supper is not yet religion. Its remains—that is, a corpse—are to be relieved. After the resurrection, the erection of the church of stone [of Peter] will properly institute religion. But the stone itself will give rise there to another fracture, another ruin, another mourning, another relief.

So we must concern ourselves with both Christ's immortality and what passes through his mouth.

The immortality of the one who is God's anointed, who is a being (*Wesen*) only as the son of God, this immortality, the glorious resurrection of his body, consists in letting itself be thought. To think is to think being, and to think being as immortal is to think its life. To think being as life in the mouth, that is the *logos*. Being, life, father, and son are equal in the infinite unity of the *logos*.

Hegel recalls that Jesus often says that the one who speaks through his mouth is in him and at the same time greater and higher than he. He calls himself thus—the Son of God. His Father goes through him and beyond him. And this filiation, which constitutes his *Sein*, his *Wesen*, can be revealed, attested, declared only by the Father. When Peter [*Pierre*] recognizes the one in whose favor God has given evidence, the son of Life, Jesus tells him: it is not your finitude, it is my father who has revealed this to you. Only the infinite—the Father—can name the bond of the finite to the infinite. What binds Hegel determines here as life. The bond (*Band*) holds God and Jesus together, the infinite and the finite; of this life Jesus is a part, a member (*Glied*), but a member in which the infinite whole is integrally regrouped, remembered. Such is life's secret (*Geheimnis*), the remembrance, the inner recollection of the whole in the morsel, that mysterious and incalculable operation the Jews could not comprehend. In order to grasp the strange status that makes this unity stand, one must stop thinking human nature and divine nature apart: one must make the father enter the son and think them together, gather them together in one same elevation. That is the essence of life as reconciliation and the essence of being, essence itself as life. Being measures up to thinking-together in the inner binding [*ligature*]; being is self-equality in infinite reconciliation.

What thus stands and remains inaccessible to the Jew is not then a column, of stone, of fire or clouds—of matter—or even a

center. And it would be a snare, a supplementary decapitation, to see everything agglutinated, agglomerated around a principal sucker, be it virgin/castrated like a flower ("metamorphoses into flowers," "flowers condemned mirthlessly by notorious councils," the "huge, ridiculous water lily" of a life—sister Zoé, the "virgin"—who, "her breath taken away [*le souffle coupé*], toppled into the water"; "And from their flowery mouths the big shots spat smacking [*claquants*] gobs of spit . . .," ". . . the thought of being the mystic fiancé of the murderer who had let me have the rose that had come directly from a supernatural garden") or the whole family structure of the mother tongue properly and lovingly slit at the throat [*égorgée*], at the glottis, erected/excreted, in the depths of a grotto or a forge (sounds of "sobs [*sanglots*]," "tramps [*cloches*: also, bells]," a "bugle" making one page clack; then the following: ". . . a huge crucifix. All the kids who were being punished that day were waiting at the door for their turn to be sentenced . . ."; then the following: ". . . their unwashed asses. They would say of a youngster whose toenails were too long: 'His nails [*ongles*] are curling.' They would also say: 'Your crap basket.' 'I'm going to shake your crap basket' ('craps' when he heard it, the child adding the infamous s).").

Why would the s be a mark of infamy? What is at stake in this (hi)story of infamy

to drive the young girls of Athens mad and force them to hang themselves.

The name Erigone was given to the Virgin, a celestial constellation and the Mother of Christ.

What the four black men find when they penetrate Harcamone's body by the ear and the mouth: the Immaculate Conception and the Mystic Rose.

Like the executioners, like Our-Lady-of-the-Flowers, threatened by the feminine "'glaive'" of justice (multiplied by the "bayonets" the moment the hour of his death sounds, and which will be signified

colossos, the dead's double, but a tree, a vegetable being, a tree of life. The whole circulates in it, from the root toward the top through all the parts. The whole already resides in *le gland* [acorn, glans].

Is this a question of a comparison, a metaphor, a phallocentric figure? A phallogocentric figure? The tree is said to be essentially feminine. Is this contradictory?

A remark in a kind of appendix: "This relation of a man to God in which is found the son of God, similar to the relation of branches, of foliage and fruits to the trunk their father, had to rouse the deepest indignation of the Jews, who had maintained an insurmountable abyss between human being and divine being and had accorded to our nature no participation in the divine."

This apparent metaphoricity is life's essence or rather life as the essence of being. When one is a Jew, when one does not comprehend life, when one is cut off [*coupé*] from life, and when one no longer feels [*sent*] it, only an accessory metaphor is seen there, a rhetorical auxiliary without its own proper truth. When one feels it from the inside, one knows that life is metaphoricity, the alive and infinite bond of the whole thought in its parts.

The language [*langue*] of the Jews does not have access to this. Their language is at once capable and incapable of metaphor. Thus the evaluation of its powers will be ambiguous. The Jew is capable of metaphor, of stating metaphors; he is incapable of this to the extent he sees precisely a metaphor, only a metaphor, a finite image leaving the finite and the infinite separate. But since the language, the historic state of a language was conceived by Hegel in a teleological way, as the becoming of a kind of acorn [*gland*], as a dynamic preparation to the accomplishment of the *logos* that will fill up the Christian's mouth, its very incapacity is only a childhood. The Jewish tongue [*langue*] speaks without yet knowing how to speak, without being able to develop fully the sperm of the *logos*. It is the childhood of the tongue.

Here that consists in a certain sort of analysis: to dissociate, oppose, let the opposites hardheadedly persist in reflection, be enclosed in the limits of the understanding, without comprehending the living unity that circulates among the terms, that is childhood. It is not, as is too easily thought, the sensible and imaginative confusion that does not know how to raise itself to the intellect. Here childhood is the state of intellect (*Verstand*), but as an underdevelopment of reason (*Vernunft*). The Jews do not comprehend the metaphor of the tree, which they take for a simple metaphor because their language or culture still derives from the *gland* [acorn, glans].

The evangelists constrained, restrained by the laws of the Jewish language, felt cramped for room. They had to freeze, harden, petrify the oppositions just where it was necessary to let the unity

to him by the Presiding Judge de Sainte-Marie), Harcamone is a virgin.

At least he still is when he cuts the throat [*coupe le cou*] of a young girl as he deflowers her beside an eglantine bush: "At the age of sixteen, he was frightened by women, and yet he could not keep his flower any longer. He was not afraid of the girl. When they were near an eglantine bush, he stroked her hair. The shuddering little bitch let him do it. He probably whispered something trivial, but when he put his hand under her skirt, she defended herself and blushed, out of coquetry—or perhaps fear. Her blushing made Harcamone blush, and he got excited. He fell on top of her. . . ." The red insists, is going to flow through the text until the four black men also fall upon the red rose at the heart of Harcamone's bodily tabernacle, while also pushing back [*écartant*] some skirts.

Like the remain(s) (of a Rembrandt, for example), the scene of the Mystic Rose stands out [*se découpe*] facing a painting without one ever knowing ((no) more illustration, (no) more legend, (no) more margin, (no) more signature) whether the gallery regards the text, or whether I have nothing facing me other than a voice *off*, an invisible night light [*veilleuse*], describing or clarifying a picture. In any case all that is twisted in the bottom of a cradle: "When we were in our shirts, we embraced again. The mattress was warm. We pulled the brown woolen blankets over our heads, and for a moment we lay still, as in the cradles

of the divine sap flow [*couler*], the unity of the infinite life engulfing these oppositions. The evangelists had, in spite of themselves, to speak the language of childhood.

Such is the case with John's text. Hegel accords it a very particular interest: "Pure life is being (*Sein*). . . . This pure is the source (*Quelle*) of all separate lives, pressures, and acts. . . . In the determinate situation in which he appears, the man can appeal only to his origin (*Ursprung*), to the source (*Quelle*) from which every shape of restricted life flows to him (*ihm fliesst*); he cannot appeal to the whole, which he now is, as to an absolute. He must call on the Most High, on the Father (*an das Höhere, an den Vater appellieren*) who lives immutable in all mutability. Since the divine is pure life, anything and everything said of it must be free from any opposition. And all reflection's expressions about the relations of the objective or about the activity for the sake of the objective action itself must be avoided, since the working of the divine is only a unification of spirits. Only spirit grasps and encloses spirit in (it)self. Expressions such as command, teach, learn, see, recognize, make, will, come (into the Kingdom of Heaven), go, express only relations of objectivity. . . . Hence it is only in inspiration (*Begeisterung*) that the divine can be spoken of. . . . John is the Evangelist who has the most to say about the divine and Jesus' bonding (*Verbindung*) with it. But the Jewish culture, so poor in spiritual relationships, forced him to avail himself of objective bondings and a language of actuality (*Wirklichkeitssprache*) for expressing the highest spiritual things, and this language thus often sounds harsher than when feelings are supposed to be expressed in the trading style. The Kingdom of Heaven; entry into the Kingdom; I am the door; I am the true food (*rechte Speise*), whoever eats my flesh, etc. (*wer mein Fleisch isst usw.*)—into such bondings (*Verbindungen*) of dry actuality is the spiritual forced (*ist das Geistige hineingezwängt*)."

So John is led, compelled to force his way into Jewish culture, to make the best of its form, to be sure, but to do violence to it in order to slide [*glisser*] the Christian semanteme into it, even at the risk of wounding it. In so doing, can he be said to have violated childhood?

Yes and no. Jewish culture does indeed have something of the underdeveloped childhood. But it is, nevertheless, perverse enough to have lost the deep charm of childhood. Jewish culture has neither maturity nor innocence. It has never been fully formed, never reached puberty, has only been deformed. Neither culture nor nonculture, but misculture (*Missbildung*). It is a monstrous acorn [*gland*]: "The state of Jewish culture cannot be called the state of childhood, nor can its language be called an undeveloped, childlike language. There are a few deep, childlike tones (*Laute*) retained in it, or rather reintroduced into it, but the remainder,

where Byzantine painters often confine the Virgin and Child. And after we had taken our pleasure twice, Divers kissed me and fell asleep in my arms. What I had feared occurred: I remained alone." That's the end.

Then begins the elaboration of Harcamone's dream. Like the executioners, like Our-Lady-of-the-Flowers, like every flower, Harcamone is a virgin. And his dream, on the eve of his death, repeats the trial [*procès*] of Our-Lady threatened by the feminine "'glaive'" of justice. It also has to do with a miracle: "In a hamlet, the name of the flower known as 'queen of the fields' made a little girl who was thinking of Our-Lady-of-the-Flowers ask:

"'Mommy, is she someone who had a miracle?'

"'There were other miracles that I haven't time to report. . . .'"

In writing's spacing, during the trial of the narrative [*récit*], the vertical lines (necktie, rain, glaive, cane or umbrella tip [*éperon*]) cut the horizontal lines of the newspaper or the book, of the wings or the spokes of the umbrella. Language cuts, decollates, unglues, decapitates. The sentences coil around a direction like liana along a truncated column. The direction—in reverse, everything has to be reread in reverse—takes us back to a cradle: what I am (following) is always the Immaculate Conception. "Thus,

with its forced and constrained (*gezwungene*) mode of expression, is rather a consequence of the supreme miseducation (*Missbildung*) of the people. A purer being (*ein reineres Wesen*) has to fight with this miseducation, and he suffers under it when he has to present himself (*sich darstellen*) in its forms (*Formen*); and he cannot dispense with them, since he himself belongs to this people."

Where does John take place? Who has signed his text? On the one hand, he is born of the Jewish people; he is Jewish; he is part of what "*zu diesem Volke gehört*." He undergoes its cultural and linguistic constraints; he is *formed* as a Jew. A Jew writes, accusing himself in his own tongue.

For simultaneously he also represents the "*reineres Wesen*," the purer being that breaks into the Jewish world. He must "fight" his own proper belonging.

Now he can fight his belonging only in using the arms it places at his disposal. He must steal his categories, his values from it, in order to annul them or turn them back against their own proper nature, against their congenital essence. These stolen categories, are they language's or thought's?

John writes in Greek. The Gospel undersigned John is by a Greek Jew. How have the Jewish categorial constraints been able to ligate, to make obsolete [*vieillir*] in advance the writing of the good news?

Au commencement était le logos, in the beginning was the *logos*. Here I write in French and English the translation of a Greek text that its apparent signer, transcribing it in a breath neither Greek nor Jewish, had to continue, to a certain extent, to think in the tongue of his childhood while printing it in the foreign one.

Im Anfang war der Logos, that is what interests Hegel. Among the four Gospels, the one he attends to the most, the most philosophically, the most dialectically, remains apart. The original written text, the only one we possess, with its marks of Hellenism (of Philonism or Hermetism) poses every kind of problem for the philologists and exegetes. Are these Hellenic traits accidental, prophetic, or essential?

This reading problem can unfold itself only on a family stage, in a family scene.

What interests Hegel is that the most Greek of the Gospels still keeps the revelation of the *logos* back within the Judaic limit and yet already begins to free it from that limit. The beginning of John's Gospel is produced, to be sure, "in a more appropriate language (*in eigentlicherer Sprache*)," at once because later and because it is Greek. But it still remains all bound up within analytic, intellectualistic formality. Scissionist. So one must distinguish between the essential content of sense and the formal appearance through which it is to be intended [*viser*]. *Im Anfang war der Logos* has only the appearance of a thetic proposition, of a judicative statement positing both

the newspapers were disturbing, as if they had been filled only with columns of crime news [*faits divers*], columns as bloody and mutilated as torture stakes. And though the press has very parsimoniously given to the trial, which we shall read about tomorrow, only ten lines, widely enough spaced to let the air circulate between the over-violent words, these ten lines— more hypnotic than the fly of a hanged man, than the words 'hempen collar,' than the word 'a gay'—these ten lines quickened the hearts of the old women and jealous children. Paris did not sleep. She hoped that the following day Our-Lady would be condemned to death; she desired that (man) [*le*]."

That (man)? What? Who? *What* Paris desires is *he and that* he be condemned to death. She desires *that (man) insofar as* condemned to death and condemns him to death in desiring that (man). In a word, she makes *that (man)* desirable and decollatable.

Let us space. The art of this text is the air it causes to circulate between its screens. The chainings are invisible, everything seems improvised or juxtaposed. This text induces by agglutinating rather than demonstrating, by coupling and decoupling, gluing and ungluing [*en accolant et en décollant*] rather than by exhibiting the continuous, and analogical, instructive, suffocating necessity of a discursive rhetoric.

"The hearing. . . . The courtroom is not majestic, but it is very high, so that it gives a general impres-

existence and a copula relation of subject to predicate. The true sense, the set *Anfang-Logos*—archeology or logoarchy—the spiritual and luminous life that passes through this set and gathers it together, this must not, should not have been analyzed into several terms. One should not have divided, judged (*urteilen*), distributed into subject, predicate, temporal modes modifying the pure presence. At once through naiveté and reflexivity [*réflexivité*], two accomplices, is the imperfect used; through concretism [*chosisme*] one says of the *logos* that it *was in God* (war bei *Gott*), that God *was* the *logos*, that in him *was* life. The coarseness of these statements results from division, the relation of inherence as well, introducing finitude (as if something could be *in* God) and abstraction (as if being and living could be universal predicates). Predicative division, the simple judicative copulation goes here in the wrong direction, goes to nonsense [*à contre-sens*]; it is "*widersinnig.*" If the true sense and the inadequate judgment are brought into relation, there is a feeling of contradiction: what is posited must be immediately annulled, what is in God is not in God, what was was not but still is, and so on. This disorder, this contradiction (*Widerspruch*) are formal and finite only for the understanding; and for those content to read, or rather who read badly because they are content to read, because they do not animate the objectivity of the dead language. Hegel takes into account the textual fact, but also the necessity of relieving it: if the reader passively receives the gospel text, without spiritual activity, without living repetition, the reader will see in it only formal contradictions, but if the reader, on the contrary, knows how to read (no longer just being content to read), matters will go completely otherwise. Everything depends on the reader's spirit: "This always objective language hence attains sense and weight only in the spirit of the reader." The variations, the diversity depend here on the reader's degree of consciousness and on what the reader can think of the living relations, as of "the opposition of the living and the dead."

The family theatre organizes this theory of judgment whose schema is already fixed for the whole future of Hegelian logic. It is dominated by the Johannine values of life (*zōē*) and light (*phōs*), that is, truth. In effect there are two ways of conceiving *logos* in John's Gospel. Both are insufficient and one-sided. The one Hegel qualifies as more "objective" consists in making the *logos* some thing, an individual actuality; the other, the "subjectivist," determines *logos* as reason, universality, as being-thought. But this division represents the "Jewish principle" of the opposition between thought and actuality, rationality and the sensible, the division of life, a relation of death between God and the world. Such a scissionist operation presupposes, as its unthought or unreflected, just what it gives the form of reflection to: the one, the unique (*das Einige*) in which no partitioning (*Teilung*) and thus no objectifying

sion of vertical lines, like lines of quiet rain. Upon entering, one sees on the wall a big painting with a figure of justice, who is a woman, wearing big red drapings. She is leaning with all her weight upon a saber, here called a 'glaive,' which does not bend. Below are the platform and table where the jurors and the presiding judge, in ermine and red robe, will come to sit in judgment on the child. The presiding judge is called 'Mr. Presiding Judge Vase de Sainte-Marie.'"

At this table (the *Miracle of the Rose* also sets out a "Holy Table" scene before putting Harcamone to death), the Presiding Judge who, under his red robe, is stiff like justice (a woman "wearing big red drapings," leaning on the glaive) and bears the name of the Virgin, simultaneously takes the place of God and, like Our-Lady, of the thirteenth one: "The twelve jurors are twelve decent men suddenly become sovereign judges. So, the courtroom had been filling up since noon. A banquet hall. The table was set."

They are going to eat and drink the *pharmakos*, but it is already clear that each figure occupies all places at once, circulates from one to the other, just as the necktie will shortly do.

judgment (*Urteil*) could take place. Simultaneously it must presuppose the possibility of division, of the infinite separation of the one, then the unity of unity and separation, of reality and thought, and so on. God and *logos* are one. But different insofar as God is the content (*Stoff*) in the form (*Form*) of the *logos*. Only understanding requires such a distinction, and only understanding can thus oppose them. "The *logos* itself is with God (*bei Gott*); they are one . . . all things are through the *logos*."

Through the *logos*: the mediation of *logos* interrupts all emanationism. If actuality were an emanation of God, it would be thoroughly and immediately divine. Hegel vigorously excludes this possibility. And yet, he directly adds, as actuality, it is an "emanation," a part, a morsel (*Teil*) of the infinite partitioning (*Teilung*).

This apparent contradiction is thinkable only through the familial determination of the concept of emanation. Here emanation is not what its name seems to indicate: the continuous production flowing from the source naturally [*coulant de source*]. A relation of living to living, emanation lets itself be worked (over) by discontinuity, division, negativity. Life and division go together, and with them sight, since the dehiscence of the living being is just what opens it to the light and thus to the truth (*phōs*, *alētheia*).

Hegel follows John to the letter: "Yet, as actual, the actual is an emanation, a part of the infinite partitioning, though at the same time (*zugleich*) in the part (ἐν αὐτῷ is better taken with the immediately preceding οὐδὲ ἓν ὃ γέγονεν), or in the one who partitions ad infinitum (if ἐν αὐτῷ is taken as referring to λογος), there is life." So life is at once the part and the partitioning, the morsel and the whole, its own proper difference, its own proper self-opposition. Each living part is the whole. Life is that strange division producing wholes.

Here the "metaphor" of the tree turns up again as a family metaphor: the genealogical tree in a radical sense.

So the individual, the singular, the limited, inasmuch as it is opposed to the primordial unity of the living, as dead, is a morsel of life, a branch in the tree of life. Branch is said *Zweig*. Like the two,

But to see it there must be a judas. "At the edge of a gulf bristling with bayonets, Our-Lady is dancing a perilous dance. . . . The public comes here only insofar as a word may result in a beheading [*décollation*] and as it may return, like Saint Denis, carrying its severed head in its hands. . . . Here death is only a black wing [*une aile noire*] without a body, a wing made with some cuttings of black stamin [*coupons d'étamine noire*] supported by a thin framework of umbrella ribs . . ."

Etamine [stamin, stamen], if you were pressed to dispose of the cutting, in order to restitch [*recoudre*] it somewhere else, as with each piece of material or each flower of the text, you would find it again in the *Thief's Journal*, over the cunt of a Spanish whore.

But the erection has to be elaborated very slowly; cutting and sewing proceed by themselves, without visible application. ". . . umbrella ribs, a pirate banner without a staff. This wing of stamin floated over the Palace, which you are not to confuse with any other, for it is the Palace of Justice [*Palais de Justice*]."

If you displaced the tongue, in effect, the palate [*le palais*] would not be the same any more.

the bough [*le rameau*] is produced by division; this dead something (*Totes*) is at the same time (*zugleich*) "a branch of the infinite tree of life (*ein Zweig des unendlichen Lebensbaumes*). Each part, to which the whole is external, is at the same time (*zugleich*) a whole, a life." The incomprehensible, what the understanding does not understand, what the Jew is deaf to, is this *zugleich*, this structural at once (*simul*) of the living whole and morsel. Reflected upon and divided, considered from the viewpoint of the partitioning (*Teilung*) at once dividing and making possible the object of a judgment (*Urteil*), life is at once subject and predicate, the synthesis of existence and thought universality: at once life (ζωή) and life thought, grasped (*aufgefasstes*), light (φῶς), truth (*Wahrheit*). Life is life, life is light, life is truth.

Hegel translates John into German but also, following a dialectical law, into a family syllogism. The light's new coming into the world, life's coming into the light of truth follows a process such that the recognition, the conscious grasp [*la prise de conscience*] of a revelation already there, the bringing to light of the light, the truth of the light in the light of truth, the truth of truth, comes down to recognizing God and recognizing ourselves (*sich erkennen*) as children of God (*als Kinder Gottes*). This process is a process of family reappropriation. The question is recognizing what returns to the father.

The light is in the world, in the ordered beauty of the *kosmos*. "Though John was not himself the light," the light was, in every man who enters the world of men, equivalent. The *kosmos*, a more restricted notion than *panta*, designates the totality of human relations. The light does not accidentally befall the *kosmos*; the *kosmos* is in the light insofar as the *kosmos* is human and is the work of the *anthrōpou phōtos* or of the *anthrōpos phōtizomenos*. The light of truth never blooms, never lights up, and nothing lights up in it—before the anthrope [*l'anthrope*]. Now there is in man something before man, and in his light something that rejects the light. Man began by closing himself to what was nonetheless his most own, what was most proper and closest (*sein Eigenstes* (ἴδιον)), most related to him. He treated his own properness as a stranger (*als fremd*). Since the light properly his own is also the light of life, not to receive it is to cut himself off from life. Those in return who receive it, those who recognize themselves in it as at home, give

"It [*Elle*]/the wing [*aile*] of stamin/enveloped it in its folds and had detached a green crepe de Chine necktie to represent It in the courtroom. The necktie, which lay on the Judge's table, was the only piece of evidence. Death, visible here, was a necktie, and this fact pleases me: it was a light Death."

It is too soon to consider the *étamine*.

But wing, the Death that floats above the Palace, is *represented* by a necktie. It "had detached a necktie to represent It. . . ." A fabric is represented by a fabric. The necktie that passes around the neck is the weapon of the crime and, in the hands of God, of the Virgin Mary, of the Apostles, of Judas, will become, in an instant, what it will always have been in the hands of Our-Lady, namely Christ, Christ himself, a phallus. That's too self-evident, and there would be no need to insist on it. Nor is it in any way what interests us in this representation of a text by a text. What does interest us is the fact that the textile that always represents never represents anything. And we like it so: the simulacrum of the represented is the lightness of Death. There are only representatives. Death is nothing. But its representatives are even less than nothing. And yet everything is written for Death, from Death, to the address of the Dead. I write for the dead, he says everywhere. Read the Letters to Roger Blin, the Studio of Alberto Giacommetti, read every-

themselves a power (*Macht*) that is not a new force (*neue Kraft*) but one degree (*Grad*) more in the equality or inequality (*Gleichheit oder Ungleichheit*) of life.

In doing so, they do not become others; "they know God and recognize themselves as children of God, as weaker than he, yet of a like nature (*von gleicher Natur*) in so far as they become conscious of that relation (*Beziehung* (ὄνομα)) of the ἄνθρωπος as φωτιζόμενος φῶτι ἀληθινῳ [lighted by the true light]. They find their essence (*Wesen*) in no stranger, but in God."

What Hegel translates by relation, relationship, is the name. What man discovers more proper within himself, in his own proper name, in his most appropriating relation, is God and God as his father. So truth comes to the world, or rather reveals itself as the structure of the *kosmos* in the nomination of the filial relation. The name, the relation, the spirit (Hegel sometimes translates *onoma* by *spirit*) is the structure of what returns to the father.

This nomination is not an event. Not simply. This is an event insofar as it is new, the absolutely new. But this new illuminates only the light; it brings the light of day to light, gives birth to the light [*met le jour au jour*].

The sign that this nomination of truth as filiation is not absolutely new, that it *already* repeats, and that the spirit always repeats, is the sign. That sign—of newness as repetition—is a linguistic sign. The family or filial syntagm did not upsurge with the good news. As if by chance, by contingency, *zufällig*, he says, the Jewish tongue has this at its disposal. It was one of those rare and naturally happy expressions that awaited their fertilization, their true fulfilment, their full reference.

John has nothing to do with this. He introduced the concrete, individual, existential reference into the discourse of truth. "John bore witness, not of the φῶς alone (verse 7), but also of the individual (verse 15)." Thus has the generic relation replaced the

thing. But he specifies: for the dead who have never been alive. The *glas* is for (no) one. (No) one. It announces or recalls nothing. It hardly sounds, it sooner resounds, before ever having touched the material of any sign. That (*ça*) resounds. Why call that (*ça*) death? Why call for one's death? Because that (*ça*) has *already* (déjà) taken place.

This strange *already* (déjà) has to be deciphered.

What sends a representative (wing, floating death) is nothing, but as a past that has never been present, has never taken place. We do not await death, we only desire it as a past we have not yet lived, that we have forgotten, but with a forgetfulness that has not come to cover over an experience, with a memory more ample, more capable, older than any perception. This is why there are only traces here, traces of traces without tracing, or, if you wish, tracings that only track and retrace other texts, wing/necktie again, hymen and

déjà, already. Death has already taken place, before everything. How is one to decipher this strange anteriority of an *already* that is always shouldering you with a cadaver? You have remarked that he is always in the act of palming off his cadaver on you. He wishes you never to be able to get rid of the very stiff body his literature, his funeral rite, will have banded erect for you. How does one seduce, how does one win love without telling you *I am dead*? Not just "pay attention, I am going to die," "I am mortal," which would only have a relative and provisional effect, but "I am *already* [déjà] dead," even before living. Who does it better? Who says it better? And if, as I have demonstrated elsewhere (*Speech and Phenomena*, *Glas in Phenomen* in its Slovene translation), *I am* and *I am dead* are two statements indistinguishable in their sense, then the *already* [déjà] that I am (following) [*je suis*] sounds its own proper *glas*, signs itself its own death sentence [*arrêt de mort*], regards you in advance, sees you advance without any comprehension of what you will have loved, following, in a column, the funeral march of an erection everyone will intend to have available from now on.

A more or less argot translation of the *cogito*: "I am therefore dead." This can only be written. After friends, "new and old, those to whom I am 'Jeannot with the Pretty Neckties,'" were evoked, it is written: "I am therefore dead. I am a dead man who sees his skeleton in a mirror, or a dream character who knows that he lives only in the darkest region of a being whose face he will not know when the dreamer is awake."

discourse on man in general and truth in general. "The most commonly cited and the most characterizing (*bezeichnendste*) expression of Jesus' relation to God is his calling himself the son of God and contrasting himself as son of God with himself as the son of man. The characterizing (*Bezeichnung*) of this relation is one of the few natural expressions (*Naturlaute*) remaining by accident (*zufällig übriggeblieben war*) in the Jewish speech of that time, and therefore it is to be counted as part of their happy expressions (*glücklichen Ausdrücke*)."

This remark [*propos*] belongs to the whole Hegelian system of expression's good fortune in the naturally speculative language-effects.

Why doesn't the Jew comprehend, in sum, what he says, what his language [*langue*] says in advance in his place? More precisely, why doesn't he say what he can say?

Literally, one cannot maintain that the Jew does not comprehend, does not grasp what he says. On the contrary, he conceives what he utters, what his tongue places in his mouth. That is his limit: he conceives. He remains no further than the order of the concept. Now the father-son relation is inconceivable, at least in terms of universal generalities, of "thoughts." The unity of son and father is not conceptual, for every conceptual unity lives on opposition, is finite. Now life is infinite. If the living relation of father to son is life as a nonconceptual unity, every conceptual unity presupposes that relation, implies that nonconcept as the concept's production, the concept's nonconceptual conception. The living conception is the relation of father to son. This conception forms a contradiction in the logic of the understanding, here of the Jew, who cannot master it—precisely because he intends to master. One masters only finite life—or death.

"The relation of a son to his father is not a unity, a concept (as, for instance, unity or harmony of disposition, equality of principles, etc.), a unity which is only a unity in thought and is abstracted from life. On the contrary, it is a living relation of living beings, a likeness of life (*gleiches Leben*); simply modifications of the same life, not the opposition of essence, not a plurality of absolute substantialities. Thus the son of God is the same being (*Wesen*) as the father. . . ."

This unity cannot be stated in the analytic and finite logic of the understanding. In the all but inconceivable judgment, "the son is the father," "the father is the son," there is neither formal tautology nor empiric heterology. This *a priori* infinite synthesis is the condition of all synthetic *a priori* judgments.

Since this unity cannot be stated in the understanding's abstract language, it requires a kind of metaphoricity. Beyond the concept, this metaphoricity also hands over [*livre*] every determinate concept's condition of possibility.

screen that one finally breaks open at the end "for nothing." It was only that, and they make so many (hi)stories. The Mother breaks the last one. There is a whole "theory" of the event there—by theory I understand *theater*, of course—sewn from the same filial filaments, and a whole theory of the immemorial as well. But theory—always blind on this point—seduces us less than the event that slips away unraveling [*se défile*], in the studio, in the text, in the scene, on the stage. This other logic of the event and of time you would find enunciated in his letter (to Roger Blin), even though the signer lacks "the time to go into the matter at greater length," or elsewhere, everywhere else. In *The Studio*, for example: "I understand badly what in art they call an innovator. Should a work be understood by future generations? But why? And what would that signify? That they could use it? For what? I do not see. But I see much better—even though very darkly—that every work of art, if it wishes to attain the most grandiose proportions, must, with an infinite patience and application from the moments of its elaboration, descend the millennia, rejoin, if it can, the immemorial night peopled by the dead who are going to recognize themselves in this work.

"No, no, the work of art is not destined for generations of children. It is offered to the innumerable population of the dead. Who accept it. Or refuse it. But the dead of whom I was speaking have never been alive. Or I forget the fact."

I do not see. But I see much better—even though very darkly . . . The whole *Studio* describes the viewpoint of Oedipus.

For whom does one write, who accepts or refuses? For whom is this gift that never becomes present?

The metaphor still remains natural, physical, seemingly vegetable. Still the tree, a tree with three branches: "It is true only of objects, of dead things, that the whole is other than the parts; in the living thing, on the other hand, the part of the whole is one and the same as the whole. If particular [separate, cut off, *besonderen*] objects, as substances, are grasped together while each of them at the same time (*zugleich*) retains its property as an individual (numerically), then their ensemble, their unity, is only a concept, not an essence (*Wesen*), not something being (*Seiendes*). Living things, however, are essences as separate (*Abgesonderte*), and their unity is as well an essence. What is a contradiction (*Widerspruch*) in the realm of the dead (*im Reich des Toten*) is not one in the realm of life. A tree which has three branches makes up *one single* tree (einen *Baum*) with them; but every son of the tree, every branch (and also its other children, leaves and blossoms) is itself a tree. The fibers bringing sap to the branch from the trunk are of the same nature (*gleichen Natur*) as the roots. If a tree is set in the ground upside down it will put forth leaves out of the roots in the air, and the boughs (*Zweige*) will root themselves in the ground. And it is just as true to say that there is only *one single* tree here as to say that there are three."

on the same page, the example of the Arab: a son of the Koresh tribe, among the Arabs, is the whole tribe. Whence the form of warfare that "natural, undivided" peoples (*natürlichen ungeteilten Volke*) develop: the individuals do not count here; they are massacred with the greatest cruelty. In Europe on the contrary—and this time Hegel seems to see a decline in this—the individual has no organic bond (*Band*) with the whole, only a bond of abstract thought. War, then, is a relation between state totalities. "As with any genuinely free people (*wie bei jedem echt freien Volk*), so among the Arabs, each one is a part and at the same time the whole (*ein Teil, aber zugleich das Ganze*)."

The possibility of turning upside down, of the upside-down erection [*de l'érection à l'envers*], is inscribed in the cycle of the family standing up [*stance*]. The son is son only in his ability to become father, his ability to supply or relieve the father, in his occupying his place by becoming the father of the father, that is, of the son's son. A father is always his grandfather and a son his own grandson.

The movement of the upside-down erection describes the structure of the concept's nonconceptual conception.

This "metaphor" marks itself twice and simultaneously occupies two places. Through its semantic tenor, it stands, like life, beyond the concept, as you understand, beyond the dead concept, beyond the understanding's finite analysis, beyond the objectifying determination. But this life is not the one the metaphoric "vehicle" designates; the life of the spirit is named through the natural life in

The Studio and the remain(s). It *describes* the viewpoint of Oedipus, surveys its surface of blindness from the point of a style that you will never know whether the style belongs or not to the surface described. The point certainly touches that surface. But one has to know how to read this point of contact.

That is not only true of *The Studio* in which we are and to which we shall return (it is precisely contemporary with the "event" recounted in "What Remained. . ."), but of all the rest, the whole remain(s): which is always written, not *within* the Oedipus, but in Oedipus, just as a piece of music is composed *in*, a book written in—these or those letters. More precisely, since the syncategoremes assume importance, the whole remain(s) is written *on* Oedipus, mounted on Oedipus, as on a mounting, an easel [*chevalet*], a pedestal, or a ring. A slab. And the one who mounts—listen to the laughter of the avant-garde and the innovators—knows full well this cavalier operation of the painter, the sculptor, or the jeweler, is no more for Oedipus than against Oedipus, inside him than outside him. And if the Oedipal event was something, it would be what here gives him the force to mount Oedipus, to fuck you, to unhorse [*désarçonner*] you when you want to interpret, judge, decide. You are still inside the *Palais*. In(side) the mother tongue.

You always have the necktie in your hands, and you don't really know what to do with it.

which it grows [*végète*]. But between the two lives, analogy makes metaphor possible. Between the two, there is the concept and death. This double mark is found again across all history and the whole system; it even describes the structure of all life, the living organization of the Hegelian system.

An index, among many others, but to that privileged place, the end of the greater *Logic*. In the last section of the "Subjective Logic" ("The Idea"), life is inscribed both as a syllogism and as the moment of a syllogism. The first of three chapters on the Idea precisely treats life. The Idea's first determination is life; the second, cognition and will (the idea of the true and the good); the third, the absolute Idea in which the spirit recognizes itself in its infinite, "absolute truth," in and for (it)self. In this syllogism of the Idea, life first appears as a natural and immediate determination: the spirit outside self, lost in naturality, in natural life that itself constitutes a "smaller" syllogism. The immediate Idea has the form of life. But the absolute Idea in its infinite truth is still determined as Life, true life, absolute life, life without death, imperishable life, the life of truth.

Between the two lives, as their hyphen [*trait d'union*], their contract or contraction—death. But also the space of metaphoric play and the analogy that interests us here under the title of [*au titre de*] filiation.

Does "life" have, here or there, its own proper, literal sense? One does not have to choose. Life does not have, here or there, its own proper(ty), its own literalness; life produces itself as the circle of its own reappropriation, the self-return before which there is no proper self. Nothing precedes the return. "The absolute Idea, as the rational concept that in its reality meets only with itself, is by virtue of this immediacy of its objective identity, on the one hand the return to *life* (*die Rückkehr zum* Leben); but it has no less relieved (*aufgehoben*) this form of its immediacy, and contains within itself the highest degree of opposition." The Idea, immediate and natural life, relieves, abolishes and preserves, itself, dies in raising itself to the spiritual life. So life develops itself in contradiction and negativity; the metaphor between the two lives is only this movement of relieving negativity. "The concept is not merely *soul* (Seele), but free subjective concept that is for itself and therefore possesses

The other paragraph: Our-Lady enters the courtroom. "Nevertheless, I shall make so bold as to say that all eyes could read, graven in the aura of Our-Lady-of-the-Flowers, these words: 'I am the Immaculate Conception.'"

Who will have the necktie?

Our-Lady, virgin born of a virgin, who announces himself—he is an archangel—and who says to us, in sum, "I conceive myself without a father, I am generated [*je nais* as Genet] of myself or of the operation of the Holy Spirit," I am my father, my mother, my son, and myself, Our-Lady has killed. With a verge. He has put a necktie into play, but in the beginning he did not even own this necktie. And no one wants it, no one is even able to keep it.

Word for word: "Have I mentioned the fact that the audience was made up mostly of men? But all of them, darkly dressed, with umbrellas on their arms and newspapers in their pockets, were shakier than a bower of wisteria [*glycine*], than the lace curtain of a crib. Our-Lady-of-the-Flowers was the reason why . . ."

I have no right to operate like this; let us, however, select, let us section in the two pages that follow so as to join the necktie that lies about (". . . Punch and Judy show . . . glory . . . the lovely crevice . . . thousand precursors of Our-Lady, an annunciatory angel of this virgin,

"Our-Lady, an annunciatory angel of this virgin": Our-Lady is therefore not only another name for the Virgin Mary, for the Presiding Judge, for the Christ, and for the entire Holy Family, he is also the angel announcing the virgin, as another *first name* for the mother.

personality—the practical, objective concept determined in and for itself which, as person, is impenetrable atomic subjectivity—but which, none the less, is not exclusive individuality, but for itself *universality* and *cognition*, and in its other has its own objectivity for its object (*seine eigene Objektivität zum Gegenstande*). All else is error, confusion, opinion (*Meinung*), tendency, arbitrariness, and transitoriness (*Vergänglichkeit*); the absolute Idea alone is *being* (Sein), imperishable life (*unvergängliches* Leben), *self-knowing truth*, and is *all truth*."

The same movement in the *Encyclopedia*, at the end, concerning *Sa*. The third term returning to immediacy, this return to simplicity being brought about by the relief of difference and mediation, natural life occupies both the end and the beginning. In their ontological sense, the metaphors are always of life; they put rhythm into the imperturbable equality of life, of being, of truth, of filiation: *phusis*.

Thus the Hegelian system commands that it be read as a book of life. The categories of reading must first bend to that. To speak of several states of Hegelian thought, of a youthful Hegel or an accomplished Hegel, is at once both Hegelian and anti-Hegelian. Thus Bourgeois's book on Hegel at Frankfurt applies Hegel's most preformationist categories to its subject. It opposes, to be sure, the "arrival of the mature Hegelianism" to the "incipient Hegelianism," but precisely states that the latter "is engaged on the path of Hegelianism properly so called, on which he will formulate at Jena the ingenious intuition in writing that the absolute must be conceived as the 'identity of identity and nonidentity.'" In this one sees Hegel "anticipating . . . future themes," "the philosophy of the concept; that is, of Hegelianism," of "Hegelianism itself"—"Hegelianism," the title of the book's third chapter being presented as the conclusion of a syllogism in which "Judaism" and "Christianity" (the other two titles) would be the first two terms. "Early Hegelianism," "incipient Hegelianism," "mature Hegelianism," "accomplished Hegelianism," "Hegelian philosophy properly so called," "Hegel become fully adult as a speculative philosopher," realizing what he "aspired to since his adolescence," and so on—all these categories reflect, double

"in seinem Anderen." The "its other" is the very syntagm of the Hegelian proper; it constitutes negativity in the service of the proper, literal sense. When life becomes its own proper object for (it)self, the objectivity of natural life dies and puts itself "opposite" the Idea, as a particular thing, on the subject of which something can be said. In truth, life is what always speaks of (about) itself, of its life and its death, again of its life

before Jena, the "Fragment of a System (1800)" takes up again the essential point of the theses on Christianity: "*das Leben sei die Verbindung der Verbindung und der Nichtverbindung,*" in other words, the copula or the ligament of the ligament and the nonligament in which life in the same stroke [*du même coup*] bands and unbands itself erect. Now, life is being

In *Our-Lady-of-the-Flowers*, Divine loves Gabriel, surnamed the Archangel. To guide him into love, she puts a little of her urine into whatever she gives him to eat or drink. That is how dogs are kept attached, she had heard. She draws him into her attic, where she arranges a funereal atmosphere (darkness, incense, *glas*): "She was bound to have Gabriel up sooner or later. As the curtains are drawn, he finds himself in a darkness the more massive for having been mildewed for years (as by a scent of chilled [*glacé*] incense) by the subtle essence of the farts that had blossomed there [*éclos là*]." When he penetrates her, Gabriel makes "his verge quiver like a shying horse." Once he penetrates her, supposing that he somewhere bears the same first name as that whoring mother, it is true that he merely recovers his form and his place. Divine had told him: "'I love you as if you were inside my belly,' and also:
"'You're not my sweetheart, you're myself. My heart or my sex. A branch of me.'
"And Gabriel, thrilled, though smiling with pride, replies:
"'Oh! you little hussy!'"

a blond young boy ('Girls blond as boys . . .' I shall, indeed, never weary of this phrase, which has the charm of the expression: 'a French guardswoman') whom I used to watch in gymnasium groups. He depended upon the figures that he helped to form, and, thus, was only a sign. . . . on the floor . . . nun pushing aside her veil . . . poem (or fable) that was born of it (recurring miracle of Anne Boleyn: from the steaming blood sprang a bush of roses, that might have been white, but were certainly fragrant), the necessary sifting was done in order to disengage the truth scattered beneath the marble. . . . With a stroke of the knife [*D'un coup de couteau*], he had put out his eye. . . . On the table, the lithe little Death lay inert and looked quite dead. . . . The Court entered by a hidden door that was cut out of the wallpaper behind the jurors' table. . . . just as, on Palm Sunday, the clergy, who usually leave the sacristy by a side door near the choir, surprise the faithful by appearing from behind their backs [*dos*] [the plays open this way—from behind

Hegel's teleological discourse. It is normal, the truth of Hegelianism being conceived only at the end of the course, that philosophical narration be produced in the future. Bourgeois's book says all the time: Hegel will think, Hegel will have to, Hegel will come to, and so on. Frankfurt is only the to-come of the completed system. It is also normal that the logical reading be constantly accompanied by a biographical narrative [*récit*] (the young Hegel, the adult Hegel, etc.).

Nothing more Hegelian. But nothing less Hegelian: in distinguishing the old from the young, one sometimes dissembles the systematic chains of the "first" texts; and above all one applies a dissociating and formal analysis, the viewpoint of the understanding in a narration that risks missing the living unity of the discourse; how does one distinguish philosophically a before from an after, if the circularity of the movement makes the beginning the end of the end? And reciprocally? The Hegelian tree is also turned over; the old Hegel is the young Hegel's father only in order to have been his son, his great-grandson.

The risk, then, is the Jewish reading.

What do the Jews make of Hegel? What do they do with him? What do they do when they hear it said that the son is one with the father? When the unity of essence (*Weseneinheit*) of father and son is presented to them? Or even the upside-down erection?

They count up, they add up the accounts. They cry out scandal. How can Jesus identify himself with God, regard himself equal to God, and believe that possible by naming God his father? They understand this unity in terms of numeric equality, what Hegel never stops denouncing, even concerning the Trinity. Consequently the father/son relation becomes impossible, unthinkable for them. They consider the family nomination of the relation of God to men or to Jesus as images (*Bilde*), in the most external sense, as ways of speaking or imagining. Thus do they disqualify what essential the advent of Christianity can include in the history of the spirit. Understanding the father/son relation at once as purely conceptual and as purely imaginative, they miss its schema and are doubly mistaken. ". . . Jesus continually appealed, especially in John, to his oneness (*Einigkeit*) with God, who has granted to the son to have life in (him)self, just as the father has life in himself. He and the father are one; he is bread come down from heaven, and so forth. These are hard words (σκληροὶ λόγοι), and they are not softened (*milder*) by being interpreted [declared, ex-

[*de dos*] and in the text—on their structure, almost always, see the onset [*attaque*] of the maids] . . . . Our-Lady had a foreboding that the whole session would be faked and that at the end of the performance his head would be cut off by means of a mirror [*de glaces*] trick. . . . M. Vase de Sainte-Marie was wearing a monocle . . .").

There is given then the necktie at the Last Supper scene. However, who is there, who has it, this hanging counterpart.

"The Presiding Judge had the soft tie in his fingers, a tie like a piece of ectoplasm, a tie that had to be looked at while there was still time, for it might disappear at any moment or stiffen [*bander roide*] in the dry hand of the Judge, who felt that if it did actually become

everything is always attacked *de dos*, *from the back*, written, described from behind. *A tergo*. I am *already* [déjà: also, D.J.] (dead) signifies that I am *behind* [derrière]. Absolutely behind, the *Derrière* that will have never been seen from the front, the *Déjà* that nothing will have preceded, which therefore conceived and gave birth to itself, but as a cadaver or glorious body. To be behind is to be before all—in a rupture of symmetry. I cut myself off, I entrench myself—behind—I bleed [*je saigne*] at the bottom of my text. "The author of a beautiful poem is always dead" (*Miracle of the Rose*).

At the same time, by cutting myself off, by entrenching myself, by withdrawing my presence, by dying, I escape the blows [*coups*] in advance. The Behind and the Already, the *Derrière* and the *Déjà*, protect me, make me illegible, shelter me on the text's verso. I am accessible, legible, visible only in a rear-view mirror. Also read, as forms of repression, all the rhetorical flowers in which I disperse my signature, in which I apostrophize or apotropize myself. It is a matter of repulsing the worst threat, and, to do so, of cutting oneself off beforehand, by oneself from oneself: the *genêt* is thus a kind of *reseda morbis*, an incantation of one thing in order to hide behind the other, to be shut up in its enclosure.

In silence fallen into the prison of the other.

"And I, having only the name Divers as a visible, prehensible asperity for grasping the invisible, shall contort it to make it enter mine, mingling the letters of both. Prison, particularly a State prison, is a place which makes things both heavier and lighter [*allège*]. Everything that pertains to it, people and things alike, has the weight of lead and the sickening lightness of cork [*l'écœurante légèreté du liège*]. Everything is ponderous because everything seems to sink, with very slow movements, into an opaque element. One has 'fallen,' because too heavy. The horror of being cut off from the living precipitates us—the word

plained: *erklärt*] as imagery (*für bildliche*) or by slipping conceptual unities behind them instead of taking them spiritually as life. Of course, as soon as understanding's concepts are opposed to imagery (*Bildlichem*) and taken as dominant, every image must be set aside as only play (*Spiel*), as a by-product (*Beiwesen*) of imagination (*Einbildungskraft*) without truth; and instead of the life of the image, nothing remains but the objective."

The Jew stands by this objectivism that, incapable of leaving the finite closure of the understanding or the imagination, also remains a subjectivism. Enclosed in this double nondialectic one-sidedness, he has access neither to the divine nor to the spiritual sense of filiation. For the spirit has not yet spoken in him. He has not yet become an adult in himself. At bottom no matter how much the Jew strives to be [*a beau être*] a kind of executioner, he is also a child. And what characterizes childhood is that it cannot think childhood as such, filiation as such. As long as he is child, the son is blind to the father/son relation. To see it he must become adult. He becomes son for-(it)self only in becoming adult, then in identifying himself with the father. Only a father can become a son, and a son can think himself as such only in identifying himself with the father. This strange indifferent difference opens up spiritual filiation, relieves the genealogy of the natural family. Hegel articulates this in a play on words that must not be considered an imaginal *Beiwesen*. The Jew is not filial (*kindlich*) because he is puerile (*kindisch*). Not at all childlike, but childish. If the Jew accuses Jesus of blaspheming when he says his father has entered him, that is because the Jew understands neither the finite nor the infinite, neither the measured nor the immeasurable, neither the part nor the whole. More precisely, what the Jew does not understand is neither this nor that, but the commensurability or the passage between the two, the presence of the immeasurable in the determinate, the beauty and the immanence of the infinite in the finite.

Castration and the prison: "The Jewish multitude was bound to wreck his attempt to give them the consciousness of something divine, for faith (*Glaube*) in something divine, something great, cannot make its home in excrement [mud, mire, *Kote*]. The lion has no room in a nest, the infinite spirit none in the dungeon (*Kerker*) of a Jewish soul, the whole of life none in a withering leaf. The mountain and the eye which sees it are object and subject, but between man and God, between spirit and spirit, there is no such cleft (*Kluft*) of objectivity; one is to the other only one and an other in that one recognizes the other. One branch [corollary, *Zweig*] in taking the relation of son to father objectively, or rather in its form considering the will, is the discovery of a connection (*Zusammenhang*) for itself with God in the connection between the separate human and divine natures thus conceived and reverenced in Jesus,

erect or disappear, he would be covered with ridicule. He therefore calls for precipice (remark the number of words relating to prison that evoke falling, fall itself, etc.)."

hastened to pass the instrument of the crime to the first juror, who passed it to his neighbor, and so on, without anyone's daring to linger over recognizing it, for each of them seemed to be running the risk of being metamorphosed before his own eyes into a Spanish dancer."

The "and so on" of this circulation of the phallus that kills—an attack again on one and the same neck, in one and the same stroke [*d'un seul et même cou*], tighten the necktie—always comes down to the movement of the virginal flower (varginal: between verge and vagina of the virgin, little stone [*petite pierre*] or clitoral bell [*cloche*]), of the phallus taken from the Holy Mother, and that no more belongs to the Presiding Judge de Sainte-Marie than to Our-Lady-of-the-Flowers ("I am (following) the Immaculate Conception").

The phallus could seem to belong to the victim (of the theft or the murder) since it is his own necktie. Now the victim ought to give up as lost what should have returned to him like the phallus to the virgin mother.

Precisely the indignation of Vase de Sainte-Marie when Our-Lady—himself—reveals to him that it is the murdered man—himself—who gave him the thing and the idea for the crime (He "was wearing a necktie that squeezed his neck. He was all red.").

is the hope for a love between two total unequals (*Ungleichen*), a love of God for man which might at best be a form of sympathy. Jesus' relation to God, as the relation of son to father, is a childlike (*kindliches*) relation, since in essence, in spirit, the son feels himself one with the father who lives in him. This has no resemblance to that childish (*kindischen*) relation in which a man might bind himself with the rich overlord of the world whose life he feels wholly alien to him and with whom he connects himself only through presents showered on him, only through the crumbs falling from the rich man's table."

One does not bind oneself to the father with scraps [*reliefs*], by calculating exchanges. The bond to the father is incalculable. Jesus' being, his essence (*Wesen*), insofar as it couples him to his Father, "can be truly grasped only by *Glauben*"; *Glauben*, the act of faith, has here an infinite, ontological force. This results from the fact that, unlike finite cognition (relating a spirit to a determinate object that remains heterogeneous to it), *Glauben* is of/by a spirit for a spirit. Whence the "metaphor" of harmony: "The relation of a spirit to a spirit is the feeling of harmony, is their unification (*Vereinigung*); how could heterogeneity be unified?"

The homogeneous, then, that born of the same, in its self-sameness [*en soi-même*], such is the harmonious element of *Glauben*. The one that believes in this element of the same does not believe in any other thing, rediscovers itself in its *Glauben*, "rediscovers . . . its own nature (*seine eigene Natur wiederfindet*)." The musical metaphor of the homogeneous has its analog in the anthropo-photological metaphor. The proper nature of man the bearer of light becomes clear. Man does not bring the light to bear as one bears a torch. The light and life are within him. He is in the light and in life, rather he is borne by them. In every sense of this word, he belongs to, is part of, the light, "he is the property of the light (*er ist das Eigentum des Lichts*)." If man is the light's (truth's, being's, and so on) property, ownness, he does not receive the light from the outside; he is ablaze in it; he catches fire [*s'embrase*] in the homogeneity of its element and in the act of *Glauben*. The light's brightness [*éclat*] (*Glanz*) is not foreign to him; it benumbs all his substance and all the glory of his body. "He is the property of the light. He is not illumined by a light in the way in which a dark body is when it borrows a brightness not its own (*nur fremden Glanz*); on the contrary, his own inflammability (*sein eigener Feuerstoff*) takes fire and he burns with a flame that is his own (*eine eigene flamme*)."

That is what Jesus explains to Simon: the divine in you has recognized me as divine. We are the same, born of the same. My essence "has re-echoed in yours (*in dem deinigen wiedergetönt*)." Then of Simon, son of Jonah, he made Peter (*Pierre*), transformed him into "the rock (*zum Felsen*) on which his community will be

The effort to *render* the flower can only fail. No circular and proper course: letter *seing* of the Mother hidden and lost in all the proper names of the erianthus. The flower is nothing, never takes place because it is never natural or artificial. It has no assignable border, no fixed perianth, no being-wreathed. Which is why proper names, which are always surnames of *classification*, violently imposed, operations of class, which ring to call to the work of mourning, to expropriation, always come down to (Our-Lady-of-the-) flowers.

Is the work [*travail*] of mourning work, a kind of work? And will thanatopraxis, the technique of the funeral rite taught today in institutes, giving rise to diplomas of qualification, be limited to one corporation among others, within a social economy? Is not all work a work of mourning? and, by the same appropriative stroke [*coup*] of the more or less of loss, a *classic* operation? a violent operation of class and classification? a decollation, an ungluing, of what keeps the singular for itself? This work of mourning *is called* — glas. It is always for/of the proper name. The *glas* is first of all (*clas, chiasso, classum, classicum*) the signal of a trumpet destined to *call* (*calare*), convoke, gather together, reassemble as such, a *class* of the Roman people. There is given then *glas* in classical literature, but also in the class struggle: class

in what psychoanalysis strictly determines as such, the work-of-mourning would merely devour more quickly, in the course of a single meal, the gathered time of a Last Supper [*Cène*], a bigger bit [*mors*]

"**classicus** bürger der ersten
klasse (in Rom).

"Daraus entlehnt nfr. *classique* adj. '(author) who is of
the most eminent rank, who merits being imitated the

founded." The power conferred on him is essentially that of "binding and loosing (*binden und lösen*)."

Peter's faith still represents only the first step [*marche*] (*die erste Stufe*) of this procession toward the light in the light. John: "'Until you have light, you must believe in the light in order to become sons of the light.'" To believe in the light, to testify in its favor, as John the Baptist, is not yet to be, such as Jesus, an "individualized light." Undoubtedly his disciples are united in Jesus, in his flame, as the vine shoots (*Ranken*) are united in the vinestock (*Weinstock*). But they will have a life of their own and will at the same time let themselves be penetrated fully with the divine spirit only after the disappearance of Jesus, of their master, of the one who still occupied the individual place of a center or a vinestock. When the stock will be, as it were, cut, what still separates them from God, the partition [*la cloison*], the diaphragm (*Scheidewand*) between the Father and his children, will fall. Jesus is the diaphragm of the divine light. His body subtly seals off its passage. So his death is indispensable. John remarked on this: streams can gush from the body only *after* cutting the vinestock itself. In the future. "When Jesus says (John 7:38−39): 'If someone believes in me, from his body *will gush* streams of life (werden *Ströme des Lebens quellen*),' John remarks that this is understood only of what, in the future, will be through and through animated by the Holy Spirit." Jesus has not yet been transfigured; only through death will he be. In the interval, he is a man among men; he is set over against and individualized only opposite the Jewish character. "John says (2:25) of Jesus that he knew what was in man; and the truest mirror (*Spiegel*) of his beautiful *Glauben* in nature is his discourse at the sight of immaculate nature." Not soiling this nature or becoming a child ("in my name," *in meinem Namen*) is the same thing. What will be done to the one who soils the uncorrupted nature? He will be drowned "in the depths of the sea (*im tiefsten Meere*)." After a stone is attached to him, "a millstone (*Mühlstein*) . . . round his neck [*cou*]." He will be like a hanged man at the bottom of the sea.

One is chastised for no longer being child enough.

What is the difference between this immersion and baptism's?

John is the only one able to explain it to us. It was his "habit" to "immerse (*unterzutauchen*)" into the water the one who had been raised to his spirit. "Nothing analogous is known to have been done by Jesus." Now this habit of John has a "symbolic signification (*ist eine bedeutende symbolische*)." In order to understand something about this Johannine symbol, what "being immersed" means (to say) must be known.

That is, what is a child and what an angel does.

The angels contemplate the face of my father in the sky. This proposition is very rich: "Unconsciousness (*das Bewusstlose*), undeveloped unity, being (*Sein*), and life in God, are here severed

most' (1548), 'man of the first rank, whose example would have to be followed' (ca. 1550), nfr. '(author) taught in classes' (seit Cotgr 1611): 'what is related to the teaching of Greek and Latin languages, literatures' (seit Ac 1798).

"Ablt.—Nfr. *classicisme* 'system of exclusive advocates of ancient writers or classic writers of the 17th cent.' (seit Besch 1845).

"Lt. CLASSICUS 'bürger der ersten klasse' wird einmal, von Gellius, als adj. gebraucht: *vel oratorum aliquis vel poetarum, id est classicus assiduusque aliquis scriptor, non proletarius.* Es wird im 16. jh., bei der übernahme ins fr., zum adj. gemacht. Zuerst erscheint es bei Th. Sebillet, Art poétique (1548): *la lecture des bons et classiques poétes françois comme sont entre les vieux Alain Chartier et Jean de Meun.* Es wird also mit bezug auf französische dicter verwendet. Da die Pleiade die ältere französische literatur verleugnet, macht ihr sieg die anwendung des wortes auf die französische literatur unmöglich. Sein sinn wird nun umgebogen zu einer ablt. von *classe* 'schulklasse': *classique* bedeutet jetzt '(autor) der in der schule gelesen und interpretiert wird'; die einschränkung auf die literatur des Altertums hängt unmittelbar damit zusammen. Erst im 18. jh. wurde das adj. auch auf die nun als vorbilder betrachteten autoren des 17. jhs. ausgedehnt (erster beleg Voltaire 1761), gegen ende des 18. jhs. auch auf andere dinge, die in ihrer art als vorbild, als vornehmster vertreter gelten können (*terre classique de la liberté*). Zur zeit der Romantik wird *classique* zum kennzeichen des literarischen programms der gegner der neuen bewegung. Im einzelnen müssen diese entw. noch an hand der texte untersucht werden.

"**classis** abteilung.

"1. Mfr. *clas* m. 'fleet' (1530); *classe* f. (1560, Pold. d'Albenas, Antiquités de Nîmes 205, Db—Mon 1636).
"2. a. Mfr. nfr. *classe* 'category of Roman citizens in the political, civil order' (seit Bersuire); übertragen nfr. 'rank on which persons of the same profession are placed, according to their merit' (seit Rich 1680); 'category of sailors that can be called to service in the State navy' (seit 1670); nfr. 'category of citizens distinguished according to their social condition' (seit 1792, Frey).—Ablt. Nfr. *classer* un matelot 'to record in one's class of military registration' (seit 1767, Brunot 6).

from God because they are supposed to be represented as a modification of divinity in existing children; but their being (*Sein*), their act (*Tun*) is an eternal contemplation of God." Bound to God and unbound from him, the angels are not Platonic souls that, first immersed in the intuition of the divine, later, in "their later life on earth," have only an obscure consciousness of the divinity. Jesus binds and unbinds otherwise. A man must not purely and simply be "immersed into the intuition of the sun (*ganz in die Anschauung der Sonne versunken*)": therefore he would be merged with a simple luminous feeling. A man immersed in the intuition of another man would be only that other, and so on. Division, *Entzweiung*, then is necessary. But what is divided in two (*entzweit*) reunifies itself, returns to itself, and that is true childhood. The communion granted by the father consists neither in being immersed into the elementary nor in being uprooted. It reimmerses.

The reimmersion is consonant. It is consonant with consonance and with the name. Onomastic symphony: "Jesus represents this union (*Einigkeit*) in another way (v. 19): when two among you will unite together to ask (*bitten*) something of me, the Father will grant you it. The expressions ask (*bitten*), grant (*gewähren*), strictly relate to an accord (*Vereinigung*) in respect of objects (πράγματα); it was only for an accord of this kind that the language-of-actuality (*Wirklichkeitssprache*) of the Jews had expression. But here the object in question can be nothing but the reflected unity (the συμφωνία τῶν δυοῖν ἤ τριῶν [agreement of two or three]); as object it is a being-beautiful, but subjectively it is the accord (*Vereinigung*); for spirits cannot be one in objects proper. The beautiful, the union of two or three of you, is also in the harmony of the whole (*in der Harmonie des Ganzen*), is a sound (*Laut*), a consonance (*Einklang*) in that harmony and granted or accorded by it. It *is* because it is in it (in this consonance), because it is something divine. In this communion (*Gemeinschaft*) with the divine, those who are at one are at the same time (*zugleich*) in communion with Jesus. Where two or three are united in my spirit [or in my name] (εἰς τὸ ὄνομα μοῦ, as in Matthew 10:41), in that respect in which being (*Sein*) and eternal life fall to me, in which I *am*, then I am in the midst of them (*in ihrer Mitte*), and so is my spirit."

When Jesus explains to his disciples that he must die, that his death will not leave them orphans, but will on the contrary restore filiation to them, that they will receive as much as what they believe they lose, that is the terror. In Peter's terror (*Erschrecken*) in particular, what separates faith from its fulfillment (*der Abstand des Glaubens von der Vollendung*) is understood. They are afraid as abandoned children, but that is because they are not yet true children. Their faith still appeals to an external God. "Everything lives in the Godhead, all living things are its children, but the child carries the unity, the connection, the consonance (*Einklang*) with the

"Nfr. *déclasser* 'to remove from the class in which one was classed; remove from the class lists' (seit Boiste 1829); *déclassé* 'individual fallen from a certain social class into a lower class' (seit Lar 1869); *déclassement* 'action of *déclasser*' (seit 1863).—Nfr. *enclasser* 'to enlist (sailors) in the ranks' (Voltaire Siècle de Louis XIV; 1761, Brunot 6).

"b. Nfr. *classe* 'each of the major groups of animals, of vegetables' (seit Enc 1753).—Ablt. Nfr. *classer* 'to distribute (animals, vegetables) by classes; to place in a certain class; to place in a certain category' (seit Trév 1771); *classeur* 'portfolio or piece of furniture with compartments that serves to class documents' (seit Besch 1845); *classement* 'action of classing' (seit 1798); *inclassable* 'what cannot be classed' (seit 1890, Journ Gonc). Nfr. *classifier* 'to divide up following a classification' (seit Raym 1832); *déclassifier* v. r. 'to depart from a classification' (1876).—Nfr. *classification* 'methodical distribution of individuals by species, genera, classes, etc.' (seit Fér 1787); *classificatoire* adj. 'what is related to the classification' (seit 1874); *classificateur* 'author of classifications' (Besch 1845—1863, so Ste-Beuve. Lundis 14, 120).

"3. a. Nfr. *classe* 'category of students that follow each degree of a course of study' (seit Est 1549); 'teaching given to a class' (seit Ac 1740)[1]); 'room where this teaching is given' (seit Mon 1635, s. auch ALF 441 école; ALLo 1778); neuch. 'company of pastors'; Paris 'place where picklocks of an area wait to be employed' (Rich 1680–1863).—Ablt Ménades *quiasseux* 'schoolboy'.

"b. Nfr. *classe* 'category of young people called each year to military service' (seit 1863). Übertragen *être de la classe* 'to be of the 2nd year of service; to have experience' (seit 1888, Daud).

"Mfr. *clacyfier* 'to establish (a text) according to classifications' (ca. 1500).

"Lt. CLASSIS, ursprünglich 'aufgebot in militärischem sinn' erhält durch die von Servius Tullius getroffene einteilung der bürger in sechs gruppen die bed. 'volksklasse', sodann 'landheer' und 'flotte', endlich, zu Augustus zeit, auch 'gruppe von knaben, die geneinsam unterrichtet werden'. In verschiedenen dieser bed. ist es vom fr. entlehnt worden: 1 aus der bed. 'flotte' (wohl nur mit bezug auf das Altertum); 2 a aus der bed. 'volksklasse', zuerst auch mit bezug auf das alte Rom, dann aber auf moderne verhältnisse übertragen; dabei ist b eine sekundäre verwendung dieser bed. in der

entire harmony, undisturbed but undeveloped, in itself. It begins with faith in gods outside itself." Through new splits [scissions] and new reconciliations, the child must re-form the "circle" by which, becoming child again, it reestablishes everything: "God, the Son, the Holy Spirit!"

Thus does it reimmerse itself. When Matthew speaks of "immersing" (tauchen), he does not intend the immersion in water, what is called baptism (Taufe). The name (ὄνομα) is the relation between the split and the reconciliation. Jesus, in Matthew, asks where does John's baptism come from: from heaven or from man? In the consecration of spirit and of character, immersion must never be considered but an accessory thing (Nebensache). John himself, at least according to Luke, presents water as the supplement. Of fire. It is the moment when the people ask themselves whether he, John, is not the Christ: "I baptize you with water; but one is coming who is stronger than I, and I am not fit to untie the fastening of his shoes. He will baptize you in the Holy Spirit and in fire." In the course of the same scene, in John's Gospel, in Mark's too, the fire disappears. But not the straps of the sandals. John always feels himself unworthy to undress Jesus and even to kneel down to undo the bands encircling his feet.

But why is John fond, were it as an ersatz, of immersing the body in water? Why did he baptize Jesus in the Jordan? John's desire bears him neither into nor out of the water. He comes to terms with the liquid, engulfs the body with it in order to enjoy the streaming, gleaming, gliding emergence [l'emergence ruisselante, luisante, glissante]. He wants the plenitude of the aqueous universe, but in order to look at [regarder] that plenitude, which is possible only in regularly removing the body from it, in interrupting the effusion, the forgetting of self, in taking up again walking [la marche], standing up. "John's habit . . . has a symbolic signification. No feeling is so homogeneous (homogen) with the desire for the infinite, the longing to merge into the infinite, as the desire to immerse oneself (sich begraben) in the water's fullness (Wasserfülle). To plunge into it is to be confronted by an alien element (ein Fremdes) which at once (sogleich) flows round us on every side and which is felt at every point of the body. We are taken from the world and the world from us. We are nothing but felt water which touches us where we are, and we are only where we feel it. In the water's fullness, there is no lacuna, no restriction, no multiplicity, no determination. The feeling of it is the simplest, the least broken up [dispersed, dissipated, disbanded, unzerstreuteste]. After immersion a man comes up into the air again, separates himself from the body of water, is at once cut free from it and yet it still drips from him everywhere. As soon as the water leaves him, the world around him is determined again, and he [the one who emerges] comes back strengthened (gestärkt) to the multiplicity of consciousness.

naturwissenschaftlichen terminologie. 3 a aus der bed. 'schulklasse'; b ist daraus übertragen weil auch die jahresklasse der soldaten aus gleichaltrigen besteht.

───────

"1) In ausdrücken wie *faire ses classes, faire la classe* usw.

"**classum** lärm

"1. Afr. *glas* 'ringing noise; clamoring' (12.—13. jh., BenSMaure; Perl), *glais* (12. jh.), afr. mfr. *glai* (12.—15. jh.), pik. *glay* (Th 1564—Voult 1613), mfr. *mener grand glas* 'to make much noise' (Th 1564—Mon 1636), mfr. *clas* 'resounding' D'Aubigné, apr. 'cry, clamor'; afr. *a (un) glais* 'with a unanimous voice, all at once', apr. *a un clas*; mfr. *glai* 'chirping of birds' (15. jh.); afr. *glas* 'kind of trumpet' (Veng Al, R 56, 131), *glai* (1285), mfr. id. (1612); mfr. *claz* 'sound of trumpet to call together' (1530); mfr. *glai* 'honor, felicity' Eust Desch.

"2. Afr. *glas* 'ringing of all the bells [cloches] of a church' (13. jh., Gdf; GuernesSThomas), *glais* Chrestien, mfr. *claz* (poit. 1456), abress. *clars* pl. (Châtillon D. 1483, Ann Ain 1927), apr. *clar* (Hérault 15. jh., AM 18, 204), mfr. *glay* (1382), *clax* pl. (Rochelle 1465).

"Afr. *glais* 'slow ringing of a church's bell to announce someone's death-struggle, death, or interment' Florence, mfr. *glay* Guill Mach, Paris *glais* (1488, Gdf; Mén 1650), mfr. nfr. *glas* (seit Th 1564, doch bis Voult 1613 als speziell orl.), nfr. *glais* (Mon 1635—Trév 1771), Bonneval *glas* MAnt 2, 428, hbret. *gla*, Landujan *ya* ABret 15, 390, Loire l. *klā*, ang. *clâs*, poit. *kła*, Vendée *cliâ* (1807), bgât. *clas*, saint. *kyā*, kanad. *glas* pl., centr. *clas*, Allier *klā*, Varennes *clairs*, morv. *iâs*, Mâcon *clar*, verdch. *glia*, Côte d'Or *gyā*, Yonne *glais*, VassyP. *guiais*, Créancey *ghiai* F 279, Gr Combe *kyas*, Jura *gya*, Vaudioux *(ë)gliés* pl., Thônes *glié*, Vaux *tyâr*, Lyon *clior*, Mornant *glió*, St-Genis *lyôr*, Loire *klar*, stéph. *clo*, Cr. *gyā*, Estr. *głā*, voir. *clias*, Cordéac *klẹr*, Trém. *tšyẹr*, mdauph. *klẹ̄*, Die *clers*, HAlpes, Lallé, Barc. *klars* pl., pr. id., *kla, klas*, Nice *clar*, lang. *classes* pl., Aniane *klar* Zaun 95, Ariège, H Gar. *klases* pl., Tarn, aveyr. *klas*, Lozère id. (nordwesten), *klases* pl., vel. *clas, gla*, Aurillac *clar* Verm 317, Ytrac, St-Simon *clar*, PuyD. χ*ya*, Vinz. Chav. *kłyar*, lim. *clhar* DD, gask. *glas*. ALF 650; G de Guer 74—87; ALLo 2087.—Übertragen nfr. *glas* 'cannon shots [coups] fired at intervals at military funerals' (Boiste 1803—DG), 'noise of a bomb, of fireworks' BL 1808.

When we look out into a cloudless blue sky and into the simple, shapeless surface of an eastern horizon, we have no sense of the surrounding air, and the play of our thoughts is something different from mere gazing out. In immersion there is only *one* feeling, there is only forgetfulness of the world, a solitude which has repelled everything, extricated itself from everything."

Such is Jesus' experience after John had immersed him in the waters of the Jordan. The sky was rent, the spirit descended over him in the form of a dove, and the voice recognized him as its son. After the forty days in the desert and the temptation of Satan, the work of the split is carried out. But this split, like Jesus' death, which is analogous to it, permits the return to childhood and to the water element. In dying, in leaving his disciples, in emerging, Jesus returns to his father who is greater than he (*Heimkehr zu seinem Vater, der grösser ist als er*). He leaves the water in order to let himself be penetrated by the spirit of the one greater than he. But in the same stroke [*du même coup*], he permits his young disciples to immerse themselves in the spirit as in the water and to let themselves be penetrated by it: "'All power is given to me in heaven and on earth. Go out therefore into all nations and let this be your task as disciples to initiate them into the relation with the Father, the Son, and the Holy Spirit, so that it may flow round them and be felt round them in all the points of their being as does the water of those immersed in it, and see, I am with you for all time, even to the perfection of the world.' . . . He is with those whose being is penetrated (*durchdrungen*) by the divine spirit. . . ."

In this movement that Mark, enclosed in the "Jewish language," would have rendered badly, the emergence uproots the body from the natural element, the water or the mother, only in order to immerse the spirit in the paternal element. The father penetrates the spirit—the metaphor of the father then is the metaphor of the mother—on condition the body has broken with the mother, that is, on condition of its death. That is, of its birth, its erection, its resurrection. Birth upsurges *as such* only in resurrection. So death is this equal inequality of the father and the mother—the spiritual metaphor, Christianity, nomination, baptism, and so on. In the chain of these values, no term can be arrested as the accident, the predicate, the contracting determination of any other.

At the least, the narrow regularly gives its form to the relation of one to the other, without the least conceptual privilege. Each one is narrower than the other, none is larger than all the others, that is what forces, wounds, obliges thinking—reason.

In the glory, with the erection of the dead-born [*mort-né*] anointed one, the equal inequality of the father and the mother has just appeared. This inequality appears, is then in the phenomenon, in the light, in the glory. But what appears is stated, in the voice, as

"Ablt.—Apr. *clasejar* 'to sound the bells; to call together by sounding the *clas*', Tarn *classexá* 'to sound the *glas* at length'.

"Zuss.—Apr. *aclassar* 'to make noise' (12. jh.).—Boussac *glas d'emprunt* '*glas* for someone deceased outside the parish'. Trans *glas à bouillie* 'ringing for a baptism'.

"Von lt. CLASSICUM 'trompetenstoss; trompete' ist früh ein CLASSUM zurückgebildet worden, das durch die frühmlt. ablt. *conclassare* (= klt. *convocare classico*) bezeugt ist. CLASSUM lebt in it. *chiasso* 'lärm', emil. *stšas* (z. b. Firenzuola d'Arda, Casella 19), Rovigno *stšaso* Ive 35, sowie im gallorom. (1), wo die klt. bed. zum teil noch erkennbar ist. Aus dem fr. entlehnt me. *glase* 'trompetenstoss' Arch 109, 331. Im gallorom. wird es auf den klang der glocken eingeschränkt (2), so auch piem. *tšas* AGI 14, 363. Aus dem fr. entlehnt bret. *glâz*. Im fr. gibt es, in allen bed., neben der form mit *a* eine mit *ai*; die entstehung dieses vokals ist noch nicht abgeklärt.—Gröber ALL 1, 547; Z 15, 497; ML 1965."
V. Wartburg

The *glas* fleshes [*acharne*] a grammatological reading of Saussure, always, precisely, of that page of the *Course* that establishes linguistics in its patronage ("So signs, it can be said, that are wholly arbitrary realize better than the others the ideal of the semiological process [*procédé*]; that is why language [*langue*], the most complex and universal of all systems of expression, is also the most characteristic; in this sense linguistics can become the general patron for all branches of semiology, *although* language is only one particular semiological system."). I have underlined *although*: the violent institution of the patronate. After which is the opposition of the signifier to the symbol: the symbol is not arbitrary, not empty, "there is the rudiment of a natural bond between the signifier and the signified. The symbol of justice, a pair of scales, could not be replaced by just any other symbol, such as a chariot." But it always can be replaced: by a glaive, by a woman, etc. And its naturalness is then always already breached. And the flower, is it a symbol or a sign?

a play of liquid and solid. All this is said by the gliding [*glissement*] of a step [*marche*], the uplift, the surrection of a streaming limit, always unequal to itself.

The Hegelian reading of Christianity seems to describe a reconciliation, in order to say everything in two words: between faith and being, *Glauben* and *Sein*. "Faith presupposes a being (*Glauben setzt ein Sein voraus*)." Union, communion, reconciliation make one with *Sein*, are one with *Sein*. Here the same sign is touched, tampered with. Communion and being have equal signification: "*Vereinigung und Sein sind gleichbedeutend*."

Nevertheless the destiny of Christianity opens a new morseling. The word *destiny* already has this sense in the Hegelian context. Split and one-sidedness in love, which is *not yet* religion, then in religion itself and in the stone [*pierre*] of the church that cannot resolve in this world the painful opposition between the living and the dead, the divine and the real. The Christian religion remains sublime. Jesus has departed; leaving his disciples without present, leaving them suspended between memory and hope, he has separated himself from the world. The accusation is therefore amplified against Jesus' political passivity, against his idealism: he preferred to reconstitute in the presence of [*auprès de*] his father, in ideality, a disappointed life. He did not know how to fight, in the world, against the Jewish reality. From then on, he had, paradoxically, to repeat Judaism. Like Abraham, he was separated from his family; further, he loved no woman, begot no child. He even left his mother. In order to shun war and to announce love, he brought the glaive on the earth, set the son against his father, daughter against her mother, daughter-in-law against parents-in-law. His abandoned disciples could, like the Jews, only speak of their "absent master," pray in common, fail in their political attempts. When their enemies accused certain of their societies of the practice of "having wives in common, an accusation which they lacked purity and courage enough to deserve, or of which they had no need to feel shame." They have often lived emigrating, in waiting, in the sign. Everything happens around a sepulcher. No doubt the memory of the rotting body was first effaced in the intuition of the glory, but it has returned, was insistent, to the very extent the split continued its work. The dead body resting there in the interminable decomposition of relics, the spirit never raises itself high enough, it is retained as a kind of effluvium, of gas fermenting above the corpse. A kind of weight "draw[s]" it "down to earth (*ihn zur Erde zieht*)," and the "God is thus supposed to hover (*schweben*) midway between heaven's infinity, where there are no limits, and earth, this gathering together of plain restrictions." The spirit is still like a kind of eagle that would want to raise itself, even though some "lead (*Blei*)" weighs down its wings or its feet. Jesus now resembles Moses. He is decidedly too Jewish. One could believe him a little Greek: "like

But the strict incidence of *glas* is not, for the moment, there. The same page of the *Course* proposes a *remark* and replies to two objections. And then, as if by chance, upsurges the example of *glas*, which Saussure treats as a word ("Words like French *fouet* 'whip' or *glas* 'knell'. . ."). The remark touches upon the arbitrary, upon the word "arbitrary": "The word *arbitrary* also calls for a remark. The term should not imply that the free choice of the signifier is left entirely to the speaking subject (we shall see below that the individual does not have the power to change a sign in any way once it has become established in the linguistic community); I mean that it is *unmotivated*, i.e. arbitrary in relation to the signified, with which it has no natural connection in reality." Constraining for the subject (the "individual"), the signifier (for example, flower or *glas*), would be "unmotivated" in relation to the signified (which? where? when?), to the referent (which? where? when?). What is the individual? reality? nature? And, above all, the connection? The whole work of the *glas* could, at the least, provide material for the reelaboration of these questions: this side of the word (and hence of linguistics that always remains, even when denying it, a linguistics of the word, verily of the noun), this side of the opposition between *phusis* and its other (where does one situate the flower?), and, above all, in another logic, practico-theoretical and necktied, this side of the bit, of what remains of the detachment of the connection [*l'attache*] and always comes to add more on.

After the *remark*, Saussure's reply to two objections. They concern *onomatopoeias* and *exclamations* and should not be "dangerous for our thesis." So one wonders first how a thesis could be in danger (the answer is given elsewhere). Here, in any case, is the reply to the objection concerning onomatopoeia: "In concluding let us consider two objections that might be raised to the establishment of this Principle I:

"1) *Onomatopoeias* might be used to prove that the choice of the signifier is not always arbitrary. But they are never organic elements of a linguistic system. Besides, their number is much smaller than is generally supposed. Words like French *fouet* 'whip' or *glas* 'knell' may strike certain ears with suggestive sonority, but to see that they have not always had this character we need only go back to their Latin forms (*fouet* is derived from *fāgus*, 'beech-tree,' *glas = classicum*). The quality of their present sounds, or rather the quality that is attributed to them, is a fortuitous result of phonetic evolution.

Hercules" starting from the funeral pyre, he has taken his "soaring aloft" starting from the "tomb." But the altars and the prayers of the Greeks appeal to a god who no longer continues to fight on the earth, who no longer remains in his body. In his wandering and his teaching, the Christ stays nailed down or rotting: "monstrous connection (*ungeheure Verbindung*)."

The accusation worsens incessantly, above all politicizes itself. In encouraging utopia, one has unleashed fanatical violence. The escape into the void produces atrocity and devastation. Flight is impossible. The destiny of the too powerful world weighs not only on the Church, it acts in the Church. If this situation is not provoked by them, it is exploited by "Great hypocrites (*Grosse Heuchler*)," the false devotees, the comedians, the powerful priests. The structure of their ruse is analyzed: "They devised for every civil action {bourgeois, *bürgerliche Handlung*} or for every expression of pleasure and desire a hiding place [*einen Schlupfwinkel*, a corner, nook, a retreat, recess] in the unity in order by this fraud (*Betrug*) to maintain at once (*zugleich*) each determination and enjoy it and yet at the same time (*zugleich*) to escape it."

Such is the very great calculus to which, in history, the Lord's anointed has given rise. In its very passivity, in the miracle's and the split's *actio in distans*, in its false starts or sortings out [*faux-départs*]. The unconscious, let us say at least the unconsciousness in which this destiny operates, Hegel speaks of it, often, expressly. His reading then is double: on one side Christianity has succeeded in lifting the Jewish limitation; and the death of Christ has permitted the sons to be sons [*des fils*]; baptism has taken place. On the other side, Christianity repeats, a little higher up, the Jewish cutting [*coupure*]; the disciples remained as sheep without a shepherd; the name has not been recognized. The check [*échec*] of filiation, of the family, of the city, hypocrisy, calculus, violence, appropriation. Stones/Peters [*Pierres*].

The reading is not double, but Christianity is, and the structure of the relief, too. The analysis is unconscious of the truth of its process. This truth appears to it only in philosophy, in the future perfect, the future anterior, of absolute religion.

The Christian religion is already posited as absolute religion. Thus the cleavage stays in absolute religion; and it stays for all time and all the figures of Christianity: "In all the forms of the Christian religion which have been developed in the fatal process of the ages, there lies this fundamental characteristic of opposition in the divine which is supposed to be present in consciousness only, never in life." The representative nature of the presence of the divine that holds itself *before* consciousness and lets itself be expected in life, that leaves religion in an anticipatory posture—these are already, from these first texts, the traits the *Phenomenology of Spirit* will recognize, will have recognized in absolute religion, that is, in

"As for authentic onomatopoeias (e.g. *glou-glou*, *tic-tac*, etc.), not only are they limited in number, but also they are already chosen somewhat arbitrarily, for they are only approximate and already more or less conventional imitations of certain noises (compare the French *ouaoua* and the German *wauwau*). In addition, once these words have been introduced into the language [*langue*], they are to a certain extent drawn into the same evolution—phonetic, morphological, etc.—that other words undergo (cf. *pigeon*, from Vulgar Latin *pīpiō*, itself derived from an onomatopoeia): obvious proof that they lose something of their original character in order to assume that of the linguistic sign in general, which is unmotivated."

Let us leave those strange agglutinations of inaudibly consonant examples to work by themselves alone: the supreme question of the beech-tree and the *glas*, the becoming-whip of the beech-tree, the apparently altogether fortuitous association (it will be spoken of again) of *glou-glou* and *tic-tac*, those "authentic onomatopoeias."

Saussure therefore seems to know what "authentic onomatopoeias" are. But this knowledge supposes that one may seize the original instant at which they have not yet been "to a certain extent drawn into the . . . evolution. . . ." But where does one recognize this pure instant that alone can divide here? Another recourse to a pure origin, this time an etymological one: to the extent of their etymological affiliation can one demonstrate that *glas* and *fouet* have no onomatopoeic value. Will one trust etymology and even a narrow concept of etymology—historicist and unilinear, to analyze the functioning of a linguistic signifier and recognize its "organic" belonging to the "linguistic system"? Does an element depart from language [*langue*] when it does not conform to its presumed semantic origin?

Christianity. Jesus has finally chosen, elected (*wählte*) the split, but this gesture cannot be simple. In breaking in two and in fleeing, he has declared war in the name of reconciliation; he is divided in his own proper split, hardened [*tendu*] against division itself, multiplying it and raising it thus to infinity. So what has happened as an accident to Christianity as it must (should) have been has nothing of an accident about it. That is the very definition of destiny, and that is recognized in the fact that Jesus was not delirious nor did he even love his death. If at least he was delirious or had been made mad [*été déliré*], that was not for himself. "To every fanatic who *is* delirious for himself alone, death is welcome; but the fanatic who is delirious for the fulfilment of a great plan can feel nothing but grief in leaving the stage (*Schauplatz*) on which his plan was to have been worked out. Jesus died in the confidence that his plan would not miscarry."

This split has effects whose political analysis is hardly even begun. It is pursued in fragments of the same epoch, in particular in the *German Constitution*. Hegel begins to study the problems of political economy more closely; he reads Steuart's *Inquiry into the Principles of Political Economy*. But even if the politico-economic consequences of the first essays are not developed, they are conceptually marked. In particular concerning the place of the family. Is that to say that a saturation to come will fill in a space whose interior borders and limits will remain untouched? That is doubtful. The nearly total silence on the woman, the daughter, the sister, the mother probably points out something other than a lacuna to be filled up, within an intact field. What happens when this silence is broken, for example in the *Phenomenology*?

The most general question would now have the following form: how is the relief of religion in(to) philosophy produced? How, on the other hand, is the relief of the family structure in(to) the structure of civil (bourgeois) society produced? In other words, how, within *Sittlichkeit* (whose notion begins to be elaborated in *The Difference Between Fichte's and Schelling's System of Philosophy*, in

So what are the "organic elements of a linguistic system"? Words? But "words" can become onomatopoeic, through the grafting of function, in whole or in part, by decomposition or recomposition, detachment or reattachment. But onomatopoeias can become words, and since the process of being "drawn" has always already begun, which is neither an accident nor something outside the system, the judges, the self-proclaimed keepers of systematic criteria, no longer know what belongs to what and to whom.

The "authentic onomatopoeia" slips away and with it all the oppositions that follow or proceed. Furthermore, the concept of onomatopoeia presupposes, in the way it is handled here, a very simplified structure of imitation (between the noise of the thing and the sound of the language). In this respect, the resemblance is faint, verily nonexistent, between *glas*—and what in fact? the noise of a bell [*cloche*]?—between *fouet* and the noise of the stinging [*cinglantes*] lashes. One wonders why Saussure chose these "words" as examples of presumed *onoma*topoeias. He must rid these empirical statements of all rigor: these words "may strike" (What luck: like the *fouet* and *glas*, words "strike"; like the *fouet* and *glas*, words make noise and strike the ear. It would be as though there were morsels of *fouet* and *glas* in each word.), they "may"—possibly—"strike . . . with suggestive sonority" and only "certain ears." In other words, the examples are chosen too poorly or too well: no one can consider *fouet* and *glas* as authentic onomatopoeias. Besides, no one has done so; and besides, there is no authentic onomatopoeia. But instead of concluding that there is then no authentically arbitrary element either, instead of taking an interest in the *contaminated* effects of onomatopoeia or of arbitrariness, in the drawing-along of the language [*langue*] (with the *fouet* or *glas*), he runs ahead of the "danger" in order to save the thesis of the sign's arbitrariness.

If arbitrariness and unmotivation can supervene upon the alleged "original character" of such "authentic onomatopoeias," why couldn't a remotivation draw in the alleged arbitrary again? If the arbitrariness were pure, that would not be possible. Now it is possible, as attested at least by what Saussure wishes to contain under the heading of artificial, illusory and fortuitous *attribution*: "The quality of their present sounds, or rather the quality that is attributed to them, is a fortuitous result of phonetic evolution."

Faith and Knowledge, and in the article on *Natural Law*), is the passage from the family syllogism to the syllogism of bourgeois society carried out? These two problems intersect in a place to be determined. It is essentially indicated in the *Phenomenology*'s next-to-last chapter: absolute religion that immediately precedes its own proper truth, the *Sa*. At the end of the syllogism (natural religion, esthetic religion, revealed-manifest religion), Christianity, absolute religion, develops itself according to the following syllogism: (1) The spirit within itself: the Trinity. (2) The spirit in its alienation: the Kingdom of the Son. (3) The spirit in its plenitude: the Kingdom of the Spirit. Through the death of the mediating term, the reconciliation still remains affected by the adverse opposition of a beyond (*Gegensatze eines Jenseits*), remains distant, in the distance of a future (the Last Judgment for the religious community) and in the distance of a past (the Incarnation of God). The reconciliation is not present. Present in the heart, it is cut off [*coupée*] from consciousness, divided in two (*entzweit*). Its actuality is broken. What enters consciousness as the in-itself is reconciliation, insofar as it holds itself beyond; but what enters consciousness as presence is the world that awaits its transfiguration. Whence the partition [*partage*] between the spiritual and the political.

Now this ultimate split between presence and representation, between the for-itself and the in-itself, has the form of an inequality between the father and the mother, in the relation to the father and the relation to the mother. The passage from absolute religion to *Sa* is brewing as the relief of this inequality.

Is this an analogy? Let us leave the analogy as a seedling, some lines before "Absolute Knowing": "Just as (*So wie*) the *individual* divine man [*einzelne* is underscored: it is Jesus, the historical individual] has a father existing in (*it*)self (ansich *seienden Vater*) and only an *actual* mother (wirkliche *Mutter*), so (*so*) too the universal divine man, the community (*die Gemeinde*), has for its father its *own proper operation* (*ihr* eigenes Tun) and *knowing* (Wissen), but for its mother, *eternal love* which it only *feels* (*die sie nur* fühlt), but does not behold in its consciousness as an actual, immediate *object*."

It is too soon to read this passage. Let us retain from it only an index and a program: the stake of the passage to *Sa* resembles a transformation of the family relation. If this is called a family relation through figure or formality, its ontological reach is indisputable. In the constitution of an absolute onto-logic, family discourse would not know how to be relegated to the subordinate regions of a rhetoric, an anthropology, or a psychology. Such a family dehiscence, since it appeals to *Sa*—to philosophy—is an essential stake in the history of being's sense. The appeal to absolute knowledge is inscribed in that history. The place of this inscription

What will remain of the internal system of the language [*langue*], of the "organic elements of a linguistic system," when it will have been purified, stripped of all those qualities, of those attributions, of that evolution? What will remain of it and where will it be found? And from what standpoint are those attributed "qualities" and those "result[s] of phonetic evolution" to be considered as "fortuitous"? This word, moreover, comes as a surprise: everything happens as if the processes of remotivation, of renaturalization, escaped every necessity, while the arbitrary itself would have nothing fortuitous about its functioning. It would be fortuitous—and therefore arbitrary—to remotivate arbitrary signs. In addition, the choice of examples would be—the word is Saussure's—"arbitrary" in the allegation of onomatopoeias. One could follow at length the effects of this opposition between the arbitrary and the motivated within a logic that, presupposing the permanence of a knowledge of what freedom, consciousness, nature, necessity are, runs out of breath [*s'essouffle*] delimiting the inside and the outside of the linguistic system, framing it, with all the assurances taken out on such a frame.

And what if *mimesis* no longer allowed itself to be arraigned, to be compelled to give accounts and reasons, to subject itself to a verification of identity within such a frame. And what if it operated according to ways [*voies*] and necessities whose laws are entangled and determined otherwise. With resources that would lead within the language's [*de la langue*] system: importing *into* linguistics all the questions and all the codes of questions that are developed here, around the effects of "proper name" and "signature"; concealing, in the course of this break-in, all the rigorous criteria of a framing—between the inside and the outside; taking away the frame no less than the inside or the outside, the picture or the thing (just imagine the havoc of a theft that would only deprive you of frames and of every possibility of reframing your valuables or your art objects). And what if *mimesis* so arranged it that language's internal system did not exist, or that it is never used, or at least that it is used only by contaminating it, and that this contamination is inevitable, hence regular and "normal," makes up a part of the system and its functioning, makes up a part of it, that is, also, makes of it, which is the whole, a part of a whole that is greater than it. Saussure's conclusion: "In

is also an un-consciousness rigorously situated between the *Phenomenology of Spirit* and the greater *Logic*, in the articulation of *Sa*.

What does the family still need? And why does it need philosophy? Why does one need *Sa* only as a family [*en famille*]?

The cleavage—which attains its absolute in absolute religion—is the need of/for philosophy. Philosophy is descended, as its own proper object, from Christianity of which it is the truth, from the Holy Family which it falls under (whose relief it is) [*dont elle (est la) relève*]. "The Need of Philosophy" ("Bedürfnis der Philosophie") (that is the subtitle of a text nearly contemporaneous with *The Spirit of Christianity*) upsurges in the *between* [*entre*], the narrow gap [*écart*] of a split, a cleavage, a separation, a division in two. One divides itself in two, such is the distressing source of philosophy: "*Entzweiung ist der Quell des Bedürfnisses der Philosophie.*" Therefore reason proceeds to busy itself thinking the wound, to reduce the division, to return this side of the source, close by the infinite unity. To relieve the terms of the opposition, the effects of the division, such would be the "interest of reason," the unique interest of philosophy (*Solche festgewordene Gegensätze aufzuheben, ist das einzige Interesse der Vernunft*). The progress of culture has led oppositions of the type spirit/matter, soul/body, faith/understanding, freedom/necessity, and all those deriving from these back toward the great couple reason/sensibility or intelligence/nature, that is, "with respect to the universal concept, under the form of absolute subjectivity and absolute objectivity." Now these oppositions are posited as such by the understanding that "copies (*ahmt*)" reason. So this enigmatic relation, this rational *mimesis*, organizes the whole history of philosophy as the history of need, the history of reason's interest in relieving the two. Reason is another name for the power of unification (*Macht der Vereinigung*). When this force grows weaker or disappears, the need of/for philosophy makes itself felt.

So all the finite syntheses that, in art and religion, pretend to be absolute syntheses are only going to imitate reason's absolute operation. They are still, in this regard, "amusing games or entertainment."

Philosophy's need is not yet philosophy. There is a *not yet* of philosophy. Philosophy—already—is announced in it. Now, reason's and thus Hegelian philosophy's essential proposition: philosophy has its beginning only in itself. Philosophy is the beginning, as the beginning of (it)self, the posit(ion)ing by (it)self of the beginning. How are these two axioms to be reconciled: philosophy only proceeds from/by itself, and yet it is the daughter of a need or an interest that are not yet philosophy?

In its own proper position, philosophy *presupposes*. It precedes and replaces itself in its own proper thesis. It comes before itself and substitutes for itself. A *pro* movement: we would be tempted

summary, onomatopoeias and exclamations are of secondary importance, and their symbolic origin is in part open to dispute." (The arbitrary too, then. As for the so-called "symbolic" origin, in part open to dispute, hence in part symbolic, it comes under [*relève de*] the logic of the bit and of the antherection. Let the consequence of this be followed.)

Just after this conclusion, is §3: "*Principle II: Linear Character of the Signifier.*"

Here, once more, one reads neither objections nor questions addressed to "Saussure," but to two pillars of the *Course* that are set against each other even as they support each other in order to uphold a powerful edification. One knows that in another connection, and elsewhere, Saussure himself took into account the "relative motivation" of the sign. He distrusts everything that the reduction of language [*langage*] to "nomenclature" could imply (nomenclature—calare nomen—calls for names, classes by names, honors names and causes them to ring out, but also, in the same stroke [*coup*], by inscribing them in taxinomic networks and intersecting generalities, starts their decomposition, destroys their singular integrity as proper names). He has even attempted, in the *Anagrams*, a "remotivating" reading for which he has barely been pardoned, a kind of daydream, certainly knowledgeable and of a superior degree, but within the current frames of the scientific institution, essentially nuts, *dingue*. (Let us forewarn those crazy enough to remotivate this last word that it has no assured, etymologically affiliating relation with *dinguer*. It's really a shame, but that (*ça*) can be repaired.

For poetics: "*Dingo* . . . adj. and n.m. (Dingot, end of 19th c.; from *dingue*). *Fam.* crazy. V. *Cinglé* [lashed], *dingue*. . . ." "*Dingue* . . . adj. and n. (1915; origin unknown; perhaps from *dengue**; cf. slang *la dingue* "paludism" (1890); or from *dinguer*). *Pop.* Crazy, *dingo*. *He is a little* dingue. *You should be sent to the dingues* [loony bin]." "*Dinguer* . . . int. v. (1833; from a onomat. rad. *din-, ding-*, expressing swinging (of bells [*cloches*], etc.). *Fam.* (After a verb). To fall [*Tomber*]. '*I had a dizzy spell and began to fall* [dinguer] *at the foot of a chestnut tree*' (Gide). *Envoyer dinguer*: to repulse violently, and *fig.* to kick out tactlessly. '*If I was the one who had wanted to present them to him, how he would have kicked me out*' (Proust)."
*"*Dengue* . . . n.f. (1866 word esp. 'smirking'). Endemo-epidemic illness in the equatorial regions, an illness

to translate the fundamental concept of *Voraussetzung* by pro-position or pros-thesis, rather than by presupposition, as is usually done.

"The Need of Philosophy" gives the impression of a *limen*, a parvis, a vestibule, a march, a stair [*une marche*], a stairway, a threshold (*Vorhof*), a forestroke [*un avant-coup*]: "The need of philosophy can be expressed as its *pro-position* (Voraussetzung) if philosophy, which begins with itself, has to be furnished (*gemacht werden soll*) with some sort of forecourt (*Vorhof*)."

The question of the family, and then of religion, is pos(it)ed thus in the preamble; the family is at home only in time—in which reason has not absolutely reappropriated itself, has not found itself (close) by itself in its absolute familiarity, in which it does not yet dwell. Crossing the vestibule—family, religion—is the passage from the pro-position to the philosophical position that is its truth. Philosophical truth says: I am always following [*suis*] family and religion.

From then on the death of God, the Christian advent, the infinite grief, the unction, the trinity, calvary, the way of the cross, the resurrection play on the parvis, even form a kind of *representation*—like the elliptic glory of a tympan—*before* philosophy's erect construction, disciplined edification [*édification dressée*].

Limen of the "speculative good friday": "But the pure concept or infinity as the abyss of nothingness (*Abgrund des Nichts*) in which all being is engulfed (*versinkt*), must signify the infinite grief purely as a moment (*rein als Moment*) of the highest Idea, and no more than a moment. Formerly, the infinite grief only existed historically (*geschichtlich*) in culture. It existed as the feeling (*Gefühl*) that 'God Himself is dead,' upon which the religion of more recent times rests (the same feeling that Pascal expressed in so to speak sheerly empirical form: 'la nature est telle qu'elle *marque* partout un *Dieu perdu* et dans l'homme et hors de l'homme.' [Nature is such that it *marks* everywhere a *lost God* both within and outside man.]) By designating this feeling as a moment of the highest Idea, the pure concept must give philosophical existence to what used to be either the moral prescription (*Vorschrift*) that we must sacrifice the empirical being (*Wesens*), or the concept of formal abstraction. Thereby it must restore for philosophy the idea of absolute freedom and along with it the absolute passion, the speculative good friday that was formerly historic (*historisch*). Good friday must even be restored in the whole truth and harshness of its Godlessness (*Gottlosigkeit*). Since the more serene, less well grounded (*Ungründlichere*), and more individual style of the dogmatic philosophies and of the natural religions must vanish, the highest totality, in all its earnestness and out of its deepest ground, at once all encompassing and in the most serene freedom of its shape, can and must rise solely from this harshness."

provoked by a filterable virus and characterized by muscular and articular pain giving a stiff gait of affected appearance. . . . HOM. *Dingue.*" Robert, this time.)

But isn't remotivation, naive or subtle, always a bit crazy [*dingue*]. Isn't this what a theoretician of motivation thinks: "The restraint of demotivation—or rather the incapacity to demotivate—is one of the characteristic symptoms of aphasia. The ill [reading *malades* for *maladies*] interpret composite words as if they obeyed the rules [*règles*] of charades: dog's-tooth = dog + tooth (Goldstein).
"Remotivation accompanies every chronic mental regression. . . . Healing is accompanied by the progressive return of demotivated locutions.
"The delirious ideas of schizophrenics can be interpreted as *lived metaphors*" (Fónagy, "Motivation et Remotivation: Comment se dépasser?" in *Poétique* 11).

That is no doubt true. But what pertinent conceptual hold hands us the opposition motivation/demotivation-unmotivation, since the "chronic mental regression" of remotivation is escaped only to risk the "verbal regression" of demotivation? Six pages farther on: "It is interesting to see that the tendency to demotivation—one of the principal forces of linguistic evolution—can be at the origin of a profound verbal regression." No doubt "verbal regression" does not simply merge with "mental regression" (even though within this old code dissociating them is difficult); no doubt too the author has in view here "the language of mathematics" as the example of perfect de-motivation. But if "mathematical language" alone (is it a language?) is the "outcome" of the de-motivation process, then all "natural" language has something to do [*à voir*] with "chronic mental regression" and "schizophrenia."

That is no doubt true and why not. But the author also enters the activity of "schizophrenic patients" to the account of de-motivation! So the concept motivation is too loose and its presuppositions too obscure. They force the conclusion, according to the schemas of Con-

The family never ceases to occupy the stage [*scène*], and yet there is the impression that there is never any question of that. The philosophical object named "family" seems ceaselessly to slip away. The ontotheological premises, the infinite kernel of the family structure, of nomination, of filiation to be sure, are visible. But the whole fundamental syllogistic is controlled by the father/son relation about which we can ask ourselves whether it opens or closes the possibility of the family. This domination belongs, it seems, to the essence of the Holy Family. Now in passing to *Gottlosigkeit* (the harsh godlessness) is the Last Supper fulfilled; thus is developed speculatively what was only historic in the Last Supper. As long as one remains no further than the Holy Family, everything happens as if there was not yet any problematic of the family properly so called. Unless the Holy Family is the family properly so called, the only essential paradigm of every authentic family.

Who in effect is missing from the Holy Family? Who can be *absent* within it, and what does *absent* mean in this case? Is the father absent? Is the mother? Since Joseph is absent and Mary a virgin, the son is the son of the Father: the father and the mother are missing, one from the finite "point of view," the other from the infinite "point of view." But this dissociation between the two points of view is precisely what speculative dialectics criticizes. The relation of the Holy Family to the earthly family plays in this strange part(y) or partition between two, three, and four that works (over) the first texts and "develops itself" in the whole later system. In still speaking of development, we do nothing but name without resolving a difficulty now recognized.

The problematic of the "earthly" family has *Sittlichkeit* for its conceptual space. Now this space is *not yet* open, defined, determinate in *The Spirit of Christianity*. This does not signify that Hegel has not yet discovered or developed the concept *Sittlichkeit*: rather it shows that the concept *Sittlichkeit* could not be unfolded actually, historically, in Christianity as such. Christianity makes the family at once possible and impossible. The political limit (the divorce between spiritual action and "worldly action," the split between the beyond and the here below, the unfinished reconciliation between the Father and the Son, and so on) compromises the totality and reintroduces a new schiz [*schize*]. This new schiz must be overcome: thus one passes to the syllogism of *Sittlichkeit* that is developed in(to) the State, after the stage of the family and of bourgeois society. Here *Sittlichkeit* takes its *departure*, its *separation* [*son* départ]: at once its origin and what separated it from its origin. *Sittlichkeit issues* from Christianity, the issue of the Holy Family. Development then, and rupture: response to the question of method.

Sittlichkeit's essential traits are apparent in *The Difference Between Fichte's and Schelling's System*, *Faith and Knowledge*, the article on

dillac, Rousseau and several others, that progress is a regression (a good and/or a bad recession toward the origin, verily short of the origin): "The genesis and evolution of language [*langage*] is a permanent struggle between tendencies that push toward demotivation and others favoring remotivation. Language [*langue*] owes its birth to demotivation, but could not evolve without having permanent recourse to the remotivation of signs and structure." But what does one say then, and what are the stakes, the forms, and the forces of this struggle? Why does it fix its representation of itself in the duel between restraint and freedom, motivation and arbitrariness, nature and *thesis*.

This is not just one thesis here, but the thesis that is structurally in danger, that is motivated to demotivate. On this precise point, if de-motivation is motivated, if, in effect, "The theory *thesei* . . . the categorical disavowal of any motivation . . . is a defense, a protection against the attraction exercised by this too weakly disguised content," then the simple alternative of two opposite forces (motivation/nonmotivation) within a homogeneous field cannot account for the internal and displaced division of each force: re-motivation is also apotropaic.
No doubt a certain logic of repression is indispensable and irreducible here—and it spoils much in the modern reflections on the problem of "motivation." But a recourse to the "notions" of psychoanalysis does not suffice to resolve the problem from the start and broach a systematic classification of the elements in play. When justly concluding, for example, that "each sound of the language is a group of distinctive articulatory and acoustical traits and thereby lends itself to the representation of several drives at once," the author of the "Bases pulsionnelles de la phonation" retroactively complicates, even takes the risk of contradicting or compromising all his earlier propositions. And what would happen if the drives (what is this all about?) were not content to converge, economically, in one same phonic or acoustical "representation," but were divided instead, verily undecided between one another in their internal contradiction?
What interest

against class, *glas* of classes, even here, here and now. The lot of the same noun always in play, at stake [*en jeu*]. That (*Ça*) is written (writes itself) with detachment.

Natural Law. But the great syllogism of the *Philosophy of Right* is not visible as such in these.

Therefore it is a question of laying down a speculative science of right, a speculative concept of *Sittlichkeit*; and so to criticize simultaneously empiricism and formalism. These two demarcations are always inseparable, for essential reasons. In the course of this double critique, the family question seems to intervene only as an example. If one wants to know, for example, of what does marriage consist, that structured totality that is the conjugal union, how do we proceed? The empiricists never want to anticipate; they claim to proceed passively, faithfully, to recount, narrate, recite (*erzählen*) what they believe they see, to enumerate a certain number of predicates that come to meet them. They say: marriage is this, and then that, and yet that. This alleged concrete content is already in a situation of formal abstraction with regard to the total unity the narrator wants to recognize. But just as the narrator cannot not presuppose a principle of unity—what is called marriage—he sets apart in advance, in a noncritical way, a predicate and, with others "excluded," places it in a controlling situation. He makes it "the essence and end." He says for example that the essence of the "relation of marriage" lies in the education of children or yet in the community of goods. Which limits the concrete unity of the conjugal development (its total syllogism), and affects the "organic relation," affects it with a violent abstraction, to be sure, but also with a stain [*souillure*]: "*das ganze organische Verhältnis bestimmt und verunreinigt,*" it determines and soils the whole organic relation. Why would the empiricist's course [*démarche*] soil the essence of marriage in situating it in the education of children or in the community of goods? Perhaps in disregarding love. *Verunreinigt,* that could as well be *veruneinigt,* synonym of *entzweit*: divides, disunites, cuts through to a decision.

This example occupies only three lines, but it comes very quickly, just at the very instant the project of a philosophical science of *Sittlichkeit* is formulated. In starting from the "absolute idea," one must consider "the nature and relation of the science of the *Sittlichen* as philosophical science, and . . . its relation with what is called the positive science of law." Now when this science will be constituted, when *Sittlichkeit* will be defined from the speculative point of view, the family will form its first moment. So here it is not a question of a simple example, and its place is not fortuitous.

The two invoked traits (community of goods and the education of children) will never be disqualified as such. The critique here bears on the manner in which the empiricist carries out their deduction. Later, in the family syllogism, the first circle of the great syllogism of *Sittlichkeit*, these two predicates will organize themselves, like the second and the third of a historic totality of

For if the proper surnames return to (Our-Lady-of-the-) flowers, these flowers are cut from the mother.

Detached rather.

To detach.

Can one dispense with the word here? Detached: like the grandest style.

The cutting, the deliaison [*déliaison*], to be sure, but also the representative delegation, the sending [*envoi*] of a detachment, on a mission close by the other, close by self: "It [wing of stamin, Death] had detached a . . . necktie to represent It. . . ."

And like all fabrics, when one wants to restore the text of the Immaculate Conception, the tie detaches itself, comes loose [*se détache*].

With that detachment, to reelaborate—as a problem of the *seing*, the signature, and the mother's name—the alternative to formalism or biographism, the untellable and so classical question of the subject in literature. "Thus, in the eyes of Our bewildered Lady, the little faggots from Place Blanche to Pigalle lost their loveliest adornment: their names lost their corolla, like the paper flower that the dancer holds at his fingertips and which, when the ballet is over, is a mere iron stem.

which marriage ("*the immediate type of ethical relationship*," the natural unity of the sexes transformed into a spiritual unity) will be the first moment.

Further, above all, the division, the split, the dissolution will be conceived. It will actually produce itself and will be consum(mat)ed, after having been prepared by marriage and the community of goods, with the education of children. But, then, it will no longer be a question of *theoretically* dissolving the family, through a proceeding of empiric knowledge, through a scientific lapse. One will have to comprehend, conceive how the family *really*, *actually dissolves itself* in the education of children and the passage to bourgeois society.

The principle of internal destruction, domestic negativity does not intervene only at this precise point within the family moment. The exposure to death is the condition of every ethical totality in general, here of the *people*.

In effect the doctrine of the death penalty assures the passage from the critique of formalism to the position of absolute *Sittlichkeit*. In an interpretation that is peculiar to him, Hegel again takes up an argumentation at that time rather current, common to Rousseau and Kant for example: the death penalty is the condition of freedom. The criminal is distinguished from the animal, is posited as a free subject, assumes the identity of his name, and so on, in raising himself above life. The penalty is not a coercive or repressive punishment. An application of the universal law, the penalty manifests the freedom of those who apply it and those who submit to it. In accepting his penalty, verily in demanding it, in glorifying it, the criminal recognizes the law, and so he is free. The death penalty bears to the absolute this manifestation of freedom. The article on *Natural Law*, like the *Phenomenology* in the chapter on "Independence and Dependence of Self-Consciousness: Lordship and Bondage," makes putting natural life into play the condition of a free subjectivity.

In the center of this demonstration, a couple of concepts designating some legal [*de droit*] operations. In accepting the principle of a penalty whose end is not to punish, chastise, or mutilate, but on the contrary to raise one to the freedom of the ethical community, the singular individual becomes free, has himself recognized as such by society, is then "be*zwungen, aber nicht ge*zwungen." The French translators say this play on words is untranslatable, and they are undoubtedly not wrong. In effect the two verbs have very closely related senses, all referring to what I would call a movement of *constriction*: grip, constraint, restriction; it is a question of closing up, squeezing, containing, suppressing, subjecting, compressing, repressing, subduing, reducing, forcing, subjugating, enslaving, hemming in. But Hegel chooses to dissociate and oppose rigorously one to the other, *zwingen* to *bezwingen*, in taking up again in

here the taut iron wire [*fil*], at the fingertips, supports [*soutient*] the paper flower: in its erection and in its appearance, the time of the ballet. But it is also what remains when the flower falls (to the tomb), reduced, without adornment [*parure*] or natural color, to its real support. And to its "proper name." The faggots lose their adornment, the names their corolla the moment the clerk cries out the "proper names" of the civil state, calls, classes according to the law, redistributes the genders: "When he called: 'Berthollet Antoine,' First Communion appeared; at the call 'Marceau Eugène,' Lady-Apple appeared. Thus, in the eyes of Our bewildered Lady, the little faggots from Place Blanche to Pigalle lost their loveliest adornment." Return to natural nomination, that is, to the first classificatory violence, inversion of sex, reintroduction of the first name that comes, in all taxinomic rigor, second. Nothing remains but filial filaments [*fils*].

But the role of filial filaments can be reversed or can recover in counterproof the sense of the engraving. "The Funambulists" is a hymn to the wire [*fil*]. This time the dancer does not hold the iron wire at his fingertips; he holds—like the text—on to a wire. The wire—the subject of the text—supports him on the edge of the fall [*chute*] ("The wire will bear you better and more surely than a road."). The funambulist must love his wire as what bears [*porte*] him, but first of all as what he will have borne, given birth to or rather resuscitated, Oedipus or Jesus? "The love—a love almost desperate, fraught with tenderness—that you must show your wire will have as much strength as the iron wire shows in supporting [*porter*] you. I know objects, their malignity, their cruelty, their gratitude too. The wire was dead—or if you prefer, mute, blind. You appear: it will live and speak." The places are going to be reversed, the

part the terminology of Fichte who speaks in his *Grundlage des Naturrechts* of a *Zwangsgesetz* [coercive law]. The constriction of *bezwingen* is distinguished from the simple application of an empiric constraint, erects the empiric individual into a free subject. The very top of this erection is called death: "This negative absolute, pure freedom, is in its phenomenon (*Erscheinung*) death; and by his ability (*Fähigkeit*) to die the subject proves itself free and entirely raised (*erhaben*) above all *Zwang*. Death is the absolute *Bezwingung*." How is this to be translated? Death is the phenomenon (the shining appearing, the lustre, the glory, the gleaming brilliance [*éclat*], the *Erscheinung*) of the subject that frees itself in subjecting itself to the law's universality. Therefore the subject raises itself, stands up above a certain type of *constriction* (*Zwang*); but the subject can stand thus only to suffer the absolute increase of a counterconstriction that, to chastise it absolutely, totally frees it from the prior constriction called natural, empiric, and so on, the prior constriction that is always weaker. *Bezwingung* erects freedom in lifting the *Zwang*. Absolute—colossal in any case—increase of a counterconstriction. But what is an absolute increase? How is it taken into account? How is death taken into account in the calculus of everything one wants to erect?

What raises itself here does not simply raise itself but first relieves (itself) (*aufhebt*). So the calculus can no longer determine anything, for the relief suspends all determinateness, whether positive or negative; the relief suspends the *plus* and the *minus*. Death, freedom are an "*Aufhebung sowohl des Plus als des Minus*," a relief of the plus as of the minus. This relief, the act of *aufheben*, "can itself be grasped and expressed positively by reflection." Before the infinite law that prescribes death, the equivalence of $+A$ and of $-A$ annihilates the two determinations. Death alone permits access to this infinite that permits calculating the incalculable, annulling the calculus thus without fail, without bargaining [*faire marché*] for chastising: "Thus the penalty is the restoration of freedom. . . . It issues from freedom, and, even as constriction (*als bezwingend*), remains in freedom. If, on the other hand, the penalty is represented as constraint (*als Zwang*), it is posited merely as a specific determinateness and as something purely finite, carrying no rationality in (it)self. It falls wholly under the common category of one specific thing contrasted with another, or as an item with which something else—namely the crime—can be purchased. The State as judicial power trades in specific wares, called crimes, for sale in exchange for other specific wares, and the legal code (*Gesetzbuch*) is its pricelist (*Preiskourant*)."

Penalty *par excellence*, death escapes every judicial and suppressive calculus that would try to establish an equivalence between the ledger of the crime and that of the penalty, as if in adding up the total of the infractions on the left, that of the chastisements

wire dances and the dancer is blind; glory returns to the true subject: the wire: "You will perform your dances, your leaps and bounds—in acrobats' lingo: your heel-and-toe, kowtows, somersaults, cartwheels, etc.—not so that *you* may shine [not in order for her, the mother, to shine: "A gold spangle is a tiny gilt-metal disk with a hole in it."—this is the opening of the text, its first sentence] but that a steel wire which was dead and voiceless can at last sing. How grateful it will be if your bearing is perfect for the sake of *its* glory and not of yours!

"Let the bedazzled spectators applaud it:
"'What an amazing wire! The way it supports its dancer! And how it loves him!'

"The wire, in turn, will make you the most marvelous dancer. . . .
". . . It matters not a bit that your solitude is, paradoxically, in full light and that the darkness is composed of thousands of eyes which are judging you, and which fear and hope you will fall ["She hoped that the following day Our-Lady would be sentenced to death; she desired it."]. You will dance in and over a desertlike solitude, eyes banded blind, if you can, with your eyelids buttoned. But nothing—and above all not applause or laughter—will keep you from dancing for your image. You are an artist—alas!—you can no longer reject the monstrous precipice of your eyes. . . .
". . . it is not you who will be dancing, but the wire. But if it is the wire that dances motionless, and if it is your image that the wire bounces, then where will *you* be?"

"The Funambulists" is divided in two: paragraphs in italics, paragraphs in roman, narrative [*récit*] and apostrophe, I-it/he, I-you. The wire of the text disappears, reappears, stretches itself to the point of vibration, becomes invisible through too much rigor or too many detours, loads itself with all the names, bears Death and the dead man. Already—the vigil [*veille*]—the place of the dead man: "Death—the Death of which I speak to you—is not the death that will follow your fall, but the one which precedes your appearance on the wire. It is before mounting the wire that you die. . . . But see to it [*veille*] that you die before appearing, and that it is a dead man who dances on the wire."

on the right, then in subtracting one from the other, one could annul a debt, discharge it. Death escapes the operation of this finite debt. Not that any equivalence is produced in it. The equivalence, the reciprocity (*Wiedervergeltung*) is the rationality of every penalty. But in the death penalty, the equivalence becomes infinite, obeys an infinite law, cannot let an empiric height in arithmetical columns be the determining factor. And precisely because the equivalence between the debt and the chastisement is infinite, no determinable resemblance, no determinable commensurability, no determinable analogy lets itself be grasped between their two ledgers, their two ranges. No relation gives itself to be understood in, lays itself open to finite concepts and understanding's determinations. The equivalence is infinite and null.

Such an analysis has already ceased to treat the case of an individual subject to the death penalty. It would concern the total functioning of an ethical community: the infinite equivalence cannot produce itself in the relation between empiric finite individuals or groups. Therefore Hegel calls the absolute ethical totality the *people*. Now the people itself has access to *Sittlichkeit* and becomes free as an ethical (*sittliche*) totality only in bringing its life into play, in standing up above its natural determinations in a strict movement. *Bezwingen*, death's infinite and thus nonconstraining constriction, produces the strict: what is called spirit, freedom, the ethical, and so on. The people must risk its life, must not hesitate to let itself be destroyed as an empiric people in order to become a free people, that is, a people in the strict sense. That is possible only in war. A condition of the ethical, war no longer belongs to the order of natural phenomena (as in Rousseau for example): it manifests consciousness, spirit, culture. A people that fears war reverts to animality; it wishes to save its life, its natural and biological health; but it alters its spiritual life and its ethical health.

Of course, if it loses the war—like the criminal *after* the fall of the blade [*couperet*] and the eucharistic materials after consum(mat)ing—it becomes empiric naturality again. Also if it wins the war, and what stands up here then hangs by a thread [*fil*], never lose it from view.

So war would prevent the people from rotting; war preserves "the ethical health of peoples," as the wind agitating the seas purifies them, keeps them from decomposing, from the corruption, from the putrefaction (*Fäulnis*) with which a "continual calm (*dauernde Stille*)" and *a fortiori* a "perpetual peace" would infect that health. In this putrefaction, this return to inorganic nature, the people would lose its name and its face, its shape (*Gestalt*), its form. No longer would a people stand up straight. Hegel cites Gibbon: peace and secured mastery have acted on the Romans as a "'slow

The displacement returns unceasingly from vigil to wire, from the funambulist, reciprocally, to the old woman [*la vieille*], by a kind of alternation as regular as that of day and night: the funambulist becomes the old woman, an old tramp [*une vieille cloche*], some tatters, a postiche fleece, which becomes the funambulist from whom she somehow hides the taut wire under her ragged robes: "*Need I say it? I would not mind the funambulist's assuming, during the day, the outward appearance of a toothless old female tramp [une vieille clocharde] covered with a gray wig. Seeing her, one would know an athlete was reposing beneath the tatters, and one would respect the great distance between day and night. Appearing in the evening! And he, the funambulist, not knowing which is his higher being: the verminous tramp [clocharde pouilleuse] or the sparkling [étincelant] solitary. Or the constant movement from her to him?*"

The fête is brief, engages something other than "our world and its logic," leads us back into "that huge canvas belly," into "the monster's flank," where "Your brief tomb illuminates us."

Death takes the place of the vigil, in other words, of the Virgin. For her and in her name must the wire [*fil*] stretch itself and the funambulist fascinate ("you do not come to entertain the audience but to fascinate it"—the word *fascinate* returns three times), dance, band, band it ("And dance! But band taut. . . . Band erect. And band the audience erect."). At the moment of absolute narcissism. ("Band erect. And band the audience erect. The heat that issues from you and radiates is your desire for yourself—or for your image—a desire never satisfied [*comblé*].") To death and the vigil is the fête again given—as a present (the vigil—already—in my place). Death taking the vigil's place, denial puts in the future (that) which will never have been present. "I obviously did not mean (to say) that an acrobat who operates twenty-five or thirty feet from the ground should entrust himself to God (funambulists, to the Virgin), that he should pray and cross himself [*se signe*] before entering the ring because death is under the big top. I was speaking to the artist only, as to the poet." Not to the only artist, but to the artist only. "Were you

and secret poison (*langsames und geheimnes Gift*)'" in the vital forces of the empire, of the Roman eagle.

As all this hangs by a thread [*fil*], the ethical body must incessantly repeat the spiritual act of its upsurge, must always be reborn, must always recall itself to its name and its freedom. In this text, the name of what takes wing again [*reprend son vol*] is neither the owl nor the eagle, but the phoenix: starting from its consuming destruction, life, "as its own seed-corn (*als sein eigenes Samenkorn*)," "rise[s] (*emporhebe*) eternally . . . from its ashes to new youth." That is the representation, the execution, the interpretation (*Aufführung*), in the ethical world, of "the tragedy which the Absolute eternally plays with itself": "it eternally gives birth to itself into objectivity, submits in this form of its own to suffering and death, and rises (*erhebt*) from its ashes into glory [*Herrlichkeit*: its brilliance [*éclat*], its majesty, its sovereignity, its pomp]." In this brilliance, the phoenix's own proper instance, the absolute of this movement is tragic because it is double, absolutely double: the divine there has "immediately a nature split in two (*gedoppelte*), and its life is the absolute being-one (*Einssein*) of these natures."

> "*Sein Leben ist das absolute Einssein dieser Naturen.*" The *Einssein*, the word bursting with brilliance [*éclatant de l'éclat*], double word and one word, literally one and the other, both in the heart [*sein*] of the one, the other's difference bound within the one ("since its own proper life (*ihr eigenes Leben*) is only in its being-bound (*Verbundensein*) to the other"), *Einssein* is the absolute tragedy because of this absolute ligature. Comedy, divine and modern, consists in unbinding the absolute, in separating both members from each other. There the destiny and the combat become a shadow without essence, a farce assured of its enjoyment. What tightens the members of the *Einssein* in the "relation of one's own body (*in leibhafter Beziehung*)" has grown slack. Both members have fallen again (to the tomb) beside one another.

To this rejuvenation, to the highest instance of this flight [*vol*], all must be subject: the world of labor, need, enjoyment. Although it does not expressly place this world on the side of servility, the article on *Natural Law* clearly states the necessity of subordinating

to dance only a yard above the mat, my injunction would be the same. I meant, as you realize, the deathly solitude, the desperate and radiant [*éclatante*] region in which the artist operates. . . .

"Gothic legend tells of saltimbanques who, having nothing else, offer their stunts to the Virgin. They danced in front of the cathedrals. I don't know to what god you will address your feats of dexterity [*d'adresse*], but you need one. . . . God does not yet exist for anyone. . . . Your gestures can be withheld. . . ."

A question of *adresse* [address, adroitness], and of knowing *for whom* to sign oneself [*se signer*] again. In place of and with a view to whom, already, for whom a funambulist thus.

If you follow this wire [*fil*], or another, from the funambulist to the *Ticktack des kleinen Glücks*, to the *Klang einer Glocke* and to the self's dead sure biting (death) [*la morsure de soi*], very near the end, you have here at your disposal, as if in contraband, everything necessary for an almost complete, literally literal reading of *Zarathustra*. You can verify.

Remain(s) to (be) divide(d), detail(ed), retail(ed) one more time

Would it not have been better to have danced the entire dance with a simple wire? The question is worth examining. The faggots showed the framework that Darling [*Mignon*] discerned behind the silk and velvet of every armchair. They were reduced to nothing, and that's the best thing that's been done so far. They entered aggressively or shyly, perfumed, made up, expressed themselves with studied care. They were no longer the grove of crinkly paper that flowered on the terraces of cafés. They were mis-

the "system of the so-called political economy" and its corresponding science to the mastery (*Herrschaft*) of the ethico-political totality sanctioned by its exposure to death.

We must see to it that this hierarchy is not overturned. Here Hegel converses with Plato and Aristotle. He distinguishes between the states or "classes (*Stände*)." The *System of "Sittlichkeit"* places the aristocratic (political and military) class at the summit of the hierarchy: the aristocratic class faces death and raises itself above needs. The commercial and industrial bourgeoisie, *die erwerbende Klasse*, the class of acquisition, amasses wealth and locks itself in the ease and luxury of private life, attains the universal only in formal abstraction, and its right [*droit*] resembles the *pharmakon* of the *Republic*, cited at length by Hegel: the *pharmakon* begets more varied and serious illnesses instead of restoring health. They do not know that "'in fact they are just cutting off a *Hydra*'s head'" ("'*sie in der Tat gleichsam die* Hydra *zerschneiden*'": Ὕδραν τέμνουσιν). Finally, the third state, a peasant class that related to the concrete whole only in the sensible and felt [*sentimentale*] form of confidence.

After the possession (*Besitz*) has become property (*Eigentum*), after the institution of right and a formal ethical life, is the third stage, ethical life, absolute *Sittlichkeit*. The organizing schema of the [*Elements of the*] *Philosophy of Right* is readable, according to the problematic *already* [*déjà*] that we know: abstract right treating property, formal subjective morality (*Moralität*), ethical or objective morality (*Sittlichkeit*) rhythmed by the three totalities the family, civil or bourgeois society, the State are. "Above these two," says *Natural Law*, "is the third, the Absolute or the *ethical* (*das Sittliche*)." All that precedes this third: possession, property, labor, abstract right, formal justice, "concerns the individual and thus does not include in (it)self the danger of death."

This whole process is described through what Hegel considers natural "images." He criticizes them less than explains their necessity: the regulated relation they maintain with their spiritual sense. The animal and oriental figure of the Phoenix will be put back in its place by *Reason in History*. All the references to natural life and death imitate and deform the process of spiritual life or death. Everywhere the relation of nature to spirit is found: spirit is (outside itself) in nature; nature is spirit outside self. The finite metaphor, real organic life is impotent to receive all the spiritual divinity of *Sittlichkeit*; nevertheless it "already expresses in itself the absolute Idea, though deformed." It has within itself the absolute infinity, but "only as an imitative (*nachgeahmte*) negative independence—i.e., as freedom of the singular individual." The same goes for the Platonic metaphor of the city as immortal animal, for the perfection of the stone or the flower of the heavenly system.

ery in motley. (Where do the faggots get their *noms de guerre*? But first it should be noted that none of them were chosen by those who bore them. For me, the same does not hold. I can hardly give the exact reasons why I chose such and such a name. Divine, First Communion, Mimosa, Our-Lady-of-the-Flowers and Milord the Prince did not come to be by chance. There exists a kinship among them, an odor of incense and melting taper, and I sometimes feel as if I had collected them among the artificial or natural flowers in the chapel of the Virgin Mary, in the month of May, under and about the greedy plaster statue that Alberto was in love with and behind which, as a child, I used to hide the phial containing my jism.)"

"For me, the same does not hold," says the child to the greedy plaster.

Verily.

To be necktied [*se cravater*] with such a text.

Our-Lady who strangles with the detachment of a phallus that his victim begins by offering him, by tendering to him (his neck, his necktie), is a virgin, and conceived without sin, like his mother ("I am the Immaculate Conception"), of whom he is also the phallus. Which she gave him. He is his mother and himself, and his mother is his victim. So he strangles himself by saying, "I am the Immaculate Conception." He can say it only in the trance of a hiccup, very

The perfect mineral in effect seems to represent the being-one (*Einsein*) of an absolute totality. In the outer form of its crystallization, in the inner form of its break [*brisure*] (*Bruch*), each part seems to be the "representative of the whole (*Repräsentant des Ganzen*)." In truth, there it is a question of an external association, a reciprocity of composition (*Aussereinander*), and not of penetration. No element is "penetrated (*durchdrungen*)" by the true identity of the infinity. The mineral's senses have "no consciousness." Unlike what is produced for a spiritual sense, "its light is a single color, and cannot see." The sound it emits when struck it does not emit of itself, like a voice, but receives the sound as if from a foreign source (*Sein Ton tönt angeschlagen von einem Fremden, aber nicht aus sich*). Its taste does not taste; its smell smells nothing; its weight and its hardness feel nothing.

The brittle and rebellious rigidity of the mineral must be reduced. That is still an operation of *Bezwingung*: the elementary fluidity must penetrate. The fluidity of the ether is what first announces the absolute indifference of spirit in its negative mode and is "married" with the absolute infinity. Then there are the "higher formations," "the fellowship of leaves of plants, of sex, of the herdwise life and common labor of animals." In its absolute quantative indifference, ether is what most resembles the indifference (*Indifferenz*) of ethical life. Ether has thrown its absolute indifference outward, in "indifferences of light (*Lichtindifferenzen*)"; the ether has set its inner reason expanding, given birth to it in expelling it (*in die Expansion herausgeboren hat*): these are the "flowers of solar systems (*Blumen der Sonnensysteme*)." These "individualizations of light (*Lichtindividuen*)" have scattered themselves in multiplicity, whereas those arranged in a circle to form the "petals" of these flowers are held opposite them, in a "rigid individuality," in an exterior relation. The flower of the heavenly system resembles then the unity of the ethical system, but its elements remain foreign to one another, in a kind of abstract ideality. The heavenly flower forms an unfolding without inner unity, a juxtaposition ordered but purely spread out, unfolded, opened out, without secret or relation to self: "*die aussereinandergefaltete Blume des himmlischen Systems*." In the analogy, the difference remains essential: when the spirit is spoken of, this flower gives a good image, but its value is still rhetorical.

Potenz: this word, appearing now and then in *Natural Law*, will, some years later, furnish the most general organizing concept of the Jena philosophy of spirit. There, in effect, the analysis

close to vomiting himself. The spitting image of his mother's breast [*sein*]. The child can say, "I am the Immaculate Conception," only by wanting to fuck himself. And therefore his mother. Of whom he remains—however—the phallus, the case according to Peter, christic and dionysiac.

Not far from the crèche.

"And this fabulous impecuniousness [*dèche*] made for Our-Lady a pedestal of cloud; he was as prodigiously glorious as the body of Christ rising aloft, to dwell there alone and fixed, in the sunny noonday sky."

So the son or the phallus of the virgin sleeps immediately with his/its mother, the father that is dead (or set aside [*écarté*] by the Immaculate Conception, but because of this fact, excusing himself just as well from passing essentially through the mother, consequently engendering his son all by himself, self-inseminating himself and calling himself in him: the son that is the mother is also the father that is the mother that is the son, "and so on, without anyone's daring to linger over recognizing it," the necktie, and you can, in the course of the trial, follow the detachment) feigns to put no more obstacles in the way.

Above all do not go on thinking that I am here telling you, in the back-store of Jesus' pharmacy, the story of a *genêt* whose dye, the *pharmakon*, interests me before anything else. And it is true that I will have done nothing if I have not succeeded in affecting you with *genêt*, in coloring, smearing, gluing [*encoller*]

of consciousness will be divided or developed in three "powers":
(1) Memory and language; this is the "theoretical" power: sensation, imagination, memory. (2) The tool (*Werkzeug*), the "practical" power: desire, labor, tool. (3) Possession and family: family, struggle for recognition, passage to the people-spirit.

What is *Potenz*? A moment of the moment, a moment of the Hegelian concept of moment. The word and no doubt the concept were present in Schelling's philosophy of nature. The *Ideas for a Philosophy of Nature* describe the absolute's going outside self into nature, as nature, according to the ternary rhythm of "powers." These "powers" are at once a *dynamis* and an *energeia*, a virtuality and an act, a completed totality on which, so to speak, is hung the totality to come. One power bears the death of the other. The absolute goes out of itself into the finite, penetrates the finite with its infinity in order to make the finite come back to it. It absorbs it, resorbs it after having entered it. This movement of effusion/resorption manifests the absolute differentiating itself, going out of the night of its essence and appearing in the daylight. Such a presentation is produced in three acts, which Schelling names "powers." *Nature*, the first unity that, penetrated by the infinite, is transformed in its turn into the *ideal world*, which is transformed again into *nature*. The same schema is found again in *The Ages of the World*; this time the question concerns *natura naturans* and God. The mark of Boehme is perceptible. The abyssal absolute (*Ungrund*) is powerless (*Potenzlos*). This im-potence is its primitive germ. God goes out from this nothingness and is the being that is (*das Seiende*). Finally, the hierarchic union of being and nonbeing is the third power. As in *Natural Law*, each totality, each power proceeds to the constriction of the preceeding one, strangles it, and raises it to the following power, according to a circular process which goes, as it were, from the seed to the plant, then from the plant to the seed.

So Hegel has more than a word in common with Schelling. But the whole criticism of Schelling's triplicity is particularly indicated in the substitution, in the epoch of Jena, of the term *Moment* for the term *Potenz*. In the Jena *Realphilosophie* manuscript, an erasure preserves the trace of this substitution; but elsewhere, the word *Potenz* long remained in place.

What Hegel says of the structure of *Potenz*—and this will be true of the dialectical moment—explains for us how he, Hegel, meant to be read. What he states on each *Potenz* can be transposed to each organized totality of his text, which at once repeats and anticipates, yet marks a jump, a leap, a rupture in the repetition, and all the while ensures the continuity of passage and the homogeneity of a development.

A plurality of continuous jerks, of uninterrupted jolts—such would be the rhythm. The last two pages of *Natural Law* in effect

you, making you sensitive, transforming you, beyond all that is combined here, out of the most proper affect of this text.

But is there any? And of what text? of his? of mine?

I place this brushstroke [*touche*] here only because of the color, of a "yellow corn mush" that I no longer know where to put in my adoration.

See. It is always during the trial, of an annal style writing. Divine comes to testify for Our-Lady: ". . . I think he's very naive, very child-like. . . . He could be my son." Like the Archangel Gabriel, *remember*. The author or the narrator (always between one *seing* or the other) then explains to us how Culafroy became Divine, how his name was written Divine and, from then on, transformed him, the named one, the surnamed, into a "poem written only for himself, hermetic for whoever did not have the key to it."

by wishing also to be Gabriel's mother, she who is forenamed, surnames, (un)names [*dénomme*] him — Divine — announces in all the brilliance [*éclat*] of his identity: I am (following) my mother, my daughter, my son, and myself. The mother obstinately precedes and follows the cortège

So this is the moment to explain how the narrator, not the author—let us say, to be circumspect, *genêt*— became a name, a flower, is tailored a beautiful renown in letters. He compares himself to Divine: "In sum, this is his secret glory, like the one I have decreed upon myself so as to obtain peace at last." In effect, a fortuneteller has announced to *genêt* that he/it had genius and would be celebrated some day. On the ground of the "old need for thinking I have genius," he ennobles his name, coifs his genealogy with this virtual celebrity. He will gain this glory, will have it more glittering than all, will be crowned with it, but

describe the life and the death of "powers," for example, of those ethical totalities that "nations" are. In each particular totality, as such, the absolute totality *comes to a halt, stops itself,* stops its necessity. The particular totality then takes, as a part, a certain independence, a certain subsistence. To come to a halt, to stop itself, is here *sich hemmen. Hemmen* is often translated by inhibit, suppress. The infinite totality inhibits itself in the *Potenz.* This totality limits itself, gives itself a form, goes out from a certain *apeiron,* suspends itself, puts an end to itself, but the delay it thus takes on itself (*hemmen* also signifies delay, defer) is the positive condition of its appearing [*apparaître*], of its glory. Without the delay, without the suspensive and inhibiting constriction, the absolute would not manifest itself. So the delay is also an advance, progress, an anticipation, an encroachment on the absolute unfolding of the absolute. Whence this double archeo-teleological movement: "The absolute totality suspends itself (*hemmt sich*) as necessity in each of its powers (*in jeder ihrer Potenzen*), produces itself out of them (*bringt sich . . . hervor*) as a totality, repeats (*wiederholt*) there the preceding powers just as it anticipates (*anti-zipiert*) the succeeding ones."

The powers are linked together: the consequence from one to the other and the limitation holding the absolute in its chains. The linking together is not a serene and continuous deduction. In the conflict of forces, in war, in the struggle to the death, the most powerful power suppresses the others. But as this war expresses absolute necessity, the greatest force is not constraining the very moment it imposes itself. As a particular power, it imposes no doubt a set of limitations; but inasmuch as it expresses the infinite power held back in it, the limitation is no longer negative; it opens a set of conditions of possibility, of existence, of life, the best ones possible at a given moment. Thus water is a determinate element that can be opposed to air or to the earth: for fish, water is the only possible one, and it in no way constitutes a limit. No more than does air for the bird. No more than does an ethical totality for a man. The analogy stops there: the natural element has no history; the ethical element is historic through and through.

Now this history, although it unfolds the divinity of the *telos,* develops by discontinuous and painful jumps. The divine's penetration can obey only this rhythm. The passage from one power to the other is dialectical; it proceeds by absolute inversions and oppositions. Such is the "misfortune (*Unglück*) of the period of passage": a brusque springing up (*Sprung*), then a stay (*Verweilen*) wherein the spirit "enjoys (*geniesst*)" the new form (*Gestalt*) it has just conquered. Metaphor, of course, of the bomb, time of the explosive bomb: "Just as a bombshell at its zenith effects a jerk [*Rück:* a stopping or recoiling movement, jolt] and then rests for a moment in it, or just as metal, when heated, does not turn soft like

by hiding it in some literal, ineffable crypt, entirely illuminated from within. It is "a parchment that no one can decipher, an illustrious birth kept secret, a royal bar sinister, a mask or perhaps a divine filiation, the sort of thing that must have been felt by . . ."

However, the divine filiation with which the *genêt* is affected is an immaculate conception, permits the son to take—therefore to leave—all the places, to sleep all alone—here with the father in (it)self, there with the actual mother (*ansichseiende Vater und nur eine wirkliche Mutter,* but *nur eine* is the best) as in *absolute religion,* that is, on the (representative) threshold of absolute knowledge where the *glas* finally returns (close) by self, resounds, reflects itself for (it)self, admires its glory and is equal to itself. We are in Galilée, between 1810 and 1910 on our calendar. It is, as it was written to Roger Blin, a "gl

"Time. I know nothing very specific about time, but, if I let a heavy enough eyelid fall back on an event, any event whatsoever. . . . The first Frenchmen bombarding Algiers in 1830, if you like, bombarded themselves from Algiers about 1800. . . .

"I haven't the time to go into the matter at greater length. . . .

". . . No sooner had the stroke [*coup*] of Dey's fan been given, no sooner had the first shot [*coup*] of the cannon sounded, than 800,000 *Pieds Noirs* were already fabricating Tixier-Vignancour. Everything was very rapid, in racing terms, very strong, strong enough *to bring off an event* without beginning or end: global."

Like *class, calends, glas, calendar* comes down to *calling* (*calare*), naming, convoking, gathering together, commemorating, announcing.

wax, but all at once (*auf einmal*) springs into liquid and stays so (*in den Fluss springt und auf ihm verweilt*)—for this phenomenon (*Erscheinung*) is the passage into the absolute opposite and so is infinite, and this emergence of the opposite out of infinity or out of its nothingness is a jump (*Sprung*), and the being-there of the figure in its new-born strength at first is for itself alone, before it becomes conscious of its relation to a foreign being—so the growing individuality has both the delight (*Freudigkeit*) of the jump and also an enduring pleasure (*Genusses*) in its new form, until it gradually opens up to the negative, and in its ruin (*Untergange*) too it is all at once and like a rupture (*brechend*)."

This structure—discontinuous jump, breaking-in and allayed stay in a form open to its own proper negativity—has no outer limit. Thanks to its own inner limit, to this contraction, or this strangulation it gives *itself*, this structure avoids losing itself in abstract indetermination (here, for example, cosmopolitanism "without form" or the world republic, and so on). But its generality meets no obstacle outside. This structure regulates the relation between absolute spirit and all its "powers" or determinate figures.

And this structure organizes in the same stroke [*du même coup*] the Hegelian text. All commentary is disqualified that, as commentary, would not follow its prescription or would hang about hesitating between explication or rupture, within all the oppositional couples generally maintaining the history of the historians of philosophy. No displacement is possible of this history without displacing—this word itself must be reinterpreted—what in the text called Hegelian imposes this rule of reading, say a displacement that itself escapes the dialectic law and its strict rhythm.

We do not yet seem to be there, and that can no more be done at one go [*d'un coup*] than by a continuous approach. The event cannot be as noisy as a bomb, as garish or blazing as some metal held in the fire. Even were it still an event, here it would be—strict-ure against strict-ure—inapparent and marginal.

Glas is written here—uniquely—to celebrate, in the depths of an absolute crypt, that *calendar trick* [coup de calendrier] whose chance will have marked an epoch. And a blink of the eye [*clin d'oeil*] in "The Strange Word of . . ." or in "Plato's Pharmacy."

The place of the one who writes must always be sought, even if it is not fixed, if it lets no more than the replacement be caught. John [*Jean*] does not name himself, but does not hesitate to point to himself, under his own pen, as Christ's preferred disciple. He lies with him, in any case on his breast [*sein*]. Denunciation of Judas: "Truly truly I tell you that one of you will betray me. The disciples looked at each other, wondering which was the one he spoke of. One of the disciples, whom Jesus loved, was lying close beside the breast of Jesus; so Simon Peter nodded to this man and said to him: Tell us which is the one of whom he is speaking. So this man leaned back so that he was close to the breast of Jesus and said to him: Lord, who is it? Jesus answered: It is the one for whom I will dip a morsel of bread and give it to him." Judas takes it but does not eat it. John replaces Jesus at the side of his mother and takes her to his house. After Pilate had said, "What I have written, I have written," in the Gospel signed John (*Jean*): "But by the cross of Jesus stood his mother; and his mother's sister, Mary the wife of Clopas; and Mary the Magdalene. So Jesus, seeing his mother with the disciple whom he loved standing beside her, said to his mother: Mother, here is your son. Then he said to the disciple: Here is your mother. And from that moment the disciple took her into his own household."

Like the downshifting multiplication into a crowd of Johns (the author, the narrator, the narratee, the dead), the play of bands envelops the Gospel in its *Funeral Rites* and mimes the resurrection: "So she [Mary Magdalene] ran back until she came to Simon Peter and the other disciple, whom Jesus loved, and said to them: They have taken our Lord from the tomb, and we do not know where they have put him. So Peter and the other disciple came out, and went to the tomb. The two ran together, but the other disciple ran faster than Peter and reached the tomb first, and bent down and looked in and saw the bands lying there, but he did not go inside. Then Simon Peter came, following him, and he went into the tomb; and he saw the bands lying there, and the napkin, which had been on his head lying not with the bands but away from them and folded." You see how he writes

To read Hegel from the inside, the problematic of *Sittlichkeit*, and then, in that, of the family, can henceforth be unfolded only in a philosophy of spirit. The absolute ethical totality having been defined "people-spirit" (*Volksgeist*), its genealogy must be traced. That is the task of the first philosophy of spirit (Jena). The three "powers" of consciousness (1. Memory, language. 2. The tool. 3. Possession, family.) constitute the spirit of a people at the term of their development. From an architectonic viewpoint, the third power, the family, marking the passage to *Sittlichkeit*, occupies at the same time [*du même coup*] the first phase, forms the first moment of ethical life, its most immediate and most natural moment. That will be confirmed, if such can be said, fifteen years later, in the *Philosophy of Right*.

In effect, right after it set out the third power, the Jena philosophy of spirit describes the *transition* from the family to the people. A transition in the strong and active sense of this word: self-destructive passage. The family, through marriage, possession, and education, annihilates or relieves itself, "sacrifices" itself, Hegel says. And consequently, in the course of a struggle for recognition, the family loses and reflects itself in another consciousness: the people. The family exists in the people only "relieved" (*aufgehobene*), destroyed, preserved, debased, degraded, raised.

What is consciousness, if its ultimate power is achieved by the family?

Consciousness is the Idea's or absolute being's return to self. Absolute being takes itself back, it is *sich zurücknehmend*, it retracts itself, contracts itself, reassumes and reassembles itself, surrounds and envelops itself with itself after its death in nature, after it lost itself, "fell," Hegel literally says, outside itself in(to) nature. The philosophy of nature is the system of this *fall* [chute] and this dissociation in(to) exteriority. The philosophy of spirit is the system of the relief of the idea that calls and thinks itself in the ideal element of universality.

The *transition* from nature to spirit is also a reversal. In its highest reaches, the transition is produced in the *organic*, after the mechanical, the chemical, and the physical. The transition signifying violent self-destruction and passage to the opposite, the relief of natural life in(to) spiritual life necessarily comes about through disease and death. So disease and death are the conditions of the spirit and of all its determinations, among others, the family.

Among others only?

The last chapters of the Jena *Philosophy of Nature*—more precisely the last sections of the last chapter—concern the "process of disease." Dissolution of natural life, disease works at the transition toward the spirit. The life of the spirit thus becomes the essence, the present truth of the past, the *Gewesenheit* of natural dissolution, of natural death. "With disease the animal transgresses (*über-*

his *Funeral Rites* and the remain(s): with the assiduous gestures of a philologist, an archeologist, a mythologist bent on dispersing, destroying, crossing out whatever he finds or reconstitutes. The most critical operation. But his assiduousness is strange, as if distracted from itself. He always seems in fact to be assiduous about something else, detached from what he does. He tells you another (hi)story, you follow the narrative attentively; he shows you this or that with a finger, and yet (this hanging counterpart) fucks [*encule*] you, his eyes elsewhere. He thus fully comes [*jouit*], as in his paradigm, and thinks there "I recognize a recurrence of my childhood love [*goûts*] of tunnels. I bugger [*encule*] the world" (*Funeral Rites*). "He rams it in. So hard and calmly that anuses and vaginas slip [*s'enfilent*] onto his member like rings on a finger. He rams it in. So hard and calmly that his virility, observed by the heavens, has the penetrating force of the battalions of blond warriors who on June 14, 1940, buggered [*enculèrent*] us soberly and seriously, though their eyes were elsewhere as they marched in the dust and sun" (*Our-Lady-of-the-Flowers*).

The rings do not only glide onto the finger, as onto all the glottises pointed in erection in the text (I leave it to you to seek out the "signifiers" there, if you wish; it is full of daggers, jokes [*blagues*], algae, scabs [*gales*] elaborated under his fly); they are also stolen from the fingers of the old man who stammers like a baby. "The old man undid his chain, from which the watch [*la montre*] was hanging, and went forward to hand it to Stilitano, who took it.

"'Your rings.'

"'My rings . . .'

"The old man was now stammering. Stilitano, standing motionless in the middle of the room, pointed sharply to the objects that he wanted. I was a little behind him, to his left, with my hands in my pockets, and I regarded him in the looking glass. I was sure that he would thus be, as he faced the trembling old queer, more cruel than nature. In fact, when the old man told him that his knotted joints prevented him from removing the rings, he ordered me to turn on [*faire couler*] the water.

"'Soap yourself.'

"Very conscientiously, the old man soaped his hands. He tried to take off his two gold signet rings, but without

schreitet) the limits of its nature; but animal disease is the becoming of the spirit." In the dissociation of the natural organization, the spirit reveals itself. It was working biological life, like nature in general, from its negativity and manifests itself therein as such at the end; spirit will always have been nature's essence; nature is within spirit as its being-outside-self. In freeing itself from the natural limits that were imprisoning it, the spirit returns to itself but without ever having left itself. A procession of returning (home). The limit was within it; the spirit was chaining up, contracting, imprisoning itself *within itself*. It always repeats itself. The end of the analysis of animal disease: "*Nature exists in the spirit, as in what is its essence.*"

This joint will assure, in the circle of the *Encyclopedia*, the circle itself, the return to the philosophy of spirit. There again, after analyzing the genus animal and the sexual relationship, the last sections of the philosophy of nature treat of disease and death. Here the question would be to accomplish the teleology inaugurated by Aristotle, reawakened by Kant, the concept of internal finality having nearly been lost between them, in modern times. This internal finality, not conscious, as would be the position of an exterior end, is of the order of "instinct (*Instinkt*)" and remains "unconscious." Instinct here is a determination of pressure (*Trieb*).

The normal fulfillment of the biological process and, in it, of the generic process is death. Death is natural. And in the same stroke violent: no contradiction in that, no other contradiction than the contradiction internal to the process [*processus*].

Genus designates the simple unity that remains (close) by itself in each singular subject, in each representative or example of itself. But as this simple universality is produced in judgment, in the primordial separation (*Urteil*), it tends to go out of itself in order to escape morseling, division, and to find, meet itself again back home, as subjective universality. This process of reassembling, of regrouping, denies the natural universality that tends to lose itself and divide itself. The natural living one must then die. The necessary differentiation of genus that determines itself in species provokes the war. The species inflicts on itself a violent death. The genus naturally produces itself through its own violent self-destruction. Lamarck and Cuvier—cited at length—knew how to choose the criteria of specific differentiation: the teeth, claws, etc., the "weapons" by which the animal "establishes and preserves itself as a being-for-self, that is, differentiates itself."

Man does not escape, as living in nature, this war of species. This war is the negative face of the genus division. In its primordial partition (*Urteil*), genus divides or multiplies itself into specific morsels only in order to reassemble itself (close) by itself. The bellicose and morseling operation of the generic process (*Gattungsprozess*) doubles itself with an affirmative reappropriation. The

success. Desperate, and fearing that his fingers might be cut off [*coupât*], he gave his hand to Stilitano, with the timid anxiety of a bride at the foot of the altar. . . . Stilitano tried to pull the rings off. With one hand the old man held up the other which was being worked on. . . . As one does with babies, or as I myself would soap his one hand, Stilitano carefully soaped the old man's."
After calmly insisting, Stilitano slaps [*gifle*] the old man and gives up on the rings.

The annulus is too tight [*serré*]. Let us not give up. What I am trying to write—gl—is not just any structure whatever, a system of the signifier or the signified, a thesis or a novel, a poem, a law, a desire or a machine, but what passes, more or less well, through the rhythmic strict-ure of an annulus.

Try, one anniversary day, to push a ring around an erected, extravagant, stretched style

obal" event.

". . . the sort of thing that must have been felt by Josephine, she who never forgot that she had given birth to the child who was to become the prettiest woman in the village, Marie, the mother of Sólange—the goddess born in a hovel who had more blazons on her body than Mimosa had on her buttocks and in her gestures, and more nobility than a Chambure. This kind of consecration had kept the other women of her age (the others, mothers of men) away from Josephine. In the village, her situation was akin

singularity rejoins, repairs, or reconciles itself with itself within the genus. The individual "continues itself" in another, feels and experiences itself in another. That begins with need and the "feeling of this lack." The lack is opened with the inadequation of the individual to the genus. The genus is in the individual as a gap [écart], a tension (Spannung). Whence lack, need, pressure: the movement to reduce the wound of the gap, to close the cut [plaie], to draw together its lips. In the same stroke [du même coup], pressure tends to *accomplish* just what it strictly reduces, the gap of the individual to the genus, of genus to itself in the individual, the *Urteil*, the primordial division and judgment. This operation consisting of filling in the gap, of uniting one to the other by carrying out the *Urteil* in the most pronounced way, is *copulation*. The word for copulation or coupling, for this general play of the copula, is *Begattung*, the operation of the genus (*Gattung*), the generic and generative operation. Just as what is rightly translated by sexual relationship (*Geschlechtsverhältnis*) also designates the relationship of genus, species, or race (family, lineage) or the sex relationship as the feminine or masculine gender (*Geschlecht*).

As is often the case, the section concerning the "sexual relationship" and copulation is augmented with an "appendix" by which precisely is abridged the classic *Encyclopedia of the Philosophical Sciences in Outline*. This addition (*Zusatz*) takes up again, almost literally, the end of the Jena *Philosophy of Nature*. In it Hegel treats of the sexual difference. "The separation of the two sexes" presents a very singular structure of separation. In each sex the organic individuals form a totality. But they do not relate to those of the other sex as inorganic alterity. On each side they belong to the genus, "so that they exist only as *a single Geschlecht* (sex or gender)." "Their union is the effacement of the sexes, in which the simple genus has come into being (*Ihre Vereinigung ist das Verschwinden der Geschlechter, worin die einfache Gattung geworden ist*)." When two individuals of the same species copulate, "the nature of each goes throughout both, and both find themselves within the sphere of this generality." Each one is, as the party taking part, as the receiving party, at once a part and a whole; this general structure recuts and overlaps [recoupe] them both, passes as bisexuality in each of them. What each one is in (it)self (a single species), each one actually posits as such in copulation. "The idea of nature here is actual in the male and female couple [pair, *Paare*]; up till now their identity and their being-for-self merely were for us only in our reflection, but they are now, in the infinite reflection of both sexes, experienced by themselves within themselves. This feeling of generality is the highest to which the animal can be brought."

"Contradiction" inherent to the difference of sexes: both the generality of genus and the identity of individuals (its belonging to the genus) are "different" from their separate, particular (*besonderen*)

to that of the mother of Jesus among the women of the Galilean village. Marie's beauty made the town illustrious. To be the human mother of a divinity is a more disturbing state than that of divinity. The mother of Jesus must have had incomparable emotions while carrying her son, and later, while living and sleeping side by side with a son who was God—that is, everything and herself as well—who could make the world not be, his mother, himself not be, a God for whom she had to prepare, as Josephine did for Marie, the yellow corn mush."

Then—it is the global event of this text—the elaboration of Harcamone's dream begins.

Like Jean, Harcamone "wanted . . . to make a calendar," but he fails at it, he "was unable to have a calendar. His dead life followed its course to infinity. He wanted to flee." So repeating the murder of the little girl and thereby disguising his suicide, he kills a guard. He acts as the artist of his life. He constructs his life as a column or as a tower, but he can see it [la voir], have it [l'avoir], know [savoir] it only in putting an end to it. The structure of the tower is such that its construction returns, stone by stone, to its destruction: one tower, two towers, one is (without) the other. "He had to raise his destiny, as one raises a tower, had to give this destiny tremendous importance, towering importance, unique and solitary, and had to build it out of all his minutes. It seems to you impossible that I dare ascribe to a petty thief [un voleur sans envergure] the act of building his life minute by minute, witnessing its construction, which is also progressive destruction."

individuality. "The individual is only one of the two individuals, and exists not as unity (*Einheit*), but only as singularity (*Einzelheit*)." Sexual difference opposes unity to singularity and thereby introduces contradiction into the genus or into the process of *Urteil*, into what produces and lets itself be constituted by this contradiction. Producing the contradiction, this process resolves the contradiction: the process of copulation aims at preserving, while annulling, this difference.

Copulation relieves the difference: *Aufhebung* is very precisely the relation of copulation and the sexual difference.

The relief in general cannot be understood without sexual copulation, nor sexual copulation in general without the relief. *In general*: if one takes into account that the *Aufhebung* is described here in a strictly determinate (strangulated) moment of the becoming of the idea (the final moment of the philosophy of nature)—but also that this moment of life is re-marked at the term of the philosophy of spirit—then the *Aufhebung* of the sexual difference is, manifests, expresses, *stricto sensu*, the *Aufhebung* itself and in general.

Still in the appendix: "The activity of the animal consists in relieving this difference (*Die Tätigkeit des Tiers ist, diesen Unterschied aufzuheben*)." The process indeed has the form of a syllogism. And the "mediation or middle term" of the syllogism is the gap [*écart*] (*Spannung*), the inadequation between the individual and the genus, the necessity for the singular to look for the "self-feeling" in the other.

What are the conditions of this relieving copulation? In describing what he calls the formation of the sexual difference—or more precisely of the different sexes (*die Bildung der unterschiedenen Geschlechter*)—Hegel subjects to the most traditional, in any case Aristotelian, philosophical interpretation what he considers the assured acquisitions of the epoch's anatomical science. He found there the proof of a hierarchic-arranging dissymmetry.

The formation of the different sexes must be "different," differentiated. By reason of the "primordial identity of the formation," the sexual parts of the male and the female must certainly belong to the "same type," but in one or the other this or that part constitutes the "essential (*das Wesentliche*)." In the type's generality, all the parts then are present in each sex, but one dominates here, the other there, in order to constitute the essence of the sex. The morphological type is bisexual in its underlying and microscopic structure. Within this structure, one element's prevailing provokes the hierarchy between the sexes.

But the difference is not so simple. To say that one element dominates here, the other there, is not enough: in the female the essence consists of indifference—rather the indifferent (*das Indifferente*), in the male the essence consists in the difference, the

Like the executioners, like the convicts [*galériens*], like Our-Lady-of-the-Flowers, Harcamone is a virgin, as is true for all flowers.

And his dream—the dream of him—repeats the same process, the same trial [*le même procès*].

After some gl strokes [*coups de gl*], as always, some detours twisted in "eglantine" and "wisteria," the four black men, penetrating inside Harcamone by ear and mouth, are drawn into a furious and avid, frightened, astonished, infinitely adventurous exploration of a body bigger than they, a body that seems to have carried them inside itself even before they dream of breaking in, and whose center or issue they would rather seek. Globally mimed, glossed, parodied, all world literature of oedipal crossroads, circumnavigations, odysseys, calvaries, descents into hell, trips through pyramids, labyrinths, mausoleums, marvelous lands, crypts at the ocean bottom. One is in the element of the elements. It is sometimes a laborious march, sometimes a flight [*vol*] without obstacle; a navigation as well. I only arraisound [*arrésonne*] the stroke of the looking glass [*coup de glace*] in the labyrinth there (that reflects, among other ecplosions there [*éclats*], the regard in the Rembrandt's looking glass and the stroke of the "*je m'éc*," *échange*, *écœure* [disgust], *écoule* [flow], *écris* [write], *écoute* [listen]) that organizes its displacement [*déport*].

"Finally, all four met at a kind of crossroads which I cannot describe accurately. It led down, again to the left, into a luminous corridor lined with huge mirrors. . . .

" 'The heart—have you found the heart?'

divided-in-two, rather, the opposition (*das Entzweite, der Gegensatz*). Male and female are not opposed as two differents, two terms of the opposition, but as indifference and difference (opposition, division). The sexual difference is the difference between indifference and difference. But each time, in order to *relieve* itself, *difference* must be determined in/as *opposition*.

So difference is produced through the general identity of the anatomical type that goes on differentiating itself. In the lower animals, the difference is hardly marked at all. Certain locusts, for example the *Gryllus verruccivorus*, a kind of grasshopper, bear large testicles coming from vessels twisted into rolls like fascicles, testicles similar to large ovaries coming from egg ducts themselves rolled into fascicles. The same analogy between the testicles and the ovarian sacs of gadflies.

"The greatest difficulty": "discovering the female uterus in the male sexual parts." Unfortunately, it was thought to be recognized in the testicle sac, in the scrotum, since the testicles shape up [*s'annoncent*] precisely as what corresponds to the ovaries. Now, instead, the prostate fulfils in man a function qualified to the uterus's. In the man, the uterus lowers itself, falls to the state of a gland, in a kind of undifferentiated generality. Hegel refers here to Ackermann's *Darstellung der Lebenskräfte*. Ackermann has shown, on his hermaphrodite, the place of the uterus in the "former masculine formations." But this uterus is not only in (the) place of the prostate: the ejaculatory ducts also go through its substance and open at the *crista galli*, into the urethra. The lips of the vulva are moreover testicle sacs, and testicle formations filled the lips of the hermaphrodite. The medial line of the scrotum finally parts in the woman and forms the vagina. "In this way, the transformation (*Umbildung*) of one sex into the other is understandable. Just as in the man the uterus sinks down to a mere gland, so in the woman, the masculine testicle remains enclosed, enveloped (*eingeschlossen*) within the ovary."

An apparently anatomical description. Now in its vocabulary and its syntax, the hierarchic evaluation mobilizes the object. The testicle "*bleibt eingeschlossen*," remains enclosed, enveloped. The development, the bringing to light, the production has been insufficient, delayed, lagging behind [*en reste*]. From this teleological interpretation is drawn a very marked speculative conclusion: "On the other hand, the male testicle in the woman remains enclosed within the ovary, does not project into opposition (*tritt nicht heraus in den Gegensatz*), does not become for itself, does not become an active brain (*wird nicht für sich, zum tätigen Gehirn*), and the clitoris is inactive feeling in general."

"The clitoris is inactive feeling in general," "*der Kitzler ist das untätige Gefühl überhaupt*," in general, absolutely, chiefly, above all, principally. Who and what says *überhaupt*?

"And realizing at once that none of them had found it, they continued their way along the corridor, tapping and listening to the mirrors. They advanced slowly, cupping their ears and often flattening [*collée*] them against the wall. It was the executioner who first heard the beats [*coups frappés*]. . . . The beats were nearer and louder. Finally, the four black men came to a looking glass on which was drawn (obviously carved with the diamond of a ring) a heart pierced by an arrow."

After a first chamber, the upsurging of a young drummer whose drumstick [*baguette*] (cutting like the ring [*la bague*], inaccessible and tumultuous) fell back [*retombait*], there remains discovering the "mystery of the hidden chamber." By getting to the heart of the heart, to the Mystic Rose, the four black men, each of whom is as if within the other (judge, lawyer, chaplain [*aumônier*], executioner in the same galley or the same palace), repeat, in Harcamone's breast [*sein*], the gesture of the virgin male. Harcamone himself being unable to "keep his flower any longer" had fallen (they also fall) on a little girl next to an eglantine bush and had passed "his hand under her skirt" before slashing her throat.

Dionysus Erigone Eriopetal Reseda.

"But no sooner did one of the four realize that they were not in the heart of the heart than a door opened by itself and we saw before us a red rose of monstrous size and beauty.

This dissymmetry is not compensated for by the fall of the uterus in the man. What does not yet emerge in the woman is sexual activity. The sexual difference reproduces the hierarchical opposition of passivity to activity, of matter to form. Hegel always, expressly, determines Reason as Activity. The *Aufhebung*, the central concept of the sexual relation, articulates the most traditional phallocentrism with the Hegelian onto-theo-teleo-logy.

Production, differentiation, opposition are bound to the value activity. That is the system of virility. The clitoris, which resembles the penis, is passive; "in the man on the contrary, we have there active sensibility (*haben wir dafür das tätige Gefühl*), the overflowing swelling of the heart (*das aufschwellende Herz*), the blood rushing into the *corpora cavernosa* and into the meshes of the spongy tissue of the urethra.

who, we? magisterial we, we of *Sa*, we men? And what if it were always the same? And who-we-assists-us here

To this rushing of blood in the man corresponds then in the woman the effusion of blood." The same abundance of blood fills and rises on the one side, pours out and is lost on the other. Swelling [*gonflement*] of the heart also says erection; *Aufschwellen* often signifies turgescence, intumescence.

Man's superiority costs him an inner division. In passively receiving, woman remains one (close) by herself; she works less but lets herself be worked (over) less by negativity. "The receiving [*Das Empfangen*: this is also the conceiving of childbirth] of the uterus, as simple behavior, is in the man, in this way, divided in two (*entzweit*) into the productive brain and the external heart (*in das produzierende Gehirn und das äusserliche Herz*). The man then, through this difference, is the active (*Der Mann ist also durch diesen Unterschied das Tätige*); but the woman is the receptacle (*das Empfangende*), because she remains in her undeveloped unity (*weil sie in ihrer unentwickelten Einheit bleibt*)."

Remaining enveloped in the undifferentiated unity, the woman keeps herself nearer the origin. The man is secondary, as the difference that causes passing into the opposition. Paradoxical consequences of all phallocentrism: the hardworking and determining male sex enjoys mastery only in losing it, in subjugating itself to the feminine slave. The phallocentric hierarchy is a feminism; dialectically feminism, making man the *subject* of woman, submits itself to Femininity and Truth, both capitalized.

Subject and form: "*Coitus* must not be reduced to the ovary and the sperm as if the new formation were merely the assemblage of forms or parts of two partners, for the feminine certainly contains the material element, while the male contains the subjectivity. Conception is the contraction of the whole individual into the

"'The Mystic Rose,' murmured the chaplain.

"The four men were floored by the splendor. The rays of the rose dazzled them at first, but they quickly pulled themselves together, for such people never permit themselves to show signs of respect. . . . Recovering from their agitation [*émoi*], they rushed in, pushing back [*écartant*] the petals and crumpling them with their drunken hands, as a lecher who has been deprived of sex pushes back a whore's skirt. They were in the throes of drunken profanation. With their temples throbbing and their brows beaded with sweat, they reached the heart of the rose. It was a kind of dark pit [*puits*]. At the very edge of this hole, which was as black and as deep as an eye, they leaned forward and were seized with a kind of vertigo. All four made the gestures of people losing their balance, and they fell into that deep regard.

"I hear the clopping of the horses that were bringing the wagon in which the victim was to be taken to the little cemetery. He had been executed eleven days after Bulkaen had been shot. Divers was still sleeping. He merely grunted a few times. He farted. A singular fact: I did not go limp [*ne débandai pas*] all night long."

deep regard of a judas. This scene handed over to a multitude of *people* [*gens*] ("such people never permit themselves to show signs of respect. . . . the gestures of people losing their balance," but to what people? I have no way of knowing whether these are profaning Gentiles, goyim, Christians or Jews, who split themselves or sign themselves.) falls (to the tomb) in a deep regard. Abyssal, this regard falls (entombs), and first by not guarding coldly its sense. In painting, a *regard* is the disposition of two figures who see one another. Example from Littré: "He has a *regard* of a Christ and a Virgin in his collection." The *regard* is also the opening of a hole through which one watches over water drainage.
Double regard. Cross-eyed [*bigle*: bi-gl] reading. While keeping an eye on the corner column [*la colonne d'angle*] (the contraband), read this as a new testament.
But also as a genesis. *The Thief's Journal* that is soon going to decline its identity, as one declines one's responsibility, is presented as "my book, become my Genesis." Elsewhere, as "*my nativity*."

simple self-abandoning unity, into its representation (*in seine Vorstellung*). . . ." The seed is this simple representation itself, entirely reduced to one single "point," "as the name and the entire self." "Conception then is nothing but this: the opposed, this abstract representation become *a single one*."

This discourse on sexual difference belongs to the philosophy of nature. It concerns the natural life of differentiated animals. Silent about the lower animals and about the limit that determines them, this discourse excludes plants. There would be no sexual difference in the plants, the first "*Potenz*" of the organic process. The Jena philosophy of nature stresses this. The tuber, for example, is undoubtedly divided (*entzweit sich*) into a "different *opposition* (*differenten* Gegensatz)" of masculine and feminine, but the difference remains "formal." This difference does not produce totalities, individual plants where some would be male and others female. "The difference between male plants and female plants is only a difference of parts on the same plant, not the formation of two individuals." Hegel notes in passing that in the cryptogam in general the sexual parts are assumed to be "infinitely small."

In this sense, the human female, who has not developed the difference or the opposition, holds herself nearer the plant. The clitoris nearer the cryptogam.

There is no conceptual gap [*écart*], in this regard, between the *Encyclopedia* and the Jena philosophy. The Jena philosophy describes the generic process as "the relief of the difference": the relief of the difference opposed to the inorganic process becomes a difference of sexes and the relief of this first difference. And in a note crossed out, the figure of the circle and the point is found again: the movement of the genus [*genre*] is within itself and returns within itself; this is the "circle properly so called"; but the movement of individuality moves as a larger circle in the smaller circles of the periphery and always touches them in one point.

This relief is also the movement that causes passing from nature to spirit. In both philosophies of nature, the sections of articulation with the philosophy of spirit analyze sexual difference, disease, and death. After the naturally violent death (the negative face of the

The hanging counterpart, the decapitation of the other, however, parted in two.

"A singular fact," a fact as little singular, however, as thinking (this hanging counterpart)—a paragraph further on, in (the) place itself of Harcamone's suffering, in the severing of the phallus that falls from the breast [*sein*] under the scaffold—about his rose, the one that has carried him and that he carries within him, more or less well digested.

"In order not to suffer too much myself, I made myself as supple as possible. For a moment, I was so flabby that it occurred to me that perhaps Harcamone had a mother—everyone knows that all men who are beheaded have a mother who comes to weep at the edge of the police cordon that guards the guillotine—I wanted to dream about her and Harcamone, already parted in two; I said softly in my state of fatigue: 'I'm going to pray for your mamma.'"

And if the reading of the Bible is not as familiar to you as it is to a slightly vicious choirboy, it is useless to continue, you will not follow, you will not be in the cortège.

And if you protest against the strabismus that someone wants to inflict on you, it is enough for you to seek out why. Querelle, who also draws a benefit from his strabismus, assumes his "*incurable wound*" and, like Stilitano, Giacometti, and the whole class of one-armed, the lame, the one-eyed, thereby makes himself loved, named, sublimated, magnified. He does not get angry, on the contrary, when "*I fixed my stare on him and told him*:

"'*Do you have a slight strabismus?*'" (*Querelle*).

Deep, stereoscopic regard. To see double. Two columns, two hills [*collines*], two breasts. It is impossible. The *colpos*, between the one and the two. You then divide yourself, you feel nauseated, you want to vomit, your head turns you around. You seem more than alone, more alone than ever. Without me. But jealous of yourself, you erect yourself, if you still can. More than ever you want to. It is exactly in *Querelle*, three lines in italics, with no apparent link with what precedes or follows, between two white spaces:

"*You are alone in the world, at night, in the solitude of an endless [immense] esplanade. Your double statue reflects itself in each one of its halves. You are solitaries, and live in that double solitude of yours.*"
It is the end

generic inadequation), after copulation (the positive relationship of genus to itself), another negativity works (over) the indefinite reproduction of the genus, the nonhistoricity and the faulty infinite of natural life. The genus preserves itself only by the decline and the death of individuals: old age, disease, and spontaneous death. In disease, the total organism is divided, not just differentiated, but morseled in its relationship to the inorganic, to the inorganic *Potenz*. Entering into conflict with this inorganic *Potenz*, one of the individual's systems or organs separates itself from the whole, acquires a kind of abnormal independence that injures the "fluidity" of the whole, the circulation of inner exchanges. The cause of this is an external attack originating from the inorganic, a heterogeneous "excitement (*Erregung*)." Such an appendix, laden with an enormous culture, goes back to Herodotus and to Heraclitus's aphorisms on fever, makes use of all the medical learnings of the epoch, takes stock on syphilis, treats of the "third kind" [*genre, Art*] of diseases, those of the soul, which are peculiar to man (the *Encyclopedia* proposes a discourse on madness or insanity and refers to Pinel), which can arise from fear or grief and can go even to the point of death.

The recovery process is disease itself. As for the treatise on the remedy, it largely overlaps [*déborde*] that of the illness. Like disease, the remedy is an *Erregung*, an external and aggressive excitement [*stimulation*]. The remedy always remains difficult to assimilate, as the organism's other. A counterexcitement destined to "relieve" the first attack, the remedy ought to be analyzed under the category of digestion: by essence the remedy is indigestible, "intolerable." A medicament is not digested more or less well; as the organism's absolute other, it is never digested. This limit is that of the speculative dialectics of digestion and of interiorization. The more one is raised in(to) the differentiating hierarchy of animalness, the more the easily digestible can be heterogeneous to the organism, the more the organism is capable of assimilating foreign bodies or differentiated organic totalities. Conversely, at the bottom of the ladder, in the vegetal or animal life incapable of "difference in (it)self," the easily digestible can be only the homogeneous, homogeneous to (it)self, homogeneous in (it)self: water for the plants, mother's milk (predigested element) for the nurslings. The more differentiation increases, the more the stimulus must be differentiated and heterogeneous in (it)self for the organism to support it. The stimulus can be homogeneous to the organism only at the rate of an equal degree of heterogeneity: thus maternal milk, like water, would be badly tolerated by the adult. That is what Hegel says. Logically, this leads to food composed of meat for man. And even to anthropophagy: anthropophagy is conceptually required by speculative idealism. Speculative idealism even reaches its highest point in anthropophagy at the opening of *Sa*.

He makes himself "as supple as possible," twists around himself, *E tu, lenta ginestra*.

The line of the parting in two not only encircles the neck [*cou*] severed by the guillotine; it overlaps the edge of the cordon (of police) that separates him, detaches him from the remain(s) of his mother to which he was nonetheless (this hanging counterpart) bound again. It/she delimits the scaffold.

Remain(s)—the mother.

However, (this hanging counterpart) two pages

example of the counsels for reading I efface all the time: as I do not cease to decapitate metalanguage, or rather to replunge its head into the text in order to extract it from the text, regularly, the interval of a respiration, whoever reads *page* must gather up all that is in bed there. For example: "A while ago, in my cell, the two pimps said: 'We're making the pages.' They meant they were going to make the beds [*lits*], but a kind of luminous idea transformed me there, with my legs spread apart [*écartées*], into a husky guard or a palace groom who 'makes' a palace page just as a young man makes a chick.
"To hear this boasting made Divine swoon with pleasure, as when she disentangled—it seemed to her that she was unbuttoning a fly, that her hand, already inside, was pulling up the shirt—certain pig-latin words from their extra syllables, as an adornment [*parure*] or fancy dress [*travesti*]: edbay, allbay."

further on, at the penultimate sentence of the book, "The rest, the remain(s), is unsayable."

The medicaments (at least the allopathics: a note emphasizes homeopathy, and also hypochondria—Hegel was an expert on this—depression, hypnosis, refreshing sleep, etc.) are differentiated foods, but totally indigestible, negative, and foreign.

They are poisons. "In so far as they are *negative* stimuli, medicaments are poisons (*Gifte*)." To the organism that has, in disease, "alienated" itself so to speak, one presents, with the remedy, something that is foreign to it, from the outside (*als ein ihm* äusserliches *Fremdes*). Before this indigestible, "intolerable" stimulant, the organism retakes itself, reappropriates itself, engages a "process" that permits it to regain possession of its "self-feeling" and its "subjectivity." So the pharmaceutical intervention is effective only insofar as it is rejected, in a certain way. If the sick cannot vomit the pharmaceutical poison, and at the same time [*du même coup*] retake their own proper(ty), they die. But this death is not natural.

Will one conclude from this that every death of natural life is violent, that it gives way to war or disease? That there is not any natural death of natural life?

There is a natural death; it is inevitable for natural life, since it produces itself in finite individual totalities. These totalities are inadequate to the universal genus and they die from this. Death is this inadequation of the individual to generality; death is the *classification* itself, life's inequality to (it)self. In this sense, death also takes the figure of abstraction; it is only an abstraction, but this abstraction is a "power," a force at work in a process from which it cannot be abstracted.

Inadequation—classification and abstraction—of the generic syllogism: it has been demonstrated that inadequation placed in motion sexual difference and copulation. So sexual difference and copulation inhabit the same space; they have the same possibility and the same limit as natural death. And if the "inadequation to universality" is the "*original disease* (ursprüngliche Krankheit)" of the individual, as much ought to be able to be said of sexual difference. And if the inadequation to universality is for the individual its "inborn *germ of death* (Keim des Todes)," this must also be understood of sexual difference, and not only by "metaphor," by some figure whose sense would be completed by the word "death." *Germ of death* is almost tautological. At the bottom of the germ, such as it circulates in the gap [*écart*] of the sexual difference, that is, as the finite germ, death is prescribed, as germ in the germ. An infinite germ, spirit or God engendering or inseminating itself naturally, does not tolerate sexual difference. Spirit-germ disseminates itself only by feint. *In this feint*, it is immortal. *As* the Phoenix.

Reason in History specifies the limits it is advisable to recognize in the wingspan of the Phoenix: the Phoenix is

Then, the germ—finite germ of sexual difference, the germ of death—is it a metaphor of the infinite germ? Or the contrary?

Remain(s) is always said of the mother.

Who always wanted to re-g(u)ard the detachment as it parts. "I realize that I loved my Colony with my flesh just as, when it was reported that the Germans were preparing to leave, France realized, in losing the rigidity they had imposed on her, that she had loved them. She squeezed her buttocks. She begged the supplanter to stay inside her. 'Remain a while,' she cried. Thus, Touraine was no longer fecundated."

"These papers are their graves. But I shall transmit their name far down the ages. This name alone will remain in the future, divested of its object. . . . If I take leave of this book, I take leave of what can be related. The remain(s) is ineffable. I say no more and walk [*marche*] barefoot."

Right next to the end again, "Remain! (*SAÏD {the son} hesitates again, then leaves.*) Fire!" and "*THE MOTHER leaves last.*" She always leaves last, as the epiphany of the nearest. "*Finally, it is behind the last screen, that is, the one nearest the audience, and, tearing this last sheet of paper, appears: it is THE MOTHER.*"

The mother would present for analysis the term of a regression, a signified of the last instance, only if you knew what the mother names or means (to say), that with which she is pregnant. Now you would be able to know it only after you had exhausted all the remain(s), all the objects, all the names the text puts in her place (galley, gallery, executioner, flowers of every species are only *examples* of her). To the extent you will not have thoroughly spelled out each of these words and each of these things, there will remain something of the mother

I am (following) the mother. The text. The mother is *behind*—all that I follow, am, do, seem—the mother follows. As she follows absolutely, she always sur-

only an "image" of the spirit, an analogy drawn from the "natural life" of the body and, what's more, an "oriental image." With the image of the Phoenix and the idea of metempsychosis, oriental "metaphysics" would have reached its summit. For the Occidental, on the contrary, the spirit is younger, to be sure, in its resurrection, but it draws itself higher and into a clearer glory (*erhöht*, *verklärt*). It "enjoys itself" and "in the enjoyment of its activity it has only to do with itself."

The value of metaphor would be impotent to decide this if the value of metaphor was not itself reconstructed from this question.

"The relief of the inadequation," of sexual difference and of death, is the return to (it)self of the lost spirit, lost for a time, time itself, in nature. Natural life, in order to accomplish this "destiny," "kills itself." Suicide is natural; it is the working [*opération*] of the spirit in nature. Spirit understands itself as suicide; there it begins to resonate for itself, becomes an object for itself, consciousness of (it)self. There the spirit calls itself, names itself—spirit—recalls, recollects itself to itself. Just as the male sex activates itself by going out of the envelope that was holding it enclosed in the woman, the spirit goes out of the "dead envelope" that was still compressing it in nature: "*Über diesem Tode der Natur, aus dieser toten Hülle geht eine schönere Natur*, geht der Geist hervor." *Hülle* is the envelope, the veil, the mask, the skin, the sheath [*gaine*]. And spirit, "nature more beautiful," is then the raising of a corpse, a kind of limp erection [*érection débandée*], the glorious ascension of a "sloughed-off skin": dialectics of nature.

Such is the "concept of the philosophy of nature": the setting free of the concept that wants to reassemble itself close by itself after having organized the suicide of nature, that is, of its double, of its "mirror (*Spiegel*)," of its "reflection (*Reflex*)." The reflection captured the concept but also dispersed it in its image, in a kind of polymorphism that had to be reduced. The Proteus had strictly to be subjugated (*diesen Proteus zu bezwingen*). Nature will have asked for nothing else: "The purpose of nature is to kill itself and to break through its shell of the immediate, of the sensible, to consume itself like a Phoenix, in order to upsurge, rejuvenated, from this exteriority, as spirit."

The rhapsodic multiplicity of these figures accuses and accentuates precisely nature. The concept's spiritual unity must do violence to these figures in order to free itself from them. This operation, "this action of spirit is philosophy."

vives—a future that will never have been presentable—what she will have engendered, attending, impassive, fascinating and provoking; she survives the interring of the one whose death she has foreseen. Logic of obsequence. Such is the great genetic scene: the mother secutrix denounces, then lets the son die—whom she transforms because of that into a daughter—leaves her, because of that makes her die and simulates, the divine whore, a suicide.

See, farther on, that calculus of the mother.

What in sum she wants, she first of all: to take back the—her—*glas* from the son, masturbate her own breast, ring by herself the—her—own tocsin (what her son desires in her place). And to remain, or to leave last, when no one will have any more time. What can a mother do better?
But to the extent that she is there, to represent herself and detach herself from herself, you can always sign yourself to death [*vous crever à signer*], she transforms your act into a sin in all tongues, your text into *ersatz*, your paraph into a fake. She takes you by the hand and you always countersign.

Subject of denunciation: I call myself my mother who calls herself (in) me. To give, to accuse. Dative, accusative. I bear my mother's name, I am (following) my mother's name, I call my mother to myself, I call my mother for myself, I call my mother in myself, recall myself to my mother. I decline the same subjugation in all cases.

The calculus of the mother—that I am (following): Ah! if my mother could assist me at my interment

you will not have exhausted. As there is no object and hence no knowledge that is not of the mother, the proposition of absolute knowledge "it is the Mother" forms the screen [*le paravent*] of a tautology, verily the hymen that bursts (is bursting with) itself. Once the screen is analyzed, one guards (against) nothing. The *para* falls (to the tomb) in the wind [*vent*], or remain(s) suspended in farts.

The family has still not been met. At least not the human family, what, by a convenience more and more problematic, one would yet be tempted to call the family *properly so called*: neither the infinite Holy Family, nor the natural cell of the finite living.

The analysis of the human family now seems accessible: on coming out of nature, when the spirit takes itself back, becomes an object for itself in consciousness. The first philosophy of spirit, at Jena, inscribes the first determination of the human family in a theory of consciousness. So its organizing concepts are those of *Potenz* and *Mitte*, power and middle term, middle [*milieu*], center. The family is the third *Potenz*, the ultimate, of consciousness. It achieves itself in *Sittlichkeit* and in the people-spirit.

The spirit's return to (it)self, consciousness is the simple and immediate contrary of itself, is what it is conscious of, to wit its opposite. At once active and passive, identifying itself with its own proper opposite, consciousness separates itself from/by itself as from its object, but hems itself in as the strict unity of its own proper separation: "On the other hand (*das andre Mal*), consciousness is the contrary of this separation, the absolute being-one (*Einsein*) of the difference, the being-one of the existent difference and of the relieved difference." As such, as the two opposites *and* the movement of opposition, the differents *and* the difference, consciousness is *Mitte*, mediation, middle, medium.

Consequently, each "power" of consciousness will have the determination of a middle. And since consciousness is the relief of nature in(to) spirit, each of these middles guards within itself a natural relieved determination. Each corresponds every time to the idealization of a natural middle, and consciousness is the middle of ideality in general, then of universality in general. It is ether: absolutely welcoming transparency offering no resistance. Ether is not natural, like air, but it is not purely spiritual. It is the middle in which the spirit relates to itself, repeats itself in going through nature like the wind.

Consciousness idealizes nature in denying it, produces itself *through* what it denies (or relieves). Through: the going through and the transgression leave in the ideal middle the analogical mark of the natural middle. Thus there is a power and a middle corresponding to the air: memory and language; next, to the earth: labor and tool. In the case of the family, the third power, an essential supplementary complication: the middle through which my family produces itself is no longer *inorganic* like air or earth. It is no longer simply external to the ideal middle. More than one consequence will follow.

The rain has dispersed the spectators who run in all directions [*sens*]. What, in sum, is it all about? About citing, about reciting the *genêt* for pages at a time? About interpreting it, executing it like a piece [*morceau*] of music? Who is being mocked. What is being proposed to us. Flourishes? Flowery cadenzas? An anthology? by what right. And the complete text, is it being dissimulated from us?

Not even an anthology. Some morsels [*morceaux*] of anthology. As an invitation, if possible, to rebind [*relier*], to reread [*relire*] in any case. Inside out and right side out, while taking up again by all the ends.

Nevertheless, all these morsels cannot, naturally, be bound.

The object of the present work, and its style too, is the *morsel*.

Which is always detached, as its name indicates and so that you don't forget it, by the teeth.

The object of the present piece of work (*ouvrage*) (code of the dressmaker) is what remains of a bite, a sure death [*une morsure*], in the throat [*gorge*]: the bit [*mors*].

Insofar as it cannot, naturally, bind (band) itself (erect).

Graft itself at the very most, that it can still do.

The graft that sews itself [*se coud*], the substitution of the supplementary *seing* "constitutes" the text. Its necessary heterogeneity, its interminable network of listening lines *en allo*, in hello, that compels reckoning with the insert, the patch.

How does the family come to air and earth, that is, to language and memory, to labor and the tool?

Homogeneous and fluid, air allows showing through and resonating, seeing and hearing. Theoretico-phonic middle. The first power of consciousness is "pure theoretical existence." It determines and holds itself back as such in memory, that is, without solid assistance. The question is evidently of the pure and living memory, a memory that would be purely evanescent without language, which furnishes it stable but still completely interior and spontaneous products. But because of this interiority and this spontaneity, language is a product that effaces itself in time. In time theoretical consciousness also disappears. It cannot *posit itself*, exist as theoretical consciousness. To do that, it must then go out of itself, pass yet into its opposite, deny its own proper theoreticity, its *air*. Theoretical consciousness cannot posit itself as theoretical consciousness except by becoming practical consciousness, through the earthly element. To the memory then is chained labor, to the linguistic product of memory the tool and the product of labor. Just as language was at once the effect and the organ of memory, the tool (*Werkzeug*) serves the labor from which it proceeds. In both cases, an activity gives rise to the production of a permanence, of an element of relative subsistence.

The family presupposes the two preceding powers, but it also goes through the *organic* element, desire and sexual difference. The permanent product is the child and family goods (*Familiengut*). Family property, proprietorship, finally raises inorganic nature (earth and air) to the ideality of a universal proprietorship guaranteed by juridical rationality. Then the ether again becomes absolute, and the family accomplishes itself by disappearing, by denying its singularity in the people-spirit.

Such is the general schema. Let us regard more closely the transition from the second to the ultimate *Potenz*, that is, the origin of the family.

In language, the invisible sonorous, evanescent middle, theoretical consciousness effaces itself, denies itself, reduces itself to the punctual instant. So the theoretical freedom in that instant is negative and formal. As it is only a point, this freedom converts itself into its contrary. Its universality becomes pure singularity, its freedom caprice or hardheadedness (*Eigensinn*). The *proper sense* of this hardheaded freedom is death [*mort*]. In order to be sure to remain (close) by (it)self and not to release its hold on it [*en démordre*], theoretical consciousness renounces everything. It wants to escape the death of the inorganic, to escape the earth, but it remains in the air and dies all the more (beautiful). The purity of life is death.

To read—its march [*sa marche*] with a prosthesis. Whose noise is not dissonant, as we might, on the contrary, believe. That runs [*Ça marche*] and that sings [*ça chante*] with parentheses

("*Parenthesis* . . . n. 1. A phrase forming a distinct sense, separated from the sense of the sentence in which it is inserted. 'Those long parentheses cutting the connection between things,' BOUHOURS. . . . 'One should avoid parentheses of too great a length, and so place them that they in no way make the sentence murky, or keep the mind from seeing the sequence of correlatives,' DUMARSAIS. . . ."

"*Prosthesis* . . . n. 1. Surgical term. The part of surgical therapy whose object is to replace with an artificial preparation an organ that has been removed in whole or in part. . . . 2. Among the Greeks, altar of prosthesis, a small altar where everything necessary for the holy sacrifice is prepared." Littré)

in the body.

And if all this galley-slaving had worn itself out with emitting (the word *emitting* strikes me as interesting but unsatisfying, it would also be necessary to say anointing, inducing, enjoining, smearing)
GL
I do not say either the signifier GL, or the phoneme GL, or the grapheme GL. Mark would be better, if the word were well understood, or if one's ears were open to it; not even mark then.

It is also imprudent to advance or set GL swinging in the masculine or feminine, to write or to articulate it in capital letters. That has no identity, sex, gender, makes no sense, is neither a definite whole nor a part detached from a whole

gl remain(s) gl
falls (to the tomb) as must a pebble in the water—in not taking it even for an archigloss (since it is only a gloss morsel, but not yet a gloss, and therefore, an

So practical consciousness is at once the negation and the posit(ion)ing of theoretical consciousness. This is played out in the passage from desire to labor.

Desire is theoretical, but as such is tortured by a contradiction that makes it practical.

In effect, theoretical consciousness (death) has only to do with the dead. In the opposition constituting theoretical consciousness, its object, its opposite is not a consciousness, but a thing—a dead thing—that itself does not oppose itself, does not of itself enter into relation. The dead thing is in the relation without, itself, relating-to. So theoretical consciousness has the form of a contradiction, the form of a relation that relates itself to something that is not related, that does not relate (itself) (*Widerspruch einer Beziehung auf ein absolut nicht Bezogenes*), that absolves itself of the relation.

This changes only with desire. Desire is related to a living thing, thus to something that relates (itself). So the negation of theoretical consciousness is first of all desire. Desire perforce implies just what it denies: theoretical consciousness, memory and language.

One might be tempted to conclude from this that desire is the proper(ty) of the speaking being. In fact Hegel does not refuse desire to the animal. So the passage from animal desire to human desire supposes theoretical consciousness and speaking [*parole*] as such. As such: for there is indeed also a theoretical attitude in the animal, if the theoretical is the relation to the dead thing. Nothing more theoretical in this regard than the animal. But neither the animal nor the theoretical can *posit itself as such*. According to a long-lived tradition, the animal would be incapable of both language and labor.

Hegel at least does not refuse desire to the animal. The animal even has the power to curb or inhibit its desire. Simply, in the animal the structure of inhibition is other. No doubt the tendency to annihilate the opposed object (desire) inhibits itself (*sich . . . hemmt*). The members of the opposition must be relieved (*als aufzuhebende*) and as such are they "posited." Desire itself is posited as "*ought-to-be* annihilated." Desire holds in check the destruction of what it desires, that is, of what it desires to consum(mat)e, destroy, annihilate. It wants to keep what it wants to lose. Desire is *of/for the Aufhebung*. Inhibition and relief are inseparable; the effect of ideality that always ensues also belongs to the structure of animal desire in general.

What then distinguishes animal desire from human desire? A question of time. The moments of the operation are dissociated and external in the animal *Aufhebung*. The annihilation and the preservation juxtapose themselves, hold themselves "separated in time (*in der Zeit auseinandergerückt*)." The consum(mat)ing and the sup-

element detached from any gloss, much more than, and something other than, the *Urlaut*), for consonants without vowels, "sounding" syllables, nonvocalizable letters, on some drive base of phonation, a voiceless voice stifling a sob [*sanglot*]

first sob [*sanglot*] or first burst [*éclat*] of laughter, the full mouth defies you to decide whether the agglutinations here glue [*encollent*] signifiers or signifieds. Whence the beauty of the thing and the sob [*sanglot*] that always comes from some contraction of the windpipe, constriction or closing of the mouth [*gueule*]. The experience of the beautiful, or of what is called such, never's ec. without gl [*ne s'ec. jamais sans gl*]. I cite to appear here the expert in languages and letters: "No sooner had this canvas leaped to my eyes, than I experienced what I have called elsewhere the aesthetic sob [*le sanglot esthétique*] (that 'aesthetic' doesn't exactly please me now), well, call it a kind of spasm between the pharynx and the esophagus, and my eyes filled with tears." *Ponge*

or a clot of milk

in the throat, the tickled laughter or the glairy vomit of a baby glutton, the imperial flight of a raptor

". . . as he sees love swooping down on me—it is not mere rhetoric which requires the comparison: like a gyrfalcon—. . . ." "I felt as if I were being carried by him. It was as if he were already on top of me and had screwed me, laying me out with all his weight and also drawing me to him as the eagle drew Ganymede, as he was to do that fourth night when, better prepared, I let him enter me deeply and he swooped down on me with his huge bulk (a whole sky falling on my back), his claws digging into my shoulders and his teeth biting my nape. He was planted inside me, pushing into my soil and, above me, unfurling a bough and a leaden foliage." And further on, still in *The Thief's Journal*, Ganymede is made literally to fly [*voler*]: "Jupiter carries off Ganymede and screws him: I could have indulged in every kind of debauchery." So the gls of the eagle are at once or alternately the aerian elevation of the concept, absolute knowledge that carries you off *and* the weight of the signifier that crushes [*écrase*] you or sinks itself into you. In *Funeral Rites*, the Trinity (the church) represents [*figure*] the eagle of the Reich. The moment you name yourself, you are always in the act of making yourself screw in contraband, such is philosophy

pression are not present at the same time, do not occupy the same present. So there is no *present Aufhebung* in the animal, *a fortiori* in inorganic nature. That is the very definition, and not one predicate among others, of nature. In that sense, it is not absurd to say that there is no *Aufhebung* or dialectics of nature. At least the dialectics does not *present* itself there. The dialectics announces itself—already—according to the mode of the not-yet. Nothing more dialectical, however.

There is animality when consum(mat)ing and nonconsum(mat)ing follow one another but do not reassemble themselves. The animal as such (that is why it would have no history and would endlessly repeat itself), man as animal consum(mat)es, then does not consum(mat)e; destroys, then does not destroy; desires to destroy, then desires not to destroy; satiates itself, then stops itself; stops itself, then satiates itself; and begins again. This dissociation or this successiveness is precisely what human desire relieves. Inhibition, this time, inhabits the consum(mat)ing itself. Ideality, the effect of inhibition, *forms part* of the present of the consum(mat)ing. The *Aufhebung presently* produces itself there, in the heart of the enjoyment. "*Human* desire must be *ideal {ideell}* in the relief itself (im Aufheben selbst), it must be relieved (*aufgehoben*), and the object must equally, while (*indem*) it is relieved, remain (*bleiben*)."

So the *Aufhebung* relieves *itself* in present desire. Human desire: relief of the relief, relieving presence of the relief, relievance [*relevance*]. The truth of ideality presents itself there as such.

The *Aufhebung* is not some determinate thing, or a formal structure whose undifferentiated generality applies itself to every moment. The *Aufhebung* is history, the becoming of its own proper presentation, of its own proper differentiating determination, and it is subject to the law, to the same law as what it is the law of: it first gives itself as immediate, then mediatizes itself by denying itself, and so on. That it is subject to the law of what it is the law of, that is what gives to the structure of the Hegelian system a very twisted form so difficult to grasp.

How does desire become labor? Why does desire remain in the animal whereas it cannot not posit itself in man's labor?

In animal desire—which constitutes the animal as such—ideality is not internal to consum(mat)ing, to satisfaction; ideality only succeeds desire. "The becoming actual of the relief, the stilling (*Stillung*) of desire, is [in the animal] an immediate becoming-relieved, without ideality, without consciousness." (One could already conclude from this, against the so clear interest of this obscure humanism, that ideality, consciousness, the humanity of desire, all that is the supplementary mediatization of animal desire—neither more nor less.) Inasmuch as desire no longer has to do with a dead object and as the preserving ideality saves up desire, it is no longer a simply theoretical operation. Desire is already

that

swoops down at one go [*d'un coup*] on your nape, the gluing, frozen [*glacé*], pissing cold name of an impassive Teutonic philosopher, with a notorious stammer, sometimes liquid and sometimes gutturo-tetanic, a swollen or cooing goiter, all that rings [*cloche*] in the tympanic channel or fossa, the spit or plaster on the soft palate [*voile du palais*], the orgasm of the glottis or the uvula, the clitoral glue, the cloaca of the abortion, the gasp of sperm, the rhythmed hiatus of an occlusion, the saccadanced spasm of an eructojaculation, the syncopated valve of tongue and lips, or a nail [*clou*] that falls in the silence of the milky say [*la voix lactée*] (I note, in parentheses, that, from the outset of this reading, I have not ceased to think, as if it were my principal object, about the milk trademarks Gloria and Gallia for the new-born, about everything that can happen to the porridge, to the mush of nurslings who are gluttinous, stuffed, or weaned from a cleft breast [*sein*], and now everything catches, is fixed, and falls in galalith).

Milkstone. A kind of tombstone   galalith
of synthetic mineral, milky fake. A block of curdled milk. Galalith is a plastic material obtained by treating pure casein in formaldehyde. When Leïla lets all those objects out from under her skirt in the "Mother's house," lamp, lamp-shade, "bits of broken glass . . . or fragments . . . pieces of glass . . . debris . . . splinters [*éclats*]," she causes THE MOTHER to ask: "Everything is there? LEÏLA: Everything. THE MOTHER (*pointing to LEÏLA's bulging belly*): And that [*ça*]? LEÏLA:

practical relation. Human desire is labor. In itself. This depends on inhibition in general structuring desire in the most interior and the most essential way. Room must be made for the generality of this structure, then one must ask whether something like repression can figure a species of the genus *Hemmung* in this general structure, whether the logic of repression is compatible with the general logic of inhibition and relief. If there were a decidable response to this question, it could not be said in a word.

So Hegel must simultaneously describe the emergence of human desire and the emergence of the practical relation. There is no animal labor, and praxis is a "power" of consciousness. "The practical relation is a relation (*Beziehung*) of consciousness." This depends on annihilation of the object being, in its very simplicity, an operation that inhibits itself within itself and opposes itself to itself (*ein in sich Gehemmtes und Entgegengesetztes*). That is why desire is never satisfied, and there lies its "practical" structure itself. "Desire does not come to its satisfaction in its operation of annihilation." Its object stays, not because it escapes annihilation, keeps outside the range for annihilation, but because it stays *in* its annihilation. *Desire remains inasmuch as it does not remain.* Operation of *mourning*: idealizing consum(mat)ing. This relation is called labor. Practical consciousness *elaborates* in the place where it annihilates and holds together the two opposites of the contradiction. In this sense labor is the middle (*Mitte*) of the opposition intrinsic to desire.

This middle in its turn posits itself, gives itself permanence. Without that, it would collapse into a pure negativity, would sink like a pure activity that of itself progressively removes itself. In order to posit itself, labor must then pass into its opposite, settle outside itself in the resistance of the middle. That is the origin of the *tool* (*Werkzeug*), the *object* (producer and product) *of labor*. "Labor is itself a thing (*Ding*). The *tool* is the existing rational middle, the existing universality, of the practical process."

What is such a thing (*Ding*)? What is the being-thing of that thing-there (*Ding*)? It's an existent universality because the *generality* of the implement prevents labor from being depleted in the singular acts of an empiric subjectivity. Without the tool's universal objectivity, labor would be a one-sided experience, would destroy and carry itself off into the ineffable multiplicity of deeds and gestures. So the tool guards labor from self-destruction, is the relieving ideality of *praxis*, is at once active and passive: the remain(s) of labor that enters tradition, practical history. But practical history as the history of desire. Desire and labor disappear, with their objects, *as empiric individuals*. One desires, one consum(mat)es, one labors, it (*ça*) passes (away) and dies. As empiric individuals. So tradition (that is Hegel's word) is what resists this loss and constitutes the maintained ideality: not the finite and

That [*Ça*]? THE MOTHER: What's that? LEÏLA (*laughing*): My latest little one. THE MOTHER (*also laughing*): Got it where? . . . No one saw you? All right, put it there. (*She points to a stool drawn on the screen in* trompe-l'oeil. *With a charcoal pencil that she has taken from her pocket,* LEÏLA *draws, above the table, an alarm clock.*) . . . It's pretty. What is it? Marble or galalith? LEÏLA (*with pride*): Galalith."

The word is detached, rings all alone. The thing too. It's an alarm.   galalith
In the bulging belly, there was this plastic, bell-shaped object that itself carried in its own belly a little hammer, a mini-tocsin whose ringing can always be triggered unexpectedly. Glou-glou/Tic-tac. All that galactic material signs the fake [*signe le toc*], not only because its substance is synthetic, but because the cheap object is only sketched, moreover in trompe-l'oeil, and on a screen. Interminable obsequy of the thing itself. In front of the representative of the law, The Mother assumes in some fashion the proprietorship of the galalith, she takes the alarm clock back into her belly. Then she mimes the gestures of her son to open the belly—of the clock itself. The gendarme observes the screen: "You were seen in a looking glass, running away. . . . The clock was no longer there. (*A pause.*) Is that the one? THE MOTHER: No. The clock's always been there. . . . The clock's been there for ages. What would wake you without it? Just imagine, one day, when he was very little, Saïd took it completely apart. Completely. Piece by piece, to see what was inside, and he put all the springs on a plate. He was still a tot, and just then I entered the house. That (*ça*) was long ago, as you can imagine. I was returning from the grocer's, and what did I see on the floor? . . . (*She mimes.*) But really, like

elaborated object, but the labor tool that can yet be of service, because of its generality structure. The tool is endowed with an ideal, reproducible, perfectible identity, gives rise to accumulation, and so on. So one cannot desire without desiring to produce tools, that is, production tools.

Now the most difficult step is to be taken: marriage.

Some lines—more elliptical than ever—close the analysis of the second "*Potenz*" (the tool) and must in sum explain the upsurge of the third (the family) in its first phase. So the question is accounting for the production of marriage by the tool.

As always, this movement has the form of a production by *posit(ion)ing*: objectification, contradiction, interiorization, subjectification, idealization, setting free, relief. Marriage: relief of the implement.

The implement is solid. Resistant thus to consum(mat)ing and assuring tradition, it acts at the same time [*du même coup*] as an outer constraint. Elaborative desire gives itself the tool, to be sure, but as an external thing and in a heteronomous relation. No longer does desire freely, spontaneously, from within, refrain from consum(mat)ing the other. Ideality still remains in a certain dissociable outside. The freedom of consciousness does not fully affirm itself in inhibitory reserve.

Marriage is the relief of this constraint, the interiorization of this exteriority, the consum(mat)ing of the implement. The labor of desire without instrument. The exteriority of the tool chain has just been defined: "The freedom of consciousness relieves this need, and inhibits the annihilating in enjoyment, through consciousness itself (*durch sich selbst*); that makes the two sexes into consciousness for one another, into beings and subsisters for one another . . . in such a way that in the being-for-self of the other, each is itself. . . ."

This is the first time the Jena philosophy of spirit touches on (and tampers with) sexual desire. The philosophy of nature treats of biological sexuality. As for desire, it had not yet been specified as sexual desire, could as well be a matter of drinking and eating. So at the moment the *Aufhebung*, within enjoyment, inhibits, retains, and relieves pleasure in order not to destroy the other and so destroy itself as enjoyment; at the moment it limits in order to keep, denies in order to enjoy, as if through fear there were no need to reach, to yield to, a *too good* that would risk sweeping away what is given in its very own excess; at that furtive moment, very near and very far from itself, from its own proper present, hardly phenomenal, between night and day—the penumbra(l man) [*le pénombre*]—at that moment does Hegel determine desire as sexual desire. This secret of enjoyment that sacrifices itself, immolates itself to itself, say on the altar of enjoyment, in order not to destroy (itself), itself

some kind of vermin ready to scamper away: little wheels, little stars, little screws, little worms, little nails, gobs and gobs of thingumabobs, little springs, sparrow's wings, cigarettes, bayonets, castanets. . . ." The mechanics of the signifier, which also covers the flight of the other (Leïla), cannot be stopped any more than the ringing of the alarm; it will also have triggered that disquieting trance of the impossible partition: between the signified and the signifier, the true and the false, the living and the inanimate, the morsel and the organic whole. All those little fetuses, penises or clitorises at once living and dead, screws and worms [*vers*], crawling without tail or head, dispensing with tail and head in order to thread their way through your fingers and make their way everywhere, are encased inside one another in trompebelly [*en trompe ventre*]. Naturally the gendarme does not like galalith, does not like the *ersatz*, is in favor of the authentic and cannot make anything out of it at all: "It's galalith, or it's marble, you can bet it's galalith. The stuff that's sold in the villages and at fairs and markets nowadays! Nothing's like it used to be."

In this day and age [*au jour d'aujourd'hui*], they would sell you anything.

If gl does not suffice for you, if no enjoyment remains for you in it, if you have nothing to fuck in it, if you want to render gl, to myself or to that galleyson surnamed Gallien, one more try. Suppose that what is more properly scaffolded here is still the form of an A, in order to pass the head there and risk the

and the other, one in the other, one for the other—essential un-enjoyment and im-potence—that is what Hegel calls love. The two sexes pass into each other, are one for and in the other—this constitutes the ideal, the ideality of the ideal.

This ideality has its "middle" in marriage. The inhibition freed in desire, the desire that "frees itself from its relationship with enjoyment," is love; and love's subsistence, its duration, its staying, its elementary middle is marriage. "And the sexual relationship comes to be that in which each one is one with the other in the being of the consciousness of each one, in other words, an ideal relation. Desire frees itself from its relationship with enjoyment; it becomes an immediate being-one (*Einssein*) of both in the absolute being for-(it)self of both, i.e., it becomes *love*; and the enjoyment is in this intuiting (*Anschauen*) of oneself in the being of the other consciousness. The relationship itself becomes in the same way the being of both and a relationship as durable (*bleibende*) as the being of both, that is, it becomes *marriage*."

An appendix of the *Philosophy of Right* will distinguish marriage from concubinage by the "repression" of the natural pressure (there *Naturtrieb* is *zurückgedrängt*). Concubinage on the contrary satisfies the natural pressure.

We have again found the syllogistic deduction of love and marriage as the immediate unity of the family.

Duration, what remains (*bleibt*) of this moment that is to love what the implement is to labor, does not remain at peace. A new dialectical cycle starts up here, a new war begins to rage. The struggle to death for recognition is inscribed here within the family syllogism. A difference between the Jena analysis and the much fuller one of the *Philosophy of Right*: the first comprehends, in the development concerning the child, an explanation of the struggle to death for recognition and possession.

So marriage is the first moment of the family, its most natural and immediate moment. Marriage is monogamous: a constant implication declared later on in the *Philosophy of Right*: "Marriage, and essentially monogamy, is one of the absolute principles on which the *Sittlichkeit* of a community depends." Or again: "In essence marriage is *monogamy*."

The free inclination of both sexes, marriage excludes any contract. Such an abstract juridical bond could in effect bind persons only to (dead) things, could not by right commit two living freedoms. In marriage there can be empiric determinations, "pathological" inclinations, but that is inessential.

Against marriage's essentiality no consideration on the empiric limitations of freedom can measure up. So Hegel never takes into consideration Kant's whole pragmatic anthropology, everything in it concerning conjugal agonistics, the struggle for mastery between husband and wife. Never does the philosophy of spirit state

blow [*coup*]. Not to add it to gl (the s fallen, let fall [*l's tombé*] once more), but to write some italic

(PARANTHESIS)

Among all the seams [*coutures*] of the genetic text, six lines between parentheses and in italics.

Why do they fascinate?

What do they fascinate? Save subsequent verification with the help of thesis-reading or -writing machines, the case of such an interpolation (not truly an interpolation, being monstrous at least in size and beauty) seems rare. It is not one of those settings *en abyme* through which the author feigns to intervene, as an author, in a narrative account [*récit*], so as to play at explaining his labor to you while he is in the act of making you swallow something else that you do not yet see, that you do not even have the time to linger behind to recognize. In these six lines, the question appears to be a simple displacement of *camera* diverting the chronological line of the narrative, a process sufficiently banal to dispense with parentheses and, above all, italics. So why?

I have no intention of accounting for this, not because I keep the reason for it to myself, but rather—since it has to do with grafting in any case

anything at all about the sex difference between the spouses. Nothing more logical: everything must happen as if the spouses were the same sex, were both bisexual or asexual. The *Aufhebung* has worked.

The war begins with the child. So all discourse on the inequality of the sexes in marriage would remain empiric, not pertinent, foreign to the essence of marriage. In "Characterization," the second part of his *Anthropology*, Kant analyzes the "Character of the Sexes" in and out of marriage. He does so in terms of the struggle for domination, the complex struggle wherein mastery passes from one sex to the other according to the domains and moments. Mastery is rarely where one expects to find it. The inequality of the sexes is the condition for a harmonious union. Equality of forces would render one sex unbearable to the other. So the progress of culture must favor inequality for the protection and propagation of the species. Bent to the teleology of nature, culture produces and accentuates the heterogeneity in the disproportion of the sexes. Man must be superior by his physical force and his courage, the woman by—I cite—her "natural talent [*Naturgabe*: natural gift] for mastering (*sich bemeistern*) man's inclination toward her." This strange superiority of the woman is not natural. It depends on the culture that thus privileges the woman, since in nature all superiority "is on the man's side." If, then, culture transforms the natural situation by providing some artificial superiority to the woman, a theory of culture—what Kant here calls anthropology—must have as its privileged, if not unique, object the status of femininity. Anthropology should be a theory of the woman. ". . . the peculiarly feminine proper(ty) (*weibliche Eigentümlichkeit*), more than the masculine sex, is a subject for study by the philosopher."

Culture does not limit itself to the simple revelation of an enveloped specifically feminine characteristic.

It grafts. The cultured woman's relative superiority is a graft of man: "In the state of brute nature (*Im rohen Naturzustande*) one can no more recognize [the specifically feminine characteristics] than those of crab apples or wild pears, which disclose their multiplicity (*Mannigfaltigkeit*) only through grafting (*Pfropfen*) or innoculation (*Inokulieren*)." Here the graft transforms only in order to display natural characteristics or properties, which explains why the relative superiority the graft confers on the woman seems to overturn the natural situation, but only consists in knowing how to submit

and in every sense—because the principle of reason perhaps is no longer in use. At least, the reason cannot be asked of the one who writes.

So the operation would consist, for the moment, in merely carrying away the graft of the paranthetic organ, without knowing whether that bleeds [*ça saigne*] or not, and then—after the removal and a certain treatment that above all does not consist in curing—to put back in place, to sew up again, the whole perhaps not growing quiet in its restored constitution, but on the contrary being slashed to pieces more than ever.

This assumes that one cites at least twice.

A first time to extract

"(*Long afterward, when I ran into him in Antwerp, I spoke to Stilitano about the postiche cluster hidden in his pants. He then told me that a Spanish whore used to wear a rose of stamin pinned on at cunt level.*

"'*To replace her lost flower,*' *he told me.*)"

This is a cutting from *The Thief's Journal*. What ran on the front page [*à la une*] and across two columns:

(1) the effect: a "garment," a uniform or costume [*parure*] (like the shoes from the very first sequence of the *Screens* or the gloves with reversible fingers, the name, the occurrences and transformations orchestrate *The Maids* from the raising of the curtain on the raising of the curtain);

(2) the statement of a law of oscillation and indecision (as, for example, "What Remained of a Rembrandt," whose "neither true nor false" or the almost-false makes you follow the basting [*faufilure*] be- the Rembrandt already reflects back the literal echo sent

to man's inclination. "For culture does not introduce these peculiarly feminine characteristics," it only produces them, brings them to light, "only causes them to develop and become remarked under favorable circumstances."

Within this general anthropo-botany, Kant analyzes the war of the sexes in marriage. The woman has a taste for domestic war; the man flees it; he "loves domestic peace" and voluntarily submits to the woman's government. "The woman wants to dominate (*herrschen*), the man wants to be dominated (*beherrscht*) (particularly before marriage)." The consequence of culture, marriage frees the woman and enslaves the man; "the woman becomes free by marriage; the man loses his freedom thereby."

The simulacrum of reversal: the woman does not become the stronger, but culture makes her weakness a lever. The possibility of inverting the natural signs—femininity itself—prohibits analyzing an essence, a feminine nature. Femininity is the power to be other than what one is, to make a weapon of weakness, to remain secret. The woman has a secret (*Geheimnis*); the man is deprived of it. That is why he is easy to analyze (*Der Mann ist leicht zu erforschen*). Analysis of the woman is impossible; she does not reveal her secret, which does not prevent her, on the contrary, from regularly betraying that of others. Because she speaks: the reign of culture as the reign of the woman is also the field of speaking [*parole*]. Language [*langage*] never says anything but this perversion of nature by culture—by the woman. The feminine weapon is the tongue [*langue*]. She transforms the slave's weakness into mastery by the tongue but already, always, by that perversion of discourse that is chitchat, loquaciousness, verbosity, volubility (*Redseligkeit*). Thus does she triumph in the domestic war and love it, unlike the man who has something else to do outside. Accumulating all the rights, she triumphs in the war by ruse: sheltered behind her husband (the right of the stronger), she controls her master (the right of the weaker). The art of the lever.

Through this law of perversion that displaces the primitive hierarchy, the natural teleology continues to operate, realizes its normal, normalizing designs, through ruses and detours. The Kantian "description" doggedly restores its intention.

126

tween the two columns) remarking the flower's incessantly instantaneous reversal [*retournement*]: penis/vagina, castration/virginity, erection/relapse [*retombée*], natural organism/disarticulated artifact, total body proper/fetishized morsel, and so on.

While being written on and as a clothing artifice, flowers, the anthologic of the undecidable, lean in italics, then fall into a note on the *affect* of indecision that interests us here more than anything else.

The first sentence of the *Journal*: "Convicts' garb is striped rose and white."

So a printed textile is described, with lines and erasures, with stripes the color of a flower (the flower is promptly induced by the "rose and white" in the subsequent sentence), like a thief's journal that is going to have to be gone over [*parcourir*] in every sense and direction in order to cut [*couper*] and gather up all the flowers there.

Rose is also the first word of the *Screens*. The play [*jeu*] originates between the color and the flower, the adjective and the noun; floats like a woman's garment over the whole text; and also dissembles the sex and forms the article, but one does not know which one. The color rose (*le rose*)? the flower rose (*la rose*)?

back from the surface of the *Screens*. The Mother's laughter: "(*She roars with laughter, and it is with roars [éclats] of laughter that she says the following.*) Those are the truths . . . ha! . . . ha! . . . ha! ha! . . . that can't be demonstrated . . . ha! ha! (*Her laughter seems uncontrollable.*) Those are the truths that are false! . . . ha! ha! ha! ho! ho! ho! . . . ha! ha! . . . (*She is bent [coupée] double with laughter.*) Those are the truths you can't carry to their extremes . . . ho! ho! ho! ho! Oh! oh! Ha! ha! Ho! ho! ho! . . . without seeing them die and without seeing yourself die of laughter, that you've got to exalt. . . ."
Our - Lady - of - the - Flowers: "Don't complain about improbability [*invraisemblance*]. What's going to follow is false, and no one has to accept it as real coin. Truth is not my strong point [*fait*]. But 'one must lie in order to be true.' And even go beyond. What truth do I want to talk about? If it is really true that I am a prisoner who plays (who plays for himself) scenes of the inner life, you will require nothing other than a game."

In effect the woman resembles a "folly" of nature, the human folly of nature. But to seduce the man, to part [*écarter*] him from his natural trajectory, she accomplishes in the final count the wise design of nature. The gap has been calculated for all time; the two sexes have been carefully and implacably ordained to this grand finality, without the subjects understanding anything about it. That is why we cannot think feminine sexuality. Our categories, our aims, the forms of our consciousness are incapable of doing it, a bit like anthropomorphic metaphors in a discourse on God. In order to reach, to have access to, the "characteristic of the feminine sex," we must not regulate ourselves by the principle of our own proper finality, of "what we have devised ourselves as our end," but on "nature's end in the constitution of femininity." "Human folly" is a means with a view to this end that is "wisdom" when "the intention of nature" is considered. So the principle of the characteristic does not depend on "our own choice," but on a "higher intention": "preservation of the species," "the improvement of society and its refinement by femininity." According to what ways?

Having entrusted to the woman the "fruit of the womb" that allows the species to develop itself, nature has taken fright for the woman in which such a "pledge [*gage*]" was deposited; nature has preserved its daughter, held her under cover, has made her fearful and timid before danger. She has been assured the man's protection. The woman's fear is nature's or life's fear for itself. Social refinement obeys the same finality. In order to favor that refinement, nature has made "the feminine sex the master (*Beherrscher*) of the masculine sex." This mastery has been assured by a moralization: not in the sense of the moral, of *Moralität*, but of mores, of *Sittsamkeit*, if not of *Sittlichkeit*. *Sittsamkeit* is decency, honesty, modesty, reserve. In the space of a few lines, one sees it opposed to morality (*Moralität*). With its ease and fluency of discourse and the games of mimicry, *Sittsamkeit* is even the mask of morality (the text would be made unreadable if *Sittsamkeit* were translated by morality), the ruse that enslaves man. Man is then, because of his "own magnanimity," "imperceptibly fettered by a child." Modesty, decency, reserve, *Sittsamkeit* indeed serves as veil or "cloak (*Kleid*)" to an invisible morality. The woman is on the side of *Sittlichkeit* or *Sittsamkeit*, which Kant places below morality. Hegel will reverse the relation of *Moralität* to *Sittlichkeit*. There a chiasm(us) is given that cannot be maintained in the limits of an "anthropology."

How does the (feminine) perversion place itself at the service of the teleology hidden in marriage? And in what does this teleological problem reproduce the chiasm(us)?

The onset of the *Screens* suspends, in a pause, the article in the exclamation: "Rose! (*A pause.*) I say to you rose!"

"Convict's garb is striped rose and white. Though it was at my heart's bidding that I chose the universe wherein I delight, I at least have the power of finding therein the many meanings I wish to find: *a close relationship exists between flowers and convicts*. The fragility, the delicacy of the former are of the same nature as the brutal insensitivity of the latter.*"

The asterisk holds the veil raised.

The footnote reference is not going to make you fall into the trap of an antonymy or an antinomy, so as to paralyze you there.

On the contrary, the note states what provokes a movement that is infinite, quivering, rustling (these last two words are very studied, and they are also among the movements, the emotions of flowers).

Here is the note: "*My excitement [*Mon émoi*] is the oscillation from one to the other."

Whose excitement? The author's? the narrator's? Who signs in the margin [*en note*] and bottom of the page? Since excitement is oscillation ("My excitement is the oscillation . . ."), the *I* is carried away, divided, moved aside in(to) the trait that relates it to anything whatsoever. Undecidable it too in its signature.

The consequences of this are drawn out in two pages, always with the detachment of the grand style, seeming, that is, to be occupied with something else. Drawn like a veil that espouses, hides, and lets one guess the form of all the chains. Those of the prisoners, but also those that bind the rhetoric of veils to the concealment (and the stealing) of truth, of castration, of erection, of nomination. There the veil is remarked, refolded, overlapped, recut [*recoupe*]

In the natural state, in the Kantian sense, the man's polygamy is nearly natural. The paradigmatic structure resembles the harem's. The man naturally desires the whole sex and not one woman; he has to deal only with exemplars of femininity. He does not love, he loves any woman, no matter whom. The woman is a kind of whore. *Conversely*, in the cultural state, the woman does not indulge the pleasure of the man outside of marriage, and of monogamous marriage; but she desires all men and so becomes, in act or intention, the whore. So the Kantian man never deals with anyone but the whore. And if this categorical pornographer were asked what he prefers, whore or virgin, he would respond virgin; all the while he knows full well that nature, which leads him to this, vigilantly sees to it that that returns, at the limit, to the same. A situation that cannot be without relation to what Hegel will analyze as the beautiful soul and the unhappy consciousness.

In both cases, natural polygamy and historic monogamy, the place of the man always determines the concept. Monogamy is a man and a woman; polygamy is again a man and many women. The woman is never polygamous, neither in Kantian nature nor in Kantian society. So it appears: in truth the woman always has everything, both in monogamy and in polygamy. In the harem, for example, there is no true multiplicity and man loses every time, with every stroke [*à tous les coups*]. The women make war in order to restore the monogamous relationship and so that one among them has the whole man, at least potentially [*en puissance*]. With the result that they all have him, no one is deprived of him, and one among them also ends by reigning over him. Thus described, the harem belongs neither to nature nor to culture. Polygamy cannot be thought in this opposition. In nature there is no marriage; in true culture, it's monogamy. Kant qualifies as "barbaric" this unclassifiable phenomenon, this society that is no longer natural and not yet moral. One ought to interrogate from this "perversion" the opposition of concepts from which polygamy escapes, that of the man about which Kant speaks, that of the woman about which he says nothing.

In the harem, the woman is no longer the "domestic animal" she had to be in nature; she begins to fight and use cunning to chain up the man's drive or captivate his desire. The harem is a prison, an enclosed precinct (*Zwinger*), but the woman already knows how to establish her mastery in it. The man no longer knows any repose there amid the busy competition of the women.

Such is the "barbaric constitution" of oriental polygamy, neither natural nor civil. In the monogamy of civil (bourgeois) society, as long as culture is not too developed, the man punishes the woman if she threatens to give him a rival. But when civilization (*Zivilisierung*) is refined to the point of decadence, when it permits "gallantry" (the fact for a married woman of having lovers) and in fact a

around flowers that are at once flowers of rhetoric and what stage—and question—rhetoric. For example, just after the asterisk that holds the veil raised: "Should I have to portray a convict—or a criminal—I shall so bedeck [*parerai*] him with flowers that, as he disappears beneath them, he will himself become a flower, a gigantic and new one."

Under the necklace, the garland, the crown of artificial flowers, under the parade or the poetic bedecking [*parure*], someone promises *at once* to provoke suffocation, the embalmed disappearance under the funeral rite, and to make the erected phallus surge up. There is no choice, no disjunction or accumulation here. My excitement is the oscillation. The play (the erection falls (to the tomb)) is announced as a funereal ceremony enshrouding the other beneath the flowers, but at the same time [*du même coup*] making it band erect under the figures of rhetoric and the *voiles* of all kinds, of every gender.

All that for nothing, for no actual insemination. The (interring) anther is suitably what contains the pollen before fertilization (it surrounds the style and forms one of the two parts of the stamen). "My adventure, never governed by rebellion or a feeling of injustice, even today will be merely one long pairing [*pariade*], burdened and complicated by a heavy, strange, erotic ceremonial (figurative

it's always a matter of encircling the absent word, letting it resound as in the hollow of a bell [*cloche*], creating a void at the center of the space reserved for it, without ever writing, ever pronouncing what you are nevertheless constrained to understand, on one scene or the other, and what, conse-

mode that makes jealousy ridiculous, then the feminine characteristic "discloses itself." The gallant perversion reveals the true nature of the woman, her profound design: "with the favor of men but against them to lay claim to freedom and thereby, simultaneously, to take possession of the whole sex." This theft [*vol*], this stealing (*Eroberung*) of the man by the woman is not simply condemned by Kant. In his analysis of the feminine perversion, the complex system of phallogocentrism can be read. But this system is always precarious and neutralizes itself, *contains* what contradicts it. Here, for example, Kant incessantly effaces the moralizing connotation that nonetheless seems so massive: he often specifies that one must not succumb to the illusions of consciousness or intention. In the feminine perversion, in the cultural, symbolic, verbal ruses—all that passes through the woman's tongue, Kant has to read the text of love in the tongue of the woman who herself knows how to bind the virile energy—one must recognize a hidden natural process, a wisdom of nature. Kant's discourse, despite pronounced and ridiculous appearances, would not be, finally, the moral disqualification of a monstrosity.

But one must admit that this last proposition immediately reverses itself. If Kant does not maintain the discourse of anti-feminine morals, it is because he moralizes through and through his recourse to nature, to the providential wisdom of her who keeps vigil over the perversion. Nature is good, is a good woman, that is, in truth, by her productive force, her reason, her profound *logos* that dominates all the feminine chatterings, her imperturbable and always victorious logic, her educative resources, a father. The good woman is a father; the father is a good woman; and he is the one who speaks through none but the women, who intend to appropriate him.

Natural reserve: if, in bourgeois monogamous marriage, the woman wants to appropriate the whole sex, that is because the man (husband or father) is finite; he dies, often young, almost always before the woman, who remains, then, alone, young, widowed. And who will have had, thus, to prepare this mourning, who knows herself always threatened, in the state of lacking a man. She takes an interest, provisionally, in sex, on the maternal advice of nature. "Although this inclination is in ill repute, under the name of coquetry, it is not without a real justifiable basis. A young wife is always in danger of becoming a widow, and this leads her to distribute her charms to all men whose fortunes make them marriageable; so that, if this should occur, she would not be lacking in suitors."

This hidden teleology justifies all the dissymmetries and all the inequalities of development that Kant believes able to describe by the title of sexual difference.

ceremonies leading to jail and announcing it)."

The text of the *Journal* and the costume of the prisoners will be cut from the same material, the same flowery fabric: downy [*à poil*], veiled, fuzzy, eriopetal flowers (all this is very burdened, isn't it: too rich and in bad taste, the gendarme or the upper bourgeois would say, but as the ceremony above stands out).

You have to know how to die of laughter when practicing inversion: "Desiring to hymn them, I use what is offered me by the form of the most exquisite natural sensibility, which is already aroused by the garb of convicts. The material evokes, both by its colors and roughness, certain flowers whose petals are slightly fuzzy, which detail is sufficient for me to

quently, strikes much more strongly, so as not to be mastered in an act. What is recognized in the effects. Against this mode of writing the parry [*parade*] is not possible, since you are never shown the arm, since one feigns to hide it modestly. Immodesty is often the repression of a fear: the cards are laid on the table in a panic in order to provoke a general disarmament.

An ever apotropaic monstration. The obscene, on the contrary, is modest, bands erect the bit whose cortège you slowly follow.

The "parade" would be imposed, by reason of context, in place of pairing [*pariade*]. Parade in the double band of the word (ornament of adorning [*parure*] and protection—umbrella [*parapluie*], screen [*paravent*], parachute, and so on). One can also bet on [*parier*] a misprint. But a more open context (several pages later) also gives its chance to the pair and the partridge. Pairing is the season when partridges pair by breaking with the group, by excluding themselves from it. Among other partridges, here is the nearest detachment: "It was therefore natural for me to imagine what his penis [*verge*] would be if he smeared it for my benefit with so fine a substance, with that precious cobweb, a tissue which I secretly called *le voile du palais*. He wore an old gray cap with a broken visor. When he tossed it on the floor of our room, it suddenly became the carcass of a poor partridge with a clipped wing . . ."

The text therefore *presents itself* as the commentary on the absent word that it delimits, envelops, serves, surrounds with its care. The text *presents itself* as the metalanguage of the language that does not present itself. But the concern is only with a parade. And the one then that comes to exhibit the active hollows of the other and to pronounce the unpronounced—parade again as metalanguage—simulates the presentation, leaves blisters [*cloques*] or bells [*cloches*], air columns in its body, surrounds, excludes still other words, and

The woman wants to be a man, the man never wants to be a woman. "Whenever the refinement of luxury (*Luxus*) has reached a high point, the woman shows herself well-behaved (*sittsam*) only by compulsion (*Zwang*), and makes no secret in wishing that she might rather be a man, so that she could give larger and freer playing room (*Spielraum*) to her inclinations; no man, however, would want to be a woman." Kant does not enlarge on this last proposition, in the closing fall [*chute*] of the paragraph. It goes without saying that that's unheard of and will never be heard of. Even if by chance one believed to come across such an aberration, what would it mean (to say)? What would it mean, for a man, to want to be a woman, seeing that the woman wants to be a man in proportion to her cultivating herself? That would mean then, apart from the semblance of a detour, to want to be a man, to want to be—that is to say, to remain—a man.

Is it so simple? Does Kant say that the woman wants to be a man? He says, more precisely, that she would like, in certain situations, to adorn herself with attributes of the man in order to realize her womanly designs: to be better able to have all men. She pretends to want to be a man or to be a man in order to "extend the playing room" of her inclinations. Everything is overturned: either the man who wants to be only a man wants to be a woman inasmuch as the woman wants to be a man; so he wants to be a woman in order to remain what he is. Or else the man who wants to be a woman only wants to be a woman since the woman wants to be a man only in order to reach her womanly designs. To wit, the man. And so on.

All this happens very quickly in the penumbra(l man) where desire binds itself, if something such as that exists.

In fact, even if she truly wanted to, which is not the case, the woman could never be a man. The masculine attributes with which she adorns herself are never anything but fake [*toc*], signifiers without signification, fetishes. Are never anything but show [*montre*], but the watch [*montre*]. Badly adjusted [*réglée*] to the sun's movement. To illustrate that the woman can on no account appropriate the masculine attribute, for example or substitution, science, culture, the book, Kant denounces a kind of transvestism: "As for scholarly women, they use their *books* somewhat like a *watch*, that is, they wear the watch so it can be noticed they have one, although it is usually stopped or badly adjusted to the sun." The choice of paradigm once more confirms: "characteristic genius" cannot be thought without the unconscious.

The endless dissymmetry between the sexes is accentuated before the taboo of virginity. The woman does not desire that the man was a virgin or continent before his marriage. She even raises no question on this subject. For the man the question is "infinitely" important. Kant does not say that he requires virginity, or even associate the idea of strength and shame with what is most naturally precious and fragile. This association, which tells me things about myself, would not suggest itself to another mind [*esprit*]; mine cannot avoid it. Thus I offered my tenderness to the convicts; I wanted to call them by charming names, to designate their crimes with, for modesty's sake, the subtlest metaphor (beneath which veil I would not have been unaware of the murderer's rich muscularity, of the violence of his sexual organ). Is it not by the following image that I prefer to imagine them in Guiana: the strongest, with a horn [*qui bandent*], the 'hardest,' veiled by mosquito netting? And each flower within me leaves behind so solemn a sadness that all of them must signify sorrow, death. Thus I sought love as it pertained to the penal colony."

As it pertained to the penal colony. To Guiana, whose end is approaching. From the first pages of the journal, the death agony of Guiana is announced in full peal [*à toute volée*].

As it pertained to the penal colony: this is the place of what we shall henceforth call *antherection*: the time of erection countered, overlapped [*recoupée*] by its contrary—in (the) place of the flower. Enanthiosis.

The overlap goes over itself again indefinitely. Whence this effect of capitalization, but also of unlimited outpouring. If the erection is inhabited by contraband, by what produces it in cutting it off, if then it is in advance, already, antherection, there can, there must be a castration of castration, an antherection of antherection, and so on to infinity.

so on. So the death agony of metalanguage is structurally interminable. But as effort and as effect. Metalanguage is the life of language: it always flutters like a bird caught in a subtle lime [*glu*]

that he desires it, but that for him the question is most serious. Perhaps he can love only virginity, perhaps he can never do so, perhaps his desire is born of the overlapping [recoupe] of virginity by its contrary. All this is played out in the gap [écart] of a sign that is almost nothing and necessarily describes itself in the subtlety of nuances and of wordplays: the man is patient (duldend), the woman tolerant (geduldig), and they do not suffer, do not behave in suffering (dulden) in the same way. The man is sensible (empfindsam), feeling, the woman impressionable (empfindlich), irritable, sensitive, touchy. The economy of the man tends to acquiring, that of the woman to saving. The man is jealous when he loves; the woman is jealous also when she does not love.

This cultural theory of the difference of sexes in marriage has no possible housing in the Hegelian philosophy of spirit. Love and marriage belong to the element of the freedom of consciousness and suppose the Aufhebung of the sexual difference. The war described by pragmatic anthropology can take place in it, in fact, but only insofar as the partners are not true spouses, as the essence of marriage is not accomplished. One remains then no further than the sexual life of empiric nature, before the emergence of Sittlichkeit. What Kant will have described would be in sum a structure of empiric, "pragmatic" accidents, a structure that does not come under the [relevant du] pure concept of marriage from which by vice and perversity it strays [s'en écartant]. Kant could not think, did not begin by thinking the concept marriage. This concept being posited, Hegel on the contrary wants to deduce its development and not its regression. Once more, Kant would remain no further along than this nondialectical conjunction of an empiricism and a formalism, a conjunction denounced in the article on natural law. Without proceeding from the essential unity of marriage, one accumulates and isolates without order the descriptive traits; one joins side by side [accole] empiric violence and contractual formalism.

The speculative dialectics of marriage must be thought: the being-one (Einssein) of the spouses, the consciousness of one in that of the other, such is the medium, the middle of exchange. The sexual

The Journal opens onto the castration of the antherection. With one stroke [D'un trait], the whole antherection of the text is set on a march, but without haste, like a long procession, a long file [théorie] chased from the penal colony ever since its closing.

For, if the colony itself expressly defines a castration, the closing of the penal colony is felt as a castration of castration, a "punishment of punishment," a decapitation of the scaffold ("The heir of kings feels a like emptiness if the republic deprives him of his anointment."), the fall of a crowned head, that is, here, of a bowed head, the convict having made his crown from just what makes him bow his head: "The end of the penal colony prevents us from attaining with our living minds [conscience vive] the mythical underground regions. Our most dramatic movement has been cut [as the director sometimes clips away the author's text]: our exodus, the embarkation, the procession on the sea, which was performed with bowed head. The return, this same procession in reverse, is without meaning. Within me, the destruction of the colony corresponds to a kind of punishment of punishment: I am castrated, I am shorn of my infamy. Unconcerned about decapitating our dreams of their glories, they awaken us pre

the alarm [réveil] always sounds in order to trigger an abortive interruption. Like the galalith alarm clock that comes out of the belly, or like the steel of this jerk [le battant de cette cloche]: "The evening . . . We wanted to sleep together a whole night long, coiled up and entangled in each other until morning, but as that was impossible we invented one-hour nights, while above us, in the dormitory which was woven with tackle to which the hammocks were attached, the night light which burned like a lantern, the surge of sleeps, the steel [le battant] of the cigarette lighter striking the flint (we would say: 'Listen to the tocsin'), the whispering of a boy [un gars], the moan of a jerk [une cloche] whom the big shots called 'a poor martyr,'

opposition is relieved there. As means or mediation, this middle has two sides: the one by which the two spouses recognize one another and relieve their difference; the other, by which this consciousness must be, as middle, opposed to their own and must bear its relief.

That is the child. "It is the child in which they recognize themselves as one, as being in *one* consciousness, and precisely therein as relieved, and they intuit in the child this relief of themselves." They "produce" thus "their own death." In order to think this death, one must make the middle of consciousness intervene and must think childhood as consciousness. The natural child, as living animal, does not bear the death of its genitors. So the death of the parents *forms* the child's consciousness.

That is education. Empirico-formalism cannot think education because empirico-formalism cannot think the parents' necessary death in the child. Yet Kant speaks of the parents' death. It will be said that this is still a matter of empiric death: the preference of the father for the daughter, of the mother for the son, above all for the most insolent, the most undisciplined son, these preferences are still explained by the possibility of widowhood. The child of the opposite sex would be the better support in old age. This derisively empiric explanation nevertheless discovers the essential affect—mourning—that relates one of the parents to the child of the other sex from the death of the married partner [*conjoint*]. The mother loves the son according to the father's death; the father loves the daughter who succeeds the mother. By reason or way [*titre*] of the empiric, doesn't one thus go further than the Hegelian deduction of the parents' death, which seems rather undifferentiated and abstract from the sexual point of view? A chiasm(us) again: speculative dialectics thinks this death in its structural necessity, *thinks* it as it thinks the effacement of the sexual difference that empiricism puts forward.

What is education? The death of the parents, the formation of the child's consciousness, the *Aufhebung* of its unconsciousness in(to) the form of ideality. "In education the *unconscious unity* of the child is relieved." There is no need to hurry to identify this idealizing relief with a "repression" of the "unconscious." But the question of such a translation cannot be avoided. Education (*Erziehung*) and culture (*Bildung*) violently delimit a matter by a form containing it. This violent form is ideal, passes through the instances of language and labor, of voice and tool. Like every formation, every

and the exhalations of the night, made us castaways of a dream. Then we would unglue our mouths: it was the awakening [*réveil*]. . . ." You could verify that the word "boy" ("*gars*") often resounds near some "*cloche*." And there are many of them. Also follow the flint, or the firestone.

The separation, comma [*virgule*], between *l'émoi, et moi*, excitement, and I, on waking [*au réveil*], is equal to decollating [*décoller*] (detachment of the neck [*cou*] and of glue [*la colle*]), and decollation to a sublimating idealization that relieves what is detached. Indecision, oscillation, the trembling vibration where ideality is announced, these are always called shuddering, quivering, and so on. "That kind of shudder also exalted my happiness, for it made our trembling kiss seem to take wing [*décoller*], to be idealized. . . . that he had been on the alert all the time and that, during the embrace, he had not been roused [*ému*], for on hearing the noise he would have had slight [*légère*] difficulty, despite his quick reflexes, in shaking off the excitement, and I [*l'émoi, et moi*], who was glued to him, would have detected that slight twinge, that decollation of a subtle glue [*glu*]" (*Miracle of the Rose*).

maturely. The home prisons have their power: it is not the same."

Supplementary antherection: for Guiana's, the home prison's is going to be substituted.

Castrated from the first, the other bands erect more beautifully: ". . . it is not the same. It is minor. The elegant, slightly bent grace is banished from it. The atmosphere there is so heavy that you have to drag yourself about. You creep along. The State prisons band erect more stiffly, more darkly and severely; the solemn and slow

to test out the logic of antherection, the time of erection that endlessly abridges its stigma and resembles

imposition of form, it is on the male's side, here the father's, and since this violent form bears the parents' death, it matures [*se fait*] above all against the father. But the death of the father is only the real death of the mother, corresponds to the idealization of the father, in which the father is not simply annihilated. The relieving education interiorizes the father. Death being a relief, the parents, far from losing or disseminating themselves without return, "contemplate in the child's becoming their own relief." They guard in that becoming their own disappearance, reg(u)ard their child as their own death. And in reg(u)arding that disappearance, that death, they retard it, appropriate it; they maintain in the monumental presence of their seed—in the name—the living sign that they are dead, not that *they are dead*, but that *dead they are*, which is another thing. Ideality is death, to be sure, but to be dead—this is the whole question of dissemination—is that *to be* dead or to be *dead*? The ever so slight difference of stress, conceptually imperceptible, the inner fragility of each attribute produces the oscillation between the presence of being as death and the death of being as presence. As long as the parents are present to their death in the child's formation, as long as one keeps [*garde*] the sign or the seme of what is no longer, even were it the ashes consumed in the small morning of a penumbra(l man), the enjoyment stays, the enjoyment of just what is, even of what is dead as what is no longer. But if death is the being of what is no more, the no-more-being, death is nothing, in any case is no longer death. Its own proper death, when contemplated in the child, is the death that is denied, the death that *is*, that is to say, denied. When one says "death is," one says "death is denied"; death is not insofar as one *posits* it. Such is the Hegelian *thesis*: philosophy, death's positing, its pose.

The child-relief of the loss [*perte*]. This loss, the labor of form on matter, the forming [*mise en forme*] of unconsciousness, the economic process, production, exchange, dies away, is amortized. The *Aufhebung* is the dying away, the amortization, of death. That is the concept of economy in general in speculative dialectics.

Economy: the law of the family, of the family home, of possession. The economic act makes familiar, proper, one's own, intimate, private. The sense of property, of propriety, in general is collected in the *oikeios*. Whatever the exportation or the generalizing expropriation of the concept economy, that concept never breaks the umbilical cord attaching it to the family. Or rather yes, it always breaks the cord, but this rupture is the *deduction* of the family, belongs to the family process as that process includes a cutting [*coupante*] instance. The *Aufhebung*, the economic law of absolute reappropriation of the absolute loss, is a family concept.

And so political. The political opposes itself to the familial while accomplishing it. So the political economy is not one region of the general onto-logic; it is coextensive with it. All the more so

no other present—it presents itself—to verify everywhere the internal antagonism that undoubles and divides [*dédouble*] each column, for example the penal colony ("slow agony of the penal colony"), to see its importance with respect to the-deconstruction-of-ontology-etc., I propose that one try everywhere to replace the verb *to be* with the verb *to band erect*.

And conjugate a little.

Since one makes activity, transitivity, the object supplement come back there. Pronouns. The forename, etc.

Perhaps one will thus be introduced by another style to the metaphysics, the grammar, and the etymology of the word "to be," to the question of *casus* (πτῶσις) and *declinatio* (ἔγκλισις).
And of the *clin* (—) between the two *col* (—)

agony of the penal colony was a more perfect blossoming of abjection."

It remains [*demeure*], to say nothing more, that the place of antherection—that which bands erect and in which it is banded erect, a place necessarily closed and guarded, whatever name you may give it (Guiana, galley [*galère*], or Colony)—is always inhabited like a province detached from the mother. "When talking about the Colony I sometimes refer to it as 'The Old Lady,' or 'The Motherfucker.' These two expressions would probably not have sufficed to make me confuse it with a woman, but, in addition to the fact that they already usually designate mothers, they occurred to me in connection with the Colony, since I was tired of my solitude as a lost child and my soul called for a mother."

The breast [*sein*] of this mother steals away from all names, but it also hides them, steals them; it is before all names,

since, in the Hegelian systematics, there is never any simply hier-archic relationship between genus and species: each part represents the whole, each region is capable of everything.

So ideality, the production of the *Aufhebung*, is an onto-economic "concept." The *eidos*, the general form of philosophy, is properly familial and produces itself as *oikos*: home, habitation, apartment, room, residence, temple, tomb [*tombeau*], hive, assets [*avoir*], family, race, and so on. If a common seme is given therein, it is the guarding of the proper, of property, propriety, of one's own [*la garde du propre*]: this guarding retains, keeps back, inhibits, consigns the absolute loss or consum(mat)es it only in order better to reg(u)ard it returning to (it)self, even were it in the repetition of death. Spirit is the other name of this repetition.

Such is the cost of the child: "In education the *unconscious unity* of the child relieves itself (*hebt sich . . . auf*), articulates itself in (it)self (*gliedert sich in sich*), becomes *formed*, *cultured consciousness* (gebildeten Bewusstsein); the consciousness of the parents is its matter (*Materie*), at the cost of which (*auf deren Kosten*) it is formed; they (the parents) are for the child an unknown, obscure presenti-ment of itself; they relieve its simple, contracted (*gedrungen*) being-in-(it)self; what they give the child they lose; they die in it; for what they give it is their own consciousness."

If one cuts it off here, education could be a loss without return, a gift without a countergift, without exchange. But in truth ex-change takes place. The other consciousness, the child's, in which the parents lose theirs, is their own proper consciousness. The other and one's own proper(ty) do not oppose each other, or rather yes, they do oppose each other, but the opposition is what permits, not what interrupts, the specular, imaginal, or speculative circulation of the proper, of one's own proper(ty). The proper, one's own proper(ty), posits itself in opposing itself in the other, in dis-tancing itself from itself. The unity of the specular and the speculative is remarked in the possibility for the parents to regard, to contem-plate their own proper disappearance relieved in the mirror of the child, of the child in formation, as becoming-conscious; in the material unconscious [*l'inconscient materiel*] they would see nothing, not even their own proper death, the death wherein they are guarded, not even death, then, or only death. "*Die Eltern schauen in seinem Werden ihr Aufgehobenwerden an*": "the parents contemplate in the child's becoming their becoming-relieved."

The child's consciousness does not come to the world as to a material and inorganic exteriority. The world is already elaborated when education begins, is a culture penetrated, permeated, in-formed by the "*knowledge of his parents.*" What first faces the child as and in place of inorganic nature is inherited knowledge, already a certain ideality. So the child raises itself in(to) the "contradiction" between the real world and the ideal world. The process of educa-

as death, the mother fascinates from the absolute of an *already*. Fascination produces an excess of zeal. In other words, jealousy. Jealousy is always excessive be-cause it is busy with a past that will never have been present and so can never be presented nor allow any hope for presentation, the presently presenting. One is never jealous in front of a present scene—even the worst imaginable—nor a future one, at least insofar as it would be big with a possible theater. Zeal is only unchained at the whip of the absolute past. *Madame Edwarda* would be a bit of foolishness, running herself dry, producing her apotrope in the spectacle, *as far as she were open to a present experience*. She has a chance to be terrible only by thrusting within herself a past, an absolute already: in giving herself to be read, not seen. But going out of the "book" does not suffice for giving oneself to be seen and interrupting the reading.

So one is only jealous of the mother or of death. Never of a man or a woman as such.

So one is only jealous of a *seing* or, what comes down here to the same, of an *already*.

This is why metaphysics, which is jealous, will never be able to account, in its language, the language of pres-ence, for jealousy.

This is why the mother (whatever forename or pro-noun she may be given) stands beyond the sexual op-position. This above all is not a woman. She only lets herself, detached, be represented by the sex.

This is why the thief distinguishes between the mater-nal and the feminine. And he does so in what you call a man: ". . . not by a man's fist but by having crashed against the glass walls which cut us off from your world—[the physical appearance] evokes for me now, though it might not have done so in the past, the prison of which he seems to me the most significant,

tion consists in relieving this contradiction. That is possible only with the disappearance (relieving) of the family itself, since the family is the place of this contradiction: it's the passage to the people-spirit.

Here intervenes the struggle to death for recognition. It is most often known under the form given it by the *Phenomenology of Spirit*. Now previously three texts had treated of it: the *System of "Sittlichkeit"* (probably earlier, just a little bit, than the Jena *Philosophy of Spirit*), the Jena *Realphilosophie* (almost contemporaneous with the *Phenomenology of Spirit*), and the *Philosophy of Spirit*. This last one is the only one to explain struggle within a problematics of the family.

The struggle in the family does not oppose, as is often believed, family heads. The text gives no indication of this. Once the family is constituted, as a power of consciousness, the struggle can break out only between consciousnesses, and not between empiric individuals. From this viewpoint, the gap [*écart*] narrows between the Jena text and that of the *Phenomenology*. If the *Phenomenology* takes up [*aborde*] the family moment after the dialectic of master and slave, that is because in it the family is interrogated according to a very particular guiding thread: the passage from the ancient family and city to Roman law and formal morality. With the result, another architectonic phenomenon at first approach [*abord*] disconcerting, that in the *Phenomenology*, the moment of "morality" and of formal right follows that of the family, whereas the inverse is produced in the *Philosophy of Right*. In the *Phenomenology*, the Greek is inscribed in a general problematics of the history of the family. So there is no "evolution of Hegel's thought" there.

At the point where we are, the struggle to death for recognition opposes consciousnesses, but consciousnesses that the family process has constituted as totalities. The individual who engages in the war is an individual-family. The essence of consciousness cannot be understood without passing through the family "*Potenz*." A phenomenology of spirit, that is, according to the subtitle, an "Experience of Consciousness," cannot be described without recognizing in it the onto-economic labor of the family. There is no pure consciousness, no transcendental ego into which the family kernel might be reduced. Here is situated the principle of a critique of transcendental consciousness as the formal *I think* (thinking is always said of a member of the family), but also a critique of concrete transcendental consciousness in the style of Husserlian phenomenology. Not only is there no monadic consciousness, no sphere to which the ego properly belongs, but it is impossible to "reduce" the family structure as a common [*vulgaire*] empirico-anthropological addition of transcendental intersubjectivity. Transcendental intersubjectivity would be abstract and formal—constituted and derived—if in it the family structure was not

the most illustrious representative. I was called to him, hastened toward him, and it is now, in my desperation, that I dare be engulfed within him. The maternal element I perceived in him was not feminine. Men sometimes hail each other as follows:
" 'Well, Old Girl?'
" 'Hi, you Hen!'
" 'Is that you, Wench?'
"This mode belongs to the world of poverty and crime. Of punished crime, which bears upon itself—or within itself—the mark of a faded brand. (I speak of it as of a flower, preferably as of a lily, when the branding sign was the *fleur de lis*.) . . .
". . . *La Guyane* (Guiana) is a feminine noun. Guiana contains all those males who are called tough. . . . I aspire to Guiana. . . . She is kindly." Elsewhere: "I name the Virgin Mother and Guiana the Comforters of the Afflicted."

Guillotine is also a feminine noun

regularly gives itself its first name, Guiana, Colony, here more precisely, more silently perhaps, "Galley" lifted by the waters: "And everything that one associates with women: tenderness, slightly nauseating whiffs from the open mouth, deep bosom [*sein*] that the wave lifts, unexpected corrections, everything, in short, that makes a mother a mother."

If one fell on the mother's first name, perhaps one would see that she shines, she, and keeps watch in the depths of the night, illuminates the galley that she leads on in full sail. ". . . You can see the ample chest of women rise and fall, and in like manner the belly of the priest swelled out. . . . I endowed the Colony with all those ridiculous and disturbing attributes of the sex, until, in my mind [*esprit*], she was presented not in the physical image of a woman, but, rather, between her and me was established a union from soul to soul which exists only between mother and son,

recognized as one of its essential structures, with all the powers Hegel implies therein: memory, language, desire, labor, marriage, the proprietorship of goods, education, and so on.

Consciousness does not relate to itself, does not reassemble itself as totality, does not become for itself—does not become conscious—except as, except in the family. "In the family, *the totality of consciousness* is the same thing as what becomes *for self*; the individual contemplates himself in the other." Consciousness posits itself for itself only through the detour of another consciousness that posits itself as the same and as other. So given there, standing up face to face, are two totalities. Singular totalities, since they also make two, are two: absolute, insoluble contradiction, impossible to live with. The relationship can only be violent. The two consciousnesses structurally need each other, but they can get themselves recognized only in abolishing, or at least in relieving, the singularity of the other—which excludes it. A pure singularity can recognize another singularity only in abolishing itself or in abolishing the other as singularity. The contradiction, although not explicit here under this form, opposes more precisely knowing (the *kennen* of *erkennen*), which can deal only with universal ideality, and the singularity of the totality "consciousness," being-in-family.

The struggle to death that is triggered then between two stances seems, in its exterminating violence, more mercilessly concrete than it does in later texts. Nevertheless two conditions contain it, the concepts of which must indeed be regulated.

(1) Death, the "demonstration" that "is achieved only with death," destroys singularity, relentlessly hounds what in the other consciousness-family remains singular. This is not a matter of just death, but of the annihilation of the characteristics of singularity, of every mark of empiricalness. Is the name, for example, the stake that founders or the stake that saves itself in this war?

One will say: what remains when all of the empiricalness is abolished? Nothing, nothing that may be present or existent. To be sure. But what is present, what *is* as such when there is only singularity? Nothing. One fights to death, in any case, for nothing, such is no doubt the intention [*propos*] hidden in the shadow of the Hegelian discourse. By definition, this intention cannot be said as such, since discourse is precisely what makes the universal pass for something, gives the impression that the universal remains something, that something remains, when every singularity has been engulfed. Medusa's face watching over the Hegelian text in the penumbra(l man) that binds [*lie*] desire to death, that reads [*lit*] desire as the desire of, the desire for, death.

and which my undeceivable soul recognized. . . . Little by little, the veils [*les voiles*] fell away from her. The mother took shape. In the cell, I really and truly found her throbbing breast [*sein*] again and, with her, I engaged in real dialogues, and perhaps those avatars that made Mettray into my mother aggravated, with a feeling of incest, the love I bore for Divers, who had come from the same breast [*sein*] as I."

Thus activates itself a substitution, a detachment in chains. The Colonies, the Prisons, the State jails form that chain of chains that are all detached (in other words, chained to one another and bound to what orders [*mande*] them or bands them erect [*bande*]) from the breast [*sein*], from the real and true [*bon*] breast, from the mythic cell where "really and truly [*de bon*] . . . her breast" is found again.

But from the moment it detaches (itself), the breast [*sein*] falls and is no longer simply real and true, "really and truly . . . her breast." It is poisoned, becomes aggressive, castrates castration. But since the first "real and true breast" was already an "avatar," its case bore an annunciation of all the others. The downfall can only be aggravated, the (hi)story grow worse, all the way to the Apocalypse.

"The bishop replied: '. . . Our Lord said: Suffer the little children to come unto me. Who could be so hard-hearted as not to heed that appeal of the divine child and to prefer the black . . . bosom [*sein*] . . .'" (*Miracle of the Rose*)

Thus activates itself a substitution: the black antherection of the State prisons that succeeds—as a detachment or a damned procession—the light antherection of the penal colony. The outfit of brown homespun in the State prisons ("So that now the State jails, bloated with evil males, are black with them as with blood that has been shot through with carbonic

The question has not been answered: is the proper name of a family and of an individual *classed* in the family a pure singularity? No. Is it a pure ideality? No.

(2) Second strict, conceptual condition: the death of singularity is always an *Aufhebung*. The so frequent translation of *Aufhebung* by *abolition* or *cancellation* precisely effaces this: that death abolishes the pure and simple abolition, death without ado, death without name. "It is absolutely necessary that the totality which consciousness has reached in the family can recognize itself as the totality it is in another such totality of consciousness. In this recognition, each is for the other immediately an absolute singular (*ein absolut Einzelner*); each posits itself (*setzt sich*) in the consciousness of the other, relieves (*hebt . . . auf*) the singularity of the other, or each posits the other in its consciousness as an absolute singularity of consciousness."

One consciousness can posit itself as such only in another consciousness: in order in it to see, to know itself, to get itself recognized. As soon as the other consciousness recognizes "my own," it goes out of its empiric singularity. I must incite it to this, and the radical going outside of empiric singularity has no other name but death. Putting to death implies here speculative dialectics's whole chain of essential concepts (relief, posit(ion)ing as passage to the opposite, ideality as the product of negativity, and so on).

The destruction of singularity must leave no remain(s), no empiric or singular remain(s). It must be total and infinite. If they should happen to desire to be loved, recognized by the other's consciousness, the subjects must accept to bear or suffer (here reciprocity is the rule) a wound, an infinite injury ("the injury (*Verletzung*) of any one of his singularities is therefore infinite"). The outrage, the offense, the violation (*Beleidigung*), the collision (*Kollision*) is achieved only with death. As this collision, this violation is reciprocal (*gegenseitige*), the project of mastery, of getting-oneself-recognized must in the same stroke [*du même coup*] engage infinite desire in a risk of absolute nonmastery: the subject must admit to itself that it no longer dominates its relation to the other. There it desires. It posits its desire only in risking death.

Total and real violence: to be sure language is implicated in this, but in this affair mere words are worthless. The war is not conducted with [*à coup de*] signifiers, above all linguistic signifiers. With names perhaps, but is the proper name a linguistic signifier? Hegel insists on this: the struggle for recognition does not have its element in the tongue. The struggle is played out between bodies, to be sure, but also between economic forces, goods, real possessions, first of all the family's. The linguistic element implies an ideality that can be only the *effect* of the destruction of empiric

gas. (I have written 'black.' The outfit of the convicts—captives, captivity, even prisoners, words too noble to name us—forces the word upon me: the outfit is made of brown homespun.) It is toward them that my desire will turn. I am aware that there is often a semblance of the burlesque. . . . a brown homespun beret. They strike poses of wretched humility. (If they are beaten, something within them must nevertheless stiffen. . . .)") substitutes itself for, by detaching itself from, the costume "striped rose and white" of Guiana. A column and a textile, a style also replace the other. A thinning out [*Coupe sombre*] and castration of the sun of castration; "I secretly recompose . . . for myself alone, a colony more vicious than that of Guiana. I add that the home prisons can be said to be 'in the shade.' The colony is in the sun."

Antherection of the style *en abyme*. The one-armed Stilitano, who promptly dominates the scene of the *Journal*, implants and repeats, in his body, the substitution that at once castrates and makes band erect—

economy of the abyss and of the center. The "*mise en abyme*" can always fill the abyss by positing it, by saturating it to infinity with its own proper representation. The motif of the "*mise en abyme*" could play here or there this appeasing role, within a certain formalism. Whence its success. Like that of decentering, if the abyss were at the center and if one distanced oneself from the abyss while taking its center (while staying there) with oneself

stronger and stiffer and blacker. In arboricultural terms, it is literally a thinning out: "When a member has been removed, they told me that the one that remains grows stronger. I had hoped that the vigor of Stilitano's cut-off arm might be concentrated in his penis. For a long time I imagined a solid member, like a blackjack, capable of the most outrageous impudence, though what first intrigued me was what Stilitano allowed me to know of it: the mere crease, though curiously precise in the left leg, of his blue

singularities, an effect and not a middle of the struggle. In the *practical* war between singular forces, the injuries must bring about actual [*effectives*] expropriations. They must wrest from the other the disposition of its own body, its language, must literally dislodge the other from its possessions. The field of the word [*verbe*] does not suffice for this: "Language, explanations, promising are not this recognition, for language is only an ideal middle (*ideale Mitte*); it vanishes as it appears; it is not a real recognition, one that remains (*bleibendes*)." The insistence is very marked: linguistic idealism, linguisticism, these can always upsurge again—the temptation is too strong—to sweeten or cicatrize the injury, to make one forget that the middle of the carnage is not ideal but "actual." "No one can prove this to the other through words, assurances, threats, or promises; for language is only the ideal existence of consciousness; here, on the contrary, actual opposites confront one another, i.e., absolutely opposed opposites that are absolutely for themselves; and their relation is strictly a practical one, it is itself actual; the middle of their recognition must itself be actual. *Hence they must injure one another.* The fact that each posits itself as exclusive totality in the singularity of its existence must become actual. The violation [*Beleidigung*: outrage, rape, abuse] is necessary."

Without this *Beleidigung* no consciousness, no desire, no relationship to the other could *posit itself.* But this breaking-in that comes to injure the other's proper(ty), the other's own, does not come down to a singular initiative, to the decision of a freedom. This breaking-in is engendered by a contradiction that inhabits the proper itself, one's own own. The question here, since Hegel insists above all on the possession of things, rather than of one's own body proper, is of a contradiction in the thing itself. It is contradictory that a thing (*Ding*) be some one's or some people's proper(ty), their own. "In particular each must be dislodged from its possession (*Besitze*), for in possession there lies the following contradiction: . . ." An exterior thing, a thing, a universal reality of the earth, by essence exposed to all, cannot, without essential contradiction, stay in the power of a singularity. The contradiction must be resolved. It can be so only by the violent and total expropriation of the singularity. But if this injury were the redistribution of morsels of proprietorship, if a singular reappropriation followed, the same contradiction would persist. So the only end possible is to put to death singularity as such, the possession of proper(ty), of one's own, in general. What is said here of the body in general, of the thing of the earth, of everything that is exposed to the light, how is the exception of one's own body proper marked in this? As visibility and availability at least, the body proper is worked (over) by the same contradiction, the stake [*enjeu*] of the same struggle to death.

denim trousers. This detail might have haunted my dreams less had Stilitano not, at odd moments, put his left hand on it, and had he not, like ladies making a curtsey, indicated the crease by delicately pinching the cloth with his nails [*ongles*]."

"The one that remains grows stronger," the more that (*ça*) remains, the better that (*ça*) bands erect. Remain(s) equals band(s) erect. In every occurrence, play at replacing remain by band erect, the remain(s) by the band(s) erect. You will begin to think [*penser*] what an event is, a case, let us rather say an occurrent. The logic of antherection must not be simplified. It (*Ça*) does not erect *against* or *in spite of* castration, *despite* the wound or the infirmity, by castrating castration. It (*Ça*) bands erect, castration. Infirmity itself bandages itself [*se panse*] by banding erect. Infirmity is what, as they still say today in the old language, *produces* erection: a prosthesis that no castration event will have preceded. The structure of prosthesis belongs to intumescence. Nothing stands upright otherwise.

occurrent is said in botany "about all the partitions converging toward a central fictive axis" (Littré)

This is the stance, the stanza, of the peg in *Our-Lady-of-the-Flowers.* Listen: in a "rattle of scrap-iron," the "miracle . . . blazed forth [*éclata*]." "Closed skylight," "icy sky [*ciel glacé*]," "catastrophic horror." The miracle, however, is "radiant as the solution of a mathematical problem, frighteningly exact." "What was it all about?" he asked himself beforehand.

The peg. It is exhibited, like any prosthesis, any epithesis, any erection, any simulacrum, any apotrope, any parade, any parry, any mascarade, with

Yet death does not resolve the contradiction. To say "on the contrary" would be too simple and one-sided. One must again speak of relief: the *Aufhebung* is indeed the contradiction of the contradiction and of the noncontradiction, the unity as well of this contradiction. Here, strictly, unity and contradiction are the same.

In effect I can make an attempt on others' life—in its singularity—only in risking my own. To posit oneself (*sich setzen*) as consciousness supposes exposure to death, engagement, pawning, putting in play [*en jeu*] or at pawn [*en gage*]. "When I go for his death, I expose myself to death (*setze ich mich selbst dem Tode aus*), I put in play my own proper life (*wage ich mein eignes Leben*)." This putting (in play, at pawn) must, as every investment, amortize itself and produce a profit; it works at my recognition by/through the other, at the posit(ion)ing of my living consciousness, my living freedom, my living mastery. Now death being in the program, since I must *actually* risk it, I can always lose the profit of the operation: if I die, but just as well if I live. Life cannot stay in the incessant imminence of death. So I lose every time, with every blow, with every throw [*à tous les coups*]. The supreme contradiction that Hegel marks with less circumspection than he will in the *Phenomenology*.

I lose every time, with every blow, with every throw, on both registers. To recognize, with a light-hearted cruelty, with all the enjoyment possible, that nothing of all this is in effect viable, that all this will end in a very bad way, and that yet, on the cutting edge of this blade [*sur le fil coupant de cette lame*], more fleeting and thinner than any thing, a limit so taut in its inexistence that no dialectical concept can grasp or master or state it, a desire stirs itself. Dances, loses its name. A desire and a pleasure that have no sense. No philosopheme is attired or prepared to make its bed there. Above all not that of desire, of pleasure, or of sense in the Hegelian onto-logic. Nor, besides, is any concept. What here must be put into play without amortization is the concept that always wants to seize on something. There is on this edge [*fil*], on this blade, the instant before the fall or the cut [*coupe*], no philosophical statement possible that does not lose what it tries to retain and that does not lose it precisely by retaining it. Nothing else to say about this than what is said about it at Jena. The blow [*coup*] to the other is the fatal contradiction of a suicide. "When I go for his

daintiness. "The little hoodlum pulled back the covers daintily and asked:

" 'Will you help me off with my leg?'

"He had a wooden peg which was fastened to a stump cut off below the knee by a system of straps and buckles."

The account—frighteningly exact—lets the (sur)plus value appear, not of what should be compensated, the member missing, but of the prosthesis that bands erect all alone. The stance, the stanza, of the peg, as of a stony colossus, no longer knows repose; dispenses with the subject, survives the wearer, and shelters him from any failure; stays awake when he sleeps. When Culafroy—for whom the "infirmity" inspires as much revulsion as the "reptiles"—overcomes his disgust through a "sublime" effort, and clasps the wooden leg against his chest, "it was now a live member, an individual, like an arm or leg detached from the trunk by a surgical operation. The peg spent the night standing up, a night of vigil, leaning in a corner [*angle*] against the wall." Disquieting stance and stanza. Meanwhile the cripple dreams: oranges in one hand, cutlass in the other, "the golden globe and the scepter."

Just as *The Thief's Journal* leaves, proceeds from Guiana, expresses itself as an exit from Guiana ("that region of myself: Guiana"), so gl begins to spurt [*gicler*], to trickle [*dégouliner*], to drip [*goutter*]: out of the mouth or the tail of the stilite, of the tube of vaseline, of the nursling's esophagus. Sperm, saliva, glair, curdled drool, tears of milk, gel of vomit—all these heavy and white substances are going to glide into one another, be agglutinated, agglomerated,

death, I expose myself to death, I put in play my own proper life. I perpetrate the contradiction of wanting to affirm (*behaupten*) the singularity of my being and my possession; and this affirmation passes over into its contrary, that I sacrifice (*aufopfere*) everything I possess, and the very possibility of all possession and enjoyment, my life itself. In that I posit myself as totality of singularity, I relieve myself as totality of singularity. . . ."

If I had not absolutely engaged myself in this contradiction of the concept, I would not raise myself above life, I would not be rational. If I had engaged myself in it partially, I would be a *slave*, the word appears already. The contra*diction* can only be sharpened. It is not only of the concept and in the statement but with them. "This recognition *of the singularity of the totality thus leads to the nothingness of death*. . . .
"This recognition of singulars is thus the absolute contradiction within itself; the recognition is just the being of consciousness as a totality in another consciousness, but as far as it [the recognition] is actual, it relieves the other consciousness; at the same time the recognition relieves itself. It is not realized, but rather ceases to be, as it is (*indem es ist*). And yet, at the same time (*zugleich*), consciousness is only as a being-recognized by another, and at the same time, it is only consciousness as an absolute numerical One and must be recognized as such; but that is to say it must go for the other's death, and for its own; and it is only in the actuality of death."

Propositions of this type are numerous. They entrain the absolute equivalence or continuity of murder and suicide. I affect myself specularly by what I affect the other by. The nearly undecidable suspense about which we were speaking—the lynching rope hanging between life and death or the unstable balance of a funambulist—leaves each consciousness to an absolute solitude in the very instance of the recognition. But this suicide solitude places two lives—and the other—in play. Let us imagine rather two bodies, gripped by one another, on the edge of a cliff: it is impossible for the one who presses the other not to be *drawn* by the void. He desires this fall (his desire is the pressure of this fall), clings to it as to himself in the act of falling, tends toward it without knowing which of the two can protect [*garder*] the other—that is, see the other dead. There is no other definition of suicide. In the Jena *Realphilosophie*, in the chapter on the "Struggle for Recognition (*Der Kampf des Anerkennens*)": "There appears to consciousness as consciousness that it aims at (goes for) the other's *death*; but also at (for) its very own: it is a suicide (*Selbstmord*) as it exposes itself to *danger*."

stretched out (*on*)*to the edge* of all the figures and pass through all the canals.

The word "*glaviaux*" ["globs"] will not be uttered until later, after invisible assimilation and deglutition, after elaboration, agglutinated to "*glaïeul*" ["gladiolus"].

But even before being presented in the text and blooming there right next to the flower, the word animates with its energetic and encircled absence the description of spit. The description is caught in a veil. "Stilitano was big and strong. His gait was [*marchait d'un pas*] both supple and heavy, brisk and slow, sinuous; he was nimble. A large part of his power over me—and over the whores of the Barrio Chino—lay in the spittle Stilitano passed from one cheek to the other and which he would sometimes draw out in front of his mouth like a veil. 'But where does he get that spit,' I would ask myself, 'where does he bring it up from, so heavy and so white? Mine will never have the unctuousness or color of his. It will merely be spun glassware, transparent and fragile.' It was therefore natural for me to imagine what his penis [*verge*] would be if he smeared it for my benefit with so fine a substance, with that precious cobweb, a tissue which I secretly called *le voile du palais* [the veil of the palace, the soft palate]."

Over the "Palace that you are not to confuse with any other," *Our-Lady-of-the-Flowers* already let float a sort of veil, the wing of stamin. The glosses seem then to resound in every sense and direction under the vaults of a *palais* [palace, palate]. The glue of chance [*aléa*] makes sense. All the ca(u)ses deploy their discourses, their effects, their substance there in *voiles* of every kind or gender [veils, sails], in cobwebs or trousers. The tongue [*langue*] makes every word glide

The suspense of the *Aufhebung* is these singularities, let us not forget, that it thus holds in the air in the absolute contradiction or equivalence of the contraries, that is also to say, in indifference. In the absolute contraction of singularity, giving is taking, giving as a present steals, presenting hides, loving is the deathstrike [*la frappe à mort*]. The difference of degree falls as well as the opposition: "Every form between absolute singulars is an equivalent [*gleichgültige*: indifferent] form; for it makes no difference whether one makes another a present (*beschenken*), or one robs him (*als ihn berauben*) and strikes him dead (*totzuschlagen*); and there is no border between the least and the greatest outrage."

Indifference, that is, absolute contradiction, the infinite flow [*écoulement*] of one into the other, is gone out of only in relieving singularity in(to) the universal that determines, marks the opposition, the hierarchy, and so on. Once relieved, the singular totality becomes universal totality, absolute spirit. It still exists as singular totality—"family," "possession," "enjoyment"—but relates to itself only in an ideal mode and "proves itself as self-sacrifice." By this sacrifice, it sees itself, gets itself recognized in another consciousness, the people's. It is "saved" at the same time as lost as singularity. It lets itself dissolve what banally singularizes it, renounces its singular freedom, its "hardheadedness" ("Its singular freedom is only its hardheadedness [*Eigensinn*, proper sense, literal sense, sense proper, one's own sense, sense of property, proprietorship]—its death.") in order to present itself in the "absolute substance" as people-spirit.

Thus it erected itself to its contrary.

"Singularity is absolute singularity, *infinity*, the immediate contrary of itself. The essence of spirit is to have in (it)self infinity in a simple way, so that the opposition must immediately relieve itself."

From that moment on, death, suicide, loss, through the passage to the people-spirit as absolute spirit, amortize themselves every time, with every blow, with every *coup*, in the political: at the end of the operation, the absolute spirit records a profit in any case, death included.

The structural discrepancies and the architectonic chiasmas remaining to be taken into account, I open with one stroke [*d'un*

on its humid surface. Further on (about twenty-five pages), the agglomerate web-veil-spittle is reconstituted, but in somewhat taking on other contents. Its constraint takes on a more formal appearance.

> the reference can always, but this is never indispensable, be turned inside out like a glove. Feigning to describe this or that, the veils or the webs, of saliva for example, the text veils itself in unveiling itself, describes, with the same exhibitionistic modesty, its own proper texture. That is how, of what I am composed, with what fabric, with what spurt of saliva. But this self-reference has to remain suspended, like Stilitano's spittle, otherwise the text becomes the sole object of a univocal description: naiveté of a formalist textualism that veers immediately into the (substantialist, thetic, and semanticist) contrary of what it claims to be. The suspension of the veil or of the spit, the elaboration time of the excrement is then *also* the indecision between reference's two directions [*sens*]. Its narrow opening, its hiatus.
>
> Description of the man with style: "Rapid as my glance [*coup d'oeil*] at him was, I had time to take in Stilitano's superb muscularity and to see, rolling in his half-open mouth, a white, heavy blob of spit, thick as a white worm [*ver blanc*] [reversed image, or, inversely, counterproof of the "'spun glassware, transparent and fragile'" of the author's spit, twenty-five pages earlier], which he shifted about, stretching it from top to bottom until it veiled his mouth, between his lips." Much later, in the *Journal*, concerning the gladiolated [*gladiolé*] stylite: "I used to wonder what could possibly be hidden behind that veil of saliva, what the secret sense was of the unctuousness and whiteness of his spittle, which was not sickly but, on the contrary, thrillingly vigorous, able to stir up orgies of energy." In little jerks, the regard descends, then rises again and contemplates the same structure: ". . . between his lips. He stood barefoot in the dust. His legs were contained in a pair of worn and shabby faded blue denim trousers. The sleeves of his green shirt were rolled up, one of them above an amputated hand; the wrist, where the resewn skin still revealed a pale, rose-colored scar, was slightly shrunken."
>
> "Rose! (*A pause.*) I say to you rose!"

It is hardly useful to recall at this point that the *"voile du palais"* furnishes another title for the question of truth.

coup] the *Phenomenology of Spirit* in its middle: passage from consciousness, self-consciousness, and reason to *spirit*. Its first formation is precisely true spirit as *Sittlichkeit*. There the spirit defines itself as the "*ethical life* of a *people*."

Since the Hegel text remains to be read, I re-form here its ellipse around two foci: (the) burial (place), the liaison between brother and sister.

So Antigone will organize the scene and guide us in this abrupt passage.

The dissymmetrical opposition between the singular and the universal is found once again. With death between the two. More precisely, the two terms of the opposition are not the singular and the universal but the *law* of singularity and the *law* of universality. The opposition is determined between these forms of generality that these laws (*Gesetz der Einzelheit, Gesetz der Allgemeinheit*) are, since the opposition works within the ethical reign that is the reign of law.

To this great opposition (the law of singularity/the law of universality) is ordered a whole series of other couples: divine law/human law, family/city, woman/man, night/day, and so on. *Human* law is the law of *day*(*light*) because it is known, public, visible, *universal*; human law rules, not the family, but the *city*, government, war; and it is made by *man* (*vir*). Human law is the law of man. Divine law is the law of woman; it hides itself, does not offer itself in this opening-manifestation (*Offenbarkeit*) that produces man. Divine law is nocturnal and more natural than the law of universality, just as the family is more natural than the city. Once more, the family appears as the most *natural* degree of the ethical community. Natural, divine, feminine, nocturnal, familial, such is the predicative system, the law of singularity. In this law—this is said more precisely, in this place, of the family—the concept is "*unconscious*." The Penates are opposed to the people, to absolute spirit, to universality-producing labor. The proper end of the family, of the woman who represents the family, strictly, is the singular as such.

Then the contradiction upsurges again: in its essentiality, singularity can only disappear, can posit itself *as such* only in death. If the family thus has singularity for its own proper object, it can only busy itself *around death*. Death is its essential object. Its destination is the cult of the dead; the family must consecrate itself to the organization of the burial (place). "The deed, then, which embraces the entire existence of the blood-relation, does not concern the citizen, for he does not belong to the family, nor the individual who is to become a citizen and will *cease* to count as *this singular individual*; it has as its object and content *this* singular individual who belongs to the family, but is taken as a *universal* essence freed from his sensible, i.e. singular, actuality. The deed no longer concerns the *living* but the *dead*, the individual who, after a long succession [*Reihe*, series] of his dispersed being-there, concentrates

Like the wing of stamin (death), the membranous partition [*cloison*] that is called the soft palate, fixed by its upper edge to the limit of the vault, freely *floats*, at its lower edge, over the base of the tongue. Its two lateral edges (it has four sides) are called "pillars." In the middle of the floating edge, at the entrance to the throat, hangs the fleshy appendix of the uvula [*luette*], like a small grape. The text is spit out. It is like a discourse whose unities are molded in the manner of an excrement, a secretion. And since the question here concerns a glottic gesture, the tongue's work on (it)self, saliva is the element that also glues the unities to one another. Association is a sort of gluing contiguity, never a process of reasoning or a symbolic appeal; the glue of chance [*aléa*] makes sense, and progress is rhythmed by *little jerks*, gripping and suctions, patchwork tackling [*placage*]—in every sense and direction—and gliding penetration. In the embouchure or along the column.

luette (uvula) is sometimes derived from *u-vette* (shrubby horsetail) "with the agglutination of the article *l'uvette, luette*," and thus from *uva*, grape and uvula

". . . I secretly called the *voile du palais*. He wore an old gray cap with a broken visor. When he tossed it on the floor of our room, it suddenly became the carcass of a poor partridge with a clipped wing . . ."

Pairing is then dreamed between two *voiles* of different sex. Hardly has the *voile du palais* been named than the text, by little jerks, already rises like *une voile*, a sail, furled at first, then floating and extended, receiving and giving move-

the *little jerks* give the very rhythm of gl, the hardly strangled setting in emotion of the text, the agonizing stricture of the antherection, its jolting force of penetration, by cuts and in fits and starts [*par coupes et à coups*], the efficacy of its repeated check [*échec*],

himself [*zusammen gefasst*, reassembles himself, recovers himself, takes possession again of himself] into *a single* completed figuration (*vollendete* eine *Gestaltung*), and has raised himself out of the unrest of the accidents of life into the calm of simple universality.—But because it is only as a citizen that he is *actual* and *substantial*, the singular individual, so far as he is not a citizen (*Bürger*) but belongs to the family, is only an *inactual* impotent [*marklose*, marrowless] shadow."

The family, the natural moment of the ethical, has as its object only the singular, the essentially singular, that is, which, without reaching the universal legality of the city, strips itself of every empiric characteristic. This pure singularity, stripped but incapable of passing to universality, is the dead—more precisely the name of the dead—is the corpse, the impotent shadow, the negation of the living being-there inasmuch as that singularity has *not yet* given rise to the life of the citizen. Already dead (as empiric existence), not yet living (as ideal universality). If the family's thing is pure singularity, one belongs to a family only in busying oneself around the dead: toilette of the dead, institution of death, wake, monumentalization, archive, heritage, genealogy, classification of proper names, engraving on tombs, burying, shrouding, burial place, funeral song, and so on.

The family does not yet know the universality-producing labor in the city, only the work of mourning.

If the family figures mourning, the economy of the dead, the law of the *oikos* (*tomb*), if the house, the place where death guards itself against itself, forms a theater or funeral rite [*pompe funèbre*], if the woman assures the representation of this, it falls to the married woman to manage, strictly, a corpse. When a man *binds himself* to a woman, even were it in secret (marriage does not depend, according to Hegel, on a formal contract), it is a matter of entrusting her with his death. All the calculations, the ruses, the blackmailings can envelop themselves in this offer of a pure singularity (that loses and guards itself in the name). Entrusting with death, the guarding of a marrowless body, on the condition that the woman erect his burial place after shrouding the rigid corpse (unction, bandages, etc.), maintaining it thus in a living, monumental, interminable surrection. In herself: under the earth, but the night of the subterranean world is the woman, Hegel specifies. Freud will also have shown the reverse side of this desire: the fear of being enclosed in the maternal womb is represented in the agony of being interred alive.

What is a corpse? What is it to make a gift of a corpse?

Pure singularity: neither the empiric individual that death destroys, decomposes, analyzes, nor the rational universality of the citizen, of the living subject. What I give as a present to the woman, in exchange for the funeral rite, is my own absolutely

ment (". . . what meaning would there be in the sight that staggers me when, in a harbor, I see a sail, joltingly, by fits and starts [*à petits coups*],

". . . our yielding to the illusion that the finished melody was well worth some losses of a precious gas. By little successive jerks we have slowly but surely turned the play into something insipid. Successive jerks in order to make certain we would have a success which, in my eyes, is in the final analysis a failure [*échec*]" (*Letters to Roger Blin*).

spreading out and with difficulty rising on the mast of a ship, hesitantly at first, then resolutely, if these movements were not the very symbol of the movements of my love for Stilitano? I met him in Barcelona.").

And the spit with which the gliding mast would be smeared becomes, very quickly—the pen is dipped into a very fluid glue—some vaseline. And even, without forcing, a tube of mentholated vaseline.

Rises therefore in one sudden stroke [*d'un coup*], though very elaborated, the "tube of vaseline" that a policeman, in 1932, two pages further on, draws out of the pocket of the narrator (this word, more and more comical, transforms everything into an *ex cathedra* discourse and an eternal seminar, is edified on the presumption that there is *something* in the author's pocket, *that* the author narrates to us: an event, object, (hi)story, a sense within the reach of knowledge; so try with the tube of vaseline)

"I was dismayed when, one evening, while searching me after a raid—I am speaking of a scene which preceded the one with which this book begins—the astonished detective took from my pocket, among other things, a tube of vaseline. We dared to joke about it since it contained mentholated [*goménolée*] vaseline. . . .

proper body, the essence of my singularity. The woman receives it in the night, however long or short. But what she receives, as pure singularity, immediately passes into its contrary. The feminine burial (place) guards nothing, unless there is an instance—for example the name called proper—that tries to hold itself, that stretches itself between the opposites or the equivalents, even though they annul each other.

The erection of the burial place would be the feminine work. Against what does it stand out? And what does the woman guard thus, in succeeding the dead man, in surviving him, in keeping watch near him? Why is the woman in this? And why doesn't the name on which she lavishes her attentions come from elsewhere than herself to be engraved on the stele or the slab? Why is it inscribed there as if for the first time?

The old humanist and metaphysical theme is familiar: (the) burial (place) is the proper(ty) of (the) man. Among the most tenacious obscurantist residues, there is this terrified failure to recognize everything one would want to refuse to "animalness": with the *logos*, burial and some other complications. Hegel also thought burial is the proper(ty) of (the) man. The family and feminine operation of mourning transforms the living into consciousness and wrests its singularity from nature. This operation prevents the corpse from returning to nature. In embalming it, in shrouding it, in enclosing it in bands of material, of language, and of writing, in putting up the stele, this operation raises the corpse to the universality of spirit. The spirit extricates itself from the corpse's decomposition, sets itself free from that decomposition, and rises, thanks to burial. Spirit is the relieving repetition.

Is it thus simply a matter of struggling against a material decomposition, against a simple dissociation that causes the organic to return to the inorganic? Is the force against which the funeral rite works, under the name death, is it a mechanical and anonymous, a physical, nonconscious exteriority? The analysis would be banal. The feminine operation of burial does not oppose itself to the exteriority of a nonconscious matter; it suppresses an unconscious desire. The family wants to prevent the dead one from being "destroyed" and the burial place violated *by this desire*. Such a remark forms the systematic opening of this analysis on subsequent problematics concerning the work of mourning, anthropophagy, cannibalism, all the processes [*processus*] of incorporation and introjection. Hegel does not determine the unconscious desires against which the dead one must be guarded. The (consanguine) family interrupts the abstract material work of nature and "takes on itself (*über sich nimmt*)" destruction. "The dead individual, by having liberated his *being* from his *operation* or his negative unity, is an empty singular, merely a passive *being-for-others*, at the mercy of every lower irrational individuality and the forces of abstract mate-

"... It concerned a tube of vaseline, one of whose ends was partially rolled up. Which amounts to saying that it had been put to use. Amidst the elegant objects taken from the pockets of the men who had been picked up in the raid, it was the very sign of abjection, of that which is concealed with the greatest of care, but yet the sign of a secret grace which was soon to save me from contempt. . . . But lo and behold! that dirty, wretched object whose purpose [*destination*] seemed to the world—to that concentrated delegation of the world which is the police . . .—utterly vile, became extremely precious to me. Unlike many objects which my tenderness singles out, this one was not at all haloed, it stayed on the table a dull little gray leaden tube of vaseline, broken and livid, whose astonishing discreetness, and its essential correspondence with all the commonplace things in the record office [*greffe*] of a prison (the bench, the inkwell, the regulations, the scales, the odor), would, through the general indifference, have distressed me, had not the very content of that tube made me think, by bringing to mind an oil lamp (perhaps because of its unctuous character), of a night light [*veilleuse*] beside a coffin."

They fall, the jet, the jaculations change signs immediately. The object is abject ("the very sign of abjection"), the object falls [*tombe*] "amidst the elegant objects taken from the pockets . . ." (*elegant* is regularly associated with *gallant*, with *glove* [gant], and is turned inside out, immediately inverts its value), but is relieved thereby, by its very fall: it recovers *from* its fall [*se relève de sa chute*]. The fall from which it recovers is just what exalts it. That holds for all cases. Its *glas* is a *coup de grâce* ("yet the sign of a secret grace"). In its form, the "mentholated" object is certainly not "haloed," but the secret of the gluing, milky substance that is pressed out of the object and shines, the substance, like gold, astonishes, illuminates a catafalque, a crypt, the tomb

before the beginning of the book. It is said in the book.

The hymn that is dedicated to that tube, that transforms it necessarily into an "oil lamp" (*elaion*) or into a "night light beside a coffin," is suspended for a long paranthesis that itself encloses another paranthesis, big and crawling, gluing and fat, with gl [*une autre paranthèse grosse et grouillante, gluante et grasse, de gl*].

rial elements, all of which are now more powerful than himself: the former on account of the life they possess, the latter on account of their negative nature. The family keeps away from the dead this dishonoring operation of unconscious desires (*bewusstloser Begierde*) and of abstract essence, and posits its own operation in their place, and weds the blood-relation to the bosom of the earth (*vermählt den Verwandten dem Schosse der Erde*), to the elemental imperishable individuality. The family thereby makes him a member of a community which on the contrary prevails over and holds under its bonds (*gebunden hält*) the forces of singular matter and the lower forms of life (*Lebendigkeiten*), which sought to unloose themselves against him and to destroy him."

Enter(s) on the scene Antigone. The daughter of Oedipus cries out against human law in the name of divine or family (nonwritten) law. She cries out for a burial (place). For a brother, the sole relative that is "irreplaceable." She would have been able, she says, to replace a dead husband, a dead son, and, consequently, to let them rot on the ground in order not to go against the city's laws. But she cannot hope for another brother. Her song is raised the moment Creon gives the order to enclose her in a "rock tomb" so that she dies or lives there without seeing the sun.

Ὦ τύμβος, ὦ νυμφεῖον, ὦ κατασκαφὴς
  οἴκησις ἀιείφρουρος
"O tomb, nuptial chamber, underground dwelling,
  my prison forever. . . ."

Where does Antigone's desire lead?

The two functions of (the) burial (place) relieve the dead man of his death, spare him from being destroyed—eaten—by matter,

The tube of vaseline, "this little object," in effect induces into the text the apparition of a mother, the apparently unexpected intervention of a maternal image ("but the following image cuts in . . ."). This mother is a thief. The figure also of a substitutive and phallic mother (moon-fish). An urge to cover her with flowers and kisses (to kill-adore-kiss-embalm-band erect), to drool or vomit over her, not directly on her breast [*sein*] (or it falls (*ça tombe*), for the severing is consummated from the cradle, the executioner has grown old), but in her fleece or between her hands that had to (should have, that can only be said in English) provoke(d) the expression of the tube and bugger(ed) [*enculer*] the baby: gl that displays, cuts, retakes itself, flows from everywhere, overflows through every orifice, drowns all the figures, holds all the offices, excludes, recruits [*racole*], reassembles all the morsels, loses and disseminates itself. The place of passage is not yet named, it is the *étamine* [stamen, stamin].

". . . had not the very content of the tube made me think, by bringing to mind an oil lamp (perhaps because of its unctuous character), of a night light [*veilleuse*] beside a coffin.

"(In describing it, I recreate this little object, but the following image cuts in: beneath a lamppost, in a street of the city where I am writing, the pallid face of a little old woman [*vieille*], a round, flat little face, like the moon, very pale; I cannot tell whether it was sad or hypocritical. She approached me, told me she was very poor and asked for a little money. The gentleness of that moon-fish face told me at once: the old woman had just got out of prison.

nature, the spirit's being-outside-self, but also by the probably cannibal violence of the survivors' unconscious desires. That is, essentially, the women's, since they, as guardians of (the) burial (place) and the family, are always in a situation of survival. The law of singularity (divine, feminine, family, natural, nocturnal) protects itself as it were from itself, against itself. And in the same stroke [du même coup], against the other law, the human (virile, political, spiritual, diurnal) law. The two laws fight each other and exchange each other across differences of strata, stages, or steps (Stufen). The law of the human community, manifest law, law from on high, solar law, passes through the rule [règle] of a government (Regierung). In government the actual spirit reassembles and reflects itself. The community in government relates itself to itself so to speak in a head, a place of individuality or indivisibility. The head maintains, holds together, by its height, the scattered members of the community. But the present and real existence of the community (Realität or Dasein) remains the family. It organizes its existence with a relative independence: personal independence, independence of property (Eigentum) always bound to the family, personal right and real right (dingliche Recht) that assures possession and use of things, labor aiming at acquisition and enjoyment. Now if government—the head—authorizes and organizes this family right, the community's element and natural being-there, it is also threatened by that right. The family imperils the head. The family in effect risks settling, engrossing itself in its own private interest, in its own right of possession and enjoyment. So, in its head, the government must become the enemy of just what it governs, must suppress the family not only as natural singularity but in the judicial system proper to it: the war of city government against the family, law of day(light) against law of night, human law against divine law, law of man against law of woman. This war is not one war among others; it is *the* war. The only, in any case the best, means of preventing the family from dissolving the city is in effect to involve the community in war against another city. The government—the virile head exposed to the sun—thus rapes woman or family. Government recalls that its master is death, violent death, the struggle for recognition, the name, the phenomenon of spirit. "In order not to let them become rooted and set in this isolation, thereby breaking up the whole and letting the spirit evaporate, government from time to time (von Zeit zu Zeit) must shake them to their core by war. By this means the government must upset their established order, and violates (verletzen) their right to independence, while the individuals who, engrossed in this order, break loose from the whole and strive after the inviolable *being-for-self* and the security of the person, are made to feel by government in the labor laid on them their lord and master, death. Spirit, thanks to this dissolution of the form of subsisting, wards off

"'She's a thief [voleuse],' I said to myself. As I walked away from her, a kind of intense reverie, living deep within me and not at the edge of my mind [esprit], led me to think that it was perhaps my mother whom I had just met. I know nothing of her who abandoned me in the cradle, but I hoped it was that old thief [vieille voleuse] who begged at night."

The lunar, maternal star acts from within the text (pointed, intense, "within me") in a manner at once beneficent and maleficent: this fish that gets out of prison is then quite stupid the very moment it gives rise to pleasure [jouir], it is "round . . . like the moon," empty like a hole that begs, demands to be covered, filled, knocked up; a poor moneybox [tirelire: also, belly] that "asked for a little money" and that, always, in parantheses, I reply to.

"'What if it were she?' I thought as I walked away from the old woman. Oh! if it were, I would cover her with flowers, with gladioluses [glaïeuls] and roses, and with kisses! I would weep with tenderness over those moon-fish eyes, over that round, foolish face! 'And why,' I went on, 'why weep over it?' It did not take my mind long to replace these customary marks of tenderness by some other gesture, even the vilest and most contemptible, which I empowered to mean as much as the kisses, or the tears, or the flowers.

"'I'd be glad to drool over her,' I thought, overflowing with love. (Does the word glaïeul [gladiolus] mentioned above bring into play the word glaviaux

as always semantic necessity, giving rise to a hermeneutics, a semiotics, verily a psychoanalysis, remains undecidably suspended from the chance of an agglutination called formal or signifying. The flight, the theft [vol] of this suspense, and its necessity, derails semanticism as well as formalism. *Voleuse* takes up *veilleuse* in mid-flight [au vol] and fixes it a little farther on in *vieille voleuse*. Marvellous [merveilleuse] writing. Incredibly precious

being engulfed (*Versinken*) in the natural being-there far from the ethical being-there; and it preserves and raises consciousness's self into *freedom* and its own *force*."

This must come about only *from time to time*. Intermittence—jerking rhythm—is an essential rule. If there were only war, the community's natural being-there would be destroyed, and by its own proper human law, by the very principle of universality. So family, the community's natural being-there, must also resist war and oppose to war its "force of self-preservation." It *must* resist what it *must* do. *Must* two times: two forces of law stand up one in the other, and against the other. The community can live only on their dialectical opposition. The absolute triumph of one or the other would return the community to nothingness. So each law is a law of death.

The "force of self-preservation," at the service of the law of singularity, is the woman, is the family as it represents itself in femininity. Is the divine law of the subterranean kingdom. Like man's law, woman's law entails differences of strata and lets itself be worked (over) by an internal opposition. The two laws do not confront each other as two solid volumes or surfaces, identical to themselves, homogeneous in themselves. Each law is fissured, notched in its inside, and already by the labor of the other within it. For example, the logic of human law commanded absolutely not to do what it commanded absolutely to do: war. Each law had to take into account, record the calculus of the opposite law. The same goes for the law of the family.

Here Hegel examines the elementary structures of kinship. His classification seems limited: he does not justify its historical, sociological, ethnological model, to wit the Western Greek family. In the family, he considers only a restricted number of elements and relations: husband/wife, parents/children, brother/sister. Not grandparents, neither uncles nor aunts, neither male nor female cousins, not a possible plurality of brothers and sisters—this last relation always remains singular.

Three relationships then are held to be primitive and irreducible. They are organized according to a hierarchy with three notches. One raises oneself in the hierarchy, it seems, by appeasing, verily by annulling strictly sexual desire. Between husband and wife, the relation of recognition is the most natural and the most immediate. It dispenses with any third. Specular and sensible as the natural desire that in principle marriage does not suppress. The relationship parents/children implies a mediation: what was only an image (*Bild*) and anticipatory representation (*Vorstellung*) of spirit in conjugual (natural and immediate) desire becomes actuality of spirit. That is progress, an advance. But both relations have a common limit. Both cases are a matter of a transitory and unequal *devotion*. The mutual devotion of the spouses remains

[globs]?) To drool over her hair or vomit into her hands. But I would adore the thief who is my mother.)"

Function of the paranthesis: writing's time. The moment, presently, I write, "in a street of the city where I am writing," I open the paranthesis in order to describe, comment upon, remark the story [*récit*], the other time that is being narrated. This fiction of the "presently" of writing opens a paranthesis within the paranthesis—and this is not fortuitous, each paranthesis of a presently presenting is big with another—in order to comment on the choice of words and the agglutination of the gl's: "(Does the word *glaïeul* [gladiolus] mentioned above bring into play the word *gla*

"'. . . spat into my mouth. An almost unconscious movement of deglutition made me swallow the *glaviaud* [glob]. [The orthography of this word, which has never belonged to the French tongue, which is made to be detached from it like a glob of spit [*molardon*], remains uncertain and plastic, elastic, finally, and lactic. In *Our-Lady*, it is *glaviots*: "I envy you your glory. You would have done me in, as they say in jail [*au tombeau*], just as you did in the Mexican. During your months in the cell, you would have tenderly spat heavy *glaviots* [oysters] from your throat and nose on my memory." In *Miracle of the Rose*, it is also *glavios*: "When the big shots wanted to needle a jerk [*cloche*] or an available chicken, or a bleater (a squealer), they would go looking for him . . . would spit *glavios* [oysters] and frightful insults in his face."] . . .
"'. . . Deloffre [global event] spat in my eyes. The seven of them took their turns, in fact several times, including Divers. I received the spit in my distended mouth, which fatigue failed to close. Yet a trifle [*un rien*] would have sufficed for the ghastly game to be transformed into a courtly [*galant*] one and for me to be covered not with spit but with roses that had been tossed at me. For as the gestures were the same, it would not have been hard for destiny to change everything. . . .'" *Miracle of the Rose*.

As always, it is a violent, parodic, radiographic, profound, implacably derisory interpretation of Golgotha.

sensible and natural; it loses itself, does not come back to itself as spirit. Natural desire, as such, is destined to lose itself, to be incapable of reflecting itself in its naturalness. If natural desire were to do so, it would no longer be what it reflects—natural. In the mutual devotion of parents and children, a certain natural contingency does not let itself be reduced. This relation is still affected by a remain(s) of nonreturn. This contradicts only in appearance the movement of narcissistic and relieving reappropriation whose general logic orchestrates everything. The relief takes place, precisely, only insofar as the family goes out of itself in order to constitute itself, destroys its formal economy, its self-identity, its tautology: insofar as it posits itself, the thesis (*Setzung*) always being relieving. What then about that nonreturn that precisely must be posited, sublimated, suspended, or relieved?

The parents' devotion for the children is affected by an original emotion: knowing that its own proper actuality was exiled in the other—the child—that its own proper for-self is within others "without return." The child's consciousness does not come back to me, does not render to me the consciousness I entrusted to it. There is no "*zurückerhalten*" here: the word designates return, the return of outlaid funds, the reception in return of an outlay, amortization. The actuality of the child is foreign (*fremde*) because it is proper, one's own (*eigene*), proper to itself. The seed does not go back to the source, it no longer circulates. Likewise, the children's devotion for their parents is marked with the same cut [*coupure*]. The child knows that it attains being-for-self in separating itself from its place of emission. The "separation from the origin (*Trennung von dem Ursprung*)" in which the source "dries up."

The *Realphilosophie* nevertheless analyzes this drying up as a relief of the origin; the child is for the parents "*der sich aufhebende Ursprung*." The contradiction here is not a formal effect of philosophical discourse, but the essence of the relief.

The still apparent paradox: the limit of the conjugal relationship is the contrary of the genealogical limit. In the former the return is only specular (thus immediate, natural, and sensible). In the latter, it is expanding mediacy, an outpouring, the pouring forth without return of what flows naturally, from the source [*coule de source*]. These two relationships, still too natural, and dissymmetric, get carried away into the transitory (*Übergehen*), disequilibrium and disparity, inequality (*Ungleichheit*). That is because desire lets itself be entrained in the seminal outpouring.

Whence the infinite superiority of the bond between brother and sister. The family bond, to be sure, since blood speaks in it, but the only one that absolutely suspends all desire. No desire is level with consciousness—Hegel analyzes consciousnesses here—whereas consciousness was, in the other relations, essentially desiring. No desire, then, between singularities of the opposite sex, the

A galalith Golgotha, staged by Matthew as it is elsewhere by John (*Jean*): "and [they] knelt before him and mocked him, saying: Hail, King of the Jews! And they spat upon him and took the reed [*roseau*] and beat him on the head." It would have taken so little (phallus) [*eût fallu si peu*] . . .

"'. . . it would not have been hard for destiny to change everything: the game is organized . . . youngsters make the gesture of hurling. . . . We were in the middle of the most flowery park in France. I waited for roses. I prayed God to alter his intention just a little, to make a false movement so that the children, ceasing to hate me, would love me. They would have gone on with the game . . . but with their hands full of flowers, for it would have taken so little for love to enter Van Roy's heart instead of hate. . . . They moved closer and closer until they were very near me, and their aim got worse and worse.'"

In other words better and better: "'I saw them spread their legs and draw back, like an archer drawing a bow [*bande l'arc*], and make a slight forward movement as the gob spurted [*giclait*]. I was hit in the face and was soon slimier than a prick-head under the discharge. I was then invested with a very deep gravity.'"

No longer his mother but his mother, no longer the bad mother, the one that cannot be erected, but the phallus ejaculating on the cross, the right mother, that is, normal, square, who shines, she, forever, whose sex glistens [*reluit*] upright, trickling sperm. But the best is the worst (taken so little (phallus)), the most grave: "'I was then invested with a very deep gravity. I was no longer the adulterous woman being stoned. I was the object of an amorous rite. I wanted them to spit more and thicker slime. Deloffre was the first to realize what was happening. He pointed to a particular part of my tight-fitting pants [*culotte collante*] and cried out: "'"Oh! Look at his pussy! It's (*Ça*) making him come [*reluire*], the bitch!"'"

They were seven spitting on him, like the archangels whose names you know. They band erect their bow [*arc*], and the mother is among them: it is a man, a man of God. To come, glisten, glow, shine, appear, be present, grow (*phuein*): to band erect. The ark or the galley. In the beginning, *en archē*, that (*ça*) will have banded erect. And the archangel who bears the name of the man of God, "in the sixth month . . . was sent unto a city of Galilee" to announce to a betrothed virgin that soon a child was going "to leap in her womb [*sein*]" and that she would be "filled with the Holy Spirit."

"relationship in its unmixed form (*unvermischte Verhältnis*)." Brother and sister "do not desire one another." The for-(it)self of one does not depend on the other. So they are, it seems, two single consciousnesses that, in the Hegelian universe, relate to each other without entering into war. Given the generality of the struggle for recognition in the relationship between consciousnesses, one would be tempted to conclude from this that at bottom *there is no* brother/sister bond, there is no brother or sister. If such a relation is unique and reaches a kind of repose (*Ruhe*) and equilibrium (*Gleichgewicht*) that are refused to every other one, that is because the brother and the sister do not receive from each other their for-self and nevertheless constitute themselves as "free individualities." These for-self's recognize, without depending on, each other; they no more desire each other than tear each other to pieces.

Is this possible? Does it contradict the whole system? Is one still in the natural sphere of *Sittlichkeit* (the family) from the moment the sexual difference seems suspended, the moment desire absents itself as well as the contrary of desire in a kind of fidelity without love? But then why brother/sister and not brothers or sisters? That is because in truth a sexual difference is still necessary, a sexual difference posited as such and yet without desire. Femininity must be represented in this "relationship without desire (*begierdeloser Beziehung*)," since femininity is the familial, the law of singularity. But this representation must bear itself therein to the highest degree of naturalness, to the point where femininity, remaining femininity, detaches itself from natural desire, deprives itself of pleasure, and on this account, has a presentiment better than ever of the essence of *Sittlichkeit*, of which the family is only the first stage, the first anticipation. Femininity raises itself in this *better* as sister, *less well* as woman, wife, mother, or daughter. "Consequently, the feminine (*das Weibliche*), as sister, has the highest *presentiment* of what is ethical (*des sittlichen Wesens*)." If she does not go beyond presentiment, that is not in order to be sister, but in order to remain feminine. She raises herself higher than the mother, the daughter, or the wife, but as feminine, taken in the naturalness of the sexual difference, she can have only a presentiment of the ethical spirituality. Sister, she holds herself suspended between a desire she does not experience, of which she experiences that she does not experience it, and a universal law (nonfamilial: human, political, etc.) that stays foreign to her. The fact that she is of the same blood as her brother seems to suffice to exclude desire. Appendix of the *Philosophy of Right*: "The brother-and-sister relationship—a *nonsexual* relationship (*Geschwister—ein* geschlechtloses *Verhältnis*)." Since the question here concerns only the monogamous family, the brother and the sister are not uterine but consanguinean brother-sister, in the technical sense metaphysics gives this word (metaphysics attributes the blood only to the father). So

"The Funambulists": "But the arrival of the Angel is announced. Be alone to receive him."

viaux [globs]?)" The other present (above) in the paranthesis is already a past, has resounded from being proferred above the others, and the height of its pronouncement is what arraisounds, calls into play the word *glaviaux*, appeals against *glaïeul* to *glaviaux*.

But agglutination not only takes hold in the signifying paste (gl de-generated by losing its gender, as *son* or *sa*), it also sticks [*colle*] to the sense: the analogy flower-spit with which what one loves (to see dead) is covered, passage from the flower to spit, from phallus to sperm, from gladiolus (glaive of justice, sword of the virgin) to the seminal drool, and so on. Now, this double series, which we could track a long way, interests us and makes a text only to the extent of a remain(s) of gl

to re-elaborate, account taken of this remain(s), a thought of *mimesis*: without imitation (of a represented, identifiable, previous and repeated object), without repetition (of a thing, an event, a referent, a signified), without signification (of a sense or of a signifier). Logic of uneasy strict-ure, its simulacra and phantasms defy the terms of any analysis, but the logic rigorously accounts for the interminability.
For example (the uniqueness of the example is destroyed by itself, immediately elaborates the power of a generalizing organ), the very moment we would claim to recapture there, in a determined text, the work of an idiom, bound to a chain of proper names and singular empirico-signifying configurations, *glas* also names *classification*, that is, inscription in networks of generalities interlaced to infinity, in genealogies of a structure such that the crossings, couplings, switchings [*aiguillages*], detours, and branchings never simply come under [*relèvent . . . d'*] a semantic or formal law. No absolute idiom, no signature. The idiom or signature effect does nothing but restart—reverberate—the *glas*.

here there is a relation of consanguinity that breaks with (desiring) naturalness.

Antigone is not specifically [*proprement*] named in this passage, but the whole analysis is fascinated by the essential figure of this sister who never becomes citizen, or wife, or mother. Dead before being able to get married, she fixes, grasps, transfixes, transfigures herself in this character of eternal sister taking away with her her womanly, wifely desire.

Hegel finds this (*ça*) very good, very appeasing. Not expressly in the *Phenomenology*, but in the *Aesthetics*. In the *Phenomenology* he writes: "The brother, however, is for the sister a peaceful and equal essence in general (*das ruhige gleiche Wesen überhaupt*); her recognition in him is pure and unmixed with any natural relationship. In this relation, therefore, the indifference of the singularity (*die Gleichgültigkeit der Enzelheit*) and the ethical contingency of the latter are not present (*vorhanden*)."

Unique example in the system: a recognition that is not natural and yet that passes through no conflict, no injury, no rape: absolute uniqueness, yet universal and without natural singularity, without immediacy; symmetrical relation that needs no reconciliation to appease itself, that does not know the horizon of war, the infinite wound, contradiction, negativity. Is that the inconceivable? What the greater logic cannot assimilate? Why is this just what obtains for Hegel that feeling of infinite peace whose secret he confides? Very close to the end, in the *Aesthetics*: "Of all the masterpieces of the classical and the modern world—and I know nearly all of them and you should and can—the *Antigone* seems to me from this viewpoint to be the most magnificent (*vortrefflichste*) and appeasing (*befriedigendste*) work of art."

An odd declaration: as in the *Phenomenology*, it says appeasement, but in the tone of a personal confidence. That is rather rare; the statements in the first person, the allusions to personal readings, the pieces of advice, the various "it seems to me," can all be counted. What is happening? And why is this happening the moment the body of the system should be straining itself in a rejection phenomenon, an offshoot phenomenon [*un phénomène de rejet*]? This graft seems to have a structure that cannot be assimilated.

The confidence sounds all the stranger since it closes one of the most "Hegelian" paragraphs. War rages in it. The carnage of Sophocles's play is exhibited. The final fall or elevation receives from this all its force of displacement, the occult strangeness of its *a parte*. Hegel has just analyzed the difference between epic reconciliation and tragic reconciliation. Tragedy is still war unleashed to relieve the individual consciousness's one-sidedness. The individuals enter into the struggle to affirm themselves as totalities in their concrete "presence," so as to be themselves "in the power of what they are

The *glas* is—then (dingdong) [*donc*]—of/for the idiom or the signature.
Of/for the absolute ancestor [*l'aïeul*].
Thus it is never found here or there in the unique configuration of a text. It always lends, affects, or steals itself. The moment you think you are reading it here, commenting on or deciphering this text here, you are commented on, deciphered, observed by an other: what remained.

There is — always — already — more than one — *glas*.

Glas must be read as "singular plural" (fall of the *or* [gold, now] in the double session). It has its breaking in itself. It affects itself and immediately resounds with this literal damage.

Pas de singularité génétique: (no) step of genetic singularity. I write here (on) no singular text, no inimitable signature. Paternity, as you know, is always attributed at the end of a trial and in the form of a judgment. Hence of a generality. But the mother? Above all the mother who dispenses with the father? May one not hope for a pure genealogy from her, purely singular, immediately idiomatic? Isn't the proper finally from the mother?

No more than the *glas* that she sets ringing [*met en branle*]. The mother is a thief and a beggar. She appropriates everything, but because she has nothing that is properly hers. She gives/takes for loving/hating but is nothing. Here again the galactic law works (over), but in order to resist it, the work of the dialectical, phenomenological, ontological law.

For example (but the singularity of the example immediately lets itself be drawn into textual chains articulated to infinity), semantic concatenation is just as powerless as formal concatenation to encompass, without remains, the scene of the old beggar-woman.
Or, for example, entirely other, the same, Mallarmé's "Aumône" ["Alms"]. Suppose that, without knowing it, you did nothing, since long ago, for a long time, here and elsewhere, but decipher it, this "poem," letter by letter, syllable by syllable, word for word, verse by verse, in all its senses, in its general form, its relation to the Mallarméan "corpus," to the French language, to others, to the history of literature past and to come, to its other versions, to the infinite constraints and the infinite opening of what is so naively called a context: what would that give?

fighting." The "injury" (*Verletzen*) they inflict on others must honor what corresponds to "their own existence." "For example, Antigone lives under the political authority of Creon; she is herself the daughter of a King and the fiancée of Haemon, so that she ought to pay obedience to the royal command. But Creon too, as father and husband, should have respected the sacred tie of blood and not ordered anything against its pious observance. So there is immanent in both Antigone and Creon something that in a reciprocal way they rise up against, so that they are gripped and shattered by something that belongs to the circle of their own proper presence (*Kreise ihres eigenen Daseins*). Antigone suffers death before enjoying the bridal dance, but Creon too is punished by the voluntary deaths of his son and his wife, incurred, the one on account of Antigone's death, the other because of Haemon's death. Of all the masterpieces of the classical and the modern world—and I know nearly all of them and you should and can—the *Antigone* seems to me from this viewpoint to be the most magnificent and appeasing work of art."

The effect of focusing, in a text, around an impossible place. Fascination by a figure inadmissible in the system. Vertiginous insistence on an unclassable. And what if what cannot be assimilated, the absolute indigestible, played a fundamental role in the system, an abyssal role rather, the abyss playing an almost tran-

for the one who would grow impatient with seeing nothing come on this side, one would have to name here Christiane, Hegel's sister, or Nanette, "the young woman who lodged in the family house." If one is to believe a remark of Bourgeois, she "had inspired [in Hegel] a feeling perhaps first of love, but which the Frankfurt letters to Nanette Endel reveal as a feeling of sincere friendship." I do not know of what name Nanette was the diminutive. Nana could always play the sister. In the Phrygian legend of Attis, Nana is a kind of holy Virgin. Zeus in a dream disseminates, lets his sperm fall [*tomber*] on the rock. Agdistis, the hermaphrodite, is born from that. The other gods take hold of and castrate him. From the amputated, bleeding [*sanglant*] member there pushes up an almond tree. Nana, daughter of the rivergod Sangarios, picks a milk almond, thrusts it within herself, and brings into the world Attes, a very handsome young man who was then loved by Agdistis, the hermaphrodite become woman (according to another version, Dionysus was the one who cut off Agdistis's member).

Does Hegel know how to dance? The question is more obscure than would be thought. Like Rousseau in any case—but does one dance at them—he loved balls, and he confided this to Nanette: "I very much like balls. It is the happiest thing there is in our sorrowful times." The *Critique of Judgment* also names the ball: the example of finality for a lawn surrounded by trees, in a forest.

*Prends ce sac, Mendiant! tu ne le cajolas
Sénile nourrison d'une tétine avare
Afin de pièce à pièce en égoutter ton glas.*

*Tire du métal cher quelque péché bizarre
Et vaste comme nous, les poings pleins, le baisons
Souffles-y qu'il se torde! une ardente fanfare.*

*Eglise avec l'encens que toutes ces maisons
Sur les murs quand berceur d'une bleue éclaircie
Le tabac sans parler roule les oraisons,*

*Et l'opium puissant brise la pharmacie!
Robes et peau, veux-tu lacérer le satin
Et boire en la salive heureuse l'inertie,*

*Par les cafés princiers attendre le matin?
Les plafonds enrichis de nymphes et de voiles,
On jette, au mendiant de la vitre, un festin.*

*Et quand tu sors, vieux dieu, grelottant sous tes toiles
D'emballage, l'aurore est un lac de vin d'or
Et tu jures avoir au gosier les étoiles!*

*Faute de supputer l'éclat de ton trésor,
Tu peux du moins t'orner d'une plume, à complies
Servir un cierge au saint en qui tu crois encor.*

*Ne t'imagine pas que je dis des folies.
La terre s'ouvre vieille à qui crève la faim.
Je hais une autre aumône et veux que tu m'oublies.*

Et surtout ne va pas, frère, acheter du pain."

If we still ask ourselves about the identity of this poem, about the system of its constraints and the force of its motivations (over-motivations or over-determinations—let us rather, in order to mark the *fold*, and that it is not, in this work, a matter of accumulating wealth, call them effects of *overuse*), do not forget that that there is only the fourth state of a poem in formation ("Haine du pauvre" ["Hatred of the Poor Man"], 1862; "A un mendiant" ["To a Beggar"], 1864; "A un pauvre" ["To a Poor Man"], 1866; "Aumône" ["Alms"], 1887). The "definitive" counterblow [*coup d'arrêt*] can always be considered empirical chance. If one let oneself only be fascinated by the word *glas*, one would first of all pick out [*relèverait*] that it appears only starting in the second state:

I.   *"Ta guenille nocturne étalant par ses trous
       Les rousseurs de ses poils et de ta peau, je l'aime,
       Vieux spectre et c'est pourquoi je te jetter vingt sous."*

The citation of letters is not to be confused with the diverse operations called "biographical" that are related to "the author's life." The letters have a status apart, not only because their stuff is writing, but because they engage what we are tracking here interminably under the name signatory. Consider that I cite those letters of Hegel to Nanette, or to his fiancée named Marie, only to recall, in passing, that the signature most often makes its vowels jump in order to abridge itself, Semitically, to HGL.

"Frankfurt, February 9, 1797

"My gentle dear Nanette,
"*Meine Liebe sanfte Nanette!*
"How much I am obliged (*verbunden*) to you for having insisted on writing to me as soon as possible. . . . for being good enough to compensate (*ersetzen*) me occasionally by written conversation for the loss of your company. Indeed an imperious fate grudgingly (*neidisch*) restricts me to this alone. But it is conquered by my power of imagination, which makes good (*meine Einbildungskraft bezwingt es und ersetzt das*) what fate has withheld: the sound of your voice (*der Ton ihrer Stimme*), the soft glance of your eyes, and all else of which life (*alles übrige Leben*) boasts over written words.
"I have written more extensively to my sister of my situation, and to you I can only say that nothing remains for me to desire but the possibility of hearing from time to time in the evening an account of—soeur Jaqueline [Jaqueline Arnauld, Mother Angelica, of which Nanette, a practicing Catholic, was to speak to Hegel]. . . . Upon mature reflection I have decided not to try to improve anything in these people [the people of the city], but on the contrary to howl with the wolves. I have decided to preserve abstinence *à la* Alexis for the day my star for once leads me to Kamchatka or the Eskimos, and only then to raise my hopes of being able by my example to help these nations resist many sorts of luxury—such as the wearing of taffeta bodices, a host of rings, and such things.
"I am surrounded on all sides by objects which remind me of you. Next to my bed hangs the lovely watch chain [*porte montre*]; over my little table hangs—according to my servant's arrangement—the most darling small pouch for my toothpicks. Each 'ist' reminds me of your pronunciation. In Swabia I was still saying '*ischt.*' But ever since inhaling Palatine air I hiss (*zische*) only fine '*ists.*'
"How anybody, especially the Privy Councillor, could have the idea of calling you roguish [waggish, *schelmisch*] I do not understand at all. Against that charge brashly invoke my own testimony. Who will say of water that it is hard, of a lamb that it is impatient, of a brook that it flows upward, or of a tree that it grows downward! There is also a Catholic church here. . . . As soon as I learn that there is a high mass I will go to perform my religious duties and to lift my soul in prayer to any beautiful image of the Virgin Mary (*Marienbild*). . . ."

II. "*Pauvre, voici cent sous . . . Longtemps tu cajolas,*
   —Ce vice te manquait,—le songe d'être avare?
   Ne les enfouis pas pour qu'on te sonne un glas."

III. "*Prends le sac. Mendiant. Longtemps tu cajolas*
    —Ce vice te manquait—le songe d'être avare?
    N'enfouis pas ton or pour qu'il te sonne un glas."

The last state (the *glas* doesn't "ring [*sonne*]" there any more)

   Prends ce sac, Mendiant! tu ne le cajolas
   Sénile nourrisson d'une tétine avare
   Afin de pièce à pièce en égoutter ton glas.

takes to its highest degree of pertinence, that is, of contiguity (contact, suction, aspiration), the *glas* of what touches the breast [*sein*], to astonish or disgust whoever would still wonder (arbitrariness or motivation?) what lactiferous form to recognize in the tocsin (in the word? in the thing? in the sense?). To its highest degree of pertinence, but without reducing the decollating games [*jeux de décollement*] necessary to the sucker [*ventouse*]. To be sure, the last three states form a more homogeneous series on the surface. But "Haine du pauvre" works the fleece

("*Ta guenille nocturne étalant par ses trous*
   Les rousseurs de ses poils et de ta peau, je l'aime,

   . . .

"*Et ne vas pas drapant ta lésine en poëme.*

   . . .

"*Mets à nu ta vieillesse et que ta gueuse joue,*
   Lèche, et de mes vingt sous chatouille la vertu,
   A bas!...—les deux genoux!...—la barbe dans la boue!")

of *coutelas* [cutlass] that seems to rhyme with the first verse of the three subsequent poems (*cajolas*). It is the only rhyme in *las* and the last verse of "Haine du pauvre."
   A throw of the dice? Gold? Silver? Copper?

   Que veut cette médaille idiote, ris-tu?
   L'argent brilla, le cuivre un jour se vert-de-grise,
   Et je suis peu dévot et je suis fort têtu,

". . . I only hope this letter finds you still in Stuttgart, and serves in my place. . . . Because of your impending departure from our house, you appear to become even more separated from me. I can imagine the sadness your departure will cause my sister. . . . Do charge my sister with letting me know right away the news you will give her. . . .

"I remember having traveled through Memmingen and having come upon a nice fertile region which is in particular completely sown with hop gardens. On the banks of the Iller you will surely find nice parts. Your spiritual nourishment is surely also well provided for. I remember having been in a Franciscan monastery. I do not know whether I should say that I fear the good seed which the young Protestant clergy in Stuttgart has sprinkled into your soul may risk being choked off there, or rather that such weeds may come to be rooted out there [Matthew, Mark, Luke]. At least you must sincerely procure a rosary, prepare longer for confession, pay more respect and reverence to the saints in word and deed, etc. . . .

"Your sincere friend,
"Hgl"

"Frankfurt am Main, July 2, 1797

"Dearest friend!

"This being the first time in a long while that I have again taken pen in hand to write anyone at all a letter, let it be to pay a most oppressive debt. . . .

". . . The recollection of those days passed in the country even now ever drives me out of Frankfurt. And so as I reconciled myself there in the arms of nature with myself and with men, I thus often flee here to this faithful mother, separating myself again with her from the men with whom I live in peace, preserving myself under her auspices from their influence, forestalling an alliance (*Bund*) with them. . . .

"What my sister and the people in Stuttgart generally are doing I have no idea. . . .

"As soon as you stopped holding me to piety, it was all over. I never more than pass by churches. According to your letter, in church attendance at Memmingen you find not only no consolation for itself, but also cause for sorrow and regret in the miserable sustenance being handed out to the two-legged believers.

"July 17

"I had written this far some time ago, and would have left this sheet lying around for still some time if a higher power, my guardian spirit, had not suddenly awakened me from my lethargy. My patron himself, the blessed Saint Alexis, called out to me in symbols on the day of his celebration: Wake up, you who sleep, arise from the dead; only in friendship is life and light!

Choisis.—Jetée? alors, voici ma pièce prise.
Serre-la dans tes doigts et pense que tu l'as [quoi? qui?]
Parce que j'en tiens trop, ou par simple méprise.

C'est le prix, si tu n'as pas peur, d'un coutelas.

No more fleece in the subsequent states: a smooth face, naked, without a beard. The "*Sénile nourrison d'une tétine* [Senile nursling of a . . . teat]" is born with the version called "definitive," the fourth. "*Avare*" and "*glas*" were already there, the rhymes were not put out of order. A necessity has slowly been imposed, from piece to piece, in the formation of the poem, to the very end of what one would be tempted to call a gestation. We will not yield to this naturalistic and teleological reading, but will retain from it the hypothesis of a necessity in the march—the market—of overuses.

To attribute only one instant, one use there, the "*pièce à pièce* [coin by coin]" of the "*métal cher* [dear metal]" falls drop by drop from the "*sac* [bag]" of the "*tétine avare* [miser teat]": (the) *glas* rings [*tinte*] near (the) *tétine* [teat]. (The) *tétine* [teat] resounds and reverberates [*retentit*]. The possibility of adding the article between parentheses assumes this interval and this passage (rhythm of sucking [*ventouse*]) between uses (between, if one still wants, the use as signifier, the use as signified, the use as referent). It has to do with yielding to the necessity that associates, in the maximum of use and of over-use, the greatest number of marks, as for example *la tétine qui retentit dans un glas* [the teat that reverberates in a *glas*]. Who has ever heard that (*ça*)? That tintinnabulum there?

The fact that each version *also* works on another version—and this ought to be able to be said as well of the "first" version—always confers a fold [*pli*] or a use [*emploi*] supplementary to the whole scene, imparts a sort of lateral twist to all its referential movements. The poem is always also the active "translation" of another poem that rings within it. A little as if, at the

"Since I feel myself too unworthy to approach this Saint, he could easily regard this lack of reverence and service—which has its source in the very feeling of my baseness—as culpable negligence. He could thus deprive me of his clemency and grace. Fortune has accordingly bestowed upon me a mediatrix between saints and human beings who represents me before him, and through whom the Saint allows his grace to flow toward me.

"I accept with all due respect one of the significant symbols (bedeutenden Symbole)—the ecclesiastical collar—along with what he thereby wished to recall to me. I will guard both as a precious treasure, a relic (Reliquie), and take great care not to profane them by usage and application. The other, more beautiful, human symbol—the garland that unites parted friends—I wish to make the companion of my life. The flowers are of course dry, and life has vanished from them. But what on earth is a living thing if the spirit of man does not breathe life into it? What is speechless but that to which man does not lend his speech? This little garland will always lisp to me: There lives somewhere a small black-eyed being—a dove nonetheless—who is your friend. And as proof that I gladly allow the small garland to tell me this, I will occasionally leave a visiting card with my address, as is now the fashion in the world. One drives up, makes someone's mouth water as if he were now to get much to hear, and then simply leaves a card.

"Farewell! I am going to bathe in the Main. The waves which will cool me perhaps you yourself saw flowing by Obbach.

"Your friend,
"Hgl
"(still, as ever, 'Master' in the address)"

"Frankfurt, November 13, 1797

"Dearest friend,
"For a long time I have had an almanac on my desk that was meant for you, and that I am finally sending. I only hope it will not have lost the appeal of novelty for you because of my delay. Yet this story can be always reread from time to time. In any case, only the pleasure of repeated viewing is decisive in the beauty of a work of art—the fact that one gladly returns to it. . . .

"I do not know why I always fall into general reflections. But you will forgive a man who once was a Master, and who drags himself around with this title and its accessories as with an angel of Satan striking him with fists (2 Cor 12:7). You will still remember our way and manner from Stuttgart. I have every reason to assume that longer association with you would have liberated me more and granted me a greater capacity for merrymaking (eines frohen Spiels)."

"Frankfurt, May 25, 1798

"Dear Nanette
". . . Do not spare me. Tear me to pieces, tell me yourself how irresponsible my negligence is. You do nothing but exercise justice. Burden me with hearing masses, with telling beads, with as many rosaries as you like, I have deserved it all. Just do not do me the injustice of believing I have not appreciated the value of your gift. You consecrated it in memory. . . . this is the best treasure a person can gain. . . . But why have you,

"interior" of Mallarmé's "corpus," between Mallarmé and Mallarmé, the operation of "Bells" ["Cloches"] was reproduced each time. "Les cloches" (1872) "translate," transpose, restrike [répercutent] rather, "The Bells." Of Poe's poem they reproduce, certainly, the grand semantic organization (silver bells, golden bells, bronze bells, iron bells) and the greatest possible number of thematic motives, according to a calculus of gains and losses, of redistributions of use that the analysis, i.e., the decomposition or reduction into elements, would never be able to exhaust: not only—even here—because of the richness or the subtlety of the machinations, but, a priori, by reason of the generative transformation that feigns imitation and transposes the text into another system. The greatest correspondence is attained only in the most different element, in an entirely other organization of resources (quantity, quality, rhythm).

One must surely admit, for example, that mimesis recharges itself and operates from one text to the other, from each text to its theme or to its reference, without the words originally resembling things and without them immediately resembling each other. And yet the resemblance reconstitutes itself, superimposes or superimprints itself through and thanks to differential or relational structures. There the content is exhausted, sometimes to the point of being about to disappear. To disappear as quality, as quantity, but more rarely as rhythm (From "The Double Session" onward, the purpose would be to rethink the value of rhythm and to introduce it to a reelaboration of the graphics of mimesis. Stumbling, in "The Economic Problem of Masochism," over the logic of quantity and quality, Freud searches—very vaguely hypothetical—in the direction of rhythm.). Poe's rhymes are not preserved, of course, but on all levels, as many as possible, the beats of a rhythm, whatever their support or material surface. Besides, the word "rhyme" (Runic rhyme) is itself regularly replaced by the word rhythm (runic rhythm, rhythm of an ancient, secret, difficult writing).
Some exemplary echoes, only the most striking—among so many others, subtle or muffled:

How they tinkle, tinkle, tinkle,
In the icy air of night!

Comme elle tinte, tinte, tinte, dans le glacial air de nuit

loose child, added a butterfly to a gift offered to memory? Do you not feel the contradiction? (*Fühlen Sie nicht den Widerspruch?*) A butterfly flutters from one flower to another without recognizing the soul of either. The fleeting theft of a few sweets is the butterfly's pleasure, but it has no intuition (*Anschauung*) of what is immortal. With a base soul, memory is only a soulless impression (*seelenlose Eindruck*) on the brain, the mark (*Abdruck*) on a material that always remains different from the imprint (*Gepräge*) it possesses and never becomes one with it.

"I hear that your Babet is married. My sister no doubt attended the wedding. There must have been much merrymaking. We would have surely also danced a lot—like the evening before my departure. I have turned in circles ever since (*ich habe seitdem mich immer so im Kreise gedreht*). Have you not had any balls in Memmingen? I very much like balls. (*Ich bin den Ballen sehr gut.*) It is the happiest thing there is in our sorrowful times. . . .

"I am sending this letter to my sister for handling since I do not know where you are."

Thirteen years later—Jena and the *Phenomenology* in between—here is, for Marie (one of three), the fiancée, a poem of ten quatrains, the *Phoenix*. For example:

"March on mountain tops with me.
From clouds below tear yourself free;
Here in the ether may we stand.
In Light's colorless womb (*In des Lichtes farbelosem Schoss*)
    take my hand.

"What opinion (*Meinung*) has into sense (*Sinn*) injected—
Half from truth, half from madness collected—
Has as a lifeless mist (*leblosen Nebel*) lifted,
By the breath of life, of love, evicted.

"The valley below of contracted nothingness (*des engen
    Nichts*),
Of vain exertion repaid in an exertion endless,
With dulled senses to desire bound (*an die Begier ge-
    bunden*)—
There your heart never has been found.

. . .

"See the altar here atop mountains,
On which Phoenix dies in a flaming fountain,
Only to rise in youth everlasting—
This fruit of its ashes endlessly winning.

"Phoenix's brooding, turned back on itself alone,
Was now preserved as merely its own (*Hatte sich zu eigen es
    gespart*).
The point of its existence shall vanish (*Nun soll seines Daseins
    Punkt zerrinnen*),
And the pain of sacrifice weigh on it in anguish.

"But the feeling of striving immortal
Pushes (*Treibt's*) him beyond his self's narrow portal.
May his earthly nature quake
In flames this striving comes awake.

. . .

Keeping time, time, time,
In a sort of Runic rhyme,
To the tintinnabulation that so musically wells
From the bells, bells, bells, bells,
    Bells, bells, bells—
From the jingling and the tinkling of the bells.

allant, elle, d'accord (d'accord, d'accord) en une sorte de rythme runique, avec la "tintinnabulisation" qui surgit si musicalement des cloches (des cloches, cloches, cloches, cloches, cloches, cloches); du cliquetis et du tintement des cloches.

. . .

—how it tells
Of the rapture that impels
To the swinging and the ringing
Of the bells, bells, bells—
Of the bells, bells, bells, bells,
    Bells, bells, bells—
To the rhyming and the chiming of the bells!

qu'il dit le ravissement qui porte au branle et à la sonnerie des cloches (cloches, cloches—des cloches, cloches, cloches, cloches), au rythme et au carillon des cloches!

. . .

In a clamorous appealing to the mercy of the fire,

dans une clameur d'appel à merci du feu,

. . .

By the side of the pale-faced moon.
Oh, the bells, bells, bells!
What a tale their terror tells
Of Despair!
How they clang, and clash, and roar!
What a horror they outpour
On the bosom of the palpitating air!

aux côtés de la lune à la face pâle. Oh! les cloches (cloches, cloches), quelle histoire dit leur terreur—ce Désespoir! Qu'elles frappent et choquent, et rugissent! Quelle horreur elles versent sur le sein de l'air palpitant! encore l'ouïe sait-elle, pleinement, par le tintouin et le vacarme, comment tourbillonne et s'épanche le danger; encore l'ouïe dit-elle, distinctement, dans le vacarme et la querelle, comment s'abat ou s'enfle le danger, à l'abattement ou à l'enflure dans la colère des cloches, dans la clameur et l'éclat des cloches!

"Narrow bands (*enge Binden*) dividing us, fall away!
Sacrifice alone is the heart's true way [*Lauf*]!
I expand myself to you, as you to me.
May what isolates us go up in fire, cease to be.

. . .

"Once the spirit atop free mountains has flown [*Tritt*],
It holds back nothing of its own (*Er behält vom Eignen nichts
    zurück*).
Living to see myself in you, and you to see yourself in me,
In the enjoyment of celestial bliss shall we be (*So geniessen wir
    der Himmel Glück*)."

(13 April 1811)

Four days later, again a poem:

"You are mine! A heart as yours I may call mine.
In your look (*In Deinem Blick*) may I divine
Love's look returned (*wiederblick*), oh bliss,
Oh highest happiness (*o höchstes Glück*)!

. . .

"Yet the poverty of words I address,
Whose power love enchanted to express—
A love which from within presses with force
O'er to the heart—is frustrated in its course.

"I could envy, Nightingale,
Your throat's power (*Deiner Kehle Macht*), making mine
    pale.
Yet, spitefully, Nature has merely lent
The language of sorrow an instrument so eloquent!

"Yet if Nature did not grant the lips
Expression in speech of love's bliss,
For lovers' bond (*Bunde*) it has given with just finesse
These lips a token of greater tenderness.

"Souls touch in the kiss—more profound than speech.
My heart overflows into yours, within mutual reach."

The next day, a letter to Niethammer:

". . . I learn that if you remain you can be more active on behalf
of the university system than in your situation thus far. Since
the matter is still pending, my letter would really seem doubly
superfluous. But I have a more precise motive for writing:
namely, my bond (*Verbindung*) with a good and very dear girl.
My happiness (*Glück*) has in part been made contingent on my
faculty appointment at the University. Since the day before
yesterday I have been certain of calling this dear heart mine. I
know I have your warm wishes for my happiness. I have told
her moreover that I would first write to you and the best of
women. Her name is Marie von Tucher. . . . I spare myself a
description of how happy I feel. Supply (*supplieren Sie*) the
image of it from your own memory and present. . . . But do
not as yet tell anybody anything of this. Due to the external
conditions and her father, we cannot yet talk aloud of it. At
most Roth and his wife may be told, but they should likewise
keep it in confidence. . . ."

Yet the ear, it fully knows,
    By the twanging
        And the clanging,
    How the danger ebbs and flows;
Yet the ear distinctly tells
        In the jangling
        And the wrangling,
    How the danger sinks and swells,
By the sinking or the swelling in the anger of the bells—
        Of the bells—
    Of the bells, bells, bells, bells,
        Bells, bells, bells—
In the clamor and the clangor of the bells!

    Hear the tolling of the bells—
        Iron bells!

*Entendez le glas des cloches—cloches de fer! quel monde
de pensée solennelle comporte leur monodie! Dans le silence de la nuit que nous frémissons de l'effroi! à la mélan-
colique menace de leur ton. Car chaque son qui flotte, hors
la rouille en leur gorge — est un gémissement.*

What a world of solemn thought their monody compels!
        In the silence of the night,
        How we shiver with affright
    At the melancholy menace of their tone!
        For every sound that floats
        From the rust within their throats
            Is a groan.
        And the people — ah, the people —
        They that dwell up in the steeple,
            All alone,
        And who tolling, tolling, tolling,
        In that muffled monotone,
        Feel a glory in so rolling
            On the human heart a stone —
    They are neither man nor woman —
    They are neither brute nor human —
        They are Ghouls: —

*Et le peuple—le peuple—ceux qui demeurent haut dans
le clocher, tout seuls, qui sonnant (sonnant, sonnant) dans
cette monotonie voilée, sentent une gloire à ainsi rouler sur
le cœur humain une pierre—ils ne sont ni homme ni
femme—ils ne sont ni brute ni humain—ils sont des
Goules: et leur roi, ce l'est, qui sonne; et il roule (roule—
roule), roule un Péan hors des cloches! Et son sein content
se gonfle de ce Péan des cloches! et il danse, et il danse, et
il hurle: allant d'accord (d'accord, d'accord) en une sorte
de rythme runique, avec le tressaut des cloches—(des
cloches, cloches, cloches), avec le sanglot des cloches;
allant d'accord (d'accord, d'accord) dans le glas (le glas,
le glas) en un heureux rythme runique, avec le roulis des
cloches—(des cloches, cloches, cloches), avec la
sonnerie des cloches—(des cloches, cloches, cloches,
cloches, cloches,—cloches, cloches, cloches)—le geig-
nement et gémissement des cloches.*

Niethammer waits for a decision of the king concerning this, delays answering, apologizes for the delay, but tells Hegel his own disagreement with the procedure: "If I have understood your letter right, you want to delay not only concluding your marriage, but even publicly announcing the engagement you have made, until your nomination at Erlangen is done. In no way can I approve that. Your nomination is, according to my information, so little in doubt that I cannot question it even in the case of me abandoning my post. . . . To speak to you frankly, I consider this as a timidity as unfortunate as unjustified on your part. At a time when even kings themselves are no longer expected to prove their ancestry to win the right to court royal daughters, at a time when the personal merit and rank one has acquired on one's own without ancestry ennobles more than all proofs of hereditary nobility, there is nothing to fear from public opinion in a union such as yours. . . . So do not allow such idle worries—not to speak of a certain vanity on your part, which so ill befits a philosopher—keep you from concluding your marriage as soon as possible.

"But I have still another reason that makes it my duty to advise you against this delay. Permission for marriage, that in your capacity as civil servant you must receive directly from His Majesty the King: you will obtain it much more easily as rector at Nuremberg than in the capacity of professor at Erlangen. The reason is very simple. The principal viewpoint considered when the matter concerns granting permission to marry is the pension assured the widow, according to the practice generally in use for all servants of the State, which poses each time the question of the funds from which the said pension must be taken. Now this question is far easier to resolve for institutions already having a regular budget than for the University of Erlangen, which does not yet have any regular funds at its disposal. . . ."

Hegel, as always, late in answering:

"It is your letter's wealth of gratifying content, my dear friend, which has kept me silent for so long, and my head is still so filled with it that I can hardly put it into the usual language of a letter. Your staying on at your present post, the altered circumstances in which you are doing so, your anticipated arrival at the wedding reception, the reception itself—everything is so intertwined that it will be difficult at first to pick up a thread from such a tissue. To be sure, I see my Marie unwind many a ball of yarn, and I help her all the more diligently to look for the ends, inasmuch as completion of the trousseau and acceleration of preparations for the wedding depend on such things. For, as you know, women want to have such important matters in order from one end to the other, and do not take to the suggestion that something like that might equally be done afterwards. But I notice that these threads have taken me right to the heart of the matter, and thus continue to say that the necessary arrangements will in any case not be in place before fall. So now it is only a question of having her father—for the rest of the family has agreed—give his assurance that, even if I am to be still a gymnasium rector, the wedding will take place in the fall. The excellent explanations which you have handed on to me have not gone unused. One objective reason, namely the

And their king it is who tolls:—
And he rolls, rolls, rolls,
    Rolls
    A pæan from the bells!
And his merry bosom swells
    With the pæan of the bells!
And he dances, and he yells;
Keeping time, time, time,
In a sort of Runic rhyme,
    To the pæan of the bells —
      Of the bells:
Keeping time, time, time,
In a sort of Runic rhyme,
    To the throbbing of the bells —
    Of the bells, bells, bells —
    To the sobbing of the bells: —
Keeping time, time, time,
    As he knells, knells, knells,
In a happy Runic rhyme,
    To the rolling of the bells —
    Of the bells, bells, bells: —
    To the tolling of the bells —
Of the bells, bells, bells, bells,
    Bells, bells, bells —
To the moaning and the groaning of the bells.

What one would be tempted to isolate as a galactic segment (the moon, the tocsin, the rounded [*galbé*], winded [*soufflé*], or palpitating bosom [*sein*]—two times—the outpouring, and so on) does not even constitute a semantic or thematic, apparent or hidden chain; it is brought into indecision by the swinging or the suspended beat, the oscillation of the tongue [*battant*] (the "true" impossible theme of the morsel), remarking or restriking itself in the neither-nor of the ghouls (between man and woman, between man and nonman, language and nonlanguage, and so on). The semantic element is struck by the rhythm of its other, exposes, opens, offers itself there, in its very hiatus.

This other, which one would be tempted to isolate as a concatenation of signifiers, of identities of arbitrary elements, is unceasingly reemployed according to a mimetics that is not related to a real sound, to a full

greater difficulty of obtaining Royal authorization from Erlangen, I have not been able to use for all it is worth. For as you know, even fanatics and liars can persuade others only inasmuch as they have persuaded themselves of the reasons to be used. But undoubtedly I can go to Erlangen only if the university is organized, in which case funding will also be taken care of, and thus funding for the widow's pension as well. You moreover know people here in Nuremberg. If all imaginable reasons counsel these people from Nuremberg to buy a horse, their first deliberations always bring them to the point of buying—for the time being—a packet of horse-hair. But since the rest of the nag adheres to this hair, the whole animal must likewise little by little be drawn into the stable. Disclosure of the engagement came about by itself. Marie's father introduced me to her grandfather. He who first says *A* now goes on through the entire alphabet. We thus comport ourselves as engaged before the entire world. You know anyway that one who has founded one's cause on the goodness of women, especially in such matters, has not built on sand. . . . there has already been so much talk about Erlangen that our union has come to be completely fused with the city in our imagination, much as man and wife. The improvement of my economic situation is necessary due to my lack of means because my Marie, whose grandfather is still alive and whose father still has seven children apart from herself, can obtain an annual sum of only 100 florins beyond the dowry. . . .

"Your sincere friend Hgl"

From the summer that follows, on the eve of the marriage, there are again two letters to Marie.

"Nuremberg . . .

"Dear Marie,
"I have written to you in thought almost all night long! What was at issue in my thoughts was not this or that isolated matter between us, but rather, inevitably, the whole thought: are we thus going to make ourselves unhappy (*unglücklich*)? From the depth of my soul came the reply: This cannot, ought not, and must not be. It shall not be! (*Dies kann, dies soll, und darf nicht sein!—Es wird nicht sein!*)
"However, what I have long told you is to me summed up in the conclusion that marriage is essentially a religious bond (*Band*). To be complete, love requires a still higher moment than that in which it consists merely in and for itself. What perfect satisfaction—i.e., being entirely happy (*glücklich sein*)—means can only be completed by religion and the sense of duty; for only therein do all particularizations of the temporal self (*Selbst*) step aside, particularizations which in actuality could cause trouble. Such total satisfaction by itself remains imperfect and cannot be taken as ultimate, though it should constitute what is called earthly happiness.
"I have before me the draft of the lines which I added to your letter to my sister. My postscript, to which you certainly attached too much importance, is missing. I was thus reminded of exactly what occasioned the frame of mind in which I wrote that postscript even while recopying the draft. Had we not talked the evening before and definitely agreed that we prefer to call what we were certain to attain

content, but indeed, as the transposition makes all that appear, to relational rhythmic structures with no invariant content, no ultimate element.

There is indeed the appearance of a simple kernel, around which everything seems to be agglomerated: *gl, cl, kl, tl, fl,* and to confine ourselves to the lexical account, very insufficient in reading rhythm, we single out [*relève*] in effect *tinKLe, oversprinKLe, JinGLing, turTLe, GLoats, starTLed, CLamorous, CLang, CLash, janGLing, wranGLing, CLamor, CLangor, FLoats, GLory, CLoches, GLacial, CLigner, CLiquetis, FLotte, enFLe, CLameur, éCLat, GLas, GLoire, gonFLe, sanGLot,* the two letters recomposing their attraction elsewhere, at a distance, in the poem, according to numerous and complex games. Moreover, this appearance of a kernel is more denuded, better read and remarked by the relievo of the two versions, Poe's and Mallarmé's. Which does not mean (to say) that there is an absolute kernel and a dominant center, since rhythm does not only bind itself to words and least of all to the proximity of the contact between two letters. Nevertheless, by ignoring "Les cloches," Fónagy remains deaf to the + L effect (consonant + L), not only in those translations where it does not occur but even in the one, the German, where it does: "The main purpose of *translation* in prose is to translate, to carry over the message from the original to the target language substituting the form *a* of the original language by form *b* of the target language. . . . Contrary to this procedure the translator of poems carries over certain features of form *a* of the original into form *b* of the target language. The silvery tinkling of the bells in the icy air of night in the poem of Edgar Allan Poe is reflected also in the Hungarian and German and Italian translations by the prevailing *i* sounds and the sequences *ng, nk, nt, nd.*

How they *tinkle, tinkle, tinkle*
In the icy air of night . . .

Hal*ld*, mi*nd*, pe*nd*ül, ko*nd*ul, cse*nd*ül. . .
(Mihály Babits)

*Wie sie kling*en, kl*ing*en, kl*ing*en,
Zw*ink*ernd sich zum Reigen schl*ing*en . . .
(Th. Etzel)

Come *tintinn*ano, *tintinn*ano, *tintinn*ano
Di una cristallina del*i*zia . . .
(Frederico Olivero)."

together 'satisfaction (*Zufriedenheit*)'? And did we not say: 'There is a *blessed* (selige) satisfaction which, all illusion aside, is more than all that is called being happy'? As I wrote the words now before me, whose meaning is so dear to me— 'You may see from it how happy I can be with her for the rest of my life, and how happy winning such love, which I scarcely still hoped for in this world, has already made me'— I added, as if this happy sensation of mine and its expression had been excessive over against what we had already said: '. . . *insofar as* happiness belongs to my life's destiny (*Bestimmung*).' I do not think this should have hurt you! I remind you, dear Marie, that your deeper sense, the formation of what is higher in you, has taught you as well that in non-superficial natures every sensation of happiness is connected with a sensation of melancholy. Furthermore, I remind you of your promise to heal me of any disbelief in satisfaction that might remain in my nature, i.e., to reconcile my true inner self with the way I too frequently am toward and for the actual. I equally remind you that this point of view gives a higher dimension to your destiny, that I credit you with strength for it, that this strength must lie in *our* love. Distinguishing (*bringen eine Unterscheidung herein*) your love for me and mine for you, if I may be so emphatically explicit, would separate *our* love: this love is solely *ours*, merely this unity, this bond (*Band*). Turn away from reflection within this distinction (*Unterschied*), allow us to hold fast to this One (*diesem Einen*) that can alone be my strength as well, my new love of life. Let this trust be the basis for everything, and then all will be truly well.

"Oh, how much more I could still write—about my perhaps hypochondriacal pedantry, which led me to insist so greatly on the distinction between satisfaction and happiness (*Glück*), a distinction which is once again so useless; or about how I have sworn to you and myself that your happiness (*Glück*) shall be my dearest possession. There is still much that passes away, is forgotten, and remedied merely by not being evoked.

"One more thing: I have long doubted whether I should write to you, since everything written or spoken again depends solely on explanation; or, since I feared explanation, which once embarked upon is so dangerous. But I have overcome this fear and have the highest hope that your heart will know how to receive these words.

"Farewell until, *dear* Marie, we see each other today again untroubled. I would still like only to be able to tell you this: what feeling, how very much—my existence as much as it is—lies for me in the words: *dear Marie*.

"Your Wilhelm"

"Nuremberg . . .

". . . I have hurt you by a few things I said. This causes me pain. I have hurt you by seeming to censure moral views I can only repudiate, as if they were principles of your own thought and action. About this I now say to you only that I reject these views in part inasmuch as they abolish the difference between what the heart likes—i.e., what pleases it—and duty; or rather inasmuch as they completely eliminate duty and destroy morality (*Moralität*). But likewise—and this is the most important matter between us—please believe me when I tell you that I do not attribute these views, insofar as

If one wanted to reduce even further the apparent kernel of the +L effect (gl, cl, kl, tl, fl, pl, and so on), one would then isolate L. Now, apropos L, after a very rich analysis (so rich that it can bring no determinate result to a halt), Fónagy has to conclude, very justly (but then what becomes of his project?), that a determination, hence a motivation, hence a univocal semantics are impossible: "The complex character of the consonant L reminds us of a hardly surprising but important truth. There is no simple and exclusive correspondence between a drive and a given sound." The drive that seeks to motivate always finds something with which to be nourished and frustrated at once. Its result necessarily contradicts the drive because the drive itself, by itself, diverges [*s'écarte*] into two columns. This essential division of the so-called Cratylean motive could be demonstrated in *English Words* that necessarily submit to the law of antherection and dissemination. Examples: "G (while not being the letter that governs the greatest number of words) has its importance, signifies first a simple aspiration, toward a point where the spirit goes: this guttural, always hard when a first letter, should be followed by a vowel or a consonant. Add that desire, as satisfied by *l*, expresses with the aforesaid liquid, joy, light, etc., and that from the idea of gliding we also pass to that of an increase through vegetable growth or through some other mode; with *r* finally, there would be something like grasping the object desired with *l*, or a need to crush [*écraser*] it or grind it."

"L. . . . This Letter would sometimes seem powerless to express by itself anything other than an appetition followed by no results . . ."

To observe only the principle and the logic (not the empirical approximations within a determined language, English), one would at least note this, that L, here satisfying desire, affording grasping its object, first marks — like G — an aspiration, or an appetition, an unsatisfied desire. The object—of desire: a desire for the object—unsatisfied. The problematic of "Bases pulsionnelles de la phonation" omits, above all, an essential relay: the effect of the proper name. If Fónagy *is right* not to hurry the answer (even though he cites Mallarmé, "'With the tired finger will you press the breast / By which the woman flows in sibylline whiteness . . .'" ["'*Avec le doigt fané presseras-tu le sein / Par qui coule en blancheur sibylline la femme . . .*'"],

they have this consequence, to *you*, to your self; that I view them as lying merely within your reflection (*Reflexion*); that you do not think, know, or gain an overview of them in their logical connection; that they serve you as a way of excusing others. To justify (*rechtfertigen*) is something else, for what one may excuse in others is not therefore considered permissible in oneself. Yet what one can justify is right for everyone, and thus for ourselves as well.

"With regard to myself and my manner of explanation, do not forget that if I condemn maxims (*Maximen*), I too easily lose consciousness of the way in which they are actual in determinate individuals—in you, for instance. Nor should you forget that such maxims appear before my eyes too earnestly in their universality, in their logical consequences, extended results, and applications. Far from taking these things to be entailed for you, you give them no thought. At the same time you yourself know that, even though character and the maxims governing insight are different, what maxims govern insight and judgment is not unimportant (*gleichgültig*). Yet I know just as well that maxims, when they contradict character, are still less important in the case of women than men.

"Lastly, you know that there are evil men who torture their wives merely so that their behavior, along with their patience and love, may be constantly tested. I do not believe that I am that evil. Yet although no harm ought ever be done to such a dear human being as you, I could almost be free of regret for having hurt you. For through the deeper insight into your being that I have thus gained I feel the intimacy and depth of my love for you have increased. So be consoled that what may have been unkind and harsh in my replies will all vanish through the fact that I feel and recognize ever more deeply how thoroughly lovable, loving, and full of love you are.

"I have to go lecture (*Ich muss in die Lektion*). Farewell, dearest, dearest, most lovely Marie.

"Your Wilhelm"

After the marriage, to Niethammer to whom he had confided that he also loved Marie because of her resemblance to "the best of women" (Niethammer's), he writes:

". . . On the whole—apart from a few modifications still to be desired—I have now reached my earthly goal. For what more does one want in this world than a post and a dear wife? Those are the principal articles (*Hauptartikel*) one has to strive for as an individual. The rest (*Das Uebrige*) no longer make up chapters in themselves (*eignen Kapitel*) but perhaps only paragraphs or remarks (*Anmerkungen*). There is really not much more I wish to tell—or have to tell—about the weeks of my married life thus far. . . .

". . . I learned . . . that you had showed a little more hope than when Roth left of further upgrading the University of Erlangen this fall, and that you no longer found yourself obliged to send Ludwig elsewhere, i.e., to Heidelberg.

"Heidelberg, however, brings me to Fries and his *Logic*. Stein's bookstore knew nothing of a copy ordered for you but let on that it would receive a copy in three weeks. I have since received one from another bookstore. But my feeling in connection with it is one of sadness. I do not know whether as a married man I am mellowing, but I feel sadness that in the name of philosophy such a shallow man attains the honorable

in full analysis of the M, of the L, with reference to milk [*lait*], "the archetype of any liquid serving as nourishment," and "probably figuring as the secret link which associates the L sound with the term 'liquid,' with the color white and with the sensation of a liquid that flows sweetly in poetry," then with reference to "mama," and so on, no relation is proposed with the name Mallarmé. Nor with the name Poe, on the same page: ". . . artificial sucking [*tétée*] which releases some MOE or POE, associated with nourishment and the mother. MOE and POE would be 'synonyms' for this stage of development."), he seems to lack a decisive structural articulation in not even anticipating the theoretical site of the question

that belongs neither to one nor the other, makes them adhere somewhere to one another; that opens them up in the same stroke [*coup*], sets them in labor, but as a kind of general *sucker* [*ventouse*].

The sucker is adoration. Adoration is always of the Holy Virgin, of the Galilean mother, in whom one is conceived without a father and whom one desires be as close to the Spanish whore as possible. The Holy Virgin is comprehended — compressed, imprisoned, squeezed, banded erect—in the tube of vaseline, which she expresses, or which also expresses her as well.

the tube is (bands erect) both the Virgin and the Christ at once, vaseline is (bands erect) the latter leaving the former as a verge or as sperm, his spat out mother. He is spit out from within his mother, at least he seems so. They are (band erect), both of them, adored and exposed. The Roman soldiers are (band erect) there in legion, like an armored and compact phalanx, "strong, handsome, husky." "Lying on the table, it was a banner [*pavillon*] telling the invisible legions of my triumph over the police. I was in a cell. I knew that all night long my tube of vaseline would be exposed to the scorn—the contrary of a Perpetual Adoration—of a group of strong, handsome, husky policemen. So strong that if the weakest of them barely squeezed his fingers together, there would shoot forth, first with a slight [*léger*] fart, brief and dirty, a ribbon of gum which would continue to emerge in a ridiculous silence. Nevertheless, I was sure that this puny and most humble object would hold its own against them; by its mere presence it would be able to exasperate all the police in the world; it would draw down upon itself contempt, hatred, white and dumb rages. . . ."

position he holds in the world, and that he even permits himself to inject such scribblings with a tone of importance. On such occasions one can become angry that there is no public voice to speak with integrity in such matters, for certain circles and persons would greatly benefit from it. I have known Fries for a long time. I know that he has gone beyond the Kantian philosophy by interpreting it in the most superficial manner, by earnestly watering it down ever more, making it ever more shallow. The paragraphs of his *Logic* and the accompanying explanations are printed in separate volumes. The first volume of paragraphs is spiritless, completely shallow, threadbare, trivial, devoid of the least intimation of scientific coherence. The explanations are likewise totally shallow, devoid of spirit, threadbare, trivial, the most slovenly disconnected explanatory lecture-hall twaddle, such as only a truly empty-headed individual in his hour of digestion could ever come up with (*das saloppste erläuternde unzusammen-hängendste Katherdergewäsche, das nur ein Plattkopf in der Verdauungsstunde von sich geben kann*). I prefer to say nothing more specific about his miserable thoughts. The main discovery, for the sake of which he has written his whole system, is that logic rests on anthropological foundations and completely depends on them; that Kant, like Aristotle before him, was deeply steeped in the prejudice of the autonomy of logic, but that they were of course right about it not being based on empirical psychology, for nothing indeed can be demonstrated from experience. Yet it is still alleged to rest on anthropological foundations, and it is moreover claimed that there is a difference between demonstration and deduction. *Logic* can be deduced, and indeed can be deduced from anthropological presuppositions based on experience. So babbles on this individual about his fundamental concepts. His pure general logic in his system starts out: 'the first *means* employed by the understanding in its process of *thinking* are concepts,' as if chewing and swallowing food were a mere means of eating, and as if the understanding still did much else besides thinking. This is the sort of shallow slovenliness (*Salopperie*) with which this man babbles on—encompassing everything from *A* through *Z* twice over, if I am not mistaken, without the least precision even in matters known to everyone, such as definitions of the faculty of imagination, of memory, and so on. I heard that his lectures were not well attended because by the time one had understood a single word, he had already sputtered out (*herausgesprudelt*) twelve more. I find this quite believable. For his shallowness drives him to pour out twelve new words on top of each word he utters, so that he may drown in himself the feeling of the misery of his thoughts, and likewise drown the students in such verbiage that they become incapable of holding onto or noting any thought whatsoever. It has been said that the higher authorities have talked of calling Fries to Erlangen to have textbooks fabricated by him. Apart from the fact that I might ultimately have reason to be quite happy about this, since perhaps a slot might thereby open up for me in Heidelberg, one would have to be curious about a university in which, next to Fries, our friend Heller is called to teach philology and aesthetics, in which—as has been assured—Graser is called upon for philosophy of education, our local secretary Kiefhaber for diplomacy, the former librarian Mr. von Aretin for the humanities, and Harl for finance and public administration [*Polizeiwissenschaft*].

The pendulum movement that drags all these "objects," cloven themselves, from one value to the opposite value, is also a movement of the tongue, of the mouth, of the glottis. Adoration is first of all the effect of an *inversion* of sense. Demonstration:

(1) agglutinate: "(. . . But I would adore that thief who is my mother.)" The subsequent paragraph: "I knew that all night long my tube of vaseline would be exposed to the scorn—the inverse of a Perpetual Adoration—of a group of strong, handsome, husky policemen."

(2) glide over the bars, they are mine, leap from one to the other: "The tube of vaseline, / whose destination is well known to you, summoned up the face of her who, during a reverie that moved through the dark alleys of the city, / was the most cherished mother."

One is at a sort of rhetorical con as intubation [*entubage*] (metaphoro-metonymic, etc., if you press the executioner): the tube of vaseline of Holy Mary, glottis, clitoris or exposed Christ (the Lord's anointed) ought to be feted by the tongue ("I would like to find the newest words in the French tongue to hymn [the tube or the ribbon of gum].").

It ought to be adored, as the holy mother, and kissed, loved, "by some other gesture and even the . . . most contemptible." As the virgin Mary, and before her, already, behind her, the Immaculate Conception.

For the reading of these pages from the viewpoint of existential psychoanalysis, see what the *Saint Genet* says about a certain "'constellation' of images" and about the passage from one "theme" to another

a hundred pages further: "There I met handsome criminals, violent and somber, swearing in a savage language in which the oaths are the finest in the world.

"'I fuck the Mother of God in the ass!'

"I hope to be able to bring out my work on logic by next Easter. My psychology [*Psychologie*] will follow later. It might not be ill-advised for the authorities to wait upon further treatments of logic before sanctioning and publicly introducing for instructional purposes the old logical shambles which already in and for themselves have become flat and threadbare, but which in Fries's hands have been completely trampled and washed away like some old last-remaining, used-up paper towel. No professor at a classical or modern gymnasium in the Kingdom of Bavaria can be in such misery as to cling to such shallowness. By fall my own labors for the lecture hall may likewise result in a more popular and easily accessible form, displaying more of the tone expected both of a general textbook and of gymnasium instruction. For I feel every year more inclined to make myself accessible, especially since my marriage. At the same time, I am every year more persuaded that there might be almost too much philosophical instruction in the gymnasium. That one hour is being dropped on account of religion helps some. In the meantime there is still almost too much of a good thing. I realize, of course, that the highest authorities have decreed that instruction should consist, in part or predominantly, in practical exercises. Yet I have no clear representation as to how one could engage in practical exercises in speculative thinking. Practical exercises in abstract thinking are already extremely difficult, while due to its manifoldness empirical thinking is most dispersive. The situation is much like learning to read: one cannot start right off reading entire words as some super-clever pedagogues have wished to do, but must start with what is abstract, with individual letters. So in thinking, in logic, the most abstract is really the easiest of all, for it is completely simple, pure, and uncompounded. Only gradually, as those simple sounds have penetrated as distinct from one another, can one proceed to mental exercises in what is sensory or concrete. I just now recall that a few days ago I read an excellent lead article for a third public school curriculum, which succeeds previous ones as the third just as Christ the Lord joined the buyers and sellers as the third man in the Temple. Explanations of such excellence I call truly classical. Thank goodness simple common sense and an actual earnest will to learn something are finally to be allowed to break through. As I see from the newspapers, Mr. von Zentner is back. Thus the decision about Erlangen can probably be expected soon—namely, that it has once again been postponed . . .

"Your Hgl"

scendental role and allowing to be formed above it, as a kind of effluvium, a dream of appeasement? Isn't there always an element excluded from the system that assures the system's space of possibility? The transcendental has always been, strictly, a transcategorial, what could be received, formed, terminated in none of the categories intrinsic to the system. The system's vomit. And what if the sister, the brother/sister relation represented here the transcendental position, ex-position?

The song that climbs toward the tube goes out of the throat. All that which is beautiful "provokes, and in our throat reveals, song." All that which "makes us sing" or "sob," be it a "night light beside a coffin" or betrayal, relates to beauty, and all beauty provokes a movement to (and at) the depth of the throat. The (French) tongue then ought to sing, to fete the little tube of vaseline.

"'I bugger the wall!'"

"Aesthetic sob [*sanglot*]" again

Would the festival take place at Christmas. Strange association. It runs invisible under the page. The French tongue and the narrator give some gl strokes [*coups de gl*] ("*éclat*" ["brilliance"], "*verglas*" ["hoarfrost"], "calamity," "*gel*" ["frost"], "glory," etc.). Activates itself [*S'agit*], just after the hymn to the funerary tube, the preferred glans, that of the one-handed man on whom they will smear the strokes of unguents and of quasi testamentary chrisms.

Presently: "Now as I write, I muse on my lovers. I would like them to be smeared with my vaseline, with that soft, slightly mentholated substance; I would like their muscles to bathe in that delicate transparence without which their dearest attributes are less lovely.

"When a member has been removed, the remaining one is said to grow stronger. I had hoped that the vigor of the arm which Stilitano had lost might be concentrated in his penis. . . .

". . . In order to do justice to the one-armed Stilitano I shall wait a few pages. Let it be known from the start that he was adorned with no Christian virtue. All his brilliance [*éclat*], all his power, had their source between his legs. His verge, and that

In the figure of the sister, femininity has the highest presentiment of the ethical essence, but does not reach consciousness: the law of the family remains unconscious, enclosed, in the lower darkness, with the divine power. The sister goes further or higher than the daughter. As daughter, she loses her parents with an ethical quiet and a natural emotion. Like every child, she attains her being-for-self in losing her parents. Consequently she no longer needs her parents. Mortal or dead, they induce her only to a positive natural, merely natural relation. Which is no longer the case with the brother. With the brother (we do not speak of the sister; there has been no question of that: Hegel supposes that she would not have any sexual relationship with her sister; with her brother either; but with her sister, nondesire is not the without-desire of a nonsexual relationship, it is a desire suspended in the sexual difference), the sister engages a positive, but nonnatural, relationship of recognition. She depends on him in her for-self.

The sister goes further or higher than the mother and the wife. The mother and the wife, as such, are still bogged down in nature by the "pleasure" they take. The sister, as sister, does not take any. Then their singularity is negative: she *replaces* herself. The value of *replaceability* operates discretely and decisively in this analysis judged disconcerting by more than one commentator. The replaceable or the replacement (*Ersatz*) first seems to oppose itself to the singular. So it implies a certain universalizing initiated [*amorcée*] by the repetition of the *Ersetzen*. The wife and the mother are, on one side, rooted in singularity, but on the other side, the singular that occupies them puts on a certain contingency and "can be replaced (*ersetzt werden kann*)." If desire and pleasure are, for the wife or the mother, singulars, the fact remains that, in the ethical hearth, in the "home of ethicalness (*im Hause der Sittlichkeit*)," this singularity offers itself up to substitution. Otherwise there is perhaps family, but not ethical family. The ethical family requires that the woman no longer has to deal with this husband here, this child here, but with "*husband or children in general* (ein Mann, Kinder überhaupt)." With their disappearance, she can replace them. This possibility assures the ethical structure of its relationship with other members, its access to ideality, to conceptuality, and so on. The woman always marries just a bit a concept (man); she always conceives just a bit concepts (children). In general. "The relations of the woman are based, not on sensibility, but on the universal." This trait is determined, in this context, as an inferiority. The sister, she holds herself in singularity, but in a singular singularity: purely universal at one stroke [*coup*], without cutting [*couper*] herself from the natural bond of consanguinity.

which completes it, the whole apparel was so beautiful that the only thing I can call it is a generative organ. One might have thought he was dead . . ."

Periodically, parodically, the precious inversion of the object in an anonymous, anachronic style.

Now, without apparent transition, following an invisible and nocturnal elaboration, with a brief saccade, you are made to pass from the not very Christian fly of Stilitano to the passion of Salvador (the Savior) who "took care of me." This passion lodges in humiliated misery. The word and the signs of "*misère*" are accumulated in two pages. But "Poverty [*misère*] made us erect," just as the sick man "gets an erection [*bande*]" when he has scabies [*la gale*] or leprosy and "scratches himself [*se gratte*]." The scene is invaded by lice. Not invaded from the outside, but occupied as a familiar, if not a natural, place: "the lice, our pets, our familiars. . . .

> the *topos* of the louse [*pou*] is not only the fleece, a place of the shown/dissimulated limit between the presence and the absence of penis or hole (*trou*) (the truth is a lousy concept). It is also, for the same reasons, the neck (*cou*). A scene from the *Journal*, written to the glory of Stilitano's ass (*cul*) (of his "sober posterior" that was a "Wayside Altar [*Reposoir*]") follows the course of a louse (*pou*) over the collar (*col*), near Stilitano's neck (*cou*). There the louse (*pou*) finds its "domain—its space rather." This time the louse (*pou*) is unique, but its name, lost and found, chased on the surface of the text, borrows every object and dwells in many words at once. All this is observed, narrated in the annal style, from Stilitano's "behind" in the course of a poker game ("poker . . . blew in (*s'apporta*) . . . placed (*posa*) . . . posterior . . . rump (*croupe*) . . . posterior . . . Wayside Altar (*Reposoir*) . . . poker . . . collar . . . louse (*pou*) . . . collar . . . louse . . . collar . . . Cologne . . . neck (*cou*) . . . cut (*coupés*) . . . louse (*pou*) . . . collar . . . collar . . . neck (*cou*) . . ."). The text is indeed a fleece. Note that (no more, for example, than the word *coup* [stroke]) the word *cul* [ass] has not been written. Its hole (*trou*) is only discerned—like a louse (*pou*)—between collar (*col*) and neck (*cou*). *Miracle of the Rose*, Poem: "To the glory of the trusty: . . .

So the woman (mother-wife) posits herself in the opening of an *Ersatz*. But the man (father-husband) does too. Where is the difference? What specific is there in feminine "conceptuality"?

Its immediacy. That is understood politically. A stranger to the city as such, the woman guards an immediate relationship to the universal. She remains glued, limed in the natural, in sensibility. The man, on the contrary, dissociates and mediatizes as a member of the city, as political actor. Thus he possesses the "self-conscious force of the universal." As political force he mediatizes and negotiates his right to desire. To a desire he does not lose, whereas the woman can lose it in immediate universality: she can dream anyone in (the) place of anyone. In negotiating and mediatizing his right to desire, the man guards his freedom, his mastery, his power of substitution. Substitution here has another sense, is not immediate and undifferentiated. The man can take, let go, retake. The man "thereby buys [*erkauft . . . sich*: buys himself] the right of *desire* (*Recht der* Begierde) and thereby preserves his freedom in regard to this desire." Such is the dissymmetry: the politico-sexual instance deprives the woman of the right to desire as well as of her freedom concerning the desire. If she has a desire, she has no right to it. The man who goes out of the home and into the "bourgeoisie" (*Bürgerlichkeit*), into civil society, has the right to desire, but also the freedom to control that desire. To say that he *buys* is not to say the price that it (*ça*) costs, what the political mediatizing hides as regards the costs, or as regards unproductive investment. A desire the right of which one can buy, from which one can protect oneself, the mastery and freedom of which one can be assured, is that a desire? Is that such a good buy? Who wins in the market in question? And who runs the market [*fait marcher le marché*]?

The one who poses the transcendental question of questions on the possibility of your own proper discourse can always be referred to the sister.

one of the rare letters of Christiane Hegel to her brother; it is dated from Stuttgart, 15 January 1799: "Last night, barely before 12, our father died quietly and painlessly. I am unable to write you more. God help me!
"Your Christiane."

The greater logic is there to suspend any choice and to prevent you from cutting through to a decision between the transcendental sister and the empiric sister. Far from barring the process, the brother/sister relationship is still a moment to be passed. A moment for making the family pass outside itself. This relationship marks once more the reconciliatory transition, the passage of divine law and human law into each other. That at least is what the *Phenomenology of Spirit* means (to say). But where does one learn that, for a sister, the brother is irreplaceable? More irreplaceable than a husband, a son, a daughter, a father, or a mother? What is the axiomatic validity of

" 'When the men who are being punished see him marching in front of them, they slyly say of his round and not very mobile buttocks: "that jabbers (*ça cause*)."
" 'And then, that last stroke [*coup*], that *coup de grâce*, his neck [*cou*].' "

The lice inhabited us." The lice inhabit not a house but a body, and, in the body, the fleece, the place of the antherection. They are hunted, at night, by candlelight, in the seams [*coutures*] of Salvador's trousers. The miniscule animal is again overlapped [*recoupé*] by the logic of the antherection: prosperity/misery, shame/glory, wild/tame, improper/proper: "We liked to know—and feel—that the translucent bugs were swarming; though not tamed, they were so much a part of us that a third person's louse disgusted us. . . . The lice were the only sign of our prosperity, of the very underside of prosperity, but it was logical that by making our state perform an operation which justified it, we were, by the same token [*du même coup*], justifying the sign of this state. . . . the lice were precious. They were both our shame and our glory . . ."

Being hard up [*dèche*], in the crèche illuminated by the opening of a fly, you sleep with the savior, in other words with a kind of beggar (like the Spanish woman who was a thief), but also, in the same stroke [*coup*] of a glans turned inside out, with the Virgin Mary who erects in what leaves her, all immaculately conceived like herself, by herself, who was conceived without sin, before any sin, already.

Here is the passage, from the one-handed, to the savior that returns like his phallus to the mother:

this assertion? Empirically, it seems false. One can always have another brother. In addition, Hegel does not hold here the discourse of empiricalness; his propositions are structural, they state the legality of a typical figure. So where did he get that a brother cannot be replaced? From the mouth of Antigone, of course. She is not named, but she dictates the statements. Now what does she say, the Antigone of Sophocles?

She recalls that she leaves life "the last one of all," after she had "washed, dressed" all the bodies of the family, after she had offered the "funeral libations" for them, "looked after his corpse," Polynices's. She complains about being badly paid, but compliments herself on having been right in rendering those funeral honors, on having been right in the presence of all those who have reason, all those sensible people. If she had had children, or if the corpse of her husband had been rotting, she would have obeyed the law of the city. She would have been able to have other children by another husband. "But my father and my mother once in Hades, no other brother was ever born."

So the brother is irreplaceable—not the mother, the only family member *naturally* subtracted from every substitution. But the brother is irreplaceable only in a very determined empirical situation, determined by the factual death of Antigone's parents. Will one say that Hegel has transformed into structural and paradigmatic legality an empiric situation described in a particular text of the history of tragedies? And that for the needs of a cause—or of a sister—that is obscure?

Unless the contingency lets itself be reduced. And what if the orphanage were a structure of the unconscious? Antigone's parents are not some parents among others. She is the daughter of Oedipus and, according to most of the versions from which all the tragedians take their inspiration, of Jocasta, of her incestuous grandmother. Hegel never speaks of this generation *moreover* [de plus], as if it were foreign to the elementary structures of kinship. The model he interrogates is perhaps not as empiric as might be imagined. It does not yet have the universal clarity he ascribes to it. It holds itself, like the name, between the two. Like the orphanage.

"One might have thought he was dead, for he rarely, and slowly, got excited: he watched. He elaborated in the darkness of a well-buttoned fly, though buttoned by only one hand, the luminosity with which its bearer will be aglow.

"My relations with Salvador lasted for six months. . . . The lice inhabited us. . . . It was good that, in the depths of such misery, I was the lover of the poorest and homeliest. . . . Yet, light and brilliance [*éclat*] being necessary to our lives, a sunbeam did cross the pane and its filth, and penetrate the dimness; we had the hoarfrost [*verglas*], the silver thaw, for these elements, though they may spell calamity, evoke joys whose sign, detached in our room, was adequate for us: all we knew of Christmas and New Year's festivities was what always

the strange occurrence of the word "elaborated." Frequent and unusual usage. Truth's work, conception's work. Here what is elaborated is a "luminosity." Farther on, it will be the child. Here what is elaborated is destined to be *shown* [à se montrer] and to shine like beauty ("luminosity with which its bearer will be aglow"). Farther on, what is going to leave the belly after being elaborated there will *show itself* [se montrera] only as a "monster," but equally to be erected ("to love this monster, to love the ugliness that had come out of her belly in which it had been elaborated, and to erect it devotedly"). In the two occurrences—in others as well—the elaboration takes place under a surface, a star, a closed skin. Light and life, the watch [*la montre*] — or the alarm clock — and the monster work in a pocket, under a sheath [*gaine*]. One guesses them rather than sees them agitated, displaced, swell [*gonfler*], reverse. For example, I have often availed myself of the word "elaborate" to describe—here—textual work [*travail textuel*]. No doubt because it proceeds like that monstrous light: same movement, same place, same "object." But above all because one must set apart in the elaborated text the instrument of reading or writing, the *style* with which one treats [*traiter*]. With which *one writes*, that is, folds [*plier*] metalanguage. But the fold — the employment — of metalanguage is itself irreducible. Like a pocket, a cyst, that unceasingly reshapes itself. By generalizing, by systematizing, for example, the recourse to the word "elaborate," I make out of it a sort of concept, a rule [*règle*], a law whose extension dominates—relatively—the text from which, however, I extract it. The word "elaborate" hardly covers [*couvre*] the text, broods over [*couve*] it for a limited time. A stitched [*cousue*] pocket, cystic metatongue describes, envelops, guards and regards the work

Proof moreover, if there were any need for it, that nothing is less anoedipal, verily anti-oedipal than an orphan unconscious.

Nothing should be able to survive Antigone's death. Plus nothing more should follow, go out of her, after her. The announcement of her death should sound the absolute end of history. A glaze(d), virgin, sterile transparency. Without desire and without labor.

An end of history without *Sa*. The *Sa* cannot return to a sister. To a father, to a mother, to a son, perhaps, not to a sister.

Yet all will have just missed stopping, on the march [*en marche*], on a step [*sur une marche*], just missed stumbling or losing footing.

Like Hegel, we have been fascinated by Antigone, by this unbelievable relationship, this powerful liaison without desire, this immense impossible desire that could not live, capable only of overturning, paralyzing, or exceeding any system and history, of interrupting the life of the concept, of cutting off its breath, or better, what comes down to the same thing, of supporting it from outside or underneath a crypt.

Crypt—one would have said, of the transcendental or the repressed, of the unthought or the excluded—that organizes the ground to which it does not belong.

What speculative dialectics means (to say) is that the crypt can still be incorporated into the system. The transcendental or the repressed, the unthought or the excluded must be assimilated by the corpus, interiorized as moments, idealized in the very negativity of their labor. The stop, the arrest, forms only a stasis in the introjection of the spirit.

Antigone is a moment to be passed, a terrible and divine moment, for the brother and the sister. The two laws (divine and human, subterranean and diurnal, feminine and masculine, familial and political, and so on) are going to pass into each other, are going to let themselves be mediatized and become for each other. Are going to count for each other.

The brother/sister relation is a limit. There the family as family finds its own proper limit (*Grenze*), circumscribes itself in it. Without it, the family would not determine itself, would not be what it is. Or with it either. The limit being what it is—in Hegel—it is not what it is, gets clear of itself as soon as it attains itself. With the brother/sister relation the family is exceeded by itself. It "dissolves itself and goes out of itself." The family resolves

accompanies them and what makes them dearer to merry-makers: frost [*gel*].

". . . Poverty [*misère*] made us erect. All across Spain we carried a secret, veiled magnificence unmixed with arrogance. . . . Thus developed my talent for giving a sublime sense to so beggarly an appearance. (I am not yet speaking of literary talent.) It proved to have been a very useful discipline for me and still enables me to smile tenderly at the humblest among the dregs, whether human or material, including vomit, including the saliva I let drool on my mother's face, including your excrement. I shall preserve within me the idea of myself as a beggar.

"I wanted to be like that woman who, at home, hidden away from people, sheltered her daughter, a kind of hideous, misshapen monster, stupid and white, who grunted and walked on all fours. When the mother gave birth, her despair was probably such that it became the very essence of her life. She decided to love this monster, to love the ugliness that had come out of her belly in which it had been elaborated, and to erect it devotedly. Within herself she ordained

of the text with which it will have been big. I have elaborated elaboration. But all this must remain under the sheath [*gaine*]. If only one wishes to take more pleasure there. Must remain under the sheath [*gaine*] like the shows, the watches (monsters) [*les mon(s)tres*] of tongue. It is necessary to let guess under the swollen [*gonflée*] pocket, worked by every movement (morseling, reassembling, cuttings, agglutinations), it is necessary to let silently elaborate itself the *glas* of the tongue. If, like a cocky virgin lad, uneasy that someone may run the risk of misunderstanding his tube, you naively show what you know how to do with the tongue—to cut, recompose, displace, agglutinate, and so on—everything is misfired. It is like a premature ejaculation. Not even time to band erect. And then you believe and want to make others believe that you are the master of this work of the tongue: the tongue no longer elaborates itself, no longer bands erect. And finally it remains intact, unaffected, uninfected. There is more enjoyment [*jouissance*]—but one can always, of course, wish to deprive (oneself) of or sever (oneself) from it—in acting as if the fish remained whole, still alive, in the meshes, all the more mobile, gliding, fleeing since it knows itself to be threatened

itself in this limit, the very instant what enters into it goes out of itself, at once sensibly and insensibly, like a point in a null and infinite time, interminable. Antigone *herself*, yes, that's right (*c'est ça*), and the family, which is Antigone herself, yes, that's right (*c'est ça*), this pure passage, this trance that does not re(s)t(r)ain itself. It is re(s)t(r)ained, rather, according to the relief, only by losing it. Relieving a limit is guarding it, keeping it, but here guarding (a limit) is losing it. To guard what loses itself is to lack. The logic of the *Aufhebung* (re)turns itself at each instant into its absolute other. Absolute appropriation is absolute expropriation. Onto-logic can always be reread or rewritten as the logic of loss or of spending without reserve.

This possibility wavers or truncates itself in (the) burial (place). What is a stone monument, such is the question. But in this the stone rocks—the *what is?* The *what is?* is, like every question in general, engaged in the reappropriation process the stone threatens. The question's question-form is in advance petrified [*medusée*].

And yet there is, *il y a*, stone. What does *there is* mean (to say), as soon as what there is is removed out of reach of the *it is*, the *this is*, the *c'est*, the *ceci est*, out of reach of the exposition [*ostension*] of all presence? Apropos the propriation process (*Ereignis*), Heidegger sets free the *es gibt*, in *es gibt Sein*, of Being's all-powerful precession. The value of the *gift* (*Gabe*), a value foreign to the *there is*, the *il y a*, we wager that that value will have preoccupied all.

Then the brother departs. If he is not dead. The one who is not dead. The one who lives *as brother*. He departs. He is "the member of the family in whom its spirit becomes an individuality which turns towards another sphere, and passes over into the consciousness of universality." The brother breaks with the singular bond that holds him to the family and, for example, to Antigone. He goes toward the city, abandons the immediate, elementary, unconscious, negative form of *Sittlichkeit*, in order to become a citizen, a man of human law. He is going to go into politics.

What does Antigone do? If she does not die, she gets married. In any case, she remains, she continues to mount the family guard. After the departure of her brother toward "human law," "the sister becomes, or the wife remains, the *Vorstand* [president, directress, general] of the household and the guardian of the divine law." That, the sister becomes or the wife *remains* (*bleibt*). "In this way, the two sexes overcome (*überwinden*) their natural essence (*natürliches Wesen*) and enter into their ethical signification (*sittlichen Bedeutung*), as diversities (*als Verschiedenheiten*) that the two differences (*Unterschiede*), which the ethical substance gives itself, share between them (*unter sich teilen*)."

The sexual difference is *overcome* when the brother departs, and when the other (sister and wife) remains. There is no more sexual difference *as natural difference*. "The sexes overcome their natural

an altar where she preserved the idea of monster. With devoted care, with hands gentle despite the cal . . ."

To guard against what scaffolds itself here—it is the healthiest, the most natural reflex—one will protest: sometimes against these too-long citations that should have been cut; sometimes on the contrary (verily at the same time) against these deductions, selections, sections, suspension points, suture points—detachments. Detachments of the sign, of course. (It has not escaped you, above, what was detached, and detached, as always, in our room, was a sign, "sign, detached in our room." There is where one steals, flies [*vole*].) That the sign is detached signifies of course that it is cut away [*coupe*] from its place of emission or its natural belonging; but the separation is never perfect, the difference never consum(mat)ed. The bleeding [*sanglant*] detachment is also—repetition—delegation, mandate, delay, relay. Adherence. The detached remain(s) collared [*collé*] thereby [*par là*], by the [*par la*] glue of differance, by the a [*par l'a*]. The a of gl agglutinates the detached differentiae. The scaffold of the A is gluing.

So one will protest: you cut [*coupez*] too much, you glue [*collez*] too much, you cite too much and too little. The two charges are well known, they come under [*relèvent de*] the logic that is the object here.

difference." Once overcome, the sexual difference will have been only a natural diversity. The opposition between difference and qualitative diversity is a hinge of the greater Logic. Diversity is a moment of difference, an indifferent difference, an external difference, without opposition. As long as the two moments of difference (identity and difference since identity differs, as identity) are in relationship only to themselves and not to the other, as long as identity does not oppose itself to difference or difference to identity, there is diversity. So diversity is a moment both of difference and identity, it being understood, very expressly, that difference is the whole *and* its own proper moment. So that is also true of sexual difference: sexual difference is identity, identity is the difference, itself the whole and its own proper moment.

In overcoming the natural difference *as diversity* of the sexes, we pass on to difference *as opposition*. In *Sittlichkeit* sexual difference finally becomes a true opposition: what, furthermore, it was *called*, destined to be. The determinateness of the opposition (opposition as determinate—*bestimmte*) corresponds to determination as the vocation, the destination (*Bestimmung*) of the sexual difference. *Difference* is much too general and indeterminate a concept; one must follow the determining process of the sexual difference, distinguish at least between difference as diversity and difference as opposition, the two also being differences as identities.

The moment the brother departs, "this moment loses the indeterminateness (*Unbestimmtheit*) which it still has there, and the contingent diversity of dispositions and capacities." What is lost is the natural diversity of the sexes and difference without opposition. What is gained against this contingency, this natural multiplicity, is the determinate difference in opposition, *sexual contradiction*. This moment "is now the determinate opposition of the two sexes (*der bestimmte Gegensatz der zwei Geschlechter*) whose naturalness acquires at the same time the signification of their ethical destination (*ihrer sittlichen Bestimmung*)."

The sexual difference has only just appeared. It has only just determined itself in appearing as such, *in positing itself*, that is, in opening itself to negativity and in becoming opposition. In beginning then to sublimate itself. If the difference were destined to opposition, there was not yet any sexual difference between Antigone and her brother. Their relationship was not so unusual that one could have believed that, or between them the absence of desire.

What is the position of desire in this passage from difference-diversity to difference-opposition? Is there desire already in the former? Must one wait for opposition or contradiction to see it upsurge? There is no response to a question posed in this form. No more than the concept difference is the concept desire homogeneous and univocal. Just as there is not a sexual difference in general, but a dialectical process of sexual difference that passes, for

For those, however, who would not regard gl as a satisfactory response—since they expected some response in the first place; those for whom gl says nothing—since they believed gl was saying nothing in the first place—and who, one wonders for what meal [*repas*], would continue to drool on the spot [*sur place*], let us suggest that the theoretical question, elaborated, surely (metalanguage—that always reconstitutes itself—in the better place) by this intervention, no other word is possible today, submitted in advance to the censorship of the remain(s), after all, in the ideological field, will produce, that's how (*comme ça*) it has to be said, the following thesis: every thesis is (bands erect) a prosthesis; what affords reading affords reading by citations (necessarily truncated, clippings [*coupures*], repetitions, suctions, sections, suspensions, selections, stitchings [*coutures*], scarrings, grafts, postiches, organs without their own proper body, proper body covered with cuts [*coups*], traversed by lice).

Thus does a text become infatuated. With another. This does not happen without profit or loss for the organism that undergoes grafting after having been solicited, collared [*racoler*].

What had happened globally to the mother. To the global mother. Hardly had

"*Enticher . . . v. a.* I. To begin to spoil, to corrupt. In this sense it is commonly used only in the past participle. 2. Term of couture. When placing patterns on some material in order to cut it, one *entiche* when one of the patterns takes a little corner of the material from the pattern placed next to it; it is to encroach, with the idea of saving, on what is destined for another piece necessary for the whole. 3. Fig. To taint with something false or morally bad. Who has infatuated [*entiché*] you with that opinion? 4. *S'enticher, v. réfl.* To become infatuated (*entiché*). He was infatuated with this vice. To fall in love with someone. He fell in love with an actress and married her." (From Littré, which adds in the Etymology: "Diez and Scheler derive it from the German *anstecken*, to infect with a contagion; but one does not conceive how the s would have disappeared. The proper form is *entecher*, composed of *en* I and the old French

example, from diversity to opposition, there is not first *a desire in general* that, from diversity to opposition, *determines itself*, conforms itself to its teleological calling or appellation (*Bestimmung*), posits itself more and more as desire. By removing itself from nature, by denying nature within itself, by relieving, sublimating, idealizing itself, desire becomes more and more desiring. Thus human desire is more desiring than animal desire; masculine desire is more desiring than feminine desire, which remains closer to nature. More desiring, it is then more unsatisfied and more insatiable. But this proposition is valid only insofar, provisionally, relatively, limitedly, as femininity has not yet reached the properly ethical opposition. As soon as femininity does, the woman is in the same situation as the man (beyond nature), except in degree. In the same stroke [*Du même coup*], if there is more sublimation in the man, (natural, primordial, etc.) desire is also more inhibited, less free (naturally) than in the woman. Freer also for the same reason, with a spiritual freedom.

The (sexual) opposition that just appeared is not absolute. It does not cause the unity of the ethical substance to burst out [*éclater*] of its contradiction. On the contrary, this opposition constitutes the becoming of that unity. This becoming constructs itself according to the opposition of the sexes, in other words according to the opposition of the two laws. "The difference of the sexes and of their ethical content remains (*bleibt*), however, in the unity of the substance, and its movement is just the *remaining* becoming (*das bleibende Werden*) of that substance." Neither of the two laws posits itself alone in (it)self and for (it)self. "Human law proceeds in its living movement from the divine law, the law valid on earth from that of the nether world, the conscious law from the unconscious law, mediation from immediacy—and equally returns whence it came."

Finally, the diaphanous law of consciousness (man) and the obscure law of the unconscious (woman) must become identical at the bottom of their opposition. But then they come before the light, they appear in the light, the law of laws. The opposition of noon and midnight resolves itself into noon. Such is the *truth* of a sexual revolution whose general necessity was prescribed by *The Difference Between Fichte's and Schelling's System of Philosophy*. In the obstinacy of its good sense, its health, human understanding wants to place the terms of the opposition under each other's shelter (consciousness/unconsciousness, light/matter). Speculation, that is, the relief of the opposition, frightens human understanding, which fears the destructive character of its own operation. In fact, paradoxically, human understanding is frightened because it does not know at what point speculation destroys. If it could grasp the scope (*Umfang*) of this destruction (*Vernichten*), it would be reassured; it could no longer consider speculation as an opposing

she, devotedly, erected than the great discourse on theft [*vol*] is raised.

The morsels, which I cut [*coupe*] and sew [*couds*] in the text designated by the one named Genet, must neither destroy its form or quash its (prompting) breath (do not say its unity, the question posed here being one of knowing whether *a* text could be *one* and if such a thing exists any more than a unicorn), nor recompose or recapture [*ressaisir*] its integrity in one of those nets [*filets*]—formal or semantic—that we have feigned to throw and rethrow without counting: only in order to show or rather to draw beyond any manifestation that the net operates only insofar as it is beholden to a remain(s). It only retains remains, some monumental carcasses, and lets the remain(s) fall (to the tomb). And of this remain(s) that is not, that makes text, the fall, the defalcated case, scaffolds all the writing machines. The remain(s) is at the head and the tail, it is not a matter of bringing it in on a platter.

Even if we could reconstitute, morsel by morsel, a proper name's emblem or signature, that would only

teche, which is the same as *tache*; so *entecher* or *enticher* is identical to *entacher*. *Entecher, enticher,* must not be confused with the old verb *enticier,* to excite, *enticement,* instigation.")
Perhaps one will find that I use the dictionary a great deal. I try to do so as the signer of the *entichant* text (that is, in a genetic style) that does not hesitate to bring about poetics with Larousse: in *Querelle:* "Under the word 'pederast,' Larousse entry: 'In the quarters of one of them was found a large quantity of artificial flowers, garlands and wreaths [*couronnes*] destined, without any doubt, for use as decorations [*parures*] and ornaments in their grand orgies.'"
One does not yet conceive how the s would have disappeared

169

power (*Gegnerin*). For destruction is also a power of "highest synthesis of the conscious and the non-conscious," and requires a "destruction of consciousness itself." Speculative reason (*Vernunft*) then engulfs itself (*versenkt*) with its knowledge and its reflection of the absolute identity. Speculative reason hurls itself into its "own proper abyss (*eigenen Abgrund*)" and "in this night of mere reflection and of the calculating understanding, in this night which is the noonday of life, good sense and speculation can meet one another."

There is always no purely human family. The value family continues to transport itself on a horizon or over a theological ground. What was verified in the space of Christian infinitism is confirmed here on a Greek model. The theological ahuman is also indeed on the natural ahuman side. So the human limit is undiscoverable, always disappearing. Inasmuch as it still remains too natural, the family comes under [*relève de*] the divine law. If the Greek model places the divine on the side of the subterranean burial (place), the Judeo-Christian paradigm, celestial and sublime, opposes itself to the Greek model only insofar as the paradigm actually produces religion: the rotting of the Christic corpse will have made things drag on.

The union of opposites, of man and woman, has the form of a syllogistic copulation. More precisely, this syllogistic copulation unites two syllogisms into one single one and thus produces the ethical reign. One of the extremes, the universal spirit, conscious of itself, binds itself again to its other, the unconscious spirit, through the mediation of the man, of the man's individuality. Divine law has its individuality in the woman; the unconscious spirit of the singular has its being-there in her; the woman is the middle (*Mitte*), the means by which the spirit emerges from its inactuality, passes from the unconscious to the conscious. The union of man and woman joins up the two laws or the two syllogisms, makes of the two movements—that of the woman who sinks herself deeply into the subterranean, the danger and the experience of death; that of the man who raises himself toward the light—one single movement, pervaded by a single motive [*mobile*].

As if two motives, disposing each of their self-moving principle, starting from their opposite places, crossed or met each other in the course of a circular path, stopped short [*tombaient en arrêt*], and from the collision formed one single vehicle on an infinite circle. What is done then, and does not come undone, remains irrepresentable or unimaginable. That is what Hegel calls *Wirklichkeit*, the operation of actuality, and the power of the syllogism.

The copulation of these two "opposite movements" appeases nothing. There's no reconciliation. Here tragedy begins, and the opposition continues to rage in *Sittlichkeit*. Once the preceding syllogism has taken place, one has not yet acted; no operation (*Handlung*) has been actual in the city. The moment one is dealing

be to disengage, as from a tomb someone buried alive, just what neither Genet nor I would ever have succeeded in signing, in reattaching to the lines of a paraph, and what talks (because) of this. We do not comprehend here the text denominated Genet's, it is not exhausted in the pocket I cut [*coupe*], sew [*couds*], and refasten. That text is what makes a hole in the pocket, harpoons it beforehand, regards it; but also sees it escape the text, bear its arrow away to unknown parts. This text here (or *glas*) no more reduces to a reading of Genet—that forms neither its example nor its essence, neither its case nor its truth—than this text here allows itself to be reassembled or arrowed, with others, by my paraph. And everything in it that would tend to the singular form of the signature, of one signature or the other, guards an altogether abnormal value. It comes under [*relève d'*] no rule, nor does it procure one. The operation must be singular each time, and must run [*courir*] its risk [*chance*] uniquely.

Supposing, certainly, that there is some signature. To know-how-to-be—suspended between several *clin*—(clinic, *clinamen*, clinanthous, etc.) and several *col*—(. . .)

It would be otherwise if the signature were only a *glas*-effect, otherwise stated a classification, the network of (no) more than a name. At that point, this operation would somewhere be exemplary and normative, even scientific, if, but so timidly, preliminary: a conception hardly announced.

with acting, operating, actualizing, the contradiction upsurges again, this time under the form of fault or crime. Tragic carnage: murder no longer proceeds from a voluntary decision; it is inscribed as a fatality in the operation's structure. If the ethical substance unites the two laws, the operation always comes down to a singular individual. So the operation recreates the split, the opposition of the divine and the human, of the woman and the man. Each on his or her side, Antigone and Creon hear or read only one law; they lack and betray the other.

Every operation is *a priori* guilty, culpable. "Innocence, therefore, is merely the absence of operation (*Nichttun*), like the being of a stone, not even that of a child."

So the ethical action includes within itself the moment of the crime, is moral by dint of murder—and of playing one law against another. That is why the unconscious does not let itself be reduced. No operation can actualize itself in the (day)light of consciousness without having structurally to restrain (shall we say repress, gird, suppress, push back into darkness, un-think, un-know?) the other law. The unconscious constitutes itself, in the order of *Sittlichkeit*, from this double articulation of the law: one can never know what one does on the two sides at once, on the side of human law and on the side of divine law, that is, on the side of man and on the side of woman.

The other counts.

Oedipus is cited to appear as the example of this general necessity.

There is no operation-less unconscious. Operation is action, to be sure, but action taking into account a law, one law *or* another (human or divine), then one law *and* another, the opposition of two laws. In other words, the sexual opposition. No unconscious without sexual opposition (more or less than difference).

The law commands actually acting. But the unconscious exists, if that can be said, only insofar as action, which cannot obey the two laws in the same stroke [*du même coup*], is culpable, cuttable [*coupable*]. Culpability—relationship to the unknown or to the unconscious of the other law—comes to its prominence [*prend son relief*], the irreversible existence that comes to it from the fault, only if it enters into a relationship with the other of the consciousness that has remained, precisely, unconscious to it. What seems banal: the crime is irreversible once committed. That is less banal than the crime being necessarily and structurally unconscious, nonpresent to itself, unknown to the "author" the moment he operates. This does not lighten the culpability that remains whole (here there is no involuntary homicide, no "no one is voluntarily cruel"). The crime is unconscious, and that is why it remains whole and irreversible. Its fatal necessity is inscribed in the cleaved structure of *Sittlichkeit*. No operation-less unconscious, no lawless opera-

Unwearying, the labor [*labeur*] to reconstitute the glorious and integral corpus of a proprietorship, in the authentic and organless signature, will not have failed, always, *in the end* (will have some *seing*): what sets it in motion, its first thief [*voleur*], *volens nolens*, what causes writing, is what separates [*écarte*] and sows [*et sème*], scatters [*essaime*] signacutting and signacouture [*signacoupure et signacouture*]. What desingularizes, unseals, desiglums, opens the eyes by blinding.

The mother had hardly erected, devotedly, than the discourse celebrates the theft.

Is it an accident if the father then enters on the scene. Under his name, could one say, or almost, he who appeared so absent up to here, ineffective, inactual. Is it an accident if this movement leads toward the hymn to the proper name. If that hymn does not give a shit for the civil state. And if Genet gravely coiffs himself there with the circumflex as with a royal crown [*couronne*]. Floral corolla as well, since the accent deforms the emblem and lets one read the plant in (the) place of the animal?

Step by step [*Pas à pas*], the father returns in the gesture of the theft, between the mother's erection and the circumflex's. Rape [*Viol*] of the law, law of the theft, morality. "I [born of an unknown father: "My mother was called Gabrielle Genet. My father remains unknown."] try to charm them by moral acts, by charity first of all." *Them*, they are "unknown powers."

He then explains to us how he, Genet, gives his seat to old people, stands aside to let them pass, helps blind men cross.

171

tion, no law without double law, without opposition, thus without crime (in the sight of the other-law), no innocent ("Rousseauist") unconscious. It is as impossible to reduce the operation as to efface the crime (Mallarmé says this very well, in his own way, with the same words). But if there is always crime without knowing it, and if one wants to consider that the crime without knowing it does not take place, there is never any crime.

Oedipus—then: "Actuality therefore holds concealed within it (*in sich verborgen*) the other side which is alien to this knowledge, and does not show itself to consciousness as it is in and for (it)self: to the son it does not show the father in his offender that he slays; it does not show the mother in the queen whom he makes his wife. In this way, a power which shuns the light of day [*lichtscheue*, photophobic] ensnares the ethical self-consciousness, a power which breaks forth only (*erst*) when the operation has taken place, and seizes the self-consciousness in the act. For the accomplished operation is the relieved opposition of the knowing self and the actuality confronting it. The doer cannot deny (*verleugnen*) the crime and his culpability."

So operation relieves the opposition between the knowing self and the actuality the self does not know, between the conscious and the unconscious. But the relief does not lift [*lève*] the culpability, does not wash away [*lave*] the crime. An *after*-effect [*un effet d'*après] offers endless resistance there. The crime has taken place, the culpability remains. Even if the agent did not know what he killed, whom he killed. More than elsewhere, the unconscious here seems unamenable to simple nonconsciousness. Perhaps one could use this as the authority for removing from the *Aufhebung* the identifying marks of the meaning-(to say) of Hegel, who, in a moment, is going to reorder the *Aufhebung* to the teleology of consciousness. The few lines that comment on Oedipus's operation already announce the reappropriation, the becoming-conscious of the unconsciousness that makes the foreign one's own and reunifies the elements of the split. Like *Antigone, Oedipus at Colonus* ends in the calm equality of death, in final appeasement. Even though,

"Finally, more beautiful than this rather external sort of denouement [the *deus ex machina* of the *Philoctetes*] is an inner reconciliation which, because of its subjectivity, already borders on the modern. The most perfect classical example of this that we have before us is the eternally marvellous *Oedipus Coloneus*. Oedipus has unknowingly murdered his father, taken the Theban throne, and mounted the marriage-bed with his mother. These unconscious crimes do not make him unhappy; but the old solver of riddles forcibly extracts a knowledge of his own dark destiny and acquires the dreadful

with comic laughter, "perversity" silently wells up.

"The doer cannot deny the crime and his culpability: the operation consists precisely in moving the unmoved, in bringing out into the open what was first locked up in mere possibility, and thus tying (*verknüpfen*) the unconscious to the conscious, nonexisting to

The old and the blind, the sole examples chosen.

The circumflex (that is how I shall call what distinguishes him from the author and is raised higher than he) crochets, then draws the crèche towards the crossroads: the antherection of Mary-Jocasta that gives the text its Greek ration. The old and the blind must cross in the middle of the crossroads [*en plein carrefour*]. Naming Oedipus here does not semantize, does not inflate [*gonfle*] each textual atom with sense, but on the contrary bursts as a semantic mirage what must recently be called the myth of Oedipus.

The circumflex here gives its Greek guarantee: "The nervousness provoked by fear, and sometimes by anxiety, makes for a state akin to religious moods. At such times I tend to interpret the slightest incident. Things become signs of chance. I want to charm the unknown powers upon which the success of the adventure seems to me to depend. I try to charm them by moral acts, by charity first of all: I give more readily and more freely to beggars, I give my seat to old people, I stand aside to let them pass, I help blind men cross the street, and so on. In this way, I seem to recognize that over the act of stealing [*vol*] presides a god to whom moral actions are agreeable. These attempts to throw out a random net [*filet*] where this god of whom I know nothing will let itself be captured exhaust me, enervate me, and also favor that religious state. To the act of stealing they communicate the gravity of a ritual act."

This ritual, this passage that in the text initiates you, leads you by the hand to the fictive position of

to hold Oedipus's hand [*donner la main*]. To give Oedipus a helping hand [*Donner un coup de main*]. Is that to help him? Who can do so? From where? Why? Would have to see. The archangels, on the contrary, spit in his face. With as much acuity as gravity, the circumflex had made us remark what happens when their aim is bad, "'It's

consciousness that it has been accomplished in himself. With this solution of the riddle in his own person he has lost his happiness as Adam did when he came to the consciousness of good and evil. The seer now, he blinds himself, resigns the throne, exiles himself from Thebes, just as Adam and Eve were driven from Paradise, and wanders away a helpless old man."

After he had preferred the voice of his Fury to that of his son, after having thus overcome the inner division, appeased, reconciled in himself the cleavage (*Zwiespalt*), Oedipus knows then a kind of glorification, of radiance, of illumination in death (*Verklärung im Tode*). This luminous glory is spiritual; his blind eyes become glorious (*verklärt*), become clear (*wird hell*). In particular because of this glory, because of this transfiguration of the body (Oedipus's bones become the ramparts of the town that takes him in), could a Christic harmony be found in him. "But the Christian religious reconciliation is a glorification of the soul (*Verklärung der Seele*) which [is] bathed (*gebadet*) in the source of eternal salvation. . . ."

This reconciliation makes the heart the "grave of the heart (*Grabe des Herzens*)." In exchange for the complaint or the accusation (*Anklagen*), the body expiates the earthly fault in order to reach a purely spiritual bliss. "On the other hand, the glorification of Oedipus always still remains the classical restoration of consciousness from the injuries and the conflict of ethical powers to the unity and the harmony of this *ethical* content itself.

"What is further implied in this reconciliation is the *subjectivity* of the satisfaction, and this enables us to make the transition (*Übergang*) to the opposite sphere, the sphere of *comedy*." In the "reversal" of the tragic "plasticity," comedy will set free the "perversity (*Verkehrtheit*)" of the subjective principle. But what perverts the plasticity of classical tragedy will be the very resilience [*ressort*], the very jurisdiction [*ressort*] of modern tragedy

being." So the unconscious is a possible consciousness, a virtual truth. "In this truth, therefore, the operation is brought out into the sunlight—as something in which a conscious is bound (*verbunden*) to an unconscious, the proper, one's own (*das Eigene*), to an alien, as the cleaved essence (*entzweite Wesen*) whose other side consciousness experiences, and experiences as what is also its own, but still as the power it has violated (*verletzte*) and roused to hostility."

The analysis of an absolutely unconscious crime, which receives its sense as crime only after the blow [*coup*], reintroduces the teleological temporality of self-presence, of consciousness. This movement becomes more pronounced: if an operation is *a priori* culpable, even in its unconscious, the fault is "purer," more purely culpable, when it is conscious and known in advance as such. As in the preceding case, the operation is structurally criminal; there is no innocent operation, since one law is recommended, named as reference, against another. But the crime is more *purely* ethical when the opposition of one law to the other becomes conscious, when the operation liberates and deliberates itself. One is indeed then in the order of universality—law against law—even if the crime is committed in the name of the law of singularity. The scene of the crime being opened between two laws (singularity/universality, woman/man), being read according to its two codes [*sur ses deux tableaux*], there is no murder that is not the (ethical) effect of the sexual opposition. Every crime is a sexual and family operation.

the proper name, multiplies among fifteen pages (as if it were nothing, were about nothing) the paternal associations, verily the paternal alliances.

(*Ça*) making him come [*reluire*], the bitch!' "

Verily in effect: between the legs of Mary-Jocasta, by favor of what some tube of vaseline or other signifying substance ejaculates, one could, without deciding, make the father equal to the mother and vice versa. To make equal [*Egaler*], by pruning [*élaguant*] or loosening [*larguant*], without ever ceasing to find again the one between the other. The place of the son glides there, one more time.

The rite of the passage aims to reconstitute in the father's dwelling the law of the household—economy—as presence and total presence. Theft [*vol*] is absolute knowledge. The executioner threatens, but in (the) place of the cradle, out of which one observes and one elaborates. The scene of the theft is prepared by the insistent description of the night scene. Theft is produced while families—the "people"—sleep. The ritual act "will really be performed in the heart of darkness, to which is added that it may be rather at night, while people are asleep, in a place that is closed and perhaps itself masked in black." Then, patiently repeated, the activities of unearthing, of ransacking, the exposition of the "defenseless body," and so on.

Following the rule [*règle*] of economy, I retain only

Consequently, Oedipus is a coarse murderer, half innocent, in any case impure, since he did not know what he was doing. The pure crime, the one corresponding to the most "complete" ethical consciousness, is committed by his daughter, the small orphan consciousness. This time Antigone is named. She knew what she was doing, and here she becomes the best representative of ethical consciousness. "It can be that the right which held back in ambush is not present in its own proper figure to the doing *consciousness*, but is present only *in (it)self* in the inner culpability of the decision and the action." This is the case of Oedipus. "But the ethical consciousness is more complete (*vollständiger*), its fault purer (*reiner*), if it *knows beforehand* the law and the power which it opposes, if it takes them to be violence and injustice [only one law can be unjust, but a law's injustice is necessarily a nonjuridical contingency], to be an ethical contingency, and, like Antigone, knowingly (*wissentlich*) commits the crime. . . . The ethical consciousness must . . . decipher its opposite as its own proper operation, must recognize its fault.

"'Because we suffer we acknowledge we have erred'" (*Antigone*).

Everything stops right there, and yet nothing stops. The run is interminable, although at each step [*pas*] we are concerned with falling, stopping (absolutely) short [*tomber (absolument) en arrêt*] in the last ambush. Antigone reaches the purity of crime. But the ethical plenitude is not accomplished in the crime. The crime is pure as crime because it reveals more purely the split, the opposition of laws that constitutes the ethical. But this constitution is achieved only the moment its negativity, essential here, is totally relieved. No doubt Antigone's "recognition" of the crime has worked towards that, it corresponds indeed to the birth of ethical consciousness, to disposition (*Gesinnung*), in the ethical sense. But Antigone remains in the middle of the ascent, at the stage of "disposition": in any case, caught between two laws, she disobeys. She falls back down, entombs again. Impotent in her action, she returns to the chasm (*zugrunde*), toward the hell and the subterranean world that is her fundamental place, her own proper place. She is the figure of the fall (*Untergang*), of the decline; she marches toward the bottom and entrains with her her whole family, even including Haemon who awaits her and kills himself over her corpse. All individuality "consumes" itself in culpability. The victory of one law or the other is always a catastrophe for *Sittlichkeit*, since it opens in *Sittlichkeit* a *colpos* in which everything is regularly engulfed, each border of which, rather, rhythmically caves in. Consequently, for *Sittlichkeit* to accomplish itself, the engulfing must be engulfed and the caving-in cave in. The equilibrium (*Gleichgewicht*) between the two laws will be attained when absolute right, reconciling objective right and subjective right, will engulf the two opposites, will make their incessant fall fall (to the

the presence, the resembling of self close by self [*ressemblement de soi auprès de soi*], *parousia* in the father's dwelling, in the return of the prodigal son: ". . . the prudence, the whispering voice, the alert ear, the invisible, nervous presence of the accomplice and the understanding of his slightest sign, all concentrate us within ourselves, compress us, make of us a very ball of presence, which Guy's remark so well explains:

"'You feel yourself [*se sent*] living.'"

"But within myself, this total presence, which is transformed into a bomb of what seems to me terrific power, imparts to the act a gravity, a terminal oneness—the burglary [*le cambriolage*], while being performed, is always the last, not that you think you are not going to perform another after that one, you don't think, but because such a gathering of self [*rassemblement de soi*] cannot take place (not in life, for to push it further would be to pass out of life)—and this oneness of an act which develops" does not, like the Hegelian gathering close by self [*rassemblement auprès de soi*], have the form of some oak after the case of an acorn [*gland*]; but what comes back to the same remain(s), between parentheses, an anthological expansion: "this oneness of an act which develops (the rose its corolla) into conscious gestures, sure of their efficacy, of their fragility and yet of the violence which they give to that act, here also accords to it the value of a religious rite."

burglary [*le cambriolage*], as its name indicates, is always of a chamber or familial dwelling, here of a dark chamber. It is always the last one, that is, there never was one that counted beforehand. So it is the first, the most primitive. The obscure economy of the *camera* as archeo-eschatology. Finally, if you detach the connection (gl), in the beginning will have been the theft [*vol*]. Everything will have begun with the end, on the eve of ("The Strange Word of [*mot d'*] . . .") the obsequent "funeral mime," its strange obsequent mode [*mot d'*]. The logic of obsequence

tomb). Such will be the appeasing victory of "destiny": "Only in the downfall of both sides alike (*gleichen Unterwerfung*) is absolute right accomplished, and does the ethical substance as the negative power that engulfs [devours, swallows, gulps down, *verschlingt*] both sides, that is, omnipotent and righteous *destiny*, step on the scene."

The sister's laughter. As if she knew that these engulfing movements cannot be led as far as their extremes. But the laughter is also the mother's. This laughter wells up, does not burst out [*éclate*] all at once, and later in the scene, derision is amplified in a repercussion without origin.

Hardly accomplished, the ethical essence starts dissolving itself. Once again two laws oppose each other, but they are represented by two individuals of the same sex. By Antigone's two brothers. Eteocles and Polynices fight each other, one within the community, to defend it, the other to attack it from the outside. Antigone's brother is unique only according to the feminine law of the family community. If Antigone declares just one brother, the one she chooses and identifies or unites with is the one who fights the city, Polynices. She throws a handful [*poignée*] of earth over Polynices's corpse as a sign of (the) burial (place). Antigone is also Eteocles's enemy brother.

The two brothers have killed each other.

How is that possible?

A scandalizing question traverses the text. How, in sum, is a brother possible? How can one have two sons [*fils*]? How can one be the father of two phalli, erected one against the other? How can one have a brother? How can two beings of the same sex cohabit in one family? That is to say—the question is not as easy as one believes—in the ethical reign? Of course, in the animal's natural kingdom, that is possible. Two males can, for example, belong to the same litter. But precisely they are not brothers. Brothers are not possible in nature.

But not in culture either. So brotherhood must find accommodation between nature and culture. The figure of monstrosity:

The religious act, the anthic theft, the flower's gathering are dedicated to him—a singular individual—who has lost his member at the foot of a tree to grow there no more. Stilitano had in effect the "benefit of such homage" the first time. "I think it was by him that I was initiated, that is, my obsession with his body kept me from flinching. To his beauty, to his tranquil immodesty, I dedicated my first thefts. To the singularity too of that magnificent one-handed man whose hand, cut off at the wrist [*poignet*], was rotting away somewhere, under a chestnut tree, so he told me, in a forest of Central Europe. During the theft, my body is exposed. I know that it is sparkling with all my gestures. The world is attentive to all my movements, if it wants me to trip up [*culbute*]. I shall pay dearly for a mistake, but if there is a mistake and I catch it in time, it seems to me that there will be joy in the Father's dwelling. Or else I fall [*tombe*] . . ."

Je/*tombe*, I/fall(s), I/tomb. The play of the anth-erection by which I waken to, embark on [*nais à*], my name supposes that, in more than one stroke [*coup*], I crush [*foule*] some flowers and clear [*fraye*] the virgin thicket of erianthus toward the primitive scene, that I falsify and reap [*fauche*] the genealogy. ". . . the Father's dwelling. Or else I fall, and, woe upon woe, there is prison. But as for the savages, the convict who risked 'the Getaway' will then meet them by means of the procedure briefly described above in my inner adventure. If, going through the virgin forest, he comes upon a placer guarded by ancient

passing on to culture, brotherhood has to disappear violently. Two brothers, going head to head, can only kill themselves.

(Inasmuch) as brothers. What Antigone dies of, but not without laughing, in going out the last.

The moment (in effect) the (educated) young man goes out of his family to become a citizen, he extracts himself from the law of the family, from its whole system, from the natural and immediate ethic. Yet he still guards, keeps some adherence precisely insofar as he has a brother. The figure of two brothers can only be contingent. Because of this contingency (*Zufälligkeit zweier Brüder*), naturalness stays. And yet this irrational, inconceivable contingency—the parents should never conceive two sons, at least if they want them alive—is unusual or distressing only insofar it is not altogether natural, as would doubtless be the case for two sisters, surely for two cats. But brothers are neither sisters nor cats, because males are males inasmuch as they lay claim to rational universality, law, and right. "Each of whom with equal right (*mit gleichem Rechte*) takes possession of the community." One cannot conceive that two identical and complete individualities—so they do not complete each other—equally lay claim to one and the same thing that is a law of universality. Government (*Regierung*), the force of universal law incarnated in a "unitary soul" or in the "self of the people-spirit, does not tolerate the duality of individuality (*Zweiheit der Individualität*)." No birthright or other privilege of that type can resolve this problem. Being the first born, as well as simple duality, is a natural fact for which ethical rationality cannot take responsibility. There is no other issue but death. Since both brothers are right, have reason, as men, and since there cannot be two—two foundations, two discourses, two *logoi*, two accounts, two reasons, two heads—they are both wrong. This ends very badly, "their equal right (*gleiches Recht*) to the power of state destroys them both, for they were equally wrong (*gleiches Unrecht*)."

They must each fall (on the other) [*s'abattre l'un (sur) l'autre*].

But they die once again *as singularities*; the community, attacked and defended by two empty singularities, "maintains itself," constructs itself on the brothers' death. (Inasmuch) as brothers: but the "(inasmuch) as" disappears in its very appearing. "For individuality, which for the sake of its *being-for-self* puts the whole in peril, has expelled itself from the community and has dissolved itself within itself." The community honors the one who defends it; the government on its side punishes him in depriving him of a burial (place), in abandoning his corpse to the "dogs" and

tribes, he will either be killed by them or be saved. It is by a long, long path that I choose to go back to primitive life. What I need first is the condemnation of my race."

Enter Pépé. Pépé then occupies the entire space parting [*écartant*]—separating—from this sentence the para(gra)ph that declines the signature and the civil state, towards which we make our way by a long, long path.

Isn't Pépé, the name father or grandfather, also the diminutive of Joseph, the father excluded (in (it)self ineffective, inactual) from what was immaculately conceived? His name strikes the circumflex, no less than his devirilized characters. "'Pépé,' I said to myself, 'his name is Pépé.' And I left, for I had just noticed his delicate, almost feminine little hand. . . . 'My name is Pépé,' and he extended his hand. . . . 'It's a girl,' I thought, summoning up the image of his slender hand, and I thought that his company would bore me."

The encounter with this sort of glabrous figure had been elaborated, once more, by an opposition of black and white ("black wool"/"white wool," "black woolen cloth" of a stolen cape and "nuptial scene" between two legionnaires, a "couple veiled in tulle and decked out in a parade uniform") and, in the middle, the lifting of oppositions, toward the undecidable suspense, by the circumflex's crane-like, prostituting movement: "'Really, when you pick up a client, it's you who ought to pay him,' he told me. . . . That very evening I brought back the cape of a customs officer. . . . big cape of black woolen cloth. I wrapped myself up in it in order to return to the

Christiane Hegel had—she too—two brothers. The one called Hegel then had only one sister and only one brother (Georg Ludwig, officer in the army of Wurtemberg, who died in 1812, after the *Phenomenology of Spirit*, during the Russian campaign. Nothing is known of his burial place. He bore the father's first names.). The same year (the first volume of the greater *Logic*) is the birth and the death of Hegel's daughter, Susanna Maria (suffocating catarrh), who therefore will not have known her two brothers, born in 1813 and 1814, Karl and Immanuel. After the birth of this last one, Hegel writes to Niethammer:

"Dear friend and godfather,
". . . At the baptism I stood proxy for you. I took care to behave negatively during the ceremony, so as not to place myself between your godfathership and its effects upon him, but rather to allow everything to flow smoothly and properly without hindrance. His name, about which you inquire, is Thomas Immanuel Christian; we have taken 'Christian' from my sister, 'Thomas' from Seebeck, while 'Immanuel'—the name by which he is known—has been taken from you. He shall be known as 'Christian' because he is baptized a Christian; his name is also 'Thomas' because he shall pass over to the other extreme of unbelief. But by virtue of his middle name these extremes shall be fused in friendship and philosophy, and shall be moderated and equalized as the point of indifference (*Indifferenzpunkt*)-in-the-other.
"So far the child has not belied the blessing he has received. He is thriving, thank goodness. Although my wife is not breast-feeding, she is likewise healthy. . . ."

The response of Niethammer (in English, riveter, riveting hammer):

". . . May he not be inclined too much toward Thomas and find the point of indifference without sinking into the indifference and without ending, so to speak, in *Inani El*! With regard to the name Christian, I will confidently leave that to the spirit of my co-godmother whose name he bears, so that he does not become a Christian weak of spirit, but a Christian with a strong spirit, as is fitting to the one that begins with Thomas! May the race of weak individuals without courage, who play the comedy of Christianity with cross, blood, death, humiliation, self-degradation, etc., be abhorrent for him all his life, as it is for his godfather!"

His other eponym (the "godmother"), the aunt, Hegel's sister, Christiane, committed suicide in 1832, shortly after the death of her brother. She had been confined in 1820 in the lunatic asylum of Zwiefalten, then treated by Schelling's brother. Her "nerve troubles" began in 1814 (after the death of Georg Ludwig, when Marie Hegel is expecting her first boy):

"Nuremberg, 9 April 1814

"Your condition as described in your letter received yesterday, dear sister, touches me and my wife very deeply. There is no question as to what is to be done. If your current illness is such that a trip is enough for your diversion and recovery,

hotel, and I knew the happiness of the equivocal, not yet the joy of betrayal, but the insidious confusion which would make me deny fundamental oppositions was already being established."

Joseph "is" (bands erect) then a girl, almost, in erection ("From the opening emerged a solid neck [*cou*], as large as his head. When he turned it without moving his chest, an enormous tendon stood out [*bandait*]."), the accent circumflex(es) a blind old Oedipus who climbs to calvary supported by his daughter, but his daughter is his father for whom he takes the place of scepter or glaive or gladiolus. No [*Pas d'*] Oedipus on march without gl. So he is the phallus of his father who is at the same time his mother and his daughter. What is his mare, what does that ride [*Qu'est-ce que ça cavale*].

Already the Oedipus lodges "within himself" his derision, his parody, his simulacrum, and, as what never returns to him, the wherewithal *to be* reversed. Like all the flowers. In the program always (oracle and good news), the anthoedipus arrives each season like a flower. It spits itself behind a reseda. Thus does Stilitano take him by the hand and lead him on the staircase that speaks. The staircase always leads to death: upwards and by steps, stopovers [*escales*], with

by all means visit us. . . . My wife will be delivering this fall, and if you could lend her a hand your presence would be doubly advantageous. . . . We can set you up in a small room of your own, a type of garret-room, which is of course heatable.

"Above all put your mind at rest. . . .

"Seek your reward for your efforts in part in the vocation (*Bestimmung*) you have had to follow thus far due to your economic situation, but also in the work itself, in the physical and spiritual welfare of the children committed to your care [Christiane was governess in the house of Count von Berlichingen]. . . . For the rest consult yourself and the doctor about what is to be done for your well-being."

In November 1815, in a draft of a letter of Christiane to Hegel:

". . . I have disturbed the order of your house and am sorry about that; but not the peace of your house, and that comforts me. . . ."

Christiane then settles near her cousin, the pastor Göriz. Hegel: ". . . Greet cousin Göriz along with his wife and sister. It is a particular relief for me to know that you have in him such a true and genuine friend and counsellor. Have total confidence in him, and subject your thoughts to his well-intended advice and insights. The most important thing for a human being is to free oneself of one's idle thoughts, and to find this liberation and at once the satisfaction of one's mind in a fruitful activity for a noble cause—an activity you have found under your friend's guidance. Add to this the remembrance of, even from afar,

"Your ever-faithful brother,
"Wilhelm"

". . . I . . . likewise learn from your letters—that you are continuing with the useful occupation and activity of teaching which you had begun. The success of your undertaking truly pleases me, first because you thus have a further source of income, and second because your occupation is both beneficial to health and—through the consciousness of being useful to others—satisfying to the heart. . . . On the whole, as I said, you will find in the confidence you have found among the inhabitants of Aalen as in your beneficial activity both support and satisfaction of heart and conscience, and this motive must always be foremost in our commissions and omissions.

"I am sending you in advance the interest due on 300 florins capital along with a small supplement. . . ."

Two years later, three letters to cousin Göriz to ask him to act "in my name as a brother" the moment what a man can dread worse, the "hardest" and "most unfortunate" experience, occurs.

"Berlin, 19 March 1820
"I am, dear cousin, much obliged to you for procuring and sending my certificate of baptism. I have thus incurred a monetary debt to you as well. I would, of course, like to pay you in person, and am sure you would be willing to bear with

the support of another. Oedipus and Christ meet one another on a staircase.

It is a matter here, need this be repeated, of *stairs* [*marches*].

Stilitano says, "'Follow me!'" Stumbling block where not to stumble.

"'Follow me,' he said. 'And be quiet, the staircase is talkative.'

"Gently he led me from step to step [*de marche en marche*]. I no longer knew where we were going. A wondrously supple athlete was leading me about in the night. A more ancient and more Greek Antigone was making me scale a dark, steep calvary. My hand was confident, and I was ashamed to stumble at times against a rock or root, or to lose my footing.

"Under a tragic sky, I will have crossed [*parcourus*] the most beautiful landscapes in the world when Stilitano took my hand in the night. Of what sort was this fluid that passed from him into me, and gave me a discharge?"

To climb the staircase, "to scale a . . . calvary," is as glorious as the ascension of the body on the scaffold (you mount the scaffold: "the death on the scaffold which is our glory") and the two thieves conspire to play all roles at once. The father Oedipus (Mary-Jochrist) is led by the hand, certainly, of his child, son or daughter, toward the chamber, hotel room, simulacrum of family room and of temple, that they explore in the night as thieves. The staircase talks, causes [*cause*], and orders the whole space. "Hardly had I touched it/him [*l'*], the staircase changed: it/he [*il*] was the master of the world," he, Stilitano and not the staircase. But Stilitano is the master insofar as he supports (on) [*soutient (dans)*] the staircase. The glorious one-handed man forms a sort of truncated, castrated column around which is twined, like a

me until I visit my old fatherland. The only problem is that this might take too long, and that too much interest might accumulate. You can settle accounts through my sister.

"I am also grateful to you for the sad notification you give me of my sister's unfortunate condition. My activities kept me from replying earlier in this regard. Yesterday I finished my lectures, but even today I do not know what I am to say of this. The news has moved me deeply. Of all the things that can affect a human being, this is the hardest (*das Harteste*) to take. She recovered quickly, however, from the earlier attack that befell her when she was still in Mr. von Berlichingen's household, although she admittedly retained an unhappy, irritated mood from that experience. Is it not possible that this relapse is connected with her current age, and that the change in the female constitution—which in her case is only now appearing, though normally it should probably have happened already a few years ago—has had such an effect? You still describe her problem chiefly as hysteria, which was likewise the case then.

"The only consolation I can have in this is knowing that she enjoys your loving supervision and, as you have assured me already in your letter, that she does not want for anything. I must likewise appeal to your kind attentions and judgment to decide what further is to be done for her, and what provision and treatment are to be arranged. Since it is in the first instance the physical condition of hysteria which effects such a release [*Entbindung* is also delivery, childbirth, confinement] of the inner passions, there might still be hope for her recovery through your loving care combined with medical treatment. Because she probably retains awareness of her surrounding actual environment despite her confused frame of mind, your care is what is most beneficial for her deranged mind, which requires the respect and deference which she will have for you in order to be controlled.

"I give you once more my heartfelt thanks for all your kindness and love in this sad situation. I may still ask you for news of her from time to time, and of changes in her condition. Please remember me cordially to your family in Stuttgart. My wife and children, thank God, are well. I learned only from your greetings, however, that you have remarried. I have received no news from my sister in more than a year. So please accept my warm congratulations. May all the love you have given be returned to you in this marriage.

"Your sincere cousin and friend,
"Hegel"

"Berlin, May 13, 1820

"Dear cousin,
"At the beginning of April, I informed you in a letter of the reports reaching me from Jaxthausen of my sister's illness, and also asked you for your further assistance in this matter. According to further letters from Jaxthausen, the appointment of a guardian to oversee her financial and personal well-being seems necessary. She is indeed in Neustadt, and as she herself writes no doubt has very good accommodations. But she has already found aspects of her present situation which lead her to wish a change. From my present distance I find myself obliged to address myself to others to accomplish what I cannot do myself. And in whom could I have greater confidence than in you, my old friend and cousin!

plant, the staircase. Occurrent always around a fictive column.

Another staircase scene. This time the hotel of the holy family is shady. It's a parenthesis: "(Sometimes at night I meet a youngster and go with him to his room. At the foot of the stairs, for my trade lives in shady hotels, he takes me by the hand. He guides me as skillfully as did Stilitano.)"

What glues itself [*se colle*], along the winding staircase, to the truncated column's body is indeed a son become father. Of his father, no doubt; of whom would one be the father?

Yet his march, its step, it runs [*sa marche*]: ". . . He guides me as skillfully as did Stilitano.)

"'Watch out.'

"He mumbled these words, which were too sweet for me. Because of the position of our arms I was glued to his body. For a moment I felt the movement of his mobile buttocks. Out of respect, I moved a little to the side. We mounted, narrowly limited by a fragile wall which must have contained the sleep of the whores, thieves, pimps [*souteneurs*], and beggars of the hotel. I was a child being carefully led by his father.

as one knows, at least since Jacob, each time one dreams of a sexual act, that symbolically represents a climb or a tumble [*dégringolade*]. "Steps, ladders or staircases, or, as the case may be, walking up or down them, are symbolic representations of the sexual act" (*Traumdeutung*). The staircase [*escalier*], then, speaks. It is sonorous (wood). Like the thin walls [*cloisons*] of a hotel, like its partitions [*galandages*] (he loves the word very much, and all his literature would form a galanthus; galanthus is a milk-flower). "Separated by a thin wall [*cloison*] from Armand, who was jazzing [*couché*] with Robert, I suffered at not being in the place of either one of them or at not being with them or at not being one of them. I envied them, but I felt no hatred. I went up the wooden staircase [*escalier*] very carefully, for it was sonorous and all the partitions [*galandages*] were wooden." Insatiable jealousy, of oneself, already (I am missing [*je manque*], I miss myself): to knock down the thin walls [*cloisons*], the

179

What my sister needs is the sort of friend you have always been to her to manage her financial affairs and advise as to her situation—but at once a friend who has legal authority over her in handling such matters. I likewise need a friend who is closer by to tell me what steps I must take from a legal standpoint. Privy Councillor Count von Berlichingen of course suggests to me the Orphans' Court in Stuttgart, which is responsible for ratification of a guardianship and which exercises ultimate supervisory authority. But I cannot personally arrange for such prior legal guardianship from here, and thus can immediately accomplish the necessary steps only by proxy. So I address my request to you in this unfortunate affair—which is indeed the most unfortunate (unglücklichsten) that can befall men—to intercede and initiate the necessary steps. If a formal authorization is necessary from me beyond the fact that I hereby authorize you in this letter, I would make it over to you upon some indication from you. But my authorization for establishment of a guardianship over my sister also of necessity depends on the medical attestations and testimonies of others regarding her condition and behavior, which I will have to ask you to procure yourself, and which you either already have or can quickly get. The sort of guardianship you already have at once for itself implies the more specific authorization to apply for further legal authority. I have written today to Dr. Uhland in Neustadt, who is her doctor and who has provided for her accommodation. I have asked him to establish contact with you, in part with regard to the expenses of her stay there, since so far you have handled her financial affairs. Because her own means will not be sufficient to procure decent accommodations—the contract for room and board there amounts to 300 florins a year—I have promised a supplement of 100 to 150 florins. I should really settle accounts with you first regarding this side of the question. According to what you indicated earlier, in Aalen she was no doubt able to get by with what she had. In Neustadt she now longs to return to Aalen, but the only question is whether she can remain or be left there. On the other hand, I have asked Dr. Uhland to inform you of her condition, which will determine whether she could remain in private life or must be placed in the care of a public institution. From all that I have been told and that you have already found out yourself, an authority exercising legal power over her is indispensable to keep her quiet and submissive in private life. The other solution, a public institution, can even more clearly be decided only by a formal and official guardian.

"I thus ask you to act in my name as a brother. It is most reassuring for me to be able to see you represent me in this sacred concern.

"The mail is about to leave, and so I close with the warmest of farewells.

"Your cousin,
"Hegel"

"Berlin, 17 June 1820

"Dear cousin,
"Following kind notification from you at the end of last month, I am sending you first the enclosed draft for 300 florins to pay off the sum which I still owed my sister. It has just occurred to me that I should have added interest for

(Today I am a father led to love by his child.)"

Today, between parentheses, is writing's presently presenting: I am (following) a father. But the "I was a child" of the preceding sentence, outside parentheses, belongs to the time of the same story [récit] according to which, a page higher or a step [marche] lower, the child was the old Oedipus supported [soutenu] by his daughter (Stilitantigone) to whom he gave a "confident" hand. Who lends a helping hand [un coup de main] to whom in this (hi)story? To whom does the hand return? What sense does it have in trembling? Who emits gl, the discharge of the fluid?

clefts, the partitions [galandages] in order to occupy all the places at once, to love (oneself) in (the) place of the other, to put an end to the worst suffering (to be jealous of not being jealous enough, of not even being able to reappropriate jealousy as one's suffering, one's evil, one's very own), to swallow oneself, to touch oneself, to deliver oneself [s'accoucher], to give birth to oneself and to give oneself one's own, then to band oneself erect to death, finally to masturbate oneself or to fuck oneself by flowing out of oneself [en s'écoulant]: je m'ec, je m'enc

Stilitano, the son and daughter father to the column, the one-handed stylist, always uses, in the guise of a hook, the circumflex that lends him a hand in the surroundings of places where he elaborates his luminosity. The circumflex therefore becomes his phallus, the detached member that grows back after having rotted at the foot of a tree. "By remaining inaccessible, he became the essential sign of those whom I have named and who stagger me. I was therefore chaste. At times he was so cruel as to require that I button the waistband of his trousers, and my hand would tremble. He pretended [feignait] not to see anything and was amused. (I shall speak later of the character of my hands and of the meaning of this trembling. It is not without reason that in India sacred or disgusting persons and objects are said to be Untouchable.). . .

you, but this can be done later. A remittance to Stuttgart could not be made. But from what I hear drafts for Frankfurt are sought after in Stuttgart, and you will perhaps be able to sell it yourself in Aalen. Secondly, I am also sending a statement authorizing you to assume the guardianship you have kindly offered to undertake. This authorization can take effect, however, only if tutelage is legally granted and acknowledged. You will know best what is to be done in this regard, and will kindly take care of it.

"This formality of guardianship moreover bears on what I will be able and willing to do further for my sister's care. If she acknowledges the tutelage or allows it to be exercised willingly, well and good. But if her actions remain at her own discretion, there is no way I could consent to expenditures in support of her extravagances (*Extravaganzen*)—here is where the requested supervision of all her household effects is in order—and the costs they occasion even if I had more money available than I in fact have. Such assurance is available only through a court order by which her conduct is no longer abandoned to a willfulness on her part that refuses all good advice. The doctor in Zwiefalten likewise has absolute need of such authorization over her conduct in order to undertake treatment, though he is indeed charging a little too much in relation to the cost of board. So my express request to you is still to take the preliminary steps in your or my name at the Orphans' Court in Stuttgart.

"In thanking you in advance for your friendship in this matter, I at once ask you to express to your mother, brothers, and sisters—and especially the postal secretary—my cordial gratitude for the many troubles they have taken. I hope someday to have the opportunity of returning the favor to you and your family. Farewell.

"Your faithful cousin,
"Hegel

"Please hand over the enclosed brief letter to my sister."

On page 3 of this letter, the following proxy:
"By these presents I give full powers to my cousin, Dean M. Göriz—since my sister Christiane Hegel, according to all the information received, is found suffering from mental illness—to act in my name in the affairs that concern her, and I establish him her guardian, as far as that depends on me.

"G. W. F. Hegel
"Professor of Philosophy
"at the Royal University
"of this city.
"Berlin, 17 June 1820"

A year later, Christiane leaves the mental home at Zwiefalten:

"Berlin, August 12, 1821

"My dear sister,
"It has pleased me deeply to learn from your letter of June of the fortunate restoration of your health, and of the strengthening and recovered possession of your mind. I only wish this were the only sentiment with which your letter left me. Most of all, I could only wish that the painful and bitter feelings it awakened in me might merely have concerned the past, and not refer to the present and future. For from the strengthening of your spirit and mind it is to be hoped that you may overcome the past, the memory of your sufferings, the feeling

Stilitano was happy to have me at his beck and call and he introduced me to his friends as his right arm. Now, it was his right hand that had been amputated. I would repeat to myself delightedly that I was certainly his right arm; I was the one who took the place of the strongest limb."

Ten lines further down, royally cutting short this development, with no other apparent elaboration, at the moment when Stilitano quits the scene opened by "follow me," the circumflex opens another scene, its own, that of the accent that announces itself: this is who I am, where and how I was born, what I am named and baptize myself (John baptized Christ), I call myself, I hear myself [*je m'écoute*], surname myself flower (baptism is a second birth), I am generated once more, I deliver myself [*je m'accouche*] as a flower. The race being condemned, the circumflex consecrates itself in opening the mouth and drawing the tongue—the syllable drags a bit—elevates itself and places itself on the crowned head.

The rhetorical flower organizing this antitrope, this metonymy simulating autonymy, I baptize it anthonymy. One could also say anthonomasia. Antonomasia is a "Kind of synecdoche that consists in taking a common noun for a proper name, or a proper name for a common noun" (Littré).

of having suffered the injustice and insults of others. I may at least draw your attention first to the fact that above all you ought work within yourself to put this past behind you, and to concern yourself with your present frame of mind and behavior toward others. The more you can subdue and remove such memories from your present—both your inner present and your outer present over against others—the sounder of health your mind will become, and the friendlier your relation to others, and their relation to you. In your letter to me you found it necessary for your self-justification to return to so much that is painful. Naturally you needed to convince me of the evil treatment you have received. But consider yourself generally convinced that the repetition in recollection of this past will only be detrimental to the complete restoration of your health. What most justifies you toward others is your sensible present behavior. Justification stemming from past treatment toward you, since it inevitably assumes the form of reproaches, turns away the affection of those before whom you wanted to justify yourself far more than it is able to win them over to you. My advice for your health may principally consist in encouraging you to allow your recollection of suffered injustice to dissolve and disappear. But take this matter to be of the greatest importance.

"I of course had to expect you to write to your brother of the circumstances that contributed to making you so unhappy. But I shall thus have as little as possible cause to want to justify others or myself here and there against you, and to stir up in you and bring before you again what you are rather to consider as over and done with. So I will touch just briefly on a few points which may be of interest with respect to the future. After all you have written to me about it, it is evident you can no longer enter into a relationship with Dean Göriz. It seems increasingly clear to me that this relationship has been the cause of your illness. I see from what you still write about the idea of returning to the estate of Count von Berlichingen that—as is only natural—you have merely an imperfect representation of the effect which your behavior during your illness has had on others, and can even less grasp their behavior regarding yourself. But this makes the challenge to unburden yourself of the representations you have of these matters simply all the greater. I of course am no longer in correspondence with the Count.

"I must mention two things about my own behavior. I wrote to you in Neustadt, asking you in the letter above all to direct your soul to the thought of God, and to receive into your mind [Gemüt] strength and consolation from this higher love. I have also written to you about this in a letter to Zwiefalten. But I feel you have replied in a way I had not expected, though what I said could not have come more deeply from my heart. In short, after this letter I immediately received news from you that you want to leave Neustadt, where my second letter thus no longer reached you. I wrote to Stuttgart right away, receiving the reply that you had already left from there as well. Thus neither my exhortation nor the assistance which, at my request, my friends perhaps might have given you could reach you any longer. Whether this letter will still find you in Zwiefalten or Stuttgart I do not know. As for the other matter of giving you evidence of my concern by advancing some money, you know that I scraped up the 300 florins which I still owed, and have sent them to our cousin the Dean. I have likewise committed myself to support you in the future as

"I went back to the hotel and told Stilitano about it. He said he would attend to the matter and then left.

"I was born in Paris on December 19, 1910. As a ward of the *Assistance Publique*, it was impossible for me to know anything but my civil state. When I was twenty-one, I obtained a birth certificate. My mother's name was Gabrielle Genet. My father remains unknown. I came into the world at 22 Rue d'Assas.

"'I'll find out something about my origin,' I said to myself, and went to the Rue d'Assas. Number 22 was occupied by the Maternity Hospital. They refused to give me any information. I was raised in Le Morvan by peasants. Whenever I come across *genêt* (broom) flowers on the heaths—especially at twilight on my way back from a visit to the ruins of Tiffauges where Gilles de Rais lived—I feel a deep sense of kinship with them. I regard them solemnly, with tenderness. My emotion seems ordained by all nature. I am alone in the world, and I am not sure that I am not their king—perhaps the fairy of these flowers. They render homage as I pass, bow without bowing [*s'inclinent sans s'incliner*], but recognize me. They know that I am their living, moving, agile representative, conqueror of the wind. They are my natural emblem, but through them I have roots in that French soil which is fed by the powdered bones [*os*] of the children and youths screwed, massacred and burned by Gilles de Rais.

"Through that spiny plant of the Cevennes,* I take part in the criminal adventures of Vacher. Thus, through her whose name I bear, the vegetable kingdom is my familiar. I can regard all flowers without

much as my circumstances permit. The reimbursement of that capital has of course hampered me ever since. However, as soon as I know where you will be staying I will make an effort to contribute to it. I must regret you have not wished to retain Zwiefalten as your further place of residence—once more in view of the expenses of a trip, and of the transportation of your luggage. After all that has happened to you in Aalen, and after the impression you made during your illness, you can no longer return there. But I would have thought a small town to provide the most advantageous opportunity for you—if only because the cost of living is less. But why do you not mention at all the intention of occupying yourself again with teaching, which you did successfully and, from what you write to me, with the grateful appreciation of people of Aalen? This would provide you with a more secure subsidy than what you can expect from the assistance of others. Such a purpose, by which you can render service to others, will be the most certain means of preserving your mental and thus physical health. I can never regret enough that you gave up such a situation in Aalen, and have put yourself in a situation of dependence on people on whom you thought you could rely, which has in all probability been the cause of your illness. But once you resolve to rely on yourself, you will be most securely sheltered, both inwardly and outwardly—but on yourself at once means on a frame of mind directed toward something Higher. As for teaching, I as well earn my living from it, and honor myself with it just as it honors me in the eyes of others. How this can be accomplished for you again your friends will be able to advise on the spot. But I implore you to accept the good advice of others. At least you may believe me when I say that you have spurned and severely undercut the well-intentioned sentiment of others in your regard by not accepting their advice and assistance in your own best interest, and by not allowing yourself to be restrained from what has become and has been harmful to you.
"Accept these brotherly admonitions as they have come from my heart. May peace be in your heart!
"I must still briefly report on myself, wife, and children. The latter will make themselves heard on their own. We thank God that we find ourselves in better health this summer than last winter, when I felt poorly and when my wife was still sicker and weaker. Of my external situation there would be much to say. As satisfied as I am with it, a position in a great state is different. In my field this situation cannot always be free of apprehension and anxiousness for me—whether founded or unfounded. Farewell for now, dear sister.

"Your brother,
"Wilhelm"

Six years later, still from Berlin (1827).

"My dear sister,
". . . I have learned from your letter of the mishap with my bust; it is to be sure breakab . . ."
(The bottom half of the letter is missing.)

Four years later (the year of his death).

". . . A copper engraving of me, of which you wished two copies, can no longer be found. But since I have not only been

pity; they are members of my family. If, through them, I rejoin the nether realms—though it is to the bracken and their marshes, to the algae, that I should like to descend—I withdraw further from men.**"

"*The very day he met me, Jean Cocteau called me 'his Spanish genêt' (genêt d'Espagne—rush-leaved broom). He did not know what that country had made of me."

"**Botanists know a variety of genêt which they call winged-broom (genêt ailé)."

winged phallus, "winged prick" of the *Miracle*. In the course of *Funeral Rites*, the mother (the maid) of J. D. follows his body, "to go to the cemetery . . . she put the veil behind her by simply turning that fantastically winged hat around her head." "The horse that was drawing the hearse was weary"; the mother wanted to avoid "the cavalier posture of a very proud lady"; "she was that dead person"

So this flower name would be a cryptogram or a cryptonym. It is not proper because it is common. On the one hand,

antonomasia. This alienation, already [*déjà*], even before I return to myself, promenades my proper name in the street, *classes* it in the "natural" world, freezes [*glace*] the appellation in an exterior thing, in its name or in its form. My signature trails behind. Dereliction, errance without end. Among things, equivalent, but absolutely alone. My signature will have *caught on* [pris] according to very diverse routes [*voies*]. Their systematic analysis would be necessary. For example, in the case of the *genêt*, the constitution of the emblem is easy enough and close to consciousness—that is why this reading is very preliminary—insofar as it passes through an entire nominal form. The horse and the flower do not take the outside like Giacometti's dog: this dog detaches itself—but also pulls, like every signature, on its leash—following an entirely other trajectory. To reread "in a ball [*en boule*]": "Its rigid horizontality perfectly restituted the form that a cat keeps, even when it is *in a ball*.

engraved and sculpted but now imprinted on a medal as well, I shall send you two such medals instead. I would already have done so had I only known how. Sending them by mail would cost more than the medals themselves. I thus prefer to await a favorable occasion. . . .

". . . We are presently and—we hope—forever safe from all the current unrest. But these are still anxious times, in which everything that previously was taken to be solid and secure seems to totter. . . ."

The medal given to Hegel by his students bears on its verso a heavenly spirit, standing, and flanked by a woman on its right. She holds a cross that the spirit is going to take hold of. On the other side, a philosopher seated before a column. Above the column the owl that takes wing [vol] at the end of history. The philosopher writes in a book opened on his knees.

Almost at the same moment, Hegel is made Knight of the Order of the Red Eagle (third class) for services rendered to science and in his capacity as professor. The red eagle is not the Napoleonic eagle, the only eagle before which speculative idealism kneeled. As before the "world-spirit" that advances "like a closely drawn armored phalanx advancing with imperceptible movement, much as the sun through thick and thin." This letter to Niethammer (5 July 1816) overflows with contempt for those "ants, fleas, and bugs" that claim they set themselves opposite it and that are not even worthy, as is said in the Gospel, to untie its shoes: "They can perhaps reach the shoelaces of this colossus, and smear on a bit of boot wax or mud, but they cannot untie the laces. Much less can they remove these shoes of gods—which . . . have elastic soles or are even themselves seven-league boots—once the colossus pulls them on. . . . To edify the entire bustling zealous assemblage, one can even stand there and help daub on the cobbler's wax that is supposed to bring the giant to a standstill. For one's own amusement, one can even lend a hand. . . ." The same year (1831), Victor Cousin becomes an Officer in the Legion of Honor, itself instituted by the Empire (the other eagle). He announces this to Hegel: "Here I am, my dear friend; let's chat for a moment as if we were both still lying on your sofa three hundred leagues from intruders and affairs.

"As I had almost told you, I was made Conseiller d'Etat and Officer of the Legion of Honor; it is a little more prominence without much more work. At the right time. But for a political career, I repeat to you that I do not want to enter into one. My position as deputy [députation] tempts me itself little enough, and I remain faithful to philosophy. My place on the Council of Public Instruction is agreeable to me only through the services it permits me to render to philosophy; and between us I can say that for a year I have rendered rather extensive ones. I have constituted the Ecole Normale, that is, our true philosophical seminary, I have replaced the staff of professors; I have made some regulations, instituted competitive examinations; finally given administratively a strong impetus to the studies dear to us. That is why I joined the Council; the day I would no longer have this useful influence on philosophical studies, that day will I withdraw myself and limit myself to serving philosophy through my courses and my works.

"How astonished I am that there is an animal,—it is the only one among his figures:

"HE.—It's I. One day I saw myself in the street like that [comme ça]. I was the dog.

"If this dog was first chosen as a sign of misery and solitude, it seems to me that it was drawn as a harmonious paraph, the curve [courbe] of the spine answering to the curve of the paw, but this paraph is still the supreme magnification of solitude."

The emblem, the blazon open and close (noise and strict-ure of the valve) the jerky outpouring of a wound. The whole Studio works (over) this wound. The signature is a wound, and there is no other origin for the work of art. "There is no other origin for beauty than the wound—singular, different for everyone, hidden or visible—that every man keeps in himself [en soi], that he preserves and where he withdraws when he wishes to quit the world for a temporary but profound solitude. . . . Giacometti's art seems to me to wish to discover that secret wound of every being and even of every thing, so that the wound may illuminate them." And without apparent transition—a large blank—is the paragraph about Osiris in the "crypt of the Louvre." The signature's hidden wound, the bleeding [saignant] cryptogram, is the morseling of Osiris. But the economy of the signature never interrupts its work. It finds in the remain(s) of infirmity a supplementary apotrope, a sort of reseda. As Stilitano bands erect a little more for being one-handed. As Querelle from squinting. Oedipus will never have walked [marché] so well than after his, if one may say so, recent accident. Oedipus is classed, but because limping gives class, confers a more or less proper name. Claudication: classification. To the funambulist on the ground: "I would even go so far as to advise him to limp." "He [Giacometti] resumes his march in limping. He tells me that he was very happy when he knew that his operation—after an accident—would leave him with a limp. That is why I am going to hazard the following: his statues still give me the impression that they take refuge, finally, in I know not what secret infirmity that grants them solitude." The "secret wound" is also the funambulist's "conscience [for interieur]," "It is this wound . . . that he will inflate [gonfler], will fill."

"So, dear Hegel, put yourself well in the spirit that my whole soul belongs always to philosophy. That there is the ground of the poem of my poor life, as I was saying to you; politics fills only episodes of it."

In order to baste [*faufiler*] the whole correspondence or the whole liaison Cousin/Hegel (it is a matter of letting oneself be penetrated, verily impregnated, in the name of France, by the aquiline concept): ". . . How are you? How is the good Mrs. Hegel doing? And your children?—Your soul is at peace, Hegel. Mine is suffering. I pass my life regretting my imprisonment [Cousin had been arrested in Dresden for "'participating in German revolutionary intrigues,'" of which Hegel had always besides believed him innocent. But his incontestable "liberalism" had made the accusation plausible, as it had motivated the suspension of his courses at the Sorbonne and the Ecole Normale, closed anyway, in 1820.]. But I am not forgetting that I am not alone with you, alone, at night, on your couch; and at 300 leagues distance we cannot chat intimately. . ." (13 December 1825) . . . ". . . I want to educate myself, Hegel; so I need, as much for my conduct as for my publications, austere advice, and I await it from you. . . .
". . . There are four points in this small piece of writing: 1. Method. 2. application to consciousness, or Psychology. 3. the passage from Psychology to ontology. 4. some attempts at a historical system. Let something on these four points fall from your good mind. Be all the more merciless because, determined to be useful to my country, I will always permit myself to modify, according to the needs and state, such as it is, of this poor land, the directions of my German masters. . . . It is not a matter of creating here in a hothouse an artificial interest for foreign speculations; no, it is a matter of implanting in the country's bowels fertile seeds that develop naturally there, according to the primitive virtues of the soil; it is a matter of imparting to France a French movement that may then go by itself. . . . I will match the wind's force to the poor lamb's; but as for me, who is not a lamb, I beg the wind to blow with all its force. I feel my back strong enough to withstand that wind; I only intercede for France. Hegel, tell me the truth, then I will pass from you to my country what it can comprehend of that truth" (1 August 1826). ". . . I come to myself. I have made my choice. No, I do not want to enter business; my career is philosophy, teaching, public instruction. I have declared this once and for all to my friends, and I will sustain my resolution. I have begun in my country a philosophical movement that is not without importance; I want in time to attach my name to it, that is my whole ambition. I have that ambition, and no other. I desire in time to strengthen, to enlarge, to improve my situation in public instruction, but only in Public Instruction. What do you say about this, Hegel?—Consequently, I have asked the new administration only for my reinstatement in my chair, but with a firmer title than that of assistant professor [*professeur suppléant*]. . . . That is how I am neither an assistant nor a full professor, but an associate [*adjoint*], which is better than the first but less than the second, and endows me with independence and irremovability. . . . I need, even for here, a little success in Germany. So let's see, Hegel, if Proclus, Plato, Descartes, or the *Fragments* could not possibly secure in your *Journal* the honors of a small article. From you, Sir, that would be too much,

The studio opens on all the bordellos where the lame man tracks the virgin reserved since a night before any past, "his fingers climb and descend like those of a gardener who prunes [*taille*] or grafts a climbing rosebush."

To remark the cynical character of the paraph, one must see the photograph of the sculptor, full-face, at the beginning of the book (every trait falls [*tombe*] from it, as from a beaten dog); but above all the signature of

the other. Without believing in chance and without meaning to do it so well, they have reproduced this signature, in a bad book, at the side of a photograph of the author: he bears, standing up, that cane from which he had some difficulty, several years ago, detaching himself.
The signature is a cliché. Without rights of reproduction

but have some pages written on that by Mr. Gans or the excellent Hotho. . . .

". . . I attach to your copy another one for the person who would indeed want to take charge of making a small announcement about it in your Journal or elsewhere, for example, if that were possible . . ." (7 April 1828). "My classes have just finished, and I hasten to write you, my dear Hegel. Between us, they have had some success; they received the honor of being taken down in shorthand, and they roam the world. Have they come as far as Berlin and to you? Not being sure, I am sending you a complete copy of them, with the condition that you will choose, Sir, to tell me your opinion of them. . . . Three thousand copies of my lectures [leçons] have been sold. Now here is the other side of the picture. There has been a true insurrection of the whole materialist and industrial world. The old dodderers of the Ecole de Condillac have risen up in recognizing their ancient adversary. For lack of good reasons, the accusations and the abuses have not been absent. But I am not a man to trouble myself much about all that. On the other hand, Theology has kept a keen watch over me and regards me with an anxious eye. It takes me not for an enemy, but for a suspect. I have tried to provide it no pretext, but the supremacy of Reason and Philosophy! . . ." (15 August 1828).

on the other, it is not proper because it also leads back to the nether realms, to the marshes, verily to the depths of the sea. Above the sea, with heavy sides but carried by it, the galley. In the depths of the sea, algae. "The Galley" is moreover covered with algae ("algae of velvet," "azure algae," and so on).

Alga is a cryptogam, one of those plants that hide their

the "birds." The universal, by doing this, only "grazes lightly" the "pure tip of its pyramid" the moment it carries off its victory over the rebel principle of singularity and over divine law. That is because the continuous struggle of the "conscious spirit" with the "unconscious spirit" has not come to an end. The unconscious has not been destroyed, only "wounded," injured, offended. "The publicly manifest spirit has the root of its power, its force, in the nether world (*Unterwelt*). The *self-certainty* of a people, a self-confident and unceasingly self-reaffirming certainty, possesses the *truth* of its oath, which binds all into one (*die* Wahrheit *ihres Alle in Eins bindenden Eides*), solely in the mute unconscious substance of all, in the waters of forgetfulness. Thus it is that the fulfilment of the manifest spirit transforms itself into its contrary, and it learns that its supreme right is a supreme wrong, that its victory is rather its own downfall (*sein eigener Untergang*). The dead, whose right is injured, knows therefore how to find instruments of vengeance, which are equally effective, actual, and violent as the power that has wounded it."

So the deceased continues to act; the *deceased is wounded*, returns to the charge from the mute and unconscious substance in which one wanted to repulse, reduce, curb, restrain him. The return of the dead, the vengeance of the suppressed comes to its prominence in wild nature: the birds and the dogs eat the morsels of the corpse abandoned without burial, left to the earth's surface, and then are going to "defile" with these the altars of other communities. The morseled corpse dribbles, bleeds [saigne], and spits on the cultic places. "These forces rise up in hostility and destroy the com-

another metonymy for that "thief who is my mother"; here we have to read Genette, *Metonymy in Proust*, to let be done *en abyme*, out at sea, an infinite work crossing, dredging languages or lagoons that, in every sense, true or false, literally deepen there the threat of engulfing everything: ". . . or again, much more complex, the network of analogies and proximities that is tied up in that other passage from *The Fugitive*, in which the narrator evokes his visits to the baptistry of St Mark's in the company of his mother: 'A time has now come when, remembering the baptistery of St Mark's—contemplating the waters of the Jordan in which St John immerses Christ, while the gondola awaited us at the landing-stage of the Piazzetta—it is no longer a matter of indifference to me that, beside me in that cool penumbra, there should have been a woman draped in her mourning with the respectful and enthusiastic fervour of the old woman in Carpaccio's *St Ursula* in Venice, and that that woman, with her red cheeks and sad eyes and in her black veils, whom nothing can ever remove from that softly lit sanctuary of St Mark's where I am always sure to find her because she has her place reserved there as immutably as a mosaic, should be my mother': mosaic of the baptism, 'in keeping with the site,' where the Jordan appears as a second baptistry *en abyme* within the first; reply given to the waves of the Jordan by those of the lagoon in front of the Piazzetta, frozen [glacée] freshness that falls [tombe] over the visitors like a baptismal water, a woman in mourning similar to the one, close by, in Carpaccio's painting, itself an image *en abyme* of Venice in Venice, hieratic immobility of the maternal image in the memory of the 'sanctuary,' as of one of those mosaics that face her, and by that very means, the suggestion of an analogy between the nar-

munity which has dishonoured and shattered its own force, family piety."

What the community has killed, in order to maintain itself, they are, under the name brothers, still women—family representatives. Human law, the law of the rational community that institutes itself against the private law of the family, always suppresses femininity, stands up against it, girds, squeezes, curbs, compresses it. But the masculine power has a limit—an essential and eternal one: the arm, the weapon, doubtless impotent, the all-powerful weapon of impotence, the inalienable shot [*coup*], the inalienable blow [*coup*] of the woman, is *irony*. Woman, "[the community's] internal enemy," can always burst out [*éclater*] laughing at the last moment; she knows, in tears and in death, how to pervert the power that suppresses. The power of irony—the ironic posit(ion)ing rather—results—syllogistically—from what the master produces and proceeds from what he suppresses, needs, and returns to.

at first approach, at least, to see the figure of Cybele crop up in "The Spirit of Judaism" can seem strange, in place of, on behalf of, the infinite God opposite which there are only stony beings, without life, without right, without love for themselves. Marginal note: "The priests of Cybele, the sublime godhead which is all that is, was, and is to be, and whose veil no mortal has unveiled—her priests were castrated (*verschnitten*), unmanned in body and spirit (*an Leib und Geist entmannt*)." The logic of this rapprochement is now confirmed

Antigone is Cybele, the goddess-Mother who precedes and follows the whole process. She is at all catastrophes, all (down)falls, all carnages, remains invulnerable to them, is killed invulnerable [*y reste invulnérable*]. Her very death does not affect her.

All remains in her. She is to come after, to be followed, to be continued [*à suivre*].

"Human law in its universal being-there is the community, in its activity in general is virility, in its actual and effective activity is the government. It *is, moves*, and *preserves* itself by consuming and absorbing in(to) (it)self the separatism of the Penates, or the singularization into independent families presided over by womankind, femininity; and it keeps them dissolved (*aufgelöst erhält*) in the continuity of its fluidity. But the family is, in the same stroke (*zugleich*), in general its element, the universal acting ground of the singular consciousness. Since the community only gets its subsistence through its interference with the happiness of the family, and by dissolving self-consciousness into universal self-consciousness, it produces itself right in what it suppresses (*erzeugt es sich an dem, was es unterdrückt*) and what is in the same stroke (*zugleich*) essential to it, right in femininity in general, its internal enemy. This femininity—the everlasting irony of the community—changes by

rator's mother and Christ's. . . . But the most spectacular example is evidently *Sodom and Gommorah I*, that morsel of thirty pages entirely constructed on the parallel between the 'Jupien-Charlus conjunction' and the fertilization by a bumblebee of the duchess's orchid: a parallel carefully prepared, managed, tended, reactivated from page to page throughout the episode (and the commentating discourse it inspires), and whose symbolic function does not cease to be nourished, so to speak, by the relation of contiguity that was established in the courtyard of the Guermantes' town house (unity of place) the moment the insect and the baron enter there together (unity of time) while humming in unison; so it is not enough that the miraculous (or at least then judged so by the heroes) encounter between the two homosexuals is 'like' the miraculous encounter of an orchid and a bumblebee, that Charlus enters while 'whirring *like* a bumblebee,' that Jupien is immoblized under his regard and 'takes root *like* a plant,' etc.: the two encounters must also take place 'at the same instant,' and in the same location, the analogy thus appearing only as a kind of secondary effect, and perhaps an illusory one, of *concomitance*."

sexual organs. Like ferns, which in general multiply themselves through the dispersion of spores. Whether one remarks them or not on the surface, the text is full of them. The "ferns" of the "Man Condemned to Death" are "rigid." Certain brackens unfold their fronds several meters below the ground. Cryptogams are evidently not flowers.

Antheridium names the male organ of most cryptogams.

So the association of algae and ferns in anthonomasia would dream the desire for vegetative cryptogamy (I am removed [*je m'écarte*], "I withdraw further from men") under a floral phaneronymy. Phanerogams are traditionally opposed to cryptogams.

intrigue the universal end of the government into a private end, transforms its universal activity into a work of some determinate individual, and perverts the universal property of the State into a possession and ornament (*Putz*) for the family. Woman in this way turns to ridicule the earnest wisdom of mature age which, dead to singularity—to pleasure and enjoyment as well as to actual activity—only thinks of and cares for the universal. She makes this wisdom an object of derision for raw and irresponsible youth and unworthy of their enthusiasm. In general, she maintains that it is the power, the force, of youth that really counts: the worth of the son lies in his being the lord and master of the mother who bore him, that of the brother as being one in whom the sister finds man on a level of equality, that of the young man as being one through whom the daughter, freed from her dependence, obtains the enjoyment and dignity of wifehood (*Frauenschaft*).—The community, however, can only preserve itself by suppressing (*durch Unterdrückung*) this spirit of singularity, and, because it is an essential moment, all the same produces (*erzeugt*) it and precisely by taking a suppressive attitude toward it as a hostile principle."

So suppression produces just what—the singularity of the unconscious, the irony of femininity—it suppresses as its own "essential moment." It traps itself, and glues, limes itself in its own essence. Whence the eternal burst [*éclat*] of laughter of the unconscious—or of the woman, the exclamation that indefinitely harasses, questions, ridicules, mocks the essence, the truth (of man).

Thus does the family collapse, cave in, "engulf itself," "gulp itself down." The family devours itself. But let one not go and see in this, precipitantly, the end of phallocentrism, of idealism, of metaphysics. The family's destruction constitutes a stage in the advent of *Bürgerlichkeit* (civil and bourgeois society) and universal property, proprietorship. A moment of infinite reappropriation, the most reassuring metaphysical normality of idealism, of interiorizing idealization. A ruse of reason or the woman's eternal irony, each able to take itself for the other and *to play the other*. If God is (probably) a man in speculative dialectics, the godness of God—the irony that divides him and makes him come off his hinges—the infinite disquiet of his essence is (if possible) woman(ly).

And among the phanerogams, which show them, their sexual organs, and which make flowers, gymnosperms lay their seeds bare, while angiosperms squeeze them into a vase, a vessel, a reservoir. Gymnosperms appear midway, it seems, between vascular cryptogams (for example, ferns) and angiosperms. In the case of vascular cryptogams, the spore engenders a prothallus separated from the mother plant. Fertilization forms on the prothallus. By contrast, the fertilized ovule of angiosperms remains on the mother plant, and the seed is sheltered by a fruit.

Cryptography then uses phanerogamy to mislead the proper. Improper then is the flower name, the accent of the *genêt* that is hardly pronounced. The circumflex with which it decks itself out is a sort of postiche head or headgear, and is stitched [*cousu*] in (the) place of a living wound that signs.

The seam [*couture*] of the postiche, of the *ersatz*, of the substitute, lets itself be overlapped [*recouper*], three pages farther on, by the episode of the grape cluster (cellulose and wadding) that Stilitano had stuck [*piquée*] inside his trousers.

Between the anthonymy and the scene of the cluster [*grappe*], a stop before a piece apparently plated or sewn into the tissue of the text: an image in the tapestry.

It begins this way after a fictive break [*cassure*] in the story [*récit*]:

"I had just broken with the army, had just shattered [*casser*] the bonds of friendship.

You have come back, without ever having left it, to the middle of the *Philosophy of Right*. Yet everything in it seems to start off again in the opposite direction. Antigone, for example, had abstract right, formal morality, and so on, before her. Now she has

"The tapestry known as 'Lady with the Unicorn' excited me for reasons which I shall not attempt to go

them behind her. What was *to come* (from the Roman world to Kant) in the phenomenology of spirit will have been *passed* in(to) the philosophy of right (that is, in the system of the encyclopedia). Antigone is of service twice, opens on both sides, but remains in the same place: the law of the family, the first moment of *Sittlichkeit*. She is even invoked in the first moment of the first moment: monogamous marriage. But this time the tragic (because of its immediacy) opposition of the two laws, Antigone's and Creon's, has another paradigmatic value; she is not the example of the dissolution of the ethical *in(to)* its negative (abstract right, etc.), but of the constitution of the ethical *against* its negative. Simultaneous effects of chiasm(us) and circle, of encircled chiasm(us).

The first of three parts (marriage) of the first of three sections (family) of the third part (*Sittlichkeit*) recalls the Antigone of the *Phenomenology*:

"The *natural* determinateness of the two sexes acquires from its rationality its *intellectual* and *ethical* significance. This significance is determined by the difference into which the ethical substantiality, as the concept, divides itself within itself in order to obtain, on the basis of this difference, its life (*Lebendigkeit*) as a concrete unity.

"§166. Thus the *one* sex is the spiritual as what divides itself (*sich Entzweiende*) into personal autonomy *for (it)self* and the knowledge and volition of *free universality*, into the self-consciousness of conceptual thought and the volition of the objective final end. The *other* sex is the spiritual conserving itself in unity as knowledge and volition of the substantial in the form of concrete *singularity* and *feeling*. In relation to the outside, the former is powerful and active, the latter passive and subjective. So man has his actual substantive life in the State, in science, and so forth, as well as in labor and struggle with the external world and with himself, so that it is only out of his interior division that he fights his way to autonomous unity with himself. In the family he has a tranquil intuition of this unity and the subjective feeling of ethical order, the family in which the *woman* has her substantive destination and, in this *piety*, her ethical disposition.

"For this reason, piety is expounded in Sophocles' *Antigone*— one of the most elevated representations of this virtue—as principally the law of woman, and as the law of a subjective and feeling substantiality, the law of interiority, an interiority that has not yet attained its full actualization, as the law of the ancient gods, the gods of the underworld, as an eternal law, and no man knows since

into here. But when I passed, from Czechoslovakia into Poland, the frontier, it was noon, summertime. The ideal line traversed a field of ripe rye [*seigle*], the blondness of which was that of the hair of young Poles; it had the somewhat buttery sweetness of Poland, about which I knew that in the course of history it was always wounded and pitied."

The motif of the limit, of the frontier, of the parting line will furrow the whole sequence. From one mother to the other.

The affect of (the) passage: the singular emotion born from penetration. Penetration is crossing a limit, that is, (with) a *march* separating two opposed places. And which, however, naturally continue, like Czechoslovakia and Poland, resemble each other, regard each other, separated nonetheless by a frontier all the more mysterious, concealed in the crossing, because it is abstract, legal, ideal: "I passed, from Czechoslovakia into Poland, the frontier, it was noon, summertime. The ideal line . . . ," that is, the invisible, artificial, nonexistent line, that you transgress without seeing, with a single step [*pas*], in a limit instant, like noon, no, that you do not pass presently but that you are going to pass, that you have passed: "Fear, and the kind of emotion I always feel when I pass over a frontier, conjured up at noon, beneath a leaden sun, the first fairyland. . . . Passing over frontiers and that emotion it arouses in me were to enable me to apprehend directly the essence of the nation I was entering."

What is it to pass from Czechoslovakia into Poland?

divine law, woman's recourse is always already there. The absolute already: the woman's side. Antigone insists: the advantage of nonwritten laws is that, not being instituted by men, they are engraved in the heart from always, their originating event cannot be determined.

Οὐ γάρ τι νῦν γε κἀχθές ἀλλ᾽ ἀει ποτε / ζῆ ταῦτα, κοὐδεις οἶδεν ἐξ ὅτου 'φάνη

Reason in History also takes its bearing from this. But only in order to see in it the sign of a profound rationality (at work on entering the threshold of the ethical, even if the law of the woman—of the already—opposes its rationality to man's). "Sophocles' Antigone says: The divine commands are not of yesterday, nor of today; no, they live without end, and no one can say whence they came."

The "eternal irony" of the woman will never let itself be reached behind the absolute entrenchment of this already, which is further back than the origin, older than birth, and attends death.

As irony, the woman is at once a *moment to be passed* and the very *form* of *Sa*. Double mark and double place. Irony (another architectonic index) defines the "culminating point" of subjectivity (at the end of the second part of the *Philosophy of Right*, at the moment of the "passage" from *Moralität* to *Sittlichkeit*, but already has, as the *form* of absolute subjectivity, the infinite power of *Sa*. In the experience of irony (which must be determined against Plato and the Romantics), "You accept a law as a matter of fact and honestly as existing in and for (it)self; I myself am also present to this law and within it (*dabei und darin*), but I am also still farther than you, I extend beyond (*ich bin auch darüber hinaus*), I can do *thus or otherwise* (*so oder so*). It is not the thing (*Sache*) that is excellent, but I who am so, and am the master of law and thing [Hegel adds by hand: Virtuosity, Genius—master of the ethical], who thus *only plays* (nur spielt) as I please, and in this ironic consciousness in which I let the highest perish *I enjoy only myself* (nur mich geniesse).—This figure (*Gestalt*) is not only the frivolity of all the ethical *content* of right, duty, laws—evil, and even universal evil in itself; this figure also adds to this the form (*Form*), the *subjective* frivolity that consists in knowing itself as this frivolity of all content and, in this knowledge, in knowing itself as the absolute."

Absolute woman, absolute irony, absolute evil lightly graze and mime *Sa*—for the form

when it appeared. This law is there displayed as a law opposed to manifest law, the law of the State. This is the supremely ethical and thus supremely tragic opposition, and that very thing is individualized in femininity and virility; cf. *Phenomenology of Spirit*, pp. 383 ff., 417 ff."

  Addition

  "Plant, animal—

  "Individuality not divided in two.

  "In (it)self difference, division in two, and universality.

  "Science, art, poetry.

Crossing the march between [*entre*] two (in a naturally continuous element: two lands, two seas separated by a name or a law) awakens then a unique affect, an "emotion" (two times in the same passage). In the opening of the *Journal*, the same word or nearly so: "My excitement [*émoi*] is the oscillation from one to the other," the undecided suspense between two opposite though continuous significations, between Czechoslovakia and Poland. Here the excitement is also l'*émoi entre*, the *excitement* (enters) *between, the self* (enters) *between*. At the punctual instant, unseizable but revolutionary (noon) where I enter [*j'entre*] (when I passed, from Czechoslovakia into Poland, the frontier) and where I grow, in a new soil, a new power, a new law, the opposition is lifted, the limit suspended, the inside and the outside pass into one another.

Like the law and the outlaw that are reciprocally covered in the same passage, in the interval of several pages: "Though the blue woolen cape I had stolen from the customs officer had already accorded me a kind of presentiment of a conclusion wherein the law and outlaw merge, one dissimulating itself beneath the other but feeling, with a bit of nostalgia, the virtue of its opposite—to Stilitano it would permit an adventure, less spiritual or subtle, but more deeply pursued in daily life, better utilized. It will not yet be a matter of treason. Stilitano was a power. His egotism sharply marked out his natural frontiers. (Stilitano *was for me* a power.)"

"Wherever women and the young rule in the State, the State rots. . . .

"Women can indeed be cultivated, but they are not made for the elevated sciences, philosophy, and certain productions of art, those things that require a universal. Women can have ideas (*Einfälle*), taste, grace, but they do not have the ideal. The difference between man and woman is that of animal and plant. . . .

"§167. In essence marriage is *monogamy*. . . ."

How does monogamy intervene in the chain, in the system opposing, rather, the two chains of the law, the masculine and the feminine? Is it only a question of a homogeneous relationship between two unequal forces, unequal but of the same nature? In an uncovered, open field in which darkness would be only a degree of light? Unconsciousness a virtual consciousness? In brief: can repression be thought according to the dialectic? Does the heterogeneity of all the restrictions, of all the counterforces of constriction (*Hemmung, Unterdrückung, Zwingen, Bezwingung, zurückdrängen, Zurücksetzung*) always define species of general negativity, forms of *Aufhebung*, conditions of the relief? Repression—what is imagined today, still in a very confused way, under this word—could occupy several places in regard to these re-(con)strictions: (1) within the series, the class, the genus, the gender, the type; (2) outside: no more as a case or a species, but as a completely other type; (3) outside in the inside, as a transcategorial or a transcendental of every possible re-(con)striction.

Can repression be thought according to the dialectic? The response is necessarily affirmative: if thinking means (to say) what thinking has meant (to say) in the history of thought. And if thought is what forms the question in general, is what imposes the question's questioning form, the copulation question/response. This copulation has an ontological, that is, dialectical, "destination." If one asks: "*what is* repression?" "*what is* the re-strict-ure of repression?" in other words, "how is that re-strict-ure *to be thought?*" the response is The Dialectic.

But to say that re-strict-ure—under its name repression—today remains a confused imagination, that is perhaps only to designate, in regard to philosophy, what does not let itself be *thought* or even arraigned [*arraisonner*] by a question. The question is already strict-uring, is already girded being.

In other words: what about the incest prohibition? What relation does it have with the constitution of each chain of legality? With the opposition of the two chains?

But we read, however—"The tapestry known as 'Lady with the Unicorn,'" which "excited me for reasons which I shall not attempt to go into here." We advance into a representation, or rather we penetrate without advancing ourselves, without breaking through, to the surface of an image pinned or sewn [*épinglée ou cousue*] into the general web of the text. Now every penetration, insofar as, with a step [*d'un pas*], it crosses a merely ideal line, suspends the opposition, does not find facing it any really opposable substance. From the moment it suspends and traverses, penetration is never of anything but an image: ". . . to apprehend directly the essence of the nation I was entering. I would penetrate less into a country than to the interior of an image. Naturally, I wished to possess it, but also by acting upon it. Military apparel [*appareil*] being that which best signifies it, this was what I hoped to alter."

Higher up, apparatus [*Appareil*] was the name for Stilitano's "generative organ," the place of elaboration for his "luminosity," his phanerogamy.

So one penetrates (oneself with) a representation. Sewn in the text or facing the text, rather regarding it impassively, severely (like the remain(s) of the Rembrandt, for example, but there are so many others).

The seam [*couture*] of what you will call *le pénêtre* (a signifier to be searched through in every sense) overlaps itself [*se recoupe*] here more than once.

First, a pictorial, representative, iconic text, the tapestry, is appliquéd on a narrative or discursive text: one piece in the other, as for example in *The Maids*.

From this perspective the concept marriage, the first moment of the family syllogism, can be interrogated. Can a certain scansion of reading make appear therein, at least by way of hypothesis, the trait that binds together the double concatenation and the interdiction of incest? What relation is there between monogamy, the incest prohibition, and the apparition of the value of objectivity (activity, virility, differentiation, reason, freedom, and so on) that forms the value of opposition in general? A slight syncope presses the question: what indeed does the relation with the object have to do with the incest prohibition?

The principle of objectivity is privileged, from the (de)parting, in the deduction of marriage. It is not privileged; it is the privilege, the very excellence of the "(de)parting point" in the inaugural act of marriage, as soon as it is analyzed as the operation of *Sittlichkeit*, of the ethical, of what is often translated by "objective morality."

How does one get married? There can be two "(de)parting points" to conjugality, the subjective and the objective. In the class of subjective (de)parting points, a class dependent on a particular, empiric, more or less contingent motivation, there are two possibilities: (1) the "*particular inclination*" of two individuals who meet by chance; (2) the "*foresight*" of parents who plan and manage things. At this moment of the text, marriage "arranged" by the parents is classed in the "subjective" category, since it seems to depend on the singular initiative of empiric individuals that are the parents. In these two cases, freedom is absent.

The good "(de)parting point" is objective; it results from a "free consent (*freie Einwilligung*)," independent at once in relation to the contingent (loving) inclination and in relation to the particular wishes of the parents. In free consent, two subjects merge into one, get rid of their natural predicates, subordinate them at least in order to become one single free person. In this marriage, one becomes person, that is, freedom. Doubtless *natural* freedom is a "self-restriction (*Selbstbeschränkung*)," but the fierce unity of the system of conjugal constraints produces in the same stroke [*du même coup*] the "liberation" of the person and permits the person to reach a "substantive self-consciousness." Thus does the person get free [*se délie*] at once from the contingent strings of love and from the authority of preceding generations.

Getting married is responding to a destination, to an objective vocation (*objektive Bestimmung*), and to the ethical duty, in the order of objective morality (*sittliche Pflicht*). Whoever does not get married remains no further than either the animal naturalness of desire or the formal subjectivity of "*Moralität*." The ethical and the political are reached only on condition of one being married. That being so, a long remark specifies that the "(de)parting point" is by nature "contingent" and depends on the "culture of reflection (*Bildung der Reflexion*)."

Next, the piece is less improperly *sewn* [cousue] this time: it has to do with a material (proper sense) backstitched [*piquée*] onto a textile (figurative sense).

Finally the content, if it can be called that, of this representative abyss, in this passage of the gold [*en or*] noon (one should note down [*relève*] the buttered gliding there of all the signifiers *en or*), is the *pénêtre* of the lady, the graft of a penis (a phallus) that hesitates to be [*être*], and to be what it is close to her, on the head of a fabulous animal: "the most terrible and the gentlest."

The encircled word is perhaps CHIMERA. Dissimulated like an animal, agile, lively, divined in the vegetation, it would have to be tracked, flushed.

The unicorn, the universal counterpoison, then reworks all the rips and all the seams [*coutures*]. The unicorn is not natural, has no natural place, has not perhaps even taken place, a frontier instantaneously passed between two tissues, two textiles, two texts, two sexes. This oscillation is my excitement. I am (following) almost (hardly) the lady with the unicorn and the lady with the unicorn is (almost) for me; I am (following) the lady and the unicorn. My mother has given birth [*accouché*] to the unicorn, and I give

"Unicorn [*Licorne*] . . . n. . . . they [the horns of the unicorn] were thought to be a universal counterpoison. . . . '. . . it is the most beautiful animal, the proudest, the most terrible and the gentlest adorning the earth,' VOLTAIRE" (Littré). *The Thief's Journal*, apropos the one-handed man: "It was no longer even the memory of him that I carried away with me but rather the idea of a fabulous being, the origin and pretext of all desires, terrible and gentle, far and near to the point of containing me . . ."

This remark discreetly introduces the decision that breaks the equilibrium or the indifference. To illustrate the "two extremes" of the (de)parting point, this remark places the parental intervention on the side of objectivity, and then of freedom, no more, as in the body of the text, on the side of subjectivity: "Here there are two extremes: the first, that the arrangements of well-intentioned parents [*wohlgesinnten*: a determining precision. The parents are well intentioned when they wish that the destination of marriage—in particular freedom—be realized; so they intervene in order to leave free. Thus act all the "good intentions," the most effective and actual, then, those that assure the most sublime mastery.] form the beginning and that the inclination in the persons destined (*bestimmt*) to union in mutual love arises from the fact that they become aware of being destined to this."

In that case, the well-intentioned parents arrange the destiny, the destined union: not that they fabricate the destiny; rather they make themselves arrangers for it, enter into its views and ways, have a preview (*Vorsorge*) of what calls (*bestimmt*) their children toward each other; and then love does not fail to be born, to arise; love was on the program. These statements must not be simplified, nor must their historic range be reduced: one is not only dealing here with a psychological deliberation in the head of a father/mother, but as well with a calculus of social class and with a probability of accommodating [*arrangeante*] meeting. That is the objective extreme. The other extreme: the inclination first appears (*zuerst erscheint*) in the persons as "infinitely particularized" individuals, in their "infinitely particularized singularity." One can ask oneself how infinite singularity can give rise to some ethical categoriality, to conjugality for example, how one can pass from one stage [*stade*] to the other. Or conversely, how an objective motivation can one day give birth to a singular affect. Yet the two are produced, and for this inconceivable fact, unintelligible to the understanding, speculative dialectics intends to account: one can get married on the basis of an infinitely unique passion, and one can, conversely, love ever since a marriage. The unintelligible—not the inconceivable—is conception, the birth of the concept from pure singularity, the engendering of the singular (infinite determination) from the concept, the subject's becoming-object, the object's becoming-subject. That's right (*c'est ça*), history, what makes history, (hi)stories, marriage in general.

With/in one stroke [*coup*], objectivity takes the advantage, and the symmetry is broken. It was said: "the (de)parting point" is contingent, indifferent; now it is said: the first extreme is better. The arrangement of the parents—the particular case of objective beginnings—is better than the singular inclination. Not absolutely, but from the ethical viewpoint: it is more ethical (*sittlich*), a better way, a more moral-objective way (*der sittlichere Weg*).

birth to it in my turn by passing the line. I give birth to myself [*Je m'accouche*], and I write myself [*je m'écris*] because of that. In plain-song. In the open field. I listen to myself [*Je m'écoute*].

That's where — here [*ici*] — I siglum ryeself or eagle myself [*je seigle ou m'aigle*].

I am first of all "squatting at the edge," and then there is the birth and the identification: "I remained a long time squatting at the edge, intently wondering what lay hidden in the field, if I crossed it what customs officers the rye [*seigles*] was hiding. Invisible hares must have been running through it. I was uneasy. At noon, beneath a pure sky, all nature was offering me a puzzle, and offering it to me sweetly.

"'If something happens,' I said to myself, 'it will be the apparition of a unicorn. Such a moment and such a place can only give birth [*accoucher*] to a unicorn.'

"Fear, and the kind of emotion I always feel when I pass over a frontier, conjured up at noon, beneath a leaden sun, the first fairyland. I ventured forth into that golden sea [*mer dorée*] as one enters the water. Standing up I traversed the rye [*seigles*]. I advanced slowly, surely, with the certainty of being the heraldic character for whom a natural blazon has been formed: azure, field of gold, sun, forests. This imagery, to enter the water, to adore the mother's blazon. In the course of the anthonomasia, above, of the *genêt*, cryptonym of the mother: "I should like to descend" to the nether realms, marshes and algae of which I was a part, was complicated by the Polish imagery.

This rupture of the symmetry reacts to romanticism, to the "philosophy of love and life," called first philosophy, to historical, literary, dramatic romanticism, controlled by the subjective principle and the value of infinite singularity.

The interest of the condemnation is that it accuses the cold and not the heat: romantic love, the lure of the false infinite, hides a deadly coldness under the ardent discourse of passion. Those who say they love one another from the infinite singularity of subjectivity do nothing but become heated, all hot and bothered; they do not love each other. Their subjective infinite is not truly infinite. The infinite in (it)self must also be objective, and is not satisfied with the secret of absolute singularity. "In the other extreme, it is the infinitely singular proper(ty) that makes good its claims and accords itself with the subjective principle of the modern world." This principle, foreign to Antiquity, proper to Christianity and Romanticism, commands "*Moralität*" and manifests itself everywhere, in historic modernity ("political constitution," "history of art, science, and philosophy"). Everywhere it imprints the mark of the reflection abstracted and frozen in the opposition. Whence the insipidity and the frigidity of the modern dramatic presentation: hardheaded falsification of the infinite, narcissistic affirmation drawing all its force from what it denies or negates, an affirmation that signifies itself with all the more apparent passion since it does not live, and hardly feigns to believe, what it says. "But the modern dramas and other artistic presentations, in which the love of the sexes is the fundamental interest, are permeated throughout by the element of icy [*glacée*] coldness (*das Element von durchdringender Frostigkeit*) disguised under the heat of the passions they present. . . ." What can be of an "infinite importance" for passion is not at all so "*in (it)self.*"

It follows from this demonstration that there is no infinite love without marriage, no marriage that does not proceed from parental objectivity, representing *Sittlichkeit*, law, universality, rational society, and so on. No marriage that is not decided by the parental instance, whatever the form of its intervention: coarse or elegant, immediate or (re)presented, straightforward or crafty [*brutale ou rusée*], conscious or unconscious.

How does this essential objectivity of marriage constitute itself? And since it is the first staging [*mise en scène*] of *Sittlichkeit* in general, how does *Sittlichkeit* engage, pawn, itself in it? How, according to what *act*, does *Sittlichkeit* become *more than* the subjectivity of feeling?

The response is difficult: no value will be recognized here in the contract. So we are going to have to find a form of objectifying engagement that does not come down to the contractual type. Besides, speculative dialectics always has the form of a general

"'In this noonday sky the white eagle should soar invisible!'

"When I got to the birches, I was in Poland. An enchantment of another order was about to be offered me. The 'Lady with the Unicorn' is to me the lofty expression of this passage over the line at noontide."

Follows the "ghost of Vacher" who cut the throats of children. In the course of the anthonomasia it was the ghost of Gilles de Rais who screwed, massacred, burned them.

The flight of the eagle [*aigle*] had been pre-elaborated by a whole gleaning of rye [*seigles*] ("The ideal line traversed a field of ripe rye . . . ," "This rye field was bounded . . . ," "the rye was hiding . . . ," "Standing up I traversed the rye.", and so on). But it is not for the word *seigle* (rye) that the reference of this note appears: "The first line of verse which to my

the eagle appears under a leaden [*plomb*] sun. You will have remarked that it always comes swooping down (on you), falling above you or hanging over [*surplomber*] you. It is a phallic sun, a lead [*plombé*] coffin, a heavy and rigid excrement that crashes down and plunges into you from behind, just as, come from above, Ganymede's eagle. (Or the angel Gabriel, flying-trying-stealing [*volant*] to make a child behind your back. He announced not only Jesus's birth to Mary, but also John's to Zachariah: "Your wife Elizabeth shall bear you a son, and you shall call his name John" (*Luke*). This is John the Baptist, about whom some wondered whether he was not the Christ (his cousin, almost) whom he baptized. So both were announced by Gabriel, but only one of the two was imprisoned and then decapitated: a request whispered [*soufflée*] by Herodias to the girl. "And the man went and beheaded John in the prison, and brought his head on a platter, and gave it to the girl, and the girl gave it to

critique of the contract, or at least of the contractual formality, of the contract in the strict sense.

The contract signature is under the jurisdiction of abstract right, always concerns just a thing, the possession or the disposition of a thing outside the persons. Isn't the seal of the contract itself in the end a thing, a remain(s) between persons, that draws its efficacy from this status? Now the union, the identification of spouses forms one single person, and for the engagement of the persons toward each other as such, without a third and without a thing, no contract can intervene. There can indeed be some "marriage contracts" bearing on the goods, the annuities, the pensions, and other similar things (even though the *Philosophy of Right* does not literally refer to them), but there is no *marriage* contract in that, no contract *of* the marriage. Such a contract horrifies. And for the one who thinks marriage under the category contract, better still to remain single: "To subsume marriage under the concept of contract is thus quite impossible; this subsumption—though infamous is the only word for it—is established by Kant ('Metaphysical Principles of the Doctrine of Right')." No contract, since the formal and the concrete are joined together in the speculative marriage: whence the condemnation immediately consequent on the so-called Platonic marriage and the monkish life that separate the sensible from the spiritual and the natural from the divine.

What then, without the contract signature, becomes of marriage's objectifying engagement, its objectifying commitment? The *Philosophy of Right* admits of an act of language, the production of a sign, the existence of a kind of formal affidavit [*constat*]. But such an attestation would not bind the two spouses to each other (between them, there could not be any objectifying sign, any seal, or any readable contract), it would give rise to marriage for the community, for the remain(s) of the family. There is left from this no less than that such a sign alone of attestation gives to marriage its actuality, its ethical reality. From this (ethical) viewpoint, one is never anything but *married*: one never gets married (since this act has not taken place for the two persons that only make one), but one is married by the others, for the others, and in the element of language, the most spiritual of all the elements. What does not pass through the others and through the tongue could not be called marriage. In a purely dual relation, if some such thing existed, no marriage, even secret, would find its place. But since monogamous marriage (without contract), the only one that can be admitted here, should be limited to the dual relation, marriage is impossible every time [*à tous les coups*]. Or then it is so only after-the-fact [*après-coup*] and never as an act.

"Just as the stipulation of the contract involves already for (it)self the genuine transfer of the proper(ty) (§79), so the solemn declaration (*feierliche Erklärung*) of consent to the ethical bond (*sittlichen*

amazement I found myself composing was the following: '*moissonneur des souffles coupés*' ('Harvester of winded breaths'). I am reminded of it by what I have written above."

her mother." *Mark*.) As the material signifying tomb(stone), as the signifying material falls [*le matériau signifiant tombe*]

I forget, in a certain way, everything I write, doubtless also, in another way, what I read. Save this or that sentence, some sentence morsel, apparently secondary, whose lack of apparent importance does not in any case justify this sort of resonance, of obsessive reverberation that guards itself, detached, so long after the engulfing, more and more rapid, of all the remain(s), of all the rest. One ought to touch there (coagulation of sense, form, rhythm) on the compulsional matrix of writing, upon its organizing affect. From what I have written, I have never retained "by heart," almost, anything but these few words, on the basis of which I am doubtless becoming infatuated here with the genetic "first verse" and some others. They are: "*l'exergue et le gisant essoufflé de mon discours*" ("the epigraph and breathless sarcophagous of my discourse") and "*en pierre d'attente. Et d'angle comme on pourra, par chance ou récurrence, le recevoir de quelques marques déposées*" ("protruding like a toothing-stone, waiting for something to mesh with. And like a cornerstone as it can, by chance or by recurrence, be gathered from the registering of certain trade-marks"). Without a comma [*virgule*] after *angle*. *Angle* is always, for me, a tomb's edge. And I understand this word, *angle*, its gl, at the back of my throat as what at once cuts off and spirits (away) from/ in me all the remain(s).

I forgot. The first verse I published: "*glu de l'étang*

Bande) of marriage, and its corresponding recognition and confirmation by the family and community (the intervention of the *Church* in this affair is a later determination not to be developed here), constitutes the formal (*förmliche*) *conclusion* and the actuality of marriage, such that this bond (*Verbindung*) is constituted as ethical only through the *preliminary* of this ceremony as the accomplishment of the *substantial* through the *sign*, language, the most spiritual being-there of the spiritual (§78). As a result, the sensible moment that belongs to natural life is posited in its ethical relation as something only consequential and accidental."

The linguistic sign, the element of sublimating spiritualization, precisely relieves the sensible formality of the operation. In the linguistic sign the signifier is found raised and accomplished. If marriage were confused with the "external formality" of the affidavit, nothing about its living spirituality would be understood. One would remain no further than the sensible outside that, as always, makes a system with formalism. To confine oneself to the signature's formality is to believe that marriage (or divorce) depends on that formality, is to deny the ethics of love and return to animal sexuality. Now of what does the ethics of love consist, the ethics that is satisfied with no bourgeois or civil prescription (*bürgerliches Gebot*)?

It consists of "the higher inhibition and the depreciation of the simple natural pressure (*die höhere Hemmung und Zurücksetzung des blossen Naturtriebs*)." To rivet oneself to the contractual formality of the signifier is then to let oneself be held back by instinct or to let nature—without restriction—take its course: the complicity of formalism and of empiricism is confirmed once again.

The essence of marriage appears in this active and sublimating inhibition that raises while depreciating, that does without the pressure, exercises over it a downward pressing in order to make it shoot up the highest; but in the same stroke [*du même coup*], marriage assuring the entrance into *Sittlichkeit*, this same movement of restriction produces ethical objectivity in general, its truth as objectivity. The upsurging of the object in(to) its truth supposes here that the natural pressure is compressed, contracted in strict bonds, dissembled, violently veiled under these fetters.

Where does this truth (the violent imposition of the veil) appear in an almost primordial way?

In shame. The truth (of marriage) is shame. Nothing fortuitous in its being named here. The spiritual produces itself under the veil prohibiting appearing nude. Shame (*Scham*), chastity (*Keuschheit* or *Zucht*), truth of the sex, finds its destination in marriage. More precisely: shame, which is *still natural*, spiritually accomplishes itself in the conjugal bond. "Such an opinion (*Meinung*) [a formalist, contractualist, naturalist one] that pretentiously claims to give the highest concept of freedom, inwardness, and perfection of

lait de ma mort noyée" ("glue of the pool milk of my drowned death").

Harvester of winded breaths. The other, "sent by God," "his name was John," had come to say "In the beginning was the Word." The latter presents himself in order to sound the *glas* of breath, to cu

after developing the radiographic negative of the testamentary chrisms and bandages (why anointing and banding in the two testaments?), after attacking, analyzing, toning their relics in a kind of developing bath, why not search there for the remains of John (*Jean*)? The Gospel and the Apocalypse, violently selected, fragmented, redistributed, with blanks, shifts of accent, lines skipped or moved out of place, as if they reached us over a broken-down teletype, a wiretap [*table d'écoute*] in an overloaded telephone exchange: "And the light shines in the darkness, and the darkness did not find it. . . . glory as of a single son from his father, full of grace and truth. John bears witness concerning him, and he cried out: This is he of whom I said: He who is coming behind me surpasses me, because he was before I was. . . . The world is turned inside out like a glove. It happens that I am the glove, and that I finally realize that on Judgment Day it will be with my own voice that God will call me: 'Jean, Jean!' . . . And some Pharisees were sent. And they questioned him: Why then do you immerse if you are not the Christ, nor Elijah or the prophet? John answered them: I immerse only in water. In your midst stands one whom you do not know, who is coming after me, and I am not fit to untie the fastening of his shoe. . . . Behind me comes a man who surpasses me, because he was before I was. . . . How can a man be born when he is old? Surely he cannot enter his mother's womb [*sein*] a second time and be born? . . . The Son cannot do anything by himself unless he sees the Father doing it. . . . The Father raises [*relève*] the dead and gives them life, the Son also gives life to whom he will. . . . You have sent to John and he has testified to the truth. . . . he was the lamp that burns and shines, and you wished to exult for a time in his light! But I have testimony greater than John's. . . . You search the scriptures, because you think they have life everlasting in them; and it is they who testify to me; and you are not willing to come to me to have life. . . . And when they were filled, he said to his disciples: Gather up the remains so that nothing will be lost. . . . As the scripture says: Streams of living water shall flow from his breast

love, denies [or disavows: *leugnet*] rather the ethic (*Sittliche*) of love, the higher inhibition and the depreciation of the simple natural pressure, which are already naturally contained in *shame* and are raised by the most determinate spiritual consciousness to *chastity* and to *modesty*."

An appendix opposes this conjugal bond to "*concubinage*," which consists "chiefly in satisfying the natural pressure, whereas this pressure is repressed (*zurückgedrängt*) in marriage."

The conjugal "repression" permits attaining a chastity that did nothing but announce itself in nature. That is the semantic content of a statement that still remains to be modalized, valorized. That things *happen in this way*, or rather *must* happen in this way, does not yet permit deciding if that is good or bad, if these things *must*, in the sense of the (motive, efficient, material) constraint, or teleological necessity, or moral prescription. In short, can it be asked if repression is good or bad? Or even, is there between repression and the opposition of values a bond that in advance makes any question on the *value*, the *validity* of repression laughable? That makes laughable *a fortiori* a whole modern preaching mounting the pulpit to condemn repression (or yet to reduce it by word of mouth to a mythology), with as much theoretical foolishness as edifying insipidity?

"Repression: that's bad." Who's speaking of what?

Hegel also condemns "repression": in the name of the freedom of spiritual consciousness, and so on. But—for the same reason—he prescribes the "repression" of animal pressures, which makes possible spiritual liberation, and so on. One repression for another, one restriction for an erection, one compresses on one side so that it (*ça*) rises on the other. Repression—here the relief—is not on one side or the other, on the left or the right: it "is" that relationship between the two accounts, the two registers, the two ledgers, the two operations of this economy.

Here the philosopher of *Sa* teaches moral philosophy [*la morale*], to be sure, which obliges him to keep the most rigorous account of repression. But can the at least apparent prescriptive mode of his discourse be regularly transformed into the descriptive mode? And if this possibility regularly presents itself, does it not belong to the very structure of the text? When Hegel says that marriage is not limited to the signifying formality and so to sensible nature, that marriage raises itself in accomplishing the repression of natural pressure, when he says the bond between raising, spirit, objective morality, objectivity, and so on, on the one hand, repression or inhibition of natural pressures on the other, is he prescribing or is he describing? Is he contenting himself with saying *how it is* (since *it is indeed* {bien} *like that* {comme ça} *that that* {ça} *happens* and that that [*ça*] *has always happened*)? Or else is

[*couleront de son sein*]. . . . Could it be that you are from Galilee too? Study the matter, and know that no prophet originates in Galilee. . . . We were not bred from promiscuity. We have only one father. . . . Jesus made mud and anointed my eyes. . . . I am the door. Whoever enters through me shall be saved. . . . It was Mary who anointed the Lord with ointment and wiped his feet with her hair. . . . And the man who had died came out, with his hands and feet bound with bandages, and his face enveloped with a shroud. . . . But six days before the Passover Jesus came to Bethany, where Lazarus was, the one Jesus had raised from the dead. So they prepared a supper for him there, and Martha served them, and Lazarus was one of those who dined with him. And Mary brought a measure of very costly ointment of nard, and anointed the feet of Jesus and wiped his feet with her hair; and the house was full of the fragrance of ointment. One of his disciples, Judas the Iscariot, who was about to betray him, said: Why was not this ointment sold for three hundred denarii and given to the poor? But he said this not because he cared anything about the poor but because he was a thief [*voleur*] and, being keeper of the purse, used to make off with what had been put into it. But Jesus said: Let her be, so that this can serve for the day of my burial. . . . One of the disciples, the one Jesus loved, was at table against Jesus' breast [*sein*]—it was the author. He, positioned thus against Jesus' chest [*poitrine*], said to him: Lord, who is it? Jesus answered: It is the one for whom I shall dip a crust [*bouchée*] and give it to him. So he took a crust and dipped it and gave it to Judas. . . . Pilate said to him: What is truth? . . . Pilate answered: I have written what I have written. . . . Then they took the body of Jesus and bound it in bandages along with the perfumes, as it is customary for the Jews to prepare bodies for burial. . . . Mary Magdalene saw that the stone had been removed from the tomb. . . . John stooped and looked in and saw the bandages lying there, but he did not go inside. Simon Peter went into the tomb. He saw the bandages lying there, and the shroud, which had been on his head, lying not with the bandages but away from them and rolled up. . . . For they had never yet known of the scripture, that he was to rise from the dead. . . . When they came out on the shore they saw a charcoal fire laid, and a small fish placed on it, and bread. Jesus said to them: Bring some of the fish that you caught just now. . . . I am alpha and omega. . . . Write down what you see into a book. . . . Write, then, what you have seen, and what is and what is to be after. . . . I shall fight them with the sword of my mouth. . . . To the victor I will give of the manna that is hidden, and I will give him a white stone [*caillou*], and upon the stone will be written a new name, which no

he implying that *it is indeed good {bien} that that {ça} happens like that {comme ça}?*

He describes a norm, a prescription. But what is describing a norm, a prescription? A simple play of quotation marks can transform a prescriptive statement into a descriptive one, and the simple textuality of a statement makes possible a placing between quotation marks. Rigorously considering writing can henceforth make the oppositions vacillate even up to those received here, for example between prescription and description. A discourse (that is or develops the) metaphysical can always be treated as if it contented itself with describing metaphysics, its norms, and its effects. That would be easy to show concerning classical philosophical statements (ontological and constative ones); it suffices, in order to complete the demonstration, to take into account the predicaments in which citationality, quotation marks, and signature place the theory of the performative.

"It is necessary" to raise-repress-sublimate, to reach-accede to chastity in marriage. To comprehend this proposition (*that says it is necessary*—) is to think according to speculative dialectics, is to relieve simultaneously sensibility and understanding that are equally shameless. So the tauto-heterological proposition of speculative dialectics can be thought only in marriage. And only in the Christian-monogamous marriage. Such can and must be done. ". . . consciousness goes out of its naturalness and subjectivity to unite itself with the thought of what is substantive and, instead of always still reserving to itself the contingency and the arbitrariness of the sensible inclination, removes the bond from this arbitrariness and restores it to the substance while engaging, committing itself to the Penates; the sensible moment it reduces to being a simple *conditioned* moment subordinated to the true and the ethics of the relation, and to the recognition of the bond as an ethical bond. It is shamelessness and the understanding buttressing it that do not permit grasping the speculative nature of the substantive relation, to which corresponds in return the incorrupt ethical feeling, as do the legislations of Christian peoples."

When it "goes out of its naturalness," monogamous conjugal consciousness escapes immodesty; which could let it be thought that immodesty is natural and that going out of nature suffices for re-covering it. And yet immodesty supposes understanding, the formal relation with the concept and the law. Immodesty is not only sensible, natural, inferior, an object more base than another; its baseness is the object of an interdict, of a repression whose counterforce (of law) does not have the form of distancing from nature, of a simple raising above animality, in the ontological hierarchy, of a negativity homogeneous to all the other forms of negativity. But nothing is ever homogeneous in the different ruptures, stances, or saltations of speculative dialectics. Is this het-

one knows, only he who receives it. . . . Who is worthy to open the book and break the seals on it? . . . And the sky shrank upon itself like a book one rolls. . . . There are mornings when all men experience with fatigue a flush of tenderness that makes them horny [*bander*]. One day at dawn I found myself placing my lips lovingly, though for no reason at all, on the icy [*glacée*] banister of the Rue Berthe; another time, kissing my hand; still another time, bursting with emotion, I wanted to swallow myself by opening my mouth very wide and turning it over my head so that it would take in my whole body, and then the Universe, until there would be nothing more than a ball of eaten thing which little by little would be annihilated; that is how I see the end of the world. . . . And I, John, I have heard and seen all these things." As his name indicates: the apocalyptic, in other words capital unveiling, in truth lays bare self-hunger. *Funeral Rites*, you recall, on the same page: "Jean was taken away from me. . . . Jean needed a compensation. . . . the . . . revelation of my friendship for Jean. . . . I was hungry for Jean." That (*Ça*) is called a colossal compensation. The absolute phantasm as an absolute self-having [*s'avoir absolu*] in its most mournful glory: to engulf (one)self in order to be close-by-(one)self, to make (one)self a mouthful [*bouchée*], to be(come) (in a word, band (erect)) one's own proper bit [*mors*]

t, to reap, to glean all expirations. To bind them afterwards, in the midst of a song, in a bouquet, in a sheaf. Sheaf is always said of what let itself be cut [*couper*].

He is astonished anyhow [*de toute façon*] at having made this verse. Perhaps he invented it in order to set it down there, but then its necessity would only be confirmed.

The rare force of the text is that you cannot catch it (and therefore limit it to) saying: *this is that*, or, what comes down to the same thing, this has a relation of apophantic or apocalyptic unveiling, a determinable semiotic or rhetorical relation with that, this is the subject, this is not the subject, this is the same, this is

erogeneity of the interdict heterogeneous to the *general* (thus homogeneous) heterogeneity of the whole set of the ontological system? Can one ever speak of a *general heterogeneity*? Does the interdictory repression only introduce a flection of heterogeneity in addition (a reflection of the alterity)? Or else a heterogeneity that no longer lets itself be interned in a reflection?

Since the concept of general heterogeneity is as *impossible* as its contrary, such a question cannot *pose itself*. The question's posit(ion)-ing is the question's annulment.

("Hegel"'s) *text* is offered (up), open to two responses, to two interpretations. It is text, textualizes itself rather, inasmuch as it lays itself open to the grip and weight of two readings, that is to say, lets itself be struck with indetermination by the impossible concept, divides itself in two.

The section concerning the incest prohibition is at once the example and the pivot [*charnière*]. The example and the pivot of the system that is contradictory within itself—with a contradiction of which one cannot say whether it operates *in* or *against*. The "opposition" plays two times and with it, each conceptual determination. An index: the incest prohibition breaks with nature, and *that is why* it conforms more to nature. What appears as formal incoherence, denegation, or "rationalization," critically denounces at the same time, but without its knowing, the absence of a concept of nature, of reason, or of freedom, and posits, but without its knowing, the necessity of accounting for "dark feelings." Thus:

"Since, in addition, marriage is produced out of the *free surrender* of that personality of both sexes infinitely proper to itself, marriage ought not to be concluded within the *natural-identical* circle, well-known to self and familiar in all its singularities, in which individuals do not have, opposite one another, any personality proper to themselves, but ought to take place between separate families and personalities diverse in origin (*ursprünglich verschiedener*). So marriage between *blood-relations* is opposed to the concept according to which marriage is an ethical action of freedom, not a liaison (*Verbindung*) of immediate naturalness and its pressures, so it is also opposed to genuine natural sensibility (*somit auch wahrhafter natürlicher Empfindung zuwider*).

"Marriage itself is sometimes grounded not in *natural right*, but simply on natural sexual pressure and is regarded as an arbitrary contract. Or, as well, monogamy is given external justifications drawn from physical relations such as the number of men and women; only dark feelings (*dunkle Gefühle*) are proposed for the interdiction of consanguineous marriage: therein is only the fashionable representation of a state of nature and of a naturalness of right, and fundamentally the absence in concept of rationality and freedom."

the other, this text here, this corpus here. There is always some question of yet something else. Rare force. At the limit, null. One would have to say the text's power, its potence [*puissance*]. As one would speak of the musculature of a tongue. But also of a mathematical expansion. But also of the enveloping of that which remains potential [*en puissance*]. At the limit, null. Nonexistent from remaining infinitely potential. From being condemned to power and remaining there.

What I wanted to write is the text's GALLOWS [*POTENCE*].

I expose myself to it, I tend toward it very much [*beaucoup*], I stretch much on it.

Anyhow, the scene will finish badly. He is going to be furious with me [*m'en vouloir à mort*]; I know from experience the law of this process [*procès*]. He will be furious with me for all sorts of reasons I will not undertake to enumerate. And at all events and cases. If I support or valorize his text, he will see in this a sort of approbation, verily of magisterial, university, paternal or maternal appropriation. It is as if I were stealing his erection from him. His death: "And the picture showing the capital execution of a convict in Cayenne made me say: 'He has stolen my death'" (*Miracle of the Rose*). And if, furthermore, I expose as a professor the Great(er) Logic of this operation, I do nothing but aggravate the case. If I was not valorizing, not "magnifying" his *glas* (but what have I done on the whole?), the ringer would fuck me again.

Dialectics of nature: it produces the incest prohibition in breaking with itself, but this rupture with (it)self is in its nature, in the nature of nature. Formally, that gives an argumentation in kettle-form: the connaturalness must be interrupted and incest interdicted (here the question is essentially of the brother and the sister; a note of the same section says the brother/sister relationship is a-sexual (*geschlechtloses*)) *and* this interdict is in nature. Whence in the marginal note, the empirico-genetic argumentation grounding shame in nature and alleviating the notorious weakness or fragility of products of consanguineous marriages: "it is well known that matings or couplings within an animal family produce weaker fruits. . . ."

So the interdict and the repression would be thinkable—as

in connection with, in the margin of the speculative remark—this is also the place of Kierkegaard and of what falls [*tombe*] to the side, after the stroke [*après coup*], in the *Concluding Unscientific Postscript to the Philosophical Fragments*: "To explain something, does this mean to abrogate it? I am well aware that the German word *aufheben* has various and even contradictory meanings; it has often enough been noted that it can mean both *tollere* and *conservare*. I do not know that the corresponding Danish word (*ophaeve*) permits of any such ambiguity, but I do know that our German-Danish philosophers use it like the German word. Whether it is a good trait in a word to admit of contrary meanings, I do not know, but anyone who desires to express himself with precision will be disposed to avoid the use of such a word in the crucial passages of his exposition. We have a simple phrase current among the people, used humoristically to indicate the impossible: 'To talk with one's mouth full of hot mush.' This is just about the trick that speculative philosophy contrives to perform, in thus using a word with opposite meanings. To make it perfectly clear that speculative philosophy knows nothing of any decisiveness, it employs a word as ambiguous as the one cited above, to signify the kind of explanation which constitutes speculative explanation. And if we look into it a little more closely, the confusion becomes still more evident. *Aufheben* in the sense of *tollere* means to do away with, to remove; in the sense of *conservare* it means to preserve unaltered, not to do anything at all to that which is preserved. If the government abrogates or abolishes a political organization it gets rid of it; if anyone keeps or preserves something for me, it is implied that he makes no change in it at all. Neither of these meanings is the meaning assigned to the philosophical *aufheben*. Speculative philosophy removes every difficulty, and then leaves me the difficulty of trying to determine what it really accomplishes by this so-called removal (*aufheben*). But suppose we let the word *aufheben* mean reduction, the status of a relative moment, as is also usually said when the decisive, the paradoxical, is reduced to a relativity; this will then mean that there is no paradox and nothing decisive, for the paradox and the decisive are what they are precisely through their irreconcilable resistance to such reduction. Whether speculative philosophy is right or not is another question . . ."

Anyhow, the signer recalled to Roger Blin a lost letter in which he had confided to Blin that his own books and plays were written against himself. But he added: "And if I do not succeed through the text itself to expose myself, then you have to help me. Against myself. . . ." Elsewhere, that his actors had to show him, he himself, naked. So, anyhow, I am judged and condemned, that is what he always sought to do: if I write for his text, I write against him, if I write for him, I write against his text. This friendship is irreconcilable.

Anyhow, he will vomit all that (*ça*) for me, he will not read, will not be able to read.

Do I write *for him*? What would I like to do to him? do to his "work"? Ruin it by erecting it, perhaps.

So that one reads it no more? So that one only reads it starting from here, from the moment I myself consign and countersign it?

effects of the relief. The *Aufhebung* would dominate this process.

And what if the *Aufhebung* were a Christian mother?

To write now, "complete unconsciousness about the *apparently formal*, but really *essential* question: how far have we got with the Hegelian *dialectic?*" or also, "necessity [for criticism] to settle accounts critically with its mother, the Hegelian dialectic," seems abruptly to open the archive of a problem in a very particular place. The third of the *Manuscripts of 1844* reproaches the German criticism of Hegel with letting itself be forestalled, taken up again, informed by the very logic it claims to criticize. That would be the case of *Das entdeckte Christentum* by Bruno Bauer. The criticism (of a logic) that reproduces within itself (the logic of) what it criticizes, that will always be—its lesson is not to be forgotten—an idealist gesticulation or antic. "After all these delightful antics of idealism (i.e., of Young Hegelianism) expiring in the guise of criticism, even now idealism has not expressed the suspicion of the necessity to settle accounts critically with its mother, the Hegelian dialectic, and even had nothing to say about its critical attitude towards the Feuerbachian dialectic."

By then Feuerbach was looked on as the sole "*serious*" critic of the Hegelian dialectic, the "true conqueror of the old philosophy." Precisely for having attacked what the *Aufhebung* permitted: the profound identity, thanks to the play of the *already* and the *not-yet*, of representation and presence, of the future perfect of truth, between true religion and speculative philosophy. "Feuerbach's great achievement is: (1) the proof that philosophy is nothing else but religion rendered into ideas and expounded by thought, i.e. another form and manner of existence of the alienation of the essence of man; hence equally to be condemned." Feuerbach in effect: "*Speculative philosophy* is the *rational* or *theoretical* elaboration and dissolution of the God that, for religion, is other-worldly and nonobjective. . . . The *essence* of speculative philosophy is nothing other than the *rationalized, realized, actualized essence of God*. Speculative philosophy is the *true, consistent, rational* theology."

Marx then sets out the critical movement of Feuerbach in its most operative instance: the questioning of the *Aufhebung* and of the negation of negation. The absolute positive, the criticism of religion or the Holy Family, these must not pass through the negation of negation, through the Hegelian *Aufhebung*, supposing there is any other kind. The speculative unity; the secular complicity of philosophy and religion—the former being the truth and the essence of the latter, the latter the representation of the former; their homogeneity or their homology, that is the process of the relief. Feuerbach knew how to oppose "to the negation of the negation, which claims to be the absolute positive, the positive positively based on itself and reposing on itself." The Third Manuscript links together: "Feuerbach explains the Hegelian dialectic

But he himself? he himself wanted to calculate the ruin: "And the ruin! I almost forgot the ruin! The ruin of the teeth cultivated with Warda's needle, and the total ruin of the play itself. I mean it: when the public leaves the theatre I want it to carry the well-known taste of ashes and an odor of decay in its mouth. And yet I want the play to have the consistency of silex. Not of solex!"

He is ungraspable because he bands erect double: for the galalith against natural milk, but for nature against the fake [*toc*].

there are always, after all, of the remain(s), two functions overlapping each other. *Le mot bande double*: the word bands erect double(s), the word double band: transitively and intransitively, nominally and verbally. In every gender and genre. Remain(s) always a bit more or less cavalier

Milk of mourning [*Lait de deuil*].

His tomb, he loves only that: *Sa* falls, it loves only *ça* [*Sa tombe, il n'aime que ça*].

Let that fall (*ça tombe*) in ruins

he loves the fake, but not just any fake, the gadget, but whose nothingness, defying economy, would be priceless, the most naturally in the world. That counts for literature, the *ersatz* in literature. The worst is the best, but one must not be deceived, the worst is not the least good. The best, one must not be deceived. One has to be expert in fake.

What I write, is it a sort of popular novel? He says that he likes that (*ça*). "I continue my reading of popular novels. It satisfies my love of hoodlums dressed up as gentlemen. Also my taste for imposture, my taste for the fake, which could very well make me write on my visiting cards: 'Jean Genet, bogus Count of Tillancourt.' . . . I read these books which are idiotic to reason, but my reason is not concerned with a book from which

(and thereby grounds the departing point of the positive, of sensible certainty) as follows:

"Hegel sets out from the alienation (in terms of Logic: from the infinite, the abstract universal) of substance, from the absolute and fixed abstraction; which means, put in a popular way, that he sets out from religion and theology.

"*Secondly*, he relieves the infinite, and posits the actual, sensible, real, finite, particular (philosophy, relief of religion and theology).

"*Thirdly*, he relieves in its turn the positive and restores the abstraction, the infinite—restoration of religion and theology.

"Feuerbach thus conceives the negation of the negation *only* as a contradiction of philosophy with itself—as the philosophy which affirms theology (the transcendent, etc.) after having denied it, and which it therefore affirms in opposition to itself.

"The positive position or self-affirmation and self-confirmation contained in the negation of the negation is taken to be a position which is not yet sure of itself, which is therefore burdened with its contrary, which is doubtful of itself and therefore in need of proof, and which, therefore, is not a position demonstrating itself by its existence—not an acknowledged position. . . . Let us take a look at the Hegelian system. One must begin with Hegel's *Phenomenology*, the true source and the secret of the Hegelian philosophy."

Just as the positive is "doubtful," needs to make sure of the contrary with which it is burdened, the young Hegelians need their "mother," Hegelian logic; they keep to "unconsciousness—about the relationship of modern criticism to the Hegelian philosophy in general and to the dialectic in particular."

The Hegelian dialectic, mother of the criticism, is first of all, like every mother, a daughter: of Christianity, in any case Christian theology. She returns to it ceaselessly as if to its *lap*. *Aufhebung* is a

"God is *God* only through the fact that he overcomes and negates matter; that is, the negation of God. And according to Hegel, it is only the negation of the negation that constitutes the true positing. And so in the end, we are back to whence we had started—in the lap of Christian theology. Thus, already in the most central principle of Hegel's philosophy we come across the principle and result of his philosophy of religion to the effect that philosophy, far from abolishing the dogmas of theology, only restores and mediates them through the negation of rationalism. The secret of Hegel's dialectic lies ultimately in this alone, that it negates theology through philosophy in order then to negate philosophy through theology. Both the beginning and the end are constituted by theology; philosophy stands in the middle as the negation of the first positedness, but the negation of the negation is again theology. At first everything is overthrown, but then everything is reinstated in its old place, as in Descartes. The Hegelian philosophy is the last grand attempt to restore a lost and defunct Christianity through philosophy, and, of course, as is characteristic of the modern era, by

poisoned, feathered phrases swoop down on me. The hand that launches them sketches, as it nails [*clouent*] them somewhere, the dim outline of a Jean who recognizes himself, dares not move, awaiting the one that, aimed at his heart in earnest, will leave him panting. I am madly in love (as I love prison) with that close [*serrée*] print, compact as a pile of rubbish, crammed with acts as bloody [*sanglants*] as linens [*linges*], as the fetuses of dead cats, and I do not know whether it is stiffly erect pricks which are transformed into tough knights or knights into vertical pricks" (*Our-Lady-of-the-Flowers*).

but as a stone, a firestone, a silex, verily an uncuttable [*inentamable*] diamond. Let that fall (*ça tombe*) to dust, but as a funerary slab, so natural that it would reconstitute itself in the earth itself, and always harder. He is Medusa [*se méduse*] to himself.

How can one be Medusa to oneself? One has to understand that *he* is not *himself* before being Medusa to himself. He occurs to himself since the Medusa. To be oneself is to-be-Medusa'd, and from then on the Medusa'd-being constitutes itself, that is, defends itself, bands itself erect, and elaborates itself only in being Medusa'd by oneself, in eating-Medusa'ing oneself, in making oneself a bit [*mors*] that gives oneself/itself up as lost [*fait son deuil*]. Dead sure of self. No *logic* is more powerful than this apotropic. No absolutely general economy, no exposition or pure expenditure: a strict-ure more or less strong.

His (*Sa*) Medusa('s), always.

"Thus lifted, raised, with body erect, he reaches the bench of the accused, facing a Special Court clad in scarlet, which is the blood that has been shed, the blood in person, demanding vengeance and getting it. It is perhaps this gift [*don*] of producing a miracle by a mere stab [*coup de couteau*] that astonishes the mob, alarms it, rouses it and makes it jealous of such glory. The murderer makes blood speak. He argues with it, tries to compound with the miracle. The murderer creates the Criminal Court and its machinery. In view of this, one thinks of the birth of Chrysaor, and of Pegasus, who sprang from the blood of Medusa.

identifying the *negation* of Christianity *with Christianity itself.* The much-extolled speculative identity of spirit and matter, of the infinite and the finite, of the divine and the human is nothing more than the wretched contradiction of the modern era having reached its zenith in metaphysics. It is the identity of belief and unbelief, theology and philosophy, religion and atheism, Christianity and paganism. This contradiction escapes the eye and is obfuscated in Hegel only through the fact that the negation of God, or atheism, is turned by him into an objective (*objectiven*) determination of God; God is determined as a *process*, and atheism as a moment within this process. But a belief that has been reconstructed out of unbelief is as little true belief—because it is always afflicted with its contrary—as the God who has been reconstructed out of his negation is a true God; he is rather a self-contradictory, an atheistic God."

Christian daughter-mother. Or else: the daughter-mother, the Christian holy mother is named *Aufhebung*. She—the relief—is the contradiction and the satisfaction of the Christian desire or of what the Third Manuscript calls the "critical Christ": desire of/for maternity *and* of/for virginity. *The Essence of Christianity* establishes an equivalence between the categories of miracle, imagination, and relief. The transformation of water into wine, of wine into blood, transubtantiation, resurrection above all are *Aufhebung* operations: what is destroyed preserves itself, what dies can be reborn. Wonderful and miraculous, *Aufhebung* is the productive imagination. Likewise, the dogma of the Virgin Mary sees its contradiction lifted, canceled [*lever*], or cleaned up, cleared [*laver*], by an *Aufhebung* that suspends what it keeps, what it guards, or reg(u)ards what it lifts, what it cancels. "Here we have the key to the contradiction in Catholicism, that at the same time marriage is holy and celibacy is holy. This simply realises, as a *practical contradiction*, the

"But as the Resurrection, which terminates the sacred history—a history (*Geschichte*) that does not have the signification of a mere recounted history (*Historie*), but of the truth itself—is a realised wish, so also is that which commences it, namely, the supernatural birth, though this has relation not so much to an immediately personal interest as to a particular subjective feeling (*Gefühl*).

"The more man alienates himself from Nature (*sich der Mensch der Natur entfremdet*), the more subjective, *i.e.*, supernatural or antinatural, is his view of things (*Anschauung*), the greater the horror he has of Nature, or at least of those natural things and processes which displease his imagination, which affect him disagreeably. The free, objective man doubtless finds things repugnant and distasteful in Nature, but he regards them as natural, inevitable results, and under this conviction he overcomes his feeling as a merely subjective and untrue one. On the contrary, the subjective man, who lives fixed only in the feelings and imagination, regards these things with a quite peculiar aversion. He has the eye of that unhappy foundling, who even in looking at the loveliest flower could pay

Self's dead sure biting (death) [*Morsure de soi*].

Stone, stele, *gisant*, patiently agglomerated concretion: I am (following) the calculus of my mother.

I counterband erect for her, after all, with the remain(s) of which I make myself a gift [*je me fait cadeau*].

I do not know if I have sought to understand him. But if he thought I had understood him, he would not support it, or rather he would like not to support it. What a scene. He would not support what he likes to do, himself. He would feel himself already entwined. Like a column, in a cemetery, eaten by an ivy, a parasite that arrived too late.

I wormed my way in as a third party, between his mother and himself. I gave him/her. I squealed on him/her. I made the blood [*sang*] speak.

"Because guards don't make a move when a deadly battle rages, you think they're brutes, and you're right. I like to think they were petrified [*médusés*] by a wrathful spectacle, the grandeur of which was beyond them. What was their petty existence compared to the radiant life of the children? For the colonists were all noble, even the jerks [*cloches*], since they were of the sacred race, if not of the sacred caste." Deviation [*Ecart*] of race, trace of deviation [*trace d'écart*], the interminable caste struggle, this is the case of reading, the castrated woman (is—band(s) erect)—falls (tomb)) in the sack. To be "Medusa'd" before "pants," a belt or a fly: the scene imposes itself in the *Journal*, the word "fascinated" as well; and in *Funeral Rites* that again names Medusa and her son Chrysaor, the man with the golden glaive who, with his brother Pegasus, the winged horse, came out of the throat of Gorgo the moment Perseus cut off her head. He was born brandishing his arm

attention only to the little 'black beetle' which crawled over it, and who by this perversity of perception had his enjoyment in the sight of flowers always embittered. Moreover, the subjective man makes his feelings the measure, the standard of what *ought to be*. That which does not please him, which offends his transcendental, supernatural, or antinatural feelings, *ought not to be*. Even if that which pleases him cannot exist without being associated with that which displeases him, the subjective man is not guided by the wearisome laws of logic and physics, but by the self-will of the imagination; hence he drops what is disagreeable in a fact, and holds fast alone what is agreeable. Thus the idea of the pure, unpolluted Virgin pleases him; still he is also pleased with the idea of the Mother, but only of the Mother who suffers no inconveniences, who already carries the infant on her arms.

"In the inmost essence of his spirit, his belief, Virginity is in and for (it)self his highest moral concept, the *cornu copiae* of his supranaturalistic feelings and ideas, his personified sense of honour and of shame before common nature. Nevertheless, there stirs in his bosom a *natural* feeling also, the compassionate feeling of maternal love. What then is to be done in this difficulty of the heart, in this conflict (*Zweispalt*) between a natural and a supernatural or antinatural feeling? The supranaturalist must unite (*verbinden*) the two, must comprise in one and the same subject two properties which exclude each other. Oh, what a plenitude of agreeable, sweet, supersensual, sensual emotions lies in this combination!

"Here we have the key to the contradiction in Catholicism, that at the same time marriage is holy and celibacy is holy. This simply realises, as a *practical contradiction*, the *dogmatic contradiction* of the *virgin Mother* or the mother Virgin. But this wondrous union of virginity and maternity, contradicting Nature and reason, but in the highest degree accordant with the feelings and imagination, is no product of Catholicism; it lies already in the twofold part which marriage plays in the Bible, especially in the view of the Apostle Paul. The supernatural conception of Christ is an *essential* doctrine of Christianity, a doctrine which expresses its inmost dogmatic essence, and which rests on the same foundation as all other miracles and articles of faith. As death, which the philosopher, the man of science (*Naturforscher*), the free objective thinker in general, accepts as a natural necessity, and as indeed all the limits of nature, which are impediments to feeling, but to reason are rational laws, were repugnant to the Christians, and were set aside by them through the supposed agency of miraculous power; so, necessarily, they had an equal repugnance to the natural process of generation, and relieved [*aufheben* came to correct *negieren* in a third version] it by miracle. The supernatural birth is not less welcome than the Resurrection to all, namely, to all believers; for the conception of Mary, not polluted by male sperm, which constitutes the contagium [contagious poison, *ansteckende Gift*] peculiar to original sin, was the first act of purification of mankind, soiled by sin, i.e., by Nature. Only because the God-man was not infected with original sin, could he, the pure one, purify mankind in the eyes of God, to whom the natural process of generation was an abomination, because he himself is nothing else but *supernatural feeling* (Gemüt).

"Even the arid Protestant orthodoxy, so arbitrary in its criticism, regarded the conception of the God-producing Virgin

No interest. All the same, I am not going to take [*prendre*] from him or teach [*apprendre*] him his mother, and the remain(s).

I am seeking the good metaphor for the operation I pursue here. I would like to describe my gesture, the posture of my body behind this machine.

What he would support with the greatest difficulty would be that I assure myself or others of the mastery of his text. By procuring—they say, distyle [*disentils*]—the rule [*régle*] of production or the generative grammar of all his statements.

No danger stepping there [*Pas de danger*]. We are very far from that; this right here, I repeat, is barely preliminary, and will remain so. (No) more names, (no) more nouns. It will be necessary to return to his text, which watches over this text here during its play.

So I am seeking the good movement. Have I constructed something like the matrix, the womb of his text? On the basis of which one could read it, that is, re-produce it?

No, I see rather (but it may still be a matrix or a grammar) a sort of dredging machine. From the dissimulated, small, closed, glassed-in cabin of a crane, I manipulate some levers and, from afar, I saw that (*ça*) done at Saintes-Maries-de-la-Mer at Eastertime, I plunge a mouth of steel in the water. And I scrape [*racle*] the bottom, hook onto stones and algae there that I lift up in order to set them down on the ground while the water quickly falls back from the mouth.

And I begin again to scrape [*racler*], to scratch, to dredge the bottom of the sea, the mother [*mer*].

I barely hear the noise of the water from the little room.

as a great, adorable, amazing, holy mystery of faith, transcending reason. But with the Protestants, who reduced and limited the speciality of the Christian to the domain of faith, and with whom, in life, it was allowable to be a man, even this mystery had only a *dogmatic, and no longer a practical significance*; they did not allow it to interfere with their desire of marriage. With the Catholics, and with all the old, uncompromising, uncritical Christians, that which was a *mystery of faith* was a *mystery of life, of morality*. Catholic morality is Christian, mystical; Protestant morality was already, in its very beginning, *rationalistic*. Protestant morality is and was a carnal mingling of the Christian with the man, the natural, political, civil, social man, or whatever else he may be called in distinction from the Christian; Catholic morality cherished in its heart the mystery of the unpolluted virginity. Catholic morality was the *Mater dolorosa*; Protestant morality a comely matron blessed with children. . . . Just because the mystery of the *Virgo Deipara* had with the Protestants a place only in theory, or rather in dogma, but no longer in life [first edition: *praxis*], they declared that it was impossible to express oneself with sufficient care and reserve concerning it, and that it ought not to be made an object of *speculation*. That which is denied [*negiert*, then *verneint*] in practice has no true basis and durability in man, is a mere spectre of imagination; and hence it is hidden, withdrawn from the understanding. Ghosts do not brook daylight.

"Even the later doctrine (which, however, had been already enunciated in a letter to St. Bernard, who rejects it), that Mary herself was conceived without taint of original sin, is by no means a 'strange school-bred doctrine,' as it is called by a modern historian. It comes much more from a natural consequence and a pious, thankful attitude toward the mother of God. That which gives birth to a miracle, which brings forth God, must itself be of miraculous divine origin and essence. How could Mary have had the honour of being overshadowed by the Holy Spirit if she had not been from the first pure? Could the Holy Spirit take up his abode in a body soiled by original sin? If the principle of Christianity, the holy and miraculous birth of the Saviour, does not appear strange to you, do not think strange the naive, simplistic, well-meaning inferences of Catholicism!"

dogmatic contradiction of the *virgin Mother* or the mother Virgin."

The *Theses on Feuerbach* and *The German Ideology* criticize Feuerbach's philosophy of religion and "intuitive" or sensualist "materialism" that "does not conceive sensuousness as practical activity." The Fourth Thesis delimits the Feuerbachian criticism of religion as a simple theoretical criticism. A theoretical criticism leaves its object in place, tampers with neither the terrain nor the structure whose elements it combines. In making religion the alienated essence of man, in bringing the religious world back to the earthly world, one changes nothing in this earthly world, in the anthropological base of the criticism, in the human family alienated—specularly—in the Holy Family. The operation remains speculative, guards and keeps an old concept of the family and of religion. The inner structure of the concept and of the reality has

The toothed matrix [*matrice dentée*] only withdraws what it can, some algae, some stones. Some bits [*morceaux*], since it bites [*mord*]. Detached. But the remain(s) passes between its teeth, between its lips. You do not catch the sea. She always re-forms herself.

She remains. There, equal, calm. Intact, impassive, always virgin.

And then I am not going to surprise his text with a toothed matrix. He only writes, only describes that: toothed matrix. It is *his* object.

Can an object comprehend what it is the object of, such is the question posed at Saintes-Maries-de-la-Mer at Easter. The remain(s) of the Rembrandt undoubtedly wanted to respond—and yes—to this question.

Yes, by reason of the strict-ure that interests and constrains us, the transcendental matrix always lets the text's remain(s) fall back (to the tomb).

He Medusa's himself. Well played. They say it, they know him to be generous, detached, spendthrift [*gaspilleur*]. He keeps [*garde*] nothing close by him. No goods. Above all, no works. But they already have their concession for perpetuity in all the national and international libraries, on the worldwide theatricality, the contract is signed, the author's rights come back or cause to come back.

He makes himself a gift. Infinite present.

not been transformed; one was content to analyze a representation, in all the senses of this word. As long as one believes one knows what a family in general is, that is, here, a human family, one does not analyze the process, the trial, of alienation or projection of the human family within the celestial family, the contradiction that constitutes and produces this process [*processus*]. One does not understand why or how to change this state of things. Now a purely theoretical criticism of the family cannot, by itself alone, transform the object named family, whose self-evidentness seems to be a matter of course. The same goes for religion inasmuch as it is family production. "Feuerbach starts out from the fact of religious self-alienation (*Faktum der religiösen Selbstentfremdung*), of the duplication (*Verdopplung*) of the world into a religious world and a secular (*weltliche*) one. His work consists in resolving the religious world into its secular basis. But that the secular basis lifts off from itself (*sich abhebt*) and establishes itself as an independent realm in the clouds can only be explained by the self-tearing (*Selbstzerrissenheit*) and intrinsic contradictoriness (*Sichselbstwidersprechen*) of this secular basis. The latter must, therefore, itself be both understood in its contradiction and revolutionised in practice. Thus, for instance, once the earthly family is discovered to be the secret (*Geheimnis*) of the Holy Family, the former must then itself be destroyed in theory and in practice."

This problematics will have been developed in the dark chamber of ideology: grappling with the question of fetishism and of truth (unveiled thought), of the status of *analogy* in the Marxist or psychoanalytic criticism of religion.

Reconstitution of a column: the continuum—or the already—of a fetish-value interests us. To found *or* to destroy religion (the family production) always comes down to wanting to reduce fetishism. Fetishism, to form against itself the unanimity of founders and destroyers, must indeed somewhere constitute the opposing unity: the unveiling of the column, the erection of the thing itself, the rejection [*rejet*] of the substitute. The same desire works (over) the Christian mother, her ancestry, and her descendants. As long as fetishism will be criticized—for or against religion, for

He keeps nothing close by him, no goods, no works, not himself: no absolute having [*avoir absolu*] as being-close-by-self. He has no place. He slips away and squanders himself. But perhaps he's the most consistent miser in all the annals of literature. He is above his work: his work, by being able in this way to cut itself off [*se couper*] and to fall from him, is not equal to him. He raises himself above the remain(s). The most consistent miser: he carries on him only liquid cash and whatever (a passport) helps identify his *seing*. According to the latest intelligence, he had

> the consequence, here (*ici*): to avoid having in order to have oneself [*s'avoir*], in order to be without that falling (*ça tombe*), without that (*ça*) cutting itself from self [*se coupe de soi*]. Not to spend money, not to put it in the bank, not even to put it in circulation, to destroy it by dint of keeping it near oneself. It, money, is already the sublime being-close-by-self of excrement. It is excrement that I can most easily keep. Absolute value, without value, the equivalent of all value. Not to deposit, then, in any case: another way of annulling it in its proper contradiction. "But who am I to talk, since I piss in the sink, I forget turds that I leave in old newspapers in the wardrobes of hotel rooms, and I don't have the guts to leave my money in my room for an hour. I walk with it, I steal with it, I sleep with it."
> (*Funeral Rites.*)

forgotten, he tells me, that Gabrielle was in the *Journal*. It's a matter of amassing an absolute treasure, withdrawn from any evaluation. Priceless. Advice to the funambulist: ". . . *Lots, lots of dough! Let him be filthy with it! And let it pile up in a corner of his hovel, let him never touch it, and wipe his ass {cul} with his finger. When evening approaches, he must wake up, must tear himself from this evil and at night dance on the wire.*

"*I also tell him:*
"'*You've got to work at becoming a celebrity.*'
"'*Why?*'
"'*In order to hurt.*'
"'*Is it absolutely necessary for me to earn all that dough?*'
"'*It is. . . .*'"

or against the family—will the economy of metaphysics, the philosophy-of-religion, have been tampered with?

Is it by chance if the father then enters on scene?

Already—Kant defined religion within the limits of simple reason in opening the question of fetishism to that of Papa (παπα) and of the crafty, violent, manipulative appropriation of priests. The teleological horizon of "true and unique religion" is the disappearance of the fetish.

Now always in the name of, on behalf of, the father, Hegel in sum reproaches Kant with remaining still no further than the fetish

what about the speculative dialectics concerning the fetish? In its strictly religious sense (that of which the President des Brosses speaks), the fetishistic type is, according to *Reason in History*, African. More precisely, this type belongs to inner Africa. That is to say, if *the logical schema* of the analysis *is extracted*, to an unconscious that does not let itself be dialectized as such, that has no history, that hardheadedly keeps itself on the threshold of the historico-dialectical process. But this nondialecticalness, this ahistoricity can always be interpreted as negativity, as resistance proper to the dialectic economy, and consequently interned in the speculative process. A certain undecidability of the fetish lets us oscillate between a dialectics (of the undecidable and the dialectical) or an undecidability (between the dialectical and the undecidable). *If the logical schema is extracted*: for Hegel's concrete description of the Negro could muddle the schema a bit. The description is composed starting from Ritter's *Geography* and missionary reports. Hegel recognizes the difficulty: to speak of the African all our "categories" would have to be abandoned, and yet they always intervene "surreptiously." This precaution taken, the discourse of *Reason in History* marches off: Africa "proper" has no history "properly so called." The Negro has come to neither consciousness properly so called nor objectivity properly so called, is a man who does not distinguish "between himself as an individual and his essential universality," is man in "his immediate existence," "a savage," "man . . . in a state of savagery and barbarism." "We cannot properly feel ourselves into his nature, no more than into that of a dog, or of a Greek as he kneels before the statue of Zeus." So one must try to gain access, not by feeling, but by thought to this state of being "unconscious of himself" and of "*innocence.*" In order to analyze "the general representation" of the African, we must turn toward African religion. Now this religion is constructed on the opposition of man and nature, nature being dominated by man. A strange interpretation: one has just been told that the Negro merges with nature, and in a moment one is going to learn that nature dominates the Negro. The threatening power of the natural elements compels him to *magic*. In that way he believes he secures himself, through the fantastic all-powerful—"The Negroes' power over nature is only an imaginary power, an imaginary authority."—a real efficacy over the elements. "They do not turn to any higher power, for they believe that they can accomplish their aims by their own efforts. To prepare themselves for their task, they work themselves into a state of frenzy; by means of singing, convulsive dancing, and

What is his class—objective, actual—situation? Yes, he is wherever that explodes (*ça saute*). He no longer inhabits the Judeo-Christian West. But—objectively, actually—the cord? The leash?

He knows that one only keeps what one loses. Self. One not only loses what one doesn't keep, one loses what one keeps. The other thing (the other

one does not touch, tamper with the *glas,* then (dingdong), without tampering with class. Nor with the economy of antherection without class struggle. But the coded, policed discourse on the class struggle, if it forecloses the question of *glas* (everything forged there, all that on which it reverberates, in particular, wherever it carries, the expropriation of the name), lacks at the least a revolution. And what is a revolution that does not attack the proper name? But then again what is *the* revolution if the proper name (glassification effect) — *already* [déjà] — is antherected, then (dingdong) *begins* by falling (to the tomb) in ruins? (Of) revolutions

band(s erect), the other sign(s), and so on) is lost because you give it up. But the thing you keep is lost because you give up the other. And the crack between the two is nothing. The crack is what one must occupy. The consistent miser analyzes the crack. And so he shuttles [*faire la navette*] between the two.

Navette is the word.

First, it is the one I was looking for above to describe, when a gondola has crossed the galley, the grammatical coming-and-going between *langue* [tongue, language] and *lagune* [lagoon] (*lacuna*).

Manipulation of perforated cards would be necessary to know whether the word *navette* appears, as such (as such, otherwise a machine with teeth so fine and so numerous that it surely does not yet exist will be required; a text like this one here is only a slightly more evolved, more subtle mechanical reader. Each

intoxicating roots or potions, they reach a state of extreme trance in which they proceed to issue their commands. If they do not succeed after prolonged efforts, they decree that some of the onlookers—who are their own dearest relations—should be slaughtered, and these are then devoured by their fellows. In short, man considers himself the highest commanding authority. The priest will often spend several days in this frenzied condition, slaughtering human beings, drinking their blood, and giving it to the onlookers to drink." We are not far, are we, from the other Last Supper scene? Fetishism corresponds to the *second moment* of the African religions. The Negro provides himself an intuition and a representation of his power, an "image" ("an animal, a tree, a stone, or a wooden image"). But this "fetish" is not "objective," does nothing but represent, without opposing itself to, the arbitrariness (*Willkür*) of the Negro. The fetishist remains "master of his image." That is put in the passive (arbitrariness, imagination, caprice), not in the active (freedom, autonomy of consciousness, and so on) of the Negro. That he manipulates the fetish; that he raises himself above it, at least in order to know how to produce it and to "lay it aside" wantonly, to change it (Hegel insists on this greatly) when it does not serve him, to "bind and beat the fetish" when the harvest is bad; that he ascribes to it an ambivalent signification, exalts and/or debases it—all that proves that the Negro does not raise himself above the arbitrary. The cult of the dead itself—elsewhere considered to be the inaugural stage [*stade*] of the ethical—is corrupted by fetishism: "They resort to them [the deceased] in the same way as to fetishes, offering them sacrifices and conjuring them up; but where this proves unsuccessful, they punish the departed ancestor himself, casting his bones away and desecrating him. On the other hand, they believe that the dead avenge themselves if their needs are not satisfied. . . . The power of the dead over the living is indeed recognised, but held in no great respect; for the Negroes issue commands to their dead and cast spells upon them. In this way, the substance always remains in the power of the subject. Such is the religion of the Africans, and it does not extend any farther." But if this being-subject of the substance is for once devalorized, that is because this (arbitrary, capricious, imaginary) subject is not that of consciousness.

The Negro is not even a man, since he has contempt for man. Whence—first of all—his anthropophagy. Here Hegel amasses two contradictory accusations: whereas for man there is never any pure instinct (human flesh is not meat), for the Negro, it is meat and nothing else. And yet the Negro does not consider human flesh essentially to be nourishment. He does not even kill in order to eat: "the eating of human flesh is quite compatible with the African principle; to the sensible (*sinnlichen*) Negro, human flesh is purely an object of the senses, like all flesh. It is not used primarily as food; but at festivals. . . ." Whence—secondly—slavery: "the Negroes see nothing improper about it," and "slavery has awakened more humanity among the Negroes." Doubtless "the essence of man is freedom, but he must first become mature before he can be free. Thus it is more fitting and correct that slavery should be eliminated gradually than that it should be abolished all at once." Meanwhile, the Negroes' contempt for human life continues to be marked in the ease with which "they allow themselves to be shot down in thousands in their wars with the Europeans," the absence of family feeling (consequently

word cited gives a card or a grid you can walk through the text. Each card or grid is accompanied by a schema you ought to be able to verify at each occurrent) in the so-called "complete works."

The word—*la navette*—is absolutely necessary. It will have had to be there. First, because it is a church term and everything here is hatched [*se trame*] against a church [*église*]. It concerns a small metal vessel in the form of a boat (*navis, navetta*). They keep incense in it.

And then the weaver's *navette* [shuttle]. He makes it run [*courir*]. Coming-and-going woven in a chain. The weave is in the *navette*. You see all that one could have done with that (*ça*). Isn't elaboration a weaver's movement?

Yet we have mistrusted the textile metaphor. This is because it still keeps—on the side of the fleece, for example—a kind of virtue of naturality, primordiality, cleanliness [*propreté*]. At least the textile metaphor is still more natural, primordial, proper than the metaphor of sewing, of the seam [*couture*]. The sewing metaphor still supervenes on an artifact.

the difficulty of principle is that there is no *unity* of occurrence: fixed form, identifiable theme, determinable element as such. Only *anthemes*, scattered throughout, gathered up everywhere. If, for example, the machine only selected words or themes, it could draw them all into a net [*filet*] of three, three and a half, pages: "The Fisherman of the Suquet" that I could have seemed to comment on, to surround with an interminable commentary, without ever citing it. You have only to refer to it, you would find in it this whole lexicon, this whole thematic, but that remains an *other* text

Now sewing [*couture*] is what activates itself here.

the absence of ethical law, of constitution, and of state) that results from their unbridled polygamy (Hegel does not tire of citing the 3333 wives of the king of Dahomey; the fact seems to him almost as scandalous as the reign of a woman over the Jagas [Dschacken]). Africa properly so called "has no history in the true sense of the word." "And such events as have occurred in it—i.e. in its northern region—belong to the Asiatic and European world." When the African unconscious enters history, it dialectizes itself and becomes conscious, begins to Europeanize itself, engages its arbitrariness in the teleological decision of the spiritual economy, welcomes within itself the labor of the negative, submits itself to the empire of speculative idealism. To the eagle (aigle).

What is it to speculate concerning the fetish? For such a question, the headless head [le cap sans cap] is undecidability. Despite all the variations to which it can be submitted, the concept fetish includes an invariant predicate: it is a sub-stitute—for the thing itself as center and source of being, the origin of presence, the thing itself par excellence, God or the principle, the archon, what occupies the center function in a system, for example the phallus in a certain phantasmatic organization. If the fetish substitutes itself for the thing itself in its manifest presence, in its truth, there should no longer be any fetish as soon as there is truth, the presentation of the thing itself in its essence. According to this minimal concep-tual determination, the fetish is opposed to the presence of the thing itself, to truth, signified truth for which the fetish is a substitutive signifier (from then on every fetish is a signifier, while every signifier is not necessarily a fetish), truth of a "privileged" transcendental, fundamental, central signifier, sig-nifier of signifiers, no longer belonging to the series. Some-thing—the thing—is no longer itself a substitute; there is the nonsubstitute, that is what constructs the concept fetish. If there were no thing, the concept fetish would lose its invar-iant kernel. What is called fetishism should be analyzed in a completely different [autre] place. If what has always been called fetish, in all the critical discourses, implies the reference to a nonsubstitutive thing, there should be somewhere—and that is the truth of the fetish, the relation of the fetish to truth—a decidable value of the fetish, a decidable opposition of the fetish to the nonfetish. This space of truth, the opposi-tion of Ersatz to nonErsatz, the space of good sense, of sense itself, apparently constrains all the traits of fetishism. And yet, here is the headless head, there would be perhaps, particu-larly in Freud, enough not to make fly into pieces [voler en éclats] but to reconstruct starting from its generalization a "concept" of fetish that no longer lets itself be contained in the space of truth, in the opposition Ersatz/nonErsatz, or simply in the opposition. To say there would be enough to construct such a "concept" (but what is a concept that escapes the opposition, that determines itself outside opposition, what is an undecidable concept?) is to imply that the structure of the text, Freud's in particular, includes heterogeneous state-ments, not contradictory ones, but a singular heterogeneity: that which, for example, relates in a text (but can one then speak of a text, one and the same textual corpus?) decidable statements and undecidable statements. In the essay on "Fetishism," after recalling the case of the Glanz auf der Nase of the Englishman who had "forgot" his mother tongue (shine: Glanz: glance—on/at the nose), Freud recognizes that he runs the risk of disappointing when he says that the fetish is a

What tears, what he tears — theatrically — in pieces, in plays [en pièces].

For seams [coutures], this must be stressed, do not hold at any price. They must not be, here, for ex-ample, of a foolproof solidity. This is why that (ça) works all the time. To sew up [coudre] a wound, to fight [en découdre], to resew, to be forced to sew, to be kept from sewing. Other italics between parentheses, which await us farther on: "(. . . I kept myself from learning to sew.)"

Sewing [couture] then betrays, exhibits what it should hide, dissimulacras what it signals.

Hardly has the Lady with the Unicorn vanished into the tapestry than, two pages farther on, the purest miser takes you by the sleeve [la manche] in order to prompt for you (and spirit away from you) [pour vous souffler] what he thinks about "theft," "trea-son," the "dialectic."

"substitute for the penis (*Penisersatz*)" and, "more plainly," "the substitute (*Ersatz*) for the woman's (the mother's) phallus that the little boy once believed in and—for reasons familiar to us—does not wish to give up." Whence, from the perspective of representation and not of the affect, the *Verleugnung*, the "disavowal" that protects the child against the threat of castration and maintains intact his initial belief (*Glauben*). The fetish erects itself here as a "monument," "a *stigma indelebile*," a "sign of triumph." This monumental erection of a supplementary column is a compromise solution, a counterweight solution to balance the "conflict" between the "weight (*Gewicht*)" of the "undesired perception" and "the force of the counter-wish (*Gegenwunsches*)." This sometimes permits the fetishist to do without his homosexuality: thus supplied, the woman becomes a "tolerable" sexual object. All this proceeding from the spectacle of the woman's two legs, seen from below, with, in the center of two erect members, between the two, the fleece of hair [*la toison*].

After these determinate, decidable statements, Freud broaches [*entame*] in this short article of six pages a development that seems to follow the consequence and that however does not perhaps do so so simply. In order to do this, he says he borrows a "purely speculative way." The status of the speculative can be questioned in recalling that the step [*pas*] "*Beyond the Pleasure Principle*" also advances, Freud stresses this, on a "speculative" path. Here, he will come to recognize the "divided attitude of fetishists (*zwiespältige Einstellung des Fetischisten*)" and the oscillation of the subject between two possibilities. Then, in order to ballast the speculative hypothesis, he proposes a "description." A description of very fine, "completely subtle cases (*ganz raffinierten Fällen*)." But if such cases exist, if above all recognizing them under the category of fetishism can be authorized, one must be able to give an account of them. The category must be able to receive them, to enlarge itself there, and to comprehend them.

In these very subtle cases, then, the structure, the construction (*Aufbau*) of the fetish rests *at once* on the denial and on the affirmation (*Behauptung*), the assertion or the assumption of castration. This at-once, the in-the-same-stroke, the *du-même-coup* of the two contraries, of the two opposite operations, prohibits cutting through to a decision within the undecidable. This at-once constitutes an economy of the undecidable: not that the undecidable interrupts there the efficacy of the economic principle. The at-once puts itself in the service of a general economy whose field must then be opened. There is an economic *speculation* on the undecidable. This speculation is not dialectical, but plays with the dialectical. The feint consists in pretending to lose, to castrate oneself, to kill oneself in order to cut [*couper*] death off. But the feint does not cut it off. One loses on both sides, in both registers, in knowing how to play all sides [*sur les deux tableaux*]. On this condition does the economy become general. A fetishism also unfolds itself without limit, within which the contours of a *strict* fetishism will have to be delimited: the strict fetishism in which metaphysics *as such* always struggles.—Far from generalizing the *Ersatz* or the simulacrum, strict fetishism takes an *Ersatz* for *the thing itself*.— Strict fetishism desires (nothing but) the thing itself and the *Sa* of the thing itself.
Why *general* fetishism? As soon as the economy of the un-

"For I am so poor, and I have already been accused of so many thefts, that when I leave a room too quietly on tiptoe, holding my breath [*souffle*], I am not sure, even now, that I am not carrying off with me the holes in the curtains or hangings."

All the examples stand out, are cut out [*se découpent*] in this way. Regard the holes if you can.

Then he makes you kneel before a vegetable fetish. This one is not even sewn [*cousu*]. Merely pinned [*epinglé*] on the cloth. With, lots of swaddling clothes in all that (*ça*), a "safety pin." Here is the "operation," it still bustles about very close to Stilitano's "natural frontiers":

"... excluded ... I dared not ask for further details.

"'Get started!'

"With a gesture of his lively hand, he motioned to me that he wanted to undress. As on other evenings, I kneeled down to unhook the cluster of grapes.

"Inside his trousers was pinned [*epinglé*] one of those postiche clusters of thin cellulose grapes stuffed with wadding. (They are as big as greengage plums; elegant Spanish women of the period wore them on

decidable secures for the fetish its greater solidity, as Freud recognizes, its lesser stability already presupposes some liaison to opposed interests. So the measure of solidity or stability would be the ligament between the contraries, this double bond (*doppelt geknüpft*) and the undecidable mobility of the fetish, its power of excess in relation to the opposition (true/nontrue, substitute/nonsubstitute, denial/affirmation, and so on). The argument of the *girdle*, the *sheath* [gaine], organizes the headless head of this discourse: "In very subtle cases both the disavowal and the affirmation of the castration have found their way into the construction of the fetish itself. This was so in the case of a man whose fetish was an athletic support-girdle which could also be worn as bathing drawers. This piece of clothing covered up the genitals entirely and concealed the distinction between them. Analysis showed that it signified that women were castrated and that they were not castrated; and it also allowed of the hypothesis that men were castrated, for all these possibilities could equally well (*gleich gut*) be concealed behind the girdle—the earliest rudiment of which in his childhood had been the fig-leaf on a statue. A fetish of this sort, doubly derived from contrary ideas, is of course especially solid." Same thing in the *coupeur de nattes* whose act "reconciles (*vereinigt*) two mutually incompatible affirmations"

(the word that the *Lectures on the Philosophy of World History* refer to its Portuguese origin, *feitiço*).

Jealousy is at stake.

The (Kantian) precept according to which "we can know nothing of God" is a prejudice of the time with which one must break if one wants to inaugurate a philosophy of religion. Hegel never questions that this philosophy of religion must be Christian. But he draws from it a diametrically opposed conclusion: if in piety the question is pleasing God the Father and taking pleasure in the law (Kant), is striving for perfection to that end, how would that be possible if we were enclosed in the phenomenon and left God beyond knowledge (theoretical knowledge, what Hegel does not want to distinguish here from the practical relation)? According to the formalizable law of a chiasm(us), Hegel in sum reproaches Kant with being unfaithful to reason and to Christianity, just as Kant reproaches those who believe they know God (that will have been the case with Hegel) with degrading religion to religious folly, to the delirium of arrogance, or to fetishism. "This [Kantian] standpoint must, judged by its *content*, be considered as the last stage of

their loose-brimmed, straw sun bonnets.) Whenever some queer at the Criolla, excited by the swelling, put his hand on the fly, his horrified fingers would encounter this object, which they feared to be a cluster of his true treasure, the branch on which, comically, too much fruit was hanging.

"The Criolla was not only a fairy joint. Some boys in dresses danced there, but women did too. Whores brought their pimps [*macs*] and their clients. Stilitano would have made a lot of money were it not that he spat on queers. He scorned them. He amused himself with their annoyance at the cluster of grapes. The game lasted a few days. So I unhooked the cluster, which was fastened to his blue trousers by a safety pin [*épingle de nourrice*], but, instead of putting it on the mantelpiece as usual and laughing (for we would burst out [*éclations*] laughing and joke during the operation), I could not restrain myself from keeping it in my cupped hands and laying my cheek against it. Stilitano's face above me turned hideous.

" 'Drop it (*ça*), you bitch!'

"In order to open the fly, I had squatted on my haunches, but Stilitano's fury, had my usual fervor been insufficient, made me fall to my knees. That was the position which, facing him, I used to take mentally in spite of myself. I didn't budge. Stilitano struck me with his two feet and his one fist. I could have escaped. I remained there.

" 'The key's in the door,' I thought. Through the fork of the legs that were kicking me with rage I saw it caught in the lock, and I would have liked to turn it with a double turn so as to be locked in alone with my executioner. I made no attempt to understand the reason for his anger, which was so disproportionate to its cause, for my mind [*esprit*] was unconcerned with psychological motives. As for Stilitano, from that day

the degradation of man, in which at the same time he is all the more arrogant inasmuch as he has proved to himself that this degradation is the highest possible state and his true destination." Despite the interest of this formalism that declares all save the true can be known, "this standpoint and this result are diametrically opposed to the whole nature of the Christian religion." Revelation is revelation. A revealed religion is a religion in which God reveals himself. He does not hide himself, does not hold himself back or in reserve, does not guard himself in it. The Christian religion is true, because it is the religion of truth, manifestation, and revelation.

In the encyclopedia, the third moment of the philosophy of spirit (the absolute spirit that reconciles the objective spirit and the subjective spirit in art, in revealed religion, and in philosophy), each synthesis is the truth of the past synthesis: revealed religion is the truth of art (*die schöne Kunst*). Art includes its own proper religion, which is only a stage in the spirit's liberation, and has its destination in "true religion," truth of the past art, of what art will have been. In the fine arts, the content of the idea was limited by the sensible immediacy and did not manifest itself in the universality of an infinite form. With *true* religion (the true, the Christian religion, that of the infinite God), the sensible, finite, and immediate intuition passes into the infinite of a knowing that, as infinite, no longer has any exteriority, thus knows itself, becomes present to itself. Presence (*Dasein*) that knows itself since it is infinite and has no outside, truth that announces itself to itself, resounds and reflects itself in its own proper element: the manifest, the revealed, *das Offenbaren*. If one wants to think revelation in its essence, what revealing in revealed-religion means, this *Offenbaren* must be thought: not as a finite subject would think a revelation coming to it from God (an abstract moment), but as God's infinite revelation revealing itself in its infinity: the revelation itself or the revelation of revelation, the un-veiling as the unveiling of the veil itself. To claim to think absolute, true, and revealed religion, and maintain, as Kant does, the limits of a finite subjectivity is to *prohibit* oneself from thinking what thinking is said to be, is not to think what one already thinks, is to chitchat—in the infidelity, idolatry, formalist abstraction of the understanding. "It lies essentially in the concept of religion,—the religion i.e. whose content is absolute spirit—that it be *revealed* (geoffenbart), and, what is more, revealed *by God*." Infinite, this revelation no more lets itself be contained in a historical and determinate event, as one generally imagines. Infinite truth's movement of manifestation merges with the history of spirit, the progressive revelation and reappropriation of the divine absolute. "The history of religions coincides with the world-history." The absolute presence (*Dasein*) is knowledge (*Wissen*), has itself {*s'a, savoir absolu*, absolute knowledge] and knows itself as absolute substance that manifests itself to itself,

on he stopped wearing the cluster of grapes. Toward morning, having entered the room earlier than he, I waited for him. In the silence, I heard the mysterious rustling of the sheet of yellow newspaper [*journal*] that replaced the missing windowpane.

"'That's subtle,' I said to myself.

"I was discovering a lot of new words. In the silence of the room and of my heart, in the waiting for Stilitano, this slight noise disturbed me, for before I came to understand its meaning there elapsed a brief period of anxiety. Who—or what—is calling such fleeting attention to itself in a poor man's room?

"'It's a newspaper printed in Spanish,' I said to myself again. 'It's normal that I don't understand the noise that it's making.' Then I really felt I was in exile, and my nervousness was going to make me permeable to what—for want of other words—I shall call poetry.

"The cluster of grapes on the mantelpiece disgusted me [*m'écœurait*]. One night Stilitano got up to throw it into the shithole. During the time he had worn it, it had not marred his beauty. On the contrary, in the evening, slightly encumbering his legs, it had given them a slight bend and his step [*pas*] a slightly rounded and gentle constraint, and when he walked [*marchait*] near me, in front or behind, I felt a delicious agitation because my hands had prepared it. I still think it was by virtue of the insidious power of these grapes that I grew attached to Stilitano. . . .

"I shall prudently refrain from comment upon this mysterious wearing of the cluster of grapes; yet it pleases me to see in Stilitano a queer who hates himself.

clusters hooked in order to band the eye blind [*bander l'œil*].

"They cling to loyalty as do others to virility. At noon, on a heavy, broad-rumped, hairy-legged nag that was still wearing [*couvert*] its

determines itself (*das* Selbstbestimmende *ist*). God's being is absolutely present, manifest, *there* (*da*). God is the very act of self-manifesting, of being *there*. The there, the *Da* does not supervene on him; God is *Da*, the manifest(ing) [*manifeste(r)*] of the manifestation (*schlechthin* Manifestieren).

Now the Christian religion is, in history, the only one that expressly named itself revealed religion. It calls itself the revealed (*ausdrücklich die* geoffenbarte *heisst*). No other religion is absolutely true—not for being false—but for not being of the truth, for not having made of the truth (of the unveiling) of the manifestation, of the open (and openable) its own proper essence. From then on, to claim to found Christianity in reason and to make nonetheless of nonmanifestation, of God's being-hidden, the principle of this religion is (Kant) to comprehend nothing about revelation.

Kant is Jewish: he believes in a jealous, envious God, who hides and guards his *Da*. An error all the more grave for a philosopher, since Plato, already, and Aristotle had condemned the hypothesis of an avaricious and dissembled God. Against the Nemesis, the equalizing power (gleichmachende *Macht*) conceived by the abstract understanding, they had objected that God is not "*jealous* (neidisch)." The Nemesis: on one hand, the figure of the law, of distributive, egalitarian, formal, homogeneous, at base indifferent justice, the dead and death-dealing operation of the understanding that debases the greatness and destroys the sublime. The God of Kant, death power, would have no living generosity, first by his zeal to fold back his *Da* within himself.

But the Nemesis is not only, for the Greeks, distributive justice and *nomos* (share, portion), it is also resentment before injustice, then envy, jealousy, also shame and punishment. This whole chain of significations binds together the law and jealousy or resentment, and in the same stroke [*du même coup*] a certain Greek, a certain Jew, and a certain Kant. Each time the question is of a divinity whose justice is unjust, vengeful, finite, negative, cruel, castrating, fearful. The figure of a father who would not want what he gives birth to to resemble him. Now jealousy (*phthonos*), says the *Phaedrus*, cannot be a divine attribute. It has "no place in the choir divine": this is the moment, in the myth of the procession of souls, Zeus flies on his winged chariot, followed by an army of gods and demons, while Hestia remains alone in the house of the gods (*Estia en theōn oikōi, monē*). The *Timaeus* interprets nonjealousy, in the father/son or generator/engendered relation, as the desire of resemblance: the god wants his product to resemble him. "He was good, and the good can never have any jealousy (*phthonos*) of anything. And being free from jealousy, he desired that all things should be as like himself as they could be." From its opening, the *Philosophy of Right* also draws its argument from *analogy*: "Christ says, 'Be perfect as your heavenly Father is perfect.' This lofty

"'He wants to baffle and wound, to disgust [*écœurer*] the very people who desire him,' I say to myself when I think of him. As I ponder it more carefully, I am more disturbed by the idea—which I find pregnant with meaning—that Stilitano had bought a postiche wound [*plaie*] for that most noble spot—I know that he was magnificently hung—in order to save his cut-off hand from scorn. Thus, by means of a very crude subterfuge here I am talking again about beggars and their misfortunes. Behind a real or sham physical ailment which draws attention to itself and is thereby forgotten is hidden a more secret malady of the soul. I list the secret wounds [*plaies*]:

"decayed teeth,

"foul breath,

"a cut-off hand,

"smelly feet, etc. . . .

"to conceal them and to kindle our pride we had:

"a cut-off hand,

"a gouged eye,

"a peg leg, etc.

"We are fallen [*déchu*] during the time we bear the marks of the downfall, and to be aware of the imposture is of little avail. Using only the pride imposed by poverty, we aroused pity by cultivating the most disgusting

brass and leather harness, Harcamone, riding side-saddle with his legs dangling at the left, crossed the Big Square on his way back from cartage or work in the fields. He had had the audacity to hook at the edge of his tilted cap [*calot*], near his ear and almost covering his left eye with a trembling mauve leucoma, two huge clusters of lilac. He must have been quite sure of his integrity. In the Colony, he alone could coyly adorn himself with flowers. He was a true male" (*Miracle of the Rose*).

"... First, I took the girl to my room. No one saw her going up. She wanted my lilacs.

"MAURICE: What?

"GREEN-EYES: I had a cluster of lilac between my teeth. The girl followed me. She was magnetized. . . . then she wanted to scream because I was hurting her. I choked her. I thought that once she was dead I'd be able to bring her back to life."

It is, then, the postiche, the detachable, which seduces, fascinates, attaches—the detachable. It is itself the origin of what "for want of other words—I shall call poetry." It is itself what can "'baffle and wound . . . disgust

213

demand is to the wisdom of our time an empty sound." In order to resemble God, one must know him and think him, see him reveal himself here, there, *da*, and not not know him in an incomprehensible beyond. A father cannot hide himself, cannot hold in reserve his *Da*. The nonjealousy of the generator (that these discourses do not distinguish from the father: the father has the signification of generator in any case) does not belong to him as a psychological characteristic, one trait among others. This is not an attribute: being-generative excludes envy. A father cannot be jealous as father, since he gives birth. He is good (*agathos*) inasmuch as he gives rise to *genesis*, as he causes coming to birth, to the light of day, accords birth and form. Those who say God is jealous are liars, Greeks, Jews, or Kantians. Liars or poets, but the poets are liars (Aristotle, before Nietzsche, had recalled the proverb) that comprehend nothing of the difference between day and night.

Freud is amazed when Kant compares the moral law in our heart with the spectacle of the heavenly vault above our head. This is not only because he was breathing the thick fogs of Koenigsberg whose sun does not pierce the veils. The law, the father, the God that must be pleased is a God that cannot be known, a nocturnal God: jealous, dissembling his *Da*, moral and castrating, giving himself to be seen, as the galaxy structure, only by scintillating, glimmering, twinkling on the background of night—lighted by a sun that is not seen.

Now the tradition called on—here—by Hegel is a solar and diurnal tradition, the tradition of the *agathon*, of the good god that engenders, that gives form and visibility. The unity of the values of life and truth, the unveiling to sight. Goodness, the absence of jealousy, does not consist only in giving birth, in producing life, but also in giving itself to be seen, in producing itself. The value of jealousy (*Neid*) permits merging a problematics of life and a problematics of truth as productivity. God's essence cannot be jealousy, because the essence, say the energy of the presence, the *Da*, cannot hide itself. The essence is not jealous; jealousy is not essential, or else it is only the negative of essentiality. In pure essentiality, jealousy is totally relieved. Hegel recognizes, it's true, that there was, that there will have been negativity in God (disquietude, anger that made him go out of himself, etc., torment, primordial torsion: *Qual Quelle*; as if he began *by* castrating himself *in order to* erect his *Da*, or *by* banding erect *in order to* overlap himself; as if in this simulacrum, he was Medusa'ing himself, or rather he was coming to himself, to his *Dasein*, by the medusa. The sea anemone, the jellyfish [*acalèphe*], the medusa adrift is called, Hegel does not say this, *Qualle*.); what he says of absolute religion and the nonjealous God is valid only at the term of the absolute's process of reappropriation by itself. Before term, prematurely, there is finitude and thus jealousy. But self-jealousy. Of whom could God

wounds [*les plaies les plus écœurantes*]."

[*écœurer*] [*je m'ec*] the very people who desire it.'"

Why cut off here?

If we did not read, we would have, ourselves, the imprudence to comment on this wearing of the grape cluster. We would impose new words upon this morsel, in any case words that are foreign to it. Before all the plagues [*plaies*] of Egypt, one imagines the doctors nodding their heads and psalmodizing: castration, fetishism, castration of the mother, fetishism, castration, castration I tell you, again castration.

Do not look for new words of the *navette* style. And ask yourselves why you don't need any. And what is poetry, so named for a lack of other words, if it prescribes, inscribes and comprehends and in advance overflows, engulfing in its abyss, hermeneutic and doctoral discourse?

That's subtle, I say to myself. The author who narrates himself cannot, he says, lock himself in with the key [*clé*] (the universal key, the mother's phallus, they say distyle [*disent-ils*] while nodding their heads) of his executioner. To lock himself in with the key of his lulling executioner who replaces his [*sa*] wound with another, with a detachable object that is the very one that disgusts [*écœure*] and attaches with its insidious power.

The key [*clé*]: "caught in the lock."

What remained of a Rembrandt torn into small squares and rammed down the shithole. The strange word (and mode) disgust [*écœurement*].

be jealous, except himself, except then his very own son? The Nemesis, Judaism, Kantianism are necessary, but abstract, moments of this infinite process. In *Sa*, jealousy has no place any more. Jealousy always comes from the night of the unconscious, the unknown, the other. Pure sight relieves all jealousy. Not seeing what one sees, seeing what one cannot see and who cannot present himself, that is the jealous operation. Jealousy always has to do with some trace, never with perception. Seen since *Sa*, thought of the trace will then be a jealous (finite, filial, servile, ignorant, lying, poetic) thought. The tradition since Aristotle's metaphysics: "Hence also the possession of it [of philosophy, of the supreme science] might be justly regarded as beyond human power; for in many ways human nature is in bondage, so that according to Simonides 'God alone can have this privilege' [*Simonides of Ceos*], and it is unfitting that man should not be content to seek the knowledge that is suited to him. If, then, there is something in what the poets say, and jealousy is natural to the divine power (*pephuke phthonein to theion*), it would probably occur in this case above all, and all who excelled in this knowledge would be unfortunate. But the divine power cannot be jealous (nay, according to the proverb, 'bards tell many a lie' (*polla pseudontai aoidoi*)), nor should any other science be thought more honourable than one of this sort. For the most divine science is also most honourable; and this science alone must be, in two ways, most divine. For the science which it would be most meet for God to have is a divine science, and so is any science that deals with divine objects; and this science alone has both these qualities; for (1) God is thought to be among the causes of all things and to be a first principle, and (2) such a science either God alone can have, or God above all others."

A question of filiation. A speculative staging, a speculative *mise en scène*. Legend. Kant tries to subtract his discourse from the psychoanalytic instance: "Every genealogy of morals described by psychoanalysis (parental situation, law of the father, castration, and so on) is valid perhaps in a field of phenomenal empiricalness, for particular mores, for this determinate culture, for the empiric relations between sensible fathers and sons, for finite psychological determinations, for nonuniversal, nontrue religions, for idolatries and fetishisms. Isn't Freud condemned to a crude analogism—that he ought indeed himself to admit—when he writes in the Introduction to *Totem and Taboo*: 'The difference [between the explanation of the totem and that of Taboo] is related to the fact that taboos still exist among us. Though expressed in a negative form and directed towards another subject-matter, they do not differ in their psychological nature from Kant's "categorical imperative", which operates in a compulsive fashion and rejects any conscious motives'? Freud is not careful enough about the analogy against which he puts us on guard, for example in *The Future of an Illusion*. He

In the room—impossible to lock oneself in there with the executioner who lets the key be seen between the fork of his legs—a cry for air, a missing windowpane. This windowpane, too, is replaced. But by what? by a particular and determinable object? If we had the imprudence to comment, and if we were preoccupied with psychological motives, we could predict it with certainty. You could make a thesis out of it.

What replaces the missing windowpane is only a journal, not *The Thief's Journal* that is larger than this whole scene (which is part of the *Journal*), infinitely larger, and that is also printed, in a certain way, in Spanish. No, a journal like any other, whose thief complains about not comprehending the sense, also takes pleasure in, enjoys, in the anxiety of the room, hearing only that noise which is unidentifiable but Spanish like his name. This morsel is a page detached from the thief's journal, prepared by the hands of the author, too prudent to comment on anything other than his text that always attends to something else in connection to which nothing greater can be thought.

Here again I do nothing other, can do nothing other, than cite, as perhaps you have just seen: only to displace the syntactic arrangement around a real or sham physical wound that draws attention to and makes the other be forgotten.

says: the taboo, for us, today, is the *Impératif Catégorique*, except for small differences he does not want to take in sum into account: (1) the taboo is negative, the *IC* is positive ('Though expressed in a negative form'); (2) the objects of the one and the other are different ('directed toward another subject-matter'); (3) the identity is valid only from the psychological point of view ('they do not differ in their psychological nature from Kant's "Categorical Imperative"'); (4) Taboo acts compulsively and under unconscious motivation; the *IC* gives itself at least as the very manifestation of the autonomy of conscience, freedom, and the will. Account not taken of these four differences, I am in agreement with Freud, my *IC* is his taboo, 'they do not differ.' Insofar as the *IC* would be negative—which it is not—insofar as it would have the same object—which it does not—insofar as it would be psychological, empirico-phenomenal —which it is not—insofar as it would have a heteronomic structure—which it does not—it would not be something other in effect than what Freud likens to it under the name taboo. But never a process of idealization and interiorization passing from the negative to the positive, from one object to the other, from the unconscious to the conscious, from constraint to autonomy, from the psychological to what is given as nonpsychological, non-phenomenal, never will such a process be able to give an account of the properly infinite leap that produces the object of pure morality.

unless, following a deconstructive displacement of all the oppositions on which the Kantian discourse bets, in order to make impossible in that discourse an analogical process (sensible/intelligible, phenomenal/noumenal, intuitus derivativus/intuitus originarius, and so on), psychoanalytic discourse determines—in Kantian logic—the sensible point: the point of sensibility where the two terms of the opposition touch and do without the leap [*saut*]. For example, re-*spect* of the moral law belongs to neither the rational order of the law nor the order of psychological phenomena; the *interest* of reason and in general the whole schematism of transcendental imagination is still what, raising the opposition, *suspends the leap*. There is also a Kantian analogism.
The epoch here is unanimous: the leap is good. But it is always necessary to ask oneself why and on top of what one presses to leap

"True religion—the pure morality that should ground it—breaks with all the finite determinations, criticizes fetishism, anthropomorphism, and all the sensible representations, in a word the whole phenomenal religion that organizes itself on a relation to the father or to the law as finite objects. Starting the moment the law, God the father, and so on, are no longer finite objects—that is, as well, no longer (present), no longer appear—the principle of the psychoanalytic genealogy of religion and the moral become null and void [*caduc*]."

Hegel ("the obscure Hegelian philosophy," as Freud calls it) restarts the merry-go-round. The circular repetition of the debate, its vicious circle, is what keeps an interest: "Freud is right when he

I have discovered a lot of new words, and yet I always return to the same ones for want of others.

What is poetry? What bands this text erect, seduces and troubles doctoral discourse, introduces a gap [*écart*] (a "Big Square") into the room [*pièce*] where the patient is undressed, beds down, finally says nothing, makes the master stutter in return. Some days later, the master sends a manuscript dedicated to the patient writer: with my admiration. That's good, isn't it? It's a little bit like what you do, no. The writer does not respond. He is above all not virgin enough to say that he occupies the place of the other.

The text is clustered.
Whence the permeable and seduced nervousness, on its knees, of someone who would like to take it, comprehend it, appropriate it.

The text treats of *ersatz*, in a foreign tongue, of what is posed and added instead.

The thesis (the position, the posit(ion)ing, the proposition, *Satz*) protects what it replaces, however (this hanging counterpart).

Now here is a contemporary (the fact matters a great deal) who—everything, if not his own proper *glas*, should have prepared him for reading the scene—is unsettled, who no longer wishes to see, states the contrary of what he means (to say), mounts a campaign, gets on his high horse.

everything returns to life in the hook of the cripple; the cluster, the grapnel are a kind of hooked matrix. "*Grappe . . . E.* Picardy and env. *crape*; provenç. *grapa*, hook; Spanish, *grapo*, hook; Ital. *grappo*, hook; low Latin *grapa*, *grappa* in Quicherat's *Addenda*; from the old High-German *chrapfo*, hook, mod. German *Krappen*; cp. Cymric *crap*. The cluster [*grappe*] has been so called because it has a hooked or grappled quality" (Littré)

speaks of the moral and the Kantian religion; they remain in finitude, sensible representation, psychologism, fetishism, the relations of jealousy between the hidden, invisible father and the impotent son; Kantian religion does not reach the thought of the infinite and of the true religion; it holds itself within the limits of sensible (fetishistic, anthropomorphic) religion or, what comes to the same, within the limits of a formal religion of the understanding. Now psychoanalysis can give an account of the genealogy of such a religion, but not of a religion of the concept or of speculative reason that begins, this religion, from the infinite, etc., etc., etc."

Kant: "One-upmanship of analogism! Complicity of the *Schwärmerei*, of religious folly and fetishism (God present in sensible finitude). Effacement of Christianity, infidelity, neopaganism. Speculative dialectics is more than ever subject to the psychoanalytic jurisdiction. *Confusionnisme*, misappreciation of the specificity of the religious that dissolves into the philosophical, whereas my essay on religion within the limits of reason alone carries out in this respect a movement more complex in its relation to scriptures, etc."

Hegel: "Yet you also speak there of a progress of reason. I do not propose a formal and tautological identification of the philosophical object and the religious object, but a concrete, historical, heterological, painstaking, dialectic identification. I take into consideration—actually—the shameful teleology of which your work bears the stigmas. I do, without jealousy, to be sure, certainly not, what you should have done. There is in my critique the homage of a filiation, etc."

The identity of philosophy with religion concludes a historical syllogism, a history, as Hegel specifies, whose *inner* sense must be comprehended. The proposed analogy tells us at the same time all that must not be of interest if one wants to reach the sense of the painting (and the—inner—sense in general): an external history is blind to the truth of religion. "A blind

Freud (one foot on the merry-go-round): "What happens when two philosophical systems (erect, upright, unbent paranoiac manias) confront or persecute each other by reproaching each other with comprehending nothing about religion (about the erect, upright, unbent obsessional neurosis)? What happens when two philosophical systems appealing to the truth claim they hold *at once* the truth of neurosis and that of paranoia that psychoanalysis itself claims to know all about, since psychoanalysis knows that they are, the one, the charge or the caricature (*Zerrbild*) of religion, the other of philosophy?" How can these two systems speak together and each one claim that the truth of one is in the other, of every one in every other? Will I get off this merry-go-round by diagnosing: philosophy equals "overestimation of verbal magic"? Verily.
And what makes, however, the third, the artist, or the hysteric? And which one holds the truth of the other

The *ersatz*, he says, is not good.

An alliance, not easily explicable, with Sartre. And yet: "Sartre himself noted a curious difficulty at the basis of Genet's work. Genet, the writer, has neither the power to *communicate* with his readers nor the intention of doing so. The elaboration [evidently not deliberate] of his work has the sense of a negation of those who read it. Sartre saw, though he drew no conclusions, that in these conditions the work was not entirely a work, but an *ersatz*, half way from the major *communication* at which literature aims. Literature is communication: it goes out from a sovereign author who addresses sov- / an author / ereign humanity, beyond the servitude of the isolated reader. . . .

". . . Not only has Genet no intention of communicating when he writes, but, whatever his intention may be, in that a caricature or an *ersatz* of communication would be estab- / the caricature, the *ersatz*, it's too bad, these are fakes. He likes the original edition, the seal, the *seing* of the authentic. Not the false, the true. He doesn't like the galalith. It is certainly galalith, nothing is any longer as before / lished, the author refuses his readers this fundamental similitude which the vigor of his work might risk revealing. . . . / the vigor of his work

"Genet himself never doubts his weakness. To create a work of literature can only be, I believe, a *sovereign operation*. / to create a work of literature / This is true in the sense in which the work requires its author to go beyond the pauper within himself who is not on the level / the work requires its author to go beyond the pauper within himself who is not on the level . . . yes / of these sovereign moments. . . .

". . . Not that we should stop when we read: '. . . I

person can deal with the frame, the canvas, the varnish of a picture; can know the history of painters, the fate of a picture, its price, into what hands it has fallen, and can see nothing of the picture itself.

"What obstructs religion in our epoch is that science has not been reconciled with it. Between the two is found a barrier [*cloison*]. . . ."

The identity of philosophy with religion finds its ultimate mediation in the philosophy of religion. Philosophy is the truth (the philosophy) of religion, and religion represents already (the name) (of) philosophy. "Thus religion and philosophy come to be one": "Philosophy is only explicating *itself* when it explicates religion, and when it explicates itself it is explicating religion."

The places where this unity produces itself as such are par excellence the transitions toward *Sa*, the circular passages of *Sa* to *Sa* (end of the encyclopedia: cycle of *paideia*, of the absolute spirit of God who instructs himself, who engenders himself as his very own son and enjoys then, speculatively, himself; end of the phenomenology of spirit, of the phenomenon or of the self-revelation of the spirit, passage from absolute religion to *Sa*).

In any case religion saves by/from itself.

Absolute religion is not yet what it is already: *Sa*. Absolute religion (the essence of Christianity, religion of essence) is already what it is not yet: the *Sa* that itself is already no more what it is yet, absolute religion.

The already-there of the not-yet, the already-no-more of the yet cannot agree [*s'entendre*].

They cannot agree—in several senses:

(1) The *absolute* already-there of the not-yet passes understanding, comes under [*relève de*] reason, constitutes what reason relieves absolutely. The *true* relation between philosophy and religion (or family) does not measure up to the finite-formal understanding, but to the infinite-concrete reason.

(2) The *absolute* already-there of the not-yet (or the *absolute* already-no-more of the yet) passes what, supposedly, gives itself to be understood in the time of the voice or of hearing. An unheard-of relation insofar as the *absolute* already-there of the not-yet or the *absolute* already-no-more of the yet no longer belong to time, say to the pure insensible-sensibility. They describe an eternal or intemporal circle. Their translation into a temporal grammar, into the syntax of adverbs of time and negation, is determined by Hegel as the fall [*chute*] of sense into the body, outside the circle immediately carried back into the circle, a kind of false tangent of the adverb to the verb, of the time (the tense) of the verb to the verb.

Now of this fall and this strange modification of the verb, *absolute* philosophy or *absolute* religion must give an account. The

wrote to earn money.'

and why not stop ourselves there? Who said it wasn't suitable to write for money? Who could say that? Is money evil? What exactly is it? And why not wonder how one could write that (*ça*)? Who? for whom? why? In Greek "I hear myself" is equal to "I am my first client."

The Critique of Judgment: "Art is further distinguished from *handicraft*. The first is called *free* (*freie*), the other may be called *industrial art*. . . .

". . . fine art must be free art in a double sense: i.e. not alone in a sense opposed to contract work, as not being a work the magnitude of which may be estimated, exacted, or paid for according to a definite standard, but free also in the sense that, while the mind, no doubt, occupies itself, still it does so without ulterior regard to any other end, and yet with a feeling of satisfaction and stimulation (independent of reward)."

By whom, and with what, is the "author" therefore paid? nourished? By a (free) economic authority [*instance*], represented by a (free) editorial market, a (free) minister of culture, verily by Frederick the Great, a free poet and monarch.

Unless he steals? Is this even worse or something other than writing "for money"? Is it a change of system? In any case, the liberal aesthete does not like it (*ça*)? But one sees once again that a mere nothing is enough to let the motif of the pure expenditure out of circulation reinscribe itself in the exchange of a restricted economy (here, a free one). But what happens when a mere nothing is enough? Risk (the cosy compromise too) inhabits risk. The master can always live with the sovereign

Genet's 'work as a writer' is one of those most worthy of attention. Genet himself is eager to be sovereign. But he has not seen that sover-

most worthy of attention

absolute reason of absolute (revealed, Christian, and so on) religion comprehends its own proper fall into the body and into time. Christianity's absolute privilege, religion's absolute essence: to determine itself from out of its fall (the *Sa*-tomb-falls) and its absolute relief [*sa chute (le Sa-tombe) et de sa relève absolue*].

This absolute circle that carries and relieves its tangents, that produces at once the deportation and the concentration of its other, is a family circle.

This statement requires support from neither the spirit's word [*mot d'esprit*] nor from familialism. Save specifying that the circle is of the spirit's word, of its *economy*, of the property law of the spirit that finds itself back in language, in the word in which it falls [*chute*] and that it relieves.

If one hears Hegel, understands him, if one comprehends (from inside the picture) the sense of what his text means-(to say), one cannot reduce the *absolute* already-there of the not-yet or the *absolute* already-no-more of the yet to what one believes one knows familiarly of the family. What Hegel means-(to say) is that the absolute sense of the absolute family, the family's being-family hands itself over only (in) (to) the passage between absolute religion and *Sa*, the next-to-last chapter of the phenomenology of spirit: since the absolute of the already-there of the not-yet or of the yet of the already-no-more. In order to abbreviate this syntagm and to detemporalize it, let us simplify it to *not-there* [pas-là] (the being-there (*da*) of the *not* [pas] that, being there, is not, *not there*). So the *not-there* cannot be reduced to the circle of a family about which what it is and means-(to say) would be already familiarly known. On the contrary, the absolute essence of the family can be reached only in thinking the absolute of the *not-there*. To think the family, one must think absolutely the being of the already-there of the not-yet or the yet of the already-no-more. This family between reads itself [*se lit*] inside and outside—at its [*sa*] limit—the phenomenology of spirit, at the hinge [*charnière*] of the next-to-last and the last chapter.

In effect: in absolute religion, division in two (*Entzweiung*) is *not yet* absolutely overcome by reconciliation. An opposition (*Entgegensetzung*) stays, determines itself as an anticipatory representation (*Vorstellung*). The ultimate limit of the absolutely true, absolute, revealed religion: it remains no further than the *Vorstellung*. The essential predicate of this representation is the exteriority of what presents or announces itself there. It poses in front of it(self), has a relation with an object that is pre-sent, that arrives before only inasmuch as the object remains outside. The unity of the object and the subject does not yet accomplish itself presently, actually; the reconciliation

in a crenel, unheard-of lure of a *Sa*: the Christ carrion, with some others, in sublime decomposition. In falconry terms, to be sure, the hunter sets out and fleshes the lure in a *charnière*

eignty involves the *élan* of the heart, it requires loyalty, because it is given in communication. . . .

Genet is lacking in heart. In loyalty

"GENET'S FAILURE [*ECHEC*]

"Genet's indifference to communication is at the origin of a certain fact: his *récits* are interesting, but not *enthralling*. There is nothing colder, less touching, under the glittering parade of words, than the famous passage in which

"Genet's Failure." What a title. A magical, animistic, scared denunciation. What is the sought-after effect? But hasn't Genet always calculated the "failure"? He repeats it all the time; he wanted to make a success of failure. And now, through the simple provocation of his text, he constructs a scene that obliges the other to unmask, to stammer, to become unhinged, to say what he wouldn't have wanted to, should not have said. It is this, the text (Genet) that traps, fleshes, reads the reader, judgment, criticism. Like Rembrandt. Paradigmatic scene

Genet recounts Harcamone's death. It has the beauty of a piece of jewelry: it is too rich and in somewhat cold bad taste. . . .

for bad taste, you have to look a little further on

". . . the scholar who imposes titles on people demonstrates the same stupidity as Genet, who wrote these lines concerning the time when he travelled through Spain [citation of the "palace

it would be necessary, among other constructions of the same kind, to circulate through every *palais*, in the

between the subject and the object, the inside and the outside, is left waiting. It represents itself, but the represented reconciliation is not the actual reconciliation. There is nothing fortuitous to this representative exteriority being, at the same time, time. If in the absolute religion of the absolute family, there is an already of the not-yet or a not-yet of the already (of *Sa*), that is very simply, if this can be said, because there is—yet again—time. Religion is representative because it needs time.

And if account is taken of the fact that *Sa*, as is said in the chapter that is entitled such, is at once a pure and simple deletion (*Tilgen*) and a relief (*Aufhebung*) of time, the extraordinary difficulty, if not impossibility, of this thought of *Sa* in/as its time is measured.

This barely existing limit, exceeded as soon as it is posited, is already no more what it is yet and does not even give time to think its time. This limit is what barely presents itself between absolute religion and *Sa*.

Now this limit describes an absolute family scene. Elliptically. This limit is the very ellipses in the family circle: the circle inscribes itself in an ellipse in which what is lacking (ellipsis) results from the family not managing to center itself. It has a double focus, a double home, a double hearth. This ellips(e)(is) is time—the truth of space—between the last two chapters (the last two "times") of the phenomenology of spirit: "While *in (it)self* this unity of essence (*Wesens*) and the self (*Selbsts*) has produced itself, consciousness, too, has yet (*noch*) this *representation* (Vorstellung) of its reconciliation, but as representation."

The reconciliation between being and the selfsame, between the being itself of being and the being-same of being, produces itself, to be sure, in revealed religion, but this reconciliation puts itself forward there as an object for consciousness that *has* this representation, that has this representation *in front of* it. The reconciliation has produced itself, and yet it has *not yet* taken place, is *not present*, only represented or present as remaining in front of, ahead of, to come, present as not-yet-there and not as presence of the present. But as this reconciliation of being and the selfsame (reconciliation itself) is absolute presence, absolute parousia, one has to say that in religion, in the absolute revelation, presence is present as representation. Consciousness has the representation of this presence and of this reconciliation, but as it is only a representation of what is outside consciousness (in front of or behind it, here that comes to the same), this representation remains outside it. Consciousness represents to itself the unity, but it is not there. In this does it have, it must be added, the structure of a consciousness, and the phenomenology of spirit, the science of the experience of consciousness, finds its necessary limit in this representation.

labyrinth, yes, between every *palais* (the Palace of Justice of Our-Lady, the palace of the Spanish grandee, where we are, Stilitano's "*voile du palais*," that "precious cobweb" where the gls are elaborated. One would then notice, by lingering there for a bit and working his tongue a bit, that the *palais* is precisely what I am talking about. A lot [*Beaucoup*]. I argotize, I jargon, I seem to produce new words, a new lexicon. Merely an argot, a jargon. They both come from the bottom of the throat, they linger, for a certain time, like a gargling, at the bottom of the gullet, you rasp [*racle*] and you spit.

Argot is an argot word. As with all argot words, Littré does not mention it. To argotize is to work against the lexicon. But by arguing, by elaborating, by alleging, from within its own corpus. Argot is a very old word, rooted in language and literature. Like jargon. And yet its usage is argotic first all, limited to a band or a school of which I speak (for it has no other name)"}. . . .

"The interesting aspect of Jean Genet's work does not reside in its poetic power, but in the lesson we can learn from its weaknesses. . . .

"There is, I don't know what, a fragile, cold, friable quality in Genet's writing, which does not necessarily prevent us from admiring it, but which makes us hesitate to agree with him."

I don't know what. Critique of the I don't know what. I don't know what, a fr

the heart, truly is not there

By what, despite everything, is it recognized here that one is dealing with a text by Bataille? Despite everything, despite "The Language of Flowers," despite (?) "The glas," despite

The glas
In my voluptuous bell [*cloche*]
death's bronze dances
the clapper of a prick sounds
a long libidinal swing.

So absolute religion guards yet some negativity and remains in the conflict, the split, the disquiet. The critique of antecedent religions or philosophies of religion receives some disqualification from this: they were always reproached with not going beyond division, with not attaining reconciliation.

Hegel determines the unity of being and self in effect as reconciliation: with pardon, rapprochement, and expiation. This psycho-anthropological figure of Christianity is clarified in return by its ontological sense. What consciousness seeks beyond this split is an appeasement (*Befriedigung*) by pardon. That gives to the apparently metaphorical family structure its serious weight, its weight of sin and culpability: "It [consciousness] obtains its appeasement in this, it attaches (*hinzufügt*) *externally* (*ausserlich*) to its pure negativity the positive signification of the unity of itself with the essence; its appeasement thus remains (*bleibt also*) itself burdened [affected, charged, *behaftet*] with the opposition of a beyond (*mit dem Gegensatze eines Jenseits*)." The fact of the representation, the *Vor-stellen*, forms an opposite (*Gegensatz*), an object (*Gegenstand*) that, like every object, sets itself opposite consciousness. Because it yet has an object, a desire, or a nostalgia, absolute religious consciousness remains in the opposition, the split. Reconciliation remains a beyond. The temporal motif (the movement of transcendence, relation with a nonpresent future or past, depresentation) is the truth of a metaphorically spatial motif (the "distant," the nonproximate, the nonproper). The family proper has not yet, in the absolute family, found its identity or its proximity to itself. The family has not yet reconciled itself with itself, has not yet absolutely absolved itself. This dehiscence of the family proper forms an ellipse that parts [*écarte*] the religious focus from the philosophical focus, Christianity from *Sa*. And if philosophy—*Sa*—was considered to be the myth of absolute reappropriation, of self-presence absolutely absolved and recentered, then the absolute of revealed religion would have a *critical* effect on *Sa*. It would be necessary to keep to the (opposite) bank, that of religion and the family, in order to resist the lure of *Sa*. Combinatory hypothesis.

Religion saves by/from itself.

Family time: there is no time but the family's. Time only happens in the family, as family. The opposition of the already, of the not-yet, of the already-no-more, everything that forms the time of not being present (*not-there*), everything that constitutes time as the *Dasein* of a concept that is not(-)there [*(n')est pas là*], the being-there of the not-there (one not more—not-not-there—or less), all that is a family scene.

"Its appeasement thus itself remains burdened with the opposition of a beyond. Its own reconciliation (*Seine eigene Versöhnung*) therefore enters its consciousness as something *distant* (*als ein*

Elaborations.

"The sky [ciel]
1. "Love's bronze sounds
The red clapper of your prick
In the bell of my cunt"

2. "The bald clapper of your *glas*
In the bell [*cloche*] (*crossed out: of my vagina
of my urine*)

    of the cunt
    love's bronze sounds
    the long voluptuous swing"

3. "Love's bronze dances
the long voluptuous swing
and the bald clapper of the *glas*
sounds and sounds and sounds and sounds
in my libidinal bell [*cloche*]"

4. "In my libidinal bell
death's bronze sounds
the clapper of the verge dances
the long voluptuous swing"

G. Bataille

what should have, following the general logic of his thought (the simulacrum, sovereignty as an untenable limit, transgression, loss, and so on), led him to another reading? If what must indeed be called the sententious academicism of this edifying discourse is not altogether an accident, if there is a logical effect there of blindness, of negation, of negative inversion (as the saying goes—and this is not simply, here, a figure—neurosis is the negative of perversion), perhaps it is because the system itself permits it. At any moment, everything there can turn toward the most policed predication—sinister, moral and derisively reactive. An unstable and inaccessible limit, sovereignty, with its whole system

Fernes), as something in the distant *future*, just as (*wie*) the reconciliation which the other *self* achieved appears as something in the distant *past*." So there is an analogy (*wie*) between its own proper reconciliation to come and the past reconciliation, between the past and the future, a circular analogy between the end of the world or the last judgment and God's incarnation in Christ. Also an analogy between this situation and the trinitarian family structure in general; then, within that structure, between the individual family and the family as universal community:

"Just as (*So wie*) the *individual* divine man has a father being *in (it)self* (ansich seiende Vater) and only an *actual* mother (*und nur eine wirkliche Mutter*), so (*so*) too the universal divine man, the community (*Gemeinde*), has for its father its *own proper operation* and *knowing* (*ihr* eigenes Tun *und* Wissen), but for its mother, *eternal love* which it only *feels* (*nur* fühlt), but does not behold in its consciousness as an actual, immediate *object* (Gegenstand). Its reconciliation, therefore, is in its heart, but is yet split (*noch entzweit*) with its consciousness and its actuality yet broken (*noch gebrochen*)."

The *noch* and the *nur* that punctuate these statements (only this, yet that, remains this, remains that) mark well the limit—temporal and structural—that holds absolute religion back in the opposition and separates it absolutely from *Sa*: a barely visible limit, nevertheless, a next-to-nothing that parts the present from its representation and that does that in its [*sa*] very (re)presentation.

A series of equivalent oppositions: father/mother (but these are not terms, rather already relations: relation with the father, relation with the mother, described ever since a third term, product of the operation, the son), in (it)self/for (it)self, know/feel (love, heart). How do they operate? The singular divine man—Christ—has a father in (it)self, with whom he has no actual relation. Only his relation with his mother is actual. There is no need to wonder what is his father's name: whether Joseph or the divine spirit, they are not actual since they have not actually intervened, if this can be said, with the warm semen or seed of the earth, in the conception. At the religious moment of religion, the son has a father, but the father remains beyond phenomenal actuality, invisible. The father is in (it)self, but does not present himself. The son cannot in effect interiorize, cannot actually have for himself what of the father is in (it)self. And who remains absent, transcendent, hidden, separated, severe, *not-there*. The paternal generosity, its goodness only represents itself, neither presents itself nor assimilates itself.

The incompletion then affects the reconciliation, in the son, of the father and the mother. Jesus also suffers from the divorce of his parents. The father (knowledge) is cut off [*coupé*] from actuality; the mother (affect) is too natural and deprived of [*sevrée de*] knowledge.

(simulacrum, expropriation, loss, major laughter, and so on), is always in the act of teetering [*basculer*] into metaphysics (truth, authenticity, ownership, proper(ty), mastery). Sovereignty can always be read in the code it reverses, that it more than reverses but also must reverse. For the metaphysical reading to impose itself, a mere nothing suffices, a logical or discursive or linguistic nothing: the *affect* of an intolerable identification (what is he afraid of? what is he incapable of?) provokes an interpretative decision. And so the negative comes back on the scene. Decision here is not an act of sovereign freedom. It is a position. Which cannot *see itself*, in a painting, inverted. But lets itself henceforth be observed, signed, assigned, affected from Rembrandt's place.

beyond all combinatorials, discursive versions and inversions, logico-linguistic exchanges and annulments, what signs perhaps the arrest of an interpretation, the fact of a text, that would be the affect. But the affect is classed and affected as well by its reverse, and this false opposition also falls (to the tomb), this must be known

Remember, he is the one who reads you.

So the doctors came towards him in his time and did not recognize him.

How is the cluster to be grasped?
Do the berries of this postiche form a fetish?

Let us append here the question of the fetish. Question of (the) style. Of pastiche, Gadda would say. Or

Here is the place of Gabriel, the problematic place of an Annunciation.

She makes the child without knowledge, without an actual father. The father is object, but a nonpresent object; the mother is present (phenomemom), but is not an object for consciousness; she only presents herself to the heart. There is reconciliation with the mother, but in natural, sensible, worldly immediacy. Reconciliation with reason, that of the heart and reason, of the for-(it)self and the in-(it)self, does not yet accomplish itself.

The opposition of father and mother is equivalent to all the other oppositions of the series. Equivalent, then, to *opposition itself* as it constitutes the structure of representation. What holds back this side of *Sa* while arriving there already, the null and infinite difference would therefore be sexual difference *as opposition*: what *Sa* will have relieved, to which up to there *Sa* is answerable [*relève d'*].

And if the sexual difference as opposition relieves difference, the opposition, conceptuality itself, is homosexual. It begins to become such when the sexual differences efface themselves and determine themselves as *the* difference.

This determination of the sexual difference as opposition, as opposition engaged in the whole process of opposition (*Entgegensetzung*) in general, of objectivity (*Gegenständlichkeit*), and of representation (*Vorstellen*), maintains [*entretient*] a historical and systematic essential relation with the Immaculate Conception: if not with the dogma concerning the birth of Mary, at least with its premise or its conclusion, the virginity of the mother. Indispensable to the Hegelian argumentation, to speculative dialectics, and to absolute idealism, it commands what could be called the *approach* of *Sa*.

As soon as the difference is determined as opposition, no longer can the phantasm (a word to be determined) of the *IC* be avoided: to wit, a phantasm of infinite mastery of the two sides of the oppositional relation. The virgin-mother does without the actual father, both in order to come and to conceive. The father in (it)self, the real author, subject of the conception, verily of the annunciation, does without the woman, without that in which he only passes without touching. All the oppositions that link themselves around the difference as opposition (active/passive, reason/heart, beyond/here-below, and so on) have as cause and effect the immaculate maintenance of each of the terms, their independence, and consequently their absolute mastery. Absolute mastery that they see conferred on themselves phantasmatically the very moment they are reversed and subordinated. When the virgin sees herself withdrawing the in-(it)self from the conceiving act, only then does she actually do without the father, and so on. The phantasm denounces and delimits itself as such ever since the *Sa* that makes

Warda. Question of Stilitano—antherection of the column—posed, inverted out of the sublime cold of the ice: "He [Stilitano] became the representation of a glacier. I would have liked to offer myself to the most bestial of Blacks, to the most flat-nosed and most powerful face, so that within me, having no room for anything but sexuality, my love for Stilitano might be further stylized."

For that, propose transvestism to the stilite (in whom "frigidity," "modesty," the "symbol of chastity" were just remarked).

"'Would you like me to dress up as a woman?' I murmured."

"At Stilitano's feet all was as the bounding of fauns. Robert twined his garlands about him. The cripple was the column, the other the wisteria [*glycines*]."

The style in question, the postiche held up by the diaper pin [*épingle*], is it a fetish.

This form of interrogation already supposes that one at least knows the fetish is something. Here, yes, apparently, it is a fetish: a substitute for the penis adored by the child who does not wish to renounce the mother's phallus, a monumental erection of the triumph over the threat of castration, denial, compromise, and so on. Isn't all that very recognizable?

What the stilite procures for himself is not, however, the substitute for a very beautiful and very powerful penis that he has, but already a "postiche wound [*plaie*]" (a postiche *coup*, a wound [*plaie*, plague] is always, at once [*d'un coup*], (from) a blow or stroke [*d'un coup*], as its name indicates) as much as a fetish member, in order to re-mark-compensate

one column here (*ici*)—let one think (to compensate) then the other one over there. The one shows when the other descends, but isn't the level almost constant, almost only because you count for nothing in the time

the moment of absolute religion appear as simple representation (*Vorstellen*).

Is the current concept of "phantasm" able, with some pertinence, to dominate this discourse? In fact, it is determined by and starting from that discourse. For example, phantasmatic would be the effect of mastery produced by the determination of difference as opposition (and up to the value of mastery itself), of sexual difference as sexual opposition in which each term would secure itself the domination and absolute autonomy in the *IC*: the effect—the son (rather than the daughter) comes back to me all by myself. The *check* of such a desire of the return to self, on the circle of double virginity, that would be the limit of the phantasm, that would determine the phantasm as such, at the term of the phenomenology of spirit. The phantasm is the phenomenon. The names indicate this.

But does such a check meet itself? Where? Who can speak about it? What is it to fail, to miscarry, in a case of absolute phantasm? The check's value is weak and confused. In front of what would the phantasm of the *IC* have failed? In front of "reality"? But measured by the power of the greater logic that thinks the truth of the *IC*, this notion of "reality" also remains very confusedly empiric. Who would dare say that the phantasm of the *IC* has not succeeded? Two thousand years, at least, of Europe, from Christ to *Sa*, without speaking of retroactive effects, of representations, of edging and de-bordering effects [*effets de bordure et de débordement*], of all that could be called the imperialism or the colonialisms and neocolonialisms of the *IC*. Will it be said, to determine the *IC* as phantasm, that the *IC* is not *true*, that that (*ça*) does not happen like that (*comme ça*), that this is only a myth? That would indeed be silly, and the silliness would again claim "sexual experience" as its authority. But yes, that (*ça*) happens like that (*comme ça*), and what the greater logic impeccably—this is the right word—demonstrates is that not only is this myth true, but it gives the measure of truth itself, the revelation of truth, the truth of truth. Then the (absolute) phantasm of the *IC* as (absolute) phantasm is (absolute) truth. Truth is the phantasm itself. The *IC*, sexual difference as opposition (thesis against thesis), the absolute family circle would be the general equivalence of truth and the phantasm. Homosexual enantiosis.

This difference determined as contradiction or opposition, isn't it justly the religion (the representation) resolved in *Sa*? Does *Sa*

[*mesure*] of the two heterogeneous columns. No common measure at the very moment you think you are clutching/declutching, manipulating, orchestrating, making the liquid music rise or fall by playing the pedals, by making use of fags [*en jouant des pédales*]. The columns deceive and play with you, threaten to beat on each other without leaving you any issue.

No *glas* without the interposition of machinery.

This is not handled like a pen.

No organon, any more than it can be measured against its logic, is capable of its music. Yet doesn't the organologist think that he recognizes his object there: the machine has adapted itself to every advance in Western technology (bellows action, acoustics, electronics), dispenses with breath [*souffle*], divides the body, multiplies by downshifting, powerfully supplies the gestures of the organist, comprehends in its turn *a body and a visage* (organ case and show-pipes), a *respiratory system* (bellows, wind chest), a *muscle system* (manual keyboards, pedal-boards, the valve inside the wind chest, tracker—horizontal rollers and vertical rods), a *nervous and cerebral system* (the console) with stop-handles corresponding to the "stops [*jeux*]" (timbres), combination pedals and pedals for coupling one keyboard to another and keyboards to the pedal-board (pedal couplers) and occasional fixed and free combinations of programmed registrations, and a *vocal system* (ranks of pipes that can go up to three thousand, flue pipes and reed pipes). The flue pipe has a *foot*: the air drawn in comes to hit the *languid* [*biseau*] and, passing through the *flue* [*lumière*] (an interval between the languid and the lower lip), goes on to hit the upper lip, which thereby causes the air within the pipe to vibrate. The sound is as high as the air column is long in the body: but a stopped pipe (*bourdon*) produces the effect of a pipe that is twice as long. The reed pipe has a *tongue* (a thin brass plate which strikes the reed, this brass canal shut on one side and on the other penetrating the lead kernel that makes it touch the resonant body). An iron stem, the *tuning-wire* [*rasette*], regulates, with the length of the strip, the sound's pitch.

And taking account of the "*récit* [swell organ, solo, narrative]," of the "Venetian shutters [*jalousies*]" of the "swell-box," and of the "plein-jeu" and the "grand plein-jeu," of bi-claviculation and classical, baroque or

not permit, precisely, thinking the limit of this limit, of making this limit appear as such, of *seeing* the phantasm in, as its truth [*en sa vérité*]? *Sa*, resolution of the absolute opposition, reconciliation of the in-(it)self and the for-(it)self, of the father and the mother, isn't the very *Sa* of the phantasm, is it?

Inasmuch as it implements [*opère*] the passage from representation to presence and produces the truth (present to self in knowledge) of the absolute phantasm, inasmuch as it is the truth of the absolute phantasm, its unveiled essence (*Wesen: Gewesenheit*: the phantasm having-been), *Sa* is the final accomplishment of the phantasm, the being-(close)-by-(it)self of the *logos*. The absolute phantasm: *Sa*. But do not conclude from this: *Sa*, that is nothing but—the phantasm; the truth of truth is as yet *nothing but* phantasmatic. As soon as *Sa* attains itself, everything that is equivalent to it is infinite. No longer can it be said of an infinite phantasm that it is *nothing but*. *Sa*'s discourse disqualifies the *nothing-but*.

Such would be the bar (opposition and rudder) of the religion/philosophy. Between them, *IC*'s *voiles*, its veils, its sails, virginity's or truth's, for the spirit to spirit (away), to inspire [*souffle*] there.

Knowledge, truth (of the) phantasm (of) (absolute) philosophy-(absolute) religion, this proposition delineates no limit, is the infinite proposition of hetero-tautological speculative dialectics. The infinite circle of auto-insemination that entrains the *paideia* of every seminar in(to) its phantasm. What can there be outside an absolute phantasm? What can one yet add to it? Why and how does one desire to get out of it?

romantic organs, couldn't one reconstitute an organigraphic model, a new *De organographia*

Ja dieses vielstimmige liebliche Werck begreifft alles das in sich / was etwa in der Music erdacht vnd componiret werden kan / vnd gibt so einen rechten natürlichen klang / laut vnd thon von sich / nicht anders als ein gantzer Chor voller Musicanten, do mancherley Melodeyen / von junger Knaben vnd grosser Männer Stimmen gehöret werden.   In summa die Orgel hat vnd begreifft alle andere Instrumenta musica, groß vnd klein / wie die Nahmen haben mögen / alleine in sich.   Wiltu eine Trummel / Trummet / Posaun / Zincken / Blockflöt / Querpfeiffen / Pommern / Schalmeyen / Dolzian / Racketten / Sordounen / Krumphörner / Geigen / Leyern / ꝛc. hören / so kanstu dieses alles / vnd noch viel andere wunderliche lieblichkeiten mehr in diesem künstlichem Werck haben: Also daß / wenn du dieses Instrument hast vnd höreft / du nicht anderft denckeft / du habest vnd höreft die andern Instrumenta alle miteinander.

Michael Praetorius «De Organographia» Wolfenbüttel 1619,

what would be as it were the absolute knowledge of *glas*?

But absolute knowledge, like (the) "*jalousie*," is only a piece of the machinery, a running-effect [*un effet de marche*]

an-other castration substitute, his cut-off hand, and so on. Besides, he often cuts himself ("Stilitano used to cut himself, his fingertips were finely gashed, his nail [*ongle*] was black and crushed [*écrasé*], but this heightened his beauty.").

The undecidable, isn't it the undeniable.

In remarking his supplementary castration, Stilitano seems to assert himself just as well as a male as a shameful woman or as a "queer who hates himself." A little further on, a hymn to his "rump" and to his "sober posterior," to his "Wayside Altar."

It is necessary to give oneself time. Time's remain(s).

Time's remain(s)—for the seminar(y) of *Sa*—that is nothing.

Everything that is, all time, precomprehends itself, strictly, in the circle of *Sa*, which always comes back to the circle, presupposes its beginning, and only reaches that beginning at the end (*in sich zurückgehende Kreis, der seinen Anfang voraussetzt und ihn nur im Ende erreicht*).

Trying to *think* (but this word already holds back in the circle) a remain(s) of *time* (but time already engages in the circle) that would not be, that would not come under [*relèverait d'*] a present, under a mode of being or presence, and that consequently would fall outside the circle of *Sa*, would not fall from it as *its* negative, as a negative *sound* [*comme* son *negatif*], all ready to take up again the tangent in order to remain stuck [*collé*] to the circle and let itself be drawn back in by it. The remain(s), it must be added, would not fall from it at all. Everything that falls (to the tomb) in effect yet comes under [*relève du*] *Sa*.

So would activate itself [*S'agirait*] a suspended remain(s).

Which would not be: not presence, not substance, nor essence. In general, what remains is thought to be permanent, substantial, subsistent. Here the remain(s) would not remain in that sense.

Remain(s) is also thought to be the residue of an operation (subtraction or division), a cast-off, a scrap that falls (entombed) or stays. The remain(s), here, rather, would provoke the action. The remain(s) would remain in none of these two senses. Then why this word, why keep [*garder*] a "remain(s)" that no longer corresponds to the remains of traditional semantics? Will it be said that this word keeps with this semantics a metaphorical relation? That would again be to reappropriate it to the metaphysical circulation. What remains of the "remain(s)" when it is pulled to pieces, torn into morsels? Where does the *rule* of its being torn into morsels come from? Must one still try to determine a regularity when tearing to pieces what remains of the remain(s)? A strictly angular question. The remain(s) here suspends itself.

Let us give ourselves the time of this suspense. For the moment time will be nothing but the suspense between the regularity and the irregularity of the morsels of what remains.

As soon as the thing itself, in its unveiled truth, is already found engaged, by the very unveiling, in the play of supplementary difference, the fetish no longer has any rigorously decidable status. *Glas* of phallogocentrism.

After stating the general laws and describing the essential structure of fetishism, the doctor relates, as an appendix, some "very subtle cases (*In ganz raffinierten Fällen*)" in which the fetish is split [*clivé*] by two contrary positions (*zweispältige Einstellung*).

It's the argument of the girdle (*Gürtel*, gaine).

A little earlier, one was engaged, as in *Beyond the Pleasure Principle* or whenever the logic of the unconscious forces *both* the empirical *and* the metaphysical *at once*, on a "purely speculative way." The very subtle case was that of an athletic support-girdle (*Schamgürtel*) worn as a swimsuit (*Schwimmhose*) that absolutely concealed the genital organs and hence the difference between genital organs (*Unterschied der Genitalien*). This allowed supposing *besides* "that women were castrated and that they were not castrated" and *what is more* (*überdies*) permitted the supposition (*Annahme*) of the man's castration. "*Ein solcher Fetisch, aus Gegensätzen doppelt geknüpft, hält natürlich besonders gut.*" If the fetish is all the more solid, has all the more consistency and economic resistance as it is doubly bound to contraries, the law is indicated in the very subtle case and in the appendix.

instead of citing other "cases" (Schreber again), or other contracts (the double pact, red and black, between Christopher Haitzmann and the devil with breasts): "This may not be an original thought with me, but let me restate it anyway, that the patron saint of actors is Tiresias, because of his double nature. . . . For seven years a man's

The question of time is indecipherable in the chapter of *Sa*: there it is at once annulled and relieved, suspended between the annulment (*Tilgen*) and the relief (*Aufheben*), the latter running the risk of losing itself in the annulus that risks relieving itself in(to) the circle.

Does time remain in *Sa*: for the question that is the structure of the annular. Does time remain, and if it does remain, does it remain in *Sa*? *What is it to remain* is no longer even the question: if remaining is something, remaining annuls itself in the circle. *What does remaining mean (to say)* is no longer even the question, for everything that means (to say) belongs to the circulation of *Sa*. Then, how does one get out of the annulus, and is it a matter of getting out of the annulus or of tightening (thinking) it to the closest point?

If one thinks what *logos* means (to say), if one fills with thought the words of the phenomenology of spirit and of the logic, for example, there is no means of getting out of the absolute circle. That, in any case, is what the discourse of *Sa* means (to say). If one believes or means (*meint*) to get out of it, that is pure verbalism: one cannot think what one says; one cannot conceive the signification of words that then remain void, empty.

The best example—and so the essential example—of this is the Trinity. The Trinity is truly thought only if one does not stick to the formality of the arithmetical three, to the empty signification of three. Now the trinity is intimately bound up [*a partie liée*] with the circular structure that can neither assimilate itself nor let the remain(s) fall (to the tomb).

From then on, but in order to have the "question" form no longer, the question of the time-remain(s), the question of the three, and the question of the semantic void elaborate themselves together. *Sa* fills up (with) sense [*fait le plein de sens*] in the unity without remain(s) of a triangulo-circular structure.

So what happens when Hegel's text is not read, or when it is read *badly*? What happens if one is immobilized in representation, in empty signification? Or if one deviates [*s'écarte*] from the three, the deviation, the *écart*, as its name indicates [*écart*: gap, quarter (of a shield), *é-cart*, etc.], cutting the text up and out into squares [*en carrés*] or squaring it, dividing it into quarters more or less regular, exalting it (on the contrary or thereby even) or revering the charter in it, unless the deviation deals the text out like playing cards. What about the text as remain(s)—ensemble of morsels that no longer proceed from the whole and that will never form altogether one? That is no longer a question.

For example, when he describes the approach of *Sa*, can the adverb of time (*yet*) be read, semantically accomplished, since the absolute concept? Or without it? In the first case, the adverb disappears, loses its temporal sense, is not, in a certain fashion,

The fetish's consistency, resistance, remnance [*restance*], is in proportion to its undecidable bond to contraries. Thus the fetish—in general—begins to exist only insofar as it begins to bind itself to contraries. So this double bond, this double ligament, defines its subtlest structure. All the consequences of this must be drawn.

clothing, for seven a woman's. . . . his femininity followed in close pursuit of his virility, the one or the other being constantly asserted, with the result that he never had any rest, I mean any fixed point where he could rest" (*Letters to Roger Blin*).

"The Funambulists," the blood-red glanslessness [*le sanglant* as *le sans-gland*] of the sheath: "What of your costume? Both chaste and provocative. The clinging tights of the circus. Red jersey, blood-red [*sanglant*]. It displays your muscular contours to perfection, it sheathes [*gaine*] you, it gloves you, but from the collar—open-necked, cleanly cut [*coupé*], as if the executioner were going to chip off your head this evening—from your collar to your hip sash, likewise red, but with the flaps [*les pans*] — gold-fringed — hanging loosely."

The economy of the fetish is more powerful than that of the truth—decidable—of the thing itself or than a deciding discourse of castration (*pro aut contra*). The fetish is not opposable.

It oscillates like the clapper of a truth that rings awry [*cloche*].

Like the *batail* in the throat, in other words, in the gulf of a bell [*cloche*].

I do what I do not say, almost, I never say what I do.

read. In the other case, it is deprived of its absolute conceptuality and does not let itself be truly comprehended. It is always not read. In both cases, it is read on the condition of not being read. That is because *reading* has been defined simultaneously as semantic (ful)filling and as remain(s) of semantic void.

How—for example—is one to read the Lord's anointed in the text, at the threshold of *Sa*, at the end of the next-to-last chapter of the phenomenology of spirit? How is the adverb of the *logos* to be read? One has understood that the *logos* has a father in (it)self, but only an actual mother whose eternal love it *feels* in its heart. "Its reconciliation, therefore, is in its heart but is yet split (*noch entzweit*) with its consciousness and its actuality yet broken (*noch gebrochen*). What enters its consciousness as the *in-(it)self*, or the side of *pure mediation*, is a reconciliation that lies in the beyond: but what enters it as *present* [as now: *als* gegenwärtig], as the side of *immediacy* and *being-there* (Daseins), is the world which has yet (*noch*) to await its transfiguration. The world is indeed *in (it)self* reconciled with the essence (*Wesen*), and of the *essence* it is known, of course, that it recognizes the object as no longer alienated from self but as equal to self in its love. But for self-consciousness, this immediate present (*diese unmittelbare Gegenwart*) has not yet (*noch nicht*) the figure of spirit. The spirit of the community is thus in its immediate consciousness divided from its religious consciousness, which declares, it is true (*zwar es ausspricht*), that *in (it)self* these consciousnesses are not divided, but also declares an *in-(it)self* that is not realized or that has not yet (*noch nicht*) become an equally absolute being-for-self."

What can follow what does not precede already—subsequently—this next-to-last not yet? In the chapter of *Sa*, the last then, what remains of time, to wit of not-yet, finds itself reduced, but suspended between the relief (*Aufhebung*) and the annulment (*Tilgen*). To what "time," from then on, does the "text" of *Sa*, on *Sa*, belong, the time of its repetition, of its readability—full or empty? Who reads it? Who writes it? Who frames it? Who signs it?

"*Time* is the *concept* itself that *is there* (*der da ist*) and which represents itself (*sich vorstellt*) to consciousness as empty intuition; for this reason, spirit necessarily appears (*erscheint*) in time, and it appears in time just so long (*so lange* [!]) as it has not *grasped* its pure concept, i.e. has not annulled (*tilgt*) time [*tilgen*: destroy, annihilate, efface, abolish, annul, for example a debt; *eine Schuld tilgen*: to annul, cancel, or pay off a debt, a mistake; *eine Rente tilgen*: to

For example, everything happens as if I were first working on naming, but also at founding [*fondre*] a bell [*cloche*]. In its nomenclature, making it resound and disappear at once, making it rise up to the top of some tower [*tour*], and thereby, in some turn or trick [*tour*], unhooking it with a burst [*éclat*] of laughter, making it collapse [*s'effondrer*], that's what I say I do. I describe.

Batail is first of all an old name for the clapper of a bell. Set in motion by the swing, it comes to strike the sound-bow, *la panse* (one also says *le pans*), as a kind of inner hammer. Not far from the barrel [*faussure*], the place where the bell begins to enlarge its curve, to flare. They also speak of the *faussure* (or *faulsure*) of towers.

In the towering by turns (the *tour à tour* in all genders) of the fetish—what I defer (and say I am doing) [*ce que je diffère* as *ce que je dis faire*]—the flare of a barrel [*faussure*], neither this nor that, verily neither true nor false. But the operation is not negative, it affirms with a limitless yes, immense, prodigious, inaudible. And the operation constructs, a kind of solid transverse, in order to suspend the bell between two towers. The top [*hune*], itself, this large horizontal piece of wood from which the bell is suspended, ends in two swivel pins. Wood, impassive matter but, already, the artifact. Forgotten, unperceived, deadening every resonance. Of wood. The beam. The top—she—is, already, the beam—he.

redeem an annuity]. Time is the *outer*, intuited pure self which is *not grasped* [conceptually] by the self, the merely intuited concept; when [*indem*: while, whereas, and as] this concept grasps itself it relieves its time-form (*hebt er seine Zeitform auf*), conceives this intuiting (*begreift das Anschauen*), and is a conceived and conceiving intuiting. Time, therefore, appears as the destiny and necessity of spirit that [inasmuch as it] is not complete in (it)self. . . ."

The *Da* of the concept (time) marks, at last with the stroke of time [*du coup*], its incompleteness, its inner default, the semantic void that holds it in motion. Time is always of this vacancy with which *Sa* affects itself. Because it affects itself with this, *Sa* empties itself with a view to determining itself, *it gives itself time*. It imposes on itself a gap [*écart*] in signing itself. The *Da* of *Sa* is nothing other than the movement of signification.

The philosophy of religion, working in/on the name of God, distinguishes in effect two significations of signification. One wonders there, concerning God, what the word *signify* (*bedeuten*) itself signifies. It signifies two "things"—inverse and symmetrical—that have in common such a vacuum between signification (*Bedeutung*) and representation (*Vorstellung*). Sometimes we have the representation and lack the concept, the fullness of signification (for example, when we ask ourselves, "'What does the expression God signify?'"). Conversely, we might happen to have the signification without representation, and what we call for then is an example (*Beispiel*) that "plays beside the essence," beside substantial thought. But this double signification always signifies that thought gives itself of/by itself—examples, of/by itself thought plays itself exemplarily.

It remains that, in this play, the signifying signification gap [*écart*] always permits a text to work empty, to no effect. The concept can always not come back to itself in a text. The triangle or the circle can remain open when *Sa* arrives at the text. The text then will be what *Sa* cannot always give itself, what happens [*arrive*] to *Sa*, rather than *Sa* arriving there itself.

Sa interprets the event as one of its moments, as its own proper negative under the form of naturalness, representation, empty signification. These negative values are regularly joined together themselves, for example in the first moment of the concept of absolute religion (the first of three of the last of three moments of revealed religion). This is a reading of the Trinity according to John by the phenomenology of spirit:

I write myself [*Je m'écris*] on that. On the top [*hune* as *une*: on the front page], between the two.

I hear myself say, as someone saying to me, from afar, all I write. I imitate it myself, I limit myself [*Je l'imite moi-même*], I edit myself, I apostrophize all the high and mighty tones. I deafen them.

Pendule de la hune: pendulum of the top, of the woman, the fetish oscillates—like the clapper of a truth that tilts, that cl—

The undeniable is the uncastratable.

That does not mean (to say) that there is no castration, but that this *there is* does not take place. There is that one cannot cut through to a decision between the two contrary and recognized functions of the fetish, any more than between the thing itself and its supplement. Any more than between the sexes.

The tongue remains in the sheath, the *gaine*,

so the argument of the sheath, the *gaine*, envelops everything that, like a glove or flower, turns in every sense and direction, over, inside out, upside down, without losing a certain form. That alone still permits aponeurotic tongue-effects. For poetics, one would still gain by bringing Littré into play, by drawing some disseminance from it. Of the *gaine* it is noted in Littré:

"When spirit is at first represented (*vorgestellt*) as substance in the *element of pure thought*, it is immediately simple and self-equal, eternal *essence* (*sich selbst gleiche ewige* Wesen), which does not, however, have this abstract *signification* (Bedeutung) of essence, but the signification of absolute spirit. Only spirit is not a signification, is not what is inner, but what is actual (*Wirkliche*). Therefore simple, eternal essence would be spirit only in an empty word (*leeren Worte*), if it remained no further than the representation (*Vorstellung*) and the expression (*Ausdrucke*) of the simple, eternal essence. But simple essence, because it is an abstraction, is, in fact, the *negative in its own self* and, moreover, the negativity of thought, or negativity as it is in (it)self in *essence*; i.e. simple essence is absolute *difference* (Unterschied) from itself, or its pure becoming-other. As *essence* it is only *in (it)self* or for us; but since this purity is just abstraction or negativity, it is *for its own self*, or is the *self* (*das* Selbst), the *concept*.—It is thus objective (*gegenständlich*); and since the representation apprehends and expresses as an *event* (*als ein* Geschehen) what has just been expressed as the *necessity* of the concept, it is said that the eternal essence *produces* for (it)self an other (*sich ein Anderes* erzeugt). But in this being-other it has at the same time immediately returned (*zurückgekehrt*) into itself; for the difference is the difference *in (it)self*, i.e. it is immediately different only from itself and is thus the unity that has returned into itself.

"There are thus three distinct moments: *essence*, *being-for-self* which is the being-other of essence and for which essence is, and *being-for-self* or the knowledge of itself *in the other*. Essence beholds only its own self in its being-for-self; in this alienation (*Entäusserung*) it is only close by itself (*bei sich*). The being-for-self that shuts itself out from essence is *essence's knowledge of its own self*: it is the word (*Wort*) which, when uttered (*ausgesprochen*), leaves behind, alienated and emptied (*ausgeleert zurücklässt*), the one who uttered it, but which is as immediately heard, and only this hearing of its own self is the being-there of the word (*und nur dieses Sichselbstvernehmen ist das Dasein des Wortes*). Thus the distinctions made are immediately resolved as soon as they are made, and are made as soon as they are resolved, and what is true and actual is precisely this movement circling in itself (*in sich kreisende Bewegung*).

"This movement within itself proclaims the absolute essence as *spirit*. Absolute essence that is not grasped as spirit is merely the abstract void, just as spirit that is not grasped as this movement is only an empty word. (When) (As) its *moments* are grasped in their purity, they are the restless concepts (*ruhelosen Begriffe*) which only are in being in themselves their contrary and in finding their rest in the whole. But the *representation* (Vorstellen) of the community is

"1. Case for a knife [*couteau*] or a cutting or sharp instrument. Scissors in their *gaîne*. . . . Marine term. Large hem around sails for fortifying them, before sewing on the bolt rope. *Gaîne de girouette*, a cloth band that attaches the vane to the shaft. *Gaîne de flamme*, a cloth sheath into which one passes a flaming stick. *Gaîne de pavillon*, cloth band stitched [*cousue*] in the entire expanse of the tent. 2. Architectural term. Supports of a certain kind, larger above than below, on which a bust is put; no doubt so called because the half-figure seems to rise up out of them as from a *gaîne*; they are called "terms" when the *gaîne* and the bust are of one piece. Placing the busts on the *gaînes*. 3. Botanical term. The lower part of certain leaves embracing the stem and in some way replacing the petiole. If the edges are joined, the *gaîne* is intact; if not, it is said to be cloven. 4. Anatomical term. Name given to certain parts that serve as envelopes for others; this is chiefly said of aponeuroses enveloping fleshy masses. Entomological term. In sucking insects, the tube that encloses the apparatus those insects use for sucking. In the hymenoptera, the tube in which the lip and the little tongue are contained. 5. *Gaîne de chauffe*, heating flue, in heat ventilators, in radiators, is a term used for the device that conducts the air from the heating chamber to the place to be warmed up. . . . Proverb. He who strikes with the knife will die by the *gaîne*, a proverb corresponding to: he who lives by the sword will die by the sword. . . .
"—R. The Academy, which puts a circumflex accent on *gaîne* and *gaînier*, does not put one on the composites *dégainer*, *engainer*, *rengainer*. This is an irregularity that fruitlessly complicates the orthography. . . .
"—E. Walloon, *vaimm*; Hainaut, *waine*; from the Latin *vagina*, *gaîne*. *Gaîne* is one of those examples where the Latin *v* is changed to *g*. The old form must have been *gaaine*, representing *vagīna*; but if *gaine* were found any earlier than the 14th century, one would have to think that the Latin accent had been displaced at the outset, and that it had been pronounced *vagīna*."

A question of the circumflex: of a "fruitless" complication of the orthography.

What does the *gaine* fit? To what is it going?

not this thought that *conceives*; it has the content, but without its necessity, and instead of the form of the concept it brings into the realm of pure consciousness the natural relationships of the Father and the Son."

Previously, already as regards the "actual mother" and the father "being in (it)self," these relations were presented as "drawn from natural generation." Religion, as religion, never absolutely gets beyond representation or nature. It is necessary to relieve, in(to) the concept, both the figure of natural representation (for example, that of the fall, of the son, and so on) and the arithmetic formality (for example, the number of moments). Christ's death marks at once the destruction of his natural being and the end of the abstraction of the divine essence. God himself is dead, but the knowledge of his death produces this "spiritualization" by which "substance has become subject" the moment the abstraction and the cadaveric frigidity (*Leblosigkeit*) raise themselves to the hot and glorious light of life. The triumphal moment of mourning.

At the angle of the phenomenology of spirit and *Sa* (of the greater logic), at the hinge [*charnière*], the tomb of the Son.

"'I called her Mag, when I had to call her something. And I called her Mag because for me, without my knowing why, the letter g abolished the syllable Ma, and as it were spat on it, better than any other letter would have done. And at the same time I satisfied a deep and doubtless unacknowledged need, the need to have a Ma, that is a mother, and to proclaim it, audibly. For before you say Mag you say ma, inevitably. And da, in my part of the world, means father. Besides for me the question did not arise, at the period I'm worming into now, I mean the question of whether to call her Ma, Mag or the Countess Caca, she having for countless years been as deaf as a post.'

"It is significant that Molloy, in order to replace *Mag* with some name or other, should choose, entirely by chance, the title 'Countess Caca,' as if the nickname *Mag* were a condensation of *Mama* and *caca*, with a tender softening of K into G. This G could at the same time contain an allusion to the pharyngeal contraction that accompanies the refusal of nourishment.

"In this regard, Dr. Ilse Barande has indicated to me that an American patient, a passive homosexual, one who spoke a very correct French, regularly pronounced *vaguin* instead of *vagin*. He introduced an occlusive, a hard, sharp sound, which cuts the breath, in order to replace the fricative Ž (GE), a gliding, flowing [*coulant*] sound. In this case the supplementary velar occlusive would be able to reflect a phantasy of the *vagina dentata*." Fónagy.

The remain(s) of time undecides itself between the three and the more-than-three, the fulfillment or the emptying out [*évidement*] of signification. *Sa* suffers this indecision and in that tries to find its rhythm again and as a return of seasons.

One could speak as well—the two words are closely related—of *Sa*'s saturnalia. Feasts in honor of Saturn: the Italic god had been identified with Kronos (an empty play on words, and this was the time—that one would come here to feast as *Sa* [*comme* Sa]). He is said to have taken refuge in Italy after his son had dethroned

what is it not to read Hegel or to read him badly, or rather the text *Sa*? Is this negativity comprehended, included, and at work in the text *Sa*? To admit it, it must first be read and read well. But what recourse would the text *Sa* have, and before what authority [*instance*] could it lead this nonreading or this bad preliminary reading, or all the seductions, drifts, perversions, neither real nor fictive, neither true nor false, that would entrain the text *Sa* outside itself, without subjecting themselves to its [*sa*] jurisdiction? It is impossible to *know* if such a feint is possible. Rather, such a feint can only be *known* impossible if knowledge presupposes the hierarchized opposition of the true and the false, of the infinite and the finite. A finite feint cannot remove itself from *Sa*'s infinite authority or proceedings [*instance*].
What would it mean not to comprehend (Hegel) the text *Sa*? If it is a matter of a finite failure, the failure is in advance included,

Perhaps one will find that I use Littré a great deal. I use it, that is the word I am looking for. Not to rely on it, but to play it. Genetically. The etymologistic phantasm has been discharged elsewhere and for a long time, but the word's is dying; and for poetics, if someone still cared about it today, simply to have commented on, illustrated by constant reference to [*à coups de*] dictionaries, lexicons, and encyclopedias, *the strange word of* (*l'étrange mot d'*).

comprehended in the text. If it is a matter of an infinite fault or lack, one would have to say that *Sa* does not think itself, does not say itself, does not write itself, does not read itself, does not know itself, which no longer means anything, by definition. *Sa* always ends by being full, heavy, pregnant with itself.

So the hypothesis of a bad reading, here, has no place. It has not even taken place. One must let it fall [*tomber*], in the margin or epigraph [*exergue*], as a margin or epigraph, as a remain(s) about which one does not *know* if it *works*, in view or in the service of whom of what. Like such a note at the bottom of the page of the *Concluding Unscientific Postscript to the Philosophical Fragments*, scraps of scraps [*reliefs de reliefs*] under the (last supper) scene:

"Hegel is also supposed to have died with the words upon his lips, that there was only one man who had understood him, and he had misunderstood him. . . . Hegel's statement reveals at once the defect of a direct form, and hence is quite inadequate as an expression for such a misunderstanding, giving sufficient evidence that Hegel has not existed artistically in the elusive form of a double reflection. In the second place, Hegel's mode of communication in the entire series of seventeen volumes is direct communication; so that if he has not found anyone to understand him, it is all the worse for him. It would be quite a different thing in the case of Socrates, for example, who had planned his entire form of communication to the end of being misunderstood. Regarded as a dramatic *replique* by Hegel in the hour of death, this saying is best interpreted as an attack of absent-mindedness, a piece of thoughtlessness on the part of a man who, now in death, attempts to walk paths he has never frequented in life. If Hegel as a thinker is *sui generis*, then there is no one with whom he can be compared; and if there should perhaps exist a parallel somewhere, one thing is certain: he has absolutely nothing in common with Socrates." Elsewhere: "It is presumably the witchery of this ever continuing process which has inspired the misunderstanding that one must be a devil of a fellow in philosophy in order to emancipate himself from Hegel. But this is by no means the case. All that is needed is sound common sense, a fund of humor, and a little Greek ataraxy. Outside the *Logic*, and partly also within the same, because of a certain ambiguous light which Hegel has not cared to exclude, Hegel and Hegelianism constitute an essay in the comical. Blessed Hegel has presumably by this time found his master in Socrates; and the latter has doubtless found something to

and thrown him down from the top of Olympus. He had himself sliced off the testicles of his father with the aid of his mother, Gaia. Again it is Gaia, she already, who put the sickle between her son's hands. Perhaps it is she, again, who allied herself with Zeus, her grandson, against Kronos, her son, and made him take a *pharmakon* that forced him to vomit all the children he had eaten. So Saturn would be a deposed father whose Latin reign had nevertheless left the memory of a mythic golden age. He had become the god of agriculture and more precisely, armed with a sickle and a billhook, he used to preside at the pruning of the vine. Like Dionysus-Bacchus, he was intimately bound up with wine. He would also be considered the god of the underworld.

So saturnalia corresponded with a rhythm of *season*, a word that comes no doubt, like Saturn, from *sata*, the fruits of the earth and seeds, from *serere*, to sow, or from *satus*, son. Sowing time [*semaison*] is a season; *serere* would have the same semantic origin as *semen*, *seminare*. The Greek ancestor could be named *saō* (to sift). During saturnalia, order was overturned; the law transgressed itself: time of debauchery, of licentiousness, of drunken-

Consider the title, the half or false title [*faux titre*], the apostrophe that suspends and deflects the strange word. Its mode is unusual. One waits for the word *urbanisme*, town planning, as in the first phrase ("The strange word *urbanisme*"). And in effect town planning furnishes the apparent theme of these eight pages. But through a movement of erection (still the theme of the piece), in other words of theatrical and funereal reversal, the writing obliquely describes the title itself: to wit, the word and that it is strange. And the writing does not omit, as is so often done, the always oblique aspect of the erection ("in a cemetery or very near to the crematorium with its stiff, oblique, and phallic chimney stack").

As for the strangeness of the word, here is the end of the text that this very *glas* has not ceased to accompany, to escort or precede, or betray: "Where? I read that Rome—but maybe my memory is deceiving me— had a funeral mime. What was his role? Preceding the cortege, he was in charge of miming the most important facts in the dead man's life when he—the deceased—was alive.

"Improvising gestures, attitudes?

"The words. Living (I don't know how) the French tongue dissembles and reveals the war of words— enemy brothers, they tear at each other or fall in love with one another. If tradition and treason are born from one same original and divergent impulse, each to live its singular life, how do they always know, throughout the tongue, that they are bound together in their distortion?"

What is given, handed over, betrayed by *traditio*, here, thanks to the gift of tongue and style, is at once an example and an essence, an event and a rule [*règle*]. *Traditio* is an example of the tongue's *traditio*, the example gives the gift and betrays the betrayal. The tongue proceeds by tradition and treason. In that way is the word a word.

laugh at, if Hegel otherwise remains the same. There Socrates will have found a man worth conversing with, and especially well worth asking the typically Socratic question: whether he knows anything or not. It will be remembered that Socrates proposed to ask this question of the shades in Hades. Socrates must have suffered a very great change in his nature if he permitted himself to be impressed in the slightest degree by the recitation of a series of paragraphs, and the promise that everything will become clear at the end . . ."

ness, spasmodic revolution in the course of which, says an anachronistic treatise of mythology, "the social classes were topsy-turvy," the masters becoming the slaves of their slaves that they then serve at table. The bad turn of seasons coming to put the history of spirit out of order, *Sa*'s saturnalia would then be intimately bound up with a disordering [*dérèglement*] of the *seminarium*.

To play with the four seasons: this play, this evil of *Sa*, opens this play with a gap that no longer assures it of being able to reappropriate itself in the trinitarian circle. This season disorder [*mal de saison*] neither destroys nor paralyzes absolutely the infinite concept. If it formed only the negative of this concept, it would yet confirm that concept dialectically. Rather, it puts that concept out of order, stops it, jams [*grippe*] it inconceivably. Also scratches [*griffe*] it with writing. The etymon of *Begriff* looks forward to that.

As soon as it is grasped by writing, the concept is drunk [*cuit*: or cooked]. Thus perhaps are unleashed the saturnalia of *Sa*, the drunken binge, the satiety, the satiation, the "Bacchanalian intoxication (*Taumel*)" in which the true grasps itself, sparing no "member (*Glied*)," but a delirium in which there would no longer be any surety that *Sa* introduces itself to itself in it, that *Sa* announces the delirium at the opening of the phenomenology of spirit in order to wake from it at the end, past the intoxication of a moment, the time of a part (of itself).

For one could be tempted to reduce *Sa*'s binge [*cuite*] to a typical, certainly essential, but very determinate phase of phenomenology. Does not this binge punctuate the whole phenomenology of religion? Into its three times, natural religion, esthetic religion, revealed or absolute religion?

An external index: within the phenomenology of religion one passes, for example, from the religion of flowers, next from *raw animality* (natural religion) to such "unbounded revelry of the god (*unbefestigte Taumel des Gottes*)" that must appease itself in making itself the object of esthetic religion's living work of art. This revelry or intoxication will have caused passing from the flower to the fruit and wine, to the fermented fruit, the Bacchic moment of esthetic religion: not-yet but already the bread and wine, the flesh and

"No worse lived than any other, this tongue, like others, permits crossbreeding words, like animals in heat; and what emerges from our mouths is an orgy of words that copulate, innocently or not, and give French discourse the salubrious appearance of a forest countryside where all the stray animals couple together. Writing—or speaking—in such a tongue, you say nothing. In the midst of this distracted vegetation, itself variegated by its mixed pollens, its haphazard graftings, its suckers and slips, only in its midst is a deluge of beings or, if you wish, of equivocal words, like the animals in the Fable, more permitted to swarm and jumble together.

"If someone still hopes to be able to look after a coherent discourse by means of such a proliferation—or luxuriance—of monsters, he's mistaken: at best, he can couple larval and deceitful herds resembling processions of processionary caterpillars, herds that would gladly swap their fucking to bring forth [*accoucher*] just such a carnivalesque, ephemeral, unimportant brood, coming from Greek, Saxon, Levantine, Bedouin, Latin, Gaelic, one lost Chinaman, three Mongolian vagabonds, who all speak to say nothing but to reveal by coupling a verbal orgy whose sense is lost, not in the night of time, but in the infinite of tender or brutal mutations.

"And the funeral mime?

"And the Theater in the cemetery?

"Before burying the dead man . . ."

There I leap, go see for yourselves what the dead man becomes during the feast. When "the feast is finished," one returns to the word that, without seeming to do so, lets itself be banded erect, lets itself be covered with flowers throughout the funeral ceremony. Strange death. And deceased. "When one is cunning, one can pretend to find oneself again, one can pretend to believe that words do not budge, that their sense is fixed or has budged thanks to us who become, voluntarily, one feigns to believe, if our appearance is modified just a bit, gods. As for me, when confronted with the enraged, encaged herd in the dictionary, I know that I have said nothing and will ever say nothing. And the words don't give a fuck. . . .

"So for the great parade, just before the corpse is buried, the funeral mime, if he wants to recreate the life and death of the dead man, will have to discover and dare to utter, in front of an audience, those dialectophagous words that will devour the dead man's life and death."

beats
under the sheath, gambols, cuts, cracks, re-forms,

blood of the Christian last supper scene. This phenomenological banquet is set up in the center of the center: in the middle of the esthetic religion that itself occupies a mediating position between natural religion and (absolute) revealed religion. It (*Ça*) happens, at sunset: "This *pathos* is for (it)self the essence of the *rising* sun (*Aufgangs*), but an essence which has now *set* [*couchée*] within itself (*in sich* untergegangen), and has its setting or going-down [*déclin*] (*Untergang*), i.e. self-consciousness—and hence being-there and actuality—within itself. It has here traversed the movement of its actualization. Coming down from its pure essentiality and becoming an objective force of nature and the expressions of that force, it is a being-there for the other, for the self by which it is consumed (*verzehrt wird*). The silent essence of self-less nature (*selbstlosen Natur*) in its fruit (*Frucht*) attains to that stage where self-prepared and digested, it offers (*darbietet*) itself to life (of the) self (*dem selbstischen Leben*). In its usefulness as food and drink it reaches its highest perfection; for in this it is the possibility of a higher existence and comes into contact with the spiritual being-there. In its metamorphoses, the earth-spirit (*Erdgeist*) has developed, partly into a silently powerful (*stillkräftigen*) substance, partly into a spiritual fermentation (*geistigen Gärung*): in the first case it is the feminine principle of nourishment (*weiblichen Prinzipe der Ernährung*), in the other the masculine principle, the self-impelling force (*sich treibenden Kraft*) of self-conscious being-there."

The enjoyment, here, enjoys the manifestation, the phenomenon, the light, the luminous essence (*Lichtwesen*) as it upsurges. There is a "mystery" there, but the "mystical" does not result from some dissembling (*Verborgenheit*) or from some intimate secret (*Geheimnis*) of knowledge. The mystical is the revelation, the manifestation of the self uniting itself with the essence that becomes "consumable," "an object of desire." This is the moment of the cult: "What has thus, through the cult, become manifest to self-conscious spirit within itself, is *simple* essence as the movement, partly out of its dark night of concealment (*nächtlichen Verborgenheit*) up into consciousness, there to be its silently nourishing substance; but no less, however, the movement of again losing itself in the nether darkness, in the self, and lingering above only with a silent maternal yearning. The clear pressure (*lautere Trieb*) is, however, nothing but the many-named (*vielnamige*) luminous essence of the rising sun and its undisciplined tumultuous life which, similarly let go from its abstract Being, at first enters into the objective being-there of the fruit, and then, surrendering itself to self-consciousness, in it attains genuine actuality—and now roams about as a crowd of frenzied females (*als ein Haufen schwärmender Weiber*), the unleashed (*ungebändigte*) delirium of nature in self-conscious figure."

absents, glues [*colle*], detaches, separates, alleges and delegates, argues, tightens, bands erect.

Interexhibits the dead bit but benefits from a gain of force only by retaining the inflated turbulence under the material.

Desirable if ungraspable, or close to being so.

A toilette at every instant of the bit (the dead) [*du mors*], bandaged [*pansé*], banded erect, verified, mummified.

That would be too easy otherwise.

gl remains under the sheath.

Of all the morselings; of all the reagglutinations without which the schiz could never even *be produced*—gl would be, would band erect the transcendental accomplice of skzz, the original-ly(ing) like galalith, synthetic, that closes opens the sluice, bars the outflow [*écoulement*] the very instant with a sweet explosion it forces open the floodgate [*écluse*]; of all the proliferating wounds, bites [*morsures*], breaks, sutures, borders and grafts that gl took advantage of; of all these, let appear, an infinitive scene, at the end of the operation, only the oiled surface, smooth, without ridge or scar, the calm sea of the headline [*entête*]. The title lays out, more a sign of fatigue, the appeased, glorious integrity of one entire word, the verbal body *glas*. Interposed before the disseminating mark, the vowel is seen no longer, no longer scaffolds. It sings [*chante*] or blackmails [*fait chanter*] the bit (the dead) [*le mors*].

That is where (it is necessary) to put the accent in case you desire to understand, to hear something about writing, to decipher or to decircumcise the text you sound, the text-consonant.

Such a delirium manifests only immediate spirit, the spirit of nature: bread and wine, Ceres and Bacchus. The higher gods, themselves conscious of themselves, have not appeared. Now self-consciousness presupposes the *sacrifice* of the spirit. What already announces itself in nature, in the sacrifice of bread and wine, is not yet what it announces: "the mystery of flesh and blood."

to Aulic Councilor Förster:
"*Lagrime Christi!*
"From this we can now clearly see that the tears the Lord has shed over the abuses of Catholicism have been not only salt water but bottles of liquid fire.
"And now you wish generously out of friendship to help me prepare the flow of Latin prose that I must now work up, and are going to do so by drawing on this same fire. For this I must first of all thank you. And if this poor vessel which is to distill the fiery substance does not spoil it, my amply tortured audience shall thank you for the warmth emanating from me to them.
    "B. ²²⁄₆ 30 Yours, Hegel"

"If you, dear friend, still have a sufficient supply of *Lagrimae Christi* to pour me another half dozen bottles, I will be much obliged—and indeed invigorated!—for you to put aside for me such an amount. Could you perhaps send some immediately along with the bearer of this note?
"My best compliments to your equally dear wife.
    "Yours Hgl ³⁄₁₀ 30"

The seasons, the grip(pe) of the concept, the debauch [*la saturnale*], the passage from flower to fruit, from fruit to wine, from wine to blood, the spiritual fermentation that introduces one sex into the other, so many thermal baths: heating or rather reheating phenomena. Opposition of the raw and the cooked [*cuit*], of the cold and the hot, passage from one opposite to the other, the spirit reappropriates itself in reheating itself; it recovers itself, retakes itself, in nature. Spirit had lost itself, gotten (a) cold, alienated in nature; this is not said metaphorically: the tropes here are produced by spiritual fermentation. Heating *signifies* life in general, organic life and spiritual life, the consuming destruction of life. Natural life destroys itself in order to relieve itself in(to) the spiritual life. Heating permits assimilation, digestion, nutrition, interiorization, idealization—the relief. The *Aufhebung* is a *fermentation* (*fervere, fermentum*) in nature and in natural religion, a *fervor* when religion interiorizes or spiritualizes itself. In coming back to itself in the heat, in producing itself as self-repetition, spirit raises itself, relieves itself, and like gas or effluvium holds itself in sublime suspension above the natural fermentation.

Whether it be a matter of ferment or fervor, the tumultuous opposition of the two "principles" is always at work: the feminine (night and natural silence of substance) and the masculine (light, *logos* of self-consciousness, becoming-subject of substance). This opposition, like opposition in general, will have been at once the manifestation of difference (consequently of that time-remain(s) where the void of signification deviates itself [*s'écarte*]) *and* the

There, account taken of the bit and the sublingual slaver, of caesura and agglutination, there is no sign, no tongue, no name, and above all no "primitive word" in the Cratylean sense; nor any more some transcendental privilege for an elementary couple where the analytical regression should finally stop, nor even, since no being [*étant*] or sense is represented there, a mim(s)eme [*mimême*].

Remains that: the problem of *mimesis* must be re-elaborated here, beyond the opposition of nature and law, of the motivated and the arbitrary, all the ontological couples that have rendered it, with the *Cratylus*, illegible.

gl tears the "body," "sex," "voice" and "writing" from the logic of consciousness and representation that guided those debates. While ever remaining a bit-effect (a death-effect) [*effet de mors*] among others, gl remarks in itself as well—whence the transcendental effect, always, of taking part—the angular slash [*coupure*] of the opposition, the differential schiz *and* the flowing [*coulant*] continuum of the couple, the distinction *and* the copulating unity (for example, of the arbitrary and the motivated). It is one of, only one but as a party to, the de-terminant sluices, open closed to a rereading of the *Cratylus*.

Socrates feigns to take part. For example: "And perceiving that the tongue (*glōtta*) has a gliding movement (*olisthanei*) most in the pronunciation of l (*lambda*), he made the words (*ōnomase*) *leia* (level), *olisthanein* (glide) itself, *liparon* (sleek), *kollōdes* (glutinous), and the like to conform (*aphomoiōn*) to it. Where the gliding of the tongue (*olisthanousēs tēs glōttēs*) is stopped by the power of g (*antilambanetai ē tou gamma*

235

process of its effacement or its reappropriation. As soon as difference determines itself, it determines itself as opposition; it manifests itself to be sure, but its manifestation is at the same time (that is the time of the same as the effacement of the time-remain(s) in the self (*Selbst*)) the reduction of difference, of the remain(s), of the gap [*écart*]. That is the thesis.

The religious heating, the history of religious manifestation, religion in the phenomenology of spirit, describes this effort to assimilate the remain(s), to cook, eat, gulp down, interiorize the remain(s) without remains [*le reste sans restes*]. After fermentation, the scraps [*reliefs*] of a banquet are reappropriated at the Last Supper scene.

The concept of religion fills itself up, determines itself in opposing itself to itself, then reconciles itself with itself: in three moments that fulfill the absolute spirit. In a first moment, absolute spirit finds its actual existence in religion, but in a religion whose concept yet remains empty and indeterminate. In this moment religion is *immediate* and *natural*. Spirit sees itself outside, apprehends itself as its own proper object in a natural and immediate figure. This is the moment of natural religion (sun, plant, animal, work of the artisan). The spirit loses itself and finds itself again in these external, sensible and natural objects. The last of the three (of the three and not the four, the religion of plants or flowers does not form a settled [*arrêtée*] structure, a true religion), the least natural, the artisan's work secures the mediation toward the following moment: esthetic religion. In the first moment, in natural religion, spirit has not come back to itself, is not yet (it)self (*Selbst*). In denying the natural exteriority of the sensible thing into which it had lost itself, in consum(mat)ing, interiorizing, relieving that exteriority, spirit identifies itself, finds itself again, recognizes itself as such (*Selbst*). The second moment of religion then is that of the "figure of *relieved naturalness*, or of the *Selbst*." Moment of esthetic religion: spirit contemplates itself in the object that it has itself produced, in its work. No longer does it have only consciousness of the object (sun, plant, animal, and so on) but consciousness of itself. One has passed from nature to art, as from consciousness to self-consciousness, from the object to subjectivity. This last opposition, like the one-sidedness of these two instances [*instances*], relieves itself in(to) absolute (revealed or manifest) religion. In this

dunamis) he reproduced (*apemimēsato*) the *gliskhron* (glutinous), *gluku* (sweet), and *gloiōdes* (gluey)."

So the enigma is of the sphingtor, of what will have let the sphigma pass. To squeeze (the text) so that it (*ça*) secretes, repress it with an antileptic (g), the liquid antagonism floods [*écoule*] the coming [*jouissance*]. No period after gl, a comma and yet, gl remains open, unstopped [*débouché*], ready for all concubinations, all collages. This is not an element; gl debouches toward what is called the element (an embouchure on the ocean [*la mer*], for example).

It is not a word—gl hoists the tongue but does not hold it and always lets the tongue fall back, does not belong to it—even less a name, and hardly a *pro-prénom*, a proper (before the first) name.

But may be the subject of the annunciation.

The sciences, all of them, must record here the throw of the d(ie) [*coup de dé*]. And the force of chance [*aléa*], as *clinamen*—the other collar, (that) some double fetter(s) (or understands).

Everything is moved to attach importance to the case of chance. It can never fall well and enchancre the necessary with indentations except at the undiscoverable moment when the proper name breaks into language [*langue*], destroys itself in language with an explosion—dynamite—and leaves it as a hole. Very quickly re-covered: a parasitic vegetation without memory.

ultimate relief, spirit reveals itself in its true figure, but what relieves and reveals itself here (it suffices to think of what withdraws in this veiling movement in order to see announcing itself, in the anagrammatic throw of the d(ie) [*le coup de dé anagrammatique*], the fermentation of truth) yet remains no further than figural representation. "But although in this [in revealed religion], spirit has indeed attained its true *figure* (*zu seiner wahren* Gestalt), yet the *figure* itself and the *representation* (Vorstellung) are still the unvanquished aspect (*unüberwundene Seite*) from which spirit must pass over into the *concept*, in order wholly to resolve therein the form of objectivity, in the concept which equally embraces within itself its own contrary." *Sa* has no figure, is not a figure, while absolute religion is yet (true) figure and representation.

Whence the circle of this syllogistic linking up: natural religion, the first moment of religion (immediate consciousness and sense-certainty) counts three moments whose first (the first moment of the first moment) is also, like *Sa*, at the other end, absence of figure, irrepresentable moment. The figure withdraws at the origin and the end of religion, before and after religion: whose becoming literally describes a consuming destruction of the figure, between two suns. Another jealousy of the Hegelian god who begins and ends by making disappear—in fire—its own proper figural representation. This jealousy, this *zelos* does not boil down to the passion of the Jewish God that never shows himself. Here God shows himself neither at the beginning nor at the end of times, but that is in order to show himself the whole time through his figures and in an absolute light. True, he shows himself better in not showing himself, since the determinate figures dissemble him precisely in their determination. Between the Jewish god and the Hegelian god, the problem, after all, of the remain(s) plays itself out, plays with the remain(s), under the species of an excess of zeal. The jealousy is between them.

In the first moment of natural religion, that of the luminous-essence (*Lichtwesen*), spirit is at first only its own proper concept. But this concept stays in abstract indetermination, has not yet unfolded, manifested, produced itself. It keeps itself back yet in "the night of its essence (*die Nacht seines Wesens*)." In the first split that unveils the secret (*Geheimnis*) of spirit, spirit relates to itself

Under the effect of the obliquid, the erection is always in the act of pouring forth in order to fall. Verily inverting itself.

gl protects against the schiz that gl produces.

The antherection is also that "feminine counterpart of Stilitano's cluster of grapes." No more than betrayal does transvestism furnish the theme of this *récit*; transvestism gives its range to the "literary" operation.

The feminine counterpart of the cluster is elaborated at the same time that the literary fetish abysses itself, the "literary diversion" to which "This journal I write" is not reduced.

Immediately before the transvestite sequence and after putting the "rump [*croupe*]" (Stilitano's) in chains or in the saddle with the cuttings [*coupes*], blows [*coups*], collars, necks [*cols*], lice, and other antherianthemes by now familiar, one learns that Pépé has been "arrested."

"'How long can they give him?'"

"'Life.'"

"We made no other comment.

"This journal I write is not a mere literary diversion."

The louse is detached on Stilitano's collar that it recognizes as its "domain," its "space." The collar is cut out of a whole panoply of semantic and formal variations. The turbulence of these associations calls for the false collar [*faux col*], which does not come. That is in order to bend to the flexible but tenacious force of writing, to its endless simulacrum, and to surge up again as false eyelashes [*faux-cils*] on the other page. And to get stuck [*se coller*] to the fingers, to the knuckles [*phalanges*], rather.

according to a "*simple* relation," without mediation or determination. The Being "filled (*erfüllte*)" by this concept of spirit is indeterminate; it appears, appears itself as such: pure light, simple determinability, pure medium [*milieu*], ethereal transparence of the manifestation in which nothing appears but the appearing, the pure light of the sun. This first figure of natural religion figures the absence of figure, a purely visible, thus invisible sun that allows seeing without showing itself or that shows itself without showing anything, consuming all in its phenomenon: *die Gestalt der Gestaltlosigkeit*. This figure is "the pure, all-embracing and all-filling *luminous essence*," that of the rising [*lever*] or the orient (*Lichtwesen des Aufgangs*). Nothing yet shows itself there; the orient passes here immediately into its pure being-other, absolute dark or occidentality. Analyzed as abstract subjectivity, this figureless figure, first moment of natural religion in the *Phenomenology of Spirit*, corresponds to the third moment of natural religion in the *Lectures on the Philosophy of Religion* ("Historically, the cult of light is the perspective of the religion of the Parsis [founded by Zoroaster]. The cult has its existence in this religion. They do not adore the light under the form of the sun; their adoration is not, in the strict sense, a cult of nature; but the light directly signifies the Good.").

Pure and figureless, this light burns all. It burns itself in the all-burning [*le brûle-tout*] it is, leaves, of itself or anything, no trace, no mark, no sign of passage. Pure consuming destruction, pure effusion of light without shadow, noon without contrary, without resistance, without obstacle, waves, showers, streams ablaze with light: "The movements of its own externalization, its creations in the element without obstacle of its otherness, are effusions of light (*Lichtgüsse*); in their simplicity, they are at the same time (*zugleich*) its becoming-for-(it)self and the return from its being-there, torrents of fire destructive of figuration." By very reason of this indifference—or rather of this absence of opposition—the pure content of this being is without essence. The all-burning is "an essenceless by-play, pure accessory of the substance that *rises* without ever *setting* (*ein wesenloses Beiherspielen an dieser Substanz, die nur aufgeht, ohne in sich niederzugehen*), without becoming a subject, and without consolidating through the self (*Selbst*) its differences."

A pure essenceless by-play, a play that plays limitlessly, even though it is already destined to work in the service of essence and sense. But as such, supposing that "as such" can be said of something that is not some thing, this play does not yet work, does not yet have any onto-theo-teleological horizon: fire artist without being. The word itself (*Beiherspielen*) plays the example (*Beispiel*) beside the essence. Here the pure example plays *beside* the essence so much, holds itself so diverted from [*à l'écart de*] the essence, that it has no essence: pure example, without essence, without law.

The false eyelashes of one of those mariconas who was called Pedro. This is the moment the remark "This journal I write is not a mere . . ." passes in transit to the jump of a young monkey on the shoulder of a maricona. "His eyelashes remained stuck to my knuckles; they were false. I had just discovered the existence of fakes."

One last station in the procession toward the great paranthesis.

The feminine counterpart of Stilitano's cluster is put in place, tacked in the text, only after the castration of another column has been described, and also the monumentalization of the wound re-covered with flowers.

It is the *glas* of a pissoir.

After the demolition of the shelter [*édicule*], the obsequent procession gets going, as did the convicts after the castration of Guiana. At the edge of the still smoking scar, the faggots come to place their flowers. The burial place is erected once more through the care of a delegation, a detachment of transvestites.

A blank, as always, between two antherections, an interior margin between two supplementary columns that seem detached from one another:

"Stilitano stepped back [*recula*] slowly, protected by his outstretched *moi*

you can always seek the subject. [*moi* = self]
Nothing ever bands erect, it seems, except a stump, a *moignon*. A chopped-off wrist that repulses more strongly.
Funeral Rites: "His hands were in his pockets. He was heavy and yet light, for each of his angles remained imprecise. He looked like a walking willow, each stump

Therefore without example, like God about which Hegel says that an example cannot be made, but because he, God, merges with the pure essence, pure essence is also without example. The all-burning—that has taken place once and nonetheless repeats itself ad infinitum—diverges so well from all essential generality that it resembles the pure difference of an absolute accident. Play and pure difference, those are the secret of an imperceptible all-burning, the torrent of fire that sets itself ablaze. Letting itself get carried away, pure difference is different from itself, therefore indifferent. The pure play of difference is nothing, does not even *relate* to its own blaze [*incendie*]. The light envelops itself in darkness even before becoming subject. In order to become subject, in effect the sun must go down [*décline*]. Subjectivity always produces itself in a movement of occidentalization. Now here the sun does not set—or else it sets immediately, does not know any going down, any route that leads back to self, any season, any season in the sense of cycle, just a pure season, in the sense of the seminal effusion without return. This difference without subject, this play without labor, this example without essence, devoid of self (*Selbst*), is also a sort of signifier without signified, the wasting of an adornment without the body proper, the total absence of property, propriety, truth, sense, a barely manifest unfolding of forms that straightaway destroy themselves; is a One at once infinitely multiple and absolutely different, different from self, a One without self, the other without self that means (to say) nothing, whose language is absolutely empty, void, like an event that never comes about itself.

"Its determinations [those of this pure being or this essenceless play] are only attributes which do not attain to self-subsistence (*Selbständigkeit*), but remain (*bleiben*) merely names of the many-named [empty-named, then: there is not yet any sense, time, circle] One. This One is clothed with the manifold powers of being-there and with the figures of actuality as with an ornament without self (*als mit einem selbstlosen Schmucke*); they are merely messengers, having no will of their own, messengers of its might, visions of its glory, voices in its praise."

How can the self and the for-(it)self appear? How would the sun of the all-burning breach/broach its [*sa*] course and its going down [*déclin*]?

At first approach, that the situation could change and why the void of the concept should fill itself up are not seen.

of which is lightened and thinned by an aigrette of young branches. He had a revolver."

"A posture of Erik's: his thumb was in the space between two of his fly buttons. Like Napoleon, who used to hook his thumb on his vest [*gilet*]. A sick man fearing the rush of blood to his bandaged [*bandée*] hand."

Miracle of the Rose: "Another of Harcamone's embellishments: his hand swathed in white. . . . A mere nothing would injure him. Perhaps there was nothing wrong with him and he feigned injuries! Yards of white gauze were wound around his hand. . . . Those dressings [*linges*] made him cruel, him, the gentlest of angels. . . .

"Like lots of tough guys [*mecs*], he wore on his right wrist a broad leather band . . . a 'wrist support,' but it had become an ornament, a symbol of manliness. It was laced on by a leather cord, at the bend of the wrist [*saignée*]."

Those dressings that banded the angel erect resemble the ones with which babies are swathed after circumcision. That is, all the time. Gauze swaddling and crape bandage. "And it came about, that on the eighth day they came to circumcise the baby; and they were calling him by the name of his father Zachariah. Then his mother spoke forth and said: No, but he shall be called John. And they said to her: There is no one in your kindred who is called by that name. And they made signs to his father, to learn what he wished him to be called. And he asked for a tablet and wrote, saying: John is his name. And all were amazed. But his mouth was set free at once, and his tongue. . . ." Luke's *récit* of the birth of John the Baptist.

What is necessary here: hands induced to bandage [*panser*] the column. The column is wounded, otherwise it would not be a column. It is truncated, marked, covered with scars and legends. The Stilite wears an "enormous bandage," he has his arm in a sling, but "I knew the hand was missing."

The scars are tattoos, words, and drawings incrusted in each column, notches mixing the black of the ink and the red of blood to pass the contract into the skin and treat the text. So the gl ceremony obeys, in its form, the "Order of Tattoos" whose institution is recounted in the *Miracle of the Rose*.

The tattoos also have the relievo of brilliant and cutting [*coupant*] precious stones, like those the Dayaks of Borneo used to insert, I believe, after an incision, into the surface of the penis, to increase, they say (distyle) [*disent-ils*], the woman's enjoyment.

Elsewhere, gl inserts the tattoo of a silent, precious, and brilliant antheme. " 'Bye-bye, bugger [*effleuré*].' He

How, from this consuming destruction without limit, can there remain something that primes the dialectical process and opens history? Conversely, if the process begins, how would it reduce this pure differential consuming, this pure destruction that can proceed only from fire? How would the solar outlay [*dépense*] produce a remain(s)—something that stays or that overdraws itself? How would the purest pure, the worst worst [*le pire du pire*], the panic blaze of the all-burning, put forth some monument, even were it a crematory? Some stable, geometric, solid form, for example, a *pyramis* that guards the trace of death?

Pyramis is also a cake of honey and flour. It was offered as a reward for a sleepless night [*nuit blanche*] to the one who thus remained awake. It was also a cone-shaped cake presented to the dead. The Greeks have given this name to the Egyptian monuments because of the word *pyr*, some think, since the flames end in a point, or because of this cone-shaped flour (wheat, *pyros*) cake.

If the all-burning destroys up to its letter and its body, how can it guard the trace of itself and breach/broach a history where it preserves itself in losing itself?

Here is experienced the implacable force of sense, of mediation, of the hard-working negative. In order to be what it is, purity of play, of difference, of consuming destruction, the all-burning must pass into its contrary: guard itself, guard its own movement of loss, appear as what it is in its very disappearance. As soon as it appears, as soon as the fire shows itself, it remains, it keeps hold of itself, it loses itself as fire. Pure difference, different from (it)self, ceases to be what it is in order to remain what it is. That is the origin of history, the beginning of the going down [*déclin*], the setting of the sun, the passage to occidental subjectivity. Fire becomes for-(it)self and is lost; yet worse [*pire*] since better.

Then in place of burning all, one begins to love flowers. The religion of flowers follows the religion of the sun.

The erection of the pyramid guards life—the dead—in order to give rise to the for-(it)self of adoration. This has the signification of a sacrifice, of an offer by which the all-burning annuls itself, opens the annulus, contracts the annulus into the anniversary of the solar revolution in sacrificing itself as the all-burning, therefore in guarding itself. The sacrifice, the offer, or the gift do not destroy the all-burning that destroys itself in them; they make it reach the for-(it)self, they monumentalize it. The historical placing in orbit of the consuming instant gives the instant the chance of the anni-

doesn't mean that he assumes the singer has an eglantine tattooed on his thigh or that his shoulder is branded with a fleur-de-lis, but that he hopes the child will be penetrated."

Our-Lady-of-the-Flowers thus will have prescribed the *glas* form: "The great nocturnal occupation, admirably suited for enchanting the darkness, is tattooing. Thousands and thousands of little jabs [*coups*] with a fine needle prick the skin and draw blood, and figures that you would regard as most extravagant are flaunted in the most unexpected places. When the rabbi slowly unrolls the Torah, a mystery sends a shudder through the whole epidermis, as when one sees a colonist undressing. The grimacing of all that blue on a white skin imparts an obscure but potent glamor to the child who is covered with it, as a neutral [*indifférente*], pure column becomes sacred under the notches of the hieroglyphs. Like a totem pole. Sometimes the eyelids are marked, the armpits, the hollow of the groin, the buttocks, the penis, and even the soles of the feet. The signs were barbaric and as meaningful as the most barbaric signs: pansies, bows and arrows, hearts pierced and dripping blood, overlapping faces, stars, quarter-moons, lines, swallows, snakes, boats, triangular daggers and inscriptions, mottoes, warnings, a whole fearful and prophetic literature."

In Algeria, in the middle of a mosque the colonists would have transformed into a synagogue, the Torah, brought forth from behind the curtains, is promenaded in the arms of a man or a child, and kissed or caressed by the faithful along the way. (The faithful, as you know, are enveloped in a veil. Some wear it all rolled up, like a cord, a sling, or an untied necktie around their neck. Others, more amply spread out on their shoulders and chest and trailing to the floor. Still others—and, at determined moments, everyone—on the head. Sometimes the veil is streaked in blue and white, and sometimes in black and white. Sometimes, though almost never, as if by chance or choice, it is pure white. The dead man is enveloped in his *taleth*—that is the name of the veil—after washing the body and closing all its orifices.)

The Torah wears a robe and a crown. Its two rollers are then parted [*écartés*] like two legs; the Torah is lifted to arm's length and the rabbi's scepter approximately follows the upright text. The bands in which it was wrapped had been previously undone and entrusted, generally, to a child. The child, comprehending nothing about all these signs full of sense, was to climb up into a gallery where the women, and old women especially,

versary movement from orient to occident. The chance of substance, of the *remnance* [restance] determined as subsistence. The last words of "Das Lichtwesen": "But this reeling, unconstrained [tottering, tumultuous, *taumelnde*] life must [*muss*; why must it?] determine itself as being-for-self and give its evanescent figures a stable subsistence (*Bestehen*). The *immediate being* in which this life stands in opposition to its consciousness is itself the *negative* power which dissolves [resolves, *auflöst*] its own differences. This being is thus in truth the *self* (Selbst); and spirit therefore passes on to know itself in the form of self. Pure light disseminates (*wirft . . . auseinander*) its simplicity as an infinity of forms, and offers up itself as a holocaust to the for-(it)self, so that from its substance the individual may take its subsistence."

The difference and the play of the pure light, the panic and pyromaniac dissemination, the all-burning offers itself as a holocaust to the for-(it)self, *gibt sich dem Fürsichsein zum Opfer*. It sacrifices itself, but only to remain, to insure its guarding, to bind itself to itself, strictly, to become itself, for-(it)self, (close)-by-(it)self. In order to sacrifice itself, it burns itself. The burning then burns itself and goes out; the fire appeases itself; the sun begins to go down [*décliner*], to run through the route that will lead it into the occidental interiority (the occidental, one knows this anyway, bears the sun in its heart). This sacrifice belongs, as its negative, to the *logic* of the all-burning, one could say to the double register of its accounting, accountable calculus. If you want to burn all, you must also consume the blaze, avoid keeping [*garder*] it alive as a precious presence. You must therefore extinguish it, keep it in order to lose it (truly), or lose it to keep it (truly). Both processes are inseparable; they can be read in any sense, any direction whatever, from right to left or left to right; the relief of one must value [*faire cas*] the other. A panic, limitless inversion: the word *holocaust* that happens to translate *Opfer* is more appropriate to the text than the word of Hegel himself. In this sacrifice, all (*holos*) is burned (*caustos*), and the fire can go out only stoked.

Here we are at this critical point of the anniversary where we can regard on both sides of the revolution, toward the orient and toward the occident.

What engages itself here? What is the stake at play in this column?

The gage, the engage, the stake at play [*l'enjeu*], that is indeed what is the question here. What puts itself in play in this holocaust of play itself?

were and then to pass them the ragged bands. The old women rolled them up like crape bands for infants, and then the child brought them back to the Thebah.

Meanwhile the body of the Torah was laid out on a table, and the men busied themselves, they succeed one another to it, according to the rite, for a passage, in the company of the rabbi. They used to disappear, while standing, in the movements of veils and phylacteries (*tephelin*: those little cubes of skin or parchment contain fragments of sacred texts, are affixed to the forehead and the hand with narrow bands, or rather thongs, of black leather that are pulled very tight, like a garrote, around the head, the arm and the index finger that loses all freedom of movement). As with each of the gestures consecrated by the rite, the passage—the more or less laborious reading of a morsel of text—was first auctioned off. (One of those taxing operations, in my eyes the most theatrical, consisted, as I have said, in raising the two parted columns, in bearing them at arm's length to present, from afar, the text to the crowd of the faithful, as if they could read, learn, verily purchase, at such a great distance, a book—the first—that was thick, dense, difficult, heavy, unaccented. The man was to be solid and rich, or was to let his sons support him. If, by chance, his veil, in the course of his moving, slid down his shoulders, he could not, since his hands were caught, pull it back up. One of his sons, from among the very ones who had purchased the honor for him, would put it, devotedly, back in its place.) Afterwards, they had to roll up the sacred text and wrap [*bander*] it all over again. The chant was never interrupted.

Maybe the children who watched the pomp of this celebration, even more those who could lend it a hand, dream about it for a long time after, in order to organize all the pieces and scenes of their lives.

What am I doing here? Let's put it that I am working on the origin of literature by miming it. Between the two. Read, for example, Jean Paul, *The Life of Fibel*, the
"'First Volume, containing the *fata* of the so-called Fibel in his mother's womb.'
"Marvel, all you literati of our day!
"There were still thirty-nine volumes to treat of that part of his life *after* his birth. . . .
"I readily acquired from the Judeo-Christian, at the going price, permission to lift, to tear off from these works everything that he printed, provided I spared the covers. I have thus enabled myself to guarantee, through the oaths of the Jew and through documents, certain chapters of the following biography, which have been extracted from the torn leaves and which I shall preface with the comment: *Judas*-Chapter. For our Judeo-Christian Anabaptist was called Judas; he had

This perhaps: the gift, the sacrifice, the putting in play or to fire of all, the holocaust, are under the power of [*en puissance d'*] ontology. They carry and de-border it, but they cannot not give birth to it. Without the holocaust the dialectical movement and the history of Being could not open themselves, engage themselves in the annulus of their anniversary, could not annul themselves in producing the solar course from Orient to Occident. Before, if one could count here with time, before everything, before every determinable being [*étant*], there is, there was, there will have been the irruptive event of the gift [*don*]. An event that no more has any relation with what is currently designated under this word. Thus giving can no longer be thought starting from Being [*être*], but "the contrary," it could be said, if this logical inversion here were pertinent when the question is not yet logic but the origin of logic. In *Zeit und Sein*, the gift of the *es gibt* gives itself to be thought before the *Sein* in the *es gibt Sein* and displaces all that is determined under the name *Ereignis*, a word often translated by *event*.

How is the event of an anniversary possible now? What gives itself in an anniversary?

This, perhaps: the process of the gift (before exchange), the process that is not a process but a holocaust, a holocaust of the holocaust, *engages* the history of Being but does not belong to it. The gift *is not*; the holocaust *is not*; if at least *there is some such*. But as soon as it burns (the blaze is not a being), it must, burning itself, burn its action [*opération*] of burning and begin to be. This reflection (in both senses of the word) of the holocaust engages history, the dialectic of sense, ontology, the speculative. The speculative is the reflection (*speculum*) of the holocaust's holocaust, the blaze reflected and cooled by the glass, the ice, of the mirror. The dialectic of religion, the history of philosophy (etc.), produces itself as the reflection-effect of a *coup de don* [the gift's blow, stroke, time, etc.] as/in holocaust.

But if the blazing is not yet philosophy (and the remain(s)), it cannot, nonetheless, not give rise to philosophy, to dialectical speculation, to the annulus of the exchange, to the downward [*déclinante*] course, to the circulating revolution. There is a *fatum* of the gift there, and this necessity was said in the "must" (*muss*, *doit*) we indicated above: the *Taumeln*, the vertigo, the delirium *must*

changed his old Jewish name of Judas, which the traitor Iscariot had borne, for the Christian name of Jude [the name is the same in German], an apostle who figures, as we all know, in the New Testament with its very short epistle of Saint Jude. This assonance of names, this brotherhood in milk, however, may well have made, and more than one thinks, our honest Jude continually thirsty for the baptismal waters. For, after emerging from the baptismal fonts, and having barely dried off, he got lost all over again in that common church of the two Judases, and sought to create a common asset of the Old and New Testament by associating them in a single *et Compagnie* [in French, in the text]. Nor did he ever let himself be converted." Perhaps what I am doing with you

gnon [stump], which was placed simply in front of him. The absence of the hand was as real and effective as a royal attribute, as the hand of justice.

"Those whom one of their number called the Carolinas paraded to the site of a demolished street urinal. During the 1933 riots, the insurgents tore out one of the dirtiest, but most beloved pissoirs. It was near the harbor and the barracks, and its sheet iron had been corroded by the hot urine of thousands of soldiers. When its ultimate death was certified, the Carolinas—not all, but a formally chosen delegation—in shawls, mantillas, silk dresses and fitted jackets, went to the site to place a bunch of red roses tied together with a crape veil. . . .

"When they reached the harbor they turned right, toward the barracks, and upon the rusty, stinking sheet iron of the pissoir that lay battered on the heap of dead scrap iron they placed the flowers.

"I was not in the procession . . ."

determine itself as for-(it)self and take on a stable subsistence. From the moment this constraint, this constriction of the "must" comes to press the mad energy of a gift, what this constriction provokes is perforce a countergift, an exchange, in the space of the debt. I give you—a pure gift, without exchange, without return—but whether I want this or not, the gift guards itself, keeps itself, and from then on you must-owe, *tu dois*. In order that the gift guard itself, you must-owe. You must at least receive it, already know it, recognize or acknowledge it. The exchange has begun even if the countergift only gives the receiving of the gift. I give you without expecting anything in exchange, but this very renunciation, as soon as it *appears*, forms the most powerful and most interior ligament. This bond of the for-(it)self and the debt, this contracture of sense, is already the ruse of dialectical reason at work as the negative in the holocaust. The gift can be only a sacrifice, that is the axiom of speculative reason. Even if it upsurges "before" philosophy and religion, the gift has for its destination or determination, for its *Bestimmung*, a return to self in philosophy, religion's truth. Always *already*, the gift opens the exchange, chains up, constructs its monuments, calculates on two registers the expenditures and the receipts, the debit [*doit*], the must [*doit*], the goings out, the comings in, to how much it (*ça*) is raised and how much remains.

So the gift, the giving of the gift, the pure *cadeau*, does not let itself be thought by the dialectics to which it, however, gives rise. The giving of the gift understands itself here before the for-(it)self, before all subjectivity and all objectivity. But when *someone* gives *something* to *someone*, one is already long within calculating dialectics and speculative idealization. I give *me*, I make me the gift [*je me fais cadeau*]. To whom?

If one can speak of the gift in the language [*langue*] of philosophy or the philosophy of religion, one *must say* that the holocaust, the pure gift, the pure *cadeau*, the cake [*gâteau*] of honey or fire hold on to themselves in giving themselves, are never doing anything but exchanging themselves according to the annulus. The gift for (it)self. The prototype of the gift, of the *cadeau*, is then the annulus, the ring or collar or necklace, the chain. The annulus, the chain of the annular anniversary, is not one gift among others; it hands over the gift itself, the very gift of the self (*Selbst*) for (it)self, the present for (it)self. The gift, *cadeau*, names what makes itself present.

Cadeau means *chain*. The word designates, according to Littré, the "Pen strokes [*Traits*] with which the masters of writing embellish their examples," or also, "Large letters placed at the head of acts or chapters in cursively written manuscripts." Or too, "Formerly, feast that one principally gave to women, a pleasure party." The etymology, still according to Littré, would refer to "*Catellus*,

Those roses, placed by the transvestites on the edge of a hole and on the vestigial site of a column where other flower-columns were antherected, are here transplanted, restiched [*recousues*] in the very place—it suffices to turn the page inside out—where the anthonym dresses in drag.

After extracting, one cites a second time, one resews [*recoud*] nevertheless this hanging counterpart [*cependant*], and all this, once the weaver's loom is regarded right side up, almost overlaps itself [*se recoupe*], is put back into place, the text takes time to band erect. A long paranthesis.

The flower is grafted. A question of style and taste.

"'Would you like me to dress up as a woman?' I murmured.

"Would I have dared, supported by his powerful shoulder, to walk the streets in a spangled skirt between the Calle Carmen and the Calle Mediodia? Except for foreign sailors, no one would have been surprised, but neither Stilitano nor I would have known how to choose the dress or the hair-do, for taste is required. Perhaps that was what held us back. I still remembered the sighs of Pedro, with whom I had once teamed up, when he went to get dressed.

"'When I see those rags hanging there, I get the blues! I feel as if I were going into a vestry to get ready to conduct a funeral. That's (*Ça*) got a priestish smell. Like incense. Like urine. Look at them (*ça*) hanging! I wonder how I manage to get into those damned sausage skins.'

"'Will I have to have things like that (*ça*)? Maybe I'll even have to sew [*coudre*] and cut [*tailler*] with my

"When I arrived at Fontevrault, Harcamone had been in irons for ten days. He was dying, and that death was more beautiful than his life. The death throes of certain monuments are even more meaningful than their period of glory. They blaze before going out."

small chain, from *catena*, chain . . . because of the chained form of the pen strokes. Household management teaches us that making *cadeaux* is said for making things that appear attractive but are useless, metaphorically compared to those strokes of the hand of the writing masters. From there one passes without trouble to *cadeau* in the sense of diversion, feast, and finally, present." I make me (the) present. In view of whom?

The useless, the specious, the frivolous do not escape the contractual concatenation; on the contrary they engage in it, immediately place in it the debit, the must [*le doit*]. To make themselves [*Se faire*] *cadeau*.

To give means-(to say) to give an annulus, and to give an annulus means-(to say) to guard, to keep: guard the present. (I) give (you) therefore-gift [*donc* as *don*] (I to you) give an annulus therefore-gift (I) guard, keep (you). I lose therefore-gift I win. It is necessary to place the personal pronouns between parentheses. To rethink this movement before the constitution of the *Selbst*. The annular movement re-stricts the general economy (account taken and kept, that is, not taken or kept, of the loss) into a circulating economy. The contraction, the economic restriction forms the annulus of the selfsame, of the self-return, of reappropriation. The economy restricts itself; the sacrifice sacrifices itself. The (con)striction no longer lets itself be circumscribed [*cerner*] as an ontological category, or even, very simply, as a category, even were it a trans-category, a transcendental. The (con)striction—what is useful for thinking the ontological or the transcendental—is then [*donc*] *also* in the position of transcendental trans-category, the transcendental transcendental. All the more because the (con)striction cannot not produce the "philosophical" effect it produces. There is no choosing here: each time a discourse *contra* the transcendental is held, a matrix—the (con)striction itself—constrains the discourse to place the nontranscendental, the outside of the transcendental field, the excluded, in the structuring position. The matrix in question constitutes the excluded as transcendental of the transcendental, as imitation transcendental, transcendental contraband [*contre-bande*]. The contra-band is *not yet* dialectical contradiction. To be sure, the contra-band necessarily becomes that, but its not-yet is not-yet the teleological anticipation, which results in it never becoming dialectical contradiction. The contra-band *remains* something other than what, necessarily, it is to become.

Such would be the (nondialectical) law of the (dialectical) stricture, of the bond, of the ligature, of the garrote, of the *desmos* in general when it comes to clench tightly [*serrer*] in order to make be. Lock [*Serrure*] of the dialectical.

One can follow, if one knows how to read in counter-band [*contre-bande*] (a term borrowed here from the code of blazons), the

man's help. And wear a "bow," or maybe several, in my hair.'

"With horror I saw myself decked out in enormous bows, not of ribbons, but of sausage meat in the form of obscene pricks.

"'It'll be a drooping, dangling bow,' added a mocking inner voice. An old man's droopy ding-dong. A bow limp, or impish! And in what hair? In an artificial wig or in my own dirty, curly [*bouclés*] hair?

"As for my dress [*toilette*], I knew it would be sober and that I would wear it with modesty, whereas what was needed to carry the thing off was a kind of wild extravagance. Nevertheless, I cherished the dream of sewing [*coudre*] on a cloth rose. It would emboss the dress and would be the feminine counterpart of Stilitano's cluster of grapes.

the stilite, on the contrary, "used to cut himself, his fingertips were finely gashed . . ."

"(*Long afterward, when I ran into him in Antwerp, I spoke to Stilitano about the postiche cluster hidden in his fly. He then told me that a Spanish whore used to wear a stamin rose pinned on {*épinglée*} at cunt level.*

"*'To replace her lost flower,' he said.*) . . .

"'You'll have a *toilette*, Juan.'

"I was sickened [*écœuré*] by this butcher's word (I was thinking that the *toilette* was also the greasy tissue enveloping the guts in animals' bellies). . . .

"The foot of a blond young man had got caught in the lace. I hardly had strength enough to mumble, 'Watch what you're doing.' The face of the clumsy young man, who was both smiling and excusing himself, was so pale that I blushed. Someone next to me said to me in a low voice, 'Excuse him, señora, he limps.'

"'I won't have people limping on my dress!' screamed the beautiful actress who smoldered within me. But

spiral chaining of the circle of circles. And, the logic of the anniversary, the imposition of the curve on the angle.

How far have we got?

At the limit or the mediation between the first and the second moment of natural religion, between the religion of the pure luminous essence and that of the plant or animal. This is also the passage to the for-(it)self. And, in the history of religion, the passage from sense-certainty to perception.

Why, plant and animal, plant then animal? With the becoming for-(it)self, the opposition interiorizes itself. It no longer scatters itself; it holds itself back, folds itself up, tightly clenched against (it)self, organically unified in the strict unity of the multiplicity. No opposition can form itself without beginning to interiorize itself. This organicity already binds itself again to itself in the plant, but life represents itself therein only by anticipation. The actual war, as opposition internal to the living, is not yet unchained. The plant, as such, lives in peace: substance, to be sure, and there was not yet any substantiality in the light, but peaceful substance, without this inner war that characterizes animality. Already life and self, but not yet the war of desire. Life without desire—the plant is a sort of sister.

Hegel does not say the plant religion, but the "*flower religion*," the "innocence of the *flower religion*." The plant is not the flower, but finds in the flower "*its own* self (ihr eigenes *Selbst*)." The *Encyclopedia* proposes a vast and meticulous deduction of the "vegetable organism," of flowering and fructification (the development of the anther, of the *stilus* (Griffel), of the stigma (Narbe, scar, cicatrix), and so on), modelled [*réglée*], most often, on *The Metamorphosis of Plants* (Goethe). The subjectivity of the plant is not yet for itself. The criterion for this is classic: the plant does not give itself its own proper place. The "objectivization" by which the vegetal relates itself to itself remains "entirely formal"; it is not "true objectivity." Its differentiation remains external, associative, angular, nearer geometric forms and crystalline regularity. The process of its formation, "the *inner* process of the plant's *relation to*

the people around us were laughing. 'I won't have people limping on my toilette!' I screamed to myself. Elaborated within me, in my stomach, as it seemed to me, or in the intestines, which are enveloped by the 'toilette,' this phrase must have been translated by a terrible glare. Furious and humiliated, I left under the laughter of the men and the Carolinas. I went straight to the sea and drowned the skirt, bodice, mantilla and fan. The whole city was joyous, drunk with the Carnival that was cut off [*coupé*] from the earth and alone in the middle of the Ocean. I was poor and sad.

"('Taste is required. . . .' I was already refusing to have any. I forbade myself to. Of course I would have shown a great deal of it. I knew that cultivating it would have—not sharpened me but—softened me. Stilitano himself was amazed that I was so uncouth. I wanted my fingers to be stiff: *I kept myself from learning to sew* [coudre].)"

Between the two parantheses in italics (one stitching, the other counterstitching), the one supporting within himself a terrible actress who does not want it (*ça*) limping in her dresses—the transvestite, then— renders to the Cesarean herself those toilettes that come back to him after the violent gutting of the birth. He drowns them in the sea [*mer*], he renders them to the motherwaters [*mer*]. In homage and vomit: "sickened by this word. . . ." And he needed the sea, the mother [*mer*], for this to happen beside her.

But the structure of transvestism is twisted even more.

He does not go from land to sea to render his toilettes. He is already in the sea, invested by her, like an island jutting out [*débordée*] on all sides, or almost [*presque*].

Almost: the ideal place for transvestism is,

itself" is first a relation to the outside, an exteriorization, an extra-neation, a dispossession (*Entäusserung*); its growth is a hardening, a becoming woody, verily stony (in the case of tabasheer, bamboo salt, for example). The plant is uprooted from itself, toward the outside, by the light. Now the flower sets free an advance in the movement of reappropriation and subjectivization. A moment of relief: the light no longer comes to provoke or uproot from outside; on the contrary, the light engenders itself spontaneously from inside the plant. This passage is analogous to the one that relieves the outer resonance of noise in(to) the voice. Instance of *Klang*. The *color* of the flower manifests this phenomenal auto-determination of the plant. "Consequently, the plant now engenders (*gebiert*) the light from itself, as *its own* self. It does this in the *flower*, in which the neutral color, green, is from the outset determined as a specific color."

A whole theory of colors (here again referred to Goethe and passionately anti-Newtonian) is implied here. And the sponta-neous production of the chromatic light, the interiorization of the process, the relation to self, the anthopoetic subjectivity of the plant, all that is also described as the dialectic of a *Hemmung*, of an inhibiting strict-ure. The introjection of the sun, the sublime digestion of the luminous essence, will end in "the heart of the occidental": it begins in the flower.

Flower religion is innocent insofar as the war internal to ani-mality is not yet unchained in it. The relation to self does not yet trigger the war because it does nothing but *represent itself* in the flower. Flower religion (like the flower, as the flower) mimes and anticipates the true self, contains itself in this "self-less representa-tion of the self (*selbstlose Vorstellung des Selbsts*)." The flower plays the "selfsame," does not have the power, or merely has the power to reach there. But as the flower has already begun to subjectivize the luminous essence and the plant, it no longer simply falls (en-tombed) into dissociative exteriority. The flower is neither an ob-ject nor a subject, neither a not-I nor an I, neither a pure alterity without relation to self nor a "*Selbst*." Innocent to be sure, therefore not culpable, not guilty, but its innocence is declared (what would not be done of the sun or the plant) only insofar as the flower is capable of culpability, culpable [*coupable*] of being able to become culpable, cuttable [*coupable*]. Among all these opposites, the es-sence of the flower appears in its disappearance, vacillates like all the representative mediations, but also excludes itself from the oppositional structure. The flower gives the example of every possible representation, but the circular system of the between-representation permits making the flower the trope of every representative middle or saying that every representation is antho-morphous. The flower at once cuts itself (off) by and from itself and abysses itself.

of course, *presqu'île*, almost an island, peninsula. *Péninsule*.

He becomes almost a woman on a tongue [*langue*] of lone land penetrating mid-Atlantic. The verso or the other version of a lagoon [*lagune*].

Geography writes that between land and sea, pro-cures you the more or less gratuitous passage from Barcelona to Cadiz. Barcelona is on the edge of the sea; Cadiz, which he decides to "get to," is "built in the middle of the water, though connected to the mainland by a very long jetty." Barcelona is turned to the east, on the Mediterranean, Cadiz to the setting [*couchant*] sun, in the Atlantic Ocean.

A note was enough to justify the necessary trav-esty: "While rereading this text, I find I have placed in Barcelona a scene from my life that is set in Cadiz. The phrase 'alone in the middle of the Ocean' reminds me of this. While writing, then, I committed the mistake of putting the scene in Barcelona, but into the description a detail had to slip [*glisser*], one that enables me to put it back in its true place."

The fact of the tongue that slips in its detail here is "cut off from the earth and alone in the middle of the Ocean." But under the name Cadiz "a very long jetty" was also needed.

So this mascarade (somewhere he defines feminin-ity with this word), a carnival between two counter-pointed parantheses, faces at once the East and the West, land and sea, the rising and the setting of the sun. The whole world bands erect and is incorporated in the transvestite, all kinds and genders of opposi-tions, the sun and fish on one side, the sea and night on the other. "At the outermost point of Western land, I suddenly had before me the synthesis of the Orient." The signs of Arabia in Spain, this could not happen

To adore flowers, to kneel before them, that is possible only on the threshold of culpability. The cult of animals—the totemism to which the *Phenomenology* refers—upsurges, on the contrary, in war, culpability, the struggle to death. Finally relating itself to itself, animal life destroys itself to raise itself to spiritual life, divides itself, opposes itself to itself to erect itself as spirit, in spirit. History, politics begin, in hatred, war, murder, culpability, punishment. One has left the peaceful nomenclature, the taxinomic religion completely occupied with classifying the botanic varieties. This is also the passage from pantheism to polytheism, verily to monotheism. "This pantheism which, to begin with, is the *peaceful* subsistence of these spiritual atoms (*das ruhige Bestehen dieser Geisteratome*) develops into a *hostile* movement within itself (*feindseligen Bewegung in sich selbst*)." This movement presupposes a repression of the previous structure: an internal suppression, the effect of a force that is no longer natural, instinctual, and that puts spirit in relation with the universality of the law, whence the origin of culpability. "The innocence of the *flower religion*, which is merely the self-less representation of self (*selbstlose Vorstellung des Selbsts*), passes into the earnestness of warring life, into the culpability of *animal religions*; the tranquility and impotence of contemplative individuality pass into destructive being-for-self. It is of no use to have taken from the things of perception the *death of abstraction*, and to have raised them to the essence of spiritual perception; the animation, the ensoulment (*Beseelung*), of this kingdom of spirits bears this death within it owing to the determinateness and the negativity which encroach upon the innocent indifference of plant life. Through this determinateness and this negativity, the dispersion into multiplicity of peaceful plant forms becomes a hostile movement in which the hatred of their being-for-self consumes them. The *actual* self-consciousness of this dispersed spirit is a host of separate, antagonistic national spirits who hate and fight each other to the death and become conscious of specific forms of animals as their essence; for they are nothing else than animal spirits, animal life that separates itself off from another and conscious of self without universality." In the form and the name of the totemic animal, the spirit calls, names itself, reappropriates itself, but remains yet foreign to itself, does not come back to itself, (close) by itself. The spirit is represented by a determinate, particular, finite species in which its own proper (name) exiles itself. Supplementary classification.

A structural analogy after the other: after the passage from sense-certainty to perception, the dialectic of master and slave. It develops itself in(to) the third moment of natural religion, that of the artisan (*Werkmeister*). Like every moment, that of the artisan announces (itself). Announced and announcing, it represents itself in the previous moment, becomes the representative of the

elsewhere. The fish are "caught the night before." "The sun would be rising when my fish were cooked [*cuits*]. . . . I had gathered the fish on the wharves in the darkness. It was still dark when I reached my rocks. The coming of the sun overwhelmed me. I worshiped [*rendais un culte*] it. A kind of sly intimacy developed between us. I honored it, though without, to be sure, any complicated ritual; it would not have occurred to me to ape the primitives, but I know that this star became my god. It was within my body that it rose, continued its curve and completed it. If I saw it in the sky of the astronomers, I did so because it was the bold projection there of the one I preserved within myself. Perhaps I even confused it in some obscure way with the vanished Stilitano."

So like a solar column, the cripple traverses his body, rises and sets in it. To incorporate all sexes at once—and a banquet or last supper scene is the table still depended on, the fish are "almost always" eaten "without bread or salt"—assumes the cutting [*coupure*] and the supplement within the double band. But as soon as there are two bands, by reason of the supplementary strewking, *coupture* (grafted flower), a double, undecidable at Stilitano's tip there is the nail [*ongle*]. This is all written with nails. "Stilitano used to cut [*coupait*] himself, his fingertips were finely gashed, his nail [*ongle*] was black and crushed [*écrasé*], but this heightened his beauty. (The purple of sunsets [*couchant*], according to physicists, is the result of a greater thickness of air which is crossed only by short [*courtes*] waves. At midday, when nothing is happening in the sky, an apparition of this kind would disturb us less; the wonder is that it occurs in the evening, at the most poignant time of day, when the sun sets [*se couche*], when it disappears to pursue a mysterious destiny, when perhaps it dies. The physical phenomenon that fills the sky with such pomp is possible only at the moment that most exalts the imagination: at the setting [*le coucher*] of the most brilliant of the heavenly bodies.)" In the *Miracle of the Rose*, when Harcamone appears, faces turn towards him "As sunflowers turn to the sun." The apotropaic virtue of the heliotrope: it is also a precious stone to which was attributed the singular property of making those who wore it invisible. As with the serpents in the *Inferno*, for example: "Tra questa

later and higher moment: circle and spiral. But in the moment of the artisan class, one is at the return of the return, the determinate birth of the round form, of the curve, of this particular line that figures however the totality of the process. This befalls the phallic column, according to the very example of Hegel.

So the annulus, the ring, the collar, the necklace, the chain of the gift [*cadeau*], the anniversary circle of the speculative, always turns around a phallic column, whether that column exchanges itself with a finger or an ankle, a waist or a neck [*cou*]. All that finds itself (again) wound round a cylinder, that's the right word, will have placed itself in line with the [*à la taille du*] phallus.

Simultaneously, in the moment of the *Werkmeister* and according to an inner necessity, signification begins to fill itself with voice. Merely begins: in this splendid form, the resonance (*Klang*) that the simple incidence of the light on the stone, the music of the Memnons, produces at dawn.

Let us pick up again. In the totemic war, the for-(it)self is "relieved," destroyed and preserved. It avoids pure and simple death in holding itself back in an object that survives the act of its production, the consuming destruction of its producing self. The spirit then manifests itself as artisan. The artist merely announces and represents himself in the artisan, just as esthetic religion does in the natural religion of the artisan. Spirit appears itself as artisan,

sex activates itself sheathing father and mother all at once. cruda e tristissima copia / Correvan genti nude et spaventate, / Senza sperar pertugio o elitropia."

This economic operation (an economy of undecidable death) *affects* the linguistic, the verbal, the semiotic, the rhetorical or the dialectical; it does not depend on these.

It affects them as an affect or a transvestite affects; sets them in motion, wins them, touches them, plays them, loses them, supports them, but has neither its place nor its efficacy in them, neither its force nor its remain(s).

". . . with the vanished Stilitano.

"I am indicating to you, in this way, the form that my sensibility took. Nature made me uneasy. My love for Stilitano, the roar with which he burst upon my wretchedness, and any number of other things, delivered me to the elements. But they are malicious. In order to tame them I wanted to contain them. I refused to deny them cruelty; quite the contrary, I congratulated them for having as much as they had; I flattered them.

"As an operation of this kind cannot succeed by means of dialectics, I had recourse to magic, that is, to a kind of deliberate *predisposition*, an intuitive complicity with nature. Language would have been of no help to me. It was then that things and circumstances became maternal to me, though alert within them, like the sting of a bee, was the point of my pride. (Maternal: that is, whose essential element is femininity. In writing this I do not want to make any Mazdaean allusion: I merely point out that my sensibility required that this time, by contrast, but in order that you have no fixed point where you could rest, femininity is the essential element of maternity. But it only concerns a predication. And the play of the copula is subtle. Like that of the couple in general. In fact, concerning such a

and its operation (*Tun*) makes it yet lose consciousness [*connaissance*]. Spirit produces itself as object, does not retake itself, does not recognize itself entirely. This object is not yet compared to the honey cake but to the *pyramis* whose example does not delay in coming. From the first lines, the operation is nevertheless close, according to a figure that will have become traditional, to the instinctive labor of bees constructing their cells (*ein instinktartiges Arbeiten, wie die Bienen ihre Zellen bauen*). The pyramid erects itself immediately. A lack, however, is remarked there—and thus a representation of what will appear only a little later, the curve, roundness, the curvilinear that can be produced only by the living spirit. Cold, formal, and death-dealing, the understanding proceeds geometrically, cuts [*coupe*] and secures [*arrête*] angular forms. The artisan religion is the history of a rounded angle, the passage from the pyramid to the column, from mathematics or calculus to the incommensurable grace of the spirit. And this passage is a (*re*)(*ful*)*filling*. The round and curvilinear form is more full-of-spirit. "The first form, because it is immediate, is the abstract form of the understanding, and the work (*Werk*) is not yet in its own self filled (*erfüllt*) with spirit. The crystals of pyramids and obelisks, simple combinations of straight lines with plane surfaces and equal proportions of parts, in which the incommensurability of the round is destroyed (*an denen die Inkommensurabilität des Runden vertilgt ist*), these are the works of this artisan of rigid form (*der strengen Form*). On account of the merely abstract intelligibleness (*Verständigkeit*) of the form, this form does not have its signification (*Bedeutung*) within itself, is not the spiritual self. Thus either the works receive spirit into them only as an alien, departed spirit that has forsaken its living interpenetration (*Durchdringung*) with actuality and, being itself dead, takes up its abode in the lifeless crystal; or they have an external relation to spirit as something which is itself there externally and not as spirit—they are related to it as to the dawning light, which casts its significance on them (*als auf das aufgehende Licht, das seine Bedeutung auf sie wirft*)."

One must ceaselessly go back to the philosophy of nature that dictates this interpretation of natural religion. And, in the philosophy of nature, to the relations of space and time, of light and sound in their vast and meticulous deduction. For example, in the course of repeating the "birth of sound" so "difficult to grasp" (*Die Geburt des Klanges ist schwer zu fassen*), the act by which strings, pipes, bars vibrate is described as an "alternating passage from the straight line into the arc." In the process of subjectivizing idealization that the oscillation (*Erzittern*) and the vibration (*Schwingen*) punctuate, the difference between nature and spirit corresponds to the difference between what does not resonate starting from (it)self, the bodies (*Die Körper klingen noch nicht aus sich selbst*), and what resonates with (it)self. The history of *Klang* is what reappropriates itself

it be surrounded by a feminine order. It could do so inasmuch as it could avail itself of masculine qualities: hardness, cruelty, indifference.)" The reader is then asked not to be "taken in" by words, since these fail to keep even the reflection of "bygone" states. The bygone is a "pretext-matter," it is neither the object nor the truth of the journal. And it is necessary to distinguish between what I "say" about it and the "interpretation" by which I work the bygone and play dead.

pair, why do they say a couple? "At the top of a slope, a couple (male or female?) of colonists, outlined against the sky; a thigh swelling out [*gonfle*] a pair of canvas trousers; the toughs and their open flies from which there escaped, in whiffs that turned your stomach, the scent of tea roses and wisteria [*glycines*] fading into evening." A repetition—an argument constraining, to pleasure—of the sheath [*gaine*], three lines further on, "Harcamone as a child swathed in princely poverty; the bugle [*clairon*] opening in his sleep. . . ." Ever since then, Harcamone, who "was unable to have a calendar," raises his "destiny as one raises a tower," "unique and solitary." Is it necessary to speak of a pleasure that would arise from strict-ure or sheaths of all kinds? Several pages earlier: "The word pleasure doesn't stick, isn't quite right [*ne colle pas*]."

So this happens between strewking and contra-strewking. Always, to be sure, at the limit of the good taste that "is required" when you whisper in the ears of whores or when you work in a library.

But why does he also want to stop himself from learning to sew, when he does it so well?

Here is where the argument of the sheath (*gaine*) necessarily contradicts itself—in its domestic logic, already—with a parergon that is never, as you know, internal *or* external. Whence the text's interest and difficulty. Always one letter more and less.

The stamin rose "replaces"—that's the word—the lost flower. The stamin replaces the natural rose that replaces the virginity. Detachments without chains, strewking supplements indefinitely take turns with one another and mix—such is the lapse in taste that

up to resounding *with* Klang *itself*. "*Klang* properly so called (*eigentliche*)" is in effect pure resonance (*Nachhellen*), "the unhindered inner vibration of the body freely determined by the nature of its coherence." The flux that purely and simply flows [*s'écoule*] does not resonate (*Das bloss Flüssige ist nicht klingend*). The impression freely communicates itself there to the whole, but this communication stems from the total absence of form, to the total lack (*Mangel*) of inner determination. Air and water do not spontaneously resonate, even if their capacity to communicate the *Klang* is recognized. In return, *Klang* presupposes the identity of the determination, is in itself a form. "As compact continuity and equality of matter belong to the pure *Klang*, so the metals (particularly precious metals) and glass (*Glas*) have this clear *Klang* (*diesen klaren Klang*) in themselves. These properties are developed by smelting." If, on the other hand, a bell (*Glocke*) is cracked or scratched (*einen Riss bekommen hat*), no longer is only the pure balancing swinging of the *Klang* heard, but also the noise (*Geräusch*) of the matter that obstructs, that grates, that breaks, that damages the equality of the form. The flat stones, the flagstones (*Steinplatten*) also produce a *Klang*, although they are hard, insensitive, cold, brittle (*spröde*).

In "human song," the external excitation and the vocal timbre are "homogeneous." Only in the voice is "subjectivity or independence of form present." The violin does not *resonate* (*tönt . . . nicht nach*) like the voice; it *sounds* only (*sie tönt nur*) as long as the stretched strings are rubbed.

The process of *Klang* therefore insures the passage from noise to the voice. The description of the *Encyclopedia* takes up again, in its general traits, that of the Jena *Philosophy of Nature*. In the latter, *Klang* was already recognized as that singular repercussion of interiority in exteriority. Sonority in general (*Der Ton*), in the continuity of earthly bodies, has two and only two forms: noise (*Geräusch*) and resonance (*Klang*). Noise expresses merely the immediate, *exterior*, constrained continuity of friction (*Reibung*). *Klang*, on the contrary, its *interior* continuity, by privilege in the case of metal and of glass (*Glas*). But despite this difference (exterior/interior), both, noise and *Klang*, are triggered only by a percussion *come from outside* (*nur ausserlich angeschlagen*). That is what distinguishes them from sense (*Sinn*), for example from hearing; is what also distinguishes them from the voice and above all from the reverberating interiority couple that voice and hearing form. Voice is active hearing (*das tätige Gehör*); hearing is the receptive, conceiving voice, as is said of a woman (*die empfangene Stimme*). Through this couple, the sensibility of the individual retakes itself within itself, reassembles itself, gathers itself together, comes to, contracts itself, enters into a contract with itself (*sich in sich zurücknimmt*) and constitutes itself as universal.

always concerns the sex wherever you put it—all genders, genres, genera.

Thus the stamin, *l'étamine*. *Etamine*—the whore's rose, a verge's homage to Mary and taboo of the hymen rendered to the fag petal [*pétale*]—names not only the light material in which nuns are sometimes veiled, or through which precious liquids are filtered. But *étamine*, stamen, is also the male sex organ of plants: according to the *navette* [shuttle, rape]—that's the word—running between the textile code and the botanical code. Situated around the style and its stigma, stamens generally form a thin thread [*filet*], or filaments (*stamina*). Above the thin thread, a connective with four pollen sacs (microsporangia) that "elaborate and disperse the pollen seeds": the (interring) anther. The anther can be introrse, extrorse or lateral, according to the orientation of the pollen sacs. This for bisexual flowers, where stamens constitute the androecium, while carpels (ovary, ovules, and style) form the gynoecium. Which is sometimes encased in the receptacle (an epigynous flower).

here is another stamin rose, contiguous with a column of smoke (textual effluvium): "So here she is [Divine], having decided to return, lifted by a column of smoke, to her garret, on the door of which is nailed a huge discolored stamin rose" (*Our-Lady-of-the-Flowers*).
A stamen is called abortive when it is deprived of its anther. An abortive flower: "one that falls without leaving any trace of fertilization."

The flower is hypogynous when the ovary dominates the rest [*reste*] of the flower. Sometimes the stamens are glued by their thin threads into one or more "fraternities," or else they become concrescent with petals (these are sometimes prolonged into spurs and carry nectariferous glands) or with the gynoecium: that's the case with orchids.

In the case of unisexual flowers, the fer-

the pollen of orchidaceous plants is called "agglutinated," that of rosaceous

Here in this place of the philosophy of nature, in the *Encyclopedia*, heat (the element of fermentation, then of fervor) deduces itself and deduces itself, as strange as that may seem, from *Klang*. For the current representation, sound and heat have nothing to do [*à voir*] with each other, and "it can seem striking (*es kann frappant scheinen*)" to bring them together. *Klang* is the alternation (*Wechsel*) of the reciprocal exteriority of the material parts, of their *Aussereinander, and* of its negation, of its being-denied. This negation, as always, produces ideality, but an abstract ideality. The alternation is immediately the negation of the specific exteriority and thus the real identity of cohesion and of specific gravity—what Hegel calls heat. "Sonorous bodies (*klingenden Körper*) will grow hot when they are struck (*geschlagenen*) or rubbed together, and it is in this phenomenon that heat originates with sound in conformity with the concept." There is again a process of *Aufhebung* of materiality there. The setting in motion, swinging, of the body (*Erschütterung*) is not only "relief of matter ideally [*auf ideelle Weise*] presented," it is a "real relief" through heat. Heat is the relief of the body's rigidity (*Aufheben seiner Rigidität*). "There is therefore a direct relation between sound and heat. Heat is the fulfillment (*Vollendung*) of *Klang*. . . . Yet a bell (*Glocke*) will become hot by being struck (*geschlagen*) for example, and this is a heat . . . not external to it. Not only the musician gets warm, but also the instrument."

From the dead geometric form—rectilinear and plane—the artisan class raises itself to "lifelike roundness." First this is a composite, the mediation of a "blending (*Vermischung*)" announcing the "free architecture" of esthetic religion.

What characterizes this anticipation of the artistic spirit? The hieroglyphic limit of a language insufficiently filled with signification.

This limit also results from a spatialization of language and was already marked in the fact that the sound remains exterior, produced by light, the moment the sun's ray comes to strike the stone. The sun's ray falls on a monument, to be sure, on a stone shaped by

tile pieces are similar. There is a general tendency to unisexuality among floral systems. It goes together with so-called natural selection making allogamy possible or absolutely plants, "sticky [*collant*]": it fastens onto the body of an animal attracted by the pollen or by the nectar secreted in certain glands. The bee orchid, for example, attracts, with its form, its color, and its velvet texture, drones which, thinking that they fertilize these fake bees, assure the reproduction of the orchids by passing from one bee to the other, or rather from the form of one bee to the other necessary: sexual products are conveyed from one individual to another, genotypes are mixed up or adapted, and the pollen, protected from bad weather by an impermeable sheath, lets itself be dispersed by the wind or by animal organisms.

No more than for the flower, then, is there any univocal semantic or morphological definition of *étamine*. Merely, as modern anthological science recognizes, a functional or syntactic definition.

Etamine deviates itself [*s'écarte*] from itself, bursts [*crève*] its sheath, at the risk of disseminating the pollen. This always open risk affects not only the androecium, but also the gynoecium. One must argue from the fact that the seed can always burst or remain dormant.

It is concerning the seed, a fertilized ovule, that one thinks one is literally [*proprement*] speaking of dissemination (with angiosperms or gymnosperms). The seeds are sometimes thrown in every direction [*sens*] by the bursting [*éclatement*] of the fruit. More often, they escape from it through slits or holes open in its wall; wind or animals disperse them. Germination is therefore immediate only if light and moisture permit. Otherwise, the ripe seeds stay in a dormant state for weeks or months in an exterior environment. Dormant states can be true or false. True if the seed,

the spirit, but which remains stone: white in Egypt, black in Mecca. The limit of language is determined from a certain void in signification. A sensible remain(s) prevents the three-stroke engine from turning over or running smoothly. Yet the remain(s) does nothing but promise a new anniversary.

What the artisan gives a "more lifelike form" to is a habitation (*Behausung*). His art still remains utilitarian; it only anticipates and represents the art of the artist. Nonetheless his art has passed from an unlifelike [*inanimée*] naturalness to a beginning of life and to a prefiguration of the self (*Selbst*).

How did it get there? By making matter vegetate, by bringing matter to a kind of arborescence and efflorescence. Plant-life no longer forms the object of a cult. The flower becomes usable: as an ornament. The *Aesthetics* describes at length the organic figures closest to nature the moment they have just left that nature, when the plant and the tree shoot up into stone structures. Straight up toward the sky, like a "stem," at once supple and rigid (*ein Stamm, ein schwanker Stengel*), a slight and strong liana, an erection upheld by a trunk. "The tree trunk already carries, as such, its own corolla, the blade the ear, the stem the flower." The columns derive from the most varied plant-forms (*Pflanzenbildungen*), from lotus plants for example, or onion bulbs. "Then out of this pedestal the slender stem rises up" or climbs by entwining itself (*verschlungen*) as a wreathed column, and the "capital again is a flower-like interlacing of leaves and branches (*blumenartiges Auseinandergehen von Blättern und Zweigen*)." But the imitation of plant nature is not "slavish"; the plant-forms are subject to an architectonic stylization (circle, straight line, regularity of figures): this is the moment of the *arabesque*, the root of "free architecture."

Then the plant is animalized. The artisan resorts to the "*animal form* (Tiergestalt)." The twisted, deformed plant-forms resemble animal bodies. Traversing that rigidity for which the arabesque has been reproached, the for-(it)self constitutes itself.

Recognizing *his* work, the artisan relieves this animal form. The animal form is indeed "*aufgehobene*" the moment it becomes language: first under the form of what is more primitive and subordinated, enslaved in language, to wit a nonphonetic writing: "the animal figure becomes at the same time a relieved figure and the hieroglyph of another signification (*Bedeutung*), of a thought (*Gedankens*)." The animal form makes itself a mute sign or writing the moment the human face [*visage*] appears in the dwelling, the work of the artisan. In Egyptian representations the hieroglyphic blending of animal figures and human figures indicates the specific character of this moment.

The hieroglyph was uprooted from painting, does not show some thing. In expressing a thought the hieroglyph announces language, but its mute writing does not yet reach language. The

freshly separated from the mother plant, is not fulfilled or if it is prevented by inhibiting substances that are resorbed bit by bit. False if the inhibition stems from the thickness of the tegumentary sheath and prohibits the penetration of air and water. When the seed is not dormant, it swells and nourishes itself by digesting the prothallium (for the gymnosperms) or the albumen (for angiosperms with exalbuminous seeds). The embryo of the albuminous seeds contains within itself the totality of the reserves that it consumes.

Wailing [*Vagir*] finally.

Good or bad, the cries [*vagissements*] of the thief (not of the author, and not of the narrator—neither the subject nor the question is there—let us say of the sfeigncter) unceasingly try to sheathe again, to refrain, to emparaph the seed [*semence*], to ensign the dissemination, to benumb the sperm of a signature, to reappropriate genealogy, to reconstitute the golden monument of its proper (seminary), to digest, to sluice down [*écluser*] without remain(s) his white and proper *seing*, to be the son, not the daughter, remark it well, of himself.

Here are required an executioner and a cradle (let's call it a slop-bowl [*gamelle*],

self-having, knowledge [*s'avoir*], as one is called.
Slop-bowl: his forename always resounds nearby. His forename. Which one?
Of whom? The author? the narrator? the narratee? heroes? the colossus? And of what text? "He brings with him his blankets, his slop-bowl [*gamelle*], cup, wooden bowl, and his story. At his first words I stop him. He keeps on talking, but I am no longer there.

hieroglyph lacks a self that stands there as such, carrying outside what it is inside, expressing an "inner signification." "It lacks speech," language, tongue (*Sprache*).

What is *Sprache* (*langue* or *langage*, speech or language)? An exteriorization that presents, it gives the there, the *Da-sein*, to the inner signification; but in order to move forward thus into presence, it must first let itself be filled, fulfilled, filled in, accomplished, inflated, curved [*galber*], *rounded* by the sense that penetrates it. It is the "element (*Element*) in which the sense filling itself (*der erfüllende Sinn selbst*) is present (*vorhanden ist*)."

This element is called voice: the spontaneous outside production of an inner sense filling with presence from then on the form of its emission. The spontaneity, the production of self by self gives voice. The sound, resounding ever since the blow [*coup*] struck from the outside, does not utter itself. The sound announces and represents the voice but also holds it back, too much on the outside or too much on the inside.

This moment of the half-voice [*mi-voix*] sculpts its paradigm in the statue of Memnon, son of the dawn, adored by the Ethiopians and the Egyptians. The "colossal sounding statue (*kolossale Klang-statue*)" was ringing under the first rays of the sun. The stroke [*coup*] of light on the block provokes a species of voice, extracts, evokes a voice that is not yet a voice, even when Memnon (*tönend und stimmgebend*) thanks "with its voice" the faithful who come to offer it sacrifices. Even if the work no longer has an animal shape [*figure*], the human face presented there is *tonlose*, noisy but mute: "Therefore the work [of the artisan], even when it is wholly purged of the animal element and wears only the shape of self-consciousness, is still the soundless shape which needs the rays of the rising sun in order to have sound which, generated by light, is even then merely resonance (*Klang*) and not speech (*Sprache*), and shows only an outer, not the inner, self."

The *Klang* of the stony block is *not yet* the voice that it *already* is: neither inside nor outside language, a mediation *or* an excluded middle [*tiers*]. The deciphering of Memnon follows, in the *Aesthetics*, the reading of phallic columns. The Orient, Egypt, Greece used to dedicate a cult to the general vitality (*allgemeine Lebenskraft*) of nature. The cult was directed at the representation of animal "generative organs" that were presented [*mis en scène*] and considered sacred. That above all is the case with the phallus or the *lingam* (a hieratic representation of the phallus for Indians; the word designates the mark and the genre—the class—*and* the phallus). Often cited, Herodotus recalls that on the occasion of the Dionysia, "'instead of phalli they have invented other images, a cubit long, fit with a thread.'" Phallophoric women pull on the thread, and the sex is always raised ('*sich . . . immer hebt*'), nearly as tall as the rest of the body.

" 'What's your name?'
" 'Jean.'
"That's enough. Like me and like the dead child for whom I am writing, his name is Jean. Besides, what would it matter if he were less handsome, but I have a run of bad luck. Jean there. Jean here. When I tell one of them that I love him, I wonder whether I am not telling it to myself. I am no longer there, because I am again trying to relive the few times he let me caress him. I dared all and, in order to tame him, I allowed him to have the superiority of the male over me; his member was as solid as a man's, and his adolescent's face was gentleness itself, so that when, lying on my bed, in my room, straight and motionless, he discharged into my mouth, he lost nothing of his virginal chastity. It is another Jean, here, who is telling me his story. I am no longer alone, but I am thereby more alone than ever. I mean that the solitude of prison gave me the freedom to be with the hundred Jean Genets glimpsed [*entrevus au vol*] in a hundred passers-by, for I am quite like Darling [*Mignon*], who also stole the Darlings whom a thoughtless gesture let escape from all the strangers he had brushed against; but the new Jean brings into me— as a folding fan draws in the designs on the gauze— brings in I know not what" (*Our-Lady-of-the-Flowers*).

There is always another Jean, eponym and surname, nomothete or epithet of the "first," one doubling the other (the whole parentele).

What finally is the epithet

with the remains of some gruel), the angel for banding erect the son (*slop-bowl* or throat [*gargamelle*], this (*ça*) is again announced), some talcum, if not some vaseline at fingertip to prevent any irritation in the folds or at the edge of an orifice, the glorious aura of a milky voice regurgitating sperm, as one could always contemplate it, and a song—that is, an accent—circumflexed to cover the head.

In India more than elsewhere the phallic representation is architectural: enormous columns and towers of stone larger at the base than at the top. One begins to worship them for themselves, then sets about making openings (*Öffnungen*), holes, incisions, excavations (*Aushöhlungen*) in which images of gods are inserted. They appear there. This practice is found again in the hermetic columns of Greece. The legendary representation of gods, the images, the idols, the altars come to be inscribed as tattooing on the smooth surface of these rigid columns.

Now the origin of this process [*processus*] of excavation, its *Ausgangspunkt*, is the nonperforated columns (*unausgehöhlten Phallussäulen*). The incisions would have come over columns originally unbreached. Besides, they are rather rare and tend quickly to disappear.

Later the columns are transformed into high and narrow habitations—pagodas—separated into shell and kernel.

Herodotus also mentions male columns that included, by way [*titre*] of ornament or adornment, signs of the feminine organ. He saw them only in Syria, attributes them to Sesostris, and interprets them, according to Hegel, in Greek, in true Greek, in the Greek sense: he transforms their "naturalistic signification" into "one concerned with ethical life (*Sittliche*)." "In the countries where the people were brave in battle against Sesostris during his wars, he erected columns on which he inscribed (*Inschriften*) his own name and country and how he had reduced these peoples to subjection; where, on the contrary, they submitted without a struggle he added to this inscription on the column a female *pudendum* to indicate that they had been cowardly and unwarlike.'" The properly Greek interpretation, in the Greek sense (*im griechischem Sinne*), deciphers then the ethical in the natural, and this passage from nature to *Sittlichkeit* merges with the phallocentric hierarchization. The Greek interpretation associates the positive ethical values, verily sense itself, with virility.

Then the Memnon statues upsurge. Obelisks had marked the transition. And they have the symbolic value of the sun's rays. Obelisks themselves represent luminous rays, gold ingots, or helioid genitals. Egyptian letters came at times to be engraved in the obelisk's petrified light. Heliogravure, as at Heliopolis where Mithras, god of the Medes and the Persians, let himself be enjoined, through a dream, to build obelisks, "'the sun's rays in stone (*Sonnenstrahlen in Stein*),'" and to engrave thereon letters ('*Buchstaben darauf enizugraben*') "'called Egyptian.'"

At Thebes the large statues of Memnon did not speak, although they had human shape. Some were monolithic (Strabo saw some), others were formed of two colossi seated.

How does language come to the column? By an inner sun. In

Will he have pleased [*plu*], rained [*plu*], more?

Will he have ejaculated in the galaxy?

"Botanists know a variety of *genêt which they call winged-genêt*." It describes its flight and theft in the *Journal*:

"As the theft was indestructible, I decided to make it the origin of a state of moral perfection.

"'It's cowardly, weak, dirty, low . . . (I shall define it only with words expressing shame). None of the elements composing it leaves me a chance to magnify it. Yet I do not deny this most monstrous of my sons [*fils*]. I want to cover the world with its loathsome progeny.'

"But I cannot go into great detail about this period of my life. My memory would like to forget it, would like to dim its contours, powder it with talcum, offer it a formula comparable to the milk bath which the elegants of the sixteenth century called *a bath of modesty*.

"I got my slop-bowl [*gamelle*] filled with leftover stew [*d'un reste de soupe*] and went off to eat in a corner. I preserved within me the memory of a sublime and debased Stilitano, with his head under his wing. I was proud of his strength and was strong in his complicity with the police. All day long I was sad, though sober. A kind of dissatisfaction inflated each of my acts,

the meantime, the column must be weaned from the sensible sun. The sensible sun must be denied, and the stone must do without the daylight. Therefore the phallus blinds itself, loses the outside, the light, the form, the *eidos*. The white stone becomes black. The *Behausen*—the casing or abode, *l'habitacle*, as phallus—gains the *Selbst*'s essential interiority only by plunging itself into the night, by elaborating its language in the black and formless stone.

This is the Kaaba, the black stone of Mecca: no remains; all is scraped clean, fished out, inscribed, relieved.

An interiority still negative, covering over the white stone, "cover of the inside": "Over against this outer *Selbst* [Memnon] of the figure stands the other figure which proclaims its possession of an *interior*. Nature, withdrawing into its essence, deposes its living, self-particularizing, self-entangling manifold existence to the level of an unessential casing (*unwesentlichen Gehäuse*), which is the *cover for the interior* (Decke des Inneren); and this interior is, in the first instance, still simple darkness, the unmoved, the black, formless stone."

The artisan finds himself caught in this driving contradiction between the system of the (lost and relieved) white stone and that of the black stone relieving the other only in order yet to lose true interiority by lacking voice. So the two presentations (*Darstellungen*) of the inside and the outside need to be united or reconciled. How is the artisan to elaborate this contradiction?

In an enigmatic way.

Here one has to distinguish between the enigmatic and the oracular. The oracle will be, in esthetic religion, the analog of the enigma, its voiced counterpart.

The artisan resolves the contradiction by producing enigmas composing the two contraries, nature and consciousness, inside and outside, the clear and the obscure. A spirit's word, a witticism [*mot d'esprit*], is in question: difficult to decipher, nocturnal in its form, appealing as well to the unconscious, a profound wisdom unable to give its reasons, a kind of cryptogram the Egyptians themselves, to believe the *Aesthetics* on this, did not understand. The producer of the enigma can be irresponsible, blind to what is written with his own hand. "The artisan therefore unites the two by blending the natural and the self-conscious shape, and these ambiguous essences, enigmas to themselves, the conscious wrestling with the nonconscious, the simple inner with the multiform outer, the darkness of thought mating with the clarity of utterance, these break out in the language of a profound, but scarcely intelligible wisdom."

including the most simple. I would have liked a visible, dazzling [*éclatante*] glory to be manifest at my fingertips, would have liked my potency to lift me from the earth, to explode within me and dissolve me, to shower me to the four winds. I would have rained over the world. My powder, my pollen

pollen is always threatened, exposed to the risk of being lost or destroyed. The thief remarks it when returning to Czechoslovakia. He has, again, just climbed a stairway, the police-chief's this time: "During the questioning (Why did I want to go to Czechoslovakia? What was I doing there?) I was all atremble lest my ruse be discovered. At that moment I experienced the anxious joy, fragile as the pollen on hazel blossoms, the golden morning joy of the murderer who escapes."

And pollen is not just fragile, as if fleeing before the law, it is related to yellow, falls from what is yellow, here, from the tuft of a musician: "one feels that the yellow will powder them with its pollen" (*Miracle of the Rose*).

One is not going to form the theory-procession [*théorie*] of pollen and disseminance here. From the outset, it has been another theory-procession that we follow: the logic of obsequence and of the apotropaic umbrella, under the "shower . . . to the four winds." One must always rejoin it, but after some indispensable detours and hardly calculable delays. I am always (following) the dead man. Who gives me the step [*pas*].

The galaxy does not figure the element my sperm must touch ("My powder, my pollen, would have touched the stars."), is itself a disseminal element. So it is also necessary to understand how a certain abbé in *Our-Lady-of-the-Flowers* "ejaculated a seed of constellations."

The first language properly so called is thus "double (*zwei-deutig*)," enigmatic; it brings into play the contraries between the conscious and the unconscious, on two scenes at once.

The paradigm for this is furnished by the Egyptian religion. The philosophy of religion interprets it as a "religion of enigma," of obscurity, of animal masks, of the walled-in unconscious. The Egyptian spirit lacks that unveiled transparency characterizing the Greek. Its veil *represents by anticipation* the Greek unveiling. So the representation is a veil, the veil a representation. "The most important presentation (*Hauptdarstellung*) by which the essence of this combat [between the conscious and the unconscious, the clear and the obscure, and so on] is made completely accessible to intuition (*anschaulich*) is the image of the goddess at Saïs (Neith) who was presented (*dargestellt*) veiled (*verschleiert*). It is symbolized therein and in the inscription in her temple—'I am what was, is, and shall be; my veil has been lifted by no mortal'—expressly declared that nature *is a being-differentiated in (it)self*, namely, *an other opposed to its manifestation but which immediately offers itself*, an *enigma*."

The veil does not symbolize the enigma. The enigma is the structure of the veil suspended between the contraries.

Does Hegel then construe [*fait*] a word, does he then play in a vicious way, in the Egyptian manner, on the signifiers? Citing the end of the inscription of Neith's temple in Lower Egypt, he deciphers it in Greek-German in order to read in it the whole course of the sun setting in the West and recalling itself within itself. The history of this *Erinnerung* is a family history. The spiritual sun is at once the son and the father of the sensible sun, the same and the circular inverse of the one that lighted in sum the Republic. Here its purpose is to announce the hermeneutic and teleological resolution of the enigma in the Greek (esthetic) religion, then in the Christian (revealed) religion: "It [nature] has an inner element, something that is hidden (*ein Inneres, Verborgenes*). But, it is stated further in this inscription, 'the fruit of my flesh is Helios.' This as yet hidden essence therefore expresses clearness, the sun, the becoming clear to oneself, the spiritual sun (*geistige Sonne*) as the *son* (*den* Sohn) who is born of her. It is this clearness which is attained to in the Greek and Jewish religion, in the former in art and in the beautiful human form, in the latter in objective thought. The *enigma* is solved; the Egyptian *Sphinx*, according to a deeply significant (*bedeutungsvollen*) and admirable myth, was slain by a Greek, and thus the enigma has been solved. This means that the content is *man, free, self-knowing spirit*."

The Oedipian resolution of the enigma sounds the end of natural religion in its last moment. Thought attains the clarity of its unveiled there (*Da-sein*); the artisan becomes a "spiritual laborer,"

The detours of theory-procession having to do with text, the unconscious, and obsequence, appear to be interminable. Each narrative pose, as for example here, in what could resemble a bad popular novel, inscribes theory-procession in literature. The text grips tight, bands erect each character, each name, forename, surname by bending them to its own proper rhythm, its own desire: pretext and prebend for a narrator who, like the abbé in question, dresses in travesty [*se travestit*] and enjoys their death, verily their suicide: "Ernestine's final gesture might have been performed quickly, but, like Culafroy in fact, she is serving a text she knows nothing about, a text I am composing whose *denouement* will occur when the time is ripe [*son heure*]. Ernestine is perfectly aware of how ridiculously literary her act is, but that she has to submit to cheap literature makes her even more touching in her own eyes and ours."

Ernestine, Divine's mother, knows that he is going to die and that she must simulate the suicide of her son: "'I'll say he killed himself.' Ernestine's logic, which is a stage logic [*logique de scène*], has no relationship with what is called verisimilitude, verisimilitude being the disavowal of unavowable reasons."

She gives the step [*pas*] not [*pas*] to be followed.

In fact Ernestine is going to kill her son and "curl up" on the slab of the cemetery, on its "white, slightly curved stone," like an egg or a work. She will have held the revolver "as a phallus in action," "big with murder, pregnant with a corpse."
"This book aims to be only a small fragment of my inner life." Plans at the origin of *Funeral Rites*: the source is unique, but the embouchures or the columns double. Passing from one signature to the other is necessary, the hand or tongue cannot be put on both at once.

conscious of his activity, artist. The instinctive, almost animal, elaboration is now an art.

An essentially Greek history, opened by the death of the Sphinx, the esthetic religion is developed, it too, according to the ternary rhythm of a syllogism: the *abstract* work of art, the *living* work of art, the *spiritual* work of art. This is the same rhythm, with an analogous content, as that of natural religion (indeterminate abstraction of the luminous essence, life of plants and animals, spirituality), each of the three moments dividing itself in its turn in three, according to a syllogistic structure infinitely representative of itself and always abyssal. But is the abyss saturated or hollowed out by a "*mise en abyme*"? Then, to hollow out, is that to run a risk? And in view of what?

The abstract work of art maintains the figure of the gods in the block of the spatial thing. But in this the concept strips off the angular crystal of the understanding, the blending of the inorganic and plant forms, imitation in general. The black stone is drawn out from its animal gangue; the represented figures are no longer the essences of nature but of lucid spirits, the ethical spirits of self-conscious nations. As long as they are singular national figures, Athena for example, they still keep in themselves a certain natural density, a scrap [*relief*] of nature. This naturalness must be relieved. But as long as the work does not belong to the element of the tongue, as long as it extends itself into space, it remains and falls (entombed) outside the operation of the artist. It is opposed to him. The whole of the work is cut off [*coupé*], like a remain(s), from its elaboration.

This caesura takes two contradictory and indissociable forms overlapping each other [*se recoupent*] ceaselessly. On the one hand, this is the effacement, the omission of the artist: he is sufficiently disinterested to declare that his work lives by itself, animates itself without him, removes his signature. But by removing it, the work keeps it, and under this modernic thematic [*thématique moderni-taire*], Hegel immediately discloses, on the other hand, the ruse or the dissembled, dissembling reverse, the hypocrisy of the other one-sidedness. In effect the artist verifies that the work, by being able thus to cut itself off and fall (to the tomb) from him, *is not his equal*, that it has not produced an essence equal to its author (kein ihm gleiches *Wesen hervorbrachte*). The animation proper to the work, the admiration of admirers, the offerings, verily the sacrifices it provokes and that bring it to consciousness—the artist therefore knows all that is inferior to his labor, to his elaboration, his production, precisely because that *detaches* itself from him. By his withdrawal [*retrait*] the artist consequently raises himself above his remain(s) and in the same stroke [*du même coup*] detains it as a small

Hegel to a lover of au-   part, a morsel of himself. The signature's
tographs: "Had the   omission, its nonappearance, simultane-

Such is the unique and double origin of the murder. Of the unique and double murder.

Plans [*Desseins*] that are never reduced to one alone, whence the division of glas: colpos.
The mother remains after killing because she no longer knows where to put the teat. Sketches [*Dessins*] of flowers: "The old hallucination of my childhood obtruded itself, and I can translate it only by the following image: *still flowers that do not mingle*, though they have a single source, rush into his mouth [*bouche*], which they spread [*écartent*] and fill. One of the soldiers made a slight noise." *Funeral Rites*.

gl: the strict-ure of the orifice—strangulating bottle-neck—thus informs a block of casein, for example, a belch, a fart, a remain(s) for making in any case his tomb [*sa tombe*].

But it is always the mother—now one knows this word means (to say) nothing more than what follows, obsequences, remains after killing what it gave birth to. This has just been verified for *Our-Lady-of-the-Flowers*. It can be done with *Funeral Rites*. I have often posed the question: what does *here* [ici] mean (to say) for a text and in a language in general. What is the *here and now* of a glas?

Of a remain(s)?
Of a remain(s) that would no longer be—neither relic nor remainder [*reliquat*]—of any operation.

257

ously engages an operation of mastery and the mastery of the operation. All this must be recognized as the *fact* (Tat) of the artist in his untiring strategy. If the admirers "put themselves *below* (darunter *setzen*) it and recognize in it the *essence* which dominates them, he knows himself as the master (*Meister*) of this essence."

In order to cicatrize this cut [*cicatriser cette coupure*] between the elaboration and the work, between the author and his remain(s), in order—then—to think it, the work must *remain present* to the artist, without falling from him like a thing truncated in space, like some wonderful excrement on top of which the master sits enthroned while forgetting himself. The element of art then will no longer be something in space and without consciousness; it will be time and voice. Even if—and insofar as—time is the truth of the space it relieves. The work must find time in order to become consciousness present to itself. The stone must set about speaking: "The work of art therefore demands another element of its *Dasein*, the god another process of coming forth (*Hervorgang*) than this, in which, out of the depths of his creative night, he falls into the opposite [*in das Gegenteil*—its opposing morsel—*herabfällt*], into externality, into the determination of the *thing* unconscious of itself. This higher element is *language* (Sprache)—a *Dasein* that is immediately self-conscious existence (*Existenz*). Just as the *individual* self-consciousness is there (*da ist*) in language, so is it also immediately as a *universal* contagion (*Ansteckung*)." The soul therefore exists "as soul."

The *hymn* is this presence of the universal to the singular, of inside to outside, of the production to the work, of the god to its animated figure. The religious song, the fervent flow of the religious voice gathers the singularities together in one same element of fire and water (*die Andacht, in allen angezündet, ist der geistige Strom*). It flows [*coule*] and consumes all the remains [*tous les restes*].

Yet, contrary to habit, after the hymn a remain(s) is discussed and will form the subject of a longer and more involved development. It is a question of the *oracle*: the oracle relates to the time of speaking [*parole*] as the enigma relates to the space of writing. Simple and universal, oracular propositions come from outside the community (unlike the hymn, the experience of inner communion). They are sublime, but their universality easily turns to triviality, above all in the first time of the oracle, that of natural

The response of *Funeral Rites* accuses the mother's remain(s) of having committed the murder. Let us stop close to here: ". . . faded flowers . . .? Young! No doubt about it, I said to myself, it's here . . . I stopped there. The uttering of 'here' and, even if only mentally, of the words meant to follow, 'that he was sent on his last trip,' gave to my pain a physical precision that aggravated it. The words were too cruel. Then I said to myself that the words were words and did not in any way change the facts.
"I forced myself to say over and over, inwardly, with the repetitiveness of a saw irritating the ear, He-re, He-re, He-re, He-re, He-re. My mind was being sharpened at the spot designated by 'Here.' I was no longer even witnessing a drama. No drama could have taken place in an area too narrow for any presence. 'He-re, He-re, He-re, He-re, He-re. They can trip him, can trip him, can trip him, cunt rip him, cunt rip him, cunt ripped him . . .' and I mentally composed the following epitaph: 'Here cunt ripped him.'"

Remain(s) here or (there) *glas* that can't be stopped.

That some double fetter(s) (or understands).

After Divine's death, the obsequies are then regulated by the abbé who concentrates all desires on himself. He is in travesty, a transvestite expert in break-ins and disembowelings. All words follow in silence up to the complete dispersion of the theory-procession and of the so-called seminar(y). Disintegration, defrocking, rouge and flowers.
"In the rain, this black cortege, bespangled with multicolored faces and blended with the scent of flowers and rouge, followed the hearse. The flat round umbrellas, undulating above the ambulating procession [*théorie*], held it suspended between heaven and earth. . . . The hearse had wings on its axles. The abbé emerged first into the rain singing the *dies irae*. He tucked up [*relevait*] his cassock and cope, as he had been taught to do at the seminary when the weather was bad. . . . Bear in mind that the abbé was young. You could tell that under his funereal vestments he had the lithe body of a passionate athlete. Which means, in short, that he was in travesty."

religion and of the luminous essence. In becoming for-(it)self, the oracle finds again the universal truths in a language *proper* to the community: this is, for example, Antigone's *"sure and unwritten law,"* the law of the gods who speak in the citizens' hearts. This relief of the "natural" oracle suspends chance, luck, the throw of the dice in speech [*langue*]. The natural and impulsive oracle is that fortuitous case wherein language [*langage*] falls over/upon universal truth. Whence a kind of dividing in two of the oracle: one's very own [*propre*] language and a foreign language. Socrates, for example, looks within himself for philosophy's voice, but he lets the foreign speaking of his demon inspire, prompt [*souffler*] in him unnecessary counsels, contingent precepts, tell his fortune, talk with him about the opportunity for a journey, and so on. "In the same way the universal consciousness draws knowledge of the contingent from birds, or trees, or the fermenting earth, the vapors from which deprive self-consciousness of its power of reflection. For the contingent is the unreflective and the foreign, and therefore the ethical consciousness lets itself settle such matters too, as by a throw of the dice (*wie durch ein Würfeln*), in an unreflective and foreign manner." The oracle as such, before the inner and unwritten law, is bound to the lot (*Los*). *Das Orakel oder Los.*

The petroglyph remains outside consciousness. Its antithesis, the hymn, immediately disappears, like the voice, the very moment it is produced. Like time, it is no longer *there* straightaway, immediately, as soon as it is *there*, inasmuch as it is *there* (*wie die Zeit, unmittelbar nicht mehr da, indem sie da ist*). The *Da* is posited inasmuch as it withdraws. In its counter-time [*contre-temps*]. Abstract art is made of this double one-sidedness: spatial nonmovement and temporal movement, the double loss of the divine figure, plastic art and lyric art.

This double loss is relieved in(to) the *cult*. From its beyond, the divine essence descends there as far as consciousness. The cult is first of all abstract and is announced in the fervor of the hymn that is limited to its representation: inner, secret, nonactual. This is the moment of inner purification wherein the soul does not know it is the evil. The soul purifies its surface with the waters and re-covers that surface with white linens. But the cult must not be secret; it must give rise to gestures, to actual operations: sacrifice and enjoyment, the ruse of enjoyment in the sacrifice. The act of the cult, its handling (*Handlung*), begins with abandonment (*Hingabe*), the renunciation of possessing and enjoying, without apparent benefit. But the sacrifice recaptures with one hand what it gives with the other, and its account must be kept on a double register. What is sacrificed goes up "in smoke (*in Rauch*)" as the effluvium of

"In the church—the whole funeral service having been merely a 'do this in memory of me'—approaching the altar on tiptoe, in silence, he had picked the lock of the tabernacle, parted [*écarté*] the veil like someone who at midnight parts the double curtains of an alcove, held his breath, seized the ciborium with the caution of an ungloved burglar, and finally, having broken it, swallowed a questionable host." Explore the corpus, take an inventory of all the tabernacles more or less devoid of sense, the "'secret abode [*habitacle*]'" of the *Miracle*, "'where the Captain of the galley stands,'" the hooked, fractured, disemboweled, and broken-open receptacles. In *Our-Lady-of-the-Flowers*, it is also the name of a nightclub: "All the queens of *The Tavernacle* and the neighboring bars . . ."

As he sings, transported to a fantastic Hungary (the land of Huns and Hungarians), the face of a young stranger upsurges with an extinguished butt in his mouth.

The butt is in the mouth like a word or a bit. Exquisite.

Argotic tongue, a cut [*coupé*] object almost letting its ashes fall while you still suck on it, the gloss making the abbé band erect: "The word 'butt' and the taste of the sucked tobacco made the abbé's spine stiffen and draw back with three short jerks [*coups*], the vibrations of which reverberated through all his muscles and on to infinity, which shuddered and ejaculated a seed of constellations."

would have touched the stars. I loved Stilitano. But loving him in the rocky dryness of this land, under an irrevocable sun, exhausted me, rimmed my eyelids with fire. Weeping a little would have deflated me. Or talking a lot, at great length, brilliantly, before an attentive and respectful audience. I was alone and friendless."

a consuming destruction or a decomposition. But it is retained [gardé] in the sublimity of its essence, as a spirit. The sacrificed animal becomes the sign of a god; the consum(mat)ed fruits *are* the living Ceres and Bacchus. The sacrifice reappropriates the enjoyment, but the "ruse" of the enjoyment removes itself; it consumes itself: ". . . the result, in the enjoyment, is itself robbed of its being-there (*das Resultat im* Genusse *sich selbst seines Daseins beraubt*)."

The end of enjoyment is the end of enjoyment: the final point, period. The bone or snag [*L'os*: in German, the lot, *Los*; in Latin, the mouth, *os*] of enjoyment, its chance and its loss, is that enjoyment must sacrifice itself in order to be there, in order to give itself its *there*, in order to touch, and tamper with, its *Da-sein. Telos* [*tel os*: such *os*] of enjoyment equals death—that would be the end-point (the point-of-no-end-at-all) if there were not, for the untiring desire of speculative dialectics, yet one more turn, annuli yet to be accomplished, and anniversaries to be celebrated.

The antithesis of sacrifice and enjoyment relieves itself in(to) labor, but in(to) the enjoyment of labor, in(to) the enjoyment of the durable products of the elaboration deferring the enjoyment. The dwelling and the ornament of the gods, this whole reliable pomp no longer has the naturalness of statues. And it is elaborated by man reappropriating the enjoyment of this pomp in the feast. The places and the objects of the cult, the altars, the temples, and so on, are like the hard bone [*comme l'os dur*: like the hard mouth, the hard lot] that remains from sacrifices and the consum(mat)ed enjoyment, to be sure, but they occupy the place of labor in the city. With the god the human producer shares in this all the enjoyments of the feast. "At the feast, this people adorns its own dwellings and garments, no less than its ceremonies, with graceful decorations. In this way, they receive in exchange (*Erwiderung*) for their gifts a return from the grateful god (*dankbaren Gotte*) and proofs of his favour, in which through their labor they become bound (*verband*) to him, not as a hope and in a future realization (*späten Wirklichkeit*), but rather, in witnessing to his glory and in bringing (*Darbringung*) him gifts, the nation has the immediate enjoyment of its own wealth and adornment."

This is the feast of labor and the labor of the feast in the Greek city. The sacrifice reappropriates the enjoyment lost through labor in the cult; and the cult is an exchange of labor with the god who restores to the laborers the *immediate* enjoyment of the products they have renounced, without apparent hope of return. The god pays back [*reverse*] to the laborers the sacrifice of the surplus value. Gift contra gift: I give you or sacrifice for you this here that takes on more value in being sacrificed, an object of useless ornament, lost adornment. The recognition of the addressee [*destinataire*] restores the enjoyment; and the feast, this feast at least, far from opening

What I had dreaded, naturally, reproduces itself. *Déjà.* Already. The same stage. The same stadium. Today, here, now, abandoned, me, on the endless esplanade, the debris of [*débris de*]

His hour bellringer the unction the rattle grimace(s) extreme the slab (gravestone) the basilica stands raised for the stiff king of his mother dying to close his eyelids herself.

Canopy of the upturned eye [*Dais de l'œil révulsé*].

How does he do it? He is ready. He has always had his corpse on him, in his pocket, in a matchbox. Near at hand. It (*Ça*) lights up all alone. It (*Ça*) should have, in truth. He feels himself placing obstacles in the way of his death, that is, he the living child, in the way of the sublime, immeasurable, sizeless super-elevation of his colossus. He is just a detail dividing his double, unless it be the contrary.

Always more, with a bit (a dead one) [*mors*], than with the whole of the other. Hunger for (and end of) the drive.

He is ready. How does he do it? So im-

up a pure and impossible disseminal expenditure, organizes, strictly, the circulation of enjoying in the cult. *Telos* of the cult, to speculate the enjoyment of God and to treat oneself to it.

in following the phenomenological gallery ("This becoming presents (*stellt . . . dar*) a slow-moving succession of spirits, a gallery of images (*eine Galerie von Bildern*) . . ."), from station to station, one comes back toward the *IC* and *Sa*, past the "Calvary of absolute Spirit." One finds there again, very close to the "Calvary"—to be inspected on both sides—the "certainty of his throne (*Gewissheit seines Throns*)."

It is enough in sum, only just so, to wait.

All that will have been projected, pulled to pieces, closed, nailed down, fallen (to the tomb), relieved, repeated, round about Easter.

The circle of the phenomenological gallery is reproduced and encircled in the greater *Logic* and the *Encyclopedia*. What is the difference between two editions of the same circle? Hegel, who had just learned of "the rapid sale of the second edition" of the *Encyclopedia*, confides in Winter, in 1827, his worries. He asks Winter to "commit . . . to the prompt payment of the royalty." "For the original eighteen sheets in the first edition we settled upon two-thirds of the 25 florin royalty. For the additional number of sheets we reverted to this original royalty, and for the further eighteen sheets of the second edition we agreed on 22 florins per sheet. In this agreement I reserved for myself the royalties of the first edition for the additional material contained in any new edition. . . . Whether, and by how much, this number of sheets might still be increased in the contemplated new edition I cannot yet say, since the task catches me by surprise, and since I have not yet had a chance to run through the text with this in mind. In general, however, I do not foresee undertaking any significant change or expansion. The printing remains fixed as before at a thousand copies, with eighteen complimentary author's copies, twelve on vellum and six on writing paper.

"Since I have been notified so late of the need for a new edition—Mr. Oswald's letter is dated July 13—the manuscript may be sent off later than you probably would wish. Seeing how my work has since piled up, I cannot yet say anything definite on when it will be. I shall do my best, however, to enable the edition to appear by Easter."

So he does gymnastics.

We are in the Dionysian circle. The third moment of abstract art, the religion inscribed in that moment, is already the most abstract phase of the subsequent moment, the living work of art. Through its syllogism a process of language still busies itself with the relief of the remain(s).

The first one-sided moment is the bacchic delirium, the *Taumel*, the unbounded intoxication in the course of which the god makes himself present. The ascendant luminous essence unveils itself as what it is. Enjoyment is the mystery of this revelation. For the mystical does not lie in the dissembling of a secret (*Geheimnis*) or an unknown. But what lays itself bare here still belongs to immediate spirit, to spirit-nature. The mystery of bread and wine is *not yet what* it is, *already*, that of flesh and blood. Dionysus then must pass into his contrary, appease himself to exist, not let himself be drunk and consum(mat)ed by the "crowd of frenzied females."

poverished, so naked. So many letters are missing. Not an A sounding in his name. Above all no R, not even one. No G either that a consonant, an A, or a U comes to harden or stiffen [*raidir*], stop [*arrêter*], angulate. To engrave. To keep from groaning, moaning, wailing [*vagir*]. He is all alone, with none of the good letters, she has kept them all for herself, for her forename. He also lacks I. L, he doesn't even have her, L.

L (and the little a) let fall, without making a case, without one [*un*], all naked [*nu*], just to speculate about what, without image, without knowing it, without knowledge, on his name. Without what. Otherwise. [*Sans quoi.*]

Milk of mourning [*Lait de deuil*] sealed up (coagealed, pressed, squeezed, hidden [*caché*], coagulated, curdled).

I begin to be jealous of his mother who could, to infinity, change phallus without details dividing herself. Hypothesis begodden father in (it)self not being there.

He remains light, does not cease to become

Apollo is not named, to be sure; but the antithesis, the opposite, the opposing party, the contrary stance into which the Dionysian must pass in order to "appease itself in making itself *object* (*sich zum* Gegenstande *beruhigen*)," stands up as the erect(ed) body in Greek gymnastics, the beautiful "*Körperlichkeit*." The figure of man cultivates itself in place of, on behalf of, the sculptural column of the divinity. The divine lets itself be reappropriated in the human: an exchange still of two erections, two institutions, setting in motion and renewal of life. Surplus value of the contradiction that contracts (itself) with itself, makes itself, after all, the gift of the remain(s) [*se fait du reste cadeau*].

But once more, a balancing movement, everything settles itself in the outer objectivity that was set opposite the Dionysian fiery passion [*embrasement*]. So one has two opposed morsels that contradict one another in their respective one-sidedness. The balance (*Gleichgewicht*) is unceasingly broken. In delirium, the self (*Selbst*) loses consciousness; on the stadium [*sur le stade*, in this stage] spirit is what is outside itself.

Through the spiritual work of art—language right through—reconciliation is announced: the synthesis of esthetic religion (abstraction, life, spirit). The syllogism of spiritual art (*epos*, tragedy, comedy) leads esthetic religion to revealed religion. Through comedy then.

A time to perfect the resemblance between Dionysus and Christ.
Between the two (already) is elaborated in sum the origin of literature.
But it runs to its ruin [*perte*], for it counted without [*sans*]

lighter. How to live so. All is blocked by the maternal account. Due date. So little (phallus) [*fallu si peu*] might have been needed, an A, an R, a G, for this (*ça*) to take hold some other way, stop somewhere else, drop anchor and ink in another depth, grasp or grate another surface, the same nonetheless. For this (*ça*) no longer to slip. With him, with his funeral rite, another contract. Another legacy. To pay off, to bribe the already of the absolute ancestor [*de l'aïeul absolu*].

Vor *der Sonne kamst du zur mir, dem Einsamsten.*
Wir sind Freunde von Anbeginn: uns ist Gram und Grauen und Grund gemeinsam: noch die Sonne ist uns gemeinsam.
Wir reden nicht zu einander, weil wir zu Vieles wissen—: wir schweigen uns an, wir lächeln uns unser Wissen zu. . . .
. . . was uns gemein ist,—das ungeheure unbegrenzte Ja-. . .

It is very arid on the endless esplanade, but it (*ça*) does nothing but begin, the labor, here, from now on. As soon as it (*ça*) begins to write. It (*Ça*) hardly begins. No more than one piece is missing.

It (*Ça*) grates. Rolls on the tree trunks lying down [*couchés*]. Pulleys. The greased ropes grow taut, they are all you hear, and the breathing [*souffle*] of slaves bent double. Good for pulling. Proofs ready for printing. The cracking whip [*fouet cinglant*] of the foreman. A regaining of bound force. The thing is oblique. It forms an angle, already, with the ground. Slowly bites again [*Remord*] its shadow, dead sure (death) of (it)self. So little (phallus) would have been necessary [*fallu si peu*], the slightest error of calculation, they say distyle [*disent-ils*], if it (*ça*) falls (to the tomb), if it (*ça*) is inclined and clines toward the other's bed, the machine is still too simple, the precapitalist mode of writing.

What I had dreaded, naturally, already, republishes itself. Today, here, now, the debris of [*débris de*]